CW00894888

kidsource 2

super songs for church and school
compiled by **Capt. Alan Price, CA**

We hope you enjoy *kidsource 2.* Further copies are available from your local music shop or Christian bookshop.

In case of difficulty, please contact the publisher direct by writing to:

The Sales Department
KEVIN MAYHEW LTD
Buxhall, Stowmarket, Suffolk IP14 3BW

Phone 01449 737978
Fax 01449 737834
E-mail info@kevinmayhewltd.com

First published in Great Britain in 2002 by world wide worship

Full Music ISBN 1 84003 845 4
ISMN M 57004 982 0
Catalogue No: 1470155

Combined Words ISBN 1 84003 844 6
ISMN M 57004 981 3
Catalogue No: 1470152

9 8 7 6 5 4 3 2 1 0

Cover design by Jonathan Stroulger
Music setter: Donald Thomson
Proof reader: Linda Ottewell

Printed and bound in Great Britain

Acknowledgements

The publishers wish to express their gratitude to the copyright holders who have granted permission to include their material in this book.

Every effort has been made to trace the copyright holders of all the songs in this collection and we hope that no copyright has been infringed. Apology is made and pardon sought if the contrary be the case, and a correction will be made in any reprint of this book.

Important Copyright Information

Foreword

Christ's message in all its richness must live in your hearts. Teach and instruct each other with all wisdom. Sing psalms, hymns and sacred songs; sing to God with thanksgiving in your hearts.

Colossians 3:16

God continues to inspire Christians to write quality songs for youngsters. Since the compilation of **kidsource**, new songs have been written and new writers are emerging. Alongside this, we are aware of older, traditional songs, hymns and carols that are needed to make as complete a resource as possible at any one time. Today's generation of children needs the songs which express Christian truth in words they can 'own' and in musical styles that are contemporary. Yet we as compilers have a real concern that today's children generally sing few hymns. These are the songs that connect us to our Christian forebears, that are part of our Christian 'folk culture' which reminds us of our heritage.

This is not, however, a book of hymns. It is a complementary resource book, which brings together more of the best songs that work for children of all ages. As with the first volume, the criteria for choice have been that their theological content should be biblically sound, that they should have good, memorable tunes and above all, they should be 'child-friendly'.

There are more of what we term 'cross-over' songs – those written for adults, but which are accessible to children because of their music and lyrical content. It is our belief that many adults will also find these 'children's' songs to be singable without any 'cringe-factor', thus being a collection providing a good resource for all-age worship. Of course there will be songs we have not been able to include, either through ignorance or for copyright reasons.

It is our hope that children's music is performed to the same standard and quality as 'adult' music. Those who play for adults generally rehearse much more than those who play for children. This is in some ways an insult to children, as if they are not worth the effort. So often children's music is regarded with some disdain, as if it is 'lesser' music.

Children are generally uninhibited when it comes to using their bodies in worship. Many songs have actions that reinforce the words, the worship and the celebration of being God's children. It is beyond the scope of this book to attempt to describe such actions, whether they be a simple choreography, or the use of sign language. We would encourage those who use this material to pursue this element of worship, whilst realising that many songs are best sung without physical action.

Music is a major part of life, especially for children. Apart from the almost constant 'background music' surrounding them, the educational value of music is well known as a means of reinforcing teaching. However, music is also a vital means of expressing response to God and his message. Thus **kidsource** has songs suitable for reinforcing biblical teaching on a wide range of topics, and also those songs which will enable children to express their worship and adoration and their desire to follow the Friend and Saviour, Jesus Christ.

CAPT. ALAN PRICE, CA
Compiler

JONATHAN BUGDEN
Adviser

401 A butterfly, an Easter egg *(Signs of new life)*

Words and Music: Carey Landry
arr. Norman Warren

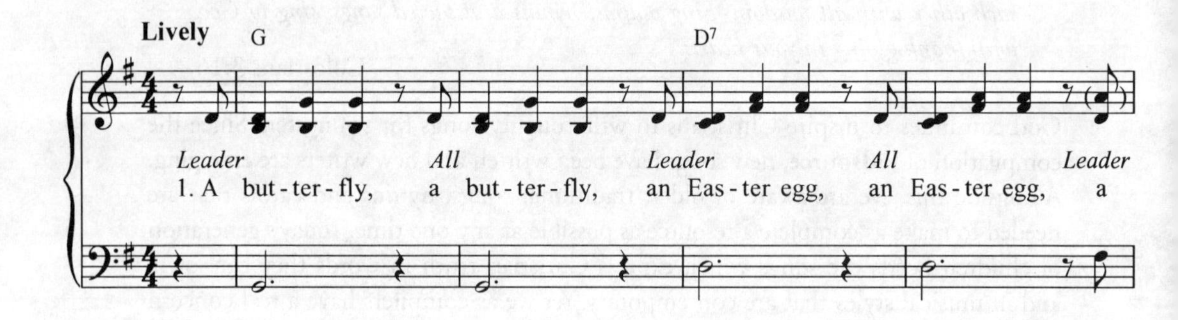
Lively
G
D7
Leader
All
Leader
All
Leader
1. A but-ter-fly, a but-ter-fly, an Eas-ter egg, an Eas-ter egg, a

G
D7
G
D7
All
foun-tain flow-ing in the park, a foun-tain flow-ing in the park.

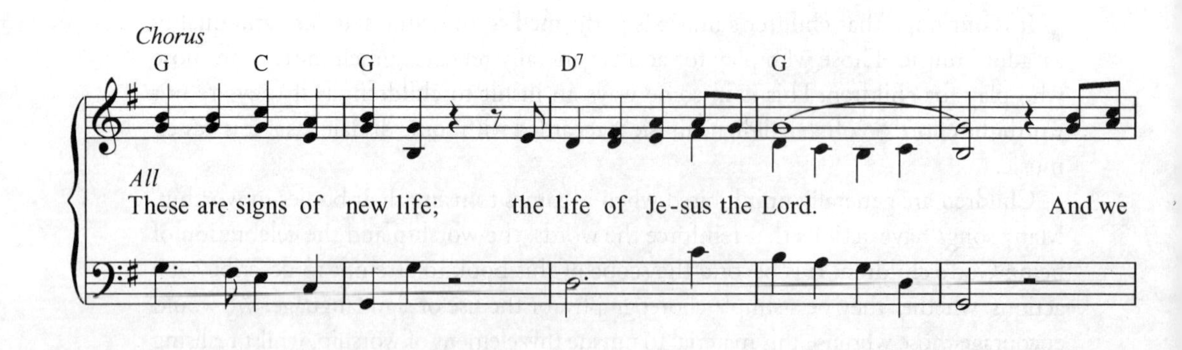
Chorus
G
C
G
D7
G
All
These are signs of new life; the life of Je-sus the Lord. And we

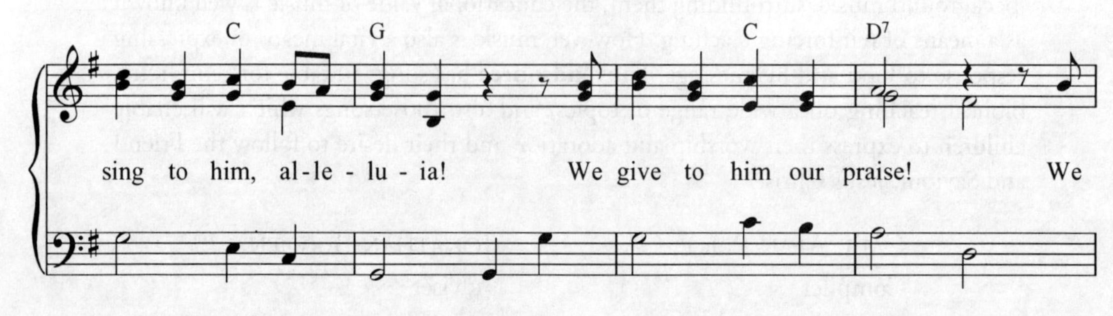
C
G
C
D7
sing to him, al-le-lu-ia! We give to him our praise! We

G C G D7
Leader
All
sing to him, al - le - lu - ia! Glo - ry be to him! Glo - ry be to

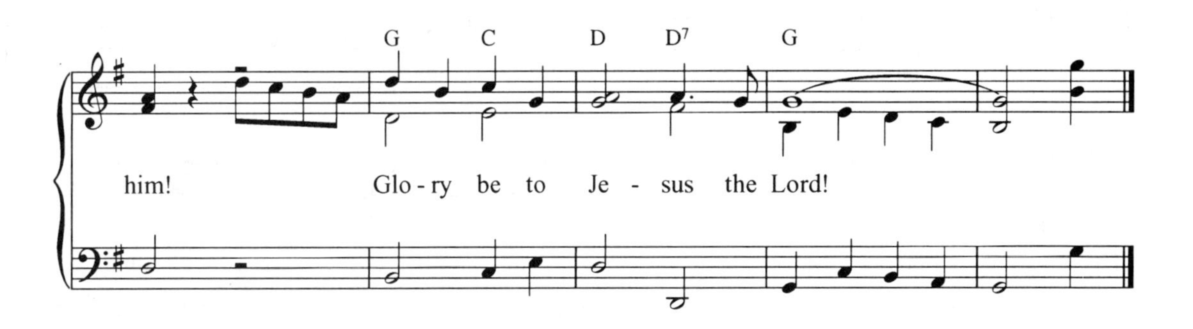
G C D D7 G
him! Glo - ry be to Je - sus the Lord!

2. A helping hand,
   a helping hand,
   a happy smile,
   a happy smile,
   a heart so full of hope and joy,
   a heart so full of hope and joy.

3. A cup of wine,
   a cup of wine,
   a loaf of bread,
   a loaf of bread,
   blest and broken for us,
   blest and broken for us.

402 All around the world

Words and Music: James Wright
arr. Chris Mitchell

Gm7 Chorus
C
Am7
All a-round the world,
all a-round the world,
Dm7
Gm7
1.
C
peo-ple are ce-le-bra-ting Christ-mas, peo-ple are
Am7
Dm7
2
C
giv-ing thanks to God.
-mas, all a-round the world.
F
Dm7
1. From the U-ni-ted King-dom
2. From the Mid-dle East to
G7
B♭
F
C/E
to Au-stra-li-a to the shores of Bra-zil,
In-do-ne-si-a to the shores of Ja-pan,

Dm7
G7
from the land of Chi - na to South Af - ri - ca,
from Co - lum - bi - a to Yu - go - sla - vi - a,
B♭
F
B♭maj7
to the streets of Se - ville. All o - ver the
to the streets of Su - dan. All o - ver the
F/A
Asus4
A7/C♯
Dm7
Cm7
F7
U S A, Phi - la - del - phi - a to L A.
world to - day peo - ple ce - le - brate this spe - cial day.
B♭maj7
F/A
Ev - 'ry na - tion, ev - 'ry tribe and tongue
Ev - 'ry coun - try, ev - 'ry tribe and tongue
1.
Gm7
B♭/C
A7sus4
A7(♯9)
D.C.
come, give him praise.
come, give him praise.

2
B♭/C
F
Dm7
Ce - le - brate, lift your hearts and sing
G7
Dm7
G7
as one. Ce - le - brate, ev - 'ry na - tion, ev - 'ry tongue,
B♭
F/A
Gm7
B♭/C
the com - ing of the Ho - ly One all a - round the world.
1.
2.
F
F
Gm7
B♭/C
Ce - le - Let the peo - ple re - joice all a - round the world,
F
Gm7
B♭/C
F
ev - 'ry tribe, ev - 'ry tongue, all a - round the world.

403 All of the people

Words and Music: Susan Sayers
arr. Andrew Moore

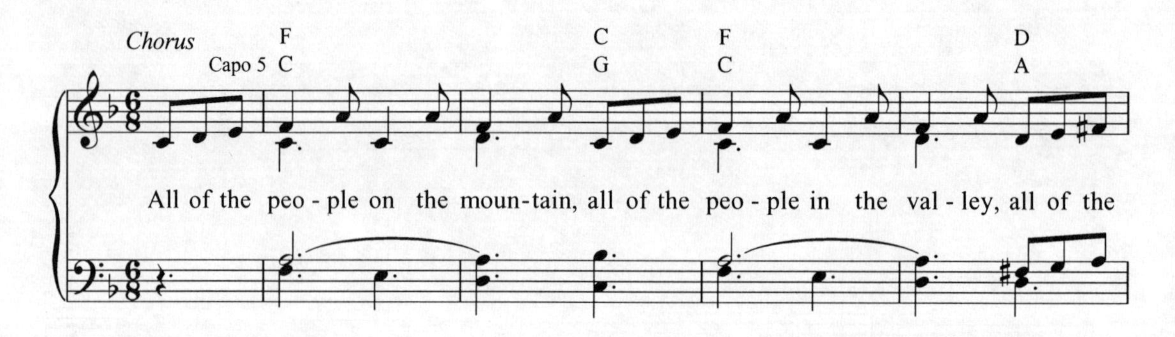
Chorus
Capo 5
F C G C D A
C
All of the peo - ple on the moun-tain, all of the peo - ple in the val - ley, all of the

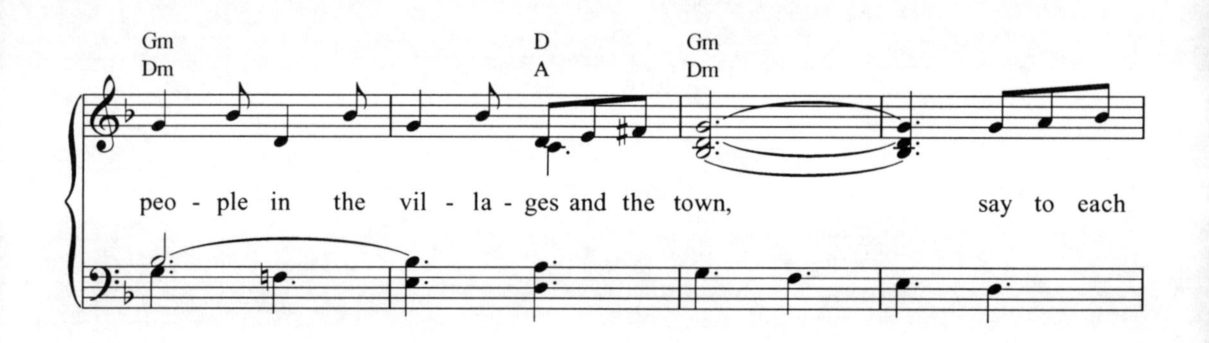
Gm Dm D A Gm Dm
peo - ple in the vil - la - ges and the town, say to each

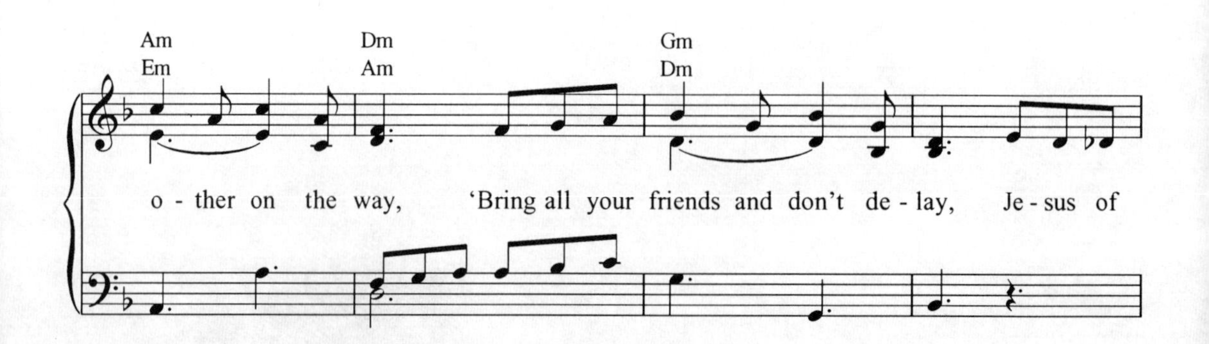
Am Em Dm Am Gm Dm
o - ther on the way, 'Bring all your friends and don't de - lay, Je - sus of

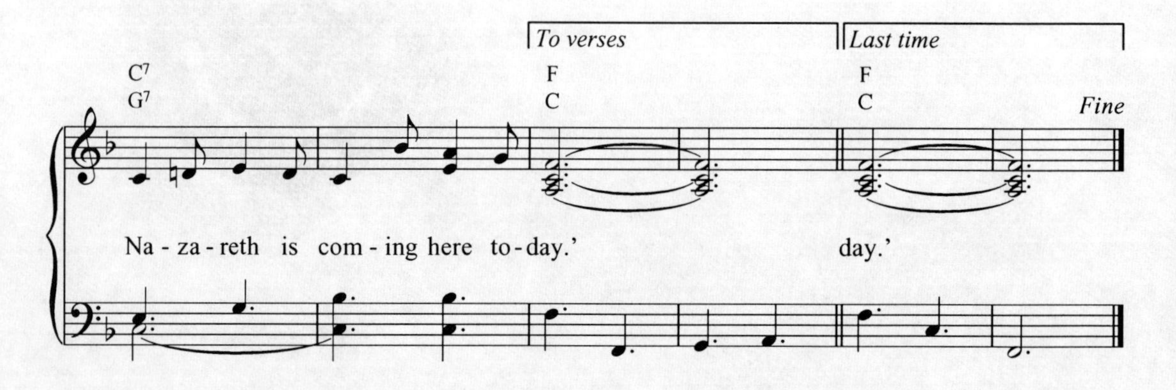
To verses
Last time
C7 G7 F C F C
Fine
Na - za - reth is com - ing here to - day.' day.'

B♭
F
Gm
Dm
F
C
Gm
Dm
1. Je - sus, Je - sus, when we are with you, it's strange, and yet it's
C
G
F
C
B♭
F
Gm
Dm
F
C
true, we start to feel that there is more to life than liv - ing as we
Gm
Dm
C
G
C7
G7
D.C.
do. It's rich - er and more sa - tis - fy - ing than we e - ver knew.

2. Jesus, Jesus, healing as you go,
your loving seems to flow
like water from a fountain,
and as we are touched we want to grow
in love towards each other –
just because you love us so!

3. Jesus, Jesus, we have come to see
that you must really be
the Son of God our Father.
We've been with you and we all agree
that only in your service
can the world be truly free!

404 And God said

Words and Music: Pamela Dew
arr. Chris Mitchell

G
E7/G#
Am
D
D7
G
1. And God said, 'Let there be light in

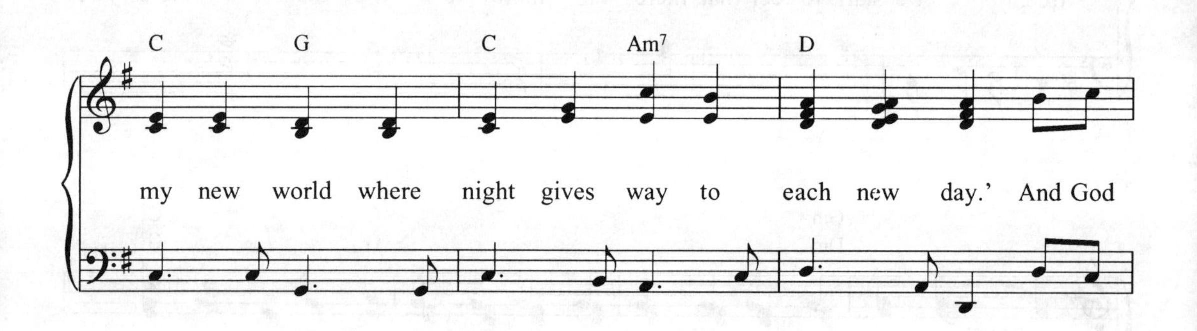
C
G
C
Am7
D
my new world where night gives way to each new day.' And God

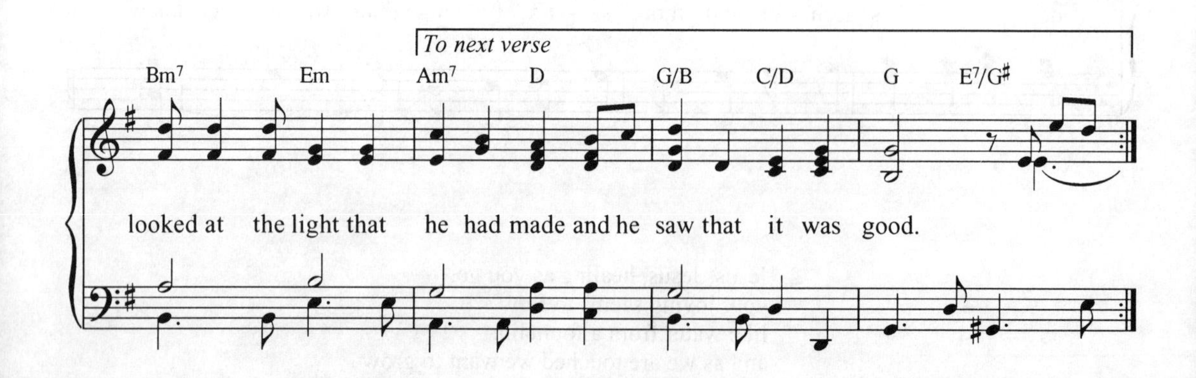
To next verse
Bm7
Em
Am7
D
G/B
C/D
G
E7/G#
looked at the light that he had made and he saw that it was good.

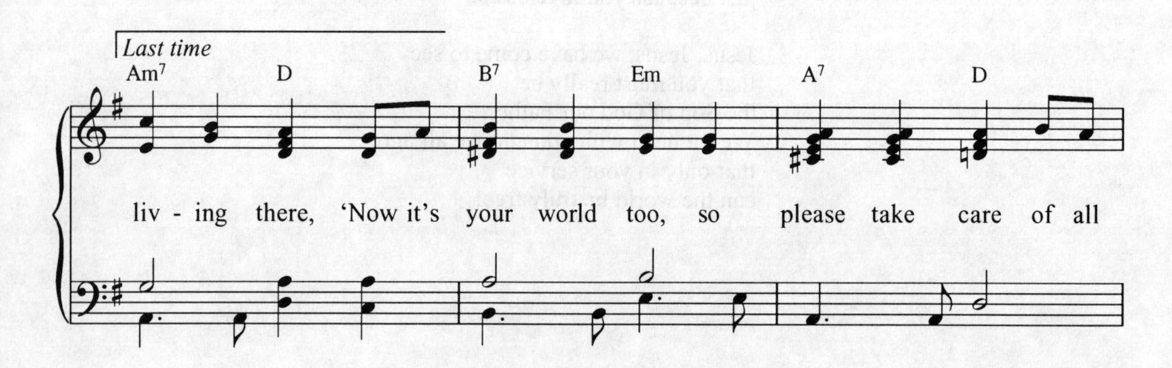
Last time
Am7
D
B7
Em
A7
D
liv - ing there, 'Now it's your world too, so please take care of all

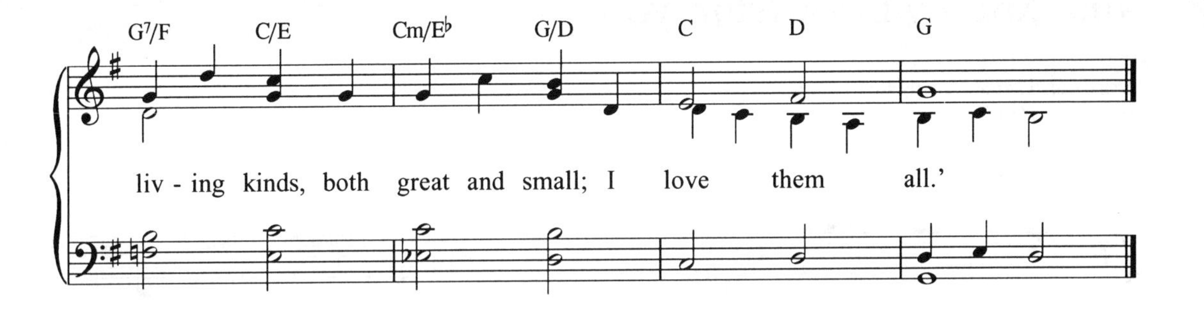
G7/F
C/E
Cm/E♭
G/D
C
D
G
liv - ing kinds, both great and small; I love them all.’

2. And God said,
   ‘Let there be space in my new world,
   a sky of blue, the deep sea too.’
   And God looked at the space that he had made
   and he saw that it was good.

3. And God said,
   ‘Let there be plants in my new world,
   with flow’rs and leaves and fruits and seeds.’
   And God looked at the plants that he had made
   and he saw that they were good.

4. And God said,
   ‘Let there be stars in my new world,
   the sunshine bright, the moon by night.’
   And God looked at the stars that he had made
   and he saw that they were good.

5. And God said,
   ‘Let there be creatures in my new world
   to run, swim, fly and multiply.’
   And God looked at the creatures he had made
   and he saw that they were good.

6. And God said,
   ‘Let there be people in my new world,
   I’d like to share my world so fair.’
   And God said to the people living there,
   ‘Now it’s your world too, so please take care
   of all living kinds, both great and small;
   I love them all.’

405 And I will worship you

Words and Music: Andy Read
arr. Chris Mitchell

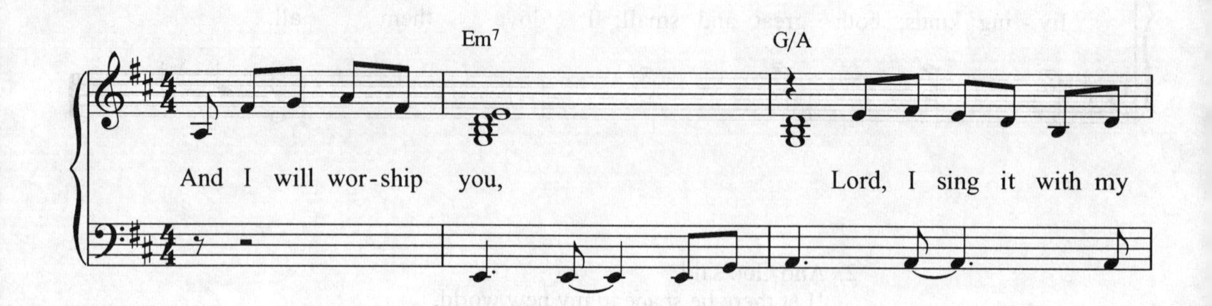
Em7
G/A
And I will wor-ship you,
Lord, I sing it with my

Dmaj7
Em7
heart.
And I will wor-ship you,

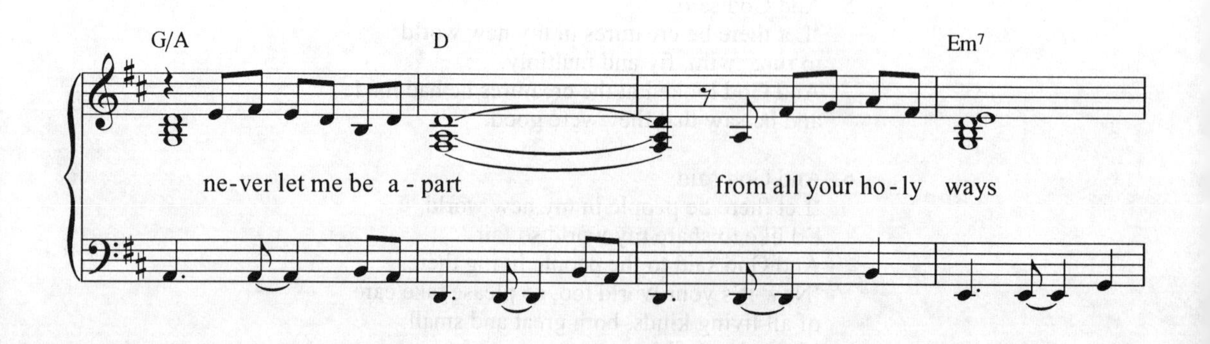
G/A
D
Em7
ne-ver let me be a-part
from all your ho-ly ways

G/A
Bm7
for I know that they are good,
so teach me how to

Em7
G/A
D
stay
close be-side you all the way.
And I will

Gmaj7
G6
F#m7
D/F#
Gmaj7
G6
F#m7
D/F#
love
you,
and I will serve
you,
and I will

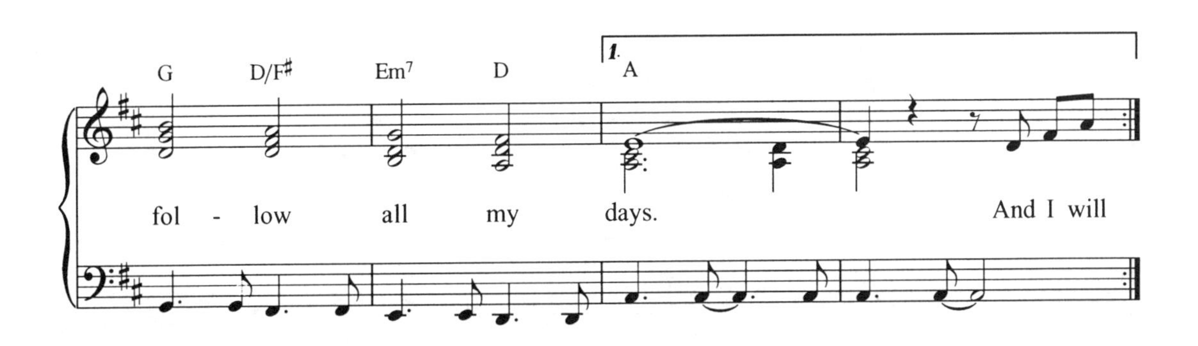
G
D/F#
Em7
D
1.
A
fol - low
all
my
days.
And I will

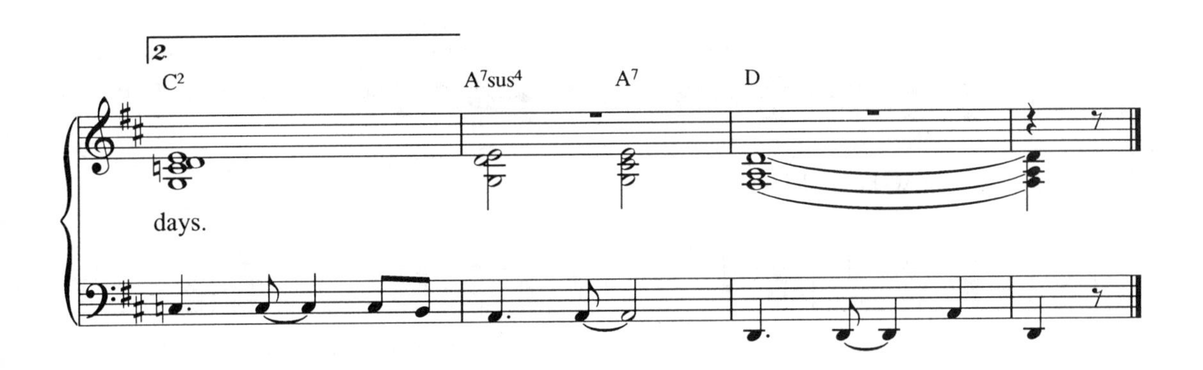
2.
C2
A7sus4
A7
D
days.

406 Angels from the realms of glory

Words: James Montgomery
Music: French or Flemish melody
arr. Richard Lloyd
IRIS 87 87 and Refrain
Capo 3
1. An - gels from the realms of glo - ry, wing your flight o'er all the earth;
ye who sang cre - a - tion's sto - ry now pro - claim Mes - si - ah's birth:
Chorus
Come and wor - ship
Christ, the new-born King; come

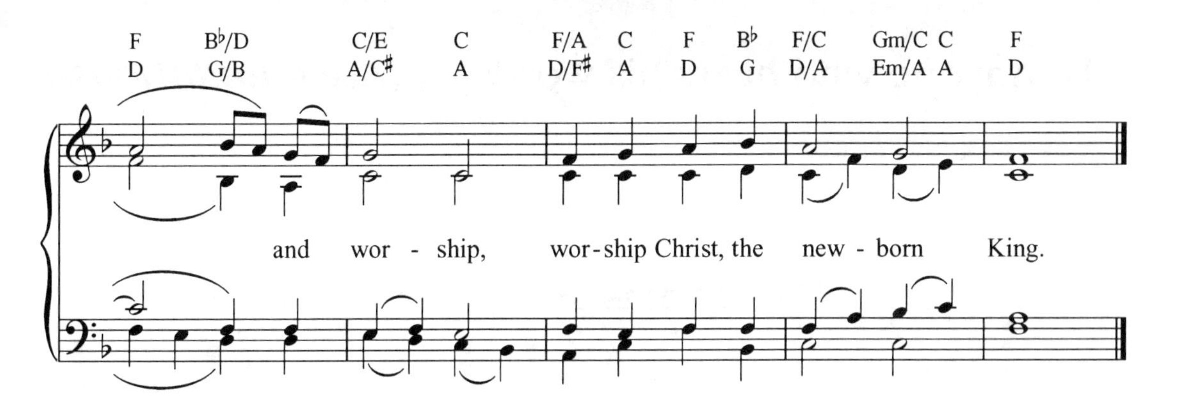
F B♭/D C/E C F/A C F B♭ F/C Gm/C C F
D G/B A/C♯ A D/F♯ A D G D/A Em/A A D
and wor - ship, wor-ship Christ, the new - born King.

2. Shepherds, in the field abiding,
   watching o'er your flocks by night,
   God with us is now residing,
   yonder shines the infant Light:

3. Sages, leave your contemplations;
   brighter visions beam afar;
   seek the great Desire of Nations;
   ye have seen his natal star:

4. Saints before the altar bending,
   watching long in hope and fear,
   suddenly the Lord, descending,
   in his temple shall appear:

5. Though an infant now we view him,
   he shall fill his Father's throne,
   gather all the nations to him;
   ev'ry knee shall then bow down:

407 Anyone who hears his words *(Ace foundations!)*

Words and Music: Dave Godfrey

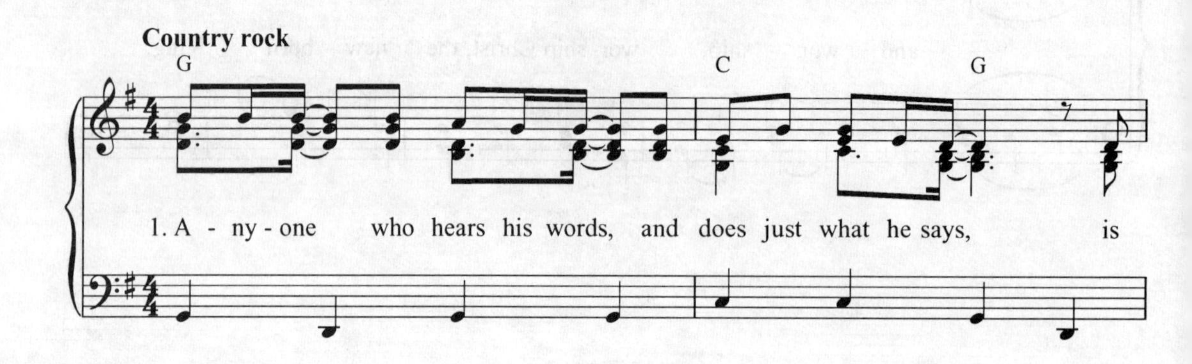
Country rock
G
C
G
1. A - ny - one who hears his words, and does just what he says, is

D
like the man who built up - on the rock. Oh, the

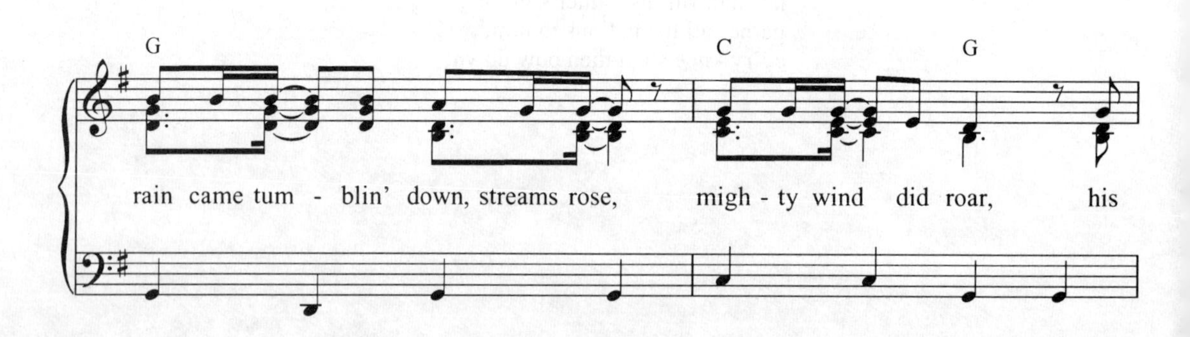
G
C
G
rain came tum - blin' down, streams rose, migh - ty wind did roar, his

D
C
G
Chorus
house stood strong, ace foun - da-tions. Wise man! He's my

C G
ace foun - da-tion, my ace foun - da - tion, I will build my life on
D G C G
him! He's my ace foun - da-tion, my ace foun - da-tion, I will

1. 2.
D C G G
build my life on Je-sus, and what he says to me! says to me!

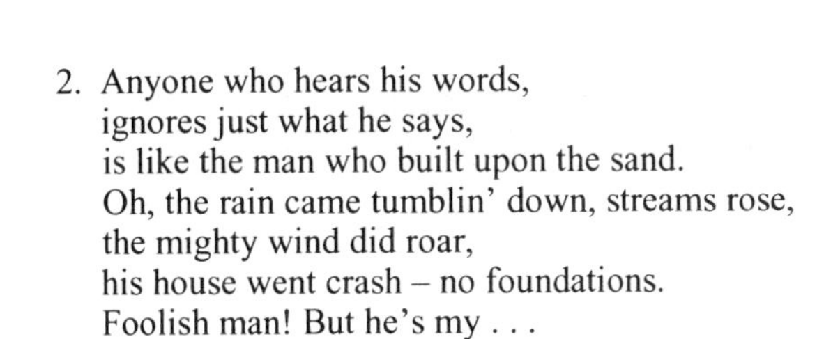

2. Anyone who hears his words,
ignores just what he says,
is like the man who built upon the sand.
Oh, the rain came tumblin' down, streams rose,
the mighty wind did roar,
his house went crash – no foundations.
Foolish man! But he's my . . .

408 Are you wired up *(Wired up)*

Words and Music: Andy Pickford

(♩ = 150)
Chorus
D
G
D
Are you wired up to the pow'r of the Lord? Are you

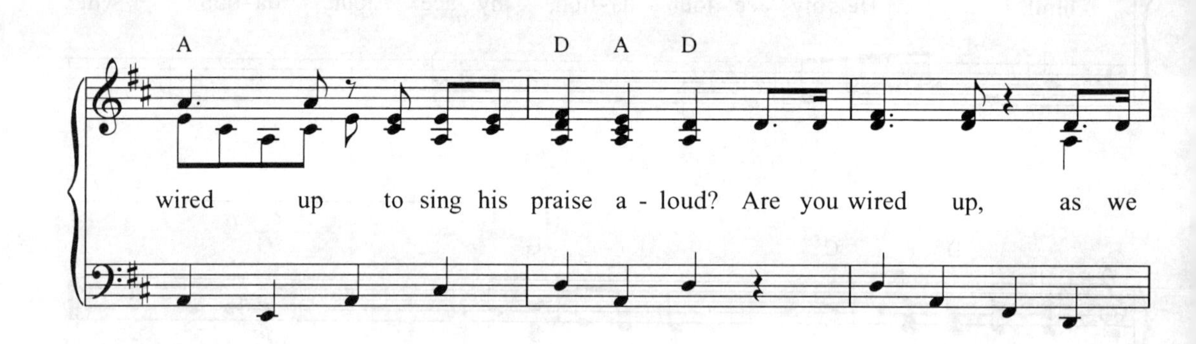

A
D A D
wired up to sing his praise a - loud? Are you wired up, as we

To repeat
To verses / Last time
G D Bm A D D
Fine
sing this song, to our won-der-ful, pow-er-ful God? Are you God?

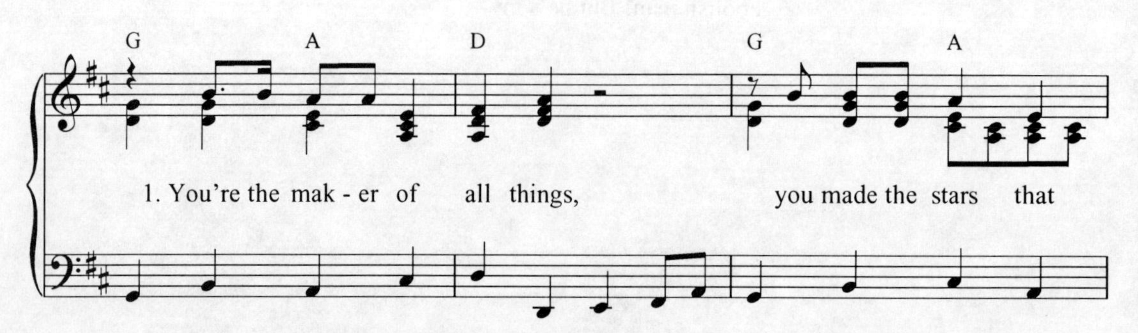

G A D G A
1. You're the mak - er of all things, you made the stars that

D
F♯m
F♯
Bm
shine:
you made the flow - ing ri - vers,

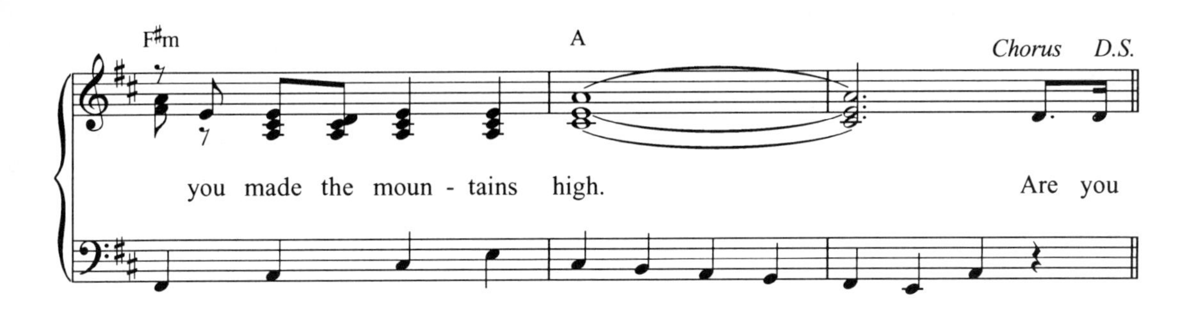
F♯m
A
Chorus D.S.
you made the moun - tains high.
Are you

2. You walked upon the water,
   you made the blind to see,
   you even fed five thousand:
   I know you care for me.

3. You're our Friend and Saviour,
   you're our loving King.
   You're the one who died for us
   and this is why we sing.

409 As I look around me *(Hi diddle de hi hi)*

Words and Music: Ian Smale
arr. Chris Mitchell

D
As I
G
D
look a-round me, this is what I see, boys and girls made as
Em7
A7
D
G
D
God made them to be. I must love them more than I love me. Sing-ing,
3
hi did-dle de hi hi,
A7
ho did-dle de ho ho,
D
G
A
D
hi did-dle de ho, did-dle de hum, did-dle de de.

410 A stranger walked along the shore

(Worship the King)

Words and Music: Roger Jones
arr. Chris Mitchell

E
A
E
1. A stran - ger walked a - long the shore of Ga - li - lee.
A/E
E
A
E
He met two fish - er - men, and then cried 'Fol - low me!'
A/E
E
D
E
They left their nets, and then he
D
E
D
taught them to catch men. They watched him as he died
A
B7sus4
B7
E
Chorus
and rose a - gain! It was the King! Wor - ship the King!

B7 E B7
Wor - ship the King!
E A E
Wor - ship the King who rules o - ver the
B7 E B7 E
world so we sing! Je - sus is King! Je - sus is King!
B7 E A E
Je - sus is King! He rules o - ver my
B7 E
To next verse
Last time
life so I sing!
2. The

2. The stranger walked along the road to Calvary.
They nailed him to a cross of wood
so cruelly.
The women watched and cried,
the blood flowed from his side,
the sun stopped shining as the Saviour died!
It was the King!

3. When Mary came to see the tomb, so early,
the stone was moved, his body gone!
'Where can it be?'
A voice came from behind,
it sounded, oh, so kind,
then suddenly it dawned upon her mind –
it was the King!

411 As we walk *(Sing this song for evermore)*

Words and Music: Andrew Rayner and Wendy Rayner
arr. Chris Mitchell

Swing (♩ = 120)
G G♯dim Am7
1.&3. As we walk the path of life, we know that God is
2. As we go through ev - 'ry day, we know we're not a -
F9 Bm7 Em7
with us, he loves us all the time, God
lone, he loves us all the time, God
A7sus4 A7 Am7/D G
loves us all the time. No mat - ter how we
loves us all the time. No mat - ter if we're
Gaug Cmaj7 C♯dim
look or feel, his love for us is al - ways real, be -
old or young, his love for us goes on and on, be -
G/D D/E E7 A7 C/D G
cause we have this cer - tain - ty we're gon - na sing this song for e - ver - more,

1, 2.
3.
E7
A7
C/D
G
Daug
we're gon-na sing his song for e-ver-more.
G
Gaug
No mat-ter what the world may say we
Cmaj7
C♯dim
G/D
know God's with us all the way; be-cause we have this
D/E
E7
cer-tain-ty we're gon-na sing this song for e-ver-more. We're gon-na
G7(♯9)
sing his song for e-ver-more, sing his song for e-ver-more
C9
G7
(echo)
sing his song for e-ver-more.
(echo)
(echo)

412 Be bold, be strong and sing

Words and Music: Alison Moon

G
D/F♯
Em
G/D
C
D
Be bold, be strong and sing to Je - sus Christ our King.

G
D/F♯
Em
G/D
Be bold, be strong and sing, for he's

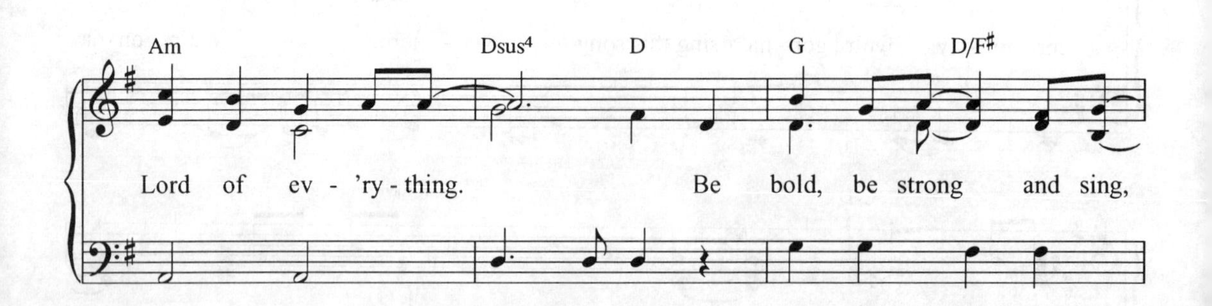

Am
Dsus4
D
G
D/F♯
Lord of ev - 'ry - thing. Be bold, be strong and sing,

Em
G/D
C
D
G
C
D
for he will ne - ver leave us. The Lord is near, we

B7 Em C D7 G
1. 2.
Fine
need not fear, there's pow - er in his name.
G7 C D G
God sent his Son to die that we might
G7 C D G G7
know just how much he cares. He
C D G D/F♯ Em
lives to give us strength and vic - to - ry, to
C Am Am/D D
D.S. al Fine
help us through each day. Be

413 Because I'm special to him

Words and Music: Susie Hare

Gently
Cmaj7
Dm7
Be-cause I'm spe-cial to him, no mat-ter how bad I have been,
G7
Cmaj7
C♯dim5
Je-sus takes all my sin, for-gives me and wash-es me clean.
Dm7
G7
Fmaj7
And he helps me be-come the
F♯dim5
C/G
C♯dim5/A
per-son that he wants to see. I'll
Dm7
G7
C
al-ways love him be-cause he is spe-cial to me.

414 Be first in my heart *(First in my heart)*

Words and Music: Sally-Ann Fatkin
arr. Chris Mitchell

Capo 1
E♭ D
Fm7 Em7
B♭ A
1. Be first in my heart as I seek to fol - low you, be
first in my heart as I choose to hon - our you, be
Cm Bm
Cm7/B♭ Bm7/A
F7/A E7/G♯
B♭sus4 Asus4
B♭ A
Gm7 F♯m7
Cm Bm
there at my side as I trust in you.
pleased with this child as I live for you.
Spi - rit with-in
A♭m Gm
Fm7 Em7
B♭sus4 Asus4
B♭ A
1.
E♭ D
A♭/B♭ G/A
cries 'Lord Je - sus, be first in my heart to - day.'
2. Be
2.
E♭ D
Chorus
Gm7 F♯m7
Cm Bm
Then I will see with your eyes

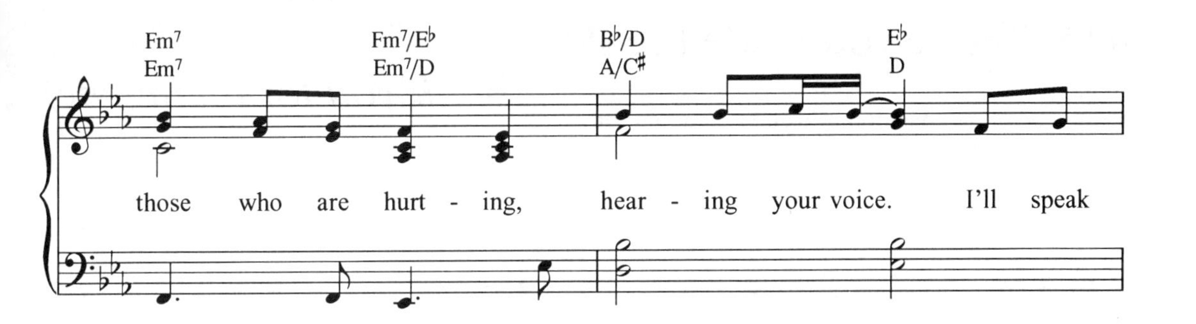

Fm7
Em7
Fm7/E♭
Em7/D
B♭/D
A/C♯
E♭
D
those who are hurt - ing, hear - ing your voice. I'll speak

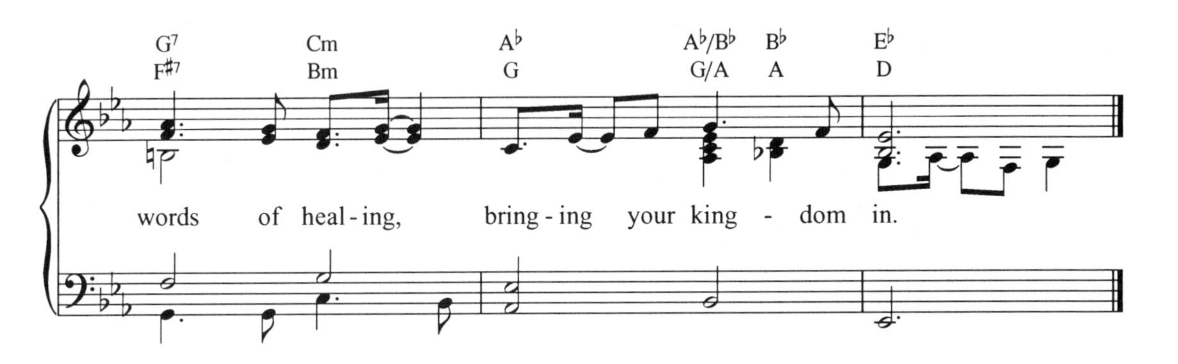

G7
F♯7
Cm
Bm
A♭
G
A♭/B♭
G/A
B♭
A
E♭
D
words of heal - ing, bring - ing your king - dom in.

415 Before you made the skies

(Thank you for loving me)

Words and Music: Mark Johnson and Helen Johnson
arr. Dave Bankhead

(♩ = 128)
E
F♯m7
A6
Bsus4
B
1. Be - fore you made the skies and sea, your
A
Bsus4
B
A/C♯
B/D♯
E
heart was full of love for me. You knew the
F♯m7
A6
G♯7
A
per - son I would be, thank you for
Bsus4
1.
E
A/E
E
2, 3, 4.
E
A/E
E
E7
lov - ing me. 2. You us.
𝄋 Chorus
F♯m7
A/B
E
C♯m
Thank you, Je - sus,

F♯m7
A/B
E
E7
thank you, my Lord.
Last time to Coda
F♯m7
A/B
E
C♯m7
Your love came down from hea - ven, come
F♯m7
B
E
after v. 4, D.S. al Coda
fill up my heart e - ver - more.
(3. Be -)
CODA
F♯m7
B
E
A/E
E
fill up my heart e - ver - more.

2. You came to earth to live like us,
   with words of life and arms of love.
   You showed the way to heav'n above,
   thank you for loving us.

3. Because God loved the world so much
   you paid the price for all of us.
   You gave your life upon a cross,
   thank you for loving us.

4. So thank you, Lord, for loving me
   today and all eternity.
   And may my song forever be,
   thank you for loving me.

416 Be holy

Words and Music: Chris Jackson
arr. Dave Bankhead

G
Em
C
Be ho - ly, be ho - ly, in all that you do;

D
G
Em
be ho - ly, be ho - ly, in

C
D
G
all that you do, just as God is ho -

Em
C
D
- ly, God is ho - ly, be ho -

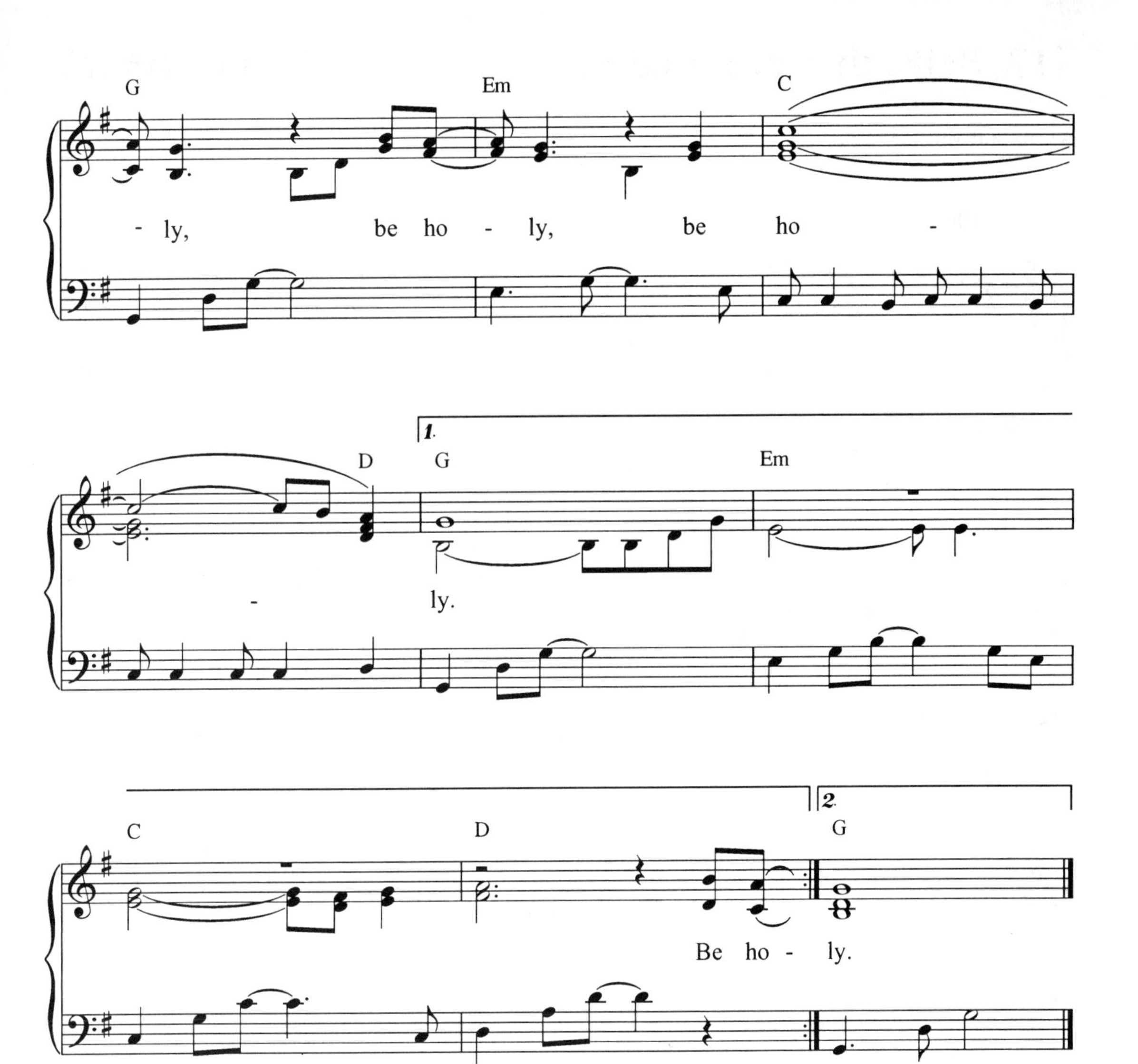
G
Em
C
-ly, be ho - ly, be ho -
D
1.
G
Em
- ly.
C
D
2.
G
Be ho - ly.

417 Bells, they are ringing *(Name over all)*

Words and Music: Jim Bailey

With energy
G
D
Em
Bells, they are ring - ing, child - ren are sing -
C
G
D
- ing, and we are ex - alt - ing the name o - ver
C
G
all. Flags, they are danc -
D
Em
C
- ing, the Church is ad - vanc - ing,
G
D
C
as we are ro - manc - ing the name o - ver all.

Chorus
G
D
Je - sus' king - dom can't be sha - ken, Je - sus'
Em7
C
G
pro - mise can't be bro - ken, Je - sus, Lord of all cre - a -
D
Csus4
C
Csus2
C
- tion, name o - ver all. Je - sus,
G
D
Em7
truth of li - be - ra - tion, Je - sus, light of our sal - va -
C
G
D
- tion, Je - sus, on - ly way to hea - ven, the name o - ver
C
G
all.

418 Best friends

Words and Music: Andy Read
arr. Chris Mitchell

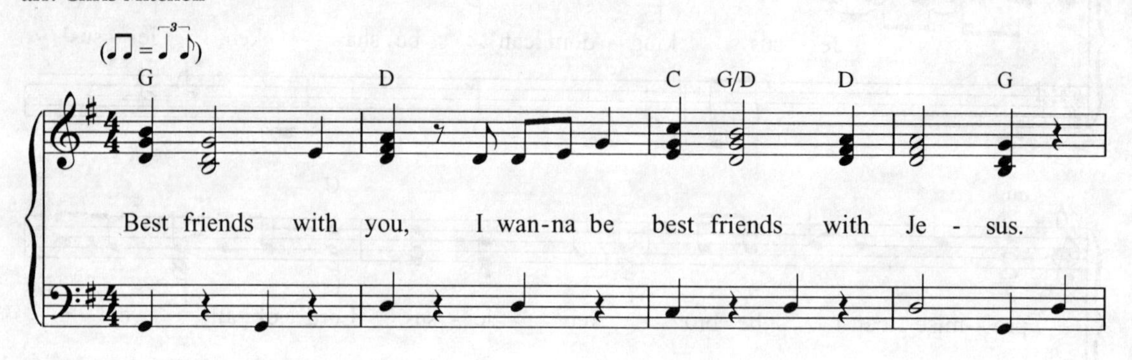
G
D
C
G/D
D
G
Best friends with you, I wan-na be best friends with Je - sus.

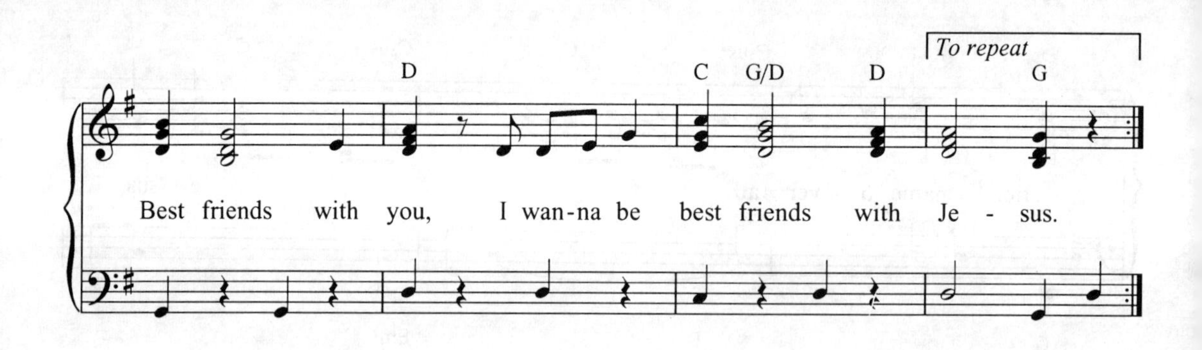
To repeat
D
C
G/D
D
G
Best friends with you, I wan-na be best friends with Je - sus.

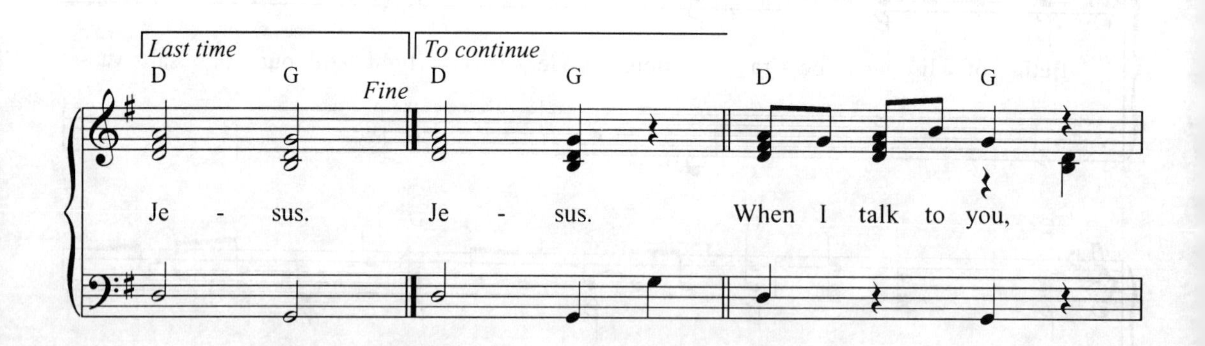
Last time
To continue
D
G
Fine
D
G
D
G
Je - sus. Je - sus. When I talk to you,

D
G
D
G
C
G
D
you can talk to me. When I walk with you, you can walk with me.

G
D
G
D
G
When I smile at you, you can smile at me. When I hold your hand, you can

C
D
D.C.
hold mine too.

419 Be strong and courageous

Words and Music: Chris Jackson

(♩ = 120)
Em
Am
Em
Bm
Em
Be strong and cour-age - ous, do not be ter - ri - fied.

Am
Em
A
B
Be strong and cour-age - ous, for the Lord is by your side.

G
D
Em
B
Do not be dis-cour - aged, do not be a - fraid;

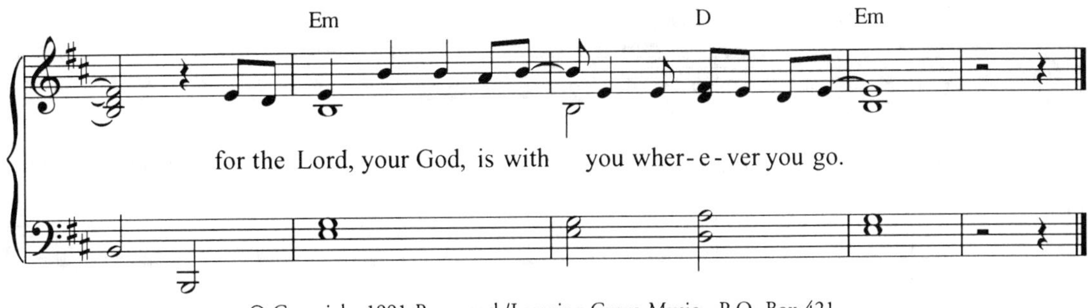
Em
D
Em
for the Lord, your God, is with you wher - e - ver you go.

420 Be strong and put on *(The armour of God)*

Words and Music: Dave Cooke

Strong 4
Capo 3
F
D
C
A
Be strong and put on the ar-mour of God. Be strong and put on the

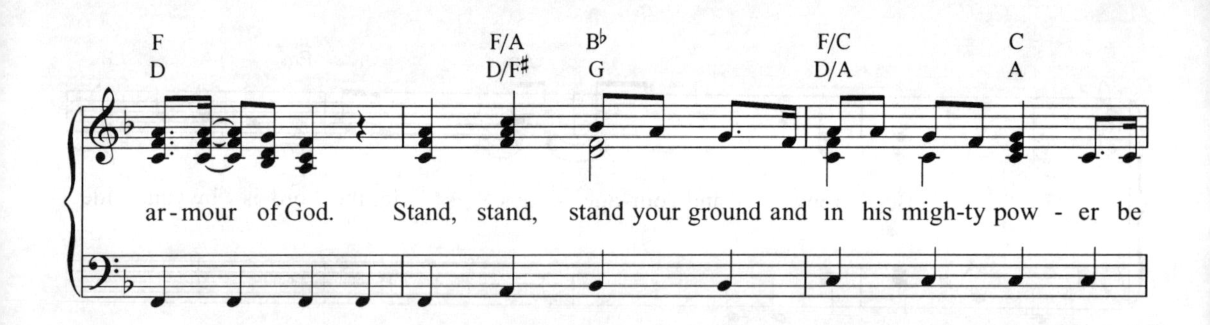
F
D
F/A
D/F♯
B♭
G
F/C
D/A
C
A
ar-mour of God. Stand, stand, stand your ground and in his migh-ty pow - er be

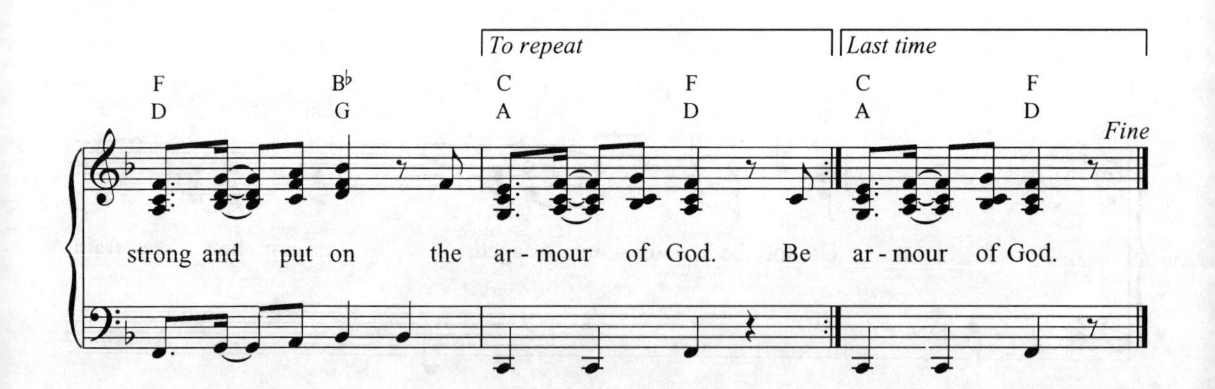
To repeat
Last time
F
D
B♭
G
C
A
F
D
C
A
F
D
Fine
strong and put on the ar-mour of God. Be ar-mour of God.

To continue
C
A
F
D
Fm7
Dm7
E♭/F
C/D
B♭/F
G/D
F
D
ar-mour of God. Put the belt of truth tight-ly round your waist. The

Fm7 Dm7 Eb/F C/D Bb/F G/D F D
breast - plate of right - eous - ness firm - ly in - to place. Pre -
Fm7 Dm7 Eb/F C/D Bb/F G/D Fm7 Dm7
pare your feet for high - ways broad and nar - row. And the
Eb/F C/D Bb/F G/D Fm7 Dm7
shield of faith, to stop those burn - ing ar - rows. And
Bb G C A F D C/E A/C# Dm Bm C A
on your head the hel - met that will save us if we fall. And the
Bb G G/B E/G# F/C D/A C A
D.S.
sword of the Spi - rit so we can stand up tall. Be

421 Be strong in the Lord *(The armour of God)*

Words and Music: Susanna Levell
arr. Dave Bankhead

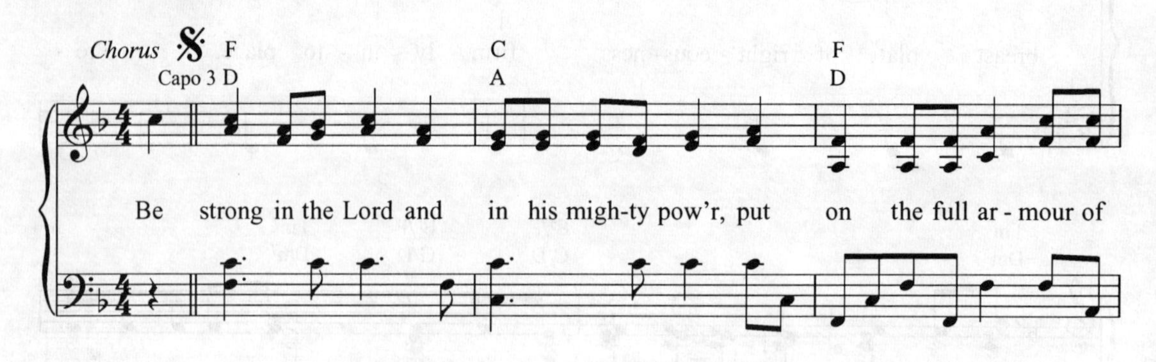
Chorus
Capo 3
F D
C A
F D
Be strong in the Lord and in his migh-ty pow'r, put on the full ar - mour of

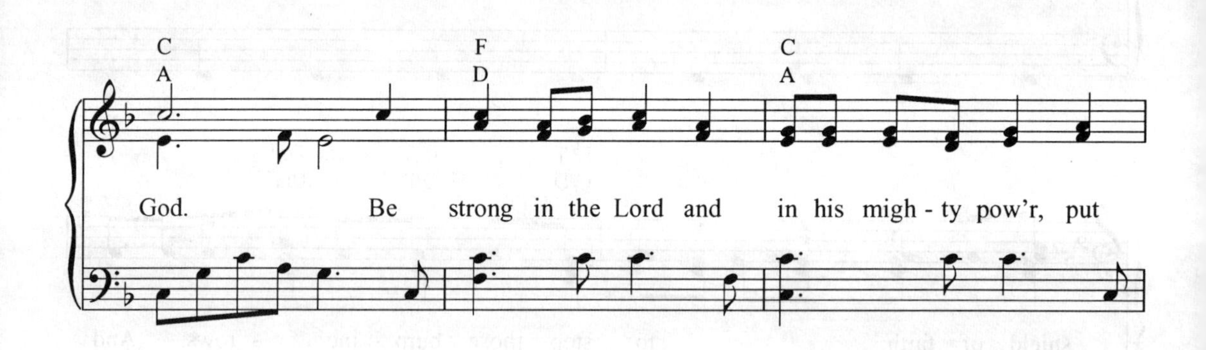
C A
F D
C A
God. Be strong in the Lord and in his migh - ty pow'r, put

Last time
To continue
B♭ G
F/C D/A
C7 A7
F D
Fine
F D
on the full ar - mour of God. God. 1. Put on the

B♭ G
F D
belt of truth that will hold your ar - mour on, know the

C
A
F
D
truth of God and he'll help you to stay strong. Put on the

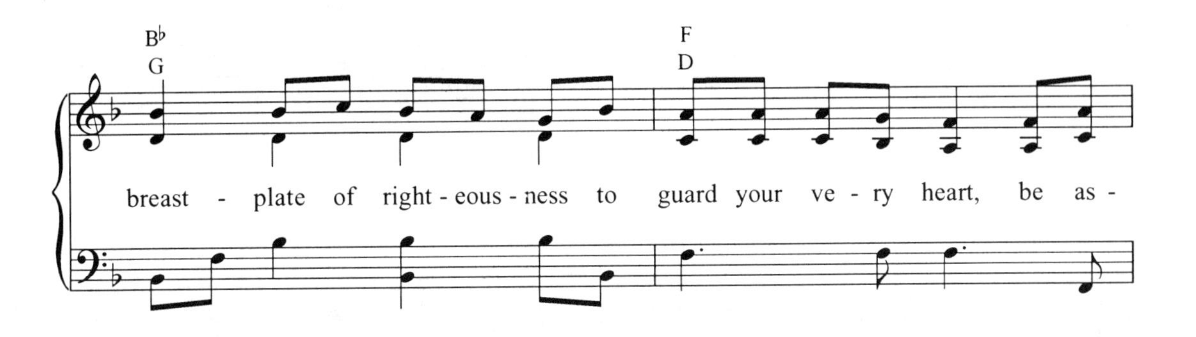
B♭
G
F
D
breast - plate of right - eous - ness to guard your ve - ry heart, be as -

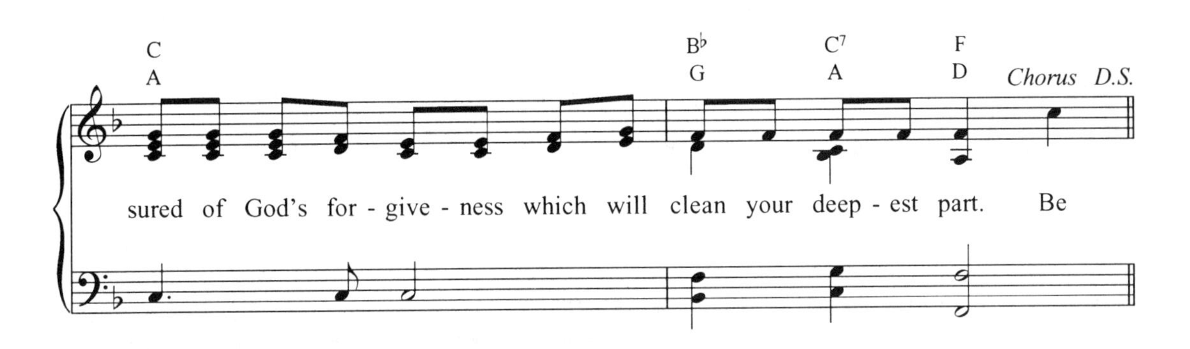
C
A
B♭
G
C7
A
F
D
Chorus D.S.
sured of God's for - give - ness which will clean your deep - est part. Be

2. Have feet of readiness
that will stand firm through the fight,
you don't want to slip and slide,
the peaceful gospel sets you right.
The shield of faith you strongly hold
which will guard you from attack,
so have faith in God alone
and nothing will you lack.

3. Put on the helmet of
salvation to protect
your mind from doubts and fears
and all the things that can infect.
Now use the sword of the Spirit
for attacking in the fight,
for God's word, it makes us strong
in the power of his might.

422 Big man

Words and Music: Graham Kendrick

Joyfully
D Em D Em
1. Big man stand-ing by the blue wa-ter-side,
2. Life was-n't ea-sy for the big fish-er-man,
D Em D G Asus4 A7 D Em
mend-ing nets by the blue sea. A-long came Je-sus, he said:
but still he fol-lowed till his dy-ing day. A-long came Je-sus, he said:
D Em D Em D G Asus4 A7
Chorus
'Si-mon Pe-ter, won't you leave your nets and come fol-low me.' 'You
'Si-mon Pe-ter, there's a place in hea-ven where you can stay.'
D G Em7 A7 G/A
don't need a-ny-thing, I've got ev-'ry-thing, but Pe-ter, it's gon-na be a

D G D
G Em7
hard way. You don't have to wor - ry now, come on and hur - ry now,
A7 G/A
1. D G D
2. D G D
I'll walk be - side you ev - 'ry day.'
day.'
3

423 Birds in the sky *(Not like the animals)*

Words and Music: Steve Burnhope

E
B
1. Birds in the air can flap their wings, fish in the sea can

E
wig - gle their fins. But they have - n't got fin - gers and they

B
E
have - n't got a chin, so they're not like you and me.

B
2. Li - ons have a migh - ty roar, e - le - phants are big - ger than

E
B
gar-age doors. But they can't just hop on one leg, that's for sure, so they're
E
Chorus
A
E
not like you and me. I'm not like the a-ni-mals, no, no, no,
B
E
A
I've got a bo-dy and a spi-rit and a soul. God made me to be
1.
2.
E
B
E
E
Fine
dif-f'rent. So I'm made in the i-mage of God.
E
B
3. Griz-zl-y bears can scratch their fleas, chim-pan-zees can

E
B
tic-kle their knees. But they can't count up to ten quick-ly
E
like you and me. 4. Cen-ti-pedes have got a
B
hun-dred feet, buy-ing new shoes is a
E
ve-ry big treat. But they're no good at bounc-ing up and
B
E
D.S. al Fine
Chorus
down to the beat. So they're not like you and me. I'm

424 Blessed are the poor in spirit *(Blessed!)*

Words and Music: Dave Godfrey

Medium rock feel
D G D A
1. Bles-sed are the poor in spi - rit: theirs, theirs is the
D G/D D
king - dom. Bles-sed are those who mourn: for
G A D G
God will com - fort them! Bles-sed are the hum - ble
A Bm A G
peo - ple: for they will in - he - rit the earth.
D G/D D G A
Bles-sed are those who hun - ger, thirst for the right - eous -

D A D
Chorus
ness, they will be filled. For
G D A D G D
these are the words that I heard him say, sat on a hill, he
Em A G A D
taught that day of bles - sings that his king - dom brings, when
Em D/F♯ G/A A D G/D
lives re - flect the glo - ry of the King!
(over to verse 2)
Last time
D A/D D G/D D A/D D
Fine

D G D A
2. Bles-sed are the mer - ci - ful: for they will be shown
D G/D D
mer - cy. Bles-sed are the pure in heart: for
G A D G
they will see our God. Bles-sed are the peace - mak -
A Bm A G
ers: for they will be his child-ren.
D G/D D G A
Bles-sed are the per - se - cu - ted, due to right-eous -
D A D
Chorus D.S.
ness, theirs is the king - dom! For

425 Bless the Lord

Words and Music: Andy Read
arr. Chris Mitchell

G
D
Em7
Bm7
Bless the Lord, O my soul, and all that

C2
G/B
C
D
is with-in me, bless his ho - ly name.

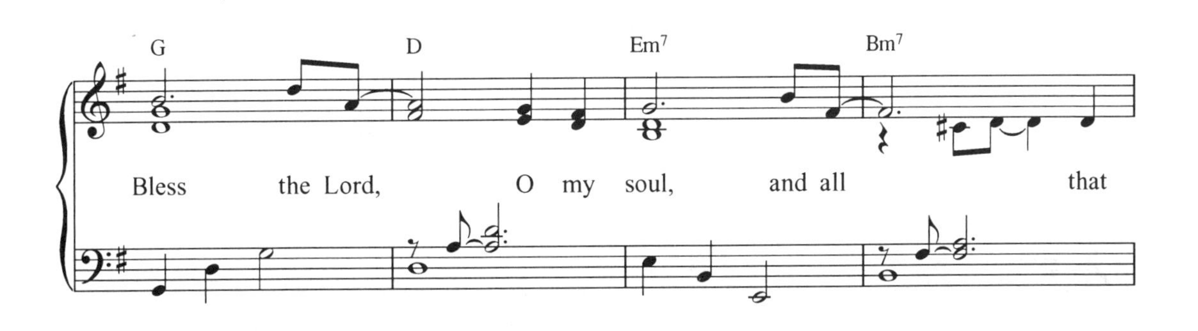
G
D
Em7
Bm7
Bless the Lord, O my soul, and all that

C2
G
C2
Dsus4
D
G
is with-in me, bless his ho - ly name.

426 Brick by brick

Words and Music: Steve Morgan-Gurr
arr. Chris Mitchell

Chorus
F C F C F C/E D7 G
Brick by brick, day by day, I will build my life this way.
F C F C F G C
Fine
When I read, when I pray, God will help me build.
F/A C F/A C Dm7 C G
1. In the Bi - ble I can see just how God wants me to be.
C F/A C F Dm7 G C
Lots of peo - ple just like me, God helped them to build.

2. How can I learn how to pray,
when I don't know what to say.
Holy Spirit, ev'ry day,
please help me to build.

427 Bring in the harvest

Words and Music: Pamela Dew
arr. Chris Mitchell

F/C
Capo 3 D/A
C7
A7
F
D
C7/G
A7/E
Bring in the har-vest, share out the har-vest,
F/A
D/F♯
F7/A
D7/F♯
B♭
G
A7
F7
Dm
Bm
God has been good to us all. There's plen-ty to eat for you and me
G7
E7
Gm7/C
Em7/A
and all the peo-ple o-ver the sea. Pick all the ap-ples, cut all the wheat down,
F7/A
D7/F♯
F/C
D/A
catch some fish from the sea. God has been good,
G7
E7
God has been good, God has been good to me.

428 Building, building

Words and Music: Capt. Alan J. Price, CA
arr. Philip Eley

Rocky (♩ = 128)
N.C.
D
G
D/F♯
G
D
G
Build - ing, build - ing, ev - 'ry - bo - dy's build - ing: like a build - ing, life
D/F♯
G
D
G
D/F♯
G
is what we're build - ing. Build - ing, build - ing, ev - 'ry - bo - dy's build - ing ev - 'ry
1, 3, 5.
2, 4, 6.
A
A
day.
day, in dif - f'rent
G
Last time to Coda
D
ways, hey, hey, hey.
When we

A
G
know what God has said, and we do just what we've read, it's like a
D
A
plan. (Like a plan.)
And if we get it wrong, then it
G
D
just won't be as strong as in the plan. (Oh man!)
Dif - fi -
G
E
cul - ties lie a - head, we don't wor - ry, but in - stead trust in God's
A
D.S.
CODA
D
plan. (Jesus – God's man!)
hey.

A
G
Ev - 'ry day, in dif - f'rent ways, hey, hey, hey.
D
A
Ev - 'ry day, come what
G
D
may, hey, hey, hey.

429 Call his name *(Mary woke with a start one night)*

Words and Music: Phil Overton
arr. Chris Mitchell

Chorus
G C Am7
Call his name, Je - sus, call his name, Sa-viour. He shall
D7 G D7
save his peo - ple from their sins. Call his
C Am7
name, Em-man - u - el, he came with us to dwell. He'll
D7
save his peo - ple from their sins.
Last time
G
Fine
To continue
G
sins.
1. Ma - ry woke with a
2. Ma - ry cried, 'How
3. Now when Jo - seph

C
Am7
start one night. A light was shi - ning bright. An
can it be? I'm on - ly a bride - to - be!' The
heard the news, he real - ly got the blues. He
D7
G
an - gel was stand - ing at her side
an - gel said, 'Lis - ten, I'll ex - plain.
thought that Ma - ry had been un - true
D7
G
and he said, 'Ma - ry, God's time has come and
God's Ho - ly Spi - rit will co - ver you. His
and he said, 'Right, I'm through with her' but
C
Am7
1, 2.
D7
you shall have a son and he will be the
pow'r will o - ver - sha - dow you. Your son will have a
God said, 'Lis - ten, sir, there's
G
Chorus
D.S.
Sa - viour of man - kind.' Call his
ve - ry spe - cial name.'

3.
D7
G
some - thing I'd like to say to you.' He said 'Now
Em
Am
Ma - ry has found fa - vour in my sight. She
D7
G
has - n't been un - true, it's quite al - right for she's
Em
A
not the un - faith - ful kind of girl and her
Am7
rit.
D7sus4
D7
D.S.
son will be the Sa - viour of the world.' Call his

430 C for the Christ Child

(Sing a song about Christmas)

Words and Music: Dave Cooke

Rocky blues
Eomit3
C for the Christ Child born in a shed.
A7
H is for He - rod who killed the boys dead.
Eomit3
R for Ro - mans who ruled the land.
B
I for Im - man - u - el, God's at hand.
Eomit3
S for shep - herds who were scared a - round ten.

A7
T for the trea - sures of the three wise men.
E
M for Ma - ry who gave birth to Je - sus.
B
A for the an - gels who sang his prai - ses.
E E7/G♯
S for the star that showed the way. It's a
A7 B7 E B
song a - bout Christ-mas we sing to-day. Sing a song a - bout
C♯m A E B A B E
Christ - mas, sing a song a-bout Christ - mas time.

431 Chicken pox and measles *(Doctor Jesus)*

Words and Music: Christine Dalton
arr. Chris Mitchell

E

1. Chick - en pox and mea - sles, mumps and flu.
2.&3. 'Doc - tor, Doc - tor Je - sus, please come quick.

My tum-my's ach - ing and I feel blue. The Bi - ble tells us
My tum-my's ach - ing and I feel sick. I know prayer can

A B *Last time to Coda* 1. E

what to do: call on Doc - tor Je - sus. 2. Say
do the trick; thank you, Doc - tor Je -

2. E A

- sus.' Well, if you're feel - ing kind - a fun - ny and your

E

nose is ve - ry run - ny, your chick - en pox are scrat - chy and your

A
face is red and pat - chy. Your mumps are big and bum - py and you're
feel - ing kind - a grum - py, here's what you should do.
F♯
B
1.
D.C. (repeat v. 1)
2.
D.C.
3. Say
CODA
E
- sus.
B
Thank you, Doc - tor Je - sus.
E
B
Thank you, Doc - tor Je - sus.
E

432 Christmas bells that bring *(Heaven's gift of love)*

Words and Music: James Wright
arr. Chris Mitchell

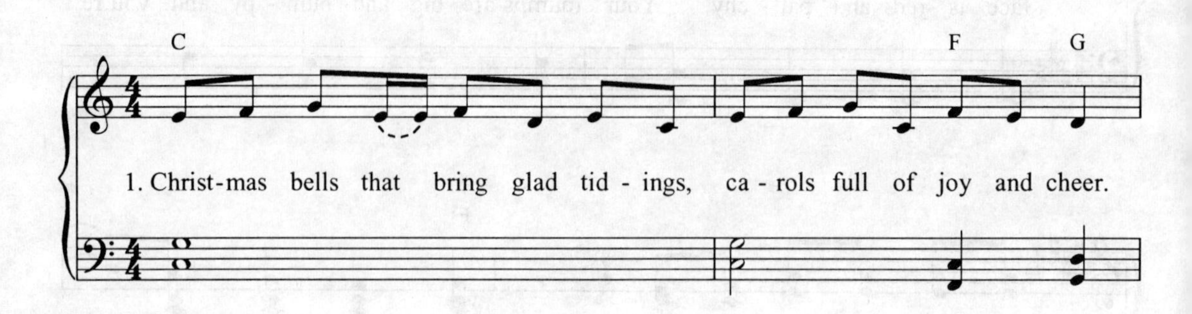
C
F
G
1. Christ-mas bells that bring glad tid - ings, ca - rols full of joy and cheer.

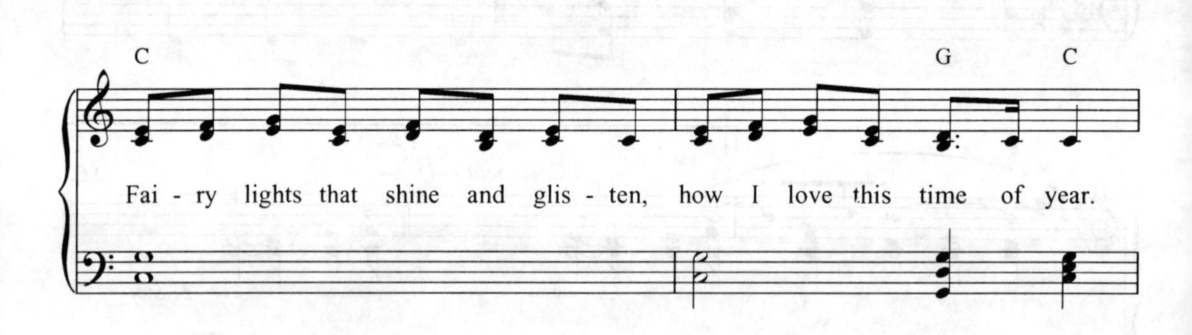
C
G
C
Fai - ry lights that shine and glis - ten, how I love this time of year.

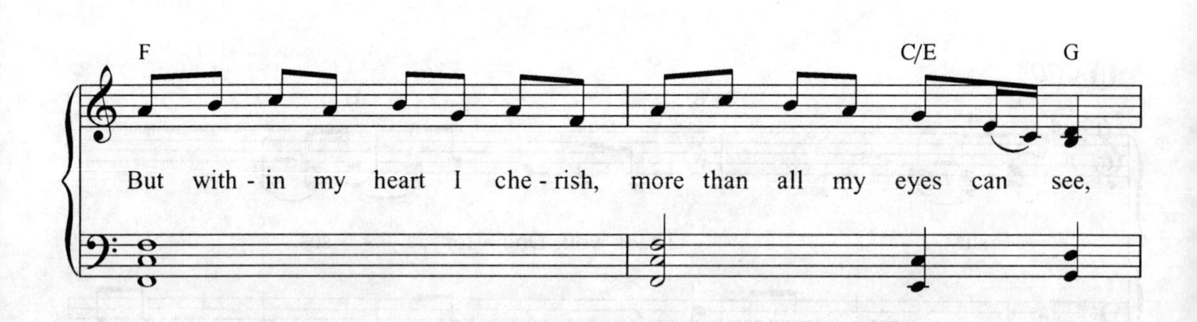
F
C/E
G
But with - in my heart I che - rish, more than all my eyes can see,

C
G7sus4
G
C
one small child laid in a man - ger, hea - ven's gift of love to me.

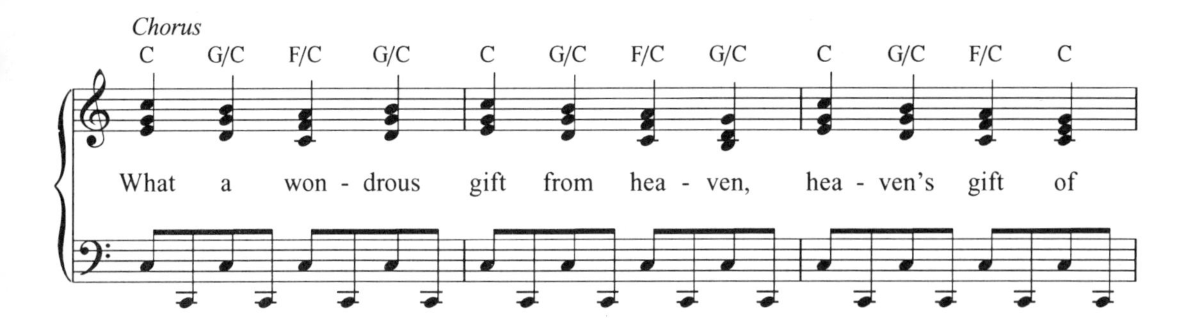
Chorus
C G/C F/C G/C C G/C F/C G/C C G/C F/C C
What a won - drous gift from hea - ven, hea - ven's gift of

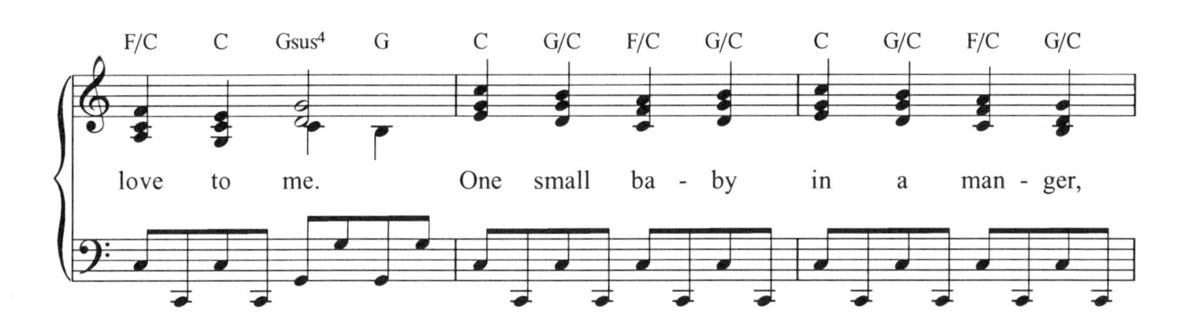
F/C C Gsus4 G C G/C F/C G/C C G/C F/C G/C
love to me. One small ba - by in a man - ger,

C G/C F/C G/C F Gsus4 G C
hea - ven's gift of love to me.

2. Christmas carols and decorations,
choc'lates on the Christmas tree.
Giving gifts to one another,
meeting friends and family.
But within my heart I cherish,
more than all my eyes can see,
one small child laid in a manger,
heaven's gift of love to me.

433 Colours of day *(Light up the fire)*

Words and Music: Sue McClellan, John Paculabo and Keith Ryecroft

Flowing
D G D A7
1. Col-ours of day dawn in - to the mind, the sun has come up, the
D G D
night is be - hind. Go down in the ci - ty, in - to the street, and let's give the
A7 D Chorus G
mes-sage to the peo-ple we meet. So light up the fire and let the flame
D A7 D
burn, o - pen the door, let Je - sus re - turn. Take seeds of his
G D A7 D
Spi - rit, let the fruit grow, tell the peo-ple of Je - sus, let his love show.

2. Go through the park, on into the town;
the sun still shines on; it never goes down.
The light of the world is risen again;
the people of darkness are needing a friend.

3. Open your eyes, look into the sky,
the darkness has come, the sun came to die.
The evening draws on, the sun disappears,
but Jesus is living, his Spirit is near.

434 Come and join in the party

Words and Music: Paul Field

(♩. = 82)
Chorus
G
C
D
Come and join in the par - ty on the king - dom's shore.

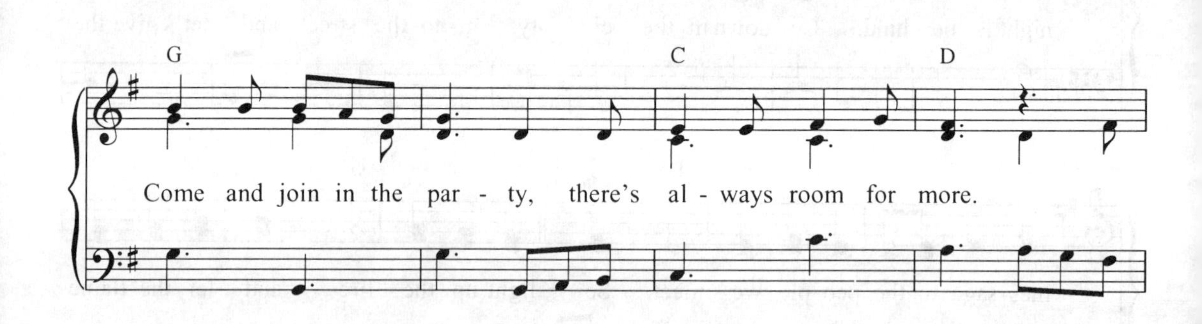
G
C
D
Come and join in the par - ty, there's al - ways room for more.

Em
D
Em
D
G
Ev - 'ry - bo - dy's in - vi - ted to find the love that's true. So

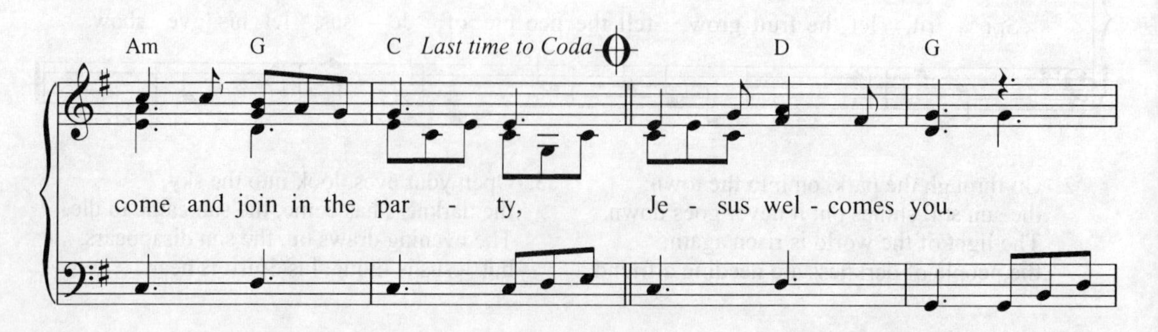
Am
G
C
Last time to Coda
D
G
come and join in the par - ty, Je - sus wel - comes you.

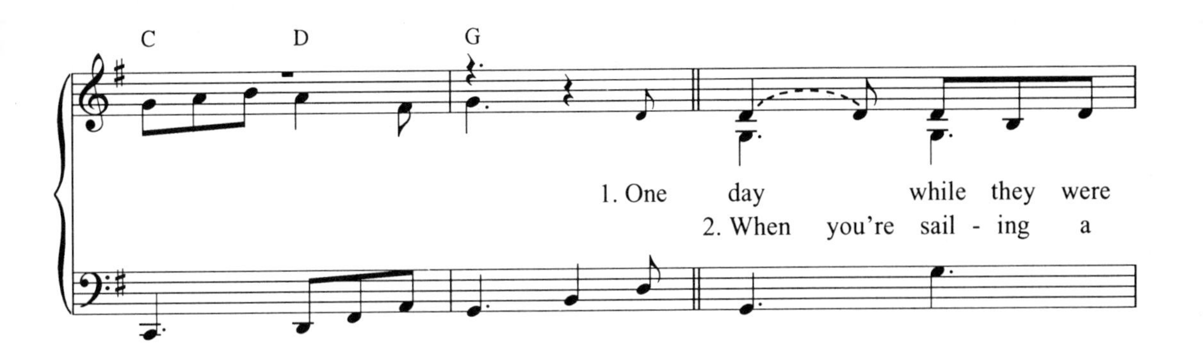
C D G
1. One day while they were
2. When you're sail - ing a
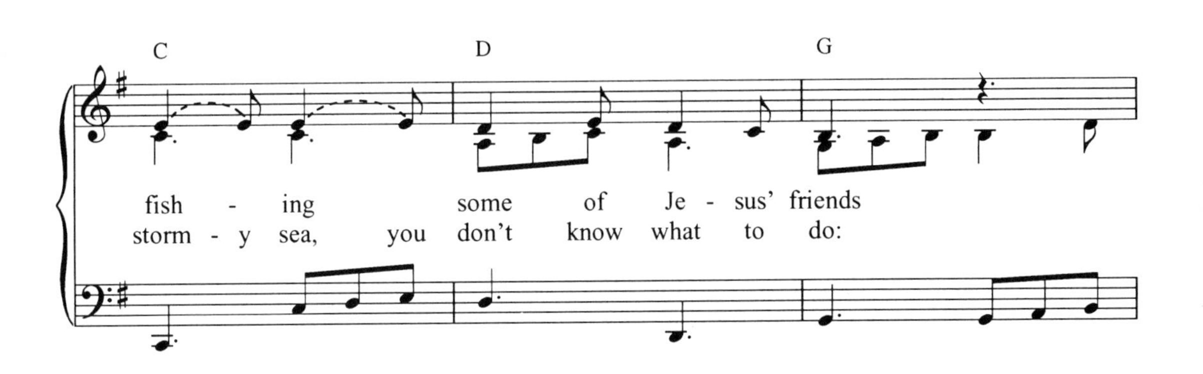
C D G
fish - ing some of Je - sus' friends
storm - y sea, you don't know what to do:
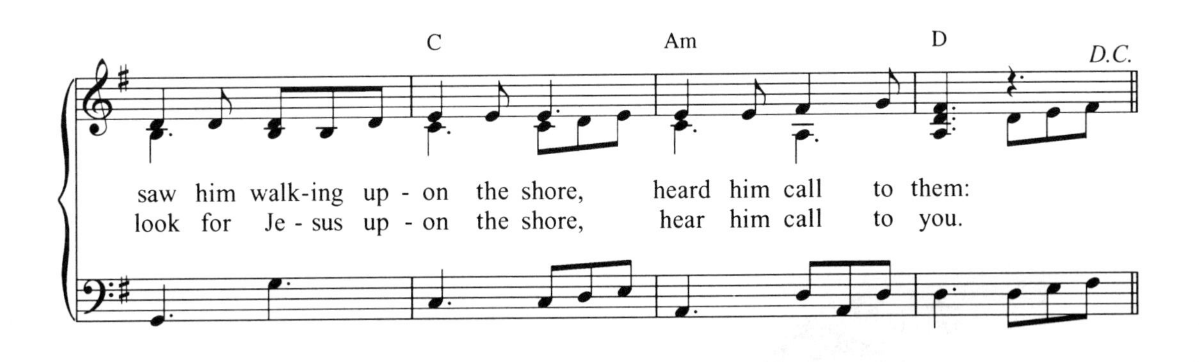
C Am D
D.C.
saw him walk-ing up - on the shore, heard him call to them:
look for Je - sus up - on the shore, hear him call to you.

CODA
C D G C D G
Je - sus wel - comes you, Je - sus wel - comes you.

435 Come, let's bow down

Words and Music: Pete Norman
arr. Chris Mitchell

D
Bm7
Come, let's bow down and wor - ship him, let's kneel
Em7
D/F#
A7sus4
D
be-fore the Lord. For he is our God, who made
Bm7
Em7
D/F#
us, we are the peo - ple un - der his care.
A7sus4
A/G
D/F#
G
And we cry, 'Ho - ly,
D/A
A7sus4
A
Em7
A7sus4
D
ho - ly, ho - ly is the Lord.'

436 Come, now is the time to worship

Words and Music: Brian Doerksen

D
Em7/D
Come, now is the time to wor - ship.
D
A
Come, now is the time to give
Em7
D/E
G
D
your heart. Come,
Em7/D
D
just as you are to wor - ship.

A
Em7
D/E
Come, just as you are be-fore your
Last time
To continue
G
D
God, come.
G
D
G
One day ev-'ry tongue will con-fess you are God, one day ev-'ry knee will bow.
D
G
Bm
Still, the great-est trea-sure re-mains for those who glad-
Em7
1.
A
2.
A
D.C.
-ly choose you now.

437 Come on and shine *(Shine out for Jesus)*

Words and Music: Dave MacGregor
arr. Chris Mitchell

(♩ = 100)
D Bm Em7 A D Bm
Em7 A D Bm
Come on and shine, shine, shine (oh, we can
G A D Bm
shine), shine out for Je - sus. Love, love, love (oh, we can
G A D Bm
love) the way he did. Live, live, live (oh, we can
G A G D A D
live), live like him al - ways. Shine out for Je - sus, live and love like him.

438 Come on, let's celebrate

Words and Music: John Hardwick

(♩ = 150)
G
Come on, let's ce - le - brate be - cause our God is great. He is

C7
G
wor - thy of our praise. Come on, let's ce - le - brate be - cause our

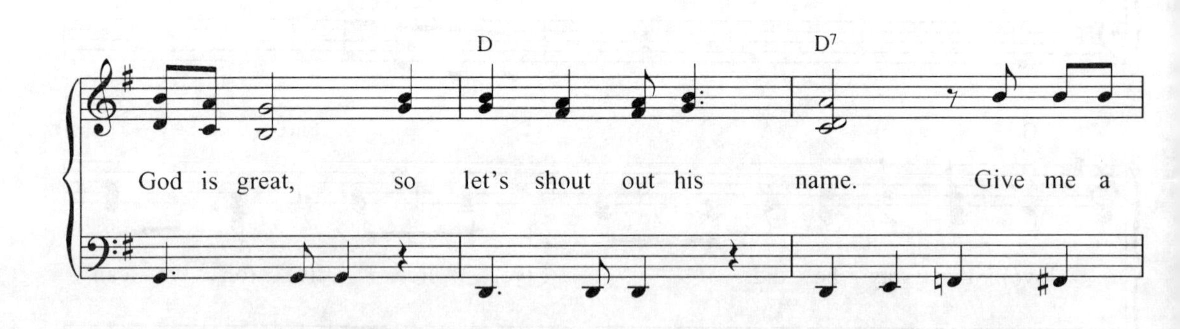

D
D7
God is great, so let's shout out his name. Give me a

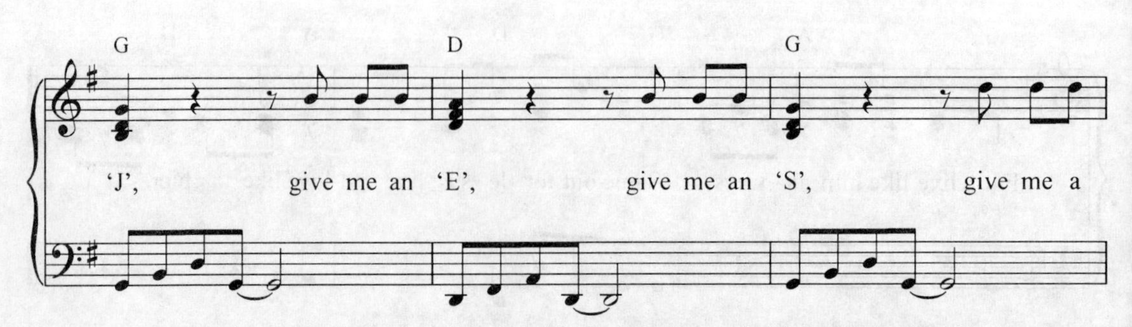

G
D
G
'J', give me an 'E', give me an 'S', give me a

C G D G
'U', give me an 'S'. Who is great? J E S U S.
Fine
D C/D G/D D
D.S.
That's who it is, Je - sus. Come on, let's

439 Come on, let's go exploring

Words and Music: Bev Gammon

With energy
Chorus G
C
Come on, let's go ex - plor - ing, let's find the truth in the Bi-ble,

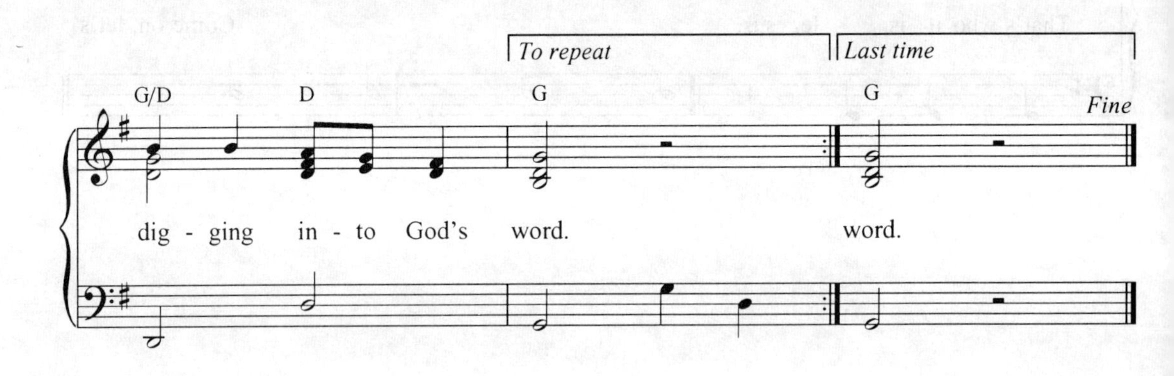
To repeat
Last time
G/D
D
G
G
Fine
dig - ging in - to God's word.
word.

To verses
G
C
word. 1. Is it on - ly for grown ups? No! No! No! Is it

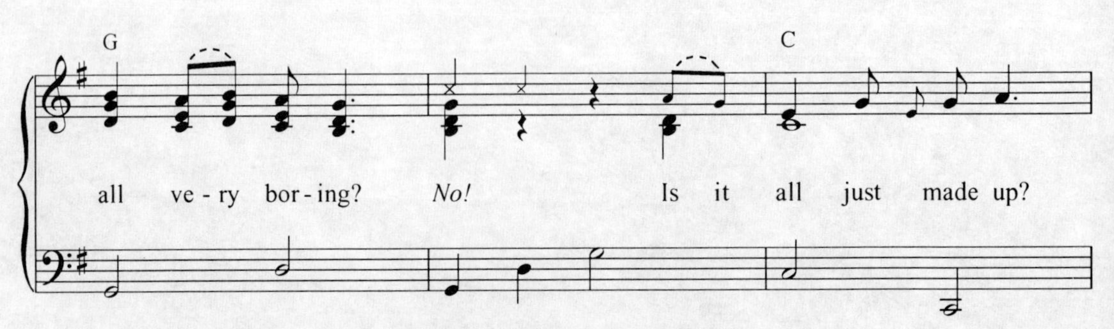
G
C
all ve - ry bor - ing? No! Is it all just made up?

D
D Am7 D
D.C.
No! No! No! Is it just fai - ry sto - ries? No!

2. Is it all about Jesus? *Yes! Yes! Yes!*
   He's our friend Jesus. *Yes!*
   Jesus who loves us. *Yes! Yes! Yes!*
   Jesus who saves us. *Yes!*

3. He's there when you're lonely. *Praise the Lord!*
   He's there when you're happy. *Praise him!*
   He's there in the night-time. *Praise the Lord!*
   He's there in the daytime. *Praise him!*

440 Come on, let's raise our voice

(Under heaven above)

Words and Music: Mark G. Rowe
arr. Chris Mitchell

A
1. Come on, let's raise our voice, let's make an awe-some noise be-cause
dance and shout be-cause the truth is out, that
D
E
A
God is in our land. Come on, let's tell the world in case they
God is in our land. Come on, let's serve our King, let's keep on
D
1.
E
have-n't heard through Je-sus we can stand. 2. Come on, let's
lis-ten-ing; we wait for his com-mand.
2.
E
Choruses
D
1. Be-fore the throne of God, be-cause he
2. For our sin is e-rased from his
E
A
E
shed his blood he's joined our hearts to-ge-ther by the
me-mo-ry, down-load-ed grace and fav-our to hu-

E/G♯
F♯m
D
E
pow'r of his love.
ma - ni - ty.
A mul - ti - col - oured peo - ple, one na -
F♯m
B7
- tion un - der hea - ven a - bove.
A
D
E
A
1.
mul - ti - col - oured peo - ple, one na - tion un - der hea - ven a - bove.
F♯m
D
E
D.S.
1. Come on, let's
2.

Repeat 3 times
D E F♯m
Je - sus Christ is Lord.
D E F♯m
Je - sus Christ is Lord.
D E F♯m
Je - sus Christ is Lord.
D E F♯m B7
Christ is Lord and King o - ver e - ve - ry land.
D E
Christ is Lord and King o - ver e - ve - ry land.
A/C♯ Cdim7 Bm7 A A♭7 A7

441 Countdown for the King

Words and Music: Andrew Rayner and Wendy Rayner
arr. Chris Mitchell

Chorus
G
A7/G
Cm6/G
Count-down for the King. Count-down for the King. The
time has come for ev - 'ry - one, for all the world to sing.
Count-down for the King. Count-down for the King.
Ev - 'ry-one a - cross the world lift your voice and sing.
To repeat
Last time
Fine
To verses
Em7
A7
C/D
1. Two thou-sand years a - go God came to earth as man,
2. Now we com - mem - o - rate a pin - na - cle of time,

G D/F♯ Em7 A7 C/D
bring - ing a hope for life and all that is to come.
then we will ce - le - brate when Christ re - turns a - gain.
1st time D.C.
Cmaj7 Cm6
No more death or mourn - ing, no more
Bm7 Em7 A7
cry - ing or pain; all old things will pass a - way.
Am7/D Cmaj7 Cm6
Ev - 'ry eye shall see him and
Bm7 Em7 A7
ev - 'ry knee shall bow. Praise and hon - our, glo - ry and
3
G/D A7/D D.C.
pow - er for e - ver.

442 Daniel knelt to say his prayers *(Why worry?)*

Words and Music: Godfrey Rust
arr. Chris Mitchell

Capo 3 A

C F C F B♭ Gm C F
A D A D G Em A D

1. Dan - iel knelt to say his prayers three times ev - 'ry day.

F D7 Gm C
D B7 Em A

Jea - lous men, they passed a law, they said,

B♭ Gm7 C7 F C F
G Em7 A7 D A D

'Dan-iel, you can't pray.' The king said, 'Dan-iel,

C F B♭ Gm B♭ C
A D G Em G A

lis-ten here, I will not be de-fied. You'll

F D7 Gm C B♭ Gm7 C7
D B7 Em A G Em7 A7

have to go in that li-ons' den.' But Dan-iel, he re-plied,

F
D
C♯dim
A♯dim
Dm
Bm
C/E
A/C♯
F
D
'Why wor - ry, God's in charge, the
B♭
G
F/A
D/F♯
Gm
Em
C
A
F
D
D7
B7
Lord of the land and sea. I'm not a - fraid of your
Gm
Em
C
A
B♭
G
Gm7
Em7
F
D
li - ons' teeth 'cos he'll take care of me.'

2. The Lord said, 'Noah, build a boat in the middle of dry land.
Make it big enough to hold a zoo and wait for my command.'
The people, they all laughed at him, 'Old Noah's lost his head,
he's building boats for pigs and goats!'
But Noah, he just said,
'Why worry, God's in charge, the Lord of the land and sea.
Wasn't that a drop of rain? Well, he'll take care of me.'

3. Goliath stood there eight feet tall, what could the people do?
The Lord said, 'David, bring your sling, I've got a job for you.'
Now when he saw that little boy, Goliath, he went wild.
He laughed till he was fit to burst, but David, he just smiled (and said)
'Why worry, God's in charge, the Lord of the land and sea.
I'll only need one little stone, 'cos he'll take care of me.'

4. Well, Daniel found the lions tame and Noah, he stayed dry.
Goliath crashed down to the ground, you know the reason why.
And God says 'Listen, I don't change, I'm still the same today.
No matter what you have to face, I want to hear you say:
'Why worry, God's in charge, the Lord of the land and sea.
I put my trust in the one who saves, and he'll take care of me.''

443 Daniel, Shadrach, Meshach, Abednego

Words and Music: Fred Chedgey
arr. Chris Mitchell

A E A E
Dan - iel, (claps) Shad - rach, (claps) Me - shach, A - bed - ne - go.
B A E A E
Dan - iel, (claps) Shad - rach, (claps)
B A B
Me - shach, A - bed - ne - go. The king said, 'Wor - ship
E C♯m A B E
on - ly me or die for your un - be - lief.' But the
A B E C♯m F♯m E
peo - ple saw God save all four from the fire and the li - ons'

B
A E A E
teeth. Dan - iel, (claps) Shad - rach, (claps)
B A B
Me - shach, A - bed - ne - go. They trust - ed in their
E C♯m F♯m A/B E
Fa - ther God and want - ed all the world to know.

444 Declare it

Words and Music: John Hardwick
arr. Chris Mitchell

Capo 3
F D Bb G C A F D
De-clare it in the north, de-clare it in the south, Je - sus Christ is Lord. De-clare
G7 E7 C A
it in the east, de-clare it in the west, Je - sus Christ is Lord. He's the
F D F7 D7 Bb G Bdim G#dim
Man of the Mil - len - ni - um; from ge - ne - ra - tion to ge - ne - ra - tion.
F/C D/A A/C# F#/A# Dm Bm Bb G C A F D
Let's de-clare it a - cross the na - tion! Je - sus Christ is Lord.

Last time
To continue
B♭ C F
G A D
Fine
B♭ C F
G A D
Je - sus Christ is Lord.
Je - sus Christ is Lord. He
C7
A7
B♭7
G7
F
D
ne - ver wrote a book or song or ap - peared on T V, yet
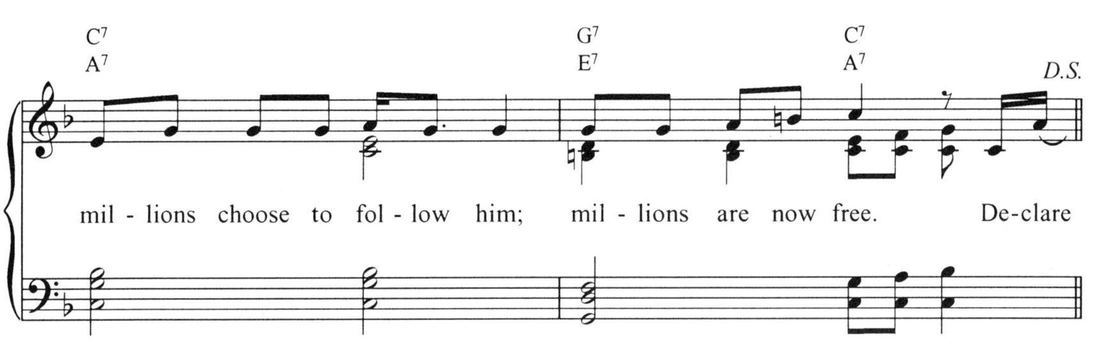
C7
A7
G7
E7
C7
A7
D.S.
mil - lions choose to fol - low him; mil - lions are now free. De-clare

445 Don't hide your light *(Topsy, turvy kingdom)*

Words and Music: Leanne Mitchell

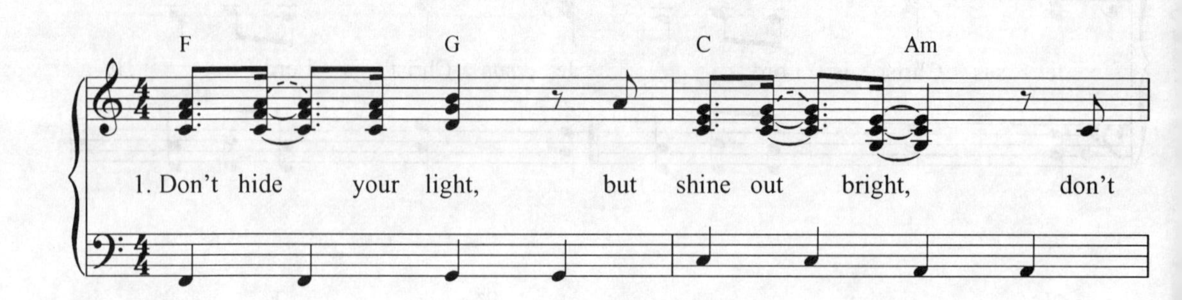

F G C Am
1. Don't hide your light, but shine out bright, don't

F G C F G
wor - ry what to wear, for like the birds of the air God will take care of you,

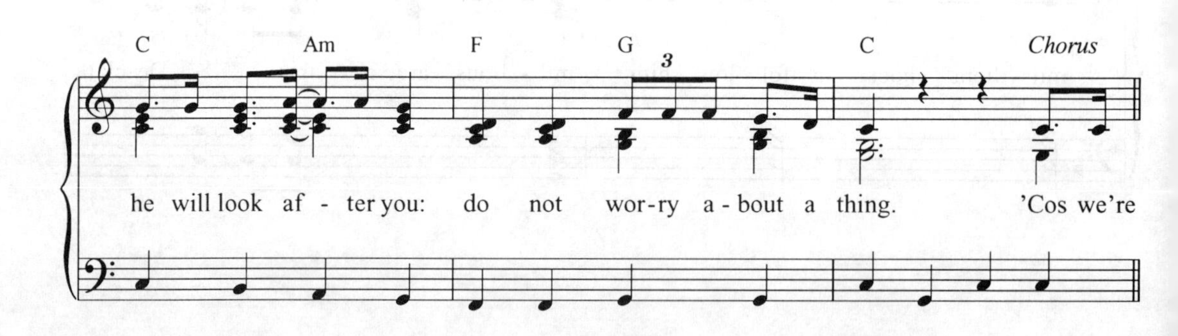

C Am F G C Chorus
3
he will look af - ter you: do not wor-ry a - bout a thing. 'Cos we're

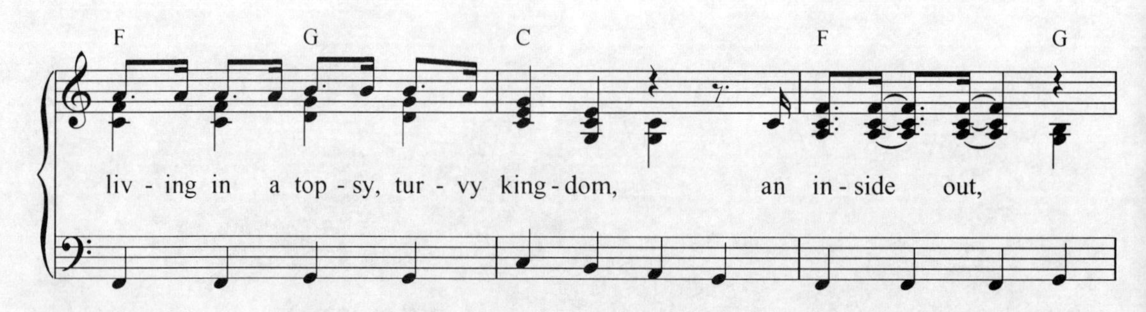

F G C F G
liv - ing in a top - sy, tur - vy king - dom, an in - side out,

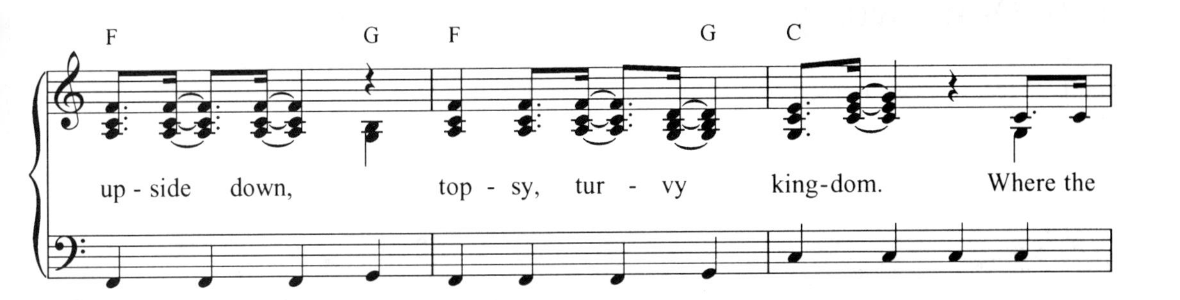
F G F G C
up - side down, top - sy, tur - vy king-dom. Where the

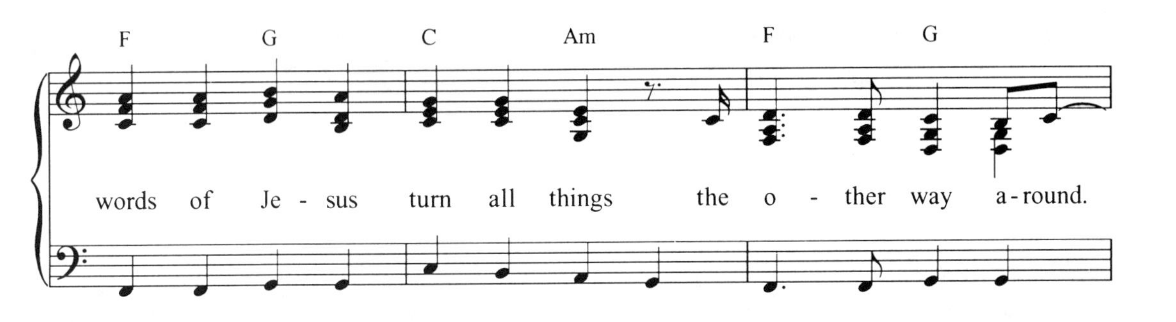
F G C Am F G
words of Je - sus turn all things the o - ther way a-round.

C F G C

2. Remember to pray every day
   for those you don't like, do not put up a fight.
   Give out lots of love like your Father above
   and you'll make a difference too.

3. Give to the poor, it says in God's law,
   be like the wise man who didn't build on the sand:
   he built on the rock, so he wasn't knocked
   when the rain came pouring down.

446 Don't worry

Words and Music: Chris Jackson
arr. Chris Mitchell

D
Don't wor - ry (don't wor - ry), don't wor - ry (don't wor - ry), don't

G A D
wor-ry a-bout a thing. Don't wor-ry (don't wor-ry), don't

G A D
wor-ry (don't wor-ry), don't wor-ry a-bout a thing. But in all your prayers

G Em7 A D
ask God for what you need,

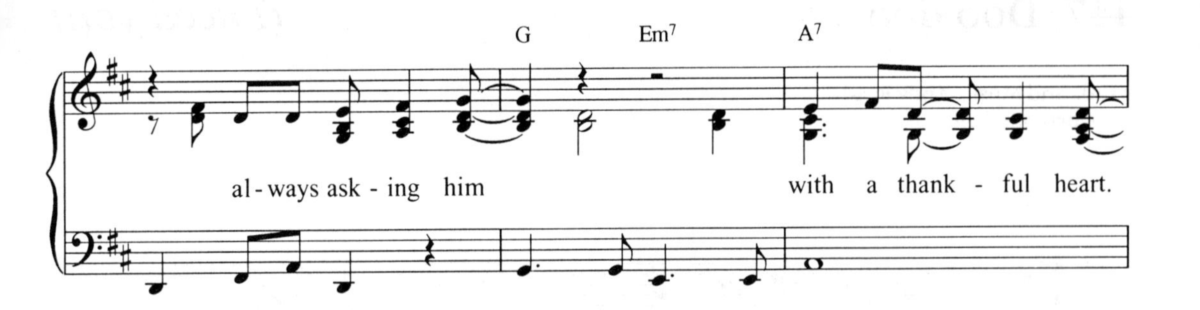
G
Em7
A7
al - ways ask - ing him
with a thank - ful heart.

D
Don't

447 Doo doo

(I need you)

Words and Music: Andy Read
arr. Chris Mitchell

(♫ = ♩♪ triplet)
Chorus
C7

Doo doo doo doo doo doo doo doo doo doo doo doo doo doo

doo doo doo doo doo doo doo doo doo doo doo doo doo doo. 1. I

need you in the morn - ing and I need you at night. I

F7

need you in the dark - ness when I'm hav - ing a fright. I

C7

hate mashed po - ta - to, but the beans are O K. I can

F7
G7
F#7
choose right from wrong, please show me the way. I need you, you,

F7
C7
C7(#9)
you, I need you.

2. I need you in my heart and I need you in my mind.
   I need you just to help me to be loving and kind.
   I hate fried rice but the chips are OK.
   I can choose right from wrong, please show me the way.

3. I need you inside for the rest of my life.
   I need to take time just to follow the light.
   I love a bit of bread and I love a bit of wine.
   Nothing like communion just to keep me in line.

448 Do what you know is right

Words and Music: Bev Gammon

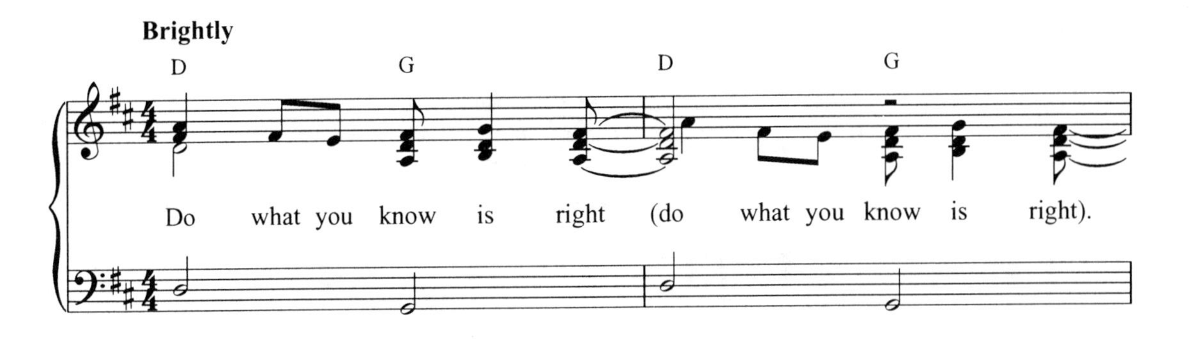
Brightly
D
G
D
G
Do what you know is right (do what you know is right).

D
G
D
Do what you know is good (do what is good).
All
If

Em
A
F♯m
Bm
G
Em
no one else does it, don't be a-fraid. Je - sus says, 'I am

A
D
Dsus4
D
with you al - ways.'

449 Do you dash *(Take a little step)*

Words: John Lane
Music: Ian Chia
arr. Chris Mitchell
C7 Bb7 C7
1. Do you dash or do you daw - dle? Do you rush or
F C7 Bb7
do you roam? Do you leap or do you wad - dle?
C7 F C7
Do you creep or do you stride? There are choi - ces
Bb7 C7 F C7
to be mak - ing; what di - rec - tion will we take? Mak - ing moves to
Bb7 C7 F
Chorus
fol - low Je - sus, not just wan - der - ing, oh no! Why don't you

Dm
C/E
Dm7
take a lit - tle step
clo - ser to Je - sus?
Take a lit - tle step

C/E
F
Em7
Am7
clo - ser to Je - sus?
Take a lit - tle step
clo - ser to Je - sus,

E♭maj7
Dm7
F/G
C
E♭maj7
Dm7
F/G
C
ne - ver let a - ny - thing keep you a - way.

2. One day kids ran up to Jesus,
   hoping he would bless them all;
   adults sniffed and snarled and snorted:
   'He's got no time for you at all!'
   Jesus' face was sad and frowning,
   'Don't you dare push kids around!
   They're most welcome in God's kingdom;
   I'm sure glad to have them round.'

Chorus 2:
   Just keep on taking little steps closer to Jesus
   taking little steps closer to Jesus,
   taking little steps closer to Jesus,
   never let anyone keep you away!

450 Do you ever wish you could fly
(Just be glad God made you 'you')

Words: Michael Forster

Music: Christopher Tambling

G Am D7 G C G
1. Do you e - ver wish you could fly like a bird, or
C G F Dsus4 D Bm Em
bur-row like a worm? Well, how ab - surd! Think of all the things that
Am D7 G A7 D7 G
you can do and just be glad God made you 'you'!

2. Do you ever wish you could swim like a duck?
Unless your feet are webbed you're out of luck!
Think of all the things that you can do
and just be glad God made you 'you'!

3. Do you ever wish you could run like a hare?
Well, wishing it won't get you anywhere!
Think of all the things that you can do
and just be glad God made you 'you'!

4. Do you ever wish you could hang like a bat?
There's really not a lot of fun in that!
Think of all the things that you can do
and just be glad God made you 'you'!

5. Do you ever wish – well, that's really enough!
To wish away your life is silly stuff!
Think of all the things that you can do
and just be glad God made you 'you'!

451 Everybody everywhere

Words and Music: Graham Kendrick
arr. Richard Lewis

(♩ = 127)
A
Asus2
Asus4
A
A/F♯
Asus2/F♯
Gsus2
A
Chorus
Asus2
Ev - 'ry - bo - dy ev - 'ry - where,
Asus4
A
A/E
A/F♯
Asus2/F♯
bless his ho - ly name.
Ev - 'ry - bo - dy ev - 'ry-where,
Gsus2
A
Asus2
for e - ver.
Ev - 'ry - bo - dy ev - 'ry - where,
Asus4
A
A/E
A/F♯
Asus2/F♯
sing a - bout his love.
Ev - 'ry bo - dy ev - ry - where,

Gsus2
Last time to Coda
for e - ver and e - ver.
1, 2.
A Asus4 A
1. I will praise you my God and King and bless your name each
2.God is kind and mer - ci - ful, he is slow to ang - er,
Asus4 E F♯m7 Gsus2
day and for e - ver. Great is the Lord, great - ly
al - ways rich in love, all that he does full of com -
G A G D/F♯ A
praise him. His great - ness knows no
pas - sion. Crea - tures and cre -
Asus4 A Asus4 E
bound - a - ries. Oh, let each ge - ne - ra - tion stand in
a - tion give you thanks, your peo - ple bless your ho - ly

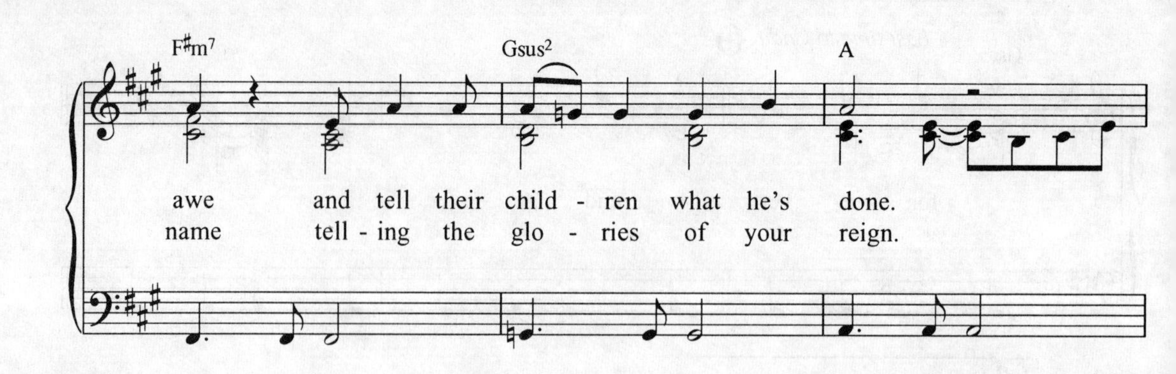
F#m7
Gsus2
A
awe and tell their child - ren what he's done.
name tell - ing the glo - ries of your reign.

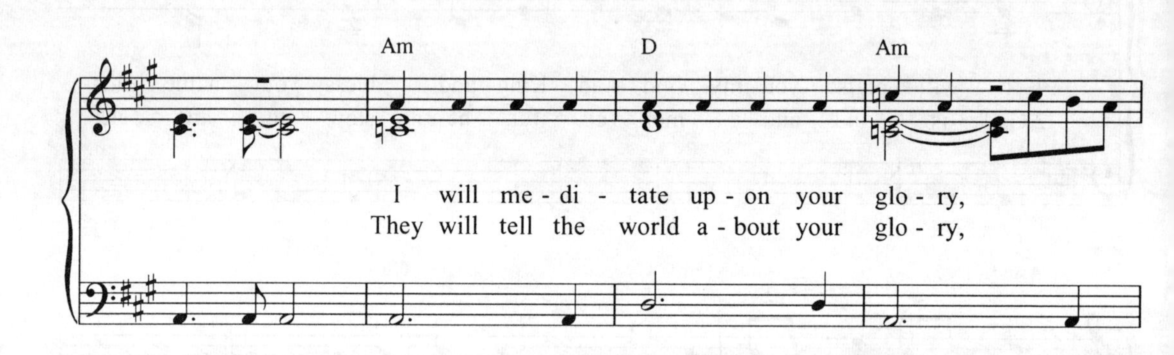
Am
D
Am
I will me - di - tate up - on your glo - ry,
They will tell the world a - bout your glo - ry,

G
D/F#
Am
D
splen - dour and ma - jes - ty, migh - ty mi - ra - cles.
splen - dour and ma - jes - ty, migh - ty mi - ra - cles,

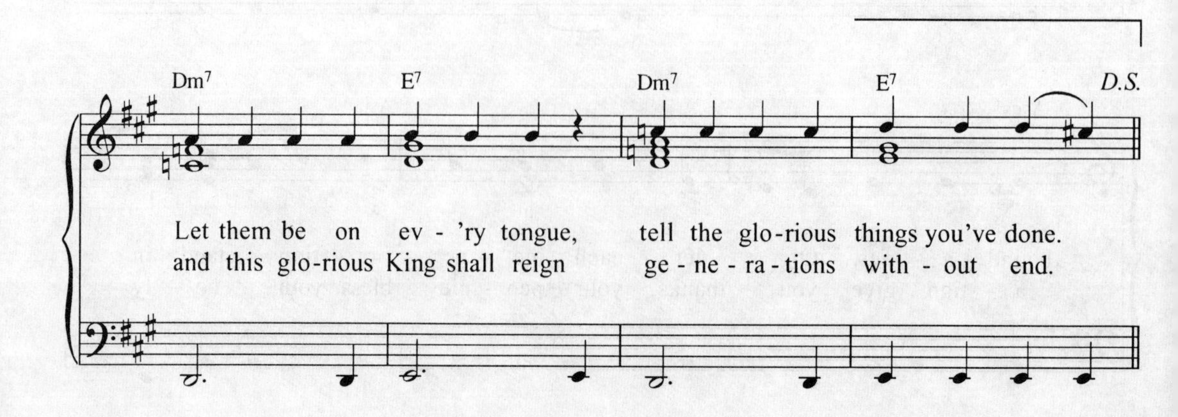
Dm7
E7
Dm7
E7
D.S.
Let them be on ev - 'ry tongue, tell the glo - rious things you've done.
and this glo - rious King shall reign ge - ne - ra - tions with - out end.

3.
Gsus2
F♯m7
Gsus2
F♯m7
3. See him lift the fal - len, share the bur - den as we
Gsus2
F♯m7
Gsus2
walk the wea - ry road. The eyes of all look up to
A
F♯m7
E/G♯
hea - ven for he is our help - er, our pro -
A
Bm7
A/C♯
G
vi - der and the source that sat - is - fies the needs of ev - 'ry liv - ing
A
Am
D
thing. The Lord is al - ways fair and full of

Am G D/F♯ Am D
kind-ness, close to all who call, seek him tru - ly.
Dm7 E7 Dm7 E7 D.S.
He ful-fils their hearts' de-sire but the wick-ed he de-stroys.
CODA
A Asus2 Asus4 A A/E
Ev-'ry-bo-dy ev-'ry-where, bless his ho-ly name.
A/F♯ Asus2/F♯ Gsus2
Ev-'ry-bo-dy ev-'ry-where, for e-ver.
A Asus2 Asus4 A A/E
Ev-'ry-bo-dy ev-'ry-where, sing a-bout his love.

A/F♯
Asus2/F♯
Gsus2
Ev-'ry-bo-dy ev-ry-where, for e-ver and e-ver,
A
for e-ver and e-ver.

452 Everybody is special to God

Words and Music: James Wright
arr. Chris Mitchell

D7 G6 D/A A7 D7 G
Ev-'ry - bo - dy is spe-cial to God, ev-'ry - bo - dy is im-
A7 D D7 G6 A7 Bm
por-tant to God, and when you think that you don't mat-ter a lot, don't for-
C G/B A7sus4 A7 D7 G6
get that you're a child of the King. Ev-'ry - bo - dy is
D/A A7 D7 G A7 D
spe-cial to God, ev-'ry - bo - dy is im - por-tant to God, and when you
D7 G6 A7 Bm7 Em7 G/A Em/D
think that you don't mat-ter a lot, don't for - get that you're a child of the King.

Last time
To continue
D
D
G6
D/A
A
Em7
D/F#
G
D/F#
Em7
D/F#
For he has called us, ev - 'ry one, to be his cho - sen
Bm7
A
Em7
D/F#
G
D/F#
daugh-ters and sons. And he has blessed us each one the same
C
G/B
Asus4
A
D.S.
with un - con - di - tion - al love. Ev - 'ry -

Rap:
Now you may be big, or you may be small,
now you may be rich, or you may be poor,
now you may be wide, or you may be thin,
but don't forget whatever shape you're in, that . . .

453 Every Christmas

Words and Music: Mark Johnson and Helen Johnson
arr. Dave Bankhead

(♩ = 138)
D
G/D
A/D
G/D
D
D
G/D
1. Ev - 'ry Christ - mas we re - mem - ber ba - by Je - sus,

A/D
D
G/A
D
G/D
A/D
G/D
D
born to the world. For this rea - son each De - cem - ber

Last time to Coda
1, 3.
2, 4.
D
G/D
A/D
D
G/A
(to v.2)
A/D
D
Chorus
is a spe - cial time for us all. true for all time. So

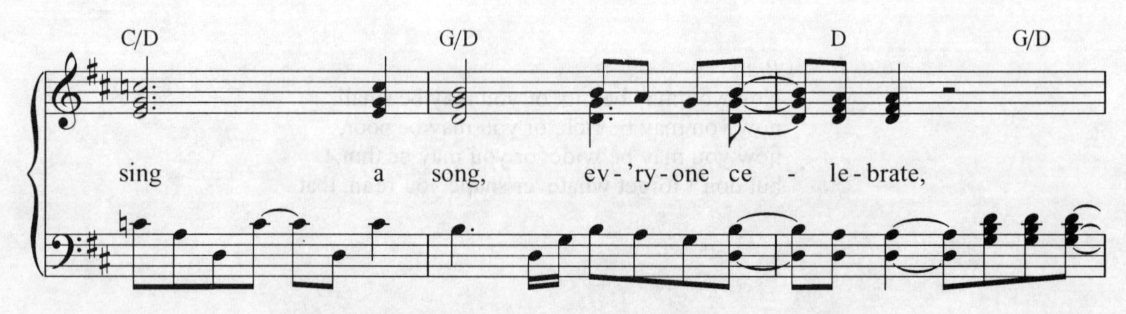
C/D
G/D
D
G/D
sing a song, ev - 'ry - one ce - le - brate,

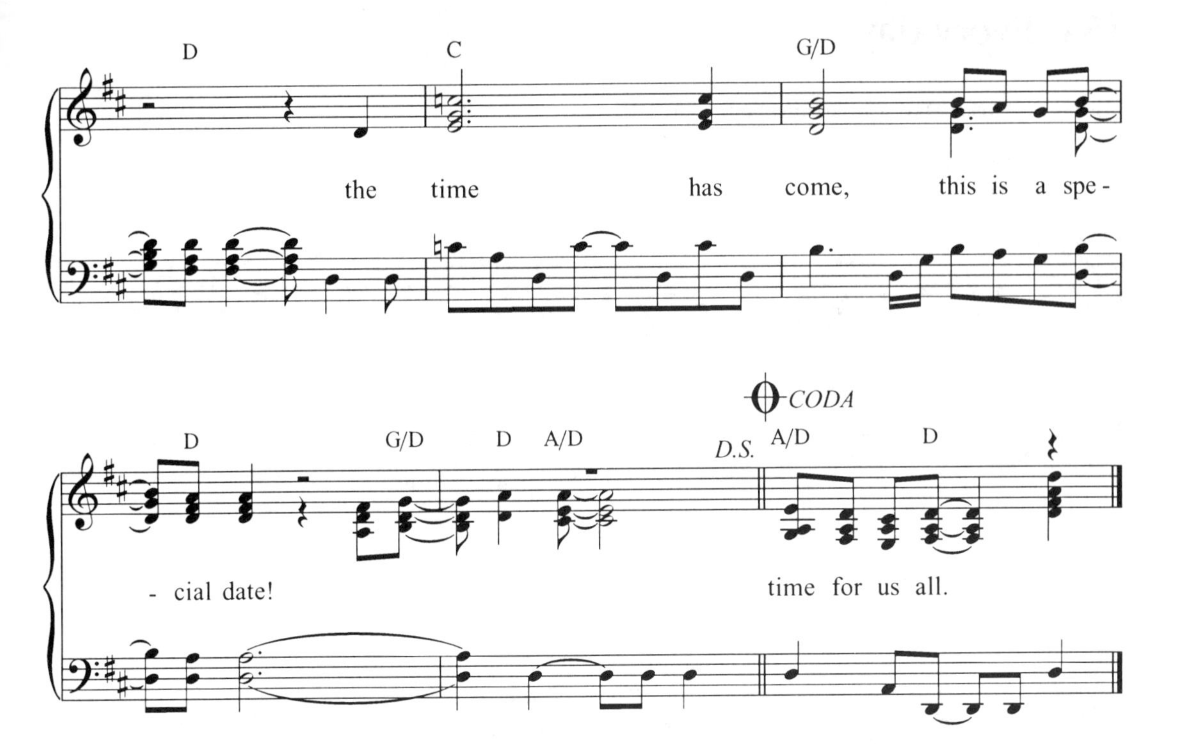
D
C
G/D
the time has come, this is a spe-
D
G/D
D
A/D
D.S.
CODA
A/D
D
- cial date!
time for us all.

2. Ev'ry Christmas we partake in
   fruit and biscuits, pudding and pies.
   But when all the food is eaten
   lies a message true for all time.

3. Ev'ry Christmas we're all busy
   buying gifts and seasonal cards.
   But behind this old tradition
   lies a present come from the past.

4. Ev'ry Christmas we have pleasure
   seeing all the glitter and lights.
   But there is a brighter treasure
   to be found in Jesus Christ.

5. Ev'ry Christmas there are parties
   fun and laughter, music and games.
   But the best place we can start is
   finding Jesus once again.

6. Ev'ry Christmas we remember
   baby Jesus born to the world.
   For this reason each December
   is a special time for us all!

454 Every day

Words and Music: Dave Cooke and Paul Field

Steadily
Chorus
E
A
E
C♯m
Ev - 'ry day let me be trust-ing you for all

A
B
E
A
I need. Ev - 'ry night I will pray:

F♯
F♯m7
E/G♯
A
F♯m7/B
E
F♯m7/E
thank you for lov - ing me ev - 'ry day.

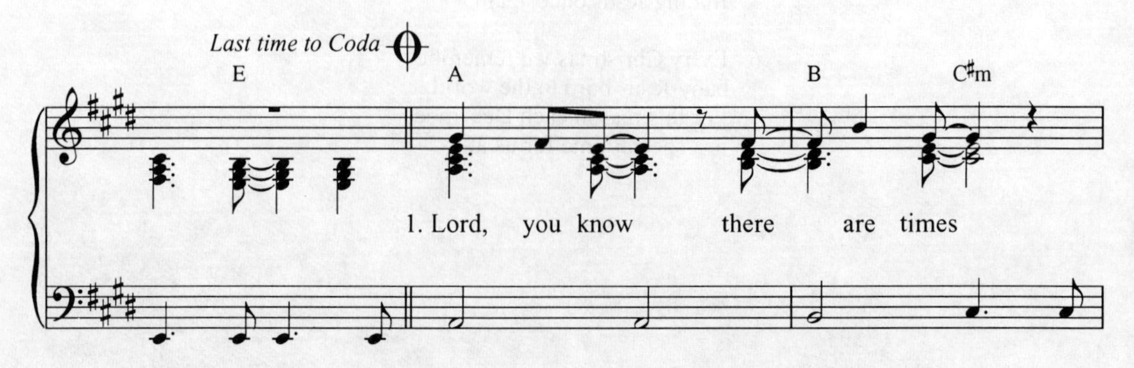
Last time to Coda
E
A
B
C♯m
1. Lord, you know there are times

A B E A
when my faith is hard to find. E - ven then you let

B C♯m F♯m7 A Bsus4 B
D.C.
me know your love won't let me go.

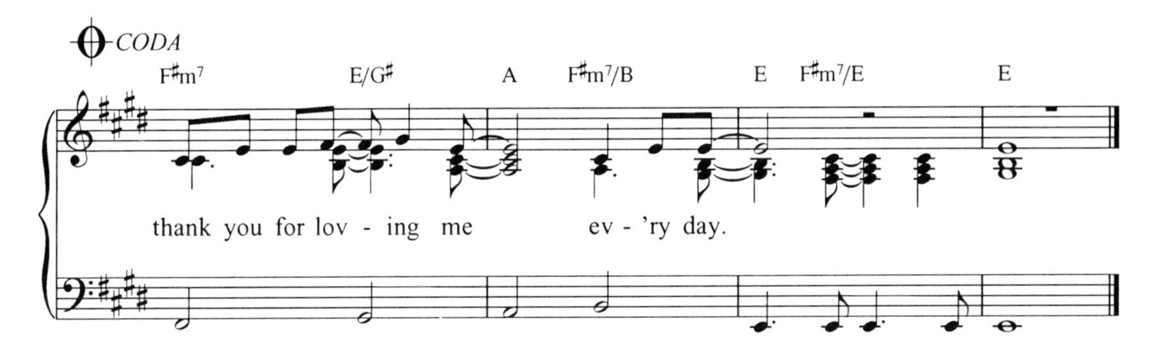
CODA
F♯m7 E/G♯ A F♯m7/B E F♯m7/E E
thank you for lov - ing me ev - 'ry day.

2. Through my joy, in my tears,
you will be throughout the years,
a faithful God whose word is true:
teach me to live in you.

455 Faith as small as a mustard seed

Words and Music: Doug Horley
arr. Dave Bankhead

D A G
Faith as small as a mus - tard seed will move moun - tains, move

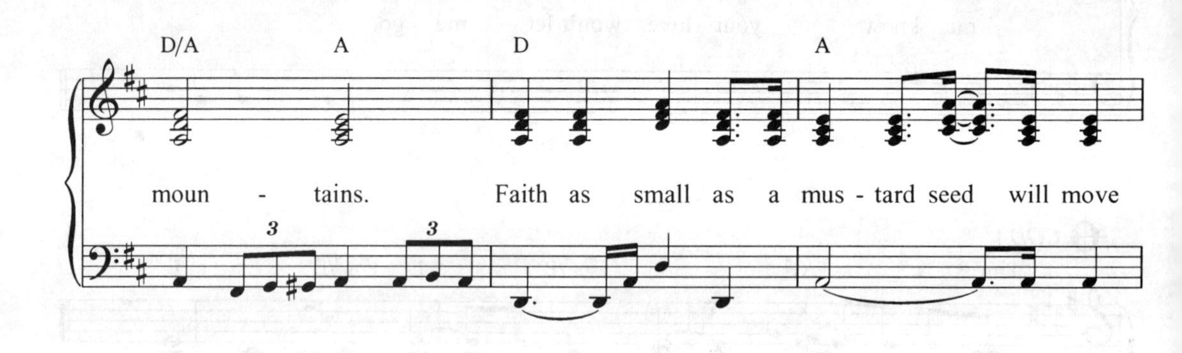
D/A A D A
moun - tains. Faith as small as a mus - tard seed will move
3
3

Last time to Coda
1.
2.
G A7 D D
moun - tains by the pow - er of God. God. Be -

G D G
lieve what Je - sus said was true, be - lieve he meant it
3

D
G
D
just for you. Wait and see what God will do, as you
A
D/A
A
D/A
A
D/A
A
D.C. al Coda
pray, pray, as you pray.
CODA
D
D
A
God. Do da do da do da do do da,
G
D/A
A
D
do da do da moun - tains. Do da do da
Last time
A
G
D/A
A
D
do da do do da do da do da mus - tard.

456 Father, I'm willing

Words and Music: Paul Crouch and David Mudie

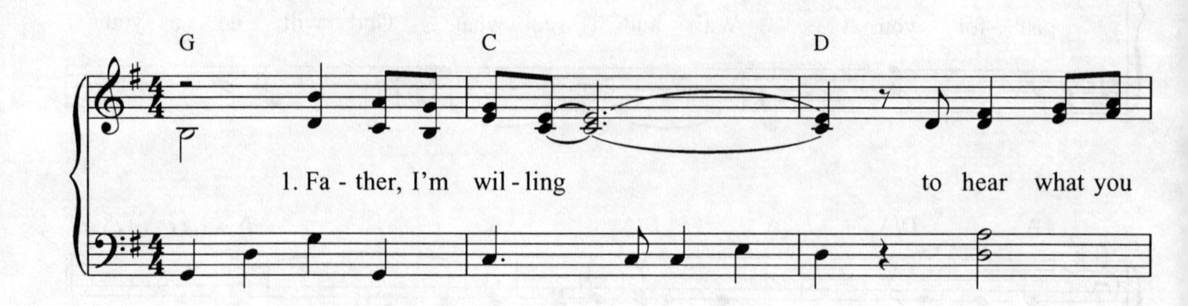
G
C
D
1. Fa - ther, I'm wil - ling
to hear what you

G
C
D
say,
give me, oh give me
a mes - sage each

G
C
D
day.
I just want to hear you,
what - e - ver I

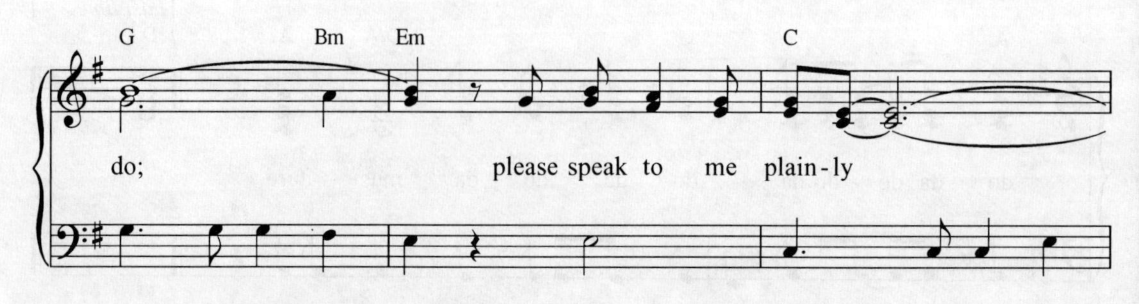
G
Bm
Em
C
do;
please speak to me plain - ly

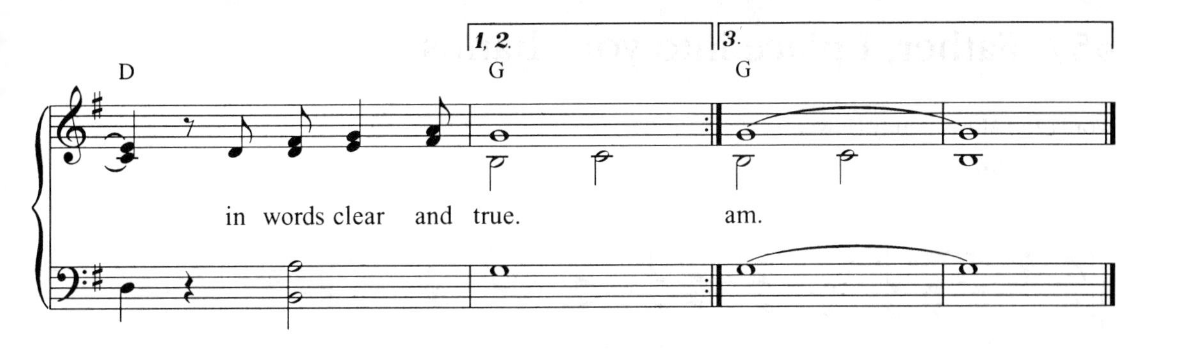
1, 2.
3.
D
G
G
in words clear and true.
am.

2. Father, forgive me when I don't want to hear,
   draw me, oh draw me until I am near.
   I want you to use me however you can,
   oh take me and use me and all that I am.

3. Father, you've given a book sent from you,
   Father, oh Father, with words clear and true.
   Oh help me to read it as much as I can,
   and then you can use me and all that I am.

457 Father, I place into your hands

Words and Music: Jenny Hewer

Gently
F
Capo 1 E
C
B
1. Fa-ther, I place in - to your hands the things I can - not do.
F
E
Fa-ther, I place in - to your hands the things that I've been through.
F7
E7
B♭
A
B♭m
Am
Fa-ther, I place in - to your hands the way that I should go, for I
F
E
C
B
F
E
know I al - ways can trust you.

2. Father, I place into your hands
my friends and family.
Father, I place into your hands
the things that trouble me.
Father, I place into your hands
the person I would be,
for I know I always can trust you.

3. Father, we love to see your face,
we love to hear your voice,
Father, we love to sing your praise
and in your name rejoice,
Father, we love to walk with you
and in your presence rest,
for we know we always can trust you.

4. Father, I want to be with you
and do the things you do.
Father, I want to speak the words
that you are speaking too.
Father, I want to love the ones
that you will draw to you,
for I know that I am one with you.

458 Father, I praise you

Words and Music: Alison Moon

D F♯m7 G Em7 A
Fa - ther, I praise you, you mean ev - 'ry-thing to
D A D F♯m7 G G/A D
me. Help me to live close to you ev - 'ry day,
1, 2. 3.
G6 G/A A D G A D
may I keep on prais-ing you. you.

2. Jesus, I serve you,
you're my Saviour and my friend.
Help me to live close to you ev'ry day,
may I keep on serving you.

3. Spirit, I love you,
you're there when I feel alone.
Help me to live close to you ev'ry day,
may I keep on serving you.

459 Father, we give you ourselves *(The Trinity blues)*

Words: Kate Abba
Music: Julia Abrahams
arr. Chris Mitchell
G7
C7
G7
1. Fa-ther, we give you our-selves to-day, a - men.
2. Je - sus, we give you our-selves to-day, a - men.
3. Spi - rit, we give you our-selves to-day, a - men.
3
C7
Fa-ther, we give you our-selves to - day, a - men.
Je - sus, we give you our-selves to - day, a - men.
Spi - rit, we give you our-selves to - day, a - men.
G7
D7
Fa-ther, we give you
Je - sus, we give you
Spi - rit, we give you

C7
G7
E♭7 D7
our-selves to-day, a - men.
our-selves to-day, a - men.
our-selves to-day, a - men.

G7
A - men,
a - men,

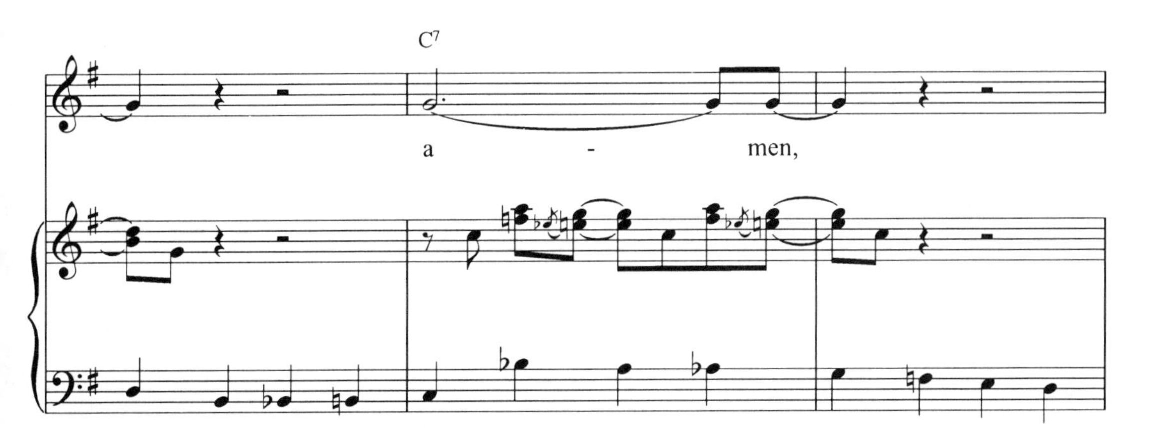
C7
a - men,

D7
a - men, a - men,

C7 G7
a - men.

460 Fisherman Peter on the sea

Words and Music: Unknown
arr. Chris Mitchell

(♩ = 100)
D
1. Fish - er - man Pe - ter on the sea, drop your

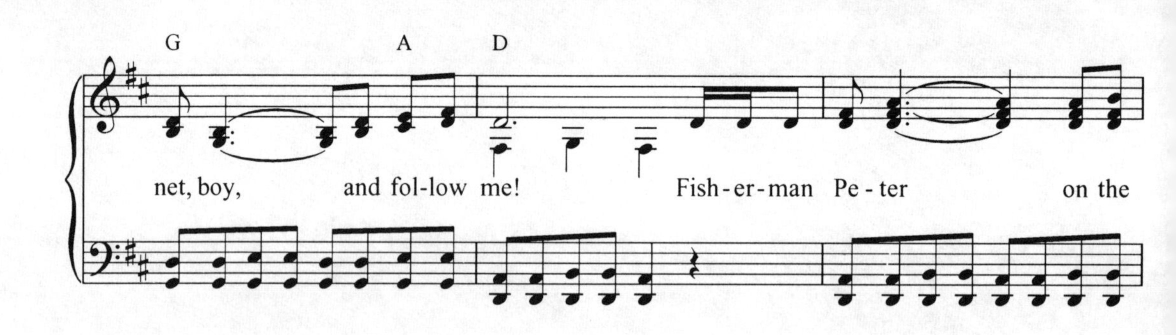
G
A
D
net, boy, and fol - low me! Fish - er - man Pe - ter on the

Last time
G
A
D
Fine
sea, drop your net, boy, and fol - low me!

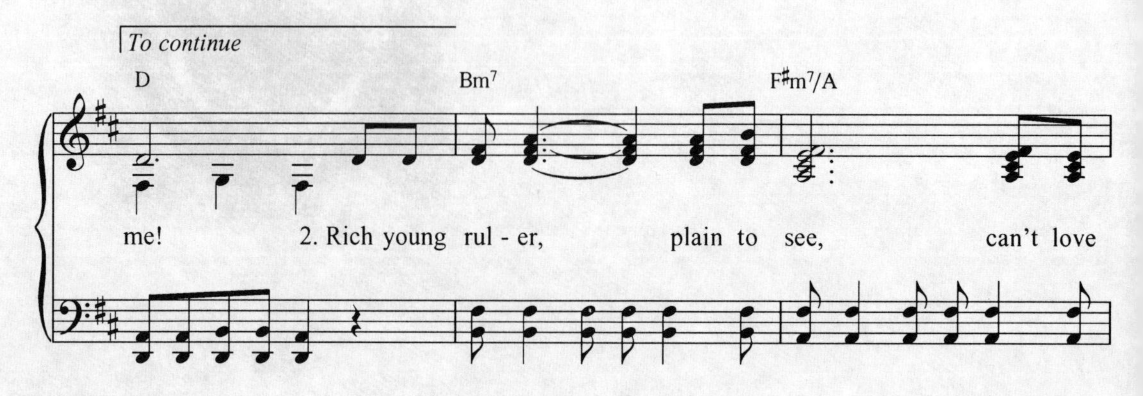
To continue
D
Bm7
F♯m7/A
me! 2. Rich young rul - er, plain to see, can't love

Gmaj7
Dmaj7/F#
Bm7
mon-ey and fol-low me! Rich young rul - er, plain to

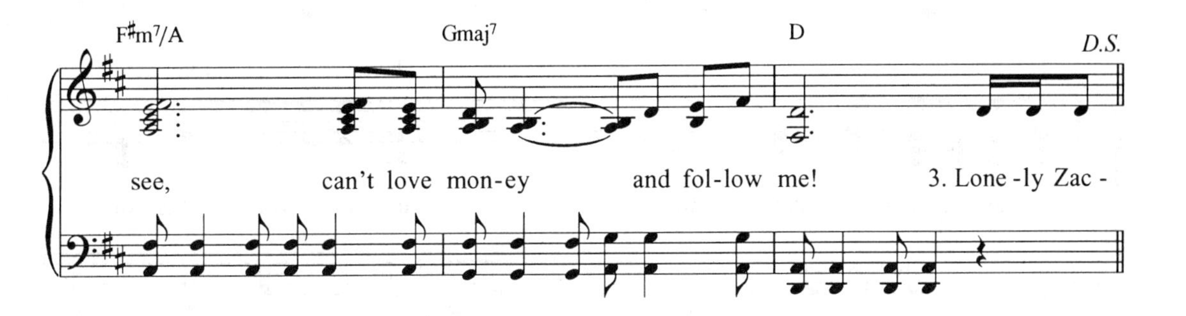
F#m7/A
Gmaj7
D
D.S.
see, can't love mon-ey and fol-low me! 3. Lone -ly Zac -

3. Lonely Zacchaeus in the tree,
   love your neighbour and follow me!
   Lonely Zacchaeus in the tree,
   love your neighbour and follow me!

4. Nicodemus, Pharisee,
   new life comes when you follow me!
   Nicodemus, Pharisee,
   new life comes when you follow me!

5. Doubting Thomas, from doubt be free,
   stop your doubting and follow me!
   Doubting Thomas, from doubt be free,
   stop your doubting and follow me!

461 Fly free

Words and Music: Mike Burn

Chorus
F/G C F C
Fly free, Spi - rit of God, fly free,
F C F Dm7
free as a dove, draw me up in your flights of
G F/G C F
love. Show me all that you see, help
C F C
me to feel what you feel, re - veal the
F G7 C
Fa - ther's heart for this land.
To verses
1. The
Last time

C G F
Spi - rit of God is brood - ing o - ver this
C G
land. The Spi - rit of God is sing - ing
F C F C/E
of the Fa - ther's plans. The Spi - rit of God is wait-
F Am7
- ing; long - ing for the day when the
F Dm7 Gsus4 G F/G
Chorus D.S.
prai - ses of God will ring loud and clear once more. Fly

2. The church of God is stirring
all through this land.
The church of God is praying,
lifting holy hands.
The church of God is rising,
rising to take her place,
joining heavenly hosts
singing praises to the Lamb.

462 For God did not

(2 Timothy 1:7)

Words and Music: Colin Buchanan

With a lilt (♩ = 144)
G C G C
G C G C
Oh! Wo oh! Wo oh!
C G C
For God (for God) did not (did not) give
G C G
us a spi-rit of ti-mi-di-ty, but a (but a) spi-rit
C G D
(spi-rit) of pow-er (of pow-er), of love and

C
G
C
of self - dis - ci - pline. 2 Ti - mo - thy, chap - ter one, verse se -
G
C
G
- ven (2 Ti - mo - thy, chap - ter one, verse se - ven), 2 Ti - mo - thy,
C
G
C
chap - ter one, verse se - ven (2 Ti - mo - thy, chap - ter one, verse se -
G
C
G
C/D
G
Oh! Wo oh! Wo oh! Oh! Wo
- ven).
C
G
1.
2.
D.S.
oh! Wo oh! For God

463 For God so loved

Words and Music: Steve Morgan-Gurr and Kay Morgan-Gurr

(♩ = 135)
C F G C F
For God so loved the world, he gave his one and on - ly Son,

G C F G Am
that all who trust him and be - lieve, have

F G C F C G C
life for-e - ver on. And if I were the on - ly one who

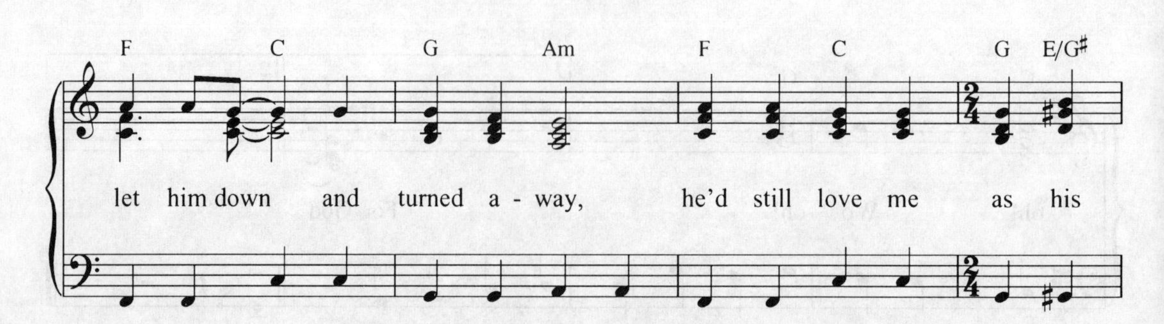

F C G Am F C G E/G♯
let him down and turned a - way, he'd still love me as his

Am
F
G
1.
C
D.S.
own,
and just for me he'd pay.
For
2.
C
F
G
1, 2, 3.
C
4.
C
And just for me he'd pay.
And

464 For God so loved the world

Words and Music: John L. Hardwick

The two halves of this song may be sung simultaneously.

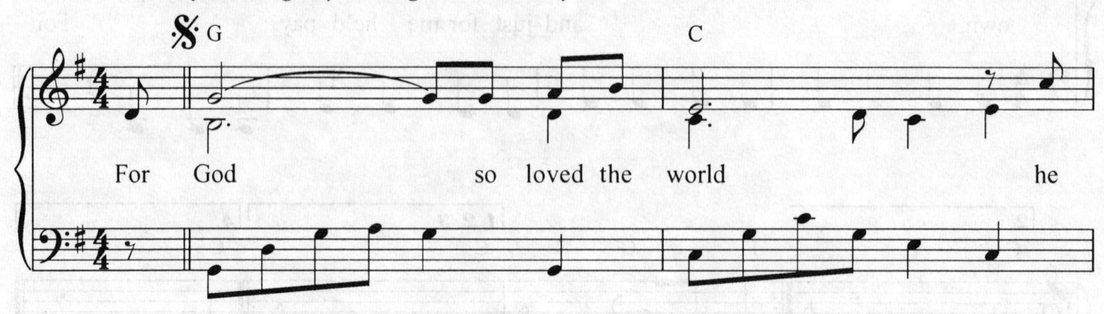
G
C
For God so loved the world he

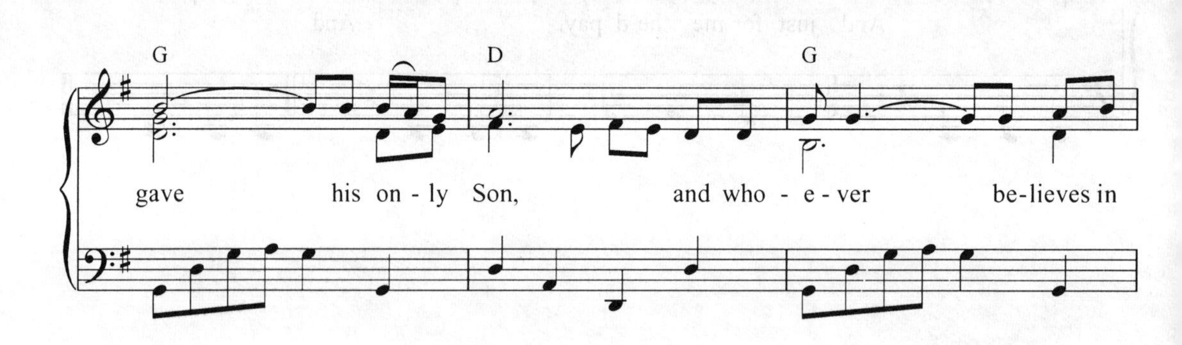
G
D
G
gave his on - ly Son, and who - e - ver be-lieves in

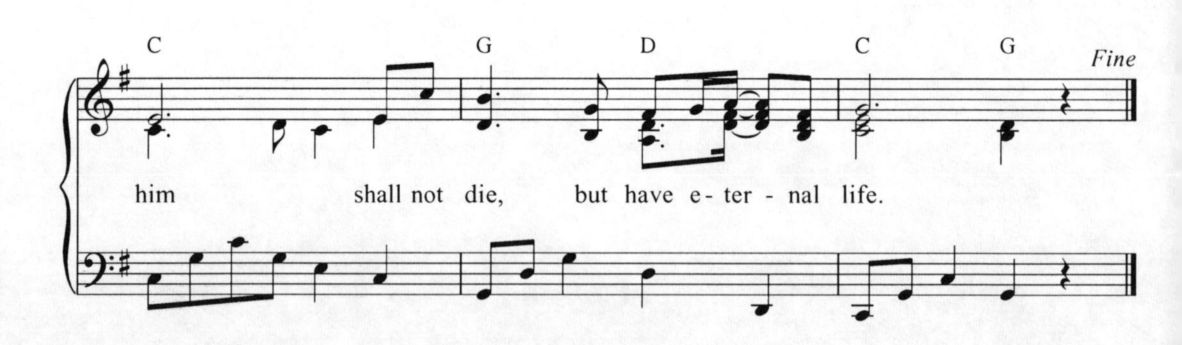
C
G
D
C
G
Fine
him shall not die, but have e - ter - nal life.

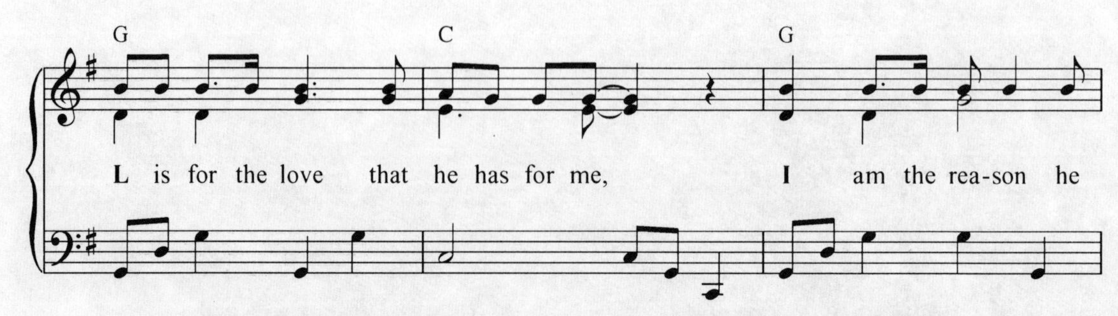
G
C
G
L is for the love that he has for me, I am the rea-son he

D
G
died on the tree,
F is for for - give - ness and

C
G
D
C
D.S.
now I am free,
E is to en - joy be-ing in his com-pa - ny. For

465 For the foolishness of God *(God's wisdom)*

Words and Music: Paul Crouch and David Mudie

Capo 3
F D
B♭ G
F D
For the fool - ish - ness of God is wis - er than man's wis - dom, and the

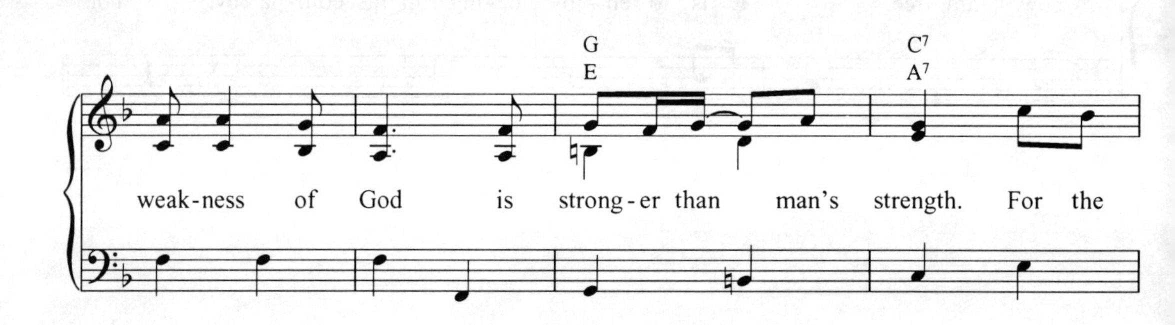
G E
C7 A7
weak-ness of God is strong - er than man's strength. For the

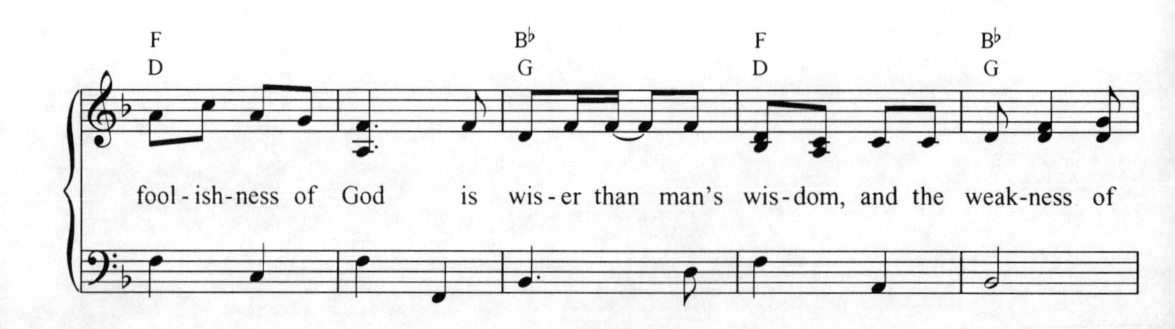
F D
B♭ G
F D
B♭ G
fool - ish - ness of God is wis - er than man's wis - dom, and the weak-ness of

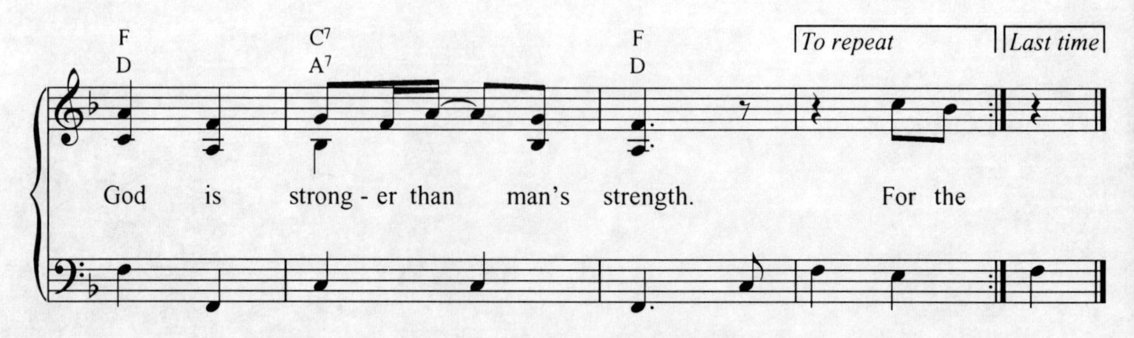
F D
C7 A7
F D
To repeat
Last time
God is strong - er than man's strength. For the

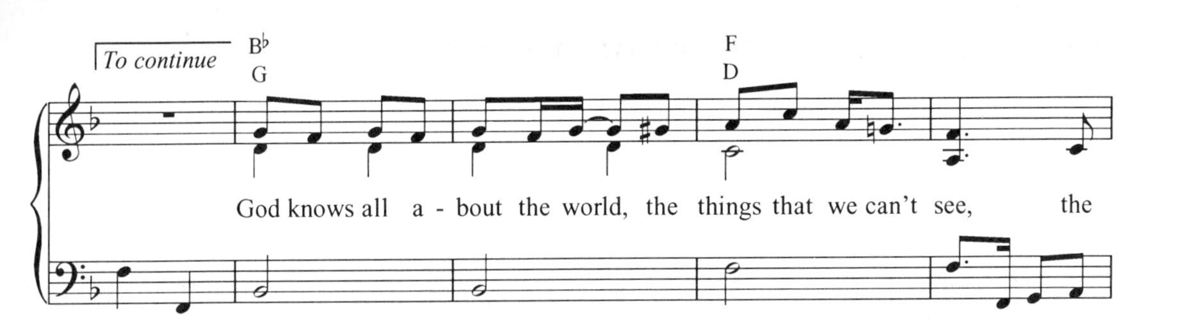
To continue
B♭
G
F
D
God knows all a - bout the world, the things that we can't see, the

B♭
G
F
D
things that we don't un - der-stand, that baf - fle you and me. His

B♭
G
F
D
C/E
A/C♯
Dm
Bm
strength is ne - ver - end - ing and we are weak and small. His

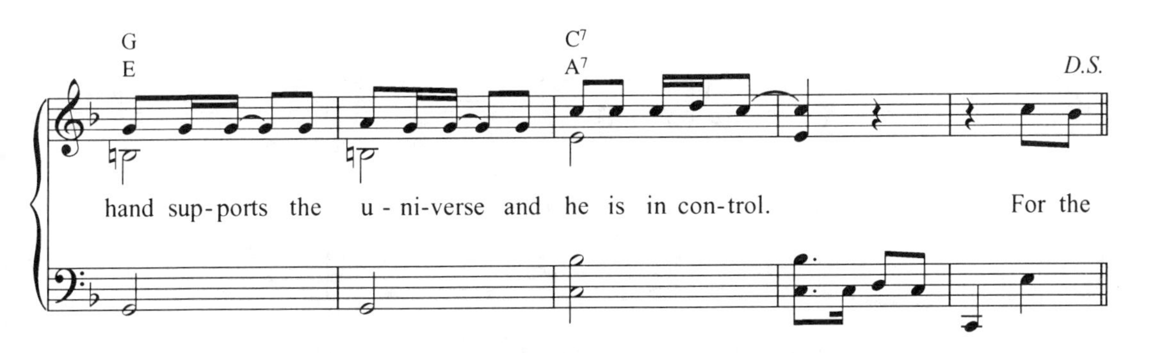
G
E
C7
A7
D.S.
hand sup - ports the u - ni - verse and he is in con - trol. For the

466 For the measure of the treasure

Words and Music: Doug Horley and Jamie Horley
arr. Dave Bankhead

G A G/A D Bm
For the mea - sure of the trea - sure that you store in hea - ven, is the
Em A D D7
mea - sure that - 'll last for - e - ver. But the
G A G/A D Bm Em A
mea - sure of the trea - sure that you store on earth might be car - ried a - way by a
Em A Em A
1.
A7/D D
thief one day, or rot when the moths get hun - gry. For the
3

2.
A7/D D A G A
hun - gry. For where your trea - sure is, that's where your
D A
heart is. For where your trea - sure is
1. 2.
G A D D
there'll be your heart. heart.

467 Friend of sinners

Words and Music: Matt Redman

Capo 2
E A B E A
D G A D G
1. Friend of sin - ners, Lord of truth, I am fall - ing in
2. Friend of sin - ners, Lord of truth, I am giv - ing my
B E A B E
A D G A D
love with you. Friend of sin - ners, Lord of truth,
life to you. Friend of sin - ners, Lord of truth,
A B E E/A E A
G A D D/G D G
I have fal - len in love with you.
I have giv - en my life to you.
Je - sus, I
B E A B E
A D G A D
love your name, the name by which we're saved. Je -

A/G B/A E/D
sus, I love your name, the
A/G B/A E/D
name by which we're saved.

468 From the top of my head

Words and Music: James Wright
arr. Chris Mitchell

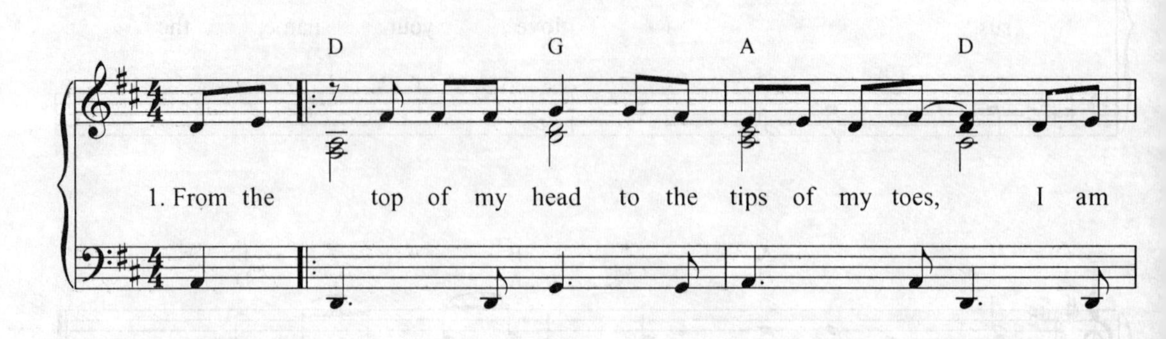
D G A D
1. From the top of my head to the tips of my toes, I am

G A D G
fear-ful - ly and won-der-f'lly made, from the col-our of my eyes to the

A D G A D/A A
shape of my nose, I am fear-ful - ly and won-der - f'lly made.

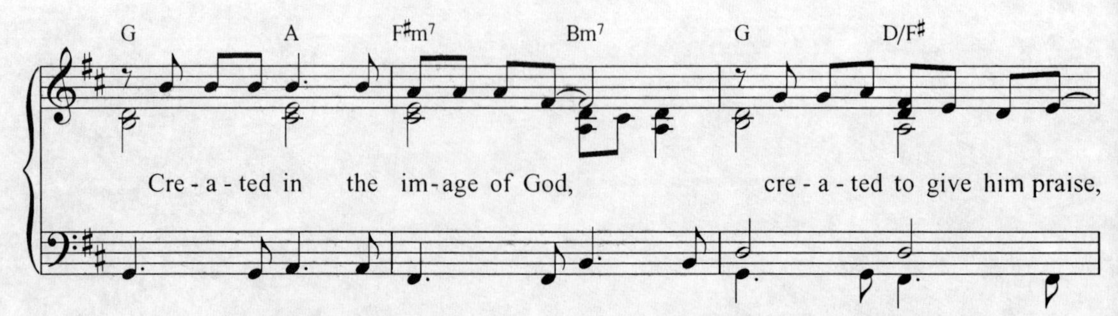
G A F♯m7 Bm7 G D/F♯
Cre - a - ted in the im-age of God, cre - a - ted to give him praise,

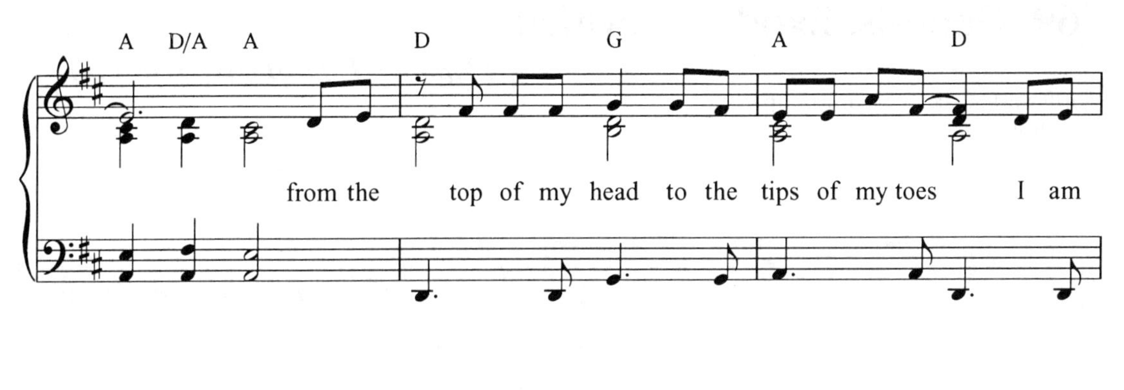

A D/A A D G A D
from the top of my head to the tips of my toes I am

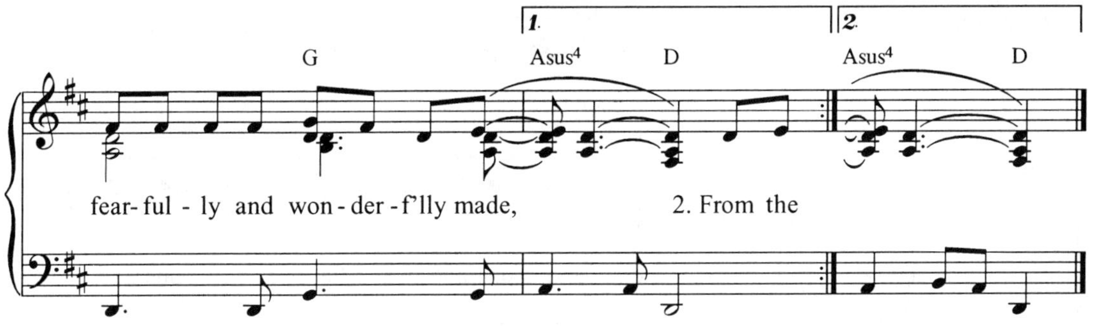

1.
2.
G Asus4 D Asus4 D
fear- ful - ly and won - der - f'lly made, 2. From the

2. From the way that I hear to the way that I talk,
   I am fearfully and wonderf'lly made,
   from the way that I see to the way that I walk,
   I am fearfully and wonderf'lly made.
   Created in the image of God, created to give him praise,
   from the way that I hear to the way that I talk,
   I am fearfully and wonderf'lly made.

469 Genesis, Exodus, Leviticus

(The Old Testament Song)

Words and Music: Steve Burnhope
arr. Chris Mitchell

(♩ = 120)
E
B
1. Ge - ne - sis, Ex - o - dus, Le - vi - ti - cus, Num - bers, Deu - te - ro - no - my,
E
Jo - shu - a, Jud - ges, Ruth and one and two Sam - u - el, one and two
B
A7
E
Kings and one and two Chro - ni - cles, Ez - ra, Ne - he - mi - ah.
B
2. Es - ther, Job and Psalms and Pro - verbs, Ec - cle - si - as - tes,

E
Song of So - lo - mon, I - sai - ah, Je - re - mi - ah, La - men - ta - tions, E-
B A7 E
ze - ki - el, Dan - iel, and Ho - se - a and Joel.
A E B E
3. A - mos, O - ba - di - ah, Jo - nah, Mi - cah,
A E B E A E
Na - hum, Hab - ba - kuk, Ze - pha - ni - ah, Hag - ga - i, Ze - cha - ri - ah,
B E A B E
Ma - la - chi, that's it, thir - ty - nine books in all.

470 Give and it shall be given!

Words and Music: Mike Burn

G
Bm7
C
1. Give and it shall be gi - ven!
Dsus4
D
G
Bm7
C
Oh, you can't out - give the Lord your
D
C
D
God. One thing is cer - tain in the
Bm
Em
Am
king - dom of hea - ven, the mea - sure you give is the
Dsus4
D
Chorus
mea - sure you'll re - ceive. And it - 'll be

G
Em
Am7
D
D7
pressed down, sha-ken to-ge-ther and o-ver-flow-

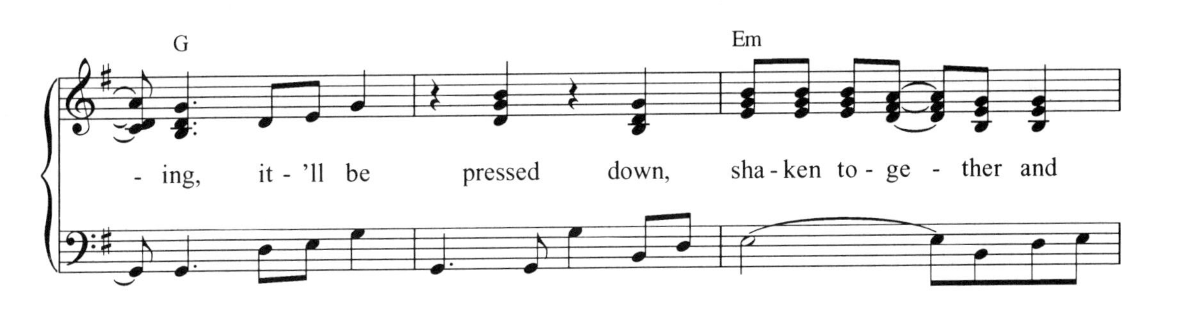
G
Em
-ing, it-'ll be pressed down, sha-ken to-ge-ther and

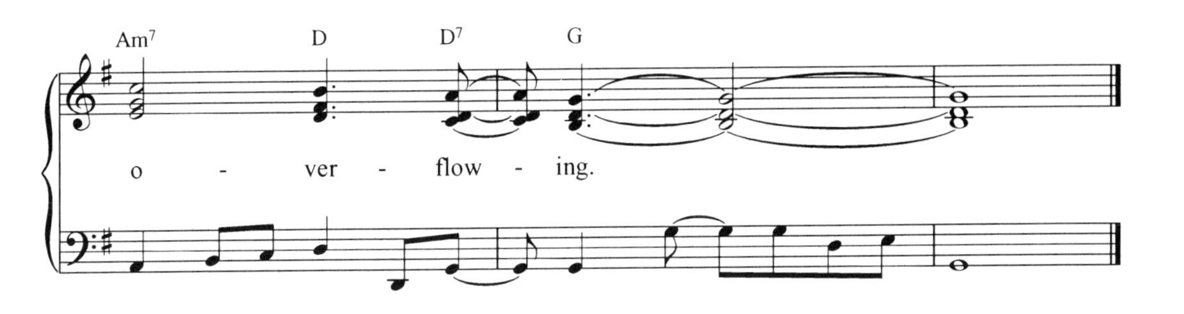
Am7
D
D7
G
o-ver-flow-ing.

2. Don't rob God of your firstfruits,
give the most you can and then some more.
He longs to open a window from heaven
and pour out a blessing so big you'll be amazed!

3. God's building now his kingdom
and his kingdom's rule will never end.
If you will give him your life, your time, your money,
you'll store up a treasure no one can steal away.

471 Give thanks to the Lord

Words: Kate Abba

Music: Julia Abrahams
arr. Chris Mitchell

(♩ = 100)
Capo 3
F7 D7
B♭7 G7
F7 D7
1. Give thanks to the Lord for he is good, hal - le - lu - jah,
thanks to the Lord for he is good, hal - le - lu - jah,
thanks to the Lord for he is good, hal - le - lu - jah,
thanks to the Lord for he is good, hal - le - lu - jah,
A7 F♯7
D7 B7
G7 E7
C7 A7
for God's love has no end, hal - le - lu - jah.
God's right hand raised me up, hal - le - lu - jah.
I am weak but you are strong, hal - le - lu - jah.
his right hand has raised me up, hal - le - lu - jah.
F7 D7
B♭7 G7
Bdim7 G♯dim7
Let all you peo - ple here, hal - le - lu - jah,
Let me sing and sing a - gain, hal - le - lu - jah,
You are God and I ex - alt, hal - le - lu - jah,
Let me sing and sing a - gain, hal - le - lu - jah,
Last time to Coda
1.
F/C D/A
Dm7 Bm7
G7 E7
B♭/C G/A
E♭ C
E C♯
F D
sing and shout for joy, shout for joy.
2. Give
4. Give

2.
E♭ C
E C♯
F D
Chorus
F7 D7
B♭7 G7
F7 D7
shout for joy. There's so ma-ny songs I want to sing,

Am7 F♯m7
Dm7 Bm7
G7 E7
B♭/C G/A
Lord, I love you, and the joy you bring.

B♭maj7 Gmaj7
B♭m7 Gm7
Morn-ing breaks an-o-ther day, and you chase the clouds a-way,

Gm7 Em7
C7sus4 A7sus4
B♭/C G/A
D.S.
Lord, I real-ly want to say, you're the good who shines my way.
3. Give

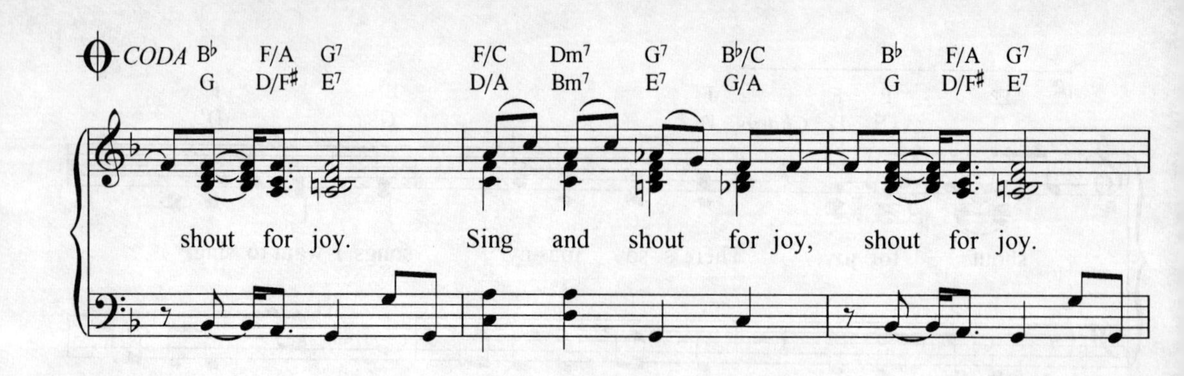
CODA
B♭ F/A G7 F/C Dm7 G7 B♭/C B♭ F/A G7
G D/F♯ E7 D/A Bm7 E7 G/A G D/F♯ E7
shout for joy. Sing and shout for joy, shout for joy.

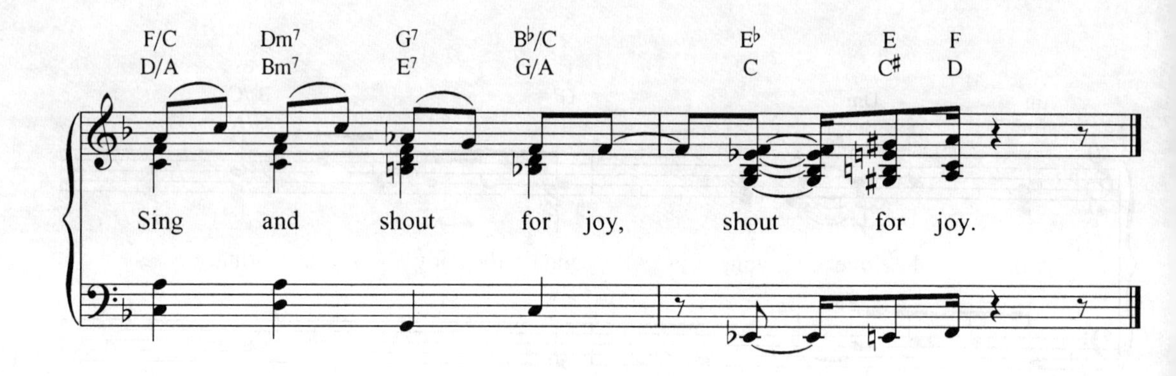
F/C Dm7 G7 B♭/C E♭ E F
D/A Bm7 E7 G/A C C♯ D
Sing and shout for joy, shout for joy.

472 God can give a very special life *(A very special life)*

Words and Music: Nick Harding

Gently
Capo 3
F D
Dm Bm
B♭ G
C A
F D
1. God can give a very special life.
Dm Bm
Gm Em
C A
That's the life I see,
F D
Dm Bm
B♭ G
and I know that if I will say 'yes'
Gm Em
C A
B♭ G
F D
God's got a plan for me.

2. God can give a very special life.
That's the greatest way,
and I know that if I will say 'yes'
I'll live for God each day.

473 God created the world

Words and Music: Susanna Levell
arr. Chris Mitchell

Chorus
Capo 3
F D
B♭ G
Gm7 Em7
God cre-a-ted the world and all he had made, he saw it was
B♭/C G/A
C7 A7
good. God is wor-thy of praise, for all he has made, it is ve-ry
good. In the be-gin-ning he made hea-vens and earth,
F/A D/F♯
now ne-ver-end-ing I will tell of his worth. God cre-a-ted the
C7sus4 A7sus4
Last time
Fine
world and all he had made, he saw it was good.

To verses
F D
B♭ G
F D
good. 1. On the first day God said, 'Let there be light' so
C7 A7
F D
part - ing light and dark - ness, he called it day and night. On the
B♭ G
F D
sec - ond day God said, 'Let there be space' so
G E
C7 A7
D.C.
se - pa - ra - ting wa - ters put the land, sea and sky in place.

2. On the third day God said,
'Let there be growth',
the land produced plantation,
the trees and flow'rs did grow.
On the fourth day God said,
'Let there be lights'.
The sun to govern daytime
and the moon and stars for night.

3. On the fifth day God said,
'Let there be life'.
He filled the sea with creatures,
and birds, they filled the sky.
On the sixth day God said,
'Let there be man'.
First animals he made, then
in his image he made man.

4. By the seventh day all
the work of his hands
was finished to completion,
his perfect, mighty plan.
On this special day God said,
'Let it be blessed'.
So he rested, made it holy
as a special day of rest.

474 God gave me fingers *(The body song)*

Words and Music: Amanda Lofts
arr. Chris Mitchell

G
G/B
D
1. God gave me fin - gers that I can wig - gle, I
C
G/B
D
G
G/B
tic - kle my friends and make them gig - gle. Fin - gers are such
D
C
D
G
use - ful things. Thank you, God, for fin - gers.

2. God gave me eyes so I can see
the lovely world that's all around me.
Flow'rs and trees of ev'ry size.
Thank you, God, for my eyes.

3. God gave me ears so I can hear
beautiful music loud and clear.
People talking far and near.
Thank you, God, for my ears.

4. God gave me a mouth so I can chew
and happily eat up all of my food.
I sing and laugh and talk and shout.
Thank you, God, for my mouth.

5. God gave me feet so I can run.
I can hop, skip and jump and have such fun.
I even walk slowly down the street.
Thank you, God, for my feet.

475 God has been good

Words and Music: Andy Read
arr. Chris Mitchell

E
B7
God has been good to me, God has been good to

E
A
me, God has been good to me and

To repeat
Last time
B7
E
E
I will live for him. him.

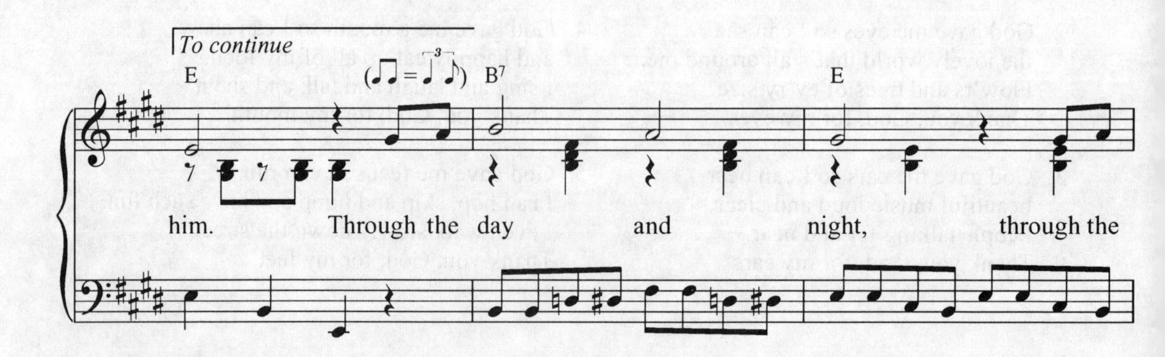
To continue
E
B7
E
him. Through the day and night, through the

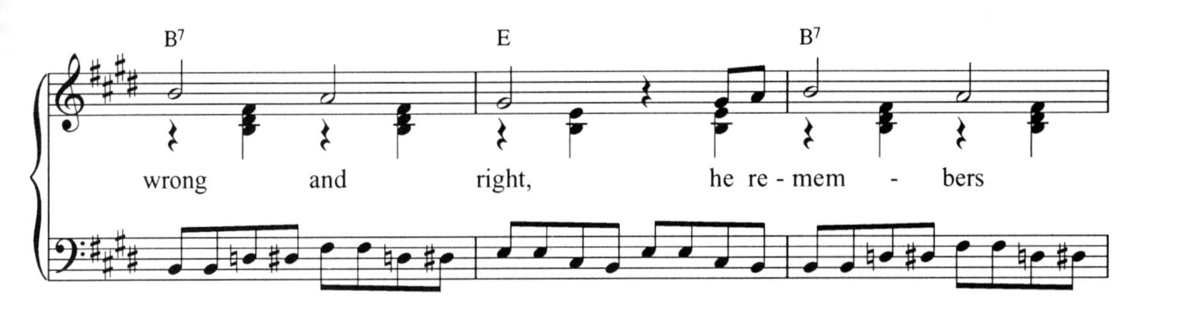
B7
E
B7
wrong and right, he re - mem - bers

(♩♫ = ♩♫)
E
F♯
B7
D.C.
me; how could I for - get the truth that

476 God has put his angels

Words and Music: Alison Moon

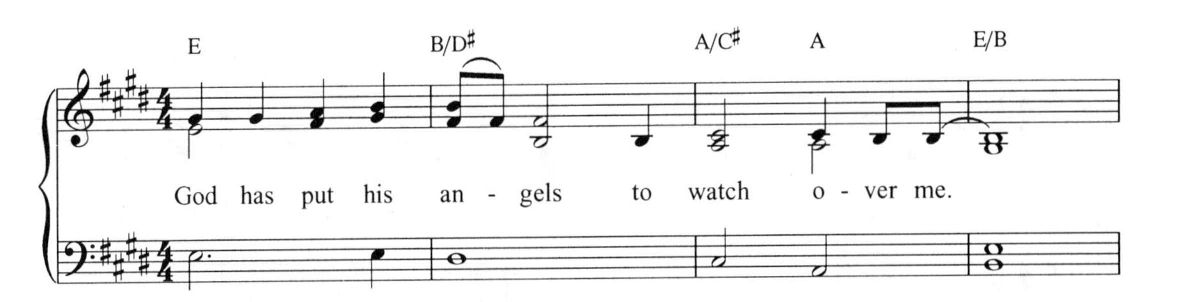
E
B/D♯
A/C♯
A
E/B
God has put his an - gels to watch o - ver me.

E
B/D♯
A/C♯
A
Bsus4
B
God has put his an - gels to pro - tect me from all harm.

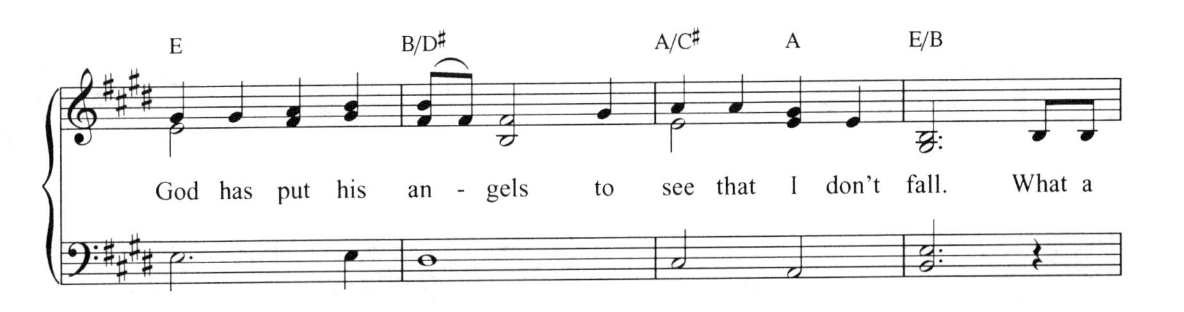
E
B/D♯
A/C♯
A
E/B
God has put his an - gels to see that I don't fall. What a

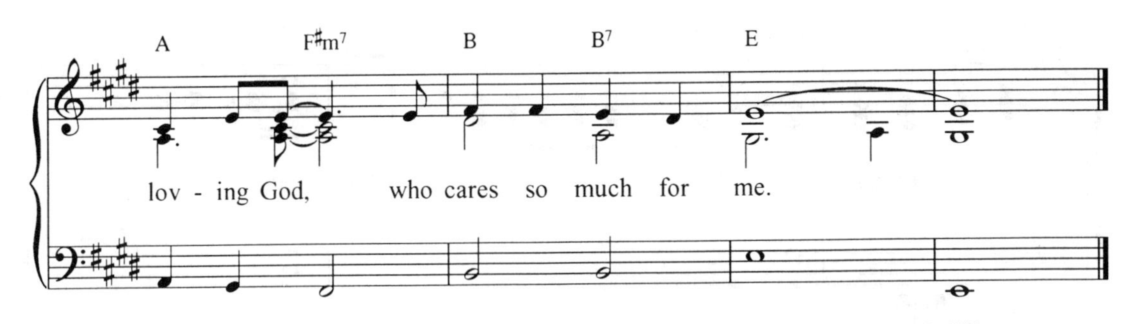
A
F♯m7
B
B7
E
lov - ing God, who cares so much for me.

477 God is good, he is great

Words and Music: Andy Read
arr. Chris Mitchell

Chorus
To repeat 3 times
G7
God is good, he is great. I will serve him all my days.
4th time
C7
F7
all my days. 1. For he is faith - ful, wise and true;
Dm7
Am7/G
G
C7
F7
wor - thy of our wor - ship, rul - er o - ver all,
Dm7
Am7/G
G
C7
ho - ly and per - fect. (Yes, God is good!)

1.
2.
D.S.
C

2. For he is mighty, strong to save,
   gen’rous, full of kindness,
   God above all gods,
   powerful in mercy.
   (Yes, God is good!)

478 God is so wonderful *(God is so clever)*

Words and Music: Jennie Flack
arr. Chris Mitchell

D
G
D/A
A
D
G
D/A
1. God is so won - der-ful, God is so cle-ver. Look at the way that God's put

A
G
D/F♯
A♯dim7
Bm7
me to - ge-ther: ears that can hear and eyes that can see.

E
A7
Oh, what a won - der-ful, won - der - ful me!

Chorus
Gmaj7
A/G
F♯m7
Bm7
Em7
I can run with my feet, I can clap with my hands, I can hug,

A7
D
Gmaj7
A/G
F#m7
I can smile, I can sing. With my mind I have learned that with-out
Bm7
Em7
A7
D
God, my Mak - er, I would - n't have all of these things.
Em7
G/A
D
Em7
G/A
D

2. God is so wonderful, God is so clever.
   Look at the way that God's put me together:
   a mind to think up things and dream lovely dreams.
   Oh, what a wonderful life it all means!

479 God knows me

Words and Music: Nick Harding
arr. Dave Bankhead

Chorus F
Capo 3 D
C/E
A/C♯
Dm
Bm
God knows me,
Gm7
Em7
B♭6/C
G6/A
F
D
C/E
A/C♯
God knows me, God knows me
Dm
Bm
Gm7
Em7
F/C
D/A
B♭6/C
G6/A
1.
F
D
bet - ter than I know my - self.
2.
F
D
C
A
B♭/C
G/A
C
A
F
D
self. 1. He knows the hair on my head,

Gm
Em
the col - our of my eyes, the
F
D
Gm7
Em7
B♭6/C
G6/A
F
D
thoughts in my mind, and things down deep in - side.
3

2. He knows me good and bad,
 happy and sad,
 frown or smile,
 he knows me all the while.

480 God loved the world so much *(John 3:16)*

Words and Music: Paul Harvey
arr. Chris Mitchell

D
G
A
God loved the world so much (so much!) that he gave his on - ly
D
Bm
G
A
Son (his Son!) so that ev - 'ry - one who be - lieves in him would
G
A
D
have e - ter - nal life (have life!). God loved the world so
G
A
D
much (so much!) that he gave his on - ly Son (his Son!) so that
Bm
G
A
G
A
D
ev - 'ry - one who be - lieves in him would have e - ter - nal life (have life!).

481 God loves me

Words and Music: Andrew Pearson and Pauline Pearson

D A D A D A
1. God loves me and ev - 'ry - thing a - bout me,
D A D A D
God loves me and all my fa - mi - ly.
A D A D A
God loves me and ev - 'ry - thing a - bout me,
D A D A D
To next verse
Last time
God loves me and all my fa - mi - ly.
ly.

2. God loves you and ev'rything about you,
God loves you and all your family. *(x2)*

3. God knows me and ev'rything about me,
God knows me and all my family. *(x2)*

4. God knows you and ev'rything about you,
God knows you and all your family. *(x2)*

482 God loves me *(Whoopah, wahey!)*

Words and Music: Doug Horley
arr. Dave Bankhead

G
D
God loves me, whoo-pah, wa-hey! God loves

G
C
G
you, whoo-pah, wa-hey! God loves us, whoo-pah, wa-hey!

D
C
1.
D
God loves you. God loves

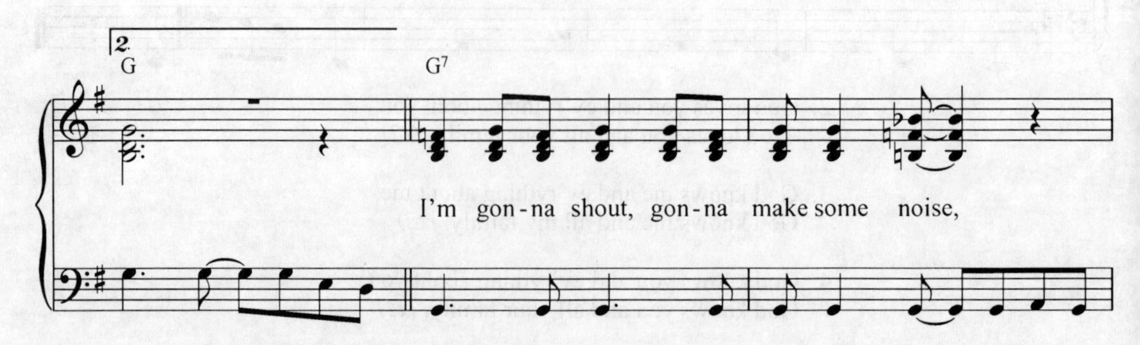
2.
G
G7
I'm gon-na shout, gon-na make some noise,

F
C
I'm gon-na sing, gon-na raise my voice,
I'm gon-na dance, gon-na
G
F
C
go a lit-tle cra-zy, will you?
Will you go, will you go?
G
F
I'm gon-na jump, gon-na jump up high,
I'm gon-na raise my hands
C
to the sky,
I'm gon-na dance, gon-na
G
1.
D.S.
D
C/D
D
go com-plete-ly loop-y, will you?
God loves

2.
G
F
Whoo, whoo - pah, way - eh - hey - eh! Whoo, whoo - pah,
C
way - eh - hey - eh! Whoo, whoo - pah, way - eh - hey - eh!
F
C
G
God loves you and no - thing you can do will ev - er change that.
D
C/D
D
G
God loves me, whoo - pah, wa - hey! God loves
G
C
G
you, whoo - pah, wa - hey! God loves us, whoo - pah wa - hey,

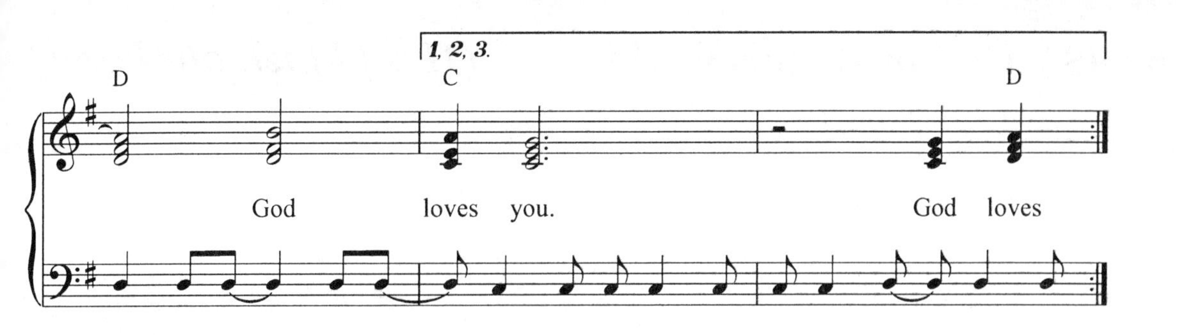
1, 2, 3.
D
C
D
God loves you. God loves

4.
C
Am
G
loves you. God loves us, whoo-pah, wa - hey!

D
C
G
God loves you.

483 God made this world *(This planet, our home)*

Words and Music: Jennifer Reay

Folk-rock feel (♩ = 132)
Capo 3
F D
B♭/F G/D
F D
B♭/F G/D
F D
C A
Dm Bm
1. God made this world and put us here: God made this
2. So much pol - lu - tion in the air, find a so -
F7 D7
B♭ G
F/A D/F♯
world for us to share. Oh what a gift for us;
lu - tion, show we care. Treat it with dig - ni - ty;
Gm Em
Csus4 Asus4
C A
F D
this pla - net, our home. Look - ing a -
this pla - net, our home. For - ests and
C A
Dm Bm
F7 D7
round we see some ways that we have spoiled this won - der - ful place;
crea - tures dy - ing out; sad - ness and suf - f'ring, there's no doubt;

B♭ G
F/A D/F♯
Gm Em
Csus4 Asus4
God has a job for us, on this pla-net, our home.
God has a job for us, on this pla-net, our home.
C A
Chorus
F D
A F♯
We'll do our best for him, oh, no-thing
Dm Bm
F7 D7
B♭ G
less for him. We're liv-ing in God's world;
F/A D/F♯
G7 E7
C A
what can we do to make it bet-ter? We'll do our
F D
A F♯
Dm Bm
best for him, oh, no-thing less for him.

F7
D7
B♭
G
F/A
D/F♯
We've got a job to do, it's up to me and you, so we'll
Gm
Em
F
D
2nd time to Coda
B♭
G
F
D
do our best for him.
B♭/C
G/A
D.S. al Coda
CODA
B♭
G
F
D
Do our best for God,
It's a place to share,
B♭
G
F
D
B♭
G
on this pla-net, our home.
on this pla-net, our home.
This pla-net, our
F
D
B♭
G
rall.
F
D
home.
This pla-net, our home.

484 God of the earth and sky *(God with a loving heart)*

Words and Music: Gill Hutchinson

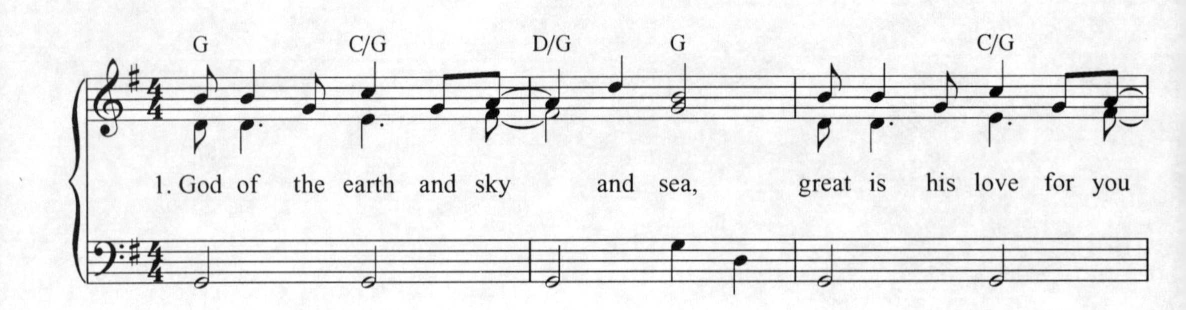
G
C/G
D/G
G
G
C/G
1. God of the earth and sky and sea, great is his love for you

D/G
G
C
D
G
and me. He is the God with a lov-ing heart.

D
G
C/G
D/G
G
C/G
He is the God whose word is true, he knows the things we say

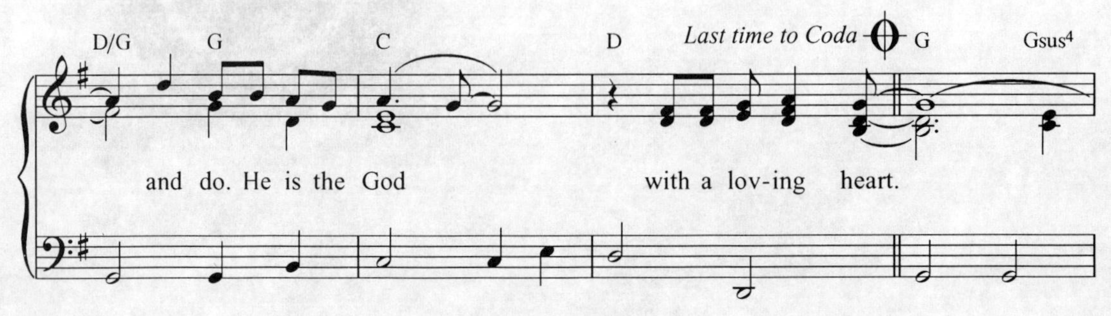
D/G
G
C
D
Last time to Coda
G
Gsus4
and do. He is the God with a lov-ing heart.

G
C
D
Em
D
He wants us all to trust him, our mak - er and our friend.
G
D
Em
Am
He's al - ways there be - side us, his love will ne - ver end.
CODA
Dsus4
D
D.C. al Coda
G
Em
He is the
C
D
G
Gsus4
G
God with a lov - ing heart.

2. He is the God who shows he cares,
   he is the one who's always there,
   he is the God with a loving heart.
   He is the God whose praise we sing,
   he is the Lord of ev'rything,
   he is the God with a loving heart,
   he is the God with a loving heart.

185 God, our Father, gave us life

Words and Music: Kathleen Middleton
arr. Noel Rawsthorne

D G Bm A D G
1. God, our Fa - ther, gave us life, he keeps us
A E A A7 G A
in his care; help us care for
D Bm D A7 D
o - thers too: Lord, hear our prayer;
A D A7 D
Lord, hear our prayer.

2. When we're frightened, hurt or tired,
there's always someone there.
Make us thankful for their love:
Lord, hear our prayer;
Lord, hear our prayer.

3. All God's children need his love,
a love that we can share.
So, we pray for ev'ryone:
Lord, hear our prayer;
Lord, hear our prayer.

486 God says 'Don't be afraid'

Words and Music: Chris Jackson
arr. Dave Bankhead

G
God says (God says), 'Don't be a - fraid,

Em
C
(don't be a-fraid), be-cause I have saved you,

D
1.
Am7
I have called you by name.'
God

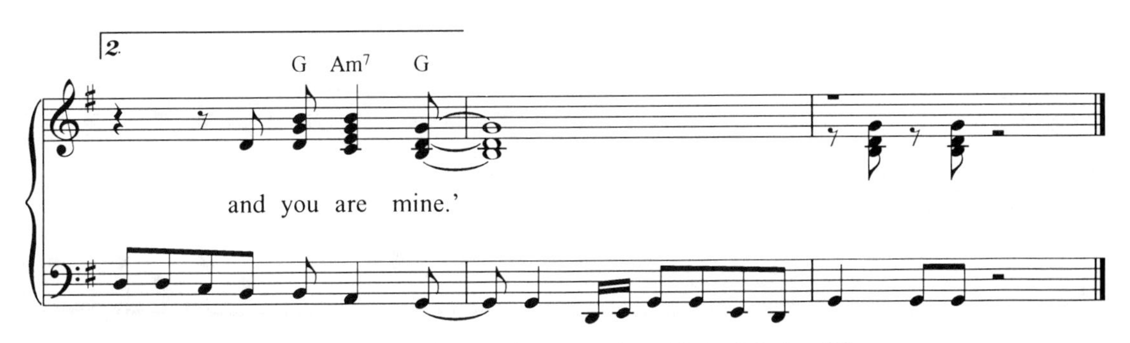
2.
G Am7 G
and you are mine.'

487 God's hands

Words and Music: Andy Read
arr. Chris Mitchell

A
E
D
God's hands, I'm in God's hands. There's no saf - er place that I can

E
A
E
be. God's hands, I'm in God's hands.

To repeat
Last time
D
E
A
A
Fine
There's no saf - er place that I can be. be.

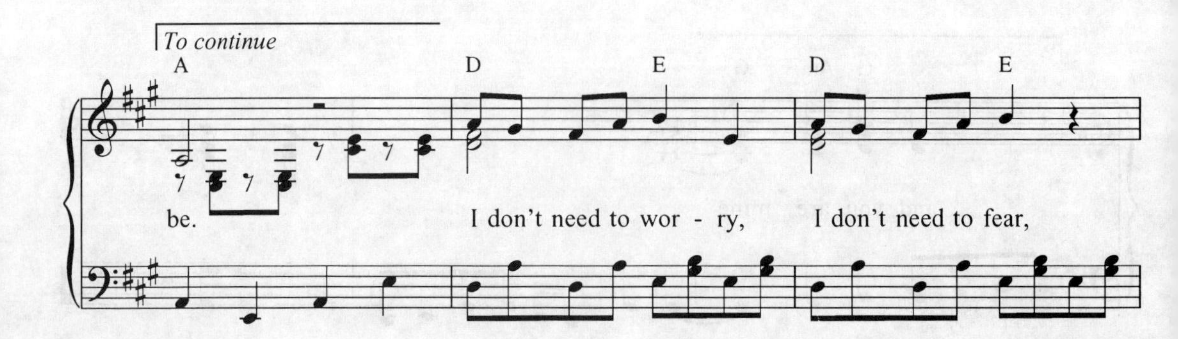
To continue
A
D
E
D
E
be. I don't need to wor - ry, I don't need to fear,

D
E
E7/G♯
A
E
all I need to do is know that God is near.

D
E
D
E
I don't need to trem - ble, I don't need to cry,

D
E
E7/G♯
A
E
all I need to do is know that God is near,

E7/G♯
A
E
E7/G♯
A
E
God is near, God is near.

488 Gonna lift you up *(Up! When I'm feeling down)*

Words and Music: Andy Read
arr. Chris Mitchell

Chorus
Am7
D7
E7
Gon-na lift you up when I'm feel-ing down. Gon-na lift you up when I'm feel-ing down, down, down. Gon-na lift you up when I'm feel-ing down.
That's the place I want to be, Ho-ly Spi-rit, set me free.
To repeat
Last time
To continue
Fine
Ho-ly Spi-rit, set me free. Ho-ly Spi-rit, set me free.

Am7
D7
E7
1. Je - sus is the name a - bove ev - 'ry name.
Am7
D7
E7
Je - sus is the one who will ne - ver change. His
Am7
D7
E7
love is faith - ful, true to the ve - ry end,
Am7
Chorus
D.S.
there is no one else who can pro - mise the same! Gon-na lift you

2. Jesus has the pow'r over ev'ry fear,
deepest kind of love that will come so near.
It's knocking at the door of your very heart,
there is no one else who can love you quite the same.

489 Gonna live for him

Words and Music: Andy Read
arr. Chris Mitchell

Capo 3
1. Gon-na live for him, gon-na live for him,
gon-na live for him for the rest of my
life. Gon-na live for
Chorus
I don't
care what I feel, I don't care what I see, I'm gon - na
shout it out a-loud: he saved me! Gon-na live for

F
D
him,
gon-na live for
him,
gon-na live for
C7
A7
1.
F
D
D.S.
him
for the rest of my
life.
2. Gon-na fol - low
2.
F
D
C7
A7
F
D
C7
A7
life,
for the rest of my
life,
for the rest of my
F
D
C7
A7
F
D
life,
for the rest of my
life.

2. Gonna follow him . . .

3. Gonna praise his name . . .

490 Goodbye, goodbye

Words and Music: Andy Pickford

Chorus
C
G
C
Good - bye, good - bye to ev - 'ry - one, good - bye, good - bye, good -

F
C
G
Am
bye. We thank you, Lord, for ev - 'ry - one, good -

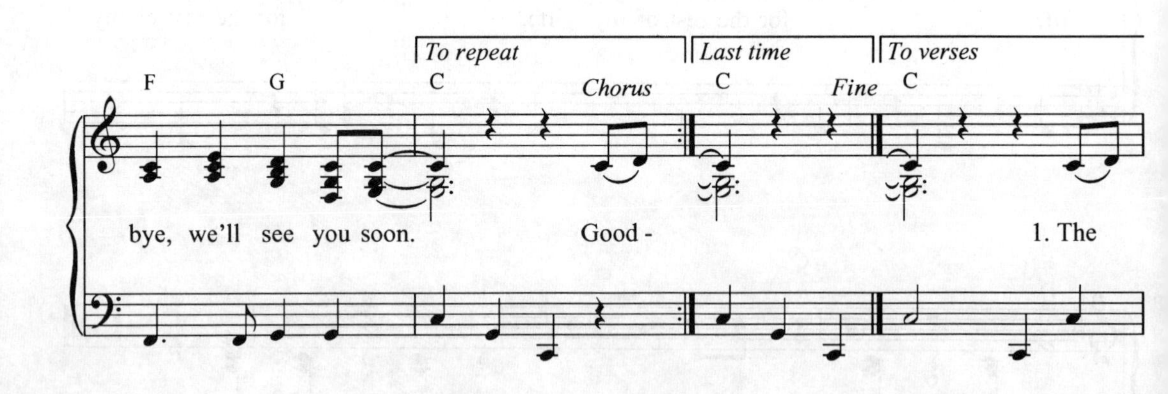
To repeat
Last time
To verses
F
G
C
Chorus
C
Fine
C
bye, we'll see you soon. Good - 1. The

G
C
F
C
G
time has come for us to go, we thank you, Lord, for be - ing here, to

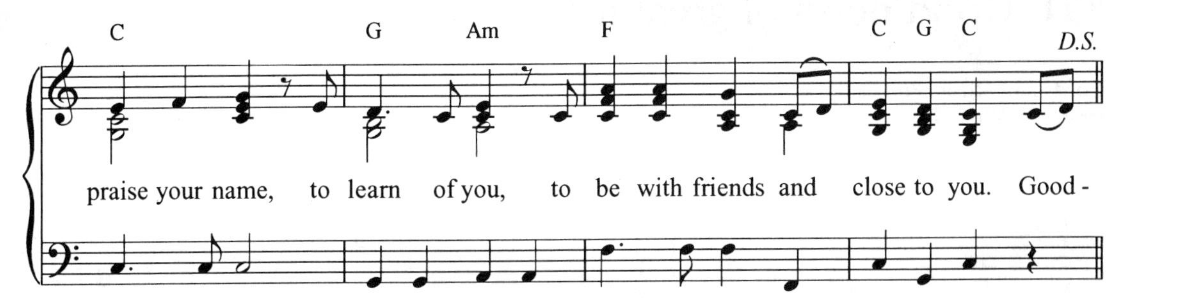
C
G
Am
F
C
G
C
D.S.
praise your name, to learn of you, to be with friends and close to you. Good -

2. This is our prayer as we go home:
   please keep us safe in all we do,
   please be with us at home and school;
   we thank you, Lord, for loving us.

491 Good news of great joy

Words and Music: Phil Chapman
arr. Chris Mitchell

PART 1
G
B
Em
A
G/D
D
Good news of great joy to all men on

G
D
G
B7
Em
A
earth. In the old town of Beth - le - hem, our

G/D
D
G
PART 2
B
Sa - viour had his birth. God's mes - sage to all sin - ful men the

Em
A
G/B
D
same as to the shep - herds then is in these joy - ful

G D G B7
words, 'A Sa - viour born in Da - vid's town' and

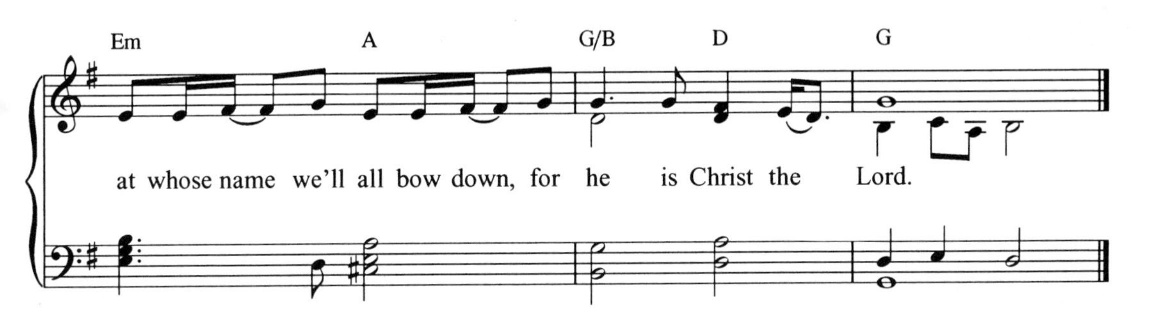
Em A G/B D G
at whose name we'll all bow down, for he is Christ the Lord.

492 Hallelu, hallelu, hallelujah

Words and Music: James Wright
arr. Chris Mitchell

Chorus
Capo 3
F C7 F B♭ F/C C7 F
D A7 D G D/A A7 D
Hal-le - lu, hal-le-lu, hal-le-lu - jah, praise ye the Lord. Hal-le-

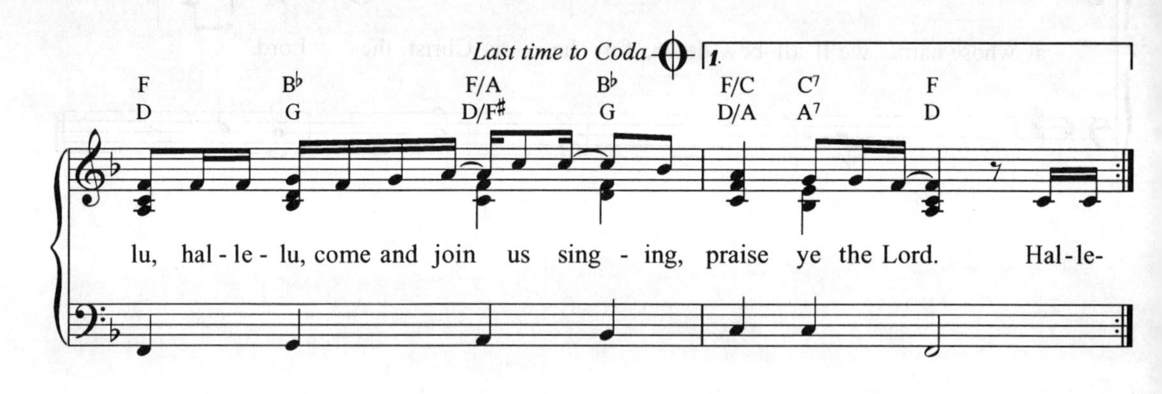
Last time to Coda
1.
F B♭ F/A B♭ F/C C7 F
D G D/F♯ G D/A A7 D
lu, hal-le-lu, come and join us sing - ing, praise ye the Lord. Hal-le-

2.
F/C C7 F
D/A A7 D
praise ye the Lord. 1. Now Je - sus was born of Ma - ry

Gm7 C7 F
Em7 A7 D
in Beth-le-hem, in a dus - ty sta - ble with a low-ly cra - dle

Gm7 C7 F B♭ F/A
Em7 A7 D G D/F♯
in Beth-le-hem. And all the a-ni-mals stand-ing in the straw must have
Gm7 Am7 D7 Gm7 F/A
Em7 F♯m7 B7 Em7 D/F♯
won-dered who he was, was he just the son of a car-pen-ter, or was
B♭ B♭/C C
G G/A A
Chorus D.S.
this the Son of God? Hal-le-
CODA
F/C C7 Dm7 G7 F/C C7 Dm7 G7 F/C C7 F
D/A A7 Bm7 E7 D/A A7 Bm7 E7 D/A A7 D
praise ye the Lord. Praise ye the Lord. Praise ye the Lord.

2. Now shepherds were sat on the hillside
   in Bethlehem,
   when a host of angels started singing praises
   in Bethlehem.
   And the night lit up with an awesome sight
   and the shepherds looked amazed,
   but the angel said, 'Please do not fear,
   your King is born this day.'

3. Now wise men travelled a long way
   to Bethlehem,
   from the Orient to the land of Israel
   to Bethlehem.
   And the star shone bright in the sky that night
   to show them where to go,
   so that they may bring gifts to the King,
   myrrh, frankincense and gold.

493 Hark, the herald-angels sing

Words: Charles Wesley, George Whitefield, Martin Madan and others, alt.

Music: adapted from Felix Mendelssohn by William Hayman Cummings

MENDELSSOHN 77 77 D and Refrain
Capo 3
F C F C F Am B♭ Gm F C
D A D A D F♯m G Em D A
1. Hark, the he - rald - an - gels sing glo - ry to the new - born
F C7 Dm F G7 Am G C F G7
D A7 Bm D E7 F♯m E A D E7
King; peace on earth and mer - cy mild, God and sin - ners re - con -
C F C7 F C F C7 F
A D A7 D A D A7 D
ciled: joy - ful, all ye na - tions rise, join the tri - umph of the
C B♭ Cm6 Gm D7 Gm C C7 F C F
A G Am6 Em B7 Em A A7 D A D
skies, with th'an - ge - lic host pro - claim, 'Christ is born in Beth - le - hem.'

B♭
G
Am Gm D Gm C C7 F C7 F
F♯m Em B Em A A7 D A7 D
Chorus
Unison
Hark, the her - ald - an - gels sing glo - ry to the new-born King.

2. Christ by highest heav'n adored,
   Christ, the everlasting Lord,
   late in time behold him come,
   offspring of a virgin's womb!
   Veiled in flesh the Godhead see,
   hail th'incarnate Deity!
   Pleased as man with us to dwell,
   Jesus, our Emmanuel.

3. Hail, the heav'n-born Prince of Peace!
   Hail, the Sun of Righteousness!
   Light and life to all he brings,
   ris'n with healing in his wings;
   mild he lays his glory by,
   born that we no more may die,
   born to raise us from the earth,
   born to give us second birth.

494 Have you ever had *(With God anything is possible)*

Words and Music: Dave Cooke

Gently
E D A E7
1. Have you e - ver had five thou-sand peo-ple to lunch, then
A7
found that you've no - thing in the fridge to munch? It's
B
ve - ry in - con - ve - nient and it's hard to ig - nore, when they're
E A B E D A
climb - ing through the win-dow and bang-ing on the door! But
E7 A7
Je - sus was teach-ing one fine day and peo-ple came to hear what he had to say:

B
E
A
B
'Love your neigh-bour, feed the poor,
pray to God, that's what your knees are for!'
A
E/G♯
F♯m
E/G♯
Chorus
With God, a - ny-thing is pos - si - ble,
with God, a - ny-thing at all. When
A
E
things ap - pear im - pos - si - ble, and pret - ty un - be - liev - a - ble,
A
E
B
to - tal - ly im - pro - ba - ble and ve - ry un - pre - dic - ta - ble,
re - mem - ber,
2nd time to Bridge
A
E
A
B
E
Fine
with God a - ny - thing is pos - si - ble,
with God a - ny - thing at all.

E D A E7
2. And he taught for hours and it got quite late, the dis -
A7
ci - ples checked their wat - ches, it was half past eight, and they
B
said to the crowd: 'Go and get some food.' But
E A B
Je - sus said: 'You feed this mul - ti - tude.' They said: 'We've
E7 A7
on - ly got five bread rolls and two lit - tle fish-es in a ve - ry small bowl.
B E A B
That's not e - nough for such a crowd.' When Je - sus stood up and said out loud:

E7
A7
'Give them to me, give them to me, I'm gon-na say grace and then you'll see.' And he
B
E
A
B
D.S.
broke the bread be - fore their eyes, then the food just start - ed to mul - ti - ply.
BRIDGE
E
D
A
E
And af - ter they had fin-ished they could eat no more, there were
A7
lots of bro - ken pie - ces all o - ver the floor, twelve
B
bags were col - lec - ted, that's no lie, when
E
E7/G#
A7
A#dim
E/B
A/B
E
E7
D.S. al Fine
Je - sus fed five thou - sand with a fish and bread pie.

495 Hear the sound of people singing

(The Christmas Child)

Words and Music: Graham Kendrick

G
F/G
G
F/G
1. Hear the sound of peo - ple sing - ing, all the bells are
In the streets the lights are glow - ing, but there is no
G
F/G
G
ring - ing for the Christ - mas Child.
know - ing of the Christ - mas Child.
Chorus
Fsus2
C/E
G
Oh, let this Child be born in your heart,
Fsus2
C/E
G
oh, let this Child be born in your heart, to -

F/G
G
F/G
night,
to - night.
To - night,
G
1.
2.
D.C.
D.S.
to - night.
3.
F/G
G
F/G
(2nd time pp)
G
F/G
1.
2.
G
Gsus2
(2nd time rall.)

2. Will our wars go on for ever,
and will peace be never
at Christmastime?
If we keep him in the manger
then there is no danger
from the Christmas Child.

496 Heaven invites you to a party

Words and Music: Graham Kendrick

Joyful, with a strong rhythm
Bsus4
B
cresc.

E
A/E
Hea - ven in - vites you to a par - ty, to ce - le - brate the birth of a

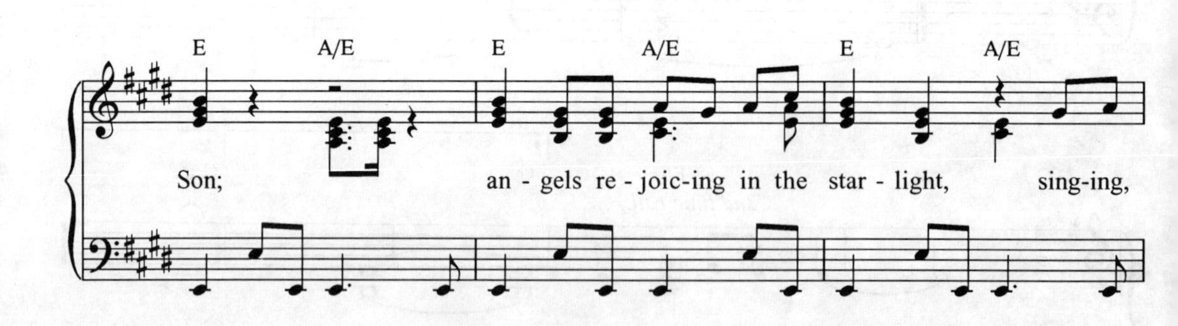
E
A/E
Son; an - gels re - joic - ing in the star - light, sing - ing,

3rd time to
1.
2.
E
A/E
'Christ your Sa - viour has come'. come.'
Leader
And it's for

E
(echo)
you (and it's for you) and it's for me (and it's for me), for all your
door (now hea - ven's door) is o - pen wide (is o - pen wide), so come on
friends (for all your friends), and fa - mi - ly (and fa - mi - ly). Now hea - ven's
in (so come on in), step in -
2.
D.S.
E A/E E
side (come step in - side). come'.
All
An - gels from the
C♯m B E
realms of glo - ry, wing your flight o'er all the earth; you who sang cre -
C♯m B E
Leader
a - tion's sto - ry, now pro - claim Mes - si - ah's birth. And it's for

E
(echo)
you (and it's for you) and it's for me (and it's for me), for all your
blast (let trum-pets blast), let mu-sic play (let mu-sic play), let peo-ple
friends (for all your friends), and fa-mi-ly (and fa-mi-ly). Let trum-pets
shout (let peo-ple shout), let ban-ners
1.
2.
wave (let ban-ners wave).
Leader
All
Come, all you peo-ple, Come, all you peo-ple,
Send in-vi-ta-tions Send in-vi-ta-tions
A/E E A/E E A/E E A/E E
Leader
All
Leader
join hands to-ge-ther, join hands to-ge-ther, bring all your neigh-bours,
to ev-'ry na-tion, to ev-'ry na-tion, come and a-dore him,
B
All
Leader
All
bring all your neigh-bours, ev-'ry-bo-dy! ev-'ry-bo-dy!
come and a-dore him,

C F B♭/F
Leader All
ev - 'ry - bo - dy! ev - 'ry - bo - dy! Hea - ven in - vites you to a
F B♭/F F B♭/F F B♭/F
par - ty, to ce - le - brate the birth of a Son;
F B♭/F F B♭/F F B♭/F
an - gels re - joic-ing in the star - light, sing-ing, 'Christ your Sa-viour has
F B♭/F F
Leader
(echo)
come.' And it's for you (and it's for you) and it's for
blast (let trum - pets blast), let mu - sic
me (and it's for me), for all your friends (for all your friends), and fa - mi -
play (let mu - sic play), let peo - ple shout (let peo - ple shout), let ban - ners
1.
2.
ly (and fa - mi - ly). Let trum - pets wave (let ban - ners wave).

497 He came in love to bring hope

Words and Music: Margaret Carpenter
arr. Dave Bankhead

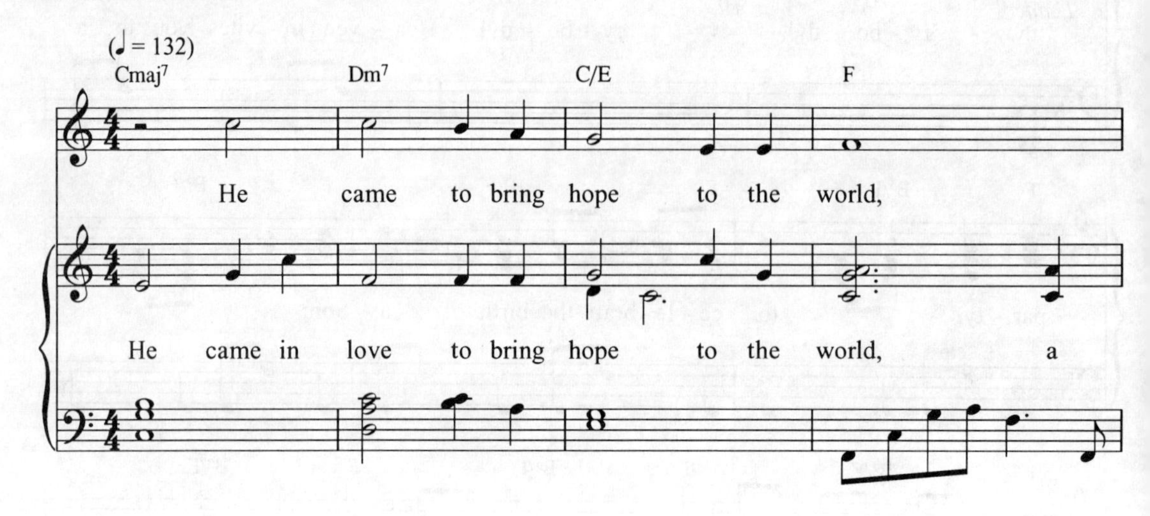

(♩= 132)
Cmaj7
Dm7
C/E
F
He came to bring hope to the world,
He came in love to bring hope to the world, a

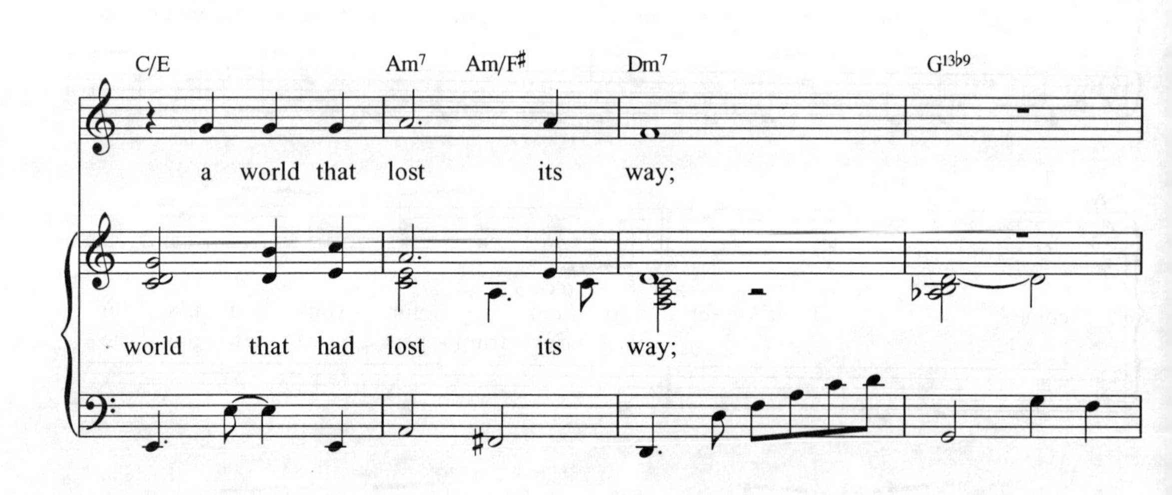

C/E
Am7
Am/F♯
Dm7
G13♭9
a world that lost its way;
world that had lost its way;

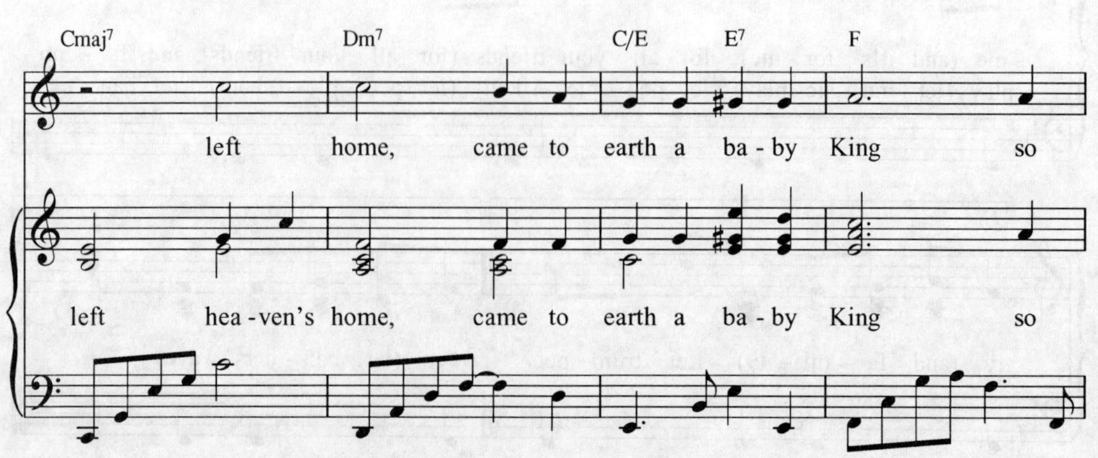

Cmaj7
Dm7
C/E
E7
F
left home, came to earth a ba - by King so
left hea - ven's home, came to earth a ba - by King so

C/G Am D9 Dm7/G G7
now, ev - 'ry Christ-mas we can glad - ly sing:
now, ev - 'ry Christ-mas we can glad - ly sing: Let the

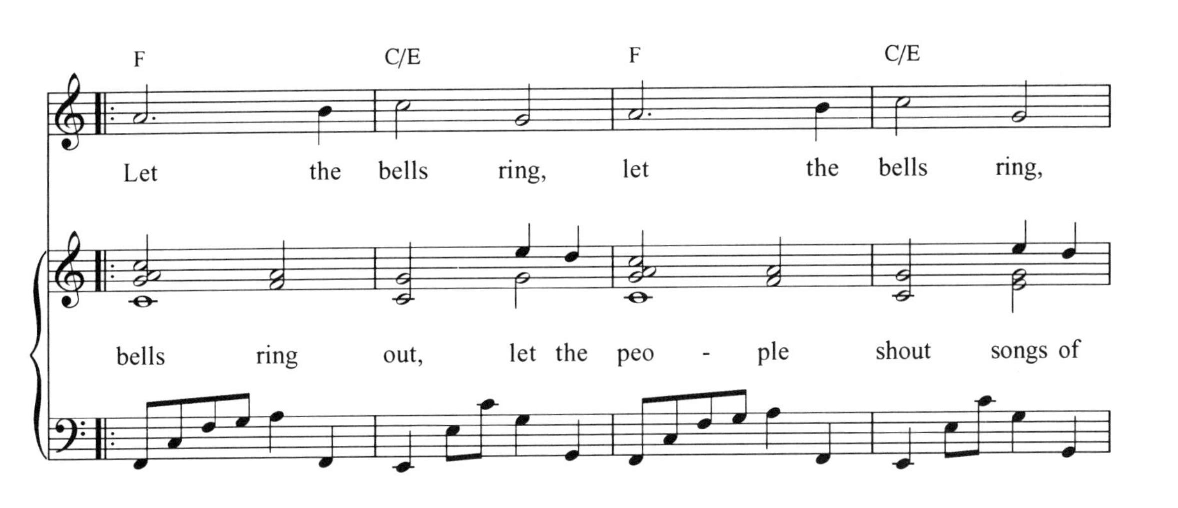
F C/E F C/E
Let the bells ring, let the bells ring,
bells ring out, let the peo - ple shout songs of

1.
F Am/F# G7sus4 G7
joy to the King, the King of kings.
joy to the King, the King of kings. Let the

2
G7
Cmaj7
Dm7
kings. Let's be first to
kings. Let's be the first to
C/E
E7
Fmaj7
2nd time to Coda
C/G
share his love on earth.
share his love on earth, for it's Christ - mas
F/G
G7
Csus4
C
D.C.
D.C.
time a - gain!
CODA
C/G
F/G
G7
C
It is Christ - mas, it's that time a - gain!
Christ - mas time a - gain!

498 He can do the impossible

Words and Music: James Wright
arr. Dave Bankhead

D
G
He can do the im-pos-si-ble, change the un-change-

D/A
A
D
-a-ble, love the un-lov-ab-le. He can cleanse the un-cleans-

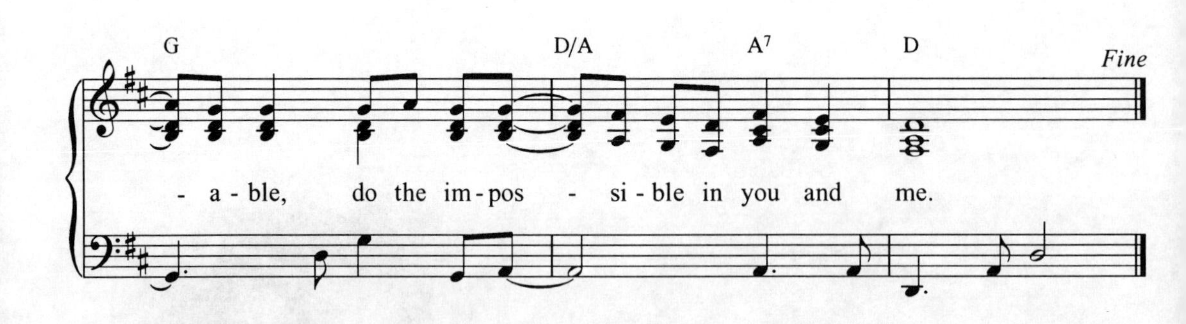
G
D/A
A7
D
Fine
-a-ble, do the im-pos-si-ble in you and me.

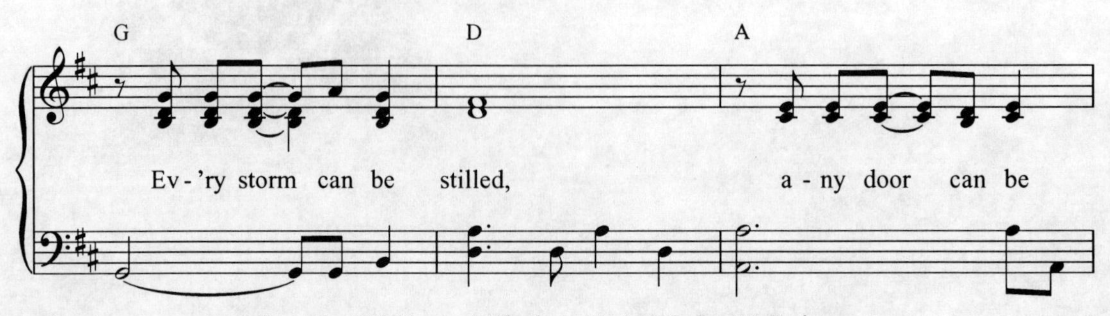
G
D
A
Ev-'ry storm can be stilled, a-ny door can be

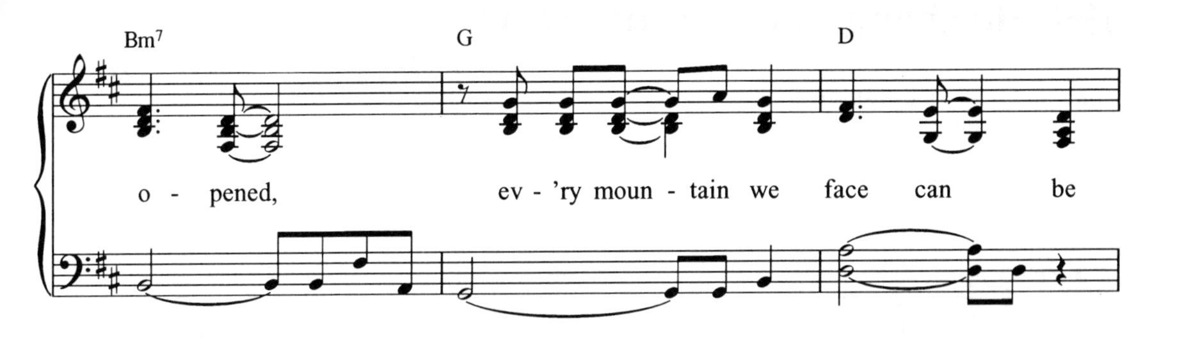
Bm7
G
D
o - pened,
ev - 'ry moun - tain we face can be

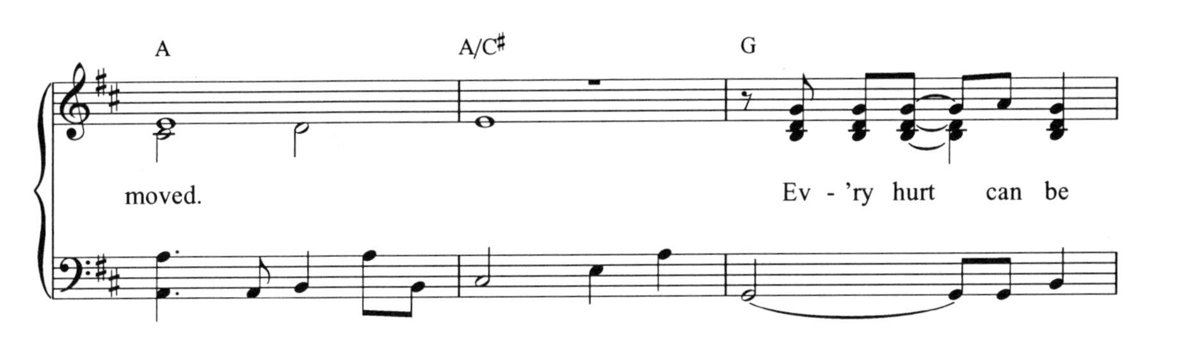
A
A/C♯
G
moved.
Ev - 'ry hurt can be

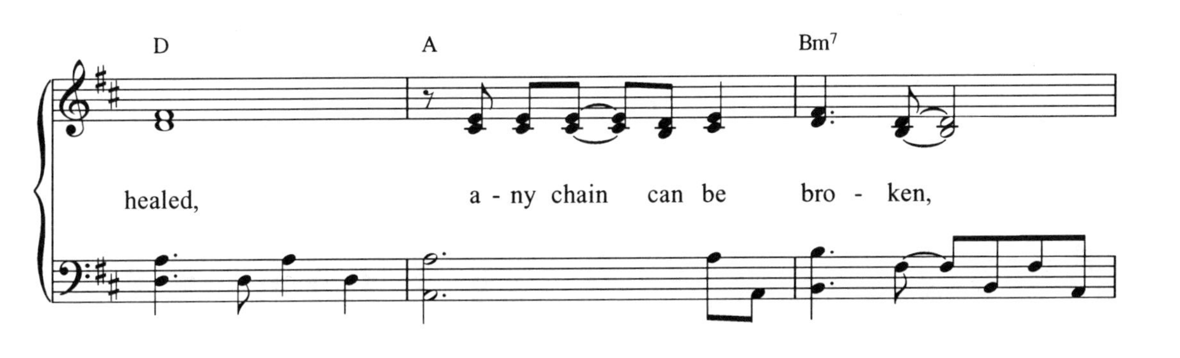
D
A
Bm7
healed,
a - ny chain can be bro - ken,

G
D
A
D.C.
in all of these things we can prove:

499 He changed water into wine

(The greatest miracle)

Words and Music: Steve Morgan-Gurr
and Kay Morgan-Gurr

Country rock (♩ = 180)
Chorus
A
He changed wa - ter in - to wine, healed the sick and
E F♯m D
cured the blind; told his friends where they would find the
E A
best fish in the sea. Mi - ra - cles his pow - er show,
E F♯m D
though it hap-pened long a - go: the great - est mi - ra - cle I know is
E A E A
what he's done for me, what he's done for me.
Fine

E
A
1. Mi - ra - cles are there to show us all who Je - sus was,

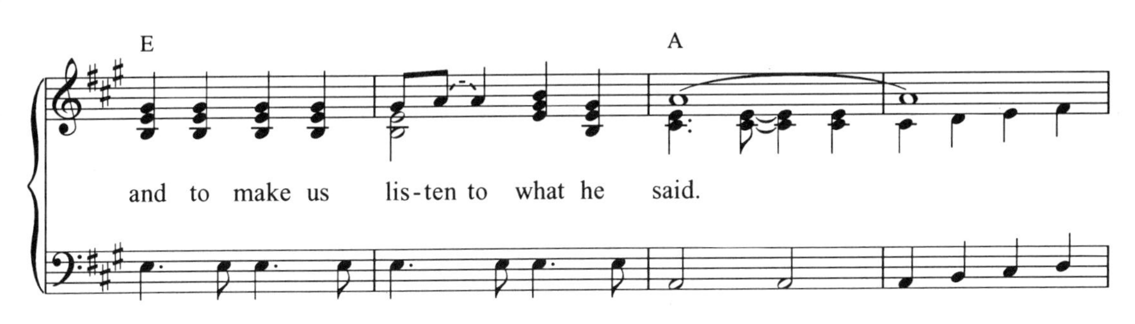
E
A
and to make us lis - ten to what he said.

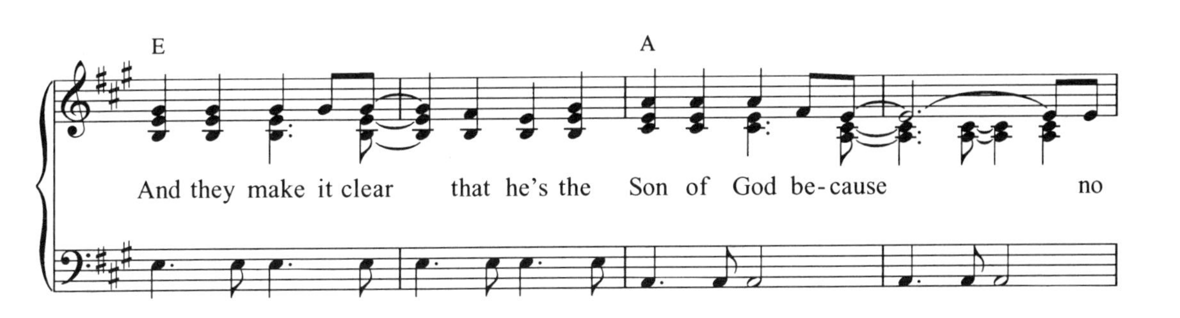
E
A
And they make it clear that he's the Son of God be - cause no

F♯m
E
D.C.
one else could give life to the dead.

2. If we turn to Jesus and are sorry for our sin,
God's word makes it plain for all to see:
from that brand new start, the greatest miracle begins,
the miracle of life eternally.

500 He gave me two ears to hear *(Two ears to hear)*

Words and Music: Andrew Pearson and Pauline Pearson

With a swing
C G C F G
He gave me two ears to hear, and one mouth to shout,
C F C G7 Am
but un - less I take time to lis - ten to God, I won't
F G C F C
know what I'm shout - ing a - bout. So I'm lis - ten - ing to what the
G C F C G
Fa - ther says, I'm lis - ten - ing to him: on - ly
F C F Em A F G C
then will I hear of his love so clear, when I'm lis - ten - ing to him.

501 He is here

Words and Music: Andy Read
arr. Chris Mitchell

C
He is here, he is here, he is here in my heart. He is

F/G
G7
C
here, he is here, he is here in my heart. He is

here, he is here, he is here in my heart and

G7
C
I will not be a - fraid. He will

F C F C
teach me what's right, he will hold me at night, he is

F C G7sus4 G7
al - ways the clo - sest to me. He will

F C F C
show me what's wrong, and will sing me this song, and

G7 C
I will not be a - fraid.

502 He is K-I-N-G

Words and Music: Brian Howard
arr. Chris Mitchell

(♩ = 120)
Chorus
G7
D7
He is K I N G. He is Lord and
Lord of lords and

G7
G7
he is King. He is
King of kings. He is K I N G of my heart,

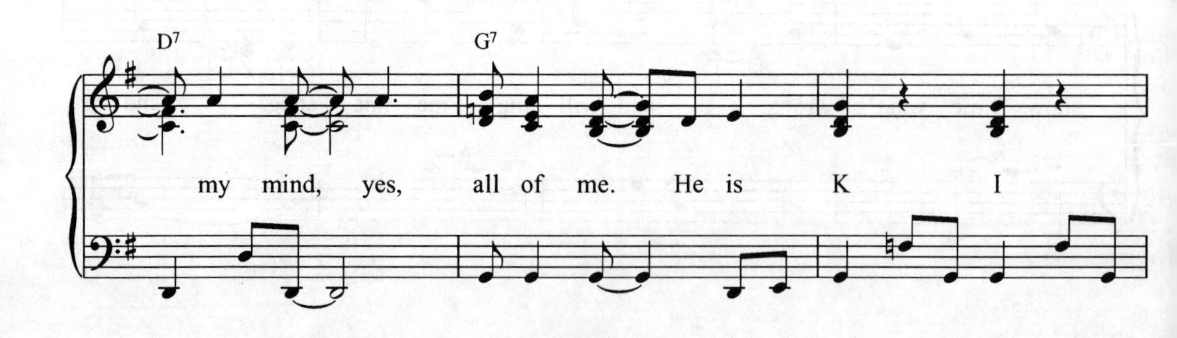
D7
G7
my mind, yes, all of me. He is K I

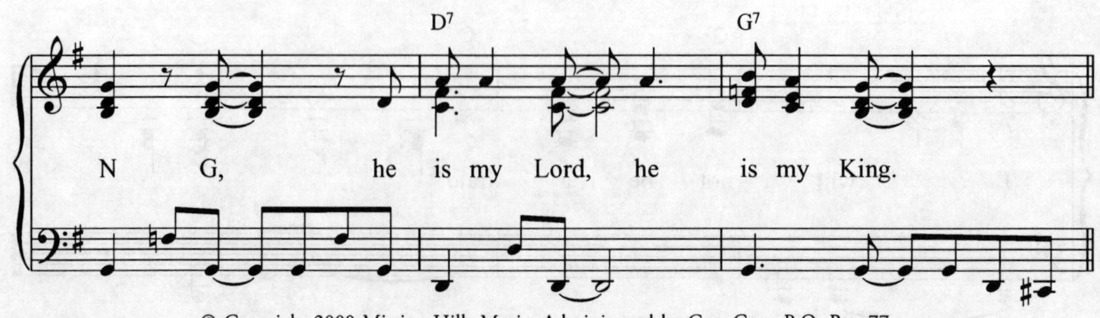
D7
G7
N G, he is my Lord, he is my King.

C7 G7 D7
1. He is Lord and he is King o - ver what has been and
2. Ev-'ry o - ther lord and king will one day
G7 C7 G7
what will be. Moun-tain tops and dark val - leys,
bend their knee. In the day of his com - ing they
A D7
high - est hea - vens and the deep-est seas.
will con - fess, he is the King of kings!
1.
K I N G, K I N G, K I N, he is
2.
K I N G.
D7(#9) G
Je - sus!

503 He is the one

Words and Music: Andrew Pearson and Pauline Pearson

Steadily
F
Capo 3 D
B♭
G
F
D
1. He is the one that sets my hands a - clap - ping, he is the one that sets

C
A
F
D
B♭
G
my hands free. He is the one that sets my hands a - clap - ping,

F
D
C
A
F
D
Chorus
he is the one for me. I wan-na tell you I'm clap - ping, I'm

B♭
G
F
D
C
A
F
D
clap - ping, I'm clap - ping, I'm clap - ping, I'm clap - ping, I'm

B♭
G
F
D
C
A
F
D
clap - ping, I'm clap - ping for my Lord.

2. He is the one that sets my feet a-dancing,
   he is the one that sets my feet free:
   he is the one that sets my feet a-dancing,
   he is the one for me.

3. He is the one that sets my voice a-singing,
   he is the one that sets my voice free:
   he is the one that sets my voice a-singing,
   he is the one for me.

4. He is the one that causes me to praise him,
   he is the one that sets me free:
   he is the one that causes me to praise him,
   he is the one for me.

Last Chorus:

I wanna tell you
I'm clapping, I'm dancing,
I'm singing, I'm praising,
I'm clapping, I'm dancing,
I'm singing for my Lord.

504 Hello, welcome

Words and Music: Andy Pickford

Moderato
G
C
G
Hel - lo,
wel - come,
in the name of the Lord,

D
G
C
Last time to Coda
(I said),
hel - lo,
wel - come,
we're

G
D
1.
G
2.
G
here to praise the Lord.
Hel - lo,

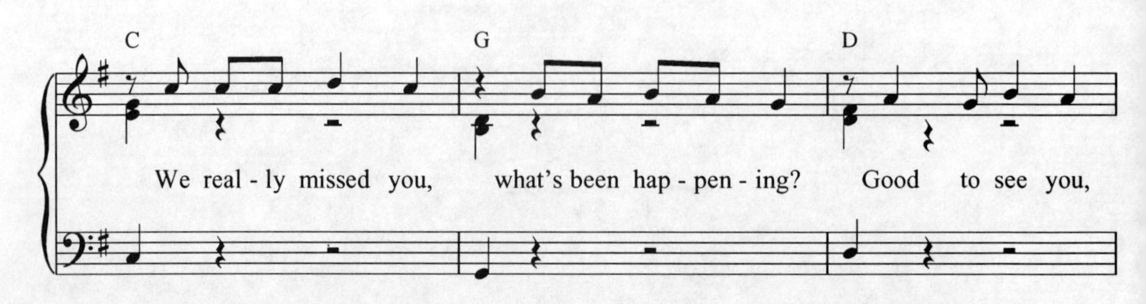
C
G
D
We real - ly missed you,
what's been hap - pen - ing?
Good to see you,

G C G
we real - ly care: we have a Fa - ther who's gon - na bless us all.

D
Now we're here to praise his name, now we're here to

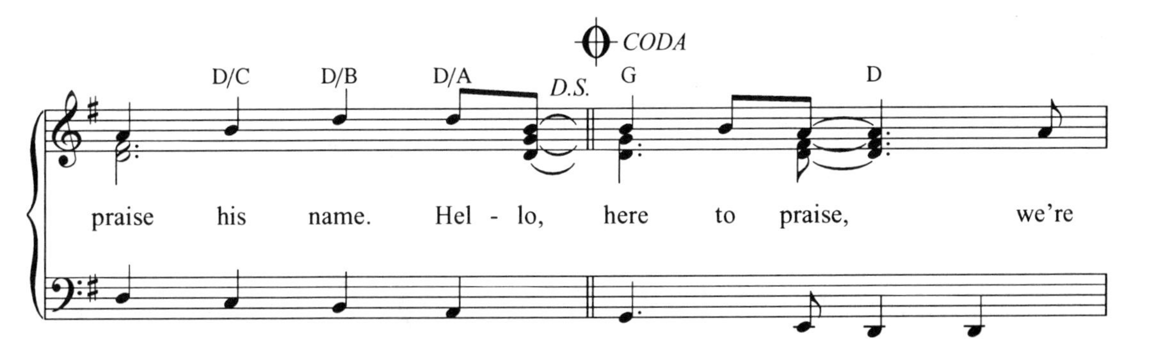
CODA
D/C D/B D/A D.S. G D
praise his name. Hel - lo, here to praise, we're

G D G D G
here to praise, we're here to praise the Lord.

505 He made the eyes of the blind man see

Words and Music: Paul Harvey
arr. Chris Mitchell

G
C
He made the eyes of the blind man see, the
D
G
Em
ears of the deaf man hear; he made the mute tongue
Am
D
G
shout for joy, the lame to leap like a deer. He made the
C
D
wind and the waves o - bey, he kept the hun - gry crowd
G
Em
Am
fed; and when they laid him in the tomb, he

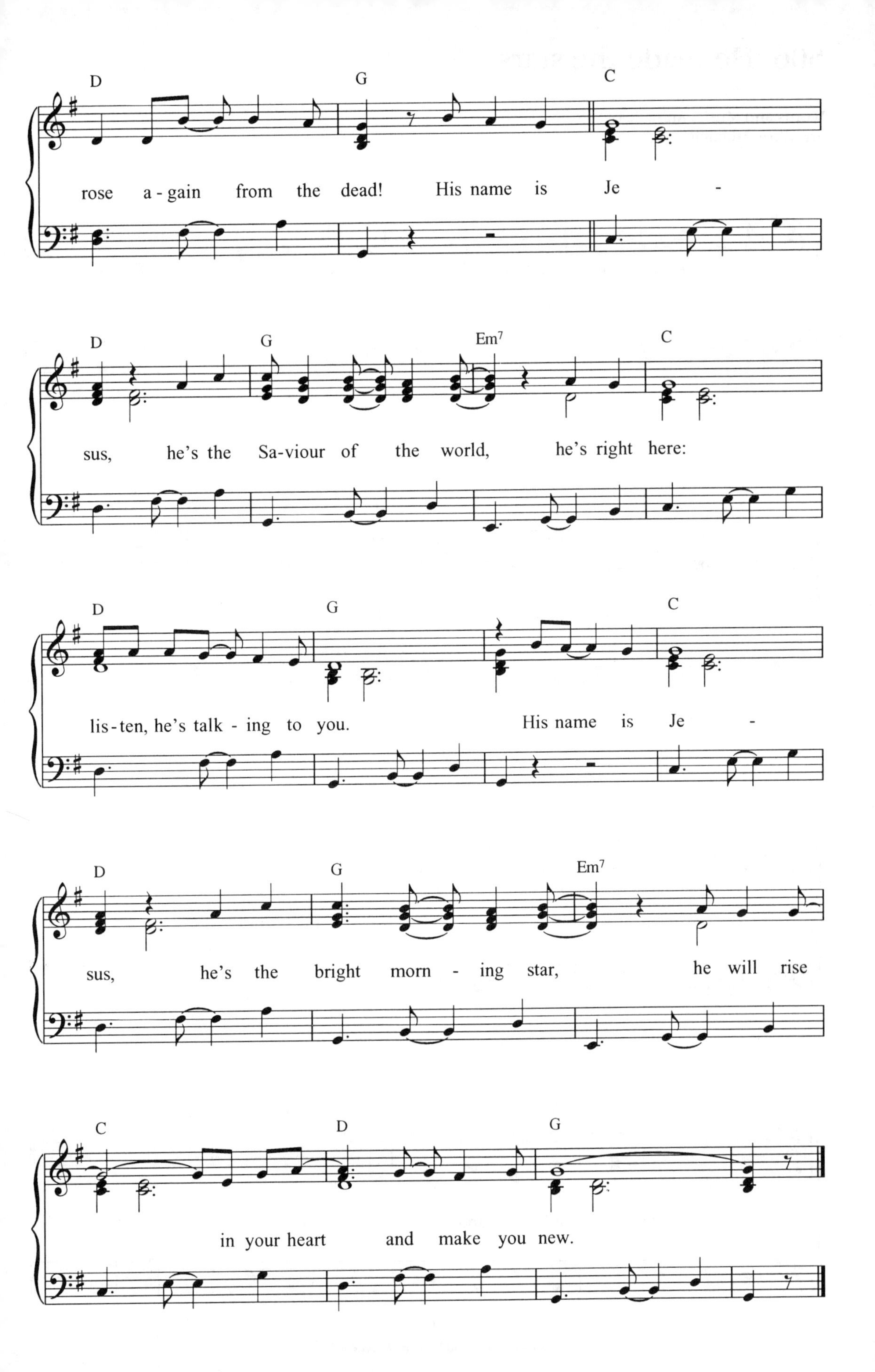
D
G
C
rose a-gain from the dead! His name is Je -
D
G
Em7
C
sus, he's the Sa-viour of the world, he's right here:
D
G
C
lis-ten, he's talk - ing to you. His name is Je -
D
G
Em7
sus, he's the bright morn - ing star, he will rise
C
D
G
in your heart and make you new.

506 He made the stars

Words and Music: Andy Read
arr. Chris Mitchell

D
A
D
A
He made the stars,
he made the trees,

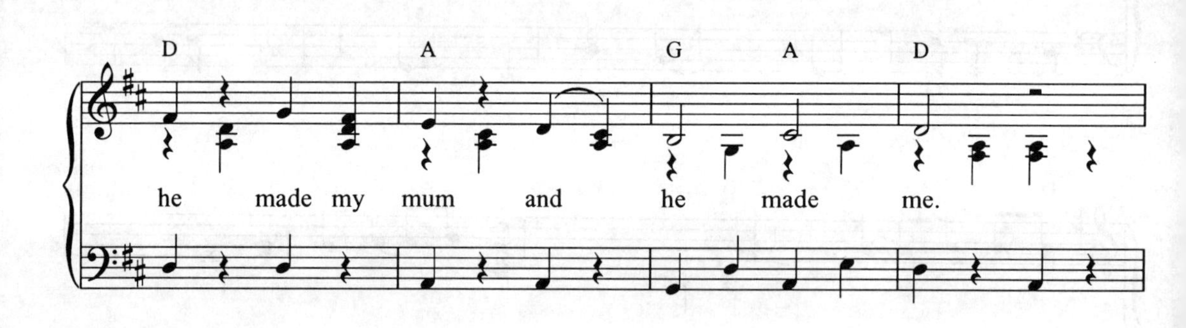
D
A
G
A
D
he made my mum and he made me.

A
D
A
He made the sun,
he made the birds,

D
A
G
A
D
he made my smile and he made me. Yes, the

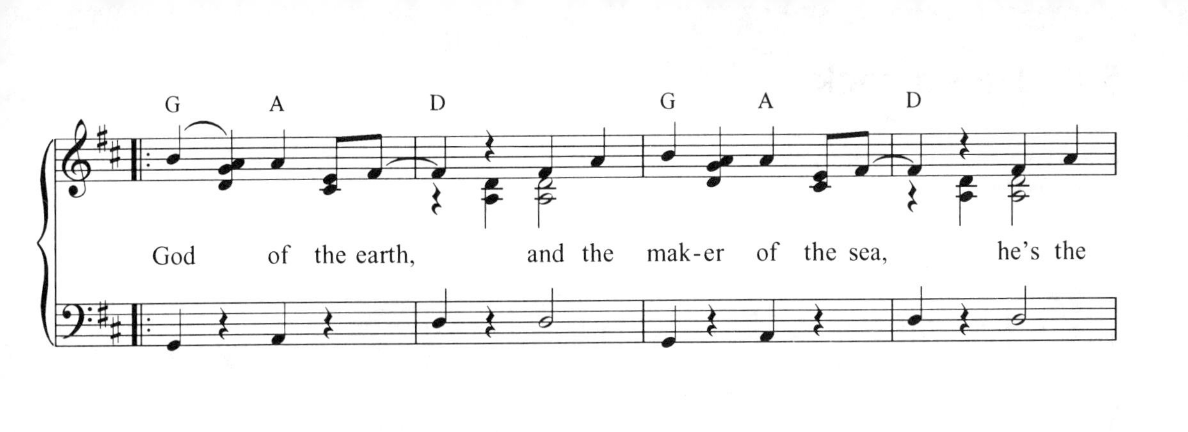
G A D G A D
God of the earth, and the mak-er of the sea, he's the

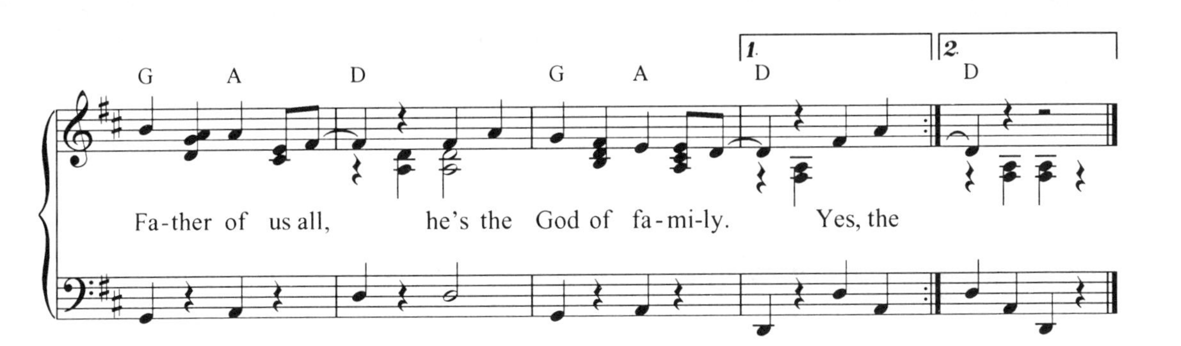
1. 2.
G A D G A D D
Fa-ther of us all, he's the God of fa-mi-ly. Yes, the

507 He's a rock

Words and Music: John Hardwick
arr. Chris Mitchell

A
He's a rock! His works are per - fect,

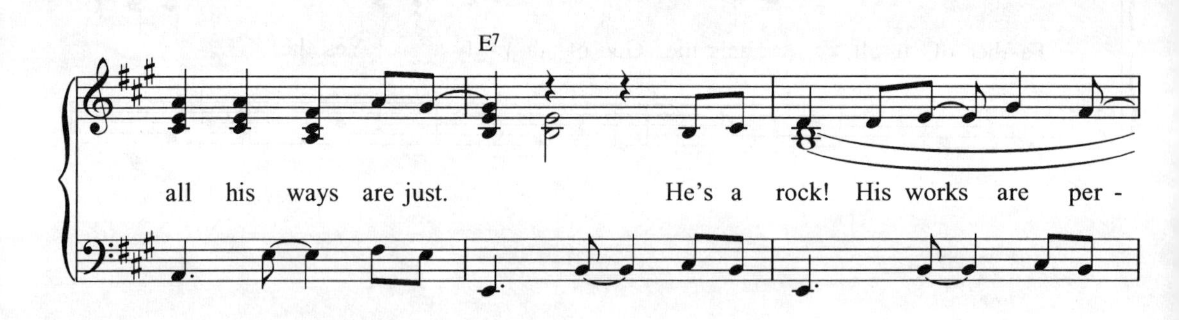
E7
all his ways are just. He's a rock! His works are per -

A
- fect, all his ways are just. He's a

faith - ful God who does no wrong; up - right and just is he!

E7
Look up chap - ter thir - ty - two, verse four
A
E7
of Deu - te - ro - no - my.
Look up chap - ter
A
thir - ty - two, verse four of Deu - te - ro - no - my.
Cha, cha, cha!

508 He's got the whole world in his hand

Words and Music: Traditional
arr. Christopher Tambling

A7
D
1. He's got the whole world in his hand. He's got the
A7
D
whole world in his hand. He's got the whole world
A7
D
in his hand. He's got the whole world in his hand.

2. He's got you and me, brother, in his hand. *(x3)*
   He's got the whole world in his hand.

3. He's got you and me, sister, in his hand. *(x3)*
   He's got the whole world in his hand.

4. He's got the little tiny baby in his hand. *(x3)*
   He's got the whole world in his hand.

5. He's got ev'rybody here in his hand. *(x3)*
   He's got the whole world in his hand.

509 He's the man who calmed the sea

(Everybody can meet him)

Words and Music: Nick Harding
arr. Dave Bankhead

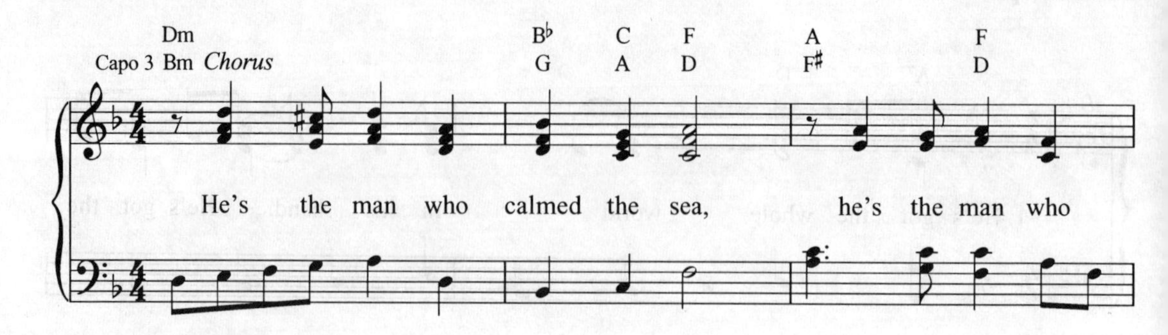
Dm
B♭ C F A F
Capo 3 Bm Chorus
G A D F♯ D
He's the man who calmed the sea, he's the man who

C A/C♯ Dm
A F♯/A♯ Bm
B♭ C F
G A D
died for me, he turned death to vic - to - ry and

A/C♯ A Dm Gm
F♯/A♯ F♯ Bm Em
Fine
ev - 'ry - bo - dy can meet him. 1. Je - sus came to

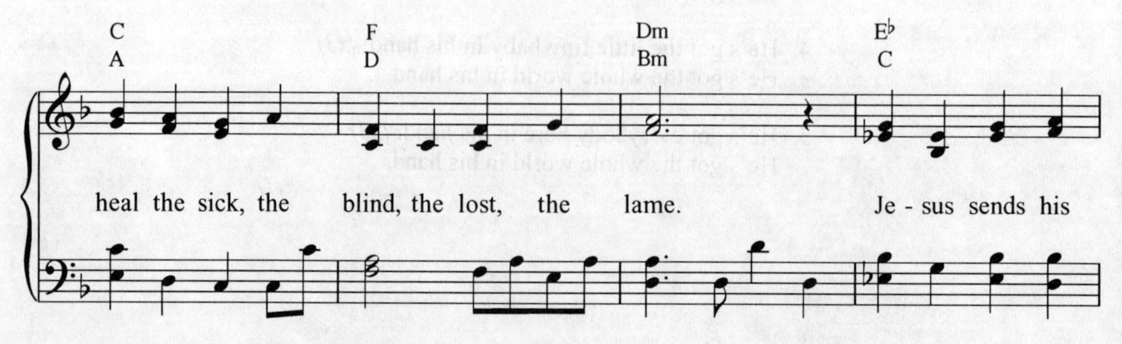
C F Dm E♭
A D Bm C
heal the sick, the blind, the lost, the lame. Je - sus sends his

Cm
Am
A/C♯
F♯/A♯
G⁷/B
E⁷/G♯
A
F♯
D.C.
Spi - rit now to help us just the same.

2. Jesus, only Son of God,
   who came to show the way.
   Jesus walks along with us
   to guide us ev'ry day.

3. There's a message for the world,
   good news for us to share.
   We can make a diff'rence now
   but only if we dare!

510 Hey! Hey! celebrate!

Words and Music: Ron Sivers
arr. Dave Bankhead

G D G C G/D D
Hey! hey! ce - le - brate! Je - sus is our Sa - viour.

To repeat / continue
Last time
G D G C C/D G C C/D G
Fine
Hey! hey! ce - le - brate! Je - sus is our King. Je - sus is our King.

D C D
Things will ne - ver be the same,

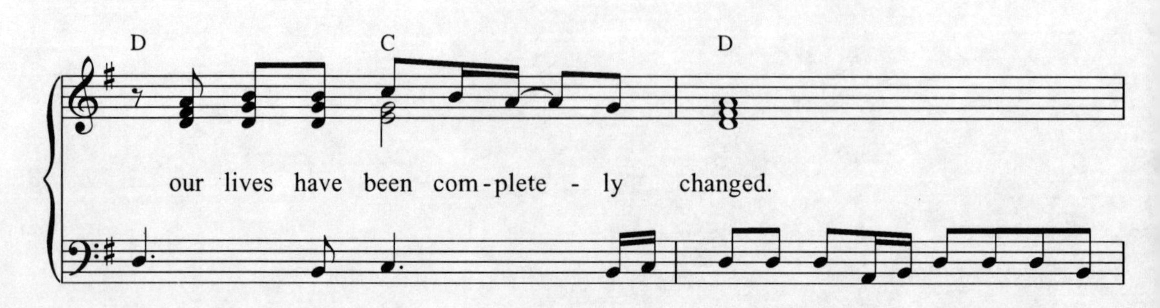

D C D
our lives have been com - plete - ly changed.

C
G
C
G
We'll give all praise to him, we will ex - alt his name,

C
G
D
D.S.
he will for e - ver reign.

511 Hey there, Mister Scarecrow

Words and Music: Philip Chapman and Stephanie Chapman
arr. Chris Mitchell

Chorus
G A D Bm7 Em G/A
Hey there, Mis-ter Scare - crow, stand-ing out in the

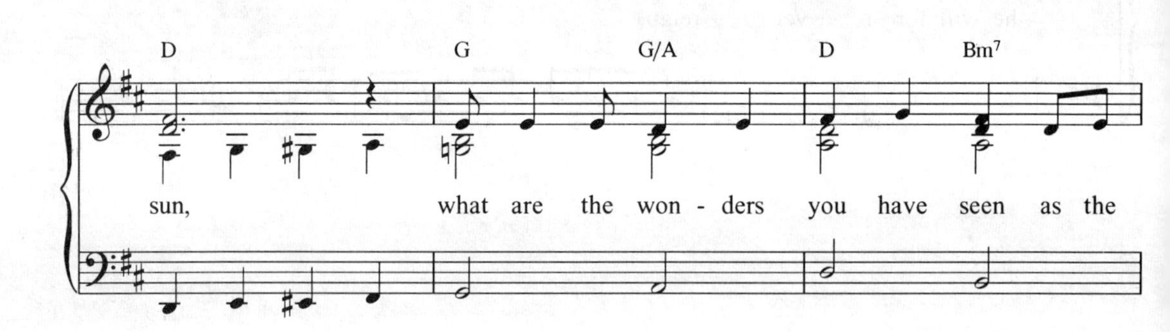
D G G/A D Bm7
sun, what are the won - ders you have seen as the

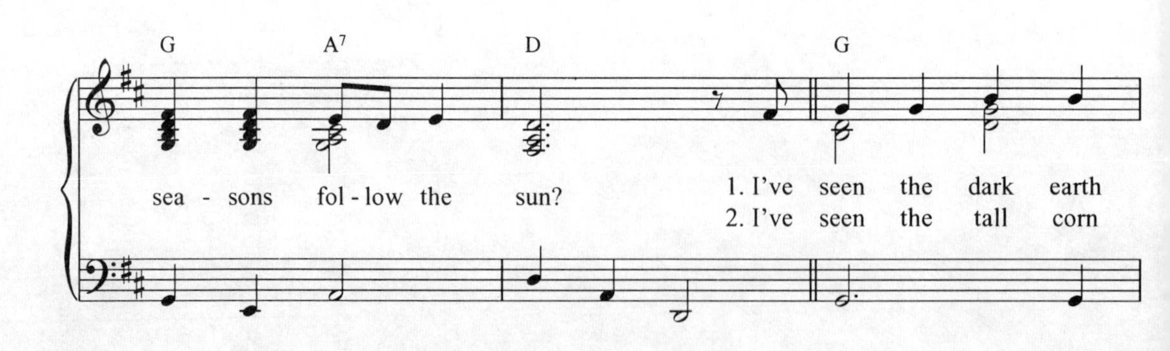
G A7 D G
sea - sons fol-low the sun?
1. I've seen the dark earth
2. I've seen the tall corn

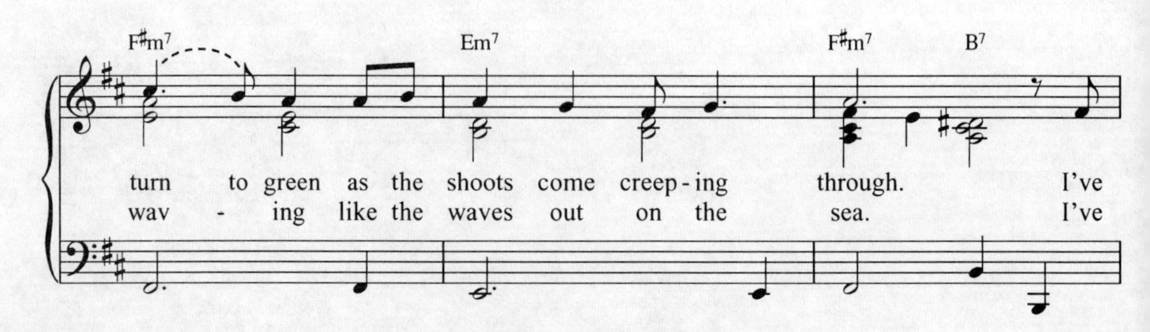
F♯m7 Em7 F♯m7 B7
turn to green as the shoots come creep-ing through. I've
wav - ing like the waves out on the sea. I've

Em7 G/A Dmaj7 Bm7 E7
felt the gen - tle rains of spring fall - ing from skies of
felt the breeze a - blow - ing and the sun that warms
A7 G F#m7
blue. I've heard the song - birds call - ing as the
me. I've heard the child - ren's voi - ces as they
Bm F#m7 Bm Em7 G/A
sun lights up the day,
laugh and as they play,
and I've known that God has
Dmaj7 Bm7 C2
made this world in a ve - ry, ve - ry, ve - ry, ve - ry,
Last time to Coda
A7 D Bm7 Em7 A7
D.C.
CODA
ve - ry spe - cial way.
way.

512 High, high, high

Words and Music: Tony Cooke
arr. Chris Mitchell

(♩ = 120)
Chorus
Capo 3
F C F C F C
D A D A D A
High, high, high, high, high, high, lift him up, lift up Je - sus
F B♭ F C F C F
D G D A D A D
high! High, high, high, high, high, high, lift him
C
A
up, lift up Je - sus high!
Last time
F
D
Fine
To verses
F
D
high! 1. The
B♭ F C F B♭ F
G D A D G D
name of the Lord, the name of the Lord is great - ly to be

C
A
B♭
G
F
D
praised! He is my strength and
C
A
F
D
B♭
G
F
D
C
A
D.C.
he is my shield, he's good in all his ways!

2. He's near to all who call on him
   and bless his holy name!
   He's good to you
   and good to me
   and good in all his ways!

513 Hi! I'm a penguin *(Hi, God made me)*

Words and Music: Brian Howard
arr. Chris Mitchell

B♭
G
1. Hi! I'm a pen - guin, God made me.
2. Hi! I'm a 'rang - u - tan, God made me.
3. Hi! I'm a child of God, God made me.
Hi! I'm a kan - ga - roo,
Hi! I'm a por - poise in the sea,
Hi! I'm a child of God, he
God made me.
God made me.
walks and talks with me.
E♭
C
Hi! I'm an
Hi! I'm an
Hi! I'm a
e - le - phant, God made me.
aard - vark, God made me.
child of God, he hears me when I pray.

B♭
G
Last time to Coda
Hi! I'm a ba - by mon - key, God made me.
Hi! I'm a pan - da bear, God made me.
Hi! I'm a child of God, and I was made in his im - age.
I'm a pen - guin and I
Well, I'm a 'rang - u - tan, and through the
walk kind of fun - ny. Can you walk like me?
trees I swing. I am a sing - ing, swing - ing 'rang - u - tan.
I'm a kan - ga - roo and I bounce
I'm a por - poise, hey, with this smile
a - round the room. Can you bounce like me?
on my face! God gave me a heart to play.

E♭
C
I'm an e - le - phant and I can
And I'm an aard - vark, and if you're
use my trunk to pick a co - co - nut from the tree. I'm a
real - ly smart, you know my name starts with two 'A's. I'm a
B♭
G
ba - by mon - key, I can climb up and down, up and down
pan - da bear, black here, white there. How do you
that co - co - nut tree.
like the lit - tle suit I wear?
CODA
F
D
B♭
G

514 Holy Spirit, fill me now

Words and Music: Bev Gammon

With feeling
C C/D D G Em C
Ho - ly Spi - rit, fill me now, I want to be like Je - sus;

Last time
Am D G Gsus4 G
show me how I can live like him.

2. Holy Spirit, teach me now,
   I want to speak for Jesus;
   tell me how I can speak for him.

3. Holy Spirit, help me now,
   I want to love like Jesus;
   show me how I can love like him.

515 Holy Spirit, Holy Spirit

Words and Music: Suzi de Faye

Format: add one numbered section on each repetition, beginning with 'Pour your power'

Rock 'n' roll
G
Ho - ly Spi - rit,
Ho - ly Spi - rit,
6.
D
C7
set me free, set me free,
5.
D
C7
bring your heal - ing, bring your heal - ing,
4.
D
C7
guide my life, guide my life,

3.
D
C7
talk to me, talk to me,
2.
D
C7
send your fire, send your fire,
1.
D
C7
Last time to Coda
pour your pow'r, pour your pow'r on me,
G
on me, on me.
CODA
G
on me, on me.

516 How does sun shine in the sky? *(How?)*

Words and Music: Nick Harding

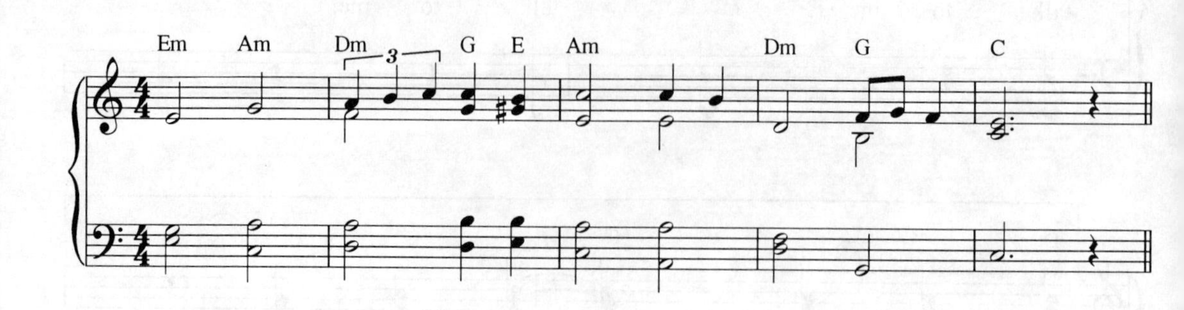
Em
Am
Dm
3
G
E
Am
Dm
G
C

C
F
G7
Em
Am
Dm
Gsus4 G
C
G
How does sun shine in the sky? How do clouds float by? How do

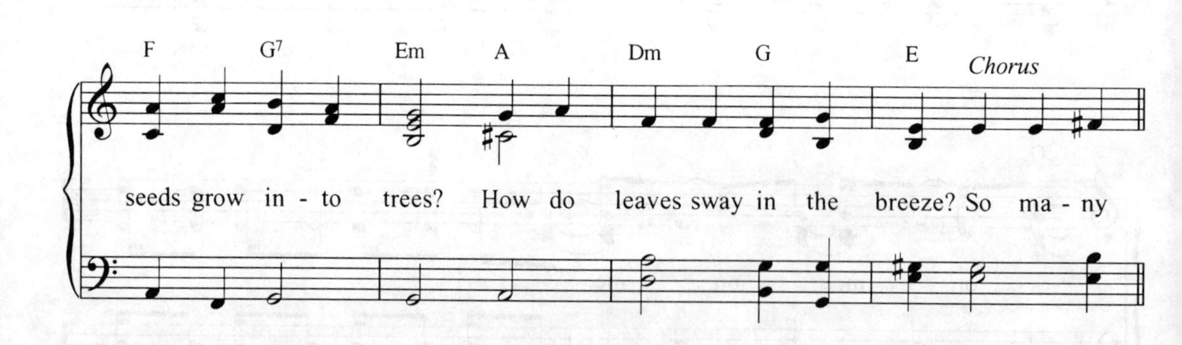
F
G7
Em
A
Dm
G
E
Chorus
seeds grow in - to trees? How do leaves sway in the breeze? So ma - ny

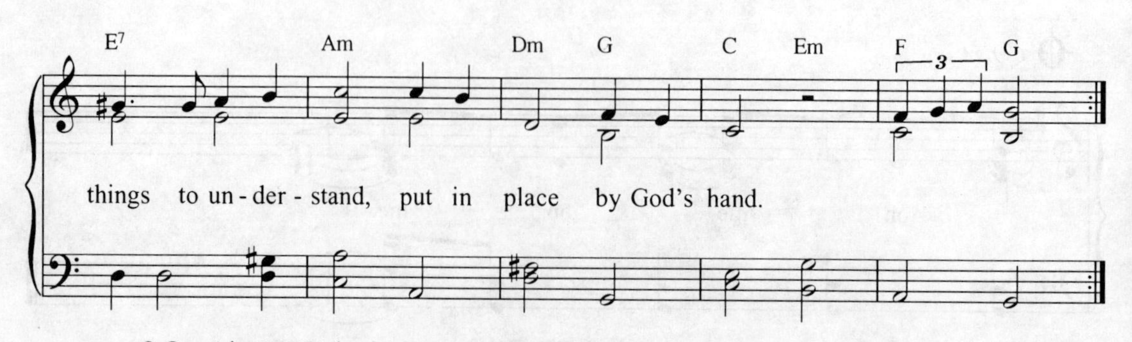
E7
Am
Dm
G
C
Em
F
3
G
things to un - der - stand, put in place by God's hand.

Last time
Em
Am
Dm
3
G
E
Am
Dm
G
C

2. How do fish live in the sea?
   How am I like me?
   How can I think what to say?
   How does night turn into day?

3. How does God teach us how to grow?
   How much can I know?
   Why does God show love and care?
   Why is Jesus always there?

517 I am H-A-P-P-Y

Words and Music: Dave Cooke
arr. Chris Mitchell

E
1. I am H A P P Y, I've got a rea-son, just
2. I can S T A N D, say that he's so

ask me why. I can S M I L E,
good to me. I can W A L K,

A7
it's ve-ry ea-sy, as you can see. I can S H
and know he's with me ev-'ry day. I can D A

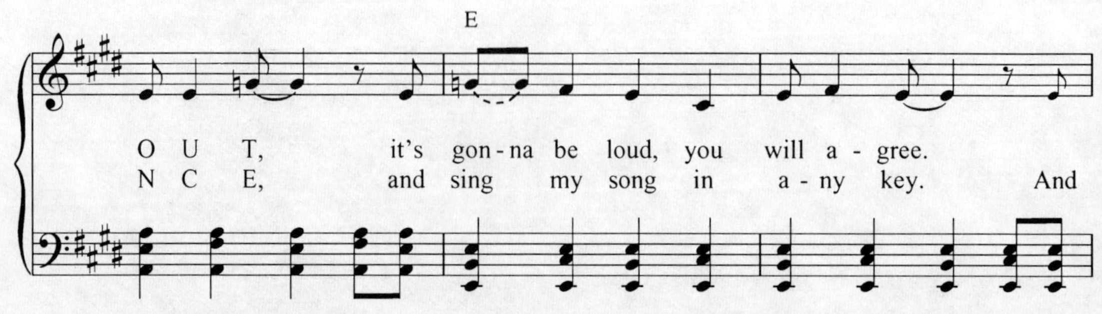

E
O U T, it's gon-na be loud, you will a-gree.
N C E, and sing my song in a-ny key. And

B7
A7
It's so G R E A T that I know him and he
I can S P E A K and tell you that he's the on-
E
knows me.
- ly way.
1.
Repeat verse
2.
Chorus
And he
A7
E
knows my name, loves me just the same; and I
want to say each and ev - 'ry day that he's a
friend of mine, to the end of time. It's so

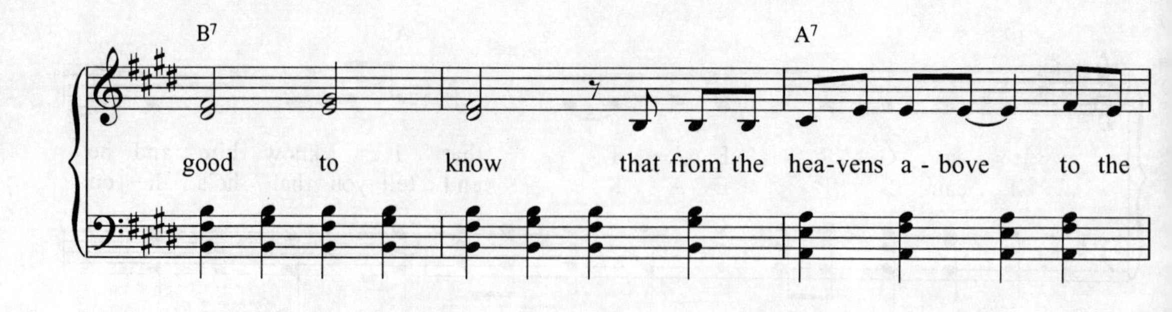
B7
A7
good to know that from the hea-vens a - bove to the

B
E
earth be-low, he loves me so.

D.C. for verse 2

518 I am loved by the Father

(Abba Father)

Words and Music: Andy Read
arr. Chris Mitchell

G2
C2
1. I am loved by the Fa - ther,
2. I am treas - ured by the Fa - ther
3. I am hugged by you, Fa - ther,
G2
D
the mak - er of cre - a - tion.
who de - lights in my life.
I'm se - cure in your arms.
G2
G/B
C2
Am7
I've been bought with a price so high
There is no se - pa - ra - tion, and no -
No harm will come to me,
G
Em7
C2
D7sus4
thing will take me a-way from his love.
*(your)

* *Verse 3 only*

G
Chorus
C
Am7
G
G/B
Ab - ba Fa - ther (Ab - ba Fa - ther), Ab - ba Fa-

C
Am7
G
G/B
C
Am7
- ther (Ab - ba Fa - ther), Ab - ba Fa - ther (Ab - ba Fa-

1, 2.
3.
G
G/B
Dsus4
D7sus4
D7
Dsus4
D
G
- ther), Ab-ba Fa - ther.

519 I am special

Words and Music: Andrew Pearson and Pauline Pearson

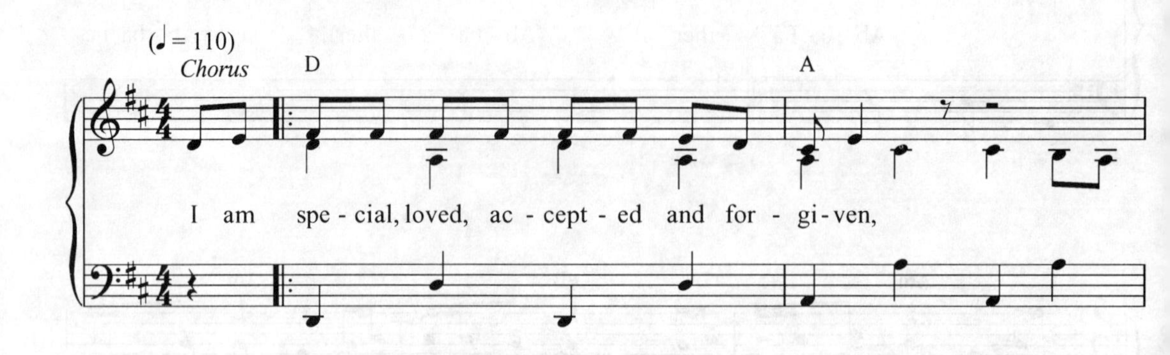

(♩ = 110)
Chorus
D
A
I am spe - cial, loved, ac - cept - ed and for - gi - ven,

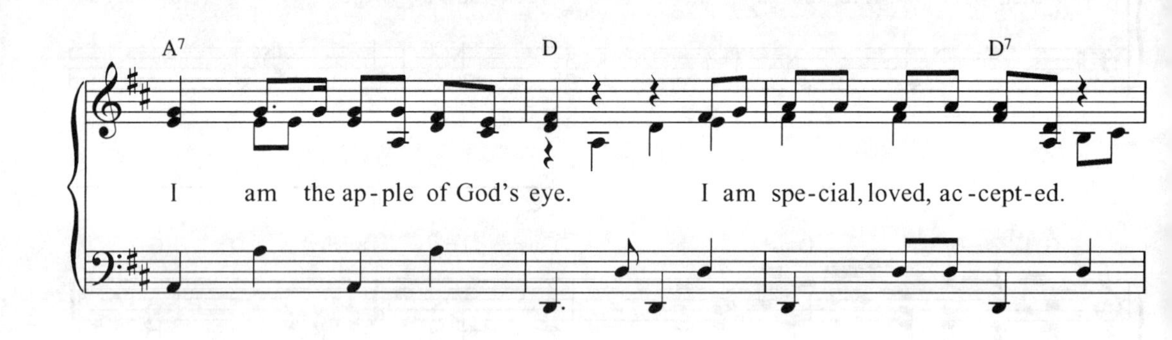

A7
D
D7
I am the ap - ple of God's eye. I am spe - cial, loved, ac - cept - ed.

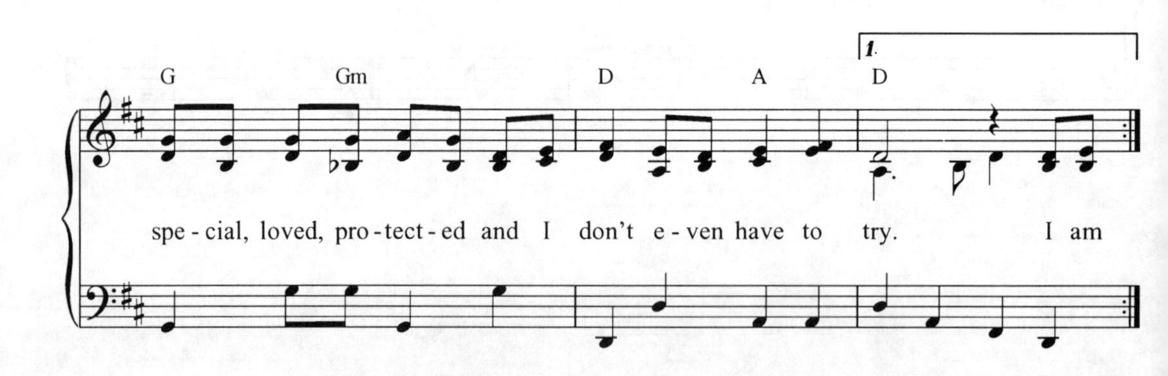

G
Gm
D
A
1.
D
spe - cial, loved, pro - tect - ed and I don't e - ven have to try. I am

2.
D
Verse
G
D
A
D
try. He loved me be - fore the world be - gan, he

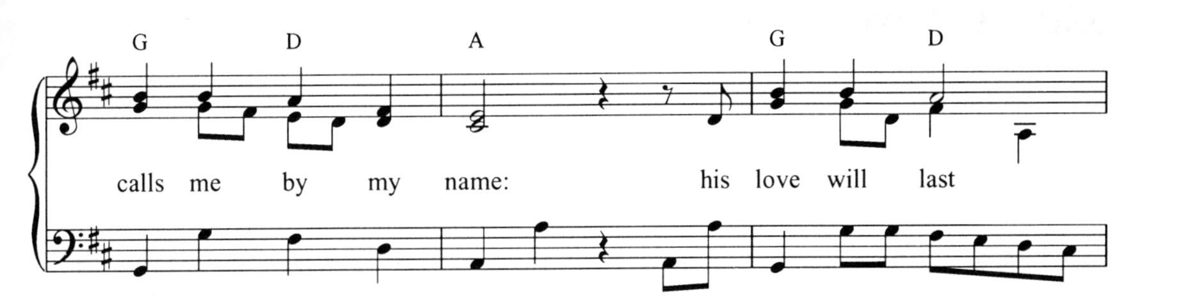
G D A G D
calls me by my name: his love will last

A D G A
for all time, and will ne - ver, e - ver change, ne - ver change.

520 I believe in God

Words: Pat Turner

Music: Pat Turner and Gareth Paul Taylor

Thoughtfully
1. I be-lieve in God the Fa - ther, I be-lieve in God the Son. I be-lieve Cal-va-ry was for-giv-ing love for me. I re-ceive, I be-lieve.
2. I be-lieve in you, my Je - sus, I be-lieve you reign a-bove. I be-lieve, Three-in-One; let your Ho-ly Spi-rit come. I re-ceive, I be-lieve.
3. I be-lieve the re - sur-rec-

A B E B A Bsus4
-tion, I be-lieve you live in me. I be-lieve
C#m G#m D C#m7 F#m E/G# A
I am known, I am called be - fore your throne. I re-ceive,
B11 C#m G#m D C#m7 F#m E/G#
I be-lieve. I am known, I am called be - fore your
A B11 E B
throne. I re-ceive, I be-lieve.
A B E B A B E

521 I believe in J-E-S-U-S

Words and Music: Iain D. Craig

D Chorus
G A D G A
I be-lieve in J-E-S-U-S. I be-lieve in J-E-S-U-S.
To verse 3
D G A D G6 A
I be-lieve in J-E-S-U-S. I be-lieve in Je - sus.
To repeat
Last time
To verses 1 and 2
D Chorus
D
Verse 1 A
I be-lieve in
1. He is
D
Sa - viour and Mes-si - ah. He is my best friend, and it's
A G A D D.S.
true, he real - ly loves me. His love will ne - ver end. I be-lieve in

Verse 2
A
2. He walked up - on the wa - ter,
D
he made the blind see.
A
And fed five thou - sand peo - ple by the shores of Ga - li - lee.
G
A
D
Chorus
D.S.
I be - lieve in
Verse 3
A
3. It was on Good Fri - day they
D
hung him on a tree,
A
but on - ly three days la - ter he rose for you and me.
G
A
D
D.S.
I be - lieve in

522 I can learn about numbers

(Jesus, I can count on you)

Words and Music: Philip Chapman
and Stephanie Chapman
arr. Chris Mitchell

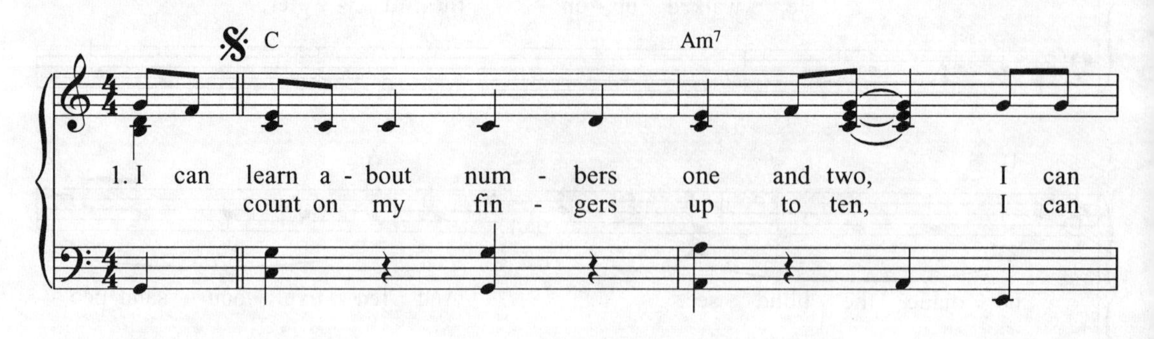
C
Am7
1. I can learn a - bout num - bers one and two, I can
count on my fin - gers up to ten, I can

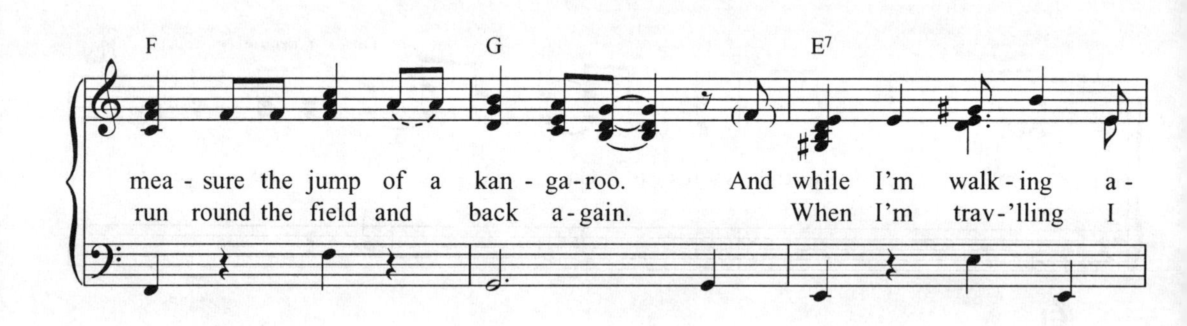
F
G
E7
mea - sure the jump of a kan - ga - roo. And while I'm walk - ing a -
run round the field and back a - gain. When I'm trav - 'lling I

Am
Dm7
D7
F/G
round the zoo I can add up the spots on a leo - pard too. But
count the cars but I run out of num - bers when I'm count - ing stars.

C
Am
D7/F#
I want some - one I can count on when - e - ver I'm hap - py or I'm

G Am Dm7(♭5) F/G G
blue. Some - one who'll al - ways love me, Je - sus I can count on
C Chorus Am Dm7 G C
you. La la la la la la, la la la la la.
E7 Am Dm7 F/G 1. C G D.S.
La la la la la la, la la la la la. 2. I can
2. C Am Dm7 G C E7
la la la la la la la, la la la la la. La la la la la
Am Dm7 F/G C
la, Je - sus, I can count on you.

523 I can sing

Words and Music: Andrew Pearson and Pauline Pearson

(♩ = 110)
C G F C F C
1. I can sing, 'La, la', I can shout, 'Hur - ray'. I can dance a - round and a-

G C G F C
round all day. I can clap my hands, I can raise them high,

F C F C F C G
when I praise, when I praise, when I praise the

C C G
Lord. 2. I can stand ve-ry still, I can

F C F C G
jump ve - ry high, I can march a - round and a - round all day, I can
C G F C F C
close my eyes, (I can) quiet - ly pray, when I praise,
F C F C G C
when I praise, when I praise the Lord.

524 I don't know why *(Let me explain)*

Words and Music: Caroline Brader

G C D
1. I don't know why a bird has to fly, why does-n't it walk like
G C
me? And I don't know how we get milk from a cow, when it
D G D
on - ly eats grass for its tea. And I am not sure what bel - ly-
C G D
but - tons are for, it's a mys - te - ry to me. The
G C D
one thing I know is Je - sus loves me, and so that's the ans - wer for

G
Chorus
D
me.
Let
me
ex - plain,
let
me

C
D
G
tell you once a - gain,
as
Je - sus' friend
you'll find his

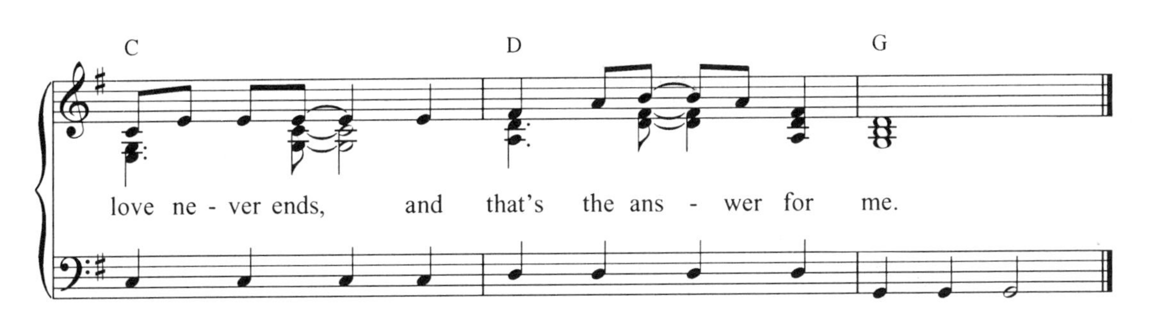
C
D
G
love ne - ver ends,
and
that's
the ans - wer for
me.

2. I don't know why my Gran's apple pie
only tastes right with ice cream.
And I don't know who
discovered sunflowers grew
all from one tiny seed.
And I don't know how
we could ever allow
repeats on our TV.
The one thing I know
is Jesus loves me
and so that's the answer for me.

525 If anyone is in Christ

Words and Music: Ian Smale

D G G7 C A A7
If a - ny - one is in Christ, he is a new cre -
D B B7 Em Am G/D D7 G
a - tion. The old has gone and the new has come.

526 If I go to the furthest place *(He'll be there)*

Words and Music: Mark Johnson and Helen Johnson
arr. Dave Bankhead

(♩ = 150)
C
1. If I go to the furth - est place that I could go,

G
C
he'll be there, he'll be there. To the east or the west, to the

G
C
C7
Chorus
sun or snow, he will al - ways be there! Oh yeah!

F
C
G
F/G
(he'll be there) oh yeah! (he'll be there) he will ne - ver leave

C
C7
F
C
me.
I know! (oh I know) he cares (how he cares)

Last time to Coda
1, 2.
G
C
G
he's the on - ly one I know who's al-ways there!

3.
C
C Chorus D.S.
CODA
C
2. In the al-ways there! Oh yeah! al-ways there!

2. In the dark of the night
or in the light of day,
he'll be there, he'll be there.
When I'm all on my own,
or I've lost my way,
he will always be there!

3. When I'm down in the dumps
and things are looking bad,
he'll be there, he'll be there.
When I'm over the moon
(when I'm really glad),
he will always be there!

527 I find my happiness

Words and Music: Phil Overton
arr. Chris Mitchell

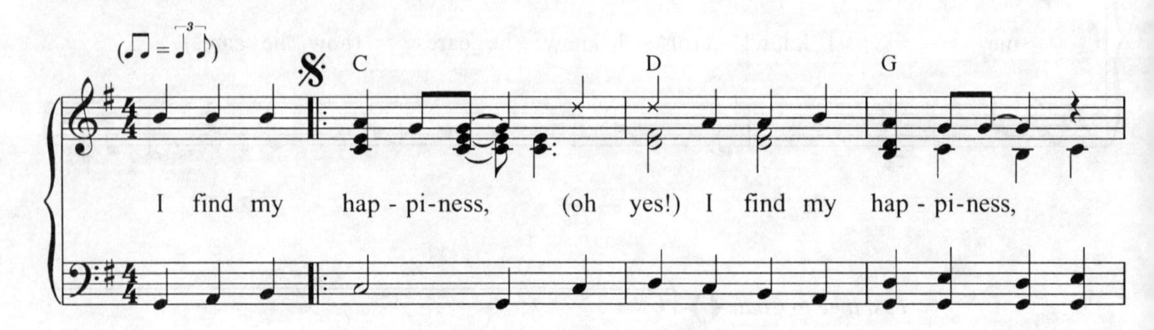

C
D
G
I find my hap - pi - ness, (oh yes!) I find my hap - pi - ness,

C
D
I find my hap - pi - ness in keep - ing your com - mands.

To repeat
G
G7
Last time
G Em
F
F♯
G
I find my

To continue
G
E7
Don't make gods of

A7
earth - ly i - dols. Don't en - vy o - thers' gain. Keep
D7
C
one day spe - cial for the Lord. Don't take his name in vain.
G
E7
Do not mur - der, do not steal. Be
A7
D7
faith - ful to your wife. Love your mo - ther
C
G
G7
D.S.
and your fa - ther. Do not cheat or lie. I find my

528 If I've been wrong

(How come I don't get what I deserve?)

Words and Music: Sammy Horner

Trad Jazz 4 feel
F
A7
1. If I've been wrong, and I've been bad,
I've been wick-ed all my days,

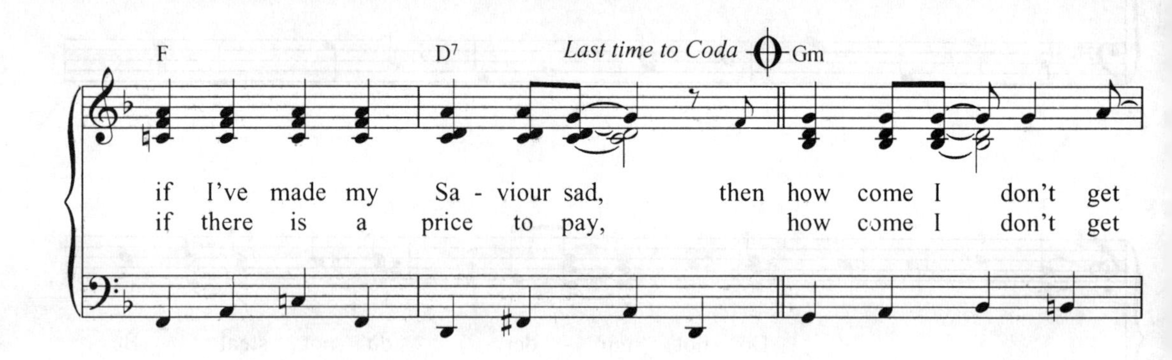
F
D7
Last time to Coda
Gm
if I've made my Sa-viour sad, then how come I don't get
if there is a price to pay, how come I don't get

C7
1.
F
C7
what I de-serve?
what I de-serve?
2. If

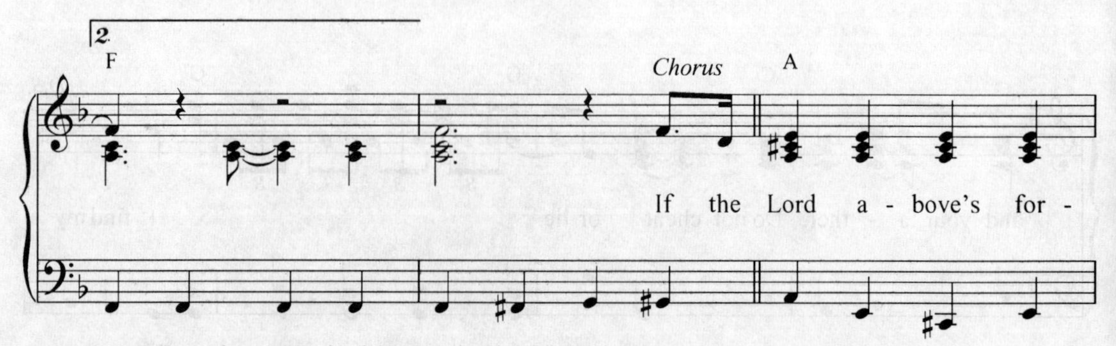
2.
F
Chorus
A
If the Lord a-bove's for-

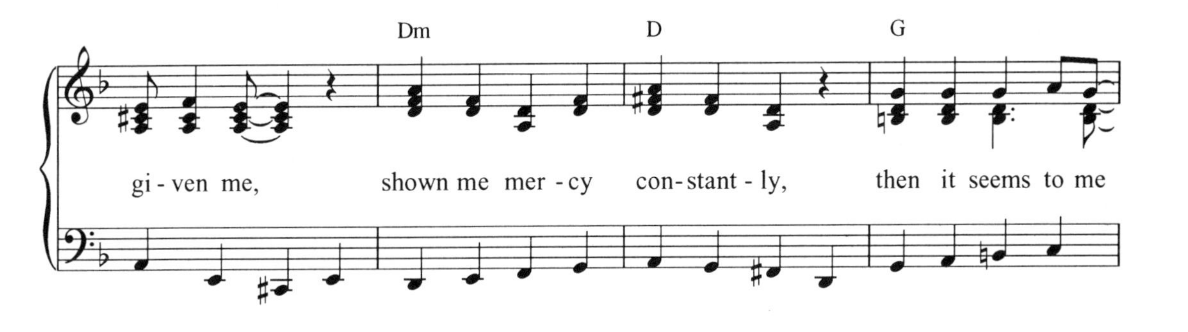
Dm
D
G
gi - ven me, shown me mer - cy con - stant - ly, then it seems to me

C
C7
D.C.
that we should do the same for o - thers con - sis - tent - ly. 3. If I've

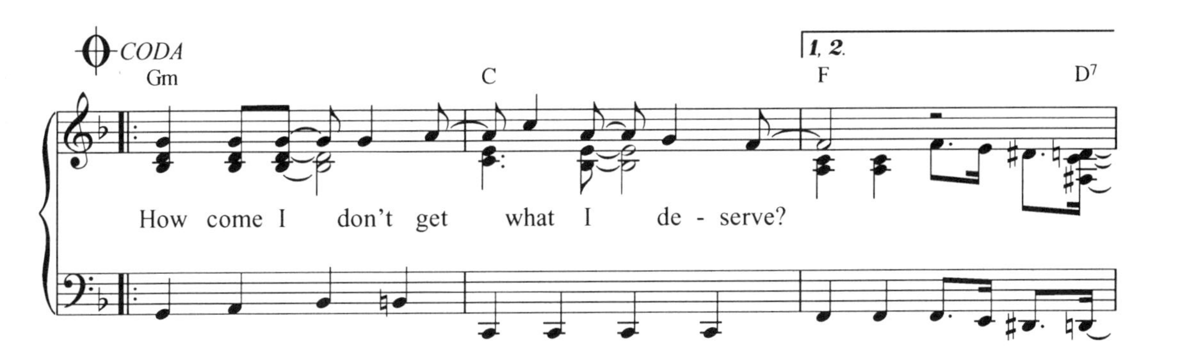
CODA
1, 2.
Gm
C
F
D7
How come I don't get what I de - serve?

3.
F
B♭/F
Fdim7
F6

3. If I've been a lying, cheating fool,
   if I treat my neighbour cruel,
   how come I don't get what I deserve?

529 If you believe

Words and Music: Mike Burn
arr. Dave Bankhead

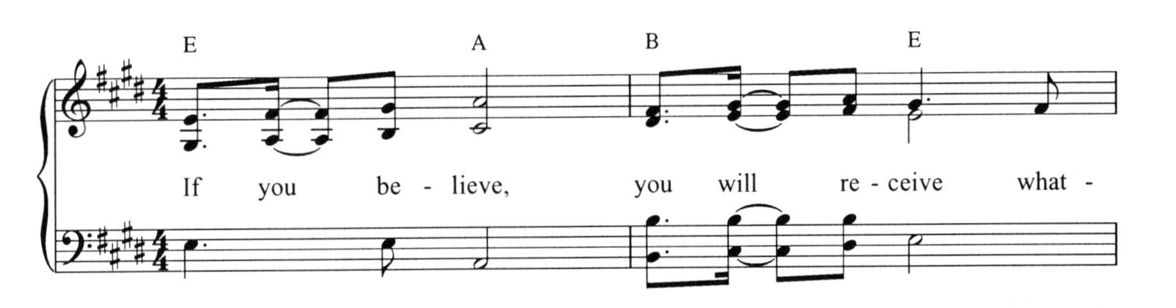
E A B E
If you be - lieve, you will re - ceive what -

A B E A
e - ver you ask for in prayer. If you be - lieve,

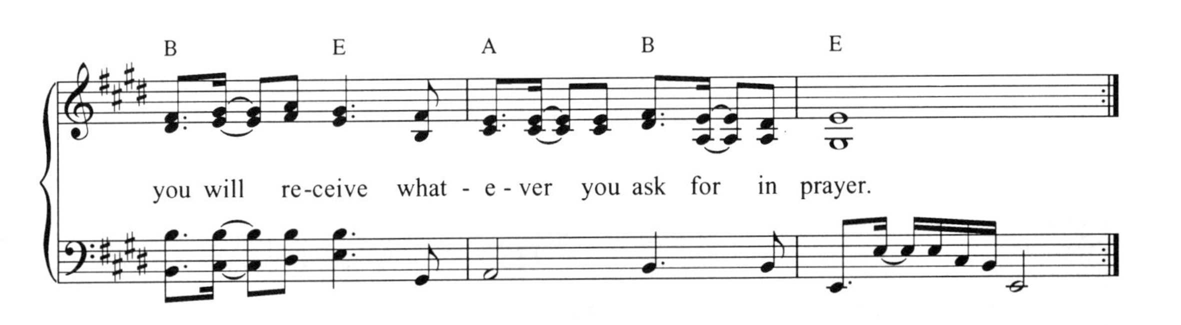
B E A B E
you will re-ceive what - e - ver you ask for in prayer.

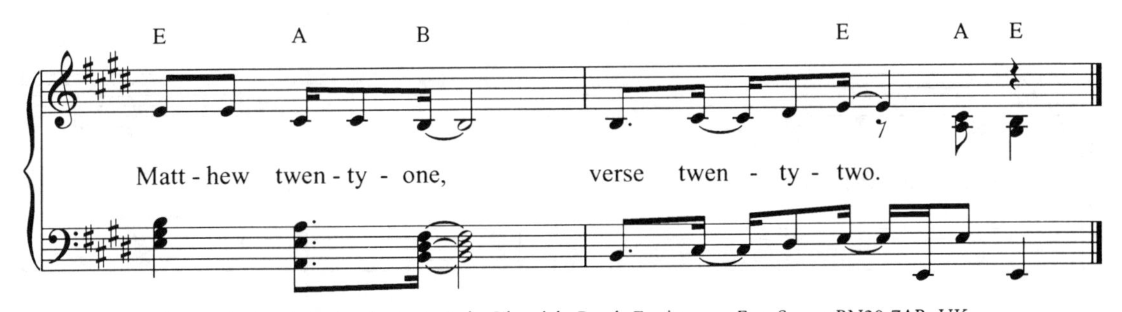
E A B E A E
Matt - hew twen - ty - one, verse twen - ty - two.

530 If you're feeling sad *(Count your blessings)*

Words and Music: Mark Johnson and Helen Johnson
arr. Dave Bankhead

Sing the whole song through in unison, then divide into groups to sing it as a round.

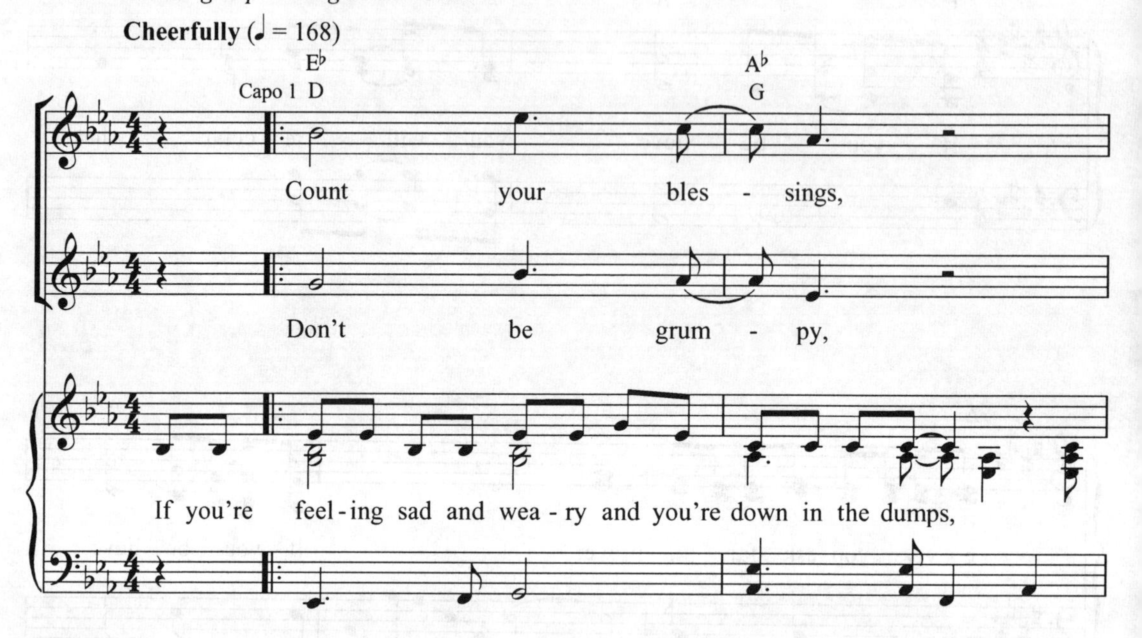
Cheerfully (♩ = 168)
E♭
Capo 1 D
A♭
G
Count your bles - sings,
Don't be grum - py,
If you're feel - ing sad and wea - ry and you're down in the dumps,

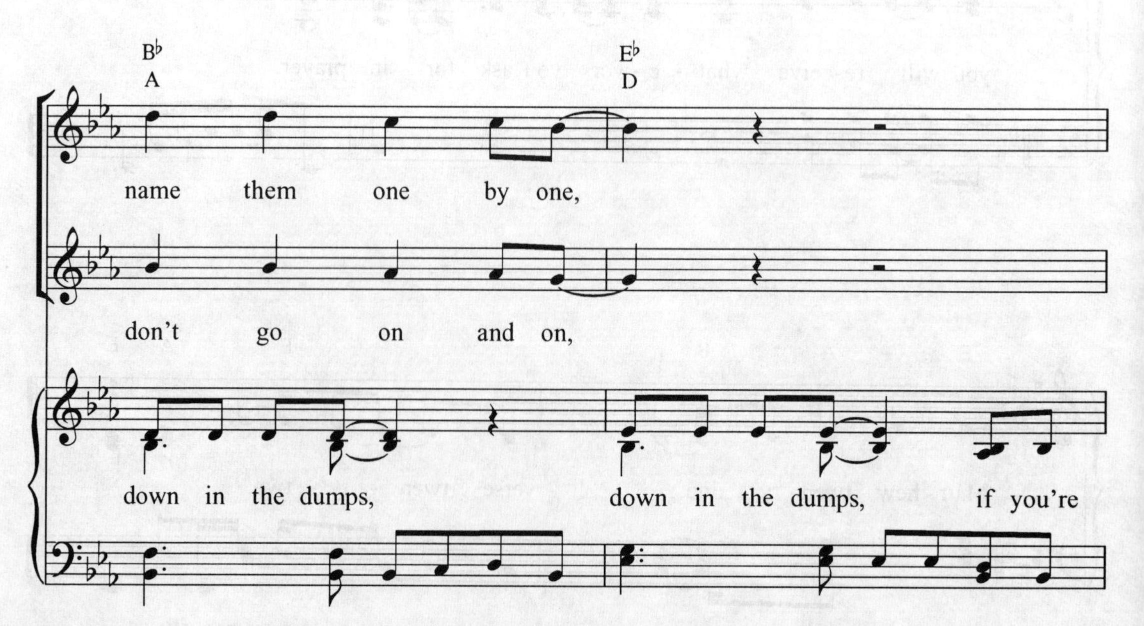
B♭
A
E♭
D
name them one by one,
don't go on and on,
down in the dumps, down in the dumps, if you're

A♭
G
count your bles - sings,
don't be grum - py,
feel - ing sad and wea - ry and you're down in the dumps, there's

To repeat
Last time
B♭
A
E♭
D
E♭
D
see what God has done!
don't you spoil the fun!
To repeat
Last time
some - thing you can do. If you're

531 If you wanna be cool

Words and Music: John Fryer

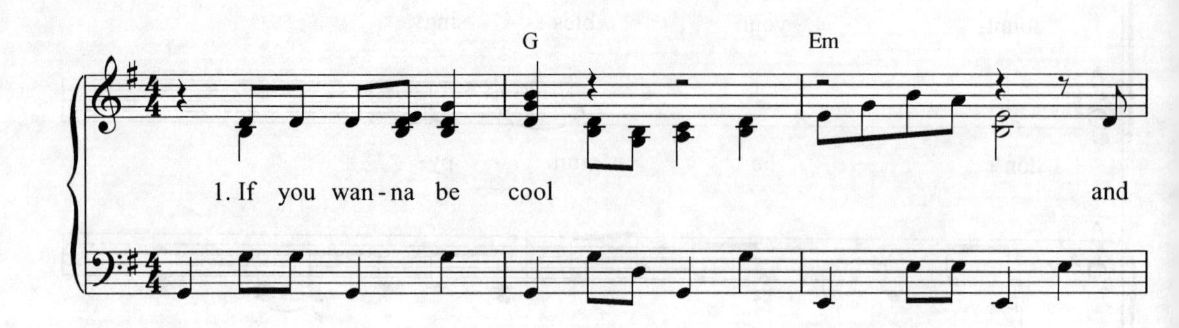
G
Em
1. If you wan-na be cool and

C
G
live in God's sight, o-bey-ing the rules

Em
C
G
and do - ing what's right, then don't be a

Em
C
fool, live in the light

Last time to Coda
1.
A7
G
D
C
D
C
and be free, free, free, free, free.
2.
G
C
Chorus
G
Je - sus said, 'If you real - ly love
C
A7
D
D.C.
me, then you will do the things I say.'
CODA
G
D
C
D
G
free, free, free, free, free.

2. If you wanna be ace and live in his way,
let the King take his place – do it today!
We're under his grace but still must obey,
to be free, free, free, free, free.

3. If you wanna be brill and live life his way,
then tell him you will (and do what you say).
With his Spirit he'll fill you ev'ry day,
to be free, free, free, free, free.

532 If you want to know why *(Bible)*

Words and Music: J.D. Bullen

(♩ = 105)
C F G
1. If you want to know why No - ah built a boat, why
C F G
Jo - seph had a ve - ry spe - cial coat, how
Am F G
God took dust and gave it life, made A - dam and then Eve, his wife. Where
F G Chorus C G
can you find all these a - maz - ing things? Look in the Bi - ble, the
Em C D G
Bi - ble, the B - I - B - L - E, the B - I - B - L - E, look in the

To next verse
C G E Am F G C
Bi - ble, the Bi - ble. God's book he's gi-ven to you and me. 2. If you
Last time
C F G C
me. God's book he's gi-ven to you and me. God's
F G C G C
book he's gi-ven to you and me.

2. If you want to know why
   Samson was long-haired,
   why Daniel with the lions was not scared,
   Jacob dreaming of a ladder,
   Moses' stick turned to an adder.
   Where can you find all these amazing things?

3. If you want to know why
   God sent plagues of flies,
   why Joshua sent out a team of spies,
   how David wrote the Psalms we sing.
   Where can you find all these amazing things?

533 I have been crucified with Christ *(Galatians 2:20)*

Words and Music: Colin Buchanan

Steady two-step (𝅗𝅥 = 100)
C
F
C

C
F
C
I have been cru - ci-fied with Christ and

F
Gsus4
G
I no long - er live, but

Last time to CODA
C
F
E
Am
F
Je - sus Christ lives in me.

C/G
G
C
I have been cru - ci - fied with Christ. The
F
C
B♭
C
life I live in the bo-dy, I live by faith in the Son of God, who
F
G
loved me and gave him - self for me, 2, 3. (Clap)
CODA
C/E
G
F
Repeat 5 times
I have been cru - ci - fied with Christ.
Become softer on each repeat.
5th time: suddenly louder.
C/G
G
C
I have been cru - ci - fied with Christ.

534 I jump up and down

Words and Music: Amanda Lofts
arr. Chris Mitchell

D
1. I jump up and down and sing, 'I love you'.
Em7
G/A
A7
D
Jump up and down and sing, 'I love you'. I jump up and down and
To next verse
Last time
Em7
A7
D
D
sing, 'I love you'. I love you, Je - sus. 2. I Je - sus.

2. I stamp my feet and sing, 'I love you'.
Stamp my feet and sing, 'I love you'.
I stamp my feet and sing, 'I love you'.
I love you, Jesus.

3. I clap my hands and sing, 'I love you'.
Clap my hands and sing, 'I love you'.
I clap my hands and sing, 'I love you'.
I love you, Jesus.

4. I hop on one leg and sing, 'I love you'.
Hop on one leg and sing, 'I love you'.
I hop on one leg and sing, 'I love you'.
I love you, Jesus.

5. I wave my arms and sing, 'I love you'.
Wave my arms and sing, 'I love you'.
I wave my arms and sing, 'I love you'.
I love you, Jesus.

6. I dance all around and sing, 'I love you'.
Dance all around and sing, 'I love you'.
I dance all around and sing, 'I love you'.
I love you, Jesus.

535 I just want to love you

Words and Music: Andy Read
arr. Chris Mitchell

E
B
C♯m7
I just want to love you,

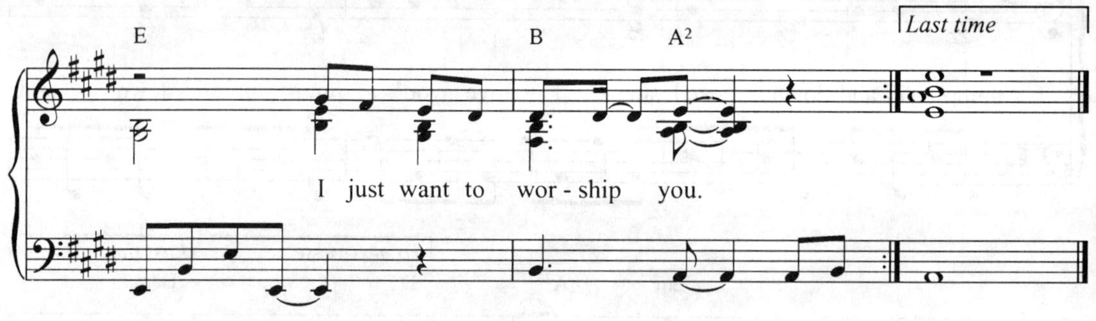
E
B
A2
Last time
I just want to wor - ship you.

E
C♯m
G♯m7
There is no-thing more I would ra - ther do than

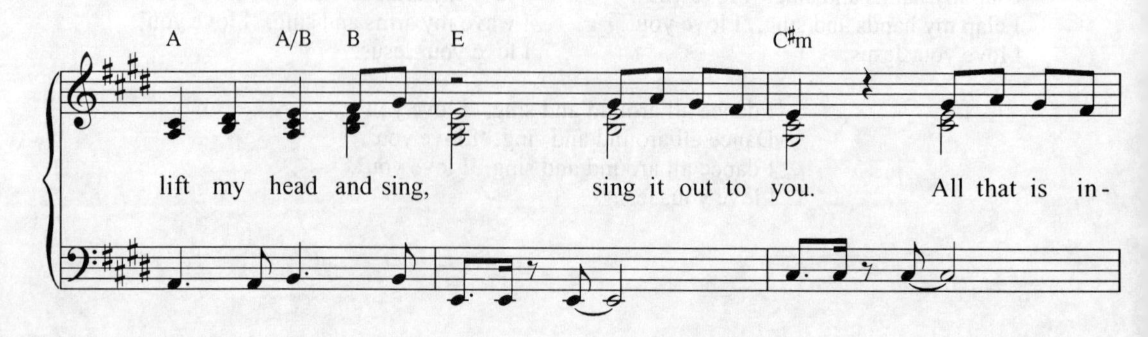
A
A/B
B
E
C♯m
lift my head and sing, sing it out to you. All that is in-

G♯m7
A
A/B
B
C♯m
side, you know my feel - ings, Lord, you are

G♯m7
A
more pow - er - ful than all

A/B
C♯m
my life. And Lord, you know
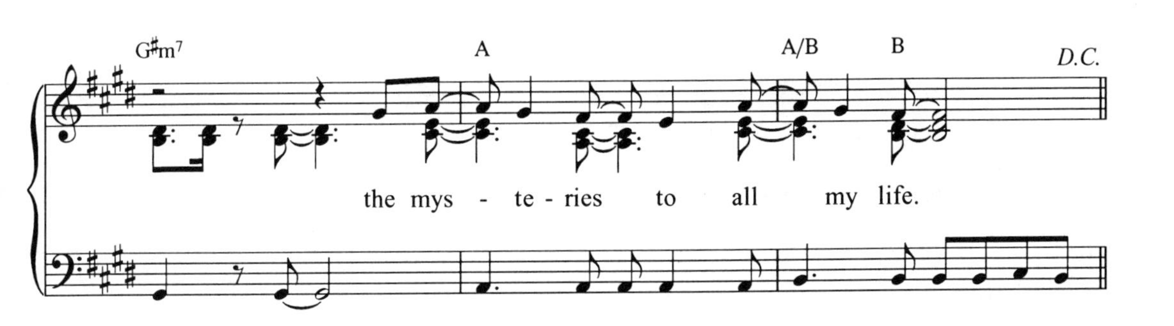
G♯m7
A
A/B
B
D.C.
the mys - te - ries to all my life.

536 I know you're here

Words and Music: Margaret Carpenter
arr. Dave Bankhead

(♩ = 67)
E♭
Capo 1 D
Descant
B♭/D
A/C♯
Cm
Bm
E♭/B♭
D/A
I know you're here be - side me,
I know you're here be - side me,
A♭
G
E♭/G
D/F♯
Fm7
Em7
B♭7
A7
with ev - 'ry breath, ev - 'ry breath I take,
with ev - 'ry breath I take,
E♭
D
B♭/D
A/C♯
Cm
Bm
E♭/B♭
D/A
when the night creeps to morn - ing,
when night - time creeps in - to morn - ing, as the

A♭
G
E♭/G
D/F♯
Fm7
Em7
B♭7
A7
A♭/C
G/B
B♭/D
A/C♯
as the sun be - gins, just be - gins to break I know you're
sun just be - gins to break, I know you're
E♭
D
E♭/G
D/F♯
A♭
G
E♭/B♭
D/A
A♭/B♭
G/A
with me, I know you're with me, I feel your smile, your
with me, I know you're with me, I feel the smile on your face, your
1.
E♭/B♭
D/A
A♭/B♭
G/A
B♭7
A7
E♭
D
B♭
A
warm em - brace, I know you are here with me.
warm em - brace, I know you are here with me.
2.
know you are here with me, here with me.
know you are here with me, here with me.

537 I'll clap, clap my hands

Words: The King's Church Creative Ministries

Music: James Wright
arr. Dave Bankhead

G C G/B Am7 G
I'll clap, clap my hands to Je - sus the King. I'll
C D G
stamp, stamp my feet be - cause I love him. I'll jump up and down, a -
To continue
Last time
C G/B Am7 G C D G G
Fine
round I will spin, I'll lift up my hands to him. Oh him.
C G D
hal - le - lu - jah, oh hal - le - lu - jah, our prai - ses we sing to the

G G7/B C G
King. Oh hal - le - lu - jah, oh hal - le - lu - jah, with

A A7 D D7 D.S.
all of my heart I praise him. I'll

538 I look forward all year *(Happy birthday)*

Words and Music: James Wright
arr. Chris Mitchell

G D/C G/B C G C G/D
1. I look for-ward all year to Christ - mas time. Oh, the joy and ex-cite-
- mas all year round for the joy of the sea-
Dsus4 G D/C G/B
- ment that is mine; Christ-mas trees in the win -
- son I have found; Christ-mas car - ols that fill
C G C G/D
- dows shine so bright like the glo - ry of God
my heart with cheer. Oh, how I real - ly love
1.
Dsus4 G D/C G/B
that shone that night. 2. I look for - ward to Christ-
this time of year.

2.
G
D
For it's King Je - sus' birth - day,
C
G
D
that we re-joice in to-day.
Two thou-sand years of grace
Am7
C/D
and pow - er and he is still migh-ty to save.
D
G Chorus
D/C
G/B
C
Hap - py birth-day,
hap - py birth-day,
G/D
1.
D/F♯ G
2.
D/F♯ G
hap - py birth-day to the King of kings.
King of kings.

539 I'm a kangaroo *(Part of God's creation)*

Words and Music: J. Macpherson

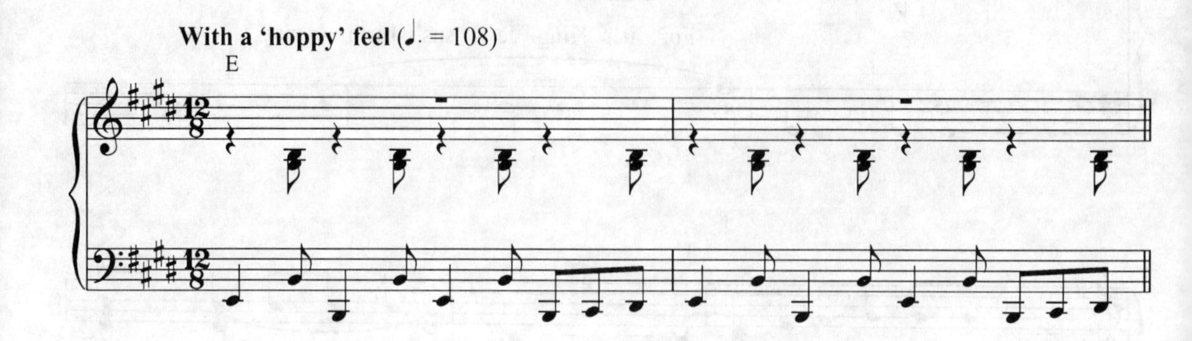
With a 'hoppy' feel (♩. = 108)
E

B
1. I'm a kan - ga - roo, liv - ing in the zoo.

E A E B E
When I get up in the morn - ing this is what I do:

B E B7 E B
hip, hop, hip - pet - ty hop, that's the way the kan - ga - roos hop.

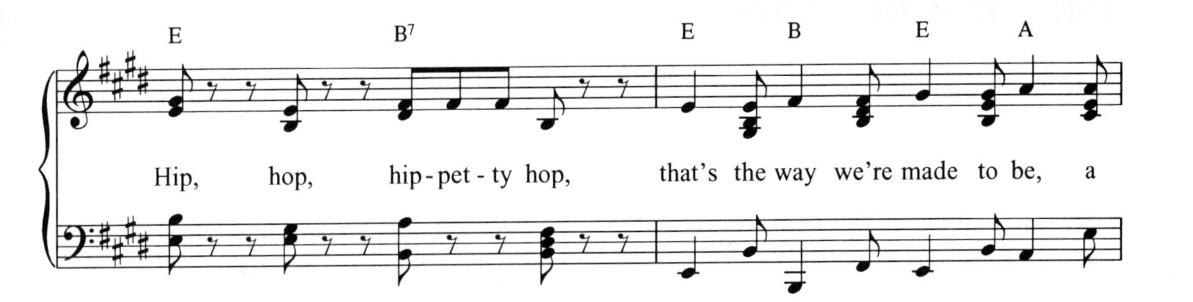
E
B7
E
B
E
A
Hip, hop, hip-pet-ty hop, that's the way we're made to be, a

To next verse
Last time
E
B
E
E
part of God's cre - a - tion.
a - tion.

2. I'm a budgie too,
 living in the zoo.
 When I get up in the morning
 this is what I do:
 tweet, tweet, tweedledee dee,
 that's the way we sing in the tree.
 Tweet, tweet, tweedledee dee,
 that's the way we're made to be,
 a part of God's creation.

3. I'm a black seal too,
 living in the zoo.
 When I get up in the morning
 this is what I do:
 flap, flap, flappetty flap,
 that's the way we cheer and clap.
 Flap, flap, flappetty flap,
 that's the way we're made to be,
 a part of God's creation.

4. I'm a hippo too,
 living in the zoo.
 When I get up in the morning
 this is what I do:
 splosh, splosh, sploshetty splosh,
 that's the way we wallow and wash.
 Splosh, splosh, sploshetty splosh,
 that's the way we're made to be,
 a part of God's creation.

5. I'm a person who
 comes from a town near you.
 When I get up in the morning
 this is what I do:
 rise, rise, rise and shine,
 say 'Hello' to a friend of mine.
 Rise, rise, rise and shine,
 that's the way we're made to be,
 a part of God's creation.

540 I may be a child

Words and Music: Capt. Alan J. Price, CA
arr. Philip Eley

(♩ = c.78)
Dm
G
F
G7
C
C
C/E
1. I may be a child, but my

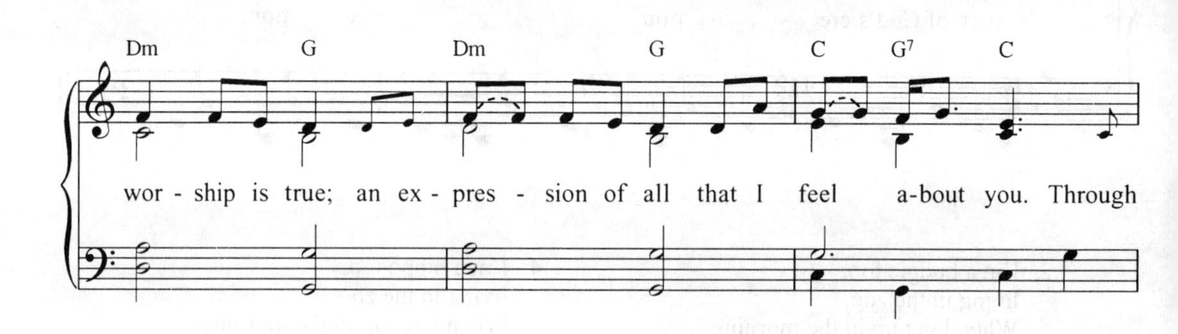

Dm
G
Dm
G
C
G7
C
wor - ship is true; an ex - pres - sion of all that I feel a-bout you. Through

F
G7
C
G7
Am
D
mu - sic and song, through words I will say: Je - sus, I'm try - ing to

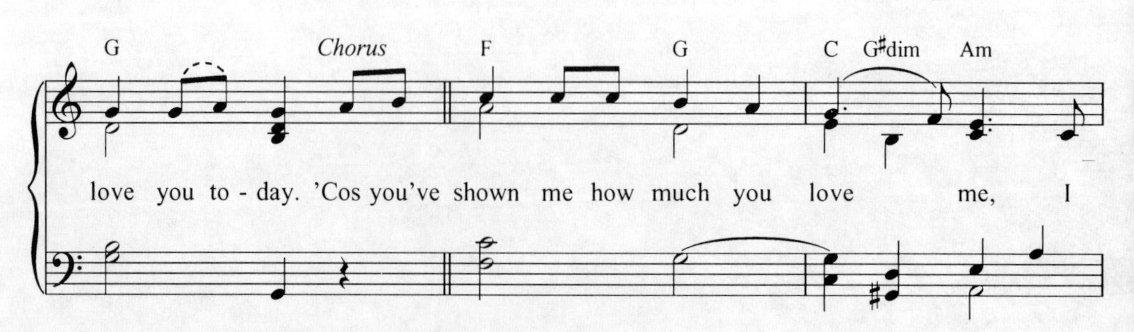

G
Chorus
F
G
C
G♯dim
Am
love you to - day. 'Cos you've shown me how much you love me, I

F G C C7 F G
know deep in - side I'm your spe - cial child. You've shown me how much you

To next verse
Last time
C G♯dim Am Dm G F G7 C F G7 C
love me, I know deep in - side I'm a child of the Lord. child of the Lord.

2. I may be a child,
   but I know what I feel,
   I want to obey you
   and show my faith is real.
   Stretch me and mould me,
   tell me what and how,
   Jesus, I want to serve you now.

3. I may be a child,
   but there's so much to know,
   it will take a lifetime
   to learn and to grow.
   But Lord, I thank you now
   for all that I can do,
   as part of your family, living for you.

541 I'm forever in your love

Words and Music: Doug Horley
arr. Dave Bankhead

E
B
E
I'm for - e - ver in your love, I'm for - e - ver saved by

A
E
B
grace. You have cho - sen me and crowned me with your love.

A
D/A
A
E
B
I'll for - e - ver trust in you, I'll for-

E
A
E
e - ver say you're good. You are King of kings and

B
A
E
I will wor-ship you.
La la la la la
B
la, just want to thank you, la la la la la
E
B
la, just want to praise you, la la la la la, that I can
1.
E
live like this for e - ver.
La la la la la
2.
B
E
live like this for e - ver.

542 I'm gonna clap *(Clap my hands)*

Words and Music: Andy Read
arr. Chris Mitchell

D7
1. I'm gon-na clap my hands and sing for joy, I'm gon-na

G7
clap my hands and sing for joy. He has tak-en

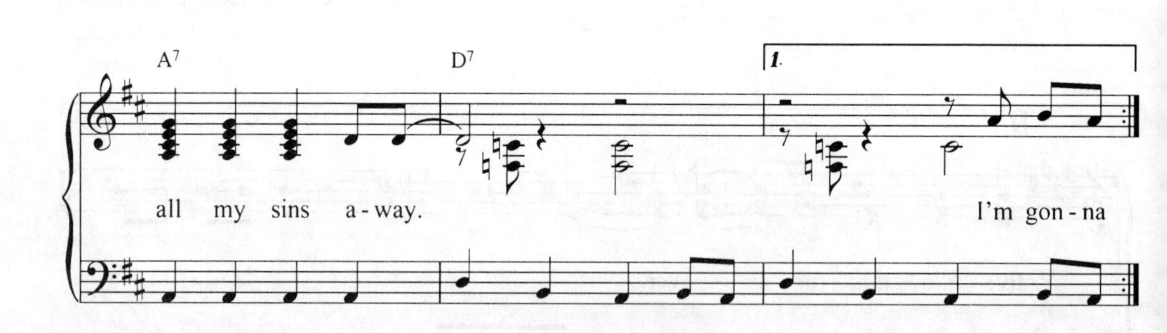

A7
D7
1.
all my sins a-way. I'm gon-na

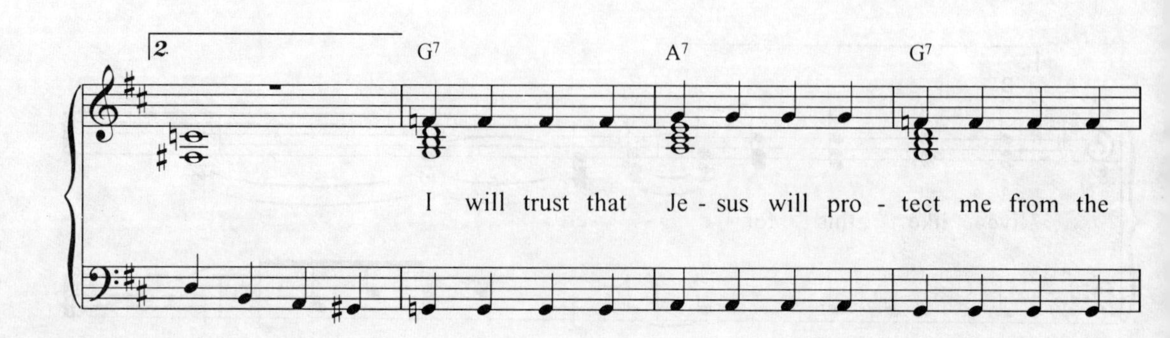

2.
G7
A7
G7
I will trust that Je-sus will pro-tect me from the

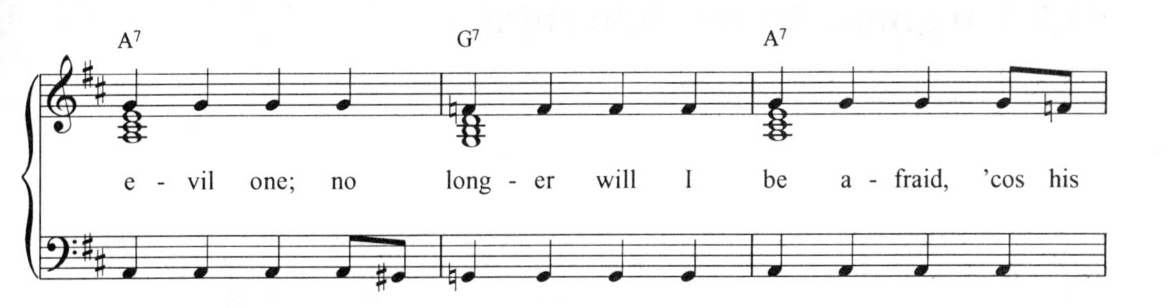
A7
G7
A7
e - vil one; no long - er will I be a - fraid, 'cos his

G7
D7
ban - ner o - ver me is won - der - ful love,

pow - er - ful love, in - cre - di - ble

love, what - e - ver you can think of.

2. I'm gonna stamp my feet and shout aloud . . .

3. I'm gonna jump and twist and wave my hands . . .

543 I'm gonna let my light shine

Words and Music: Paul Crouch and David Mudie

G
C
G
I'm gon - na let my light shine for you, let it shine for you. I'm gon - na

A
D
let my light shine for you in ev - 'ry - thing I do.

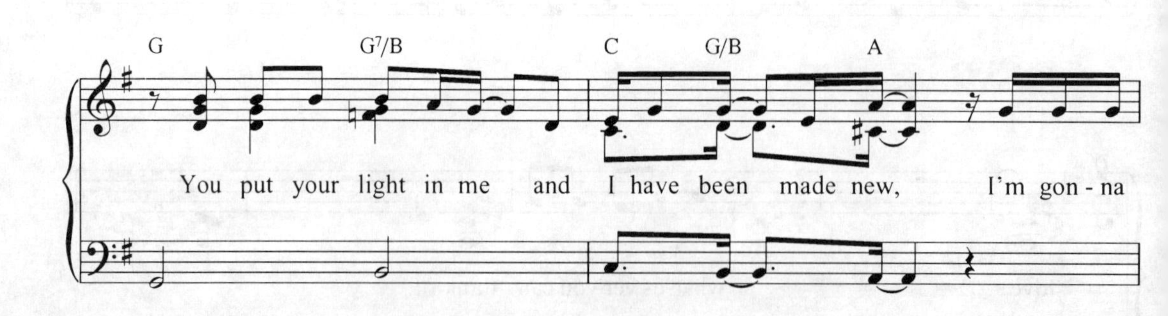
G
G7/B
C
G/B
A
You put your light in me and I have been made new, I'm gon - na

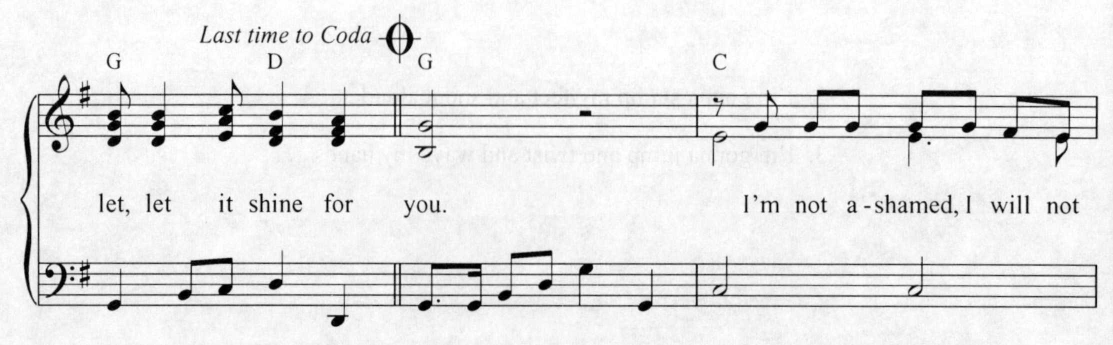
Last time to Coda
G
D
G
C
let, let it shine for you. I'm not a - shamed, I will not

G
C
G
hide it,
I'm gon - na let it blaze right out.
'Cos
C
G
Em
Je - sus is the one who has sup - plied it
and
A
D
he won't let the de - vil puff it out.
I'm gon - na
CODA
G
D
you.
I'm gon - na let, let it shine for
G
A
D
G
you.
I'm gon - na let, let it shine for you.

544 I'm gonna live for Jesus *(Live for Jesus)*

Words and Music: Martin Cooper

Chorus
A
Bm
I'm gon-na live for Je - sus,
I'm gon-na live for Je - sus,
After v.2 'Chant', repeat Chorus then end.
Last time
A/C♯
D
A
I'm gon-na live for Je - sus, gon-na do ev - 'ry-thing he says.
Bm
D
1. If he tells me I should go, then I won't say no:
If he tells me I should jump, I'll ask him how high,
F♯m
D
gon - na live for him.
gon - na touch the sky.

2. And ev'ry day I'm gonna pray,
I'm gonna live your way,
'cos I belong to you.
I'll give you ev'rything I am,
I'm gonna lift my hands,
'cos you deserve my praise.

Chant:
1, 2, 3, 4, 5, 6, 7, 8, I'm a friend of Jesus,
I think that he's really great.

545 I'm gonna say my prayers

Words and Music: Ian Smale

Brightly
Chorus
G
I'm gon - na say my prayers, read my Bi - ble ev - 'ry morn-ing, gon - na
1.
2.
D
G
G
Fine
get some fel - low - ship, wit - ness ev - 'ry day. I'm gon - na day.
1. I am gon - na pray ev - 'ry morn - ing,
1.
2.
D
G
G
D.C.
I am gon - na pray ev - 'ry day. day. I'm gon - na

2. I am gonna read my Bible ev'ry morning,
   I am gonna read my Bible ev'ry day. *(Repeat)*

3. I am gonna fellowship ev'ry morning,
   I am gonna fellowship ev'ry day. *(Repeat)*

4. I am gonna witness ev'ry morning,
   I am gonna witness ev'ry day. *(Repeat)*

546 I'm gonna walk by faith

Words and Music: Jim Bailey

Brightly
Chorus 1
G
I'm gon-na walk by faith, not by sight, I'm gon-na

D
G
G7/B
walk by faith, not by sight. I'm gon-na fol-low Je-sus, and

C
C♯dim
D
G
Verse
do what's right, I'm gon-na walk by faith, not by sight. Je-sus

C
G
said, 'If you fol-low me, you will ne-ver live in dark-ness.'

C
Am
Je - sus said, 'If you fol - low me, you will live in the light.'
D
1.
2, 3.
Chorus 2
Je - sus
I'm gon - na
G
D
watch and pray e - ve - ry day. I'm gon - na watch and pray
G
G7/B
C
C♯dim
e - ve - ry day. I'm gon - na do ev - 'ry - thing that I heard Je - sus say. I'm gon - na
D
1.
G
Verse D.S.
2.
G
watch and pray e - ve - ry day. Je - sus e - ve - ry day.

547 I might not like my ears *(Wonderfully made)*

Words and Music: Steve Burnhope
arr. Chris Mitchell

E B E A E
I might not like my ears, I might not like my

B C♯m B E B A B
nose, I might not like my two front teeth, my hair, my skin, my

E B E A E
clothes. I might think I'm too fat, I might think I'm too

B C♯m B E B
thin, too short, too tall, but warts 'n' all God

A B E A
says I'm won-der-ful-ly made. I'm won-der-ful-ly made,

E A E
I'm won - der - ful - ly made, no
C♯m A
ac - ci-dent and no mis-take, I'm won - der - ful - ly made,
B E A E
I'm won - der - ful - ly made, I'm
A E
won - der - ful - ly made, just as God the
C♯m A B E
Fa - ther planned, I'm won - der - ful - ly made.

548 I'm looking up to Jesus

Words and Music: Ian Smale

Gently
D
I'm look-ing up to Je - sus, his

G
D
face is shi-ning beau - ty. I'm feel-ing so un - wor - thy,

E
A
yet his Spi - rit leads me on. I'm

D
G
look - ing up to Je - sus, his ra - di-ance sur - rounds me.

E
I feel so pure and clean, a taste of
A
D
hea-ven on earth. I'm look-ing up to Je - sus.

549 I'm putting my trust in you

Words and Music: Andrew Pearson and Pauline Pearson

G Chorus
C
G
D
I'm put - ting my trust in you, I'm put - ting my trust in you,
G
C
G D G
I'm put - ting my trust in you, Fa - ther God.
C
G
D
1. Does - n't mat - ter how high the wind blows, does - n't mat - ter how hard it rains,
G
C
G C D G
does - n't mat - ter how loud it thun - ders, I know you're here with me.

2. Doesn't matter how big the spiders,
doesn't matter how slippy the snakes,
doesn't matter how loud the dogs bark,
I know you're here with me.

3. Doesn't matter if I'm alone,
doesn't matter if friends leave me,
doesn't matter if I trip and fall,
I know you're here with me.

550 I'm saved

Words and Music: Andy Read
arr. Chris Mitchell

Chorus
E7
I'm saved, I'm saved, it's al - right, I've been

A7
born a-gain. And I'm saved, and I'm saved, it's al -

E7
B7
B♭7
A7
right, I've been born a-gain. And I'm stand-ing on the rock

To repeat
E7
B7
Chorus
of Je - sus Christ. I'm

Last time
To verses
E7
Fine
E7
B7
G#m7
A
G#m7
1. This is the truth I be - lieve,
Je - sus him - self set me
A
G#m7
A
free
to trust and o - bey him in life.
G#m7
A
B7
D.S.
Chorus
That was the way it was meant to be.
I'm

2. This is the grace I believe;
it was his mercy to me
to show me his love and his light,
shining right into the darkest night.

551 I'm so small *(In your world)*

Words and Music: Steve Burnhope

E B G#/B# C#m7 A
I'm so small in your world, how come you e - ven no - tice

B E B G#/B#
me? I'm no-thing big, I'm just a kid,

To repeat
C#m7 A B E C#m A B
how come you are lis - ten-ing to me?

To continue
E A E B E
Je - sus, you make me feel spe-cial,

B
E
F♯m E/G♯
A
E/G♯
'cause you've al - ways time for me.
And when I pray,
A
B
C♯m7
A
I may not al - ways know what to say,
still you hear me,
B
A
B
C♯m
A
B
'cause you love me
and you made me
to be your
1.
E
B
G♯/B♯
C♯m
A
B
E
A
E
D.C.
child.
2.
E
B
G♯/B♯
C♯m
A
B
E
child.

552 I'm walking in love

Words and Music: Andy Read
arr. Chris Mitchell

Capo 3
B♭ G
E♭ C
F D
I'm walk-ing in love, I'm walk-ing in light. I'm walk-ing in the good-ness of God and the mer-cy of Je-sus Christ.
Cm7 Am7
I'm walk-ing in love, I'm walk-ing in light.
I'm walk-ing in the good-ness of God and the mer-cy of Je-sus

B♭
G
E♭
C
Christ. He has been good to me,
B♭
G
F7
D7
he has pro - tect - ed me, so why should
B♭
G
E♭
C
I be a - fraid? He is the God of all gods,
B♭
G
Gm
Em
he is the King of all kings and
B♭
G
F
D
B♭
G
right in my heart he'll stay.

553 I need your hand to guide me

Words and Music: Paul Harvey
arr. Chris Mitchell

G C D G Em7
I need your hand to guide me, your pre - sence, Lord, be -
C D G Em7 C Am7
side me; there's no one else who could e - ver take your
D Dsus4 D G
place. I need your peace to
C D G Em7 C D
still me, your Ho - ly Spi - rit to fill me;
G Em7 C Am7 D Dsus4
there's no one else who could e - ver take your place.

D G Em C D
I hide be-neath your wings, my Fa - ther,
G Em C D G Em
I owe you ev 'ry-thing, my Je - sus, send down your Spi-rit, Lord, and
C Am F D
fill my soul a - gain.
G Em C D G Em
And I will run to you, my Fa - ther, for there is none like you, my
C D G Em
Je - sus, send down your Spi - rit, Lord, and
C D G
I will praise your name.

554 Infant holy

Words: traditional Polish,
trans. Edith Margaret Gellibrand Reed

Music: Roger Jones

SUTTON COLDFIELD 87 87 88 77
Gently, with rhythm (♩ = 105)
Capo 3
F D
C/F A/D
B♭/F G/D
Csus4 Asus4
C A
A7 F♯7
Dm sus2 Dm
Bm sus2 Bm
1. In - fant ho - ly, in - fant low - ly, for his bed a cat - tle stall;
ox - en low - ing, lit - tle know - ing
Christ the Babe is Lord of all.
Swift are wing - ing

G Csus4 C A7 Dsus4 D B♭ B♭/C C
E Asus4 A F♯7 Bsus4 B G G/A A
an-gels sing-ing, no-wells ring-ing, tid-ings bring-ing,

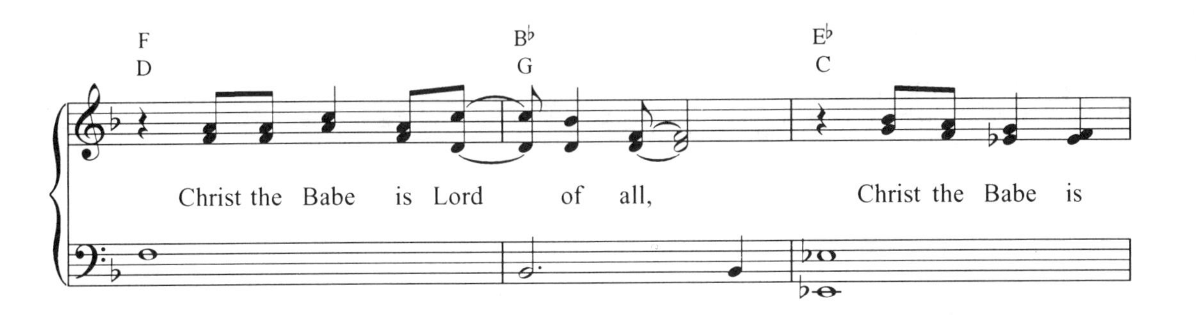
F B♭ E♭
D G C
Christ the Babe is Lord of all, Christ the Babe is

Csus4 C F C/F
Asus4 A D A/D
Lord of all.

B♭/F C/F F
G/D A/D D

2. Flocks were sleeping, shepherds keeping
vigil till the morning new;
saw the glory, heard the story,
tidings of a gospel true.
Thus rejoicing, free from sorrow,
praises voicing, greet tomorrow,
Christ the Babe was born for you,
Christ the Babe was born for you!

555 In the beginning

Words and Music: Phil Chapman
arr. Chris Mitchell

A E A7 D
In the be - gin - ning God made earth and hea - ven, let's

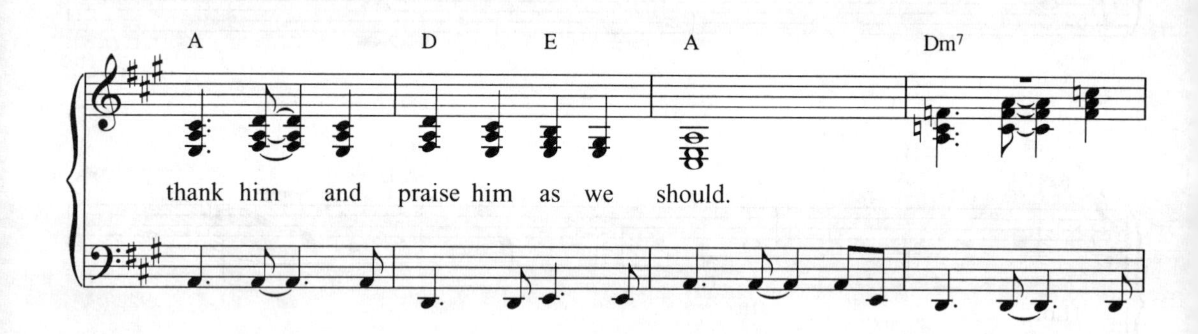
A D E A Dm7
thank him and praise him as we should.

F/G C G
In the be - gin - ning

C7 F C F
God made earth and hea - ven and God saw that it was ve - ry

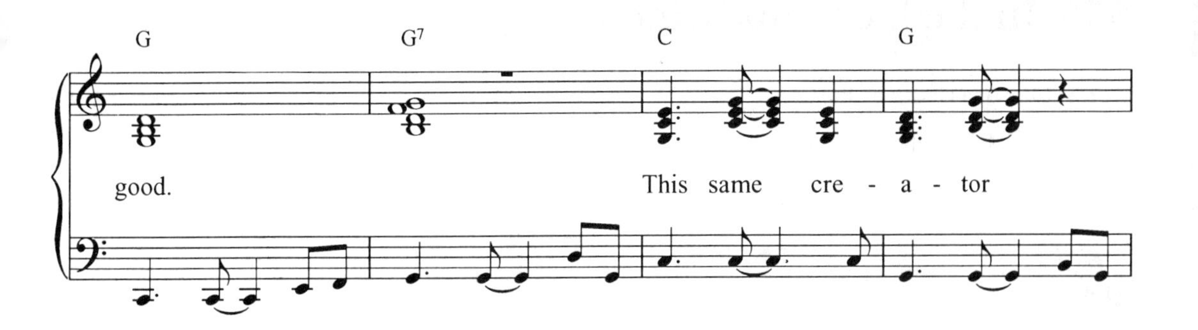
G
G7
C
G
good. This same cre - a - tor

C7
F
C
F
G
is my Lord, my Sa - viour, let's thank him and praise him as we

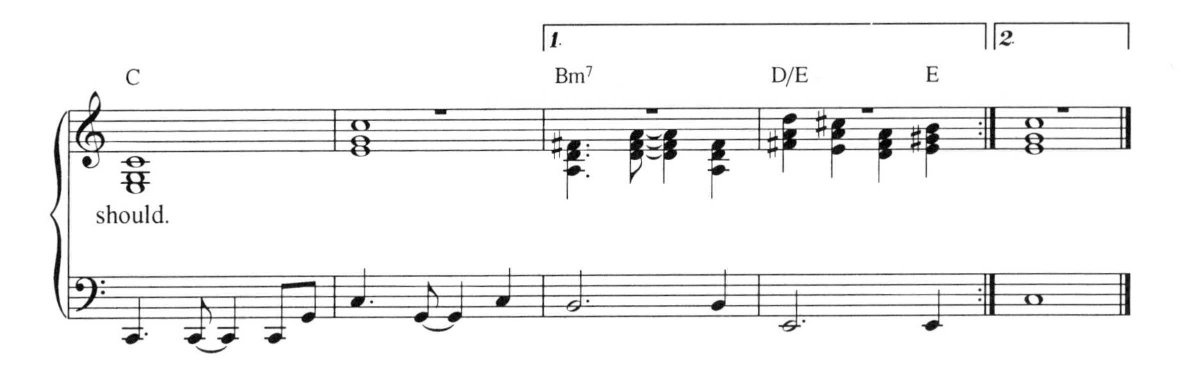
1.
2.
C
Bm7
D/E
E
should.

556 In the bleak midwinter

Words: Christina Georgina Rossetti

Music: Gustav Holst

CRANHAM Irregular
Capo 3
1. In the bleak mid - win - ter frost - y wind made moan, earth stood hard as ir - on, wa - ter like a stone; snow had fall - en, snow on snow, snow on snow, in the bleak mid - win - ter, long a - go.

2. Our God, heav'n cannot hold him
   nor earth sustain;
   heav'n and earth shall flee away
   when he comes to reign.
   In the bleak midwinter
   a stable-place sufficed
   the Lord God almighty,
   Jesus Christ.

3. Enough for him, whom cherubim
   worship night and day,
   a breastful of milk
   and a mangerful of hay:
   enough for him, whom angels
   fall down before,
   the ox and ass and camel
   which adore.

4. Angels and archangels
   may have gathered there,
   cherubim and seraphim
   thronged the air;
   but only his mother
   in her maiden bliss
   worshipped the belovèd
   with a kiss.

5. What can I give him,
   poor as I am?
   If I were a shepherd
   I would bring a lamb;
   if I were a wise man
   I would do my part,
   yet what I can I give him:
   give my heart.

557 In the morning

(Boing!)

Words and Music: Dave Godfrey

With a bounce
D
1. In the morn - ing I come down-stairs, eat my break - fast,
2. Af - ter lunch on a nor - mal day, in the play - ground,

A
D
say my prayers, get my coat on and comb my hair,
out to play, when my friends all come my way,

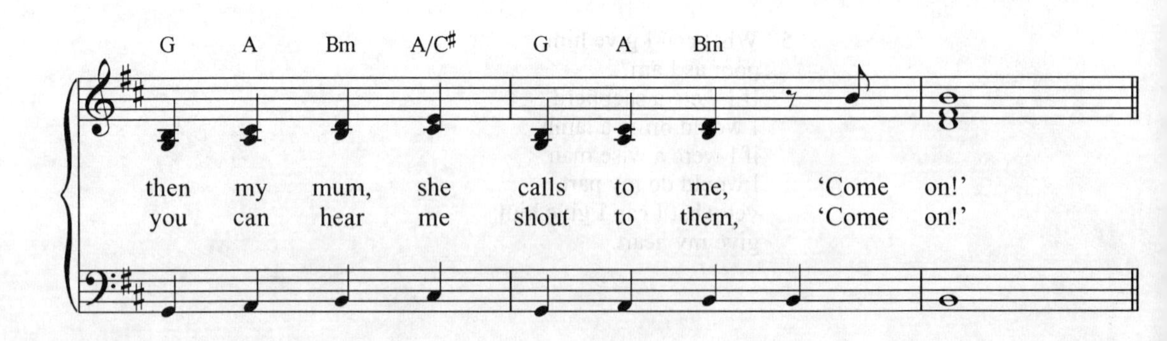
G A Bm A/C♯ G A Bm
then my mum, she calls to me, 'Come on!'
you can hear me shout to them, 'Come on!'

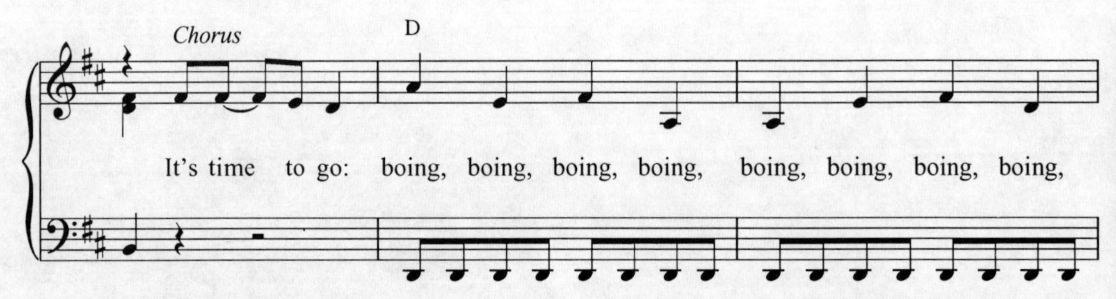
Chorus
D
It's time to go: boing, boing, boing, boing, boing, boing, boing, boing,

A
D
boing, boing, boing, boing, boing, boing, boing, boing, boing,
boing, boing, boing, boing, boing, boing, boing, boing, boing.
E
3. In the eve - ning and af - ter tea, home - work's done, I
4. Late at night as I rest my head, I read my Bi - ble
B
E
watch T. V. Lit - tle bro - ther, he jumps on me,
in my bed. I thank the Lord for what he's said,
A B C#m B/D# A B C#m
then he whis - pers in my ears: 'Come on!'
then you hear me soft - ly say: 'Come on!'

E
It's time to go:
It's time to go to Z . . .
boing, boing, boing, boing, boing, boing, boing, boing,
B
E
boing, boing, boing, boing, boing, boing, boing, boing, boing,
Last time D.S.
boing, boing, boing, boing, boing, boing, boing, boing, boing.

558 In the Spirit I rise

Words and Music: Judy Bailey
arr. Dave Bankhead

G Chorus
C
In the Spi-rit I rise, rise, I rise to your call,
G
C
G
D
in the Spi-rit I rise, rise, I rise up to your call.
G
C
In the Spi-rit I rise, rise, I rise to your call,
To verses
G
C
G
D
G
in the Spi-rit I rise, rise, I rise up to your call.

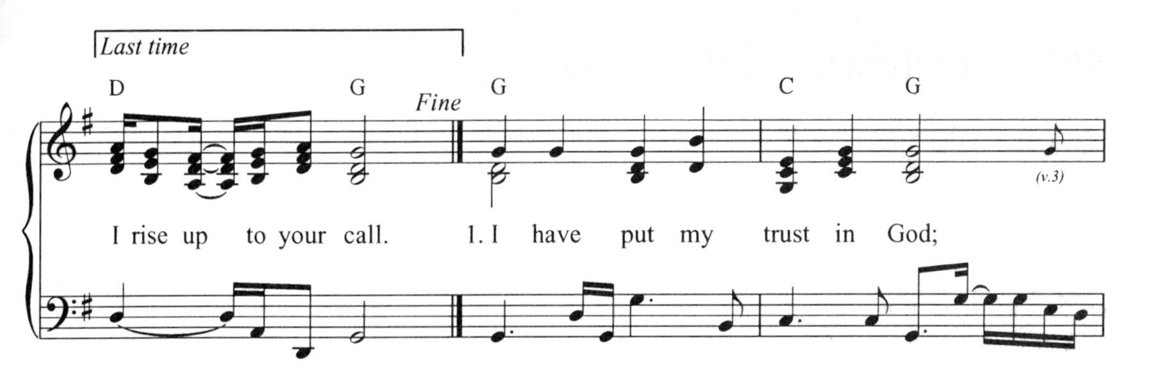
Last time
D
G
Fine
G
C
G
(v.3)
I rise up to your call. 1. I have put my trust in God;

G
D
G/B
C
G
Fa - ther, Spi - rit, Son. When he calls me to come then I

C
G
Em
D
D.C.
know I must res-pond, I rise in the Spi-rit of love.

2. When things seem too hard for me
I will not give up.
You're the strength that I need,
power when the flesh is weak
I rise in the Spirit of love.

3. I will live for you, my Lord,
my future's in your hand.
Here's my life for your plan,
take me, Jesus, here I am
I rise in the Spirit of love.

559 I really wanna thank you

Words and Music: Andy Read
arr. Chris Mitchell

G
Em7
I real - ly wan - na thank you, I wan - na find a
C2
D
G
way to show my praise. I real - ly wan - na clap you,
Em7
C2
D
I wan - na wor - ship you in dif - f'rent ways. I will sing,
G
G/F
C2
I will dance, I will lift up ho - ly hands.
Dsus4
G
G/F
I will wave be - fore you and say I want

Last time
C2
Dsus4
G
Fine
you in my, want you in my life.
To continue
C2
Dsus4
F2
you in my life. I will raise up my arms
G
F2
to be held in your arms.
G
F2
I will lis - ten, I will lis-
- ten, I will lis - ten
G
D.S.
for your voice. I real-ly wan-na

560 Is anyone in trouble?

Words and Music: Mike Burn

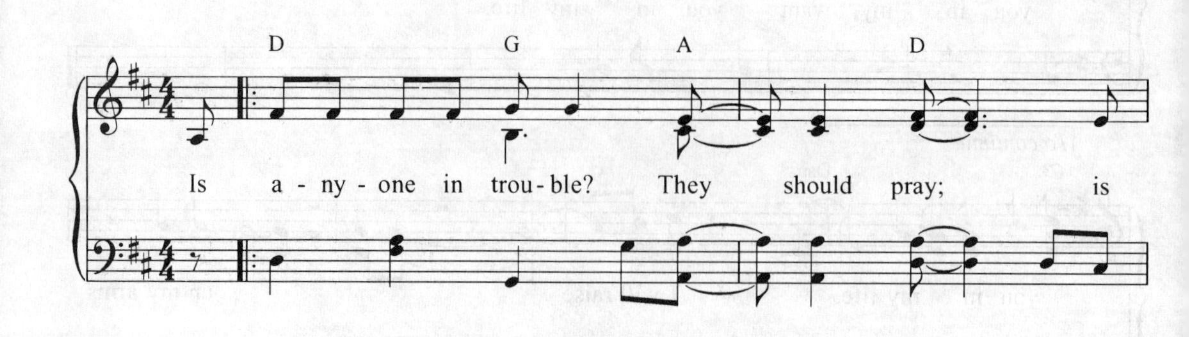
D
G
A
D
Is a - ny - one in trou - ble? They should pray; is

Bm
Em
1.
A7
D
a - ny - one hap - py? Let them sing songs of praise. Is

2.
A7
D
Bm
Em
Asus4
sing songs of praise.

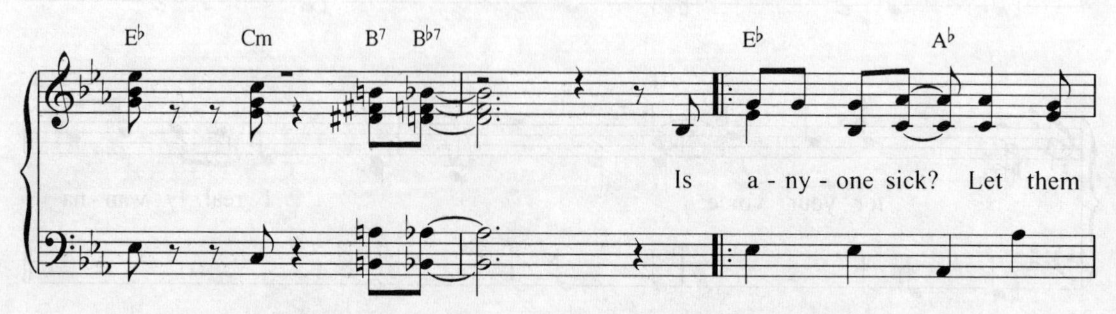
E♭
Cm
B7
B♭7
E♭
A♭
Is a - ny - one sick? Let them

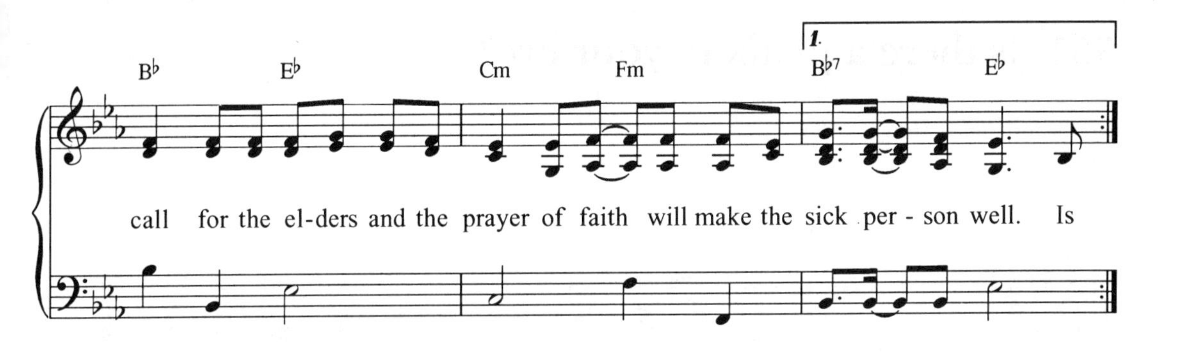
1.
B♭ E♭ Cm Fm B♭7 E♭
call for the el-ders and the prayer of faith will make the sick per - son well. Is

2.
B♭7 E♭ Cm Fm7 B♭sus4
sick per-son well.

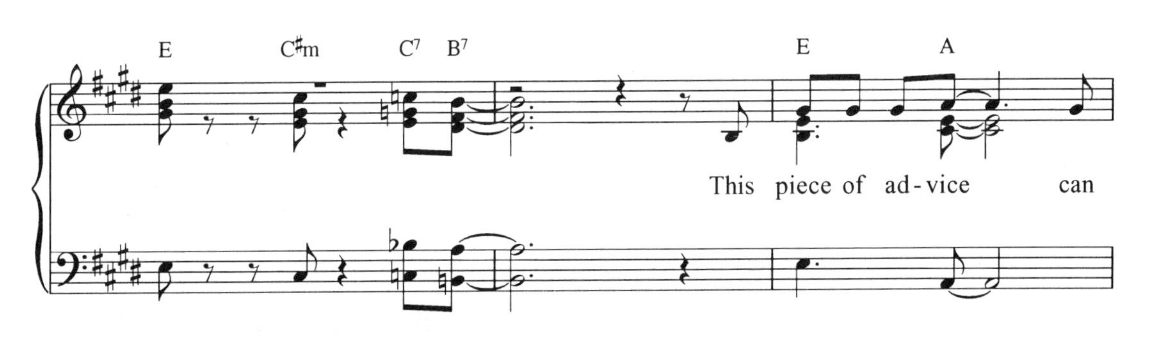
E C♯m C7 B7 E A
This piece of ad-vice can

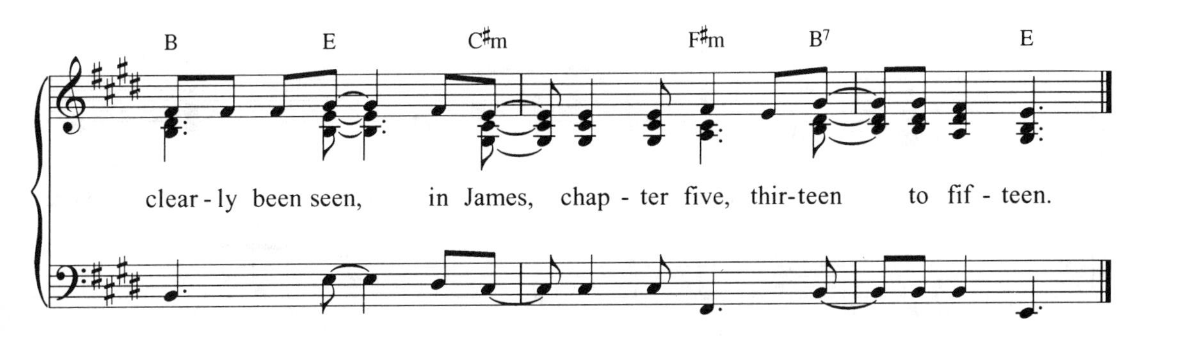
B E C♯m F♯m B7 E
clear-ly been seen, in James, chap - ter five, thir-teen to fif - teen.

561 Is there a plank in your eye?

Words and Music: Doug Horley
arr. Dave Bankhead

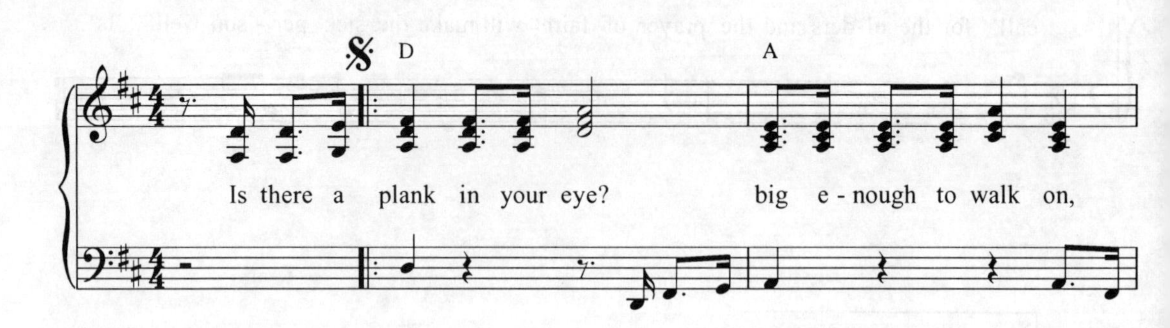
D
A
Is there a plank in your eye? big e - nough to walk on,

G
D
Em7
G/A
A
D
big e-nough to build a ship or may-be start a bon - fire. Is there a plank
3
3

Last time to Coda
1.
A
G
A
D
stuck in your eye? Stuck, stuck, stuck. Is there a

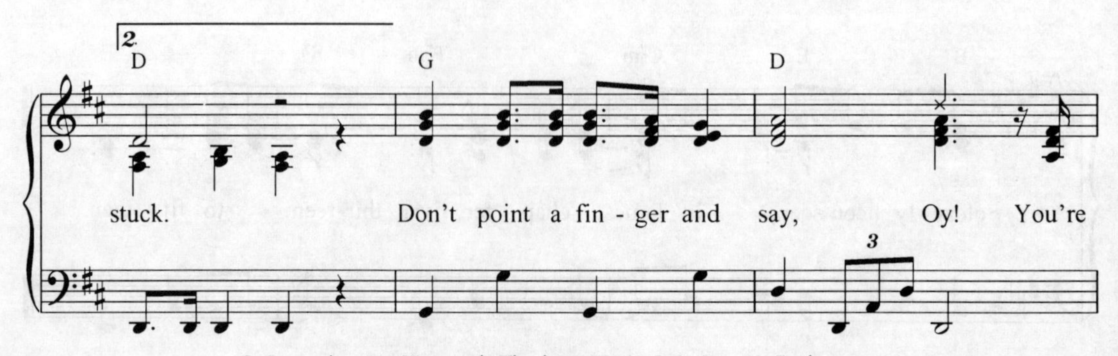
2.
D
G
D
stuck. Don't point a fin - ger and say, Oy! You're
3

A
D
G
do - ing it wrong when hey, hey, your own life is far from o -

D
A
kay. Don't point at the speck in your bro-ther's eye, when there's a

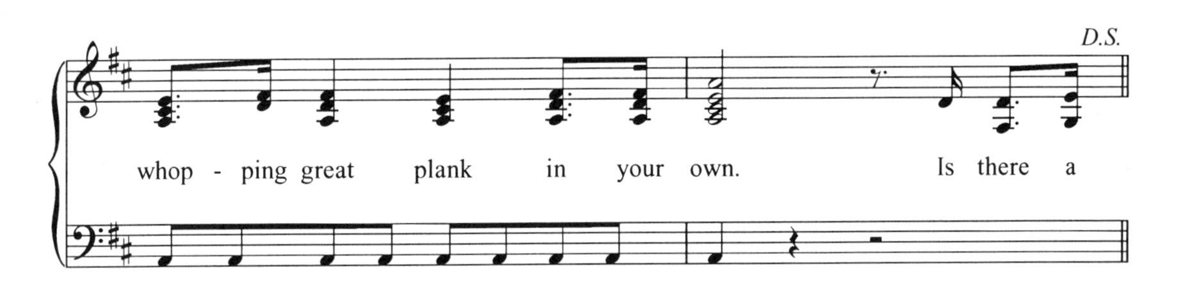
D.S.
whop - ping great plank in your own. Is there a

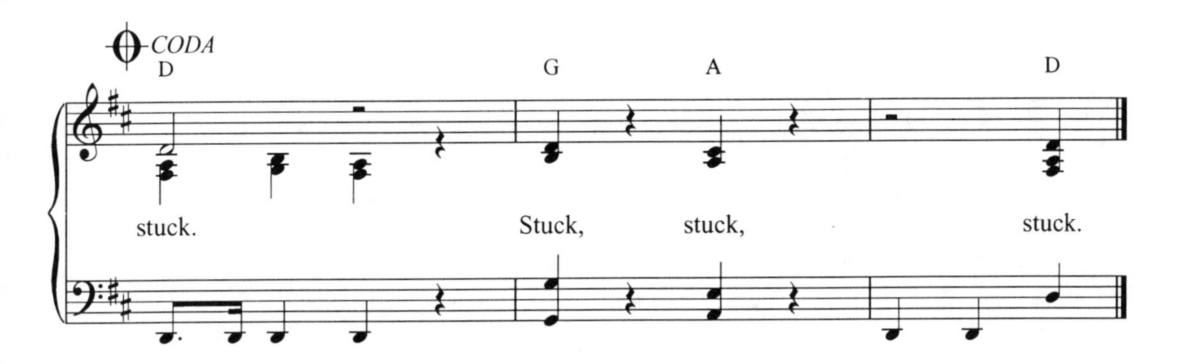
CODA
D
G
A
D
stuck. Stuck, stuck, stuck.

562 It came upon the midnight clear

Words: Edmund Hamilton Sears, alt.
Music: traditional English melody
arr. Arthur Seymour Sullivan
NOEL DCM
Capo 3
1. It came up - on the mid - night clear, that glo - rious song of old, from
an - gels bend - ing near the earth to touch their harps of gold: 'Peace
on the earth, good - will to all, from heav'n's all - gra - cious King!' The
world in sol - emn still - ness lay to hear the an - gels sing.

2. Still through the cloven skies they come,
with peaceful wings unfurled;
and still their heav'nly music floats
o'er all the weary world:
above its sad and lowly plains
they bend on hov'ring wing;
and ever o'er its Babel-sounds
the blessèd angels sing.

3. Yet with the woes of sin and strife
the world has suffered long;
beneath the angel-strain have rolled
two thousand years of wrong;
and warring humankind hears not
the love-song which they bring:
O hush the noise of mortal strife,
and hear the angels sing!

4. And ye, beneath life's crushing load,
whose forms are bending low,
who toil along the climbing way
with painful steps and slow:
look now! for glad and golden hours
come swiftly on the wing;
O rest beside the weary road,
and hear the angels sing.

5. For lo, the days are hast'ning on,
by prophets seen of old,
when with the ever-circling years
comes round the age of gold;
when peace shall over all the earth
its ancient splendours fling,
and all the world give back the song
which now the angels sing.

Still through the cloven skies they come
with peaceful wings unfurled,
and still their heavenly music floats
o'er all the weary world;
above its sad and lowly plains,
they bend on hovering wing,
and ever o'er its Babel sounds
the blessed angels sing.

Yet with the woes of sin and strife
the world has suffered long;
beneath the angel-strain have rolled
two thousand years of wrong;
and man, at war with man, hears not
the love-song which they bring;
O hush the noise, ye men of strife,
and hear the angels sing.

And ye, beneath life's crushing load,
whose forms are bending low,
who toil along the climbing way
with painful steps and slow,
look now! for glad and golden hours
come swiftly on the wing;
O rest beside the weary road
and hear the angels sing.

For lo! the days are hastening on,
by prophets seen of old,
when with the ever-circling years
comes round the age of gold;
when peace shall over all the earth
its ancient splendours fling,
and the whole world give back the song
which now the angels sing.

563 It is a thing most wonderful

Words: William Walsham How

Music: Thomas Bishop Southgate

BROOKFIELD LM
G Gaug Am D7 G C/G G
1. It is a thing most won - der - ful, al - most too
C A7/C♯ D A7/E D/F♯ D7 G C E7/B Am A7
won - der - ful to be, that God's own Son should come from
D D7/C G/B C C♯dim G/D B♭dim/D D7 G
heav'n, and die to save a child like me.

2. And yet I know that it is true:
he chose a poor and humble lot,
and wept and toiled, and mourned and died,
for love of those who loved him not.

3. I sometimes think about the cross,
and shut my eyes, and try to see
the cruel nails and crown of thorns,
and Jesus crucified for me.

4. But even could I see him die,
I could but see a little part
of that great love which, like a fire,
is always burning in his heart.

5. I cannot tell how he could love
a child so weak and full of sin;
his love must be most wonderful,
if he could die my love to win.

6. It is most wonderful to know
his love for me so free and sure;
but 'tis more wonderful to see
my love for him so faint and poor.

7. And yet I want to love thee, Lord;
O light the flame within my heart,
and I will love thee more and more,
until I see thee as thou art.

564 It really is a worry *(Right side up!)*

Words: John Lane | Music: Ian Chia

Sea shanty (♩ = 115)
D A/C♯ Bm Asus4 Gsus4 D/F♯ Gsus4 Asus4 D
1. It real-ly is a wor-ry, to
A7
stop and look a-round; there's sad-ness, hate and mad-ness, a
D
world that's up-side down! But Je-sus came to show us the
G N.C.
change when God's in charge; there's good-ness, love and jus-tice: there's a
Chorus D
new way: right side up! Oh, right side up! It's a

Em
A7
Em
A7
brand new way to live. When o - thers say 'Get e - ven!' Je - sus
D
D/F♯
D
D/F♯
says 'Love and for - give!' Oh, right side up! His
G
N.C.
love can change our hearts, he'll take out the hate, we'll all be mates, we'll
To next verse
Last time
make a brand new start! 2. When make a brand new start!

2. When people say 'Fight harder!'
he says, 'Make peace instead!'
When people say 'Act smarter!'
he says, 'Just be true instead!'
When people get too greedy,
he says 'Instead, be kind!'
When people think life's hopeless,
he says 'God is still in charge!'

3. When people say 'Look after
number one and get ahead!'
then Jesus says, 'Be happy,
obey what God has said!'
When people say 'It's nonsense!'
you gotta keep on Jesus' way.
His way will last for ever,
and it starts with us today.

565 It's amazin' what praisin' can do

Words and Music: Ian Smale

Brightly
E
B
E
A
1. It's a - maz- in' what prais - in' can do. It's a - maz - in' what prais - in' can
E
A
E
do. Join in and you'll see what it's been and done for me, it's a -
To next verse
Last time
B
E
E
maz - in' what prais - in' can do. 2. It's a - do.

2. It's amazin' what your mouth can do.
It's amazin' what your mouth can do.
It can shout, scream or cheer, as long as it's sincere,
it's amazin' what your mouth can do.

3. It's amazin' what clapping can do.
It's amazin' what clapping can do.
As my hands applaud they shout praise to the Lord,
it's amazin' what clapping can do.

4. It's amazin' what dancing can do.
It's amazin' what dancing can do.
King David employed it, and my feet enjoyed it,
it's amazin' what dancing can do.

566 It's good to be together

Words: Alison Fuggle
Music: Roger Jones
arr. Chris Mitchell
(♩ = 75)
1. It's good to be to-ge - ther in all this stor - my wea - ther, all snug - gled safe to - ge - ther in God's boat: to bob up and down all day, count-ing clouds a - bove, and pray we've fol - lowed God's in - struc - tions and we'll float!
good to be to - ge - ther, not sure if we will e - ver get off the ark and walk out on dry land! Though we've got our sea - legs now, we're all bu - sy wond' - ring how the world will start brand new as God has planned.
Chorus
It's

G
D/F#
Em
A
D
good to be to - ge - ther though we've been ra - ther cramped: you

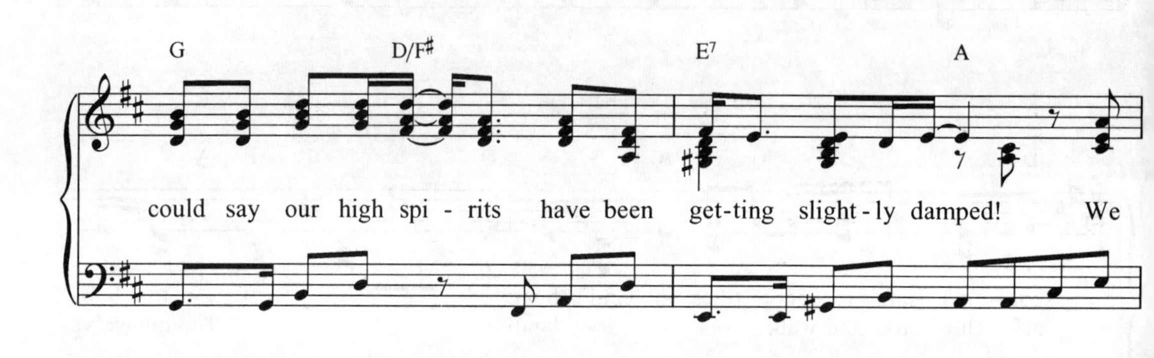
G
D/F#
E7
A
could say our high spi - rits have been get-ting slight - ly damped! We

G
D/F#
Em
A
D
hope we'll soon be land - ing: can't wait to get the nod. It's

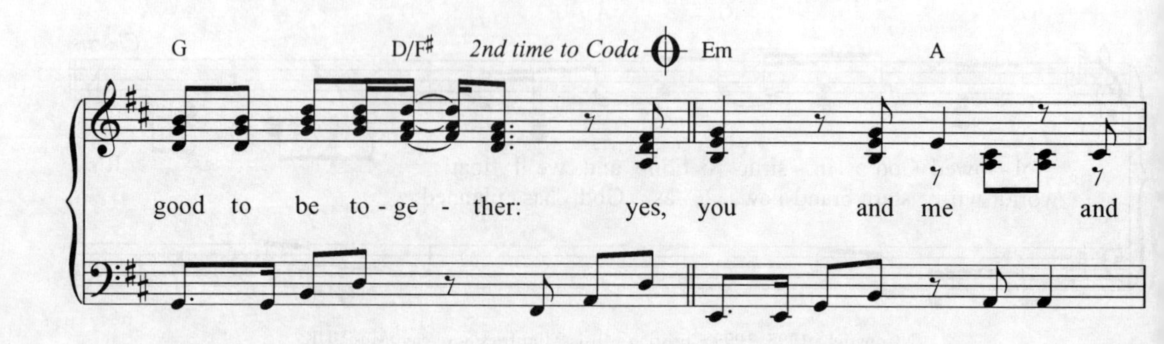
G
D/F#
2nd time to Coda
Em
A
good to be to - ge - ther: yes, you and me and

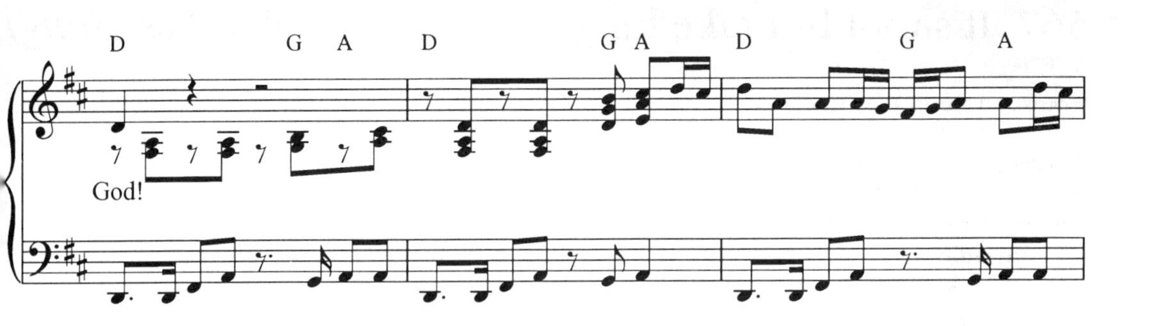
D G A D G A D G A
God!

D G A G A D
D.S.
2. It's

CODA
Em A Em A Em7 A Em7 A
you and me and you and you and you and you and you and you and you and

Em7 A G/A D G A D
you and you and Oh, I give up!
And God!

567 It shouldn't take long *(Numbers Song)*

Words and Music: Dave Cooke

This song follows a similar format to 'The Twelve Days of Christmas', counting down through the sections, starting one section later with each repetition. Finish with the Chorus.

Steadily
Chorus
Comit3 B♭omit3 Comit3
It should-n't take long to sing this song, if you tell me where we are. It's
all a-bout num-bers in the Bi - ble, just tell me where we are. From
F G
one to twelve is how it goes, sing a - long and see it grow. It
should-n't take long to sing this song, if you tell me where we are.
1
N.C.
After verse 6, D.S. for Chorus
One is for the on - ly God, the on - ly God Al - migh - ty. It

2
F
Two for the tes - ta - ments old and new.
3
G
Three for the Tri - ni - ty, three in one.
4
F
G
Four for the gos - pels (Mat - thew, Mark, Luke, John).
5
C
F
Five thou - sand
G
fed (Five loaves, two fish).
6
F
G
Six wings of the Se - ra - phim.
7
F
G
Se - ven for the days that God made.
8
F
G
Eight for the peo - ple in No - ah's Ark.
9
F
G
Nine fruits of the Spi - rit.
10
F
G
Ten for the Ten Com - mand - ments.
11
F
G
Ele - ven for the bro - thers of Jo - seph.
12
F
G
Twelve for the twelve dis - ci - ples.

568 It's Jesus' joy that fills my heart *(Jesus' joy)*

Words and Music: Brian Howard
arr. Chris Mitchell

G
verse 2: sing verse 1 lyrics
C/G
G
1. It's Jesus' joy that fills my heart; it
is your joy that fills my heart; it
D
Am7
Em
keeps me going when times get hard. On eagles' wings he lifts
keeps me going when times get hard. On eagles' wings you lift
D/F♯
G
Dsus4
me up; his grace, amazing, is
me up; your grace, amazing, is
D
To next verse
C2
D7sus4
e-nough.
e-nough.
2. It's
3. It
Last time
C2
D/C
D7sus4
D
C/E
D/F♯
G2

569 It's the time

Words and Music: James Wright
arr. Chris Mitchell

Chorus
Capo 3
F D
B♭ G
C A
F D
It's the time to start the fes - tive mu - sic,
it's the time to lift your voice and sing.
It's the time of
praise and ce - le-bra - tion,
it's the birth-day of Je - sus Christ the King.
Last time
Fine
To verses
Je - sus Christ the King.
1. Ev - 'ry - bo - dy praise him for
sending us the Son from the Fa-ther's glo - ry to
2. Ev - 'ry - bo - dy praise him for
Christ has come to earth, ev - 'ry - bo - dy praise him on

B♭ F C
G D A
earth for ev - 'ry - one. Ev - 'ry - bo - dy praise him, fill
this, the Sa - viour's birth. Ev - 'ry - bo - dy praise him, fill
B♭ F Gm7 C
G D Em7 A
1.
D.C.
up your hearts with joy, ev - 'ry - bo - dy wor - ship the King.
up your hearts with joy, ev - 'ry - bo - dy wor - ship the
2.
C B♭ F/A B♭ F/A B♭ C F
A G D/F♯ G D/F♯ G A D
King. Hal-le - lu - jah, hal-le-lu - jah the an-gels sang. Hal-le-
B♭ F/A B♭ F/A B♭ C F B♭ F/A B♭ F/A
G D/F♯ G D/F♯ G A D G D/F♯ G D/F♯
lu - jah, hal - le - lu - jah, good - will to man. Hal - le - lu - jah, hal - le - lu - jah, Em-
B♭ C F B♭ Gm7 C
G A D G Em7 A
D.C. al Fine
man - u - el, God with man to dwell.

570 It's time to say we're sorry

(Sorry Song)

Words and Music: Dave Cooke

Gently
E
B/E
E
A
C♯m
B
It's time to say we're sor - ry
for all the bad things we

A²
E
B/E
have done.
No need to wor -

E
A
C♯m
B
- ry,
God for - gives us through his Son.

A²
F♯m
It does - n't real - ly mat - ter how bad

E/G♯ A C♯m B
we've been or what we've said to each o - ther:
A E/G♯ F♯m
he can wipe the whole slate clean when we hon-est - ly ask our
C♯m B F♯m/E E F♯m/E E
Fa - ther to for - give us, for -
F♯m/E E F♯m/E E F♯m/E E
give us, for - give us,
F♯m/E E F♯m/E E F♯m/E E
for - give us.

E B/E E A C♯m
Thank you, Lord, for mak - ing us clean and send-ing Je - sus to save
B A2 E B/E
us. Thank you that no mat - ter how bad
E A E/G♯
it seems, you're there in our heart, right
F♯m A/B F♯m/E E F♯m/E E
there, al-ways rea - dy to for-give us, for -
1. 2.
F♯m/E E F♯m/E E F♯m/E E F♯m/E E
give us. give us. Thank you for for -
F♯m/E E F♯m/E E F♯m/E E F♯m/E E
giv - ing us, thank you for for - giv - ing us.

571 It was on a starry night *(A starry night)*

Words and Music: Joy Webb
arr. Chris Mitchell

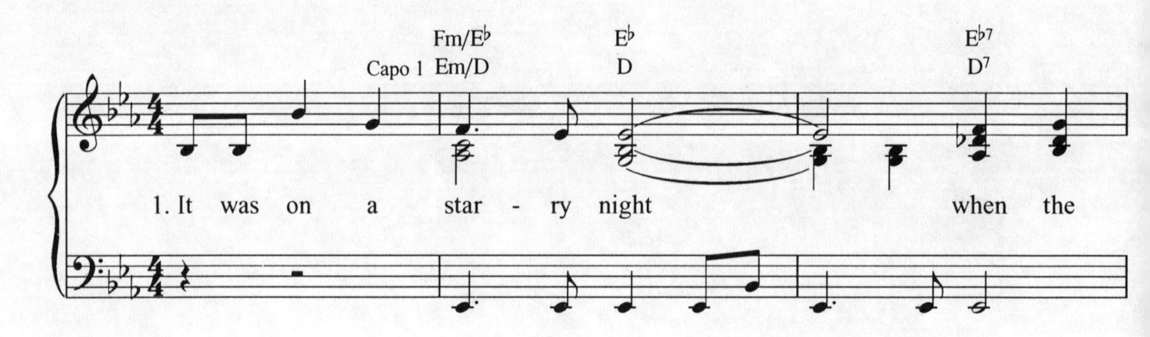
Capo 1
Fm/E♭ Em/D
E♭ D
E♭7 D7
1. It was on a star - ry night when the

A♭ G
Gm7 F♯m7
Cm7 Bm7
hills were bright. Earth lay sleep - ing,

F7sus4 E7sus4
F7 E7
A♭/B♭ G/A
B♭7 A7
Fm/E♭ Em/D
E♭ D
sleep - ing calm and still; then in a cat - tle shed,

E♭7 D7
A♭ G
E♭/B♭ D/A
in a man - ger bed a boy was born,

B♭7 A7
E♭ D
Chorus
Fm/E♭ Em/D
E♭ D
King of all the world.
And all the an - gels sang for him,
E♭7 D7
A♭ G
the bells of hea - ven rang for him;
for a boy was
E♭/B♭ D/A
B♭7 A7
E♭ D
D.C.
born,
King of all the world.
On a star - ry night,
on a star - ry night.

2. Soon the shepherds came that way,
where the baby lay,
and were kneeling,
kneeling by his side.
And their hearts believed again,
for the peace of men;
for a boy was born,
King of all the world.

572 I've got a friend called Jesus

Words and Music: Susie Hare

Fairly lively

Cmaj7 C6/G Dm7 G C/A D7
I've got a friend called Je - sus who is with me wher - e - ver I

F/G G Cmaj7 A7 Dm Fm
go. I've got a friend called Je - sus and I

C/G Dm/G G C F F♯dim
want ev - 'ry - one to know that I will ne - ver be with -

C/G Am Dm7 G C
out him, be - cause his love for me is

F
F♯dim
C/G
A
much, much high - er than the moun - tain and
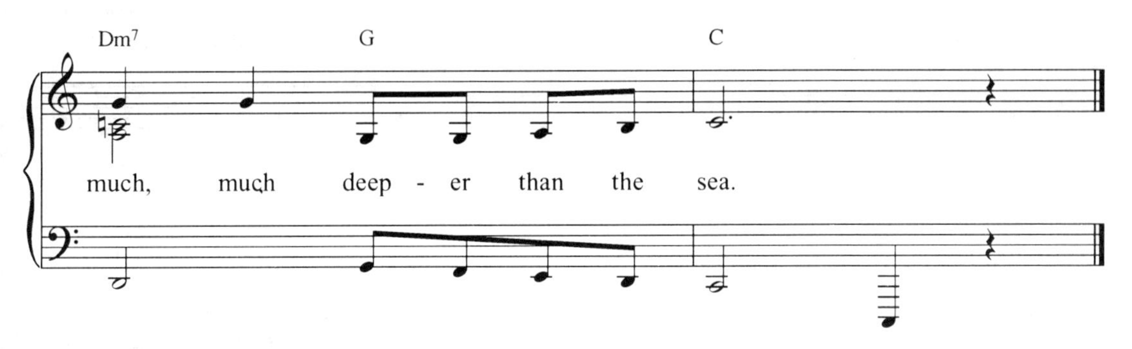
Dm7
G
C
much, much deep - er than the sea.

573 I've got that joy, joy, joy, joy

Words: G.W. Cooke

Music: Traditional
arr. Chris Mitchell

B♭
Capo 3 G
1. I've got that joy, joy, joy, joy down in my heart, (where?)

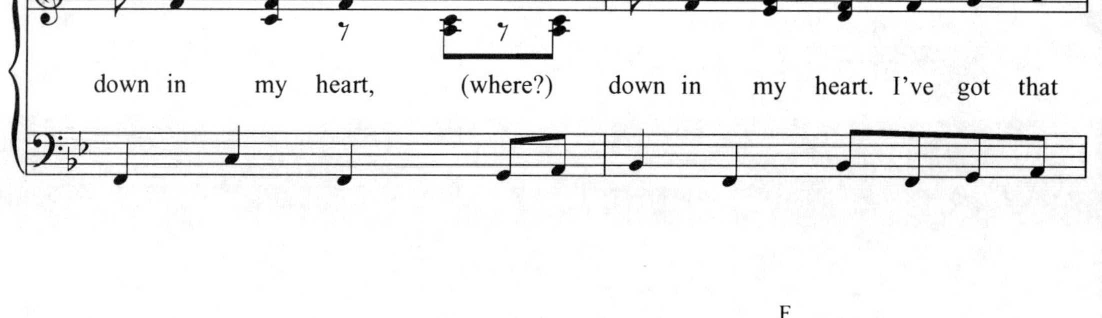
F
D
B♭
G
down in my heart, (where?) down in my heart. I've got that

F
D
joy, joy, joy, joy down in my heart, (where?) down in my heart to

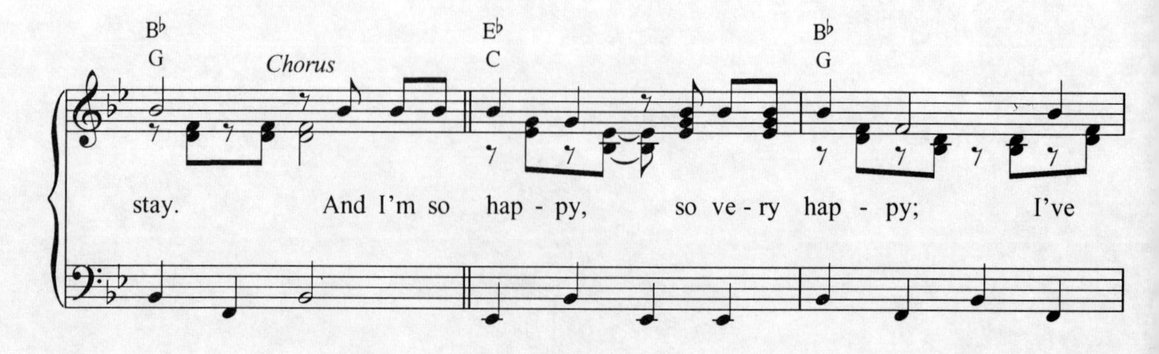
B♭
G
Chorus
E♭
C
B♭
G
stay. And I'm so hap - py, so ve - ry hap - py; I've

F7
D7
B♭
G
B♭aug/D
Gaug/B
got the love of Je - sus in my heart. And I'm so
E♭
C
B♭
G
hap - py, so ve - ry hap - py; I've
1.
2.
F7
D7
B♭
G
B♭
G
got the love of Je - sus in my heart. 2. I've got the heart.

2. I've got the peace that passes understanding
   down in my heart, (where?)
   down in my heart, (where?)
   down in my heart.
   I've got the peace that passes understanding
   down in my heart, (where?)
   down in my heart to stay.

574 I've never been to a circus *(Circus song)*

Words and Music: Phil Overton
arr. Chris Mitchell

C G C
1. I've ne - ver been to a cir - cus to
preach - er told me a - bout it, I
round has gone cra - zy. It gets
C7 F
watch the clowns per - form. I've
thought he must be mad! I
more like a cir - cus ev - 'ry day and I
G Am
ne - ver seen a tra - peze man, but I've heard
said, 'I could ne - ver keep it up' but deep in -
long to rise far a - bove it and
D D/F♯ G
a - bout it all. I've
- side I was sad. He
walk on a bet - ter way. Well,

C G C
ne - ver seen a li - on tam - er, al - though I've
said, 'You don't have to do a thing – just
Je - sus helped me to do it – all I
C7 F
heard what the child - ren say. But I'm
trust in Je - sus and pray.' So I'm
had to do was pray. And I'm
F♯dim7 C/G G7
learn-ing to walk on a tight - rope and I'm gett-ing bet-ter e - ve - ry day.
C G/B Am7 G7
Chorus
And I don't e - ven need a safe -
C G7 C
- ty net, be - cause Je - sus is watch-ing me. And al-though

G7 Am D7
I have - n't quite got it yet, I know that he's close by me.
G C G C
He throws down a line in an e - vil world for
C7 F F♯dim7
all who will trust and o - bey, and so I'm learn-ing to walk on a tight-
C/G G7 C
- rope and I'm gett - ing bet - ter e - ve - ry day.
F♯dim7 C G7
C
To next verse
D.S.
Last time
2. When a
3. The world a-

575 I wanna give you

Words and Music: Andy Read
arr. Chris Mitchell

G2
A7
I wan-na give you, I wan-na give you,
C2
C/D
I wan-na give all my love to you.
G2
I wan-na give you,
A7
I wan-na give you, I wan-na give
C2
C/D
G2
Last time
all my love to you.

To continue
G2
Walk-ing down the street, run-ning in the park,
A7
C2
swim-ming in the pool,
C/D
G2
wan-na talk to you. Ri-ding in the woods,
A7
splash-ing in the stream, play-ing in my room,
C2
C/D
G2
D.S.
I wan-na talk to you. I wan-na give

576 I want my life to be pleasing to you

(Pleasing to you)

Words and Music: Margaret Carpenter
arr. Dave Bankhead

(♩ = 88)
C
G/B
F/A
C/G
Descant
I want to please you, Je - sus,
I want my life to be pleas - ing to you,

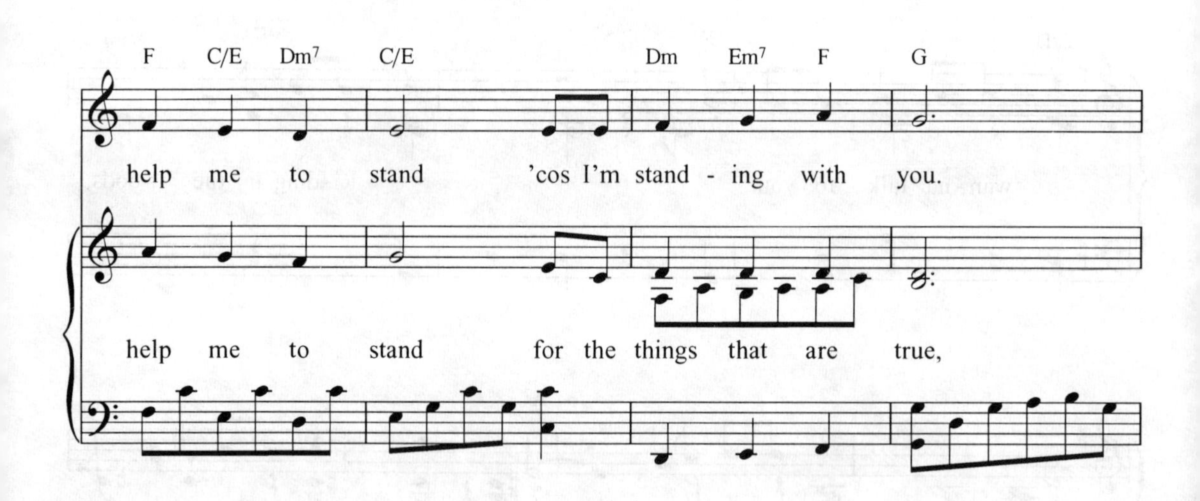
F
C/E
Dm7
C/E
Dm
Em7
F
G
help me to stand 'cos I'm stand - ing with you.
help me to stand for the things that are true,

C
G/B
F/A
C/E
Turn my back on wrong that I know,
turn - ing my back on the wrong that I know,

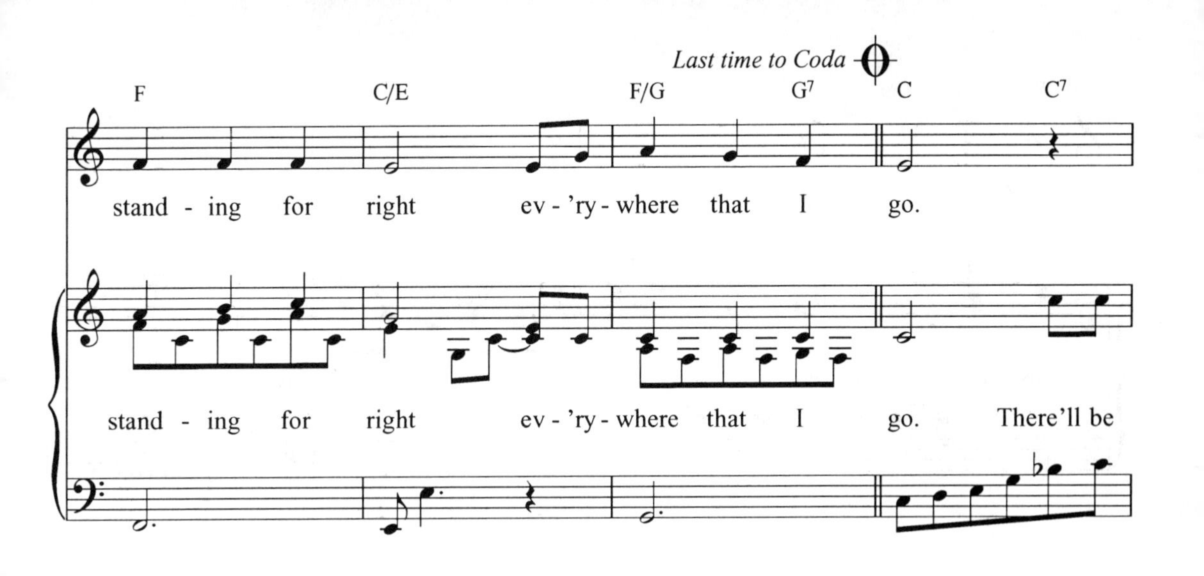
Last time to Coda
F
C/E
F/G
G7
C
C7
stand - ing for right ev - 'ry - where that I go.
stand - ing for right ev - 'ry - where that I go. There'll be

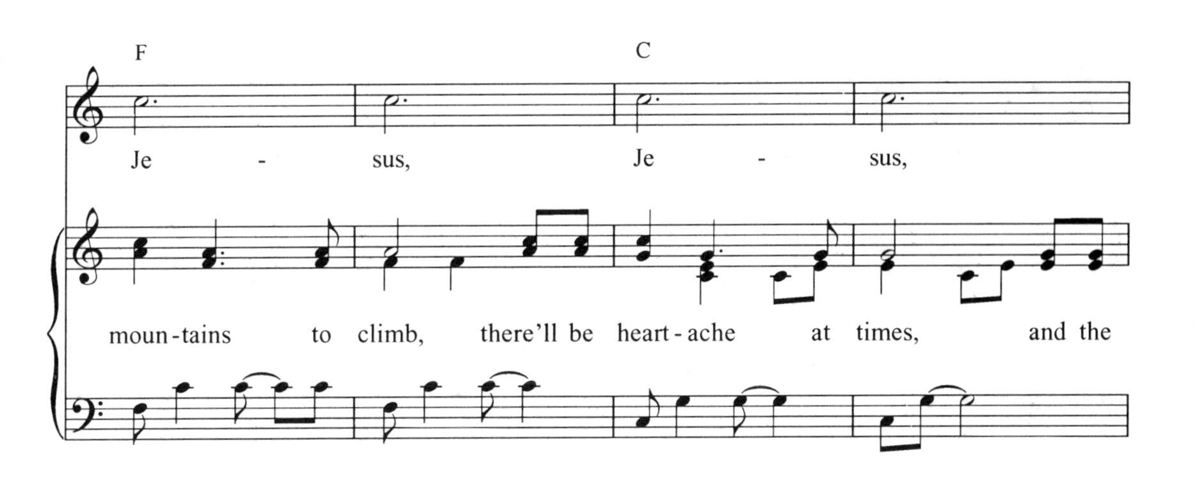
F
C
Je - sus, Je - sus,
moun-tains to climb, there'll be heart - ache at times, and the

G
C
C7
you will ne - ver leave me,
path - way won't al - ways be ea - sy, there'll be

F
C
Je - sus, Je - sus,
tears on the way but to life I will say,

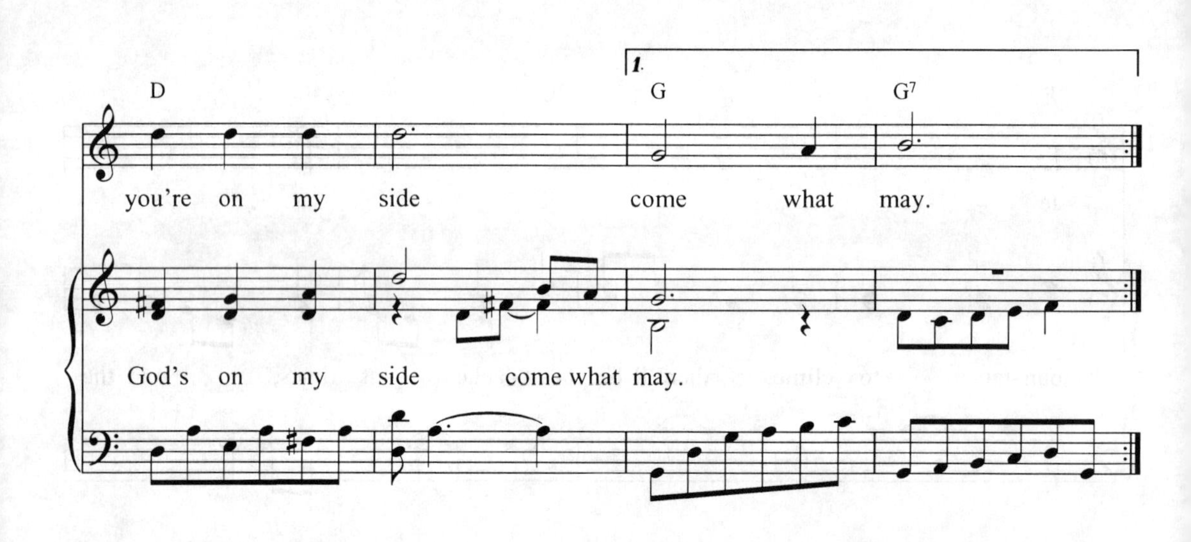
1.
D
G
G7
you're on my side come what may.
God's on my side come what may.

2
CODA
G
G/B
G
D.C.
C
what - e - ver comes my way. go.
D.C.
may. go.

577 I want to be like you, Lord Jesus

Words and Music: Chris Jackson
arr. Dave Bankhead

G D/F♯ Em D C D
I want to be like you, Lord Je - sus, I want to be like you. And

G D/F♯ Em D C D G C/G G
I want to fol-low you, Lord Je - sus, I want to fol - low you.

2. Fill me with your Holy Spirit,
 fill me with your love.
 'Cos I want to be like you, Lord Jesus,
 I want to be like you.

3. Hold me in your arms, Lord Jesus,
 keep me close to you.
 'Cos I want to follow you, Lord Jesus,
 I want to follow you.

578 I will always follow Jesus

Words and Music: Capt. Alan J. Price, CA
arr. Philip Eley

Getting faster with each repetition (𝅗𝅥 = 63)
Capo 3
F D C A F D C A
I will al - ways fol - low Je - sus,
I will al - ways fol - low him.
Ev - 'ry - thing I do for Je - sus
will bring hap - pi - ness to him.
I will make time
just for Je - sus,
I will list - en and o - bey.
I will al - ways
try to please him,
by the things I do each day.
B♭ G F/A D/F♯

579 I will believe

Words and Music: Andy Read
arr. Chris Mitchell

Chorus
E
C♯m7
A2
Bsus4
I will be-lieve in Je - sus, I will be-lieve in the cross

Bsus4
E
C♯m7
A2
where he died. I will be-lieve in Je - sus 'cos he's a -

To repeat
Last time
Fine
live!
live!

To verses
Amaj7
B
live! 1. I will trust him to be

Amaj7 B Amaj7
faith - ful and to ans - wer me when

B E Amaj7
I pray. He re - wards those

B Amaj7 B Amaj7
who will seek him and dis - co - ver

B C#m7 B/D# D.C.
his great love!

2. He will keep us and protect us
from the evil around this world.
He will fill us with the power
to tell others of his great love!

580 I will bend down and touch

Words and Music: Ian Smale
arr. Chris Mitchell

E
B7
I will bend down and touch my knees and then I'll touch my toes.

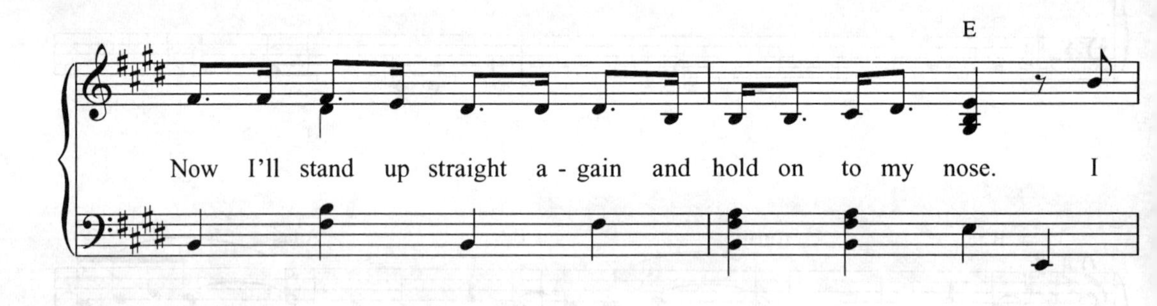
E
Now I'll stand up straight a - gain and hold on to my nose. I

B7
co - ver my eyes with my hands so I can-not see, then

E
reach my hands up in the air for God cre - a - ted me.

A E B E A
God cre-a-ted me, God cre-a-ted me. I'll reach my hands up in the air for

E B7 E
Fine
D.S.
God cre-a-ted me. I will

581 I will bless the Lord

Words and Music: Unknown

E/B E F♯m B B7
1. I will bless the Lord, he is wor - thy to be praised. I will
bless the Lord, he is wor - thy to be praised. I will
E E/B B
E F♯m B B7
bless the Lord, he is wor - thy to be praised. He is
wor - thy, wor-thy to be praised.
To next verse
E
2. I will
Last time
E
praised.

2. I will lift my voice, he is worthy to be praised. *(x3)*
   He is worthy, worthy to be praised.

3. I will lift my hands, he is worthy to be praised. *(x3)*
   He is worthy, worthy to be praised.

4. I will lift his name, he is worthy to be praised. *(x3)*
   He is worthy, worthy to be praised.

582 I will lift up the name of the Lord

Words and Music: Mike Burn

Chorus
E
I will lift up the name of the Lord, I will
B
E
A
lift up the name of the Lord, I will lift up the name of the one
E
B
B7
who lift - ed me. He
E
E7
A
took my feet from the slip - per - y clay, set them on a so - lid
C
E
B
rock to stay, I will lift up the name of the one who lift - ed

E
Verse
A
E
me. Oh, I praise you,
A
E
A
Am
Je - sus, for you al - ways hear my
E
A
E
cry. Ev - 'ry day that you
G♯
G♯7
C♯m
A
F♯m7
give me breath I'm gon-na lift your name on
Bsus4
1.
B A B♭ B
Chorus
2.
B A B♭ B
high. I will

583 I will not be afraid

Words and Music: Nick Harding
arr. Dave Bankhead

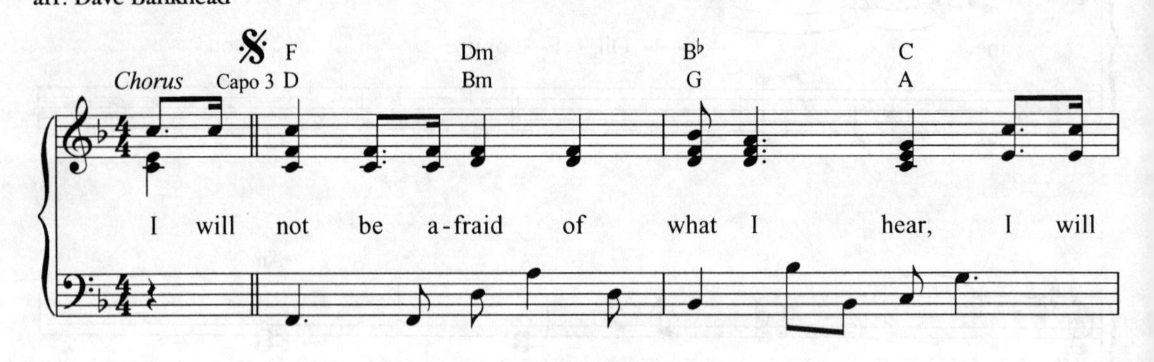

Chorus
Capo 3
F D
Dm Bm
B♭ G
C A
I will not be a-fraid of what I hear, I will

F D
Dm Bm
B♭ G
C A
F D
Dm Bm
not be a-fraid of what I see, I will not be a-fraid of

To verses
Last time
A F♯
Dm Bm
B♭ G
C A
F D
F D
Fine
an-y - thing 'cos I know God's with me. 1. Like

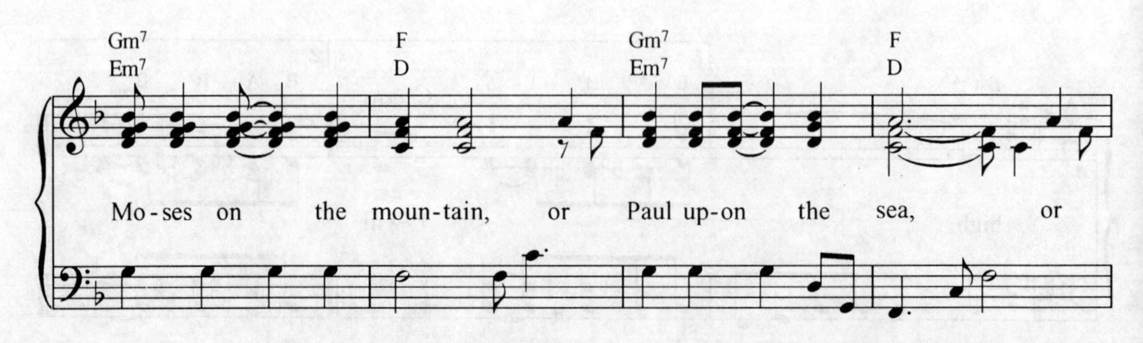

Gm7 Em7
F D
Gm7 Em7
F D
Mo-ses on the moun-tain, or Paul up-on the sea, or

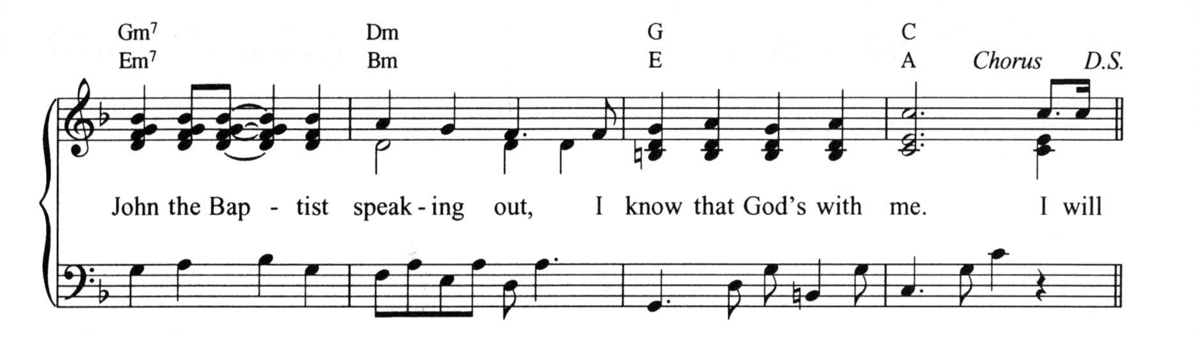
Gm7
Em7
Dm
Bm
G
E
C
A
Chorus
D.S.
John the Bap - tist speak - ing out, I know that God's with me. I will

2. Like Mary with the angel,
   or Peter when set free,
   or David hiding in a cave,
   I know that God's with me.

3. Like Noah in the flooding,
   or Joshua's victory,
   or Esther standing up for truth,
   I know that God's with me.

584 I will praise you *(Bless the Lord)*

Words and Music: Brian Howard
arr. Chris Mitchell

A♭ E♭
Capo 1 G D

I will praise you with all of my heart,

To repeat

B♭ E♭/B♭ B♭
A D/A A

soul, and mind. Oh,

Last time
B♭
A
E♭/B♭
D/A
B♭
A
Fine
mind.

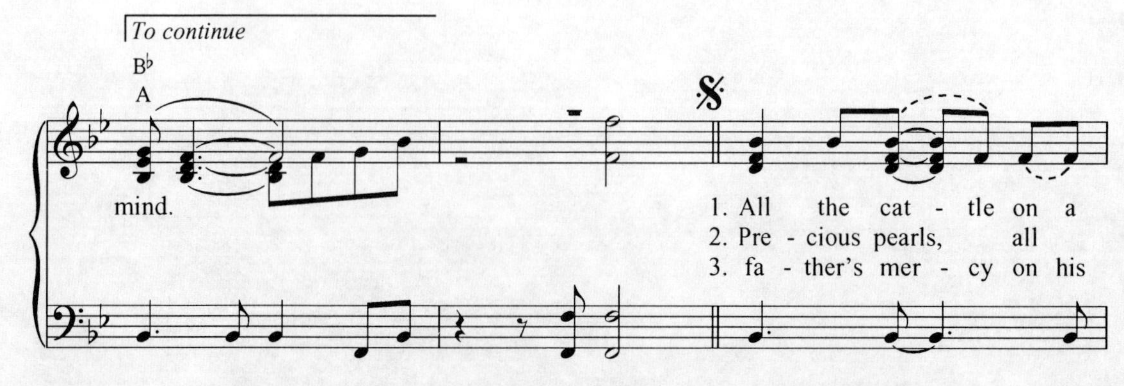

To continue
B♭
A
mind.
1. All the cat - tle on a
2. Pre - cious pearls, all
3. fa - ther's mer - cy on his

E♭ D A♭ G E♭ D
thou - sand hills,
gems and jewels,
own lit - tle ones, so the
B♭ A F E B♭ A
all the fish - es in the deep blue sea.
all the fields and all the fos - sil fuel.
Lord has shown me com - pas - sion.
F E B♭ A E♭ D
All the gold in the earth be - low,
All the cars and all the mi - cro - chips,
Why should I wor - ry, why should I fret?
A♭ G E♭ D B♭ A
all of this my
he made the things they
On my Fa - ther's love I
F E B♭ A F E B♭ A
D.S. for v.2
Last time D.C.
Fa - ther owns. All of this, yes, my Fa - ther owns.
made them with. He made the things they made them with.
can de - pend. On my Fa - ther's love I can de - pend.

F E
B♭ A
Bless the Lord now, O my soul. Bless the Lord now,
heals me and for-gives my sins. Who heals me and for-

F E
B♭ A
F E
B♭ A
O my soul. And for-get none of his be-ne-fits. And for-
gives my sins. With all of my heart now, I will praise him. With

1.
2.
F E
B♭ A
F E
B♭ A
get none of his be-ne-fits. Who
all of my heart now, I will praise him. Oh,

E♭ D
A♭ G
E♭ D
I will praise you

1.
B♭
A
E♭/B♭
D/A
B♭
A
with all of my heart,
soul and mind.

2.
B♭
A
D.S.
Oh,
mind.
3. Like a

585 Jesus, all for Jesus

Words and Music: Jennifer Atkinson and Robin Mark

E
A
B
C♯m
1. Je - sus, all for Je - sus; all I
am and have and e - ver hope to be.
1.
Last time
Fine
2.
be.
be.

E
A
E
2. All of my am - bi - tions, hopes and plans, I sur -
B
1.
C♯m
B
ren - der these in - to your hands.
2.
E
A
E
Chorus
A
hands. For it's on - ly in your will that
E
A
I am free. For it's on - ly in
E
B
D.S. al Fine
your will that I am free.

586 Jesus, baby Jesus

Words and Music: Roger Jones from *Stargazers* (1976)
arr. Chris Mitchell

Andante con moto
FINLAY 65 65 D
Dm
Je - sus,
Gm
Dm
ba - by Je - sus, you're just a small
A
Dm
Gm
babe. Je - sus, how we love you,
Dm
A7
Dm
F
though you're just a babe. Sa - viour,

C
F
as you're sleep - ing,
Sa - viour, are you

Dm
Gm
mine?
Je - sus, though a ba - by,

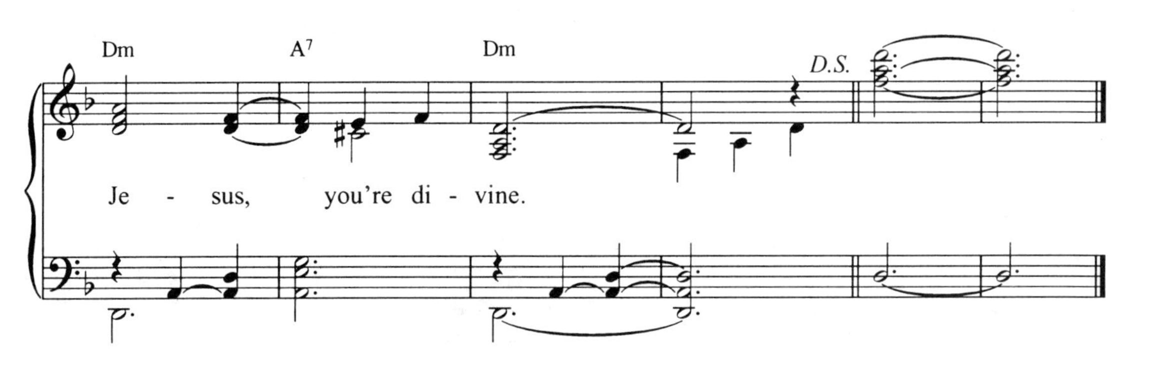
Dm
A7
Dm
D.S.
Je - sus, you're di - vine.

587 Jesus, be the centre *(Be the centre)*

Words and Music: Michael Frye
arr. Chris Mitchell

(♩ = 70)
D
Dsus4
D
Dsus4
D
Dsus4
1. Je - sus, be the cen - tre,
2. Je - sus, be the cen - tre,

D
A7sus4
G/B
be my source, be my light, Je - sus.
be my hope, be my song, Je - sus.

1.
2, 3.
D
Dsus4
D
Dsus4
D
Chorus
Be the fire

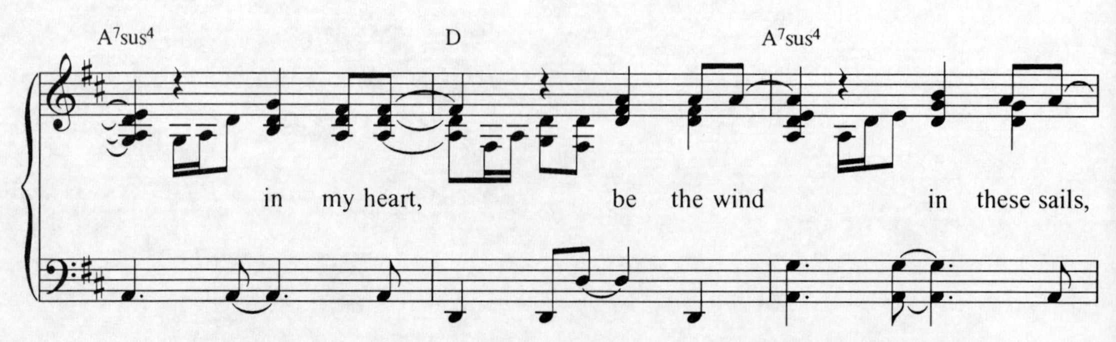
A7sus4
D
A7sus4
in my heart, be the wind in these sails,

D
A7sus4
Bm7
be the rea - son that I live,
Je - sus,

A7sus4
D
Dsus4
D
Dsus4
D.C.
D
Je - sus.

3. Jesus, be my vision,
be my path, be my guide,
Jesus.

588 Jesus bids us shine

Words: Susan Warner

Music: E.O. Excell

JESUS BIDS US SHINE 10 11 10 10
G D7/A G/B G G/D D D7 C/E D7/F♯ D7
1. Je - sus bids us shine with a pure, clear light, like a lit - tle can - dle
G C/G G Bm/D Em G/B
burn - ing in the night. In this world is dark - ness:
C G Em G/D G7/B G/D D7 G
so we must shine, you in your small cor - ner, and I in mine.

2. Jesus bids us shine
first of all for him;
well he sees and knows it,
if our light grows dim.
He looks down from heaven
to see us shine,
you in your small corner,
and I in mine.

3. Jesus bids us shine,
then, for all around;
many kinds of darkness
in the world abound:
sin, and want and sorrow;
so we must shine,
you in your small corner,
and I in mine.

589 Jesus born in Bethlehem *(The Holy Gospel)*

Words and Music: J. Macpherson

'Bush dance' style (♩ = 112)
G C G D C D G C D G C/E G/D D G D G G
1. Je - sus born in Beth - le - hem, born in a cat - tle stall.
Je - sus born in Beth - le - hem, born in a cat - tle stall.
That's the Ho - ly Gos - pel, good news for one and all.
Je - sus born in Beth - le - hem, born in a cat - tle stall.
To next verse
Last time
Lord.

2. Jesus called disciples too,
   twelve of them in all. *(x2)*
   That's the Holy Gospel,
   good news for one and all.
   Jesus called disciples too,
   twelve of them in all.

3. Jesus healed the sick and lame,
   when in faith they called . . .

4. Jesus sailed upon the sea,
   calmed the raging storm . . .

5. Jesus died upon the cross,
   carried the sins of all . . .

6. Jesus rose to life again,
   he is our living Lord . . .

590 Jesus came to make things new

Words and Music: Jennie Flack
arr. Chris Mitchell

Chorus
Capo 3
Jesus came to make things new.
He can start with you, yes he can.
Jesus came to make things new.
If you let him, he can start with you.
Last time
Fine
To continue
1. There seems to be so much wrong and

F
D
C
A
sad - ness a - round.
Peo - ple al - ways seem to spoil
F
D
B♭
G
good things.
There seems to be so much wrong and
F
D
G
E
sad - ness a - round.
Je - sus came to make things
C7
A7
Chorus
F
D
new.
Je - sus came to
Dm
Bm
F
D
C
A
make things new.
He can start with you, yes he can.

F
B♭
Bdim
F/C
C
D
G
G♯dim
D/A
A
Je - sus came to make things new. If you let him, he can start with you.

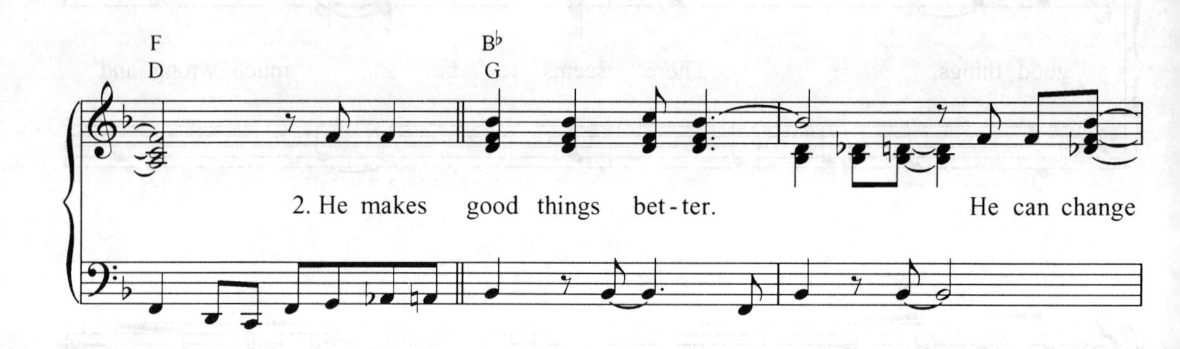
F
B♭
D
G
2. He makes good things bet - ter. He can change

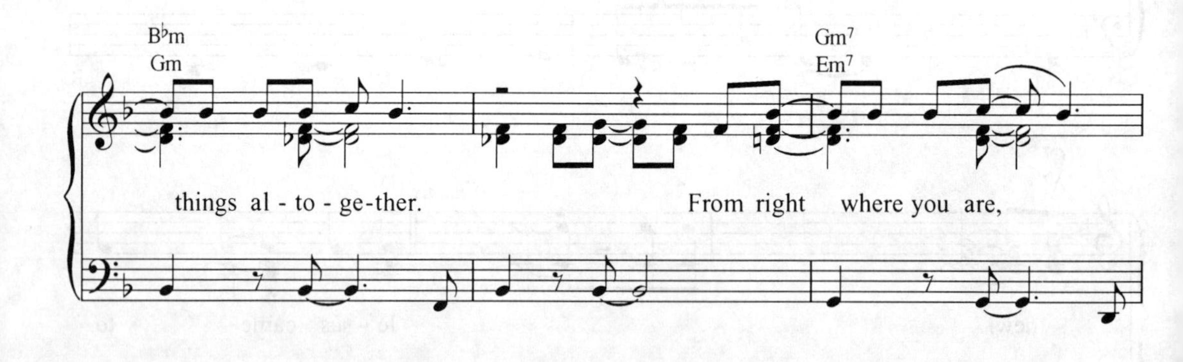
B♭m
Gm7
Gm
Em7
things al - to - ge - ther. From right where you are,

F
C7
D
A7
D.C.
he's not ve - ry far a - way.

591 Jesus, friend of little children

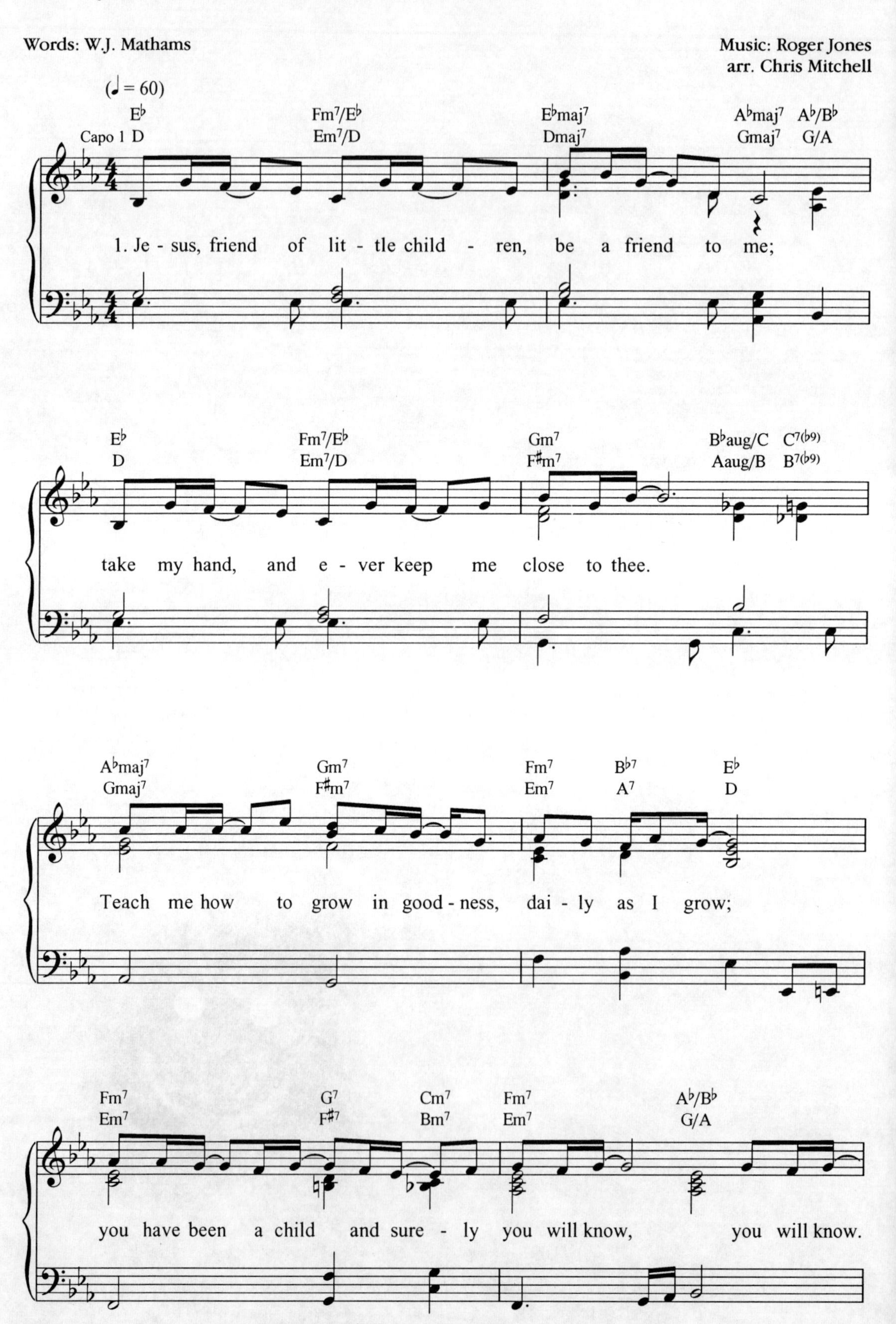
Words: W.J. Mathams
Music: Roger Jones
arr. Chris Mitchell
(♩ = 60)
Capo 1
1. Je - sus, friend of lit - tle child - ren, be a friend to me;
take my hand, and e - ver keep me close to thee.
Teach me how to grow in good - ness, dai - ly as I grow;
you have been a child and sure - ly you will know, you will know.

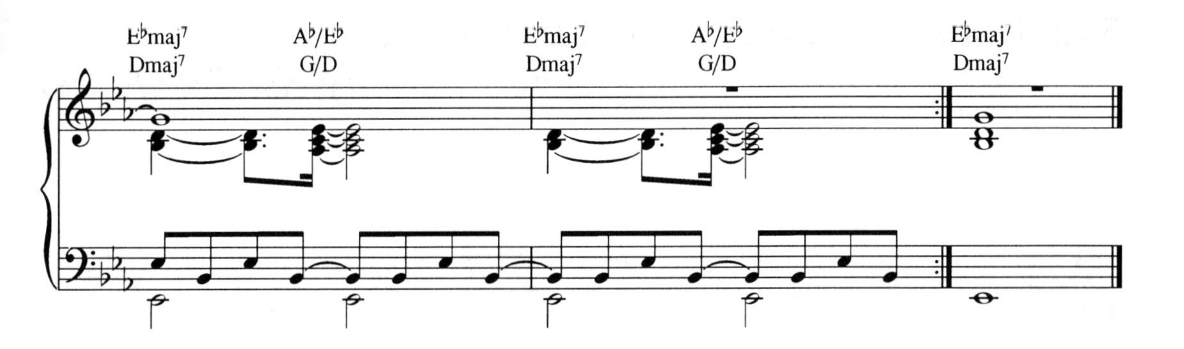
E♭maj7
Dmaj7
A♭/E♭
G/D
E♭maj7
Dmaj7
A♭/E♭
G/D
E♭maj7
Dmaj7

2. Step by step, O lead me onward,
upward into youth;
wiser, stronger, still becoming
in your truth.
Never leave me, nor forsake me;
ever be my friend;
for I need you from life's dawning
to its end, to its end.

592 Jesus gave every one of us a song
(There's nobody else like Jesus)

Words and Music: Derek Llewellyn

Em
B7
1. Je - sus gave ev - 'ry one of us a song to sing. Je - sus
C
B7
Em
B
Em
gave ev - 'ry one of us a song to sing. Je - sus
G
Am6
gave ev - 'ry one of us a song to sing. Oh! there's
To next verse
Last time
B
Em
B7
Em
Em
no - bo - dy else like Je - sus. 2. He Je - sus.

2. He loves each and ev'ry single one of us. *(x3)*
   Oh! there's nobody else like Jesus.

3. So tell ev'rybody else around the world. *(x3)*
   Oh! there's nobody else like Jesus.

4. So the whole world can come along and worship him. *(x3)*
   Oh! there's nobody else like Jesus.

593 Jesus is here *(He's everywhere)*

Words and Music: Jennie Flack
arr. Chris Mitchell

A
D
D/E
C♯m7
Je - sus is here,
Je - sus is there,

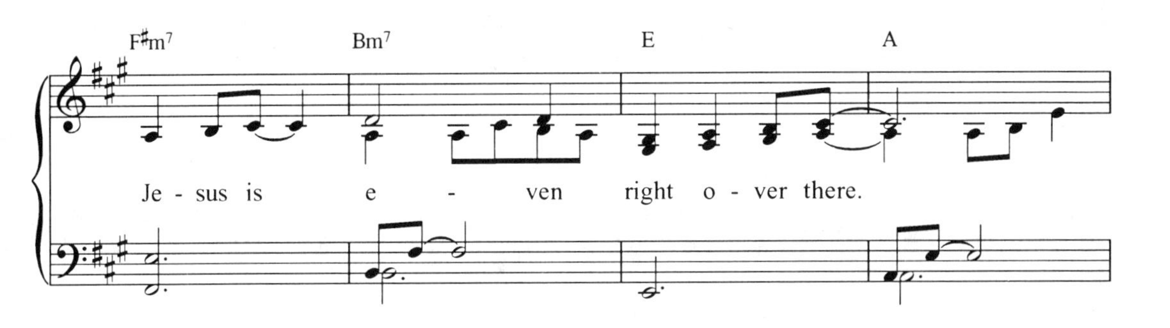
F♯m7
Bm7
E
A
Je - sus is e - ven right o - ver there.

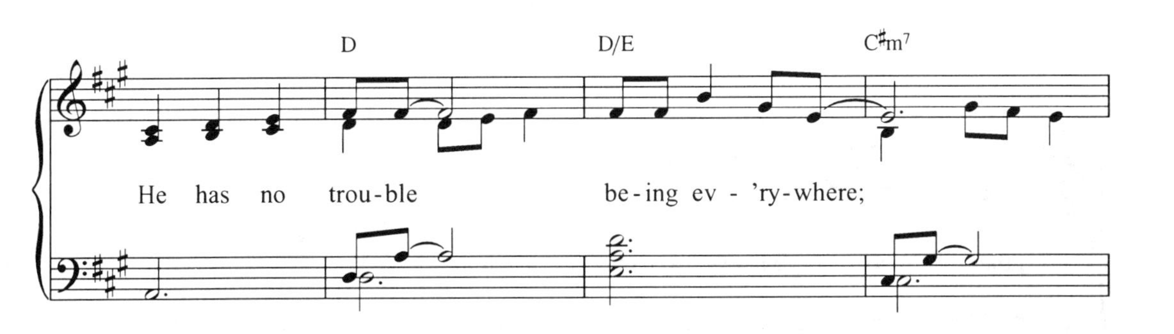
D
D/E
C♯m7
He has no trou - ble be - ing ev - 'ry - where;

F♯m7
Bm7
E7
A
that's how God meant it to be.

Dmaj7
C#m7
Bm7
Amaj7
The far - thest ga - lax - y, deep - est o - cean, the
Gmaj7
F#m7
E7sus4
E7
lone - li - est place; he is there. No -
F#m7
C#m7
Bm7
A
where in the u - ni - verse he can - not be; he is
D
E7
Asus4
A
there ev - 'ry - where lov - ing you. No
D
D/E
A
place in the sky is not high - er. No

Bm7
E7
A
hole in the earth, he's not deep-er still.
No

Dmaj7
E/D
C♯m7
F♯m7
des - ert so wide he can't stand a - stride it, he is

Bm7
D/E
A
1.
2.
there ev - 'ry - where lov - ing you.

594 Jesus is my friend

Words and Music: Steve Burnhope
arr. Chris Mitchell

E B E A/E E
Je - sus is my friend, clo - ser than a bro - ther,
B/D♯ C♯m7 A B
loves me like no o - ther, al - ways there for me.
E B E A/E E
Je - sus is my friend, he loves and pro-tects me,
B/D♯ C♯m7 A B E
ne - ver will for - get me, best friend there could be.

595 Jesus is the mighty, mighty King

Words and Music: Colin Buchanan

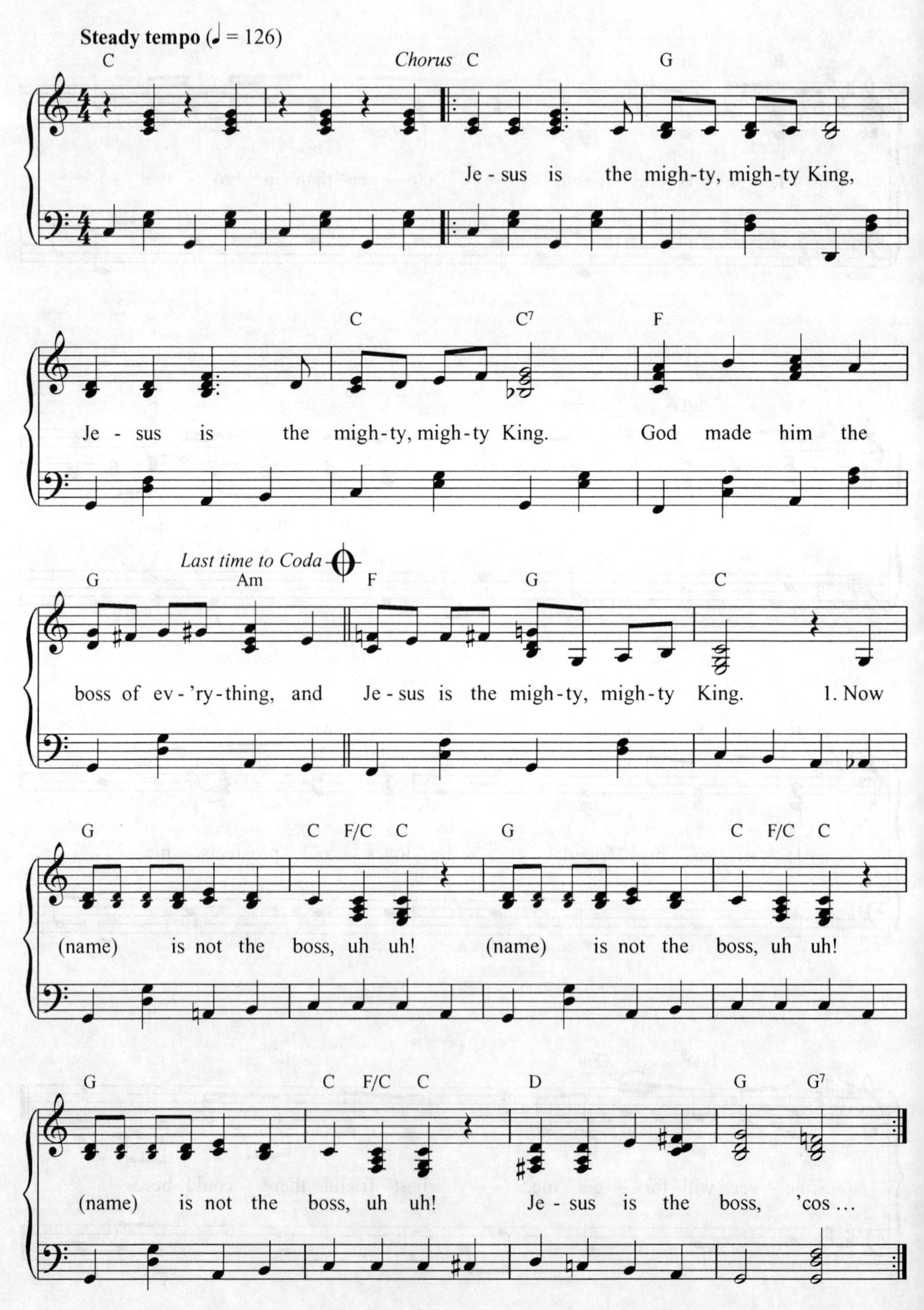
Steady tempo (♩ = 126)
C
Chorus C
G
Je - sus is the migh-ty, migh-ty King,
C
C7
F
Je - sus is the migh-ty, migh-ty King. God made him the
Last time to Coda
G
Am
F
G
C
boss of ev - 'ry-thing, and Je - sus is the migh-ty, migh-ty King. 1. Now
G
C F/C C
G
C F/C C
(name) is not the boss, uh uh! (name) is not the boss, uh uh!
G
C F/C C
D
G
G7
(name) is not the boss, uh uh! Je - sus is the boss, 'cos …

CODA
F
G
F
G
Je - sus is the migh - ty, migh - ty, Je - sus is the migh - ty, migh - ty,

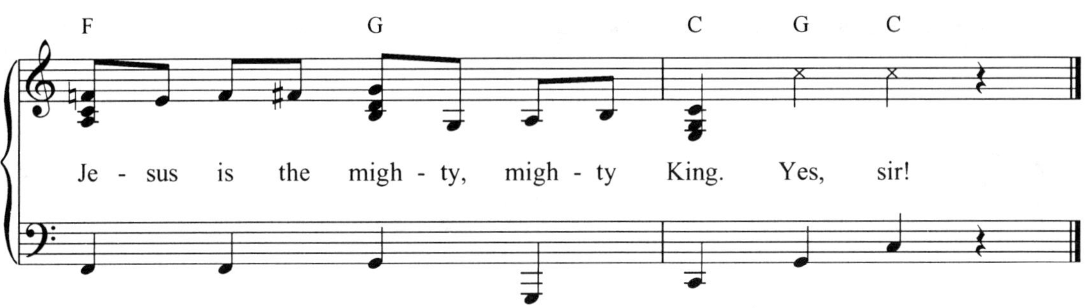
F
G
C
G
C
Je - sus is the migh - ty, migh - ty King. Yes, sir!

2. Now you are not the boss, uh uh!
   I am not the boss, uh uh!
   They are not the boss, uh uh!
   Jesus is the boss, 'cos . . .

596 Jesus is the same

Words and Music: Chris Jackson and Jill Hoffmann
arr. Dave Bankhead

Chorus
E
Je - sus is the same,
Je - sus is the same,
A
Je - sus is the same,
E
B
Je - sus is the same,
yes - ter-day, to-day,
A
E
B7
for e - ver,
Je - sus is the same.
1. He's the
E
A
heal - er and de - liv - 'rer,
he's the Sa - viour of the world.

E
O - ver all that he's cre - a - ted, he is Lord.
B
E
He's the Mas - ter and the teach - er, he's our e - ver - faith - ful friend, and his
A
A♯dim
E
B
A E/G♯ A/F♯ E
love will ne - ver, ne - ver, ne - ver end.

2. He's the Alpha and Omega,
the beginning and the end.
From the past into the future, he is Lord.
Knowing ev'rything about us,
still he loves us just the same,
so we'll give him all our love and praise his name.

597 Jesus is the Saviour

Words and Music: traditional
arr. Colin Buchanan

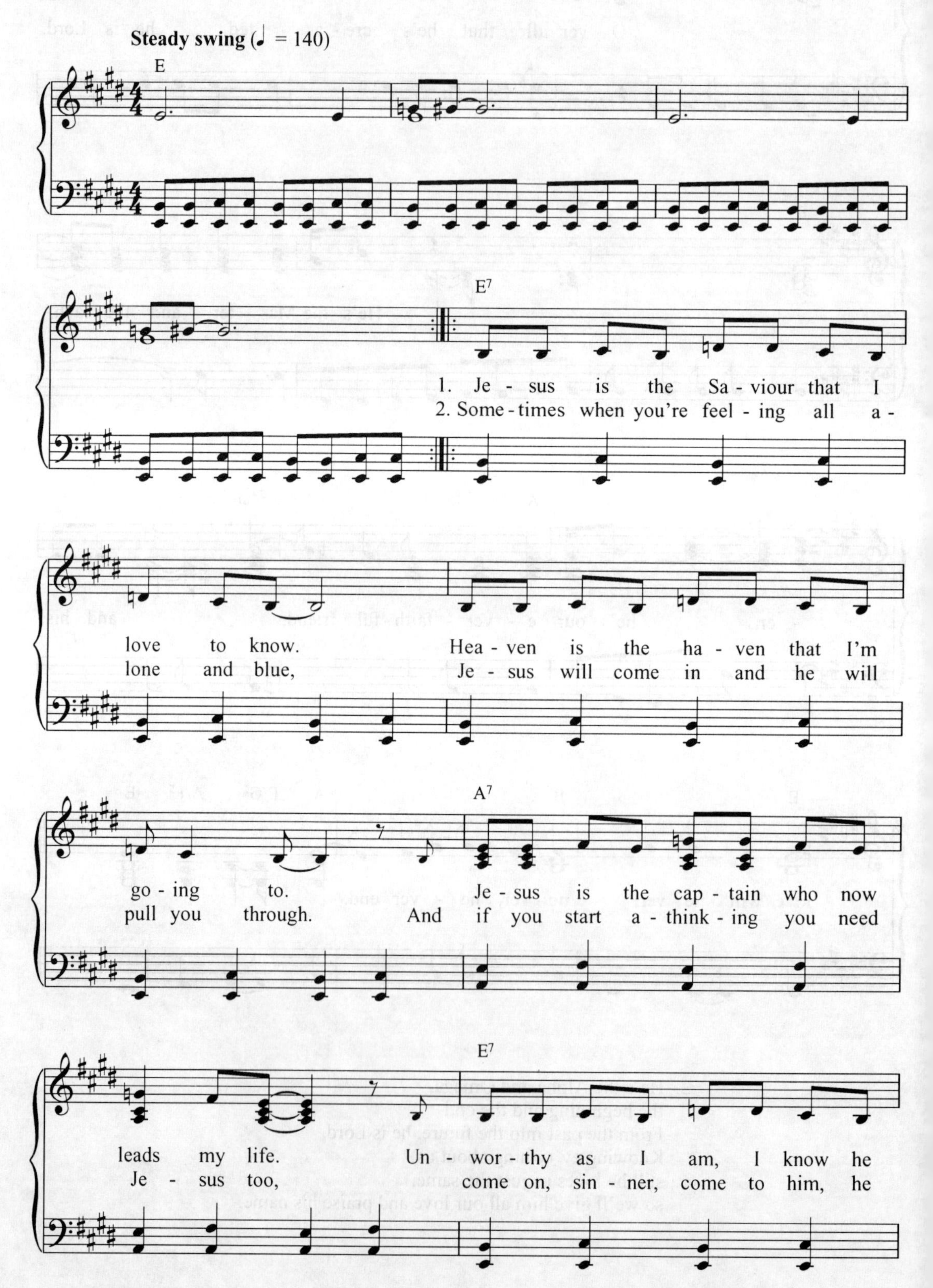

Steady swing (♩ = 140)
E
E7
1. Je - sus is the Sa - viour that I
2. Some - times when you're feel - ing all a -
love to know. Hea - ven is the ha - ven that I'm
lone and blue, Je - sus will come in and he will
A7
go - ing to. Je - sus is the cap - tain who now
pull you through. And if you start a - think - ing you need
E7
leads my life. Un - wor - thy as I am, I know he
Je - sus too, come on, sin - ner, come to him, he

Last time to Coda
B7
came to save. A sin - ner such as me, a
died for you. A sin - ner such as me, a
A7
E7
sin - ner such as you, he came to save from the
sin - ner such as you, he came to save from the
Chorus
A
grave.
grave.
For God so loved the world that he gave his
E
A7
one and on - ly Son. That who - so - e - ver be -
2nd time repeat v.1
then to Coda
B7
lieves in him should not per - ish, but have e - ver - last - ing life.

CODA
B7
A
B7
sin - ner such as me, a sin - ner such as you. A sin - ner such as me, a

A
B7
A7
sin - ner such as you. A sin - ner such as me, a sin - ner such as you. He came to

E7
save from the grave. He came to save from the grave.

598 Jesus, it's amazing

Words and Music: Capt. Alan J. Price, CA
arr. Philip Eley

(♩ = 120)
A7
D
Je - sus, it's a - maz - ing, a -
A7
maz - ing but it's true; there's no one else in his - to - ry who's
D
e - ver been like you.
1. You taught and showed what God was like, did
2. They sealed your bo - dy in a tomb, and
3. Some have died for o - thers, and
4. You're not just some great teach - er, or a
D7
G
A
no - thing else but good, but they took you and they killed you on a
thought that was 'good - bye', but God brought you back to life,
some have done great things, but Je - sus, you are dif - fe - rent,
pro - phet, that is true, you're the Son of God, the res - cu - er, and

D
Chorus
G
cross made out of wood.
ne - ver more to die.
you're the King of kings.
I be - lieve in you!
It's a shame, but it's
I'm so glad that it's

D
true; to think of all they did to try and
true; there's no one else in all the world who's

A7
G
D
get rid of you. It's a shame, but it's true; to
e - ver been like you. I'm so glad that it's true; there's

A7
D
think of all they did to try and get rid of you!
no one else in all the world who's e - ver been like you!

599 Jesus, Jesus, how you love me

Words and Music: Neil Davidson

Chorus
Capo 3
F D Bb G F D Dm Bm Gm Em C A
Je - sus, Je - sus, how you love me, Je - sus, Je - sus, how you care:
F D Bb G F D Gm7 Em7 C A F D
I will try to love and trust you, fol - low you ev - 'ry day.
Fine
Dm7 Bm7 Bb G F D Gm7 Em7 C A
1. Je - sus, you are with me each and ev - 'ry day:
2. E - ven in the play-ground, play - ing with my friends,
F D Bb G F D C A
1. 2, 3.
F D F D
D.C.
e - ven when I'm all a-lone, you will hold my hand.
I know some-one's watch-ing me, hap-py to see me here.

3. Jesus, you're my hero,
Jesus, you're my friend:
ev'ry day I grow and grow,
I'll love you even more.

600 Jesus, lover of my soul *(It's all about you)*

Words and Music: Paul Oakley

With feeling
Verse
D G A D
Je - sus, lo - ver of my soul,
G D Asus4 A D
all - con - su - ming fire is in your gaze. Je -
G A D G
sus, I want you to know I will fol - low you
D Asus4 A D G
all my days. For no one else in his - to - ry is
D G D A G
like you, and his - to - ry it - self be - longs to you.

D G Bm7 G
Al-pha and O-me - ga, you have loved me, and
D G Asus4 A
Chorus
I will share e-ter-ni-ty with you. It's all a-bout
Bm G D A Bm7
you, Je - sus, and all this is for you,
G D A Bm
for your glo - ry and your fame. It's not a-bout me,
G D G D
as if you should do things my way; you a-lone are God,
A G D
and I sur-ren - der to your ways.

601 Jesus made my body

Words and Music: Sharon E. Ward
arr. Chris Mitchell

C G7 C G7 C
Je - sus made my bo - dy, Je - sus made my soul,
D7 G Gmaj7 G7
Je - sus made my spi - rit and he made me whole.
C G7 C F Am
Je - sus made my bo - dy from my head to my feet,
Dm7 C/G G7 C
put me all to - ge - ther and he made me neat. In the
Fmaj7 Em7 Dm7 G C
im - age of the Fa - ther, the im - age of the Son,

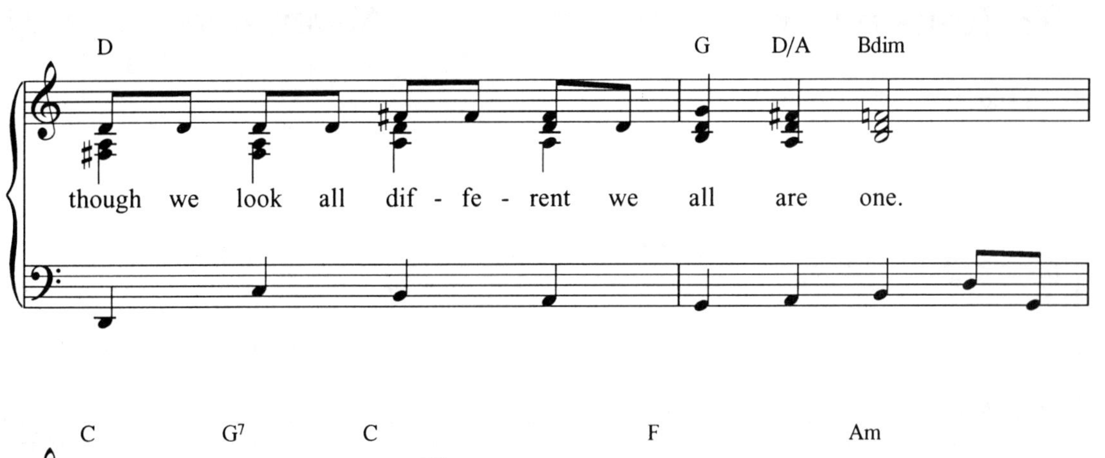
D G D/A Bdim
though we look all dif - fe - rent we all are one.

C G7 C F Am
Je - sus made my bo - dy from my head to my feet,

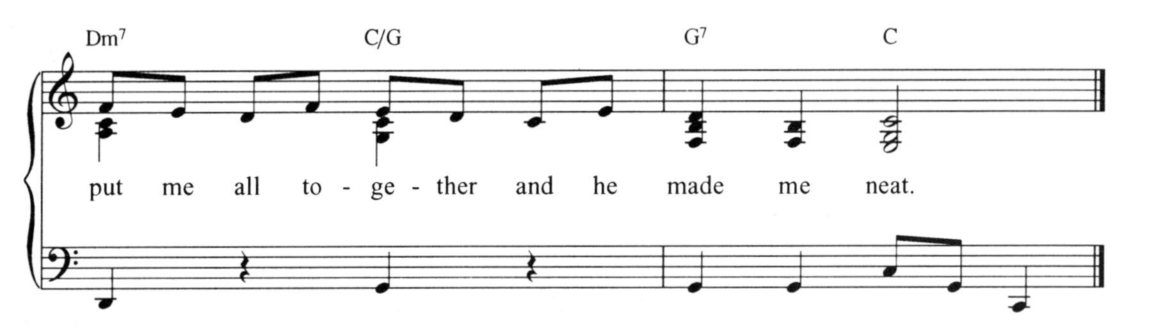
Dm7 C/G G7 C
put me all to - ge - ther and he made me neat.

602 Jesus never *(Never, never, never)*

Words and Music: John Hardwick

Joyfully (♩ = 162)
D G/D A/C♯ D G/D A/C♯ D
Je - sus ne - ver, ne - ver, ne - ver turned a - ny - one a - way. No! No! No!

G/D A/C♯ D G/D A/C♯ D
2nd time to
Je - sus ne - ver, ne - ver, ne - ver turned a - ny - one a - way. He

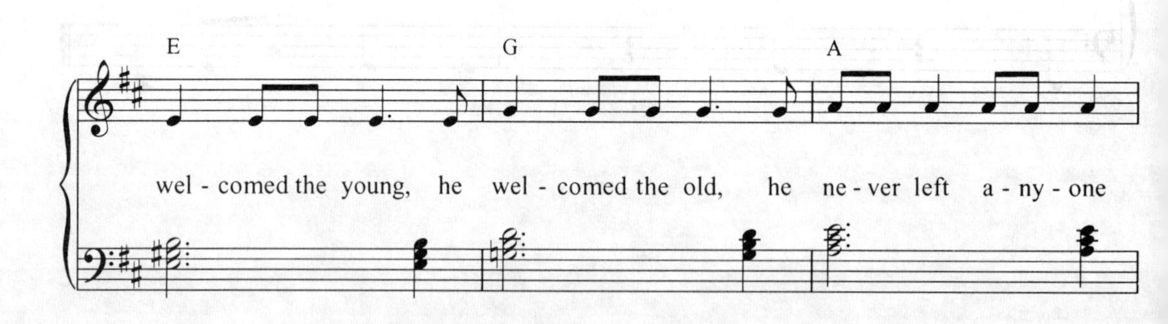
E G A
wel - comed the young, he wel - comed the old, he ne - ver left a - ny - one

E G
out in the cold. He wel - comed the hun - gry, he wel - comed the lame:

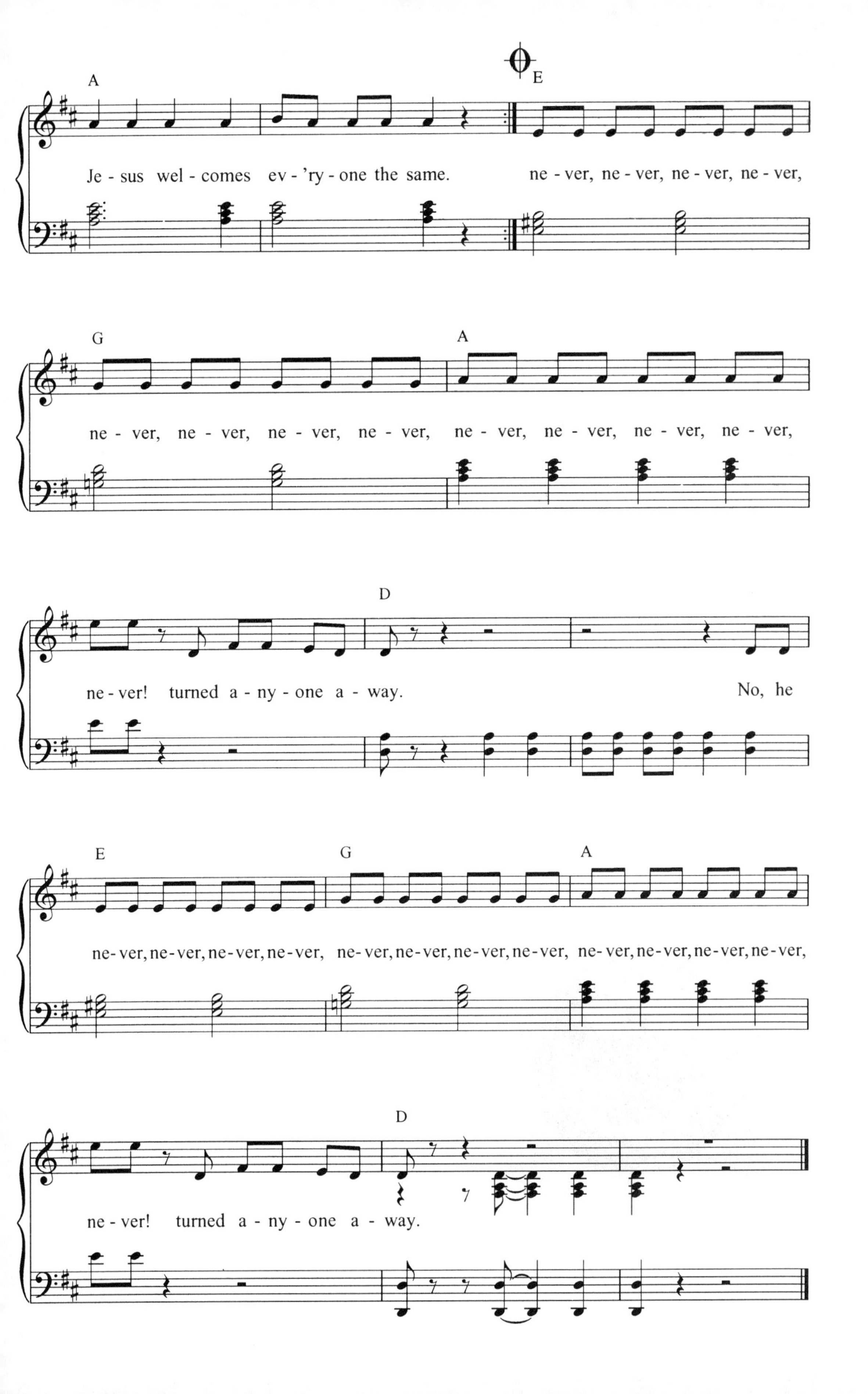
A
E
Je - sus wel - comes ev - 'ry - one the same.
ne - ver, ne - ver, ne - ver, ne - ver,
G
A
ne - ver, ne - ver, ne - ver, ne - ver,
ne - ver, ne - ver, ne - ver, ne - ver,
D
ne - ver! turned a - ny - one a - way.
No, he
E
G
A
ne - ver, ne - ver, ne - ver, ne - ver,
ne - ver, ne - ver, ne - ver, ne - ver,
ne - ver, ne - ver, ne - ver, ne - ver,
D
ne - ver! turned a - ny - one a - way.

603 Jesus said, 'I have come that they may have life'

Words and Music: Chris Jackson
arr. Dave Bankhead

A D E A
Je - sus said, 'I have come that they may have life,

D E A Asus4 A Asus4 A D
that they may have L I F E!' Je - sus said, 'I have come

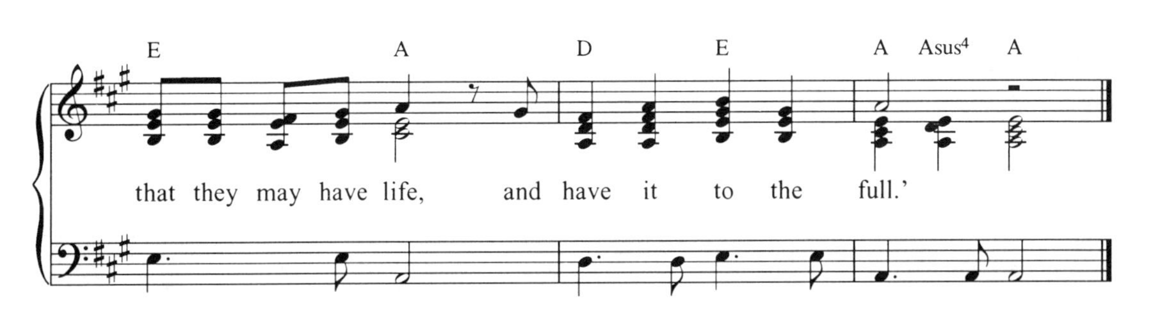

E A D E A Asus4 A
that they may have life, and have it to the full.'

604 Jesus said, 'Let little children' *(Let little children)*

Words and Music: Ian Smale

D
Je - sus said, 'Let lit - tle child - ren
come un - to me and do not e - ver hin - der them, for the
A
king - dom of God be - longs to such as these,' says the
four - teenth verse of Mark in chap - ter ten. And
D

a - ny - one who won't re - ceive the king - dom of God like a

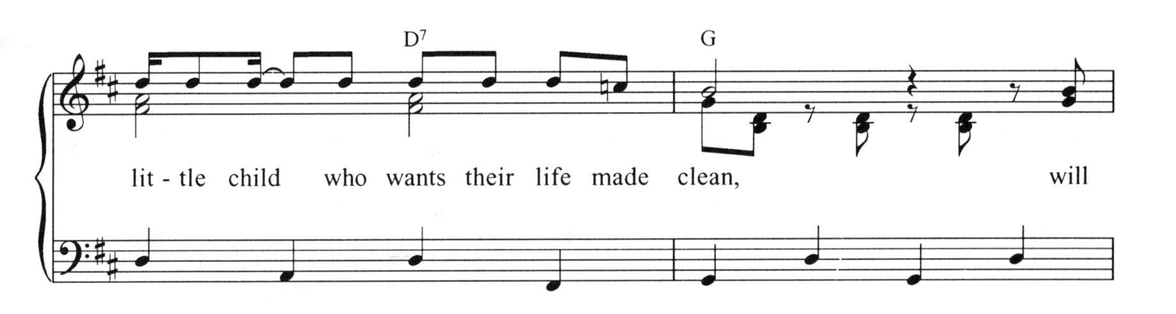
D7
G
lit - tle child who wants their life made clean, will

D
ne - ver en - ter it, is the truth that Je - sus taught. From

A
D G D
Mark in chap - ter ten and verse fif - teen.

605 Jesus said 'Let the children' *(Let the little children)*

Words and Music: John Hardwick
arr. Chris Mitchell

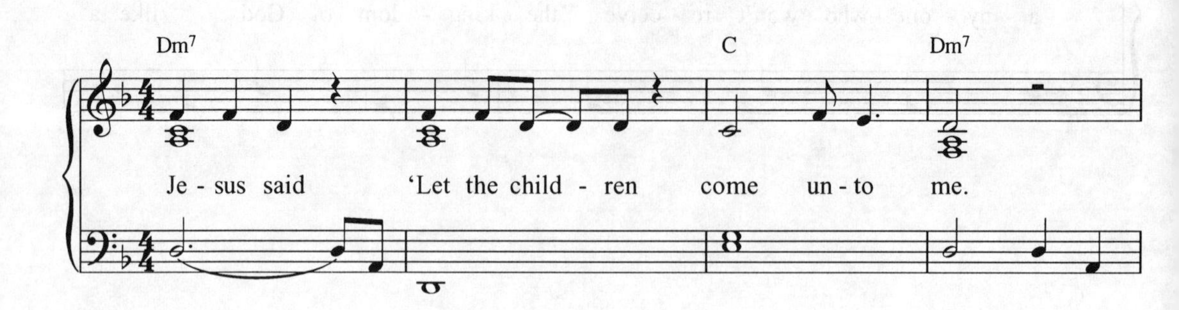
Dm7
C
Dm7
Je - sus said 'Let the child - ren come un - to me.

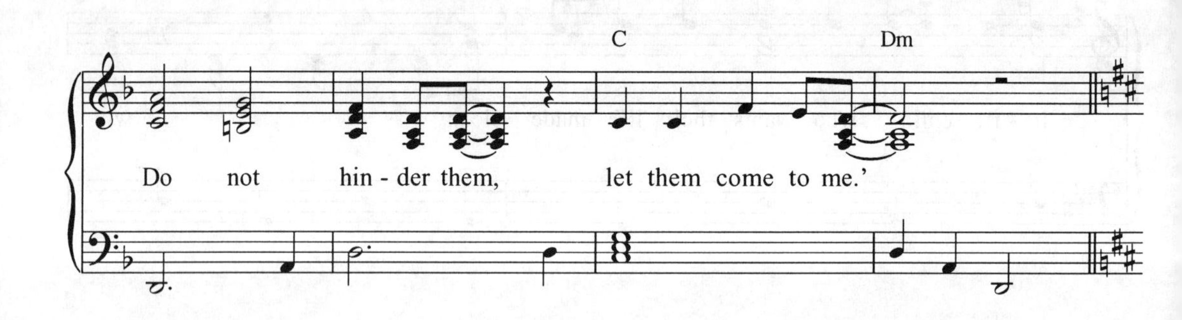
C
Dm
Do not hin - der them, let them come to me.'

D

D
G/D
D
Boys (not 1st time)
king - dom, the king - dom, the king - dom of God, yes the
Girls
Let the lit - tle child - ren,

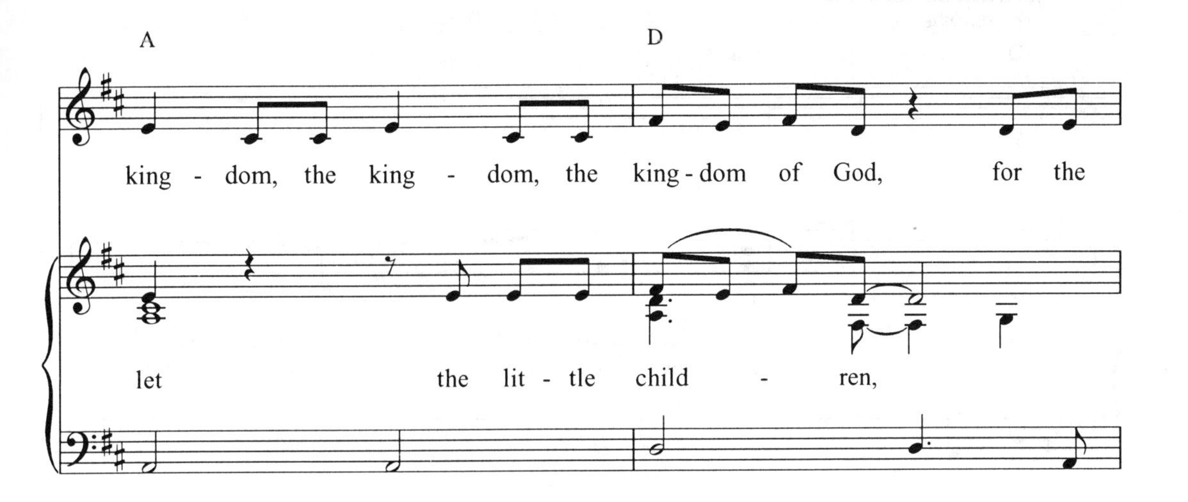
A
D
king - dom, the king - dom, the king-dom of God, for the
let the lit - tle child - ren,

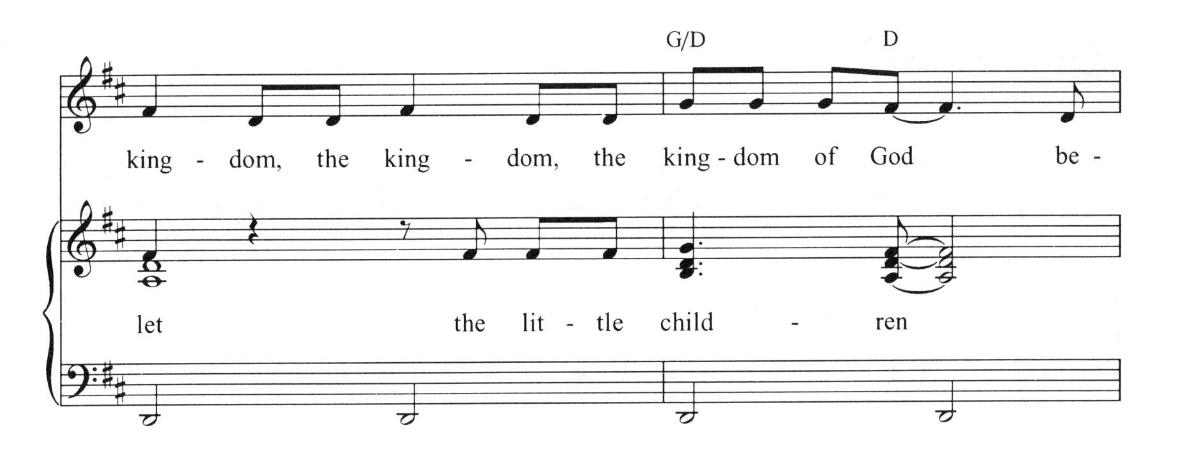
G/D
D
king - dom, the king - dom, the king-dom of God be -
let the lit - tle child - ren

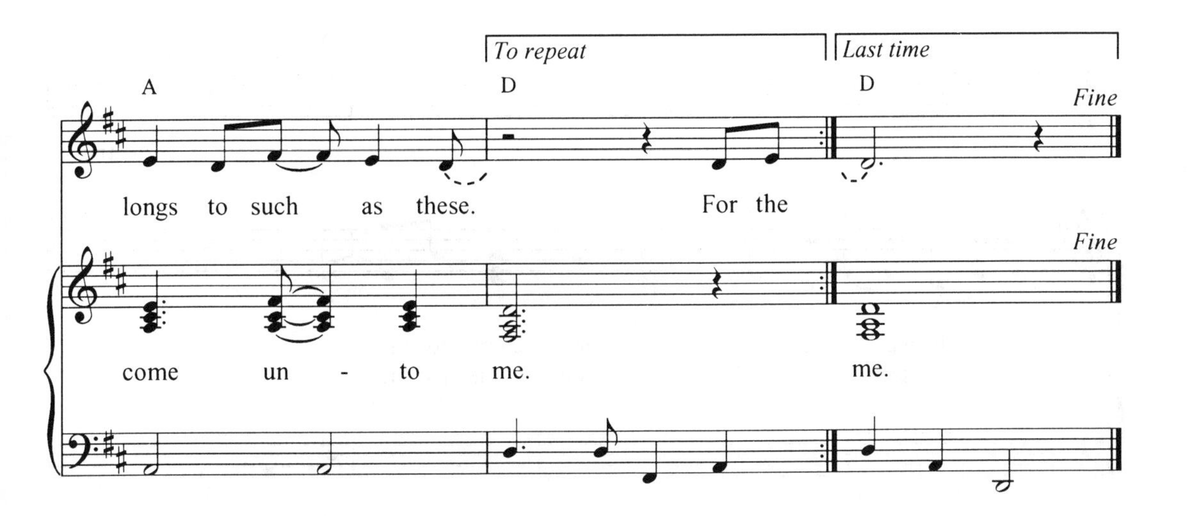
To repeat
Last time
A
D
D
Fine
longs to such as these. For the
Fine
come un - to me. me.

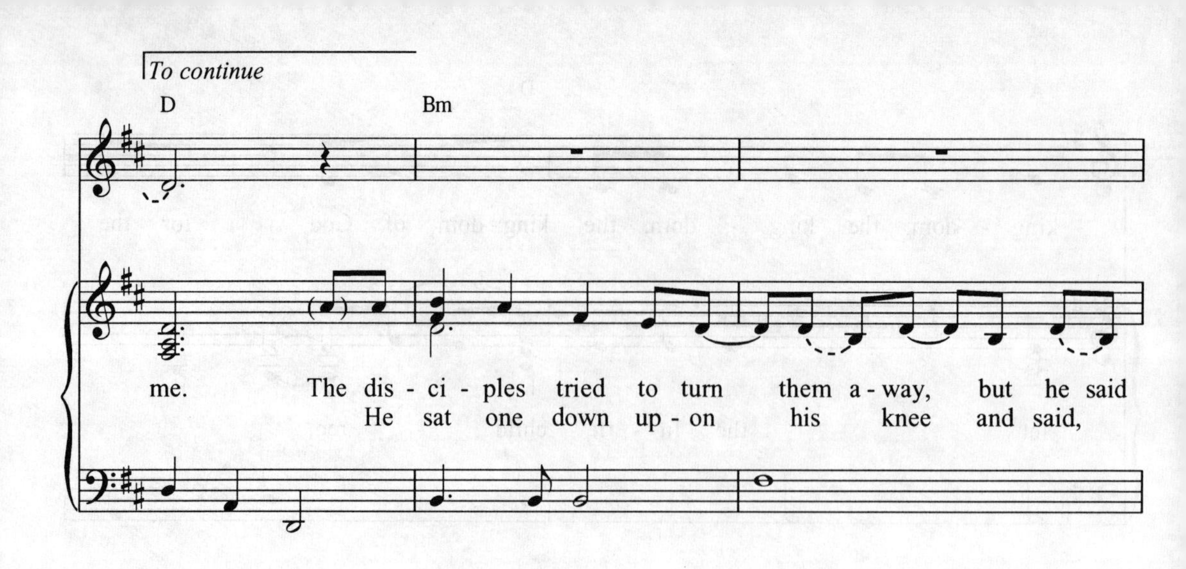
To continue
D
Bm
me. The dis - ci - ples tried to turn them a - way, but he said
He sat one down up - on his knee and said,

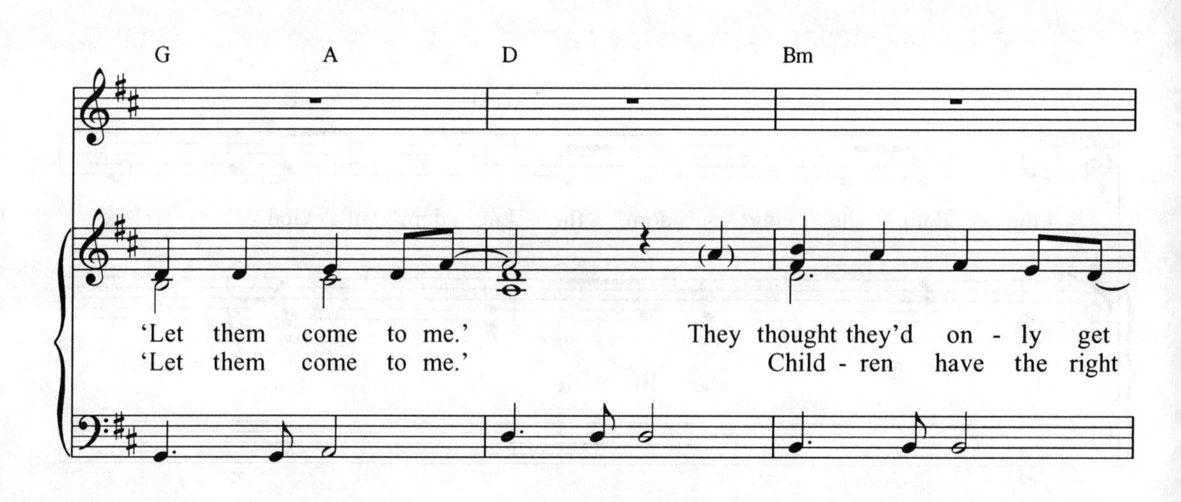
G
A
D
Bm
'Let them come to me.' They thought they'd on - ly get
'Let them come to me.' Child - ren have the right

G
A
D
Boys
D.S.
For the
D.S.
in the way, but he said 'Let them come to me.'
to see! He said 'Let them come to me.'

606 Jesus said something wonderful

(Light of the World)

Words and Music: Jennie Flack

Brightly (♩ = 132)
Capo 3
F Gm C7 F Gm
D Em A7 D Em
Je-sus said some-thing won-der-ful, Je-sus said
C7 F Gm C7 F
A7 D Em A7 D
some-thing true. What he said you should lis-ten to, 'cause
Gm C7 F Gm
Em A7 D Em
what he said was meant for you. I am the Light of the World,
C7 F
A7 D
don't live in dark-ness.
Gm C7 F
Em A7 D
I am the Light of the World, come fol-low me.

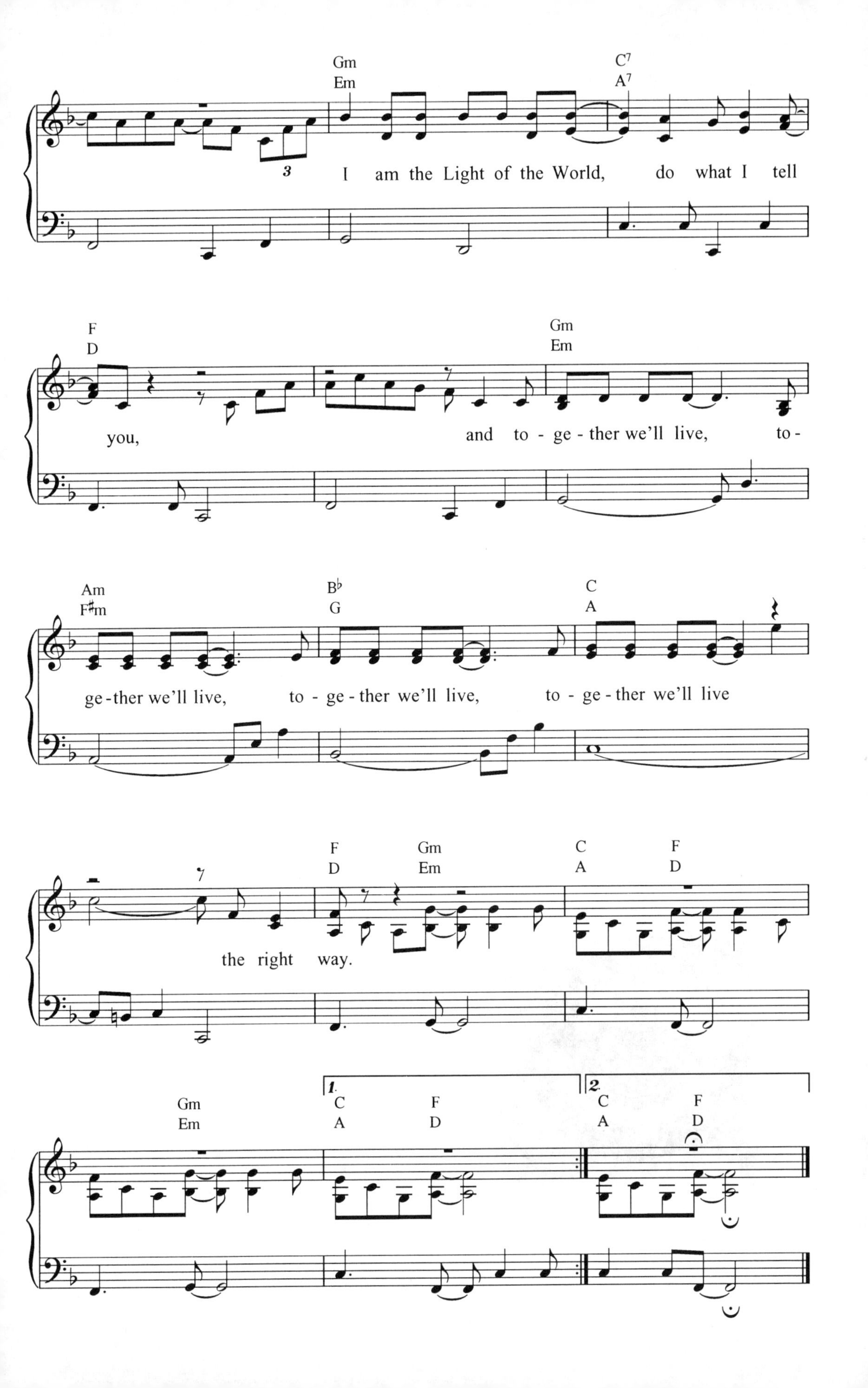
Gm Em C7 A7
I am the Light of the World, do what I tell
F D Gm Em
you, and to - ge - ther we'll live, to -
Am F♯m B♭ G C A
ge - ther we'll live, to - ge - ther we'll live, to - ge - ther we'll live
F D Gm Em C A F D
the right way.
Gm Em 1. C A F D 2. C A F D

607 Jesus wants all of me

Words and Music: Andy Read
arr. Chris Mitchell

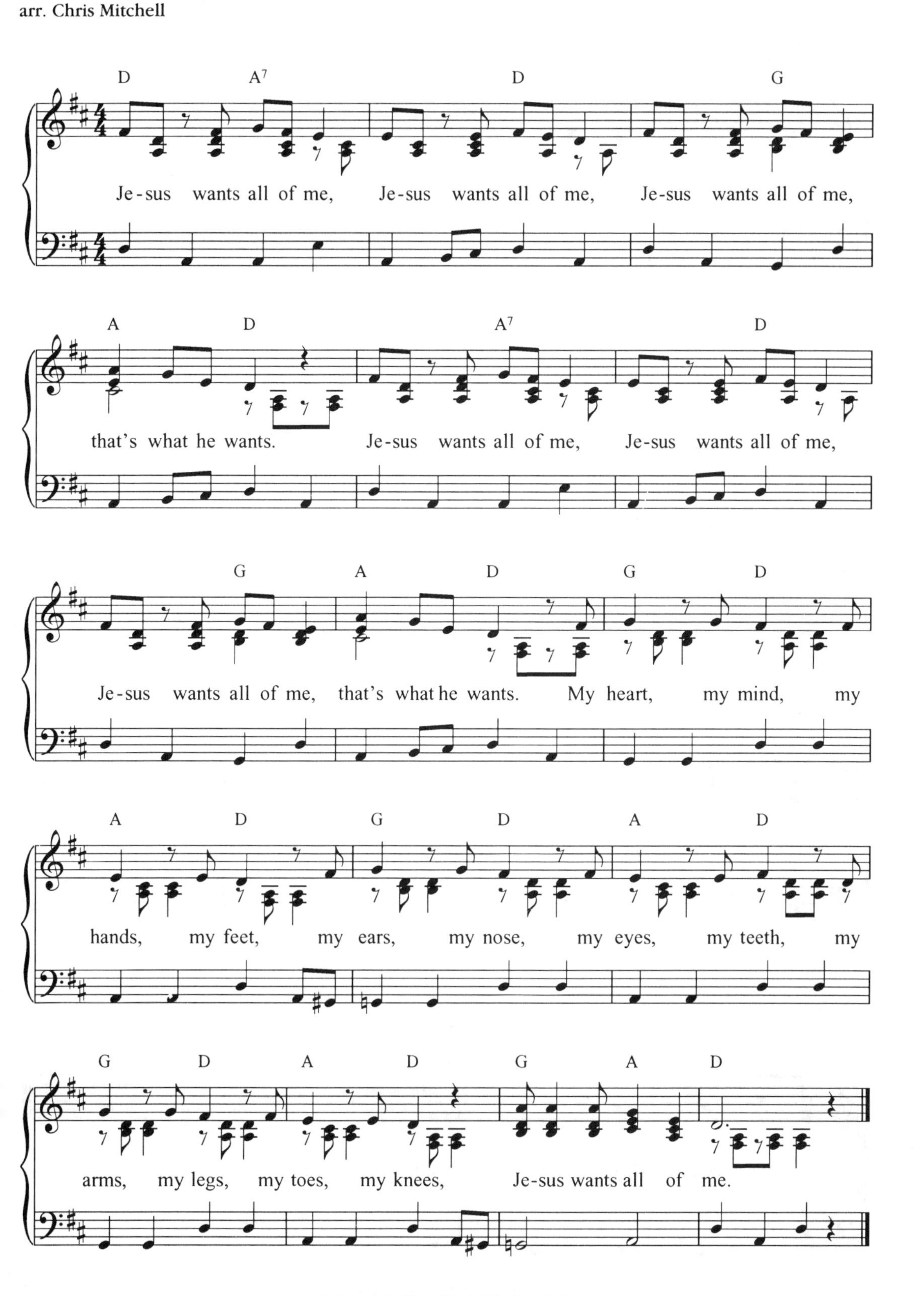
D A7 D G
Je-sus wants all of me, Je-sus wants all of me, Je-sus wants all of me,
A D A7 D
that's what he wants. Je-sus wants all of me, Je-sus wants all of me,
G A D G D
Je-sus wants all of me, that's what he wants. My heart, my mind, my
A D G D A D
hands, my feet, my ears, my nose, my eyes, my teeth, my
G D A D G A D
arms, my legs, my toes, my knees, Je-sus wants all of me.

608 Jesus was out for a walk one day

(Jesus loves the children)

Words and Music: Amanda Lofts
arr. Chris Mitchell

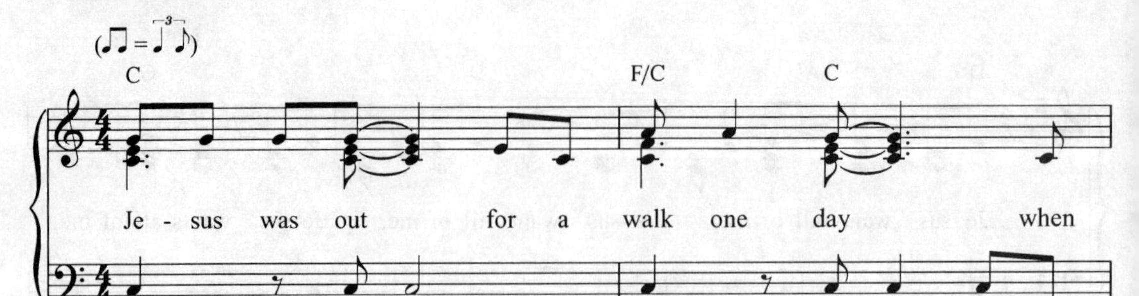
C
F/C
C
Je - sus was out for a walk one day when

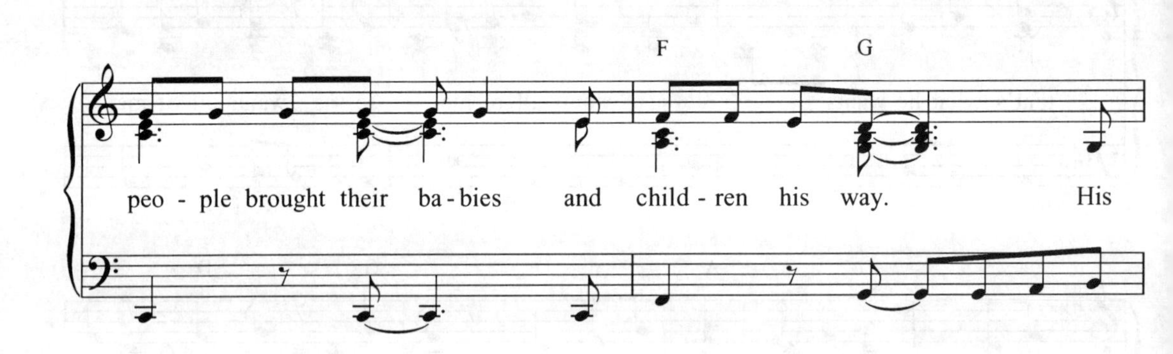
F
G
peo - ple brought their ba - bies and child - ren his way. His

C
F/C
C
friends told them off and said, 'Go a - way' but

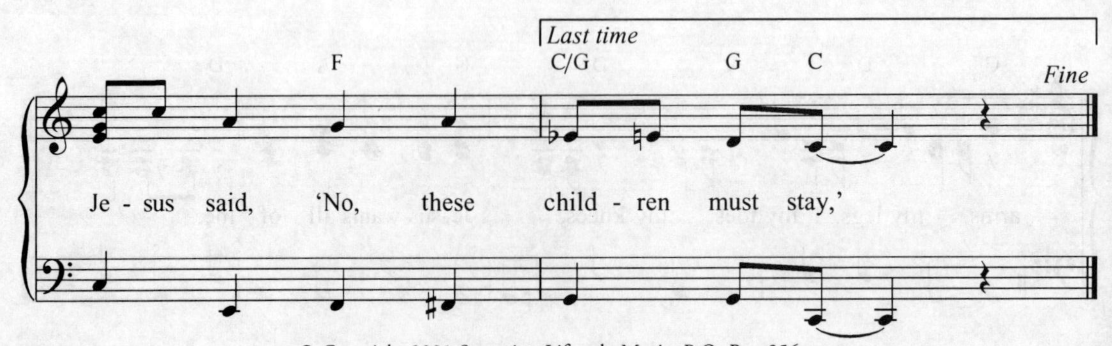
Last time
F
C/G
G
C
Fine
Je - sus said, 'No, these child - ren must stay,'

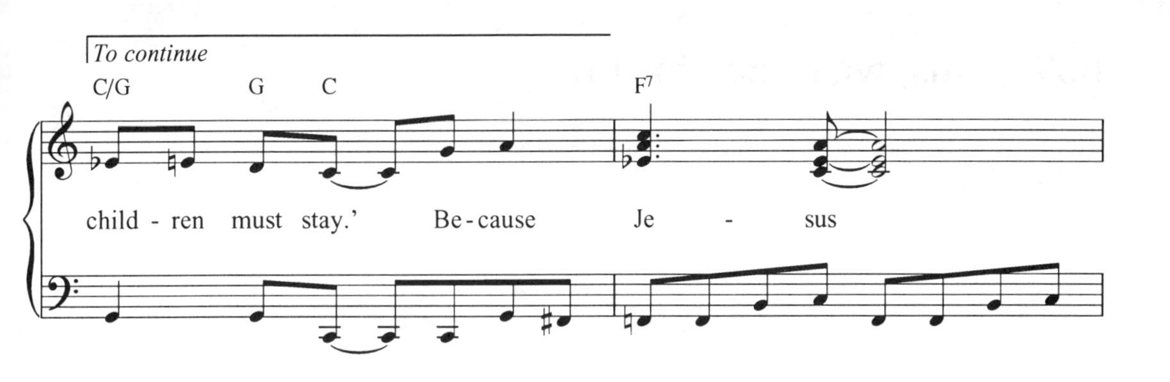
To continue
C/G
G
C
F7
child - ren must stay.' Be - cause Je - sus

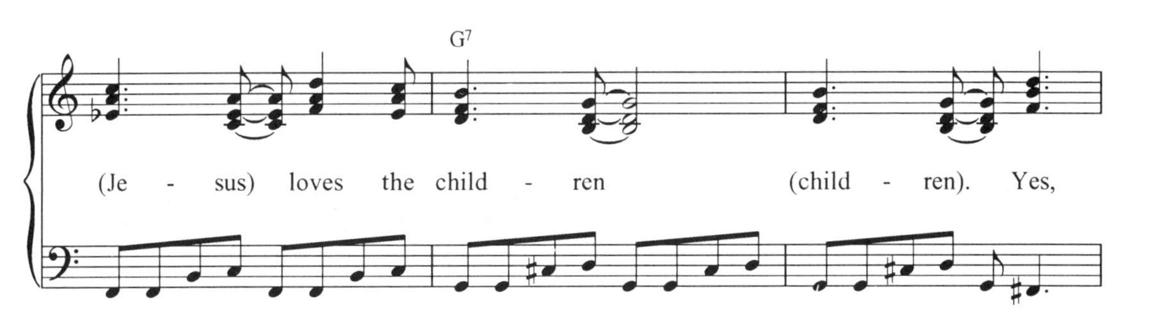
G7
(Je - sus) loves the child - ren (child - ren). Yes,

F7
G7
Je - sus (Je - sus) cares for them

F♯7
G7
D.C.
(for them).

609 Jesus, we dance for joy

Words and Music: Nick Parrans-Smith and Trish Parrans-Smith
arr. Philip Eley

(♩ = 126)
G
D
G
D
G
A
D

Chorus
G
D
G
D
G
D
Je - sus, we dance for joy, we lift our hands and we

A
G
D
G
D
praise. O Lord Je - sus, King of kings, we give you

G
A
D
Fine
hon - our and glo - ry and praise.
1. Ev - 'ry day I do so
2. Ev - 'ry day I say so

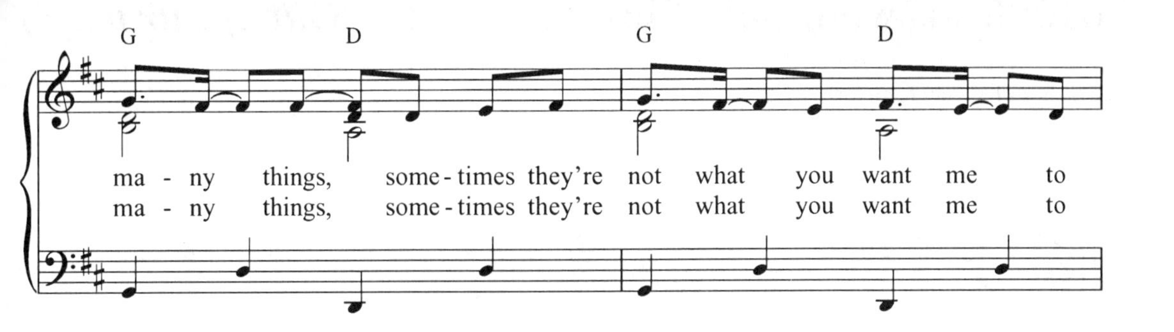
G D G D
ma - ny things, some - times they're not what you want me to
ma - ny things, some - times they're not what you want me to

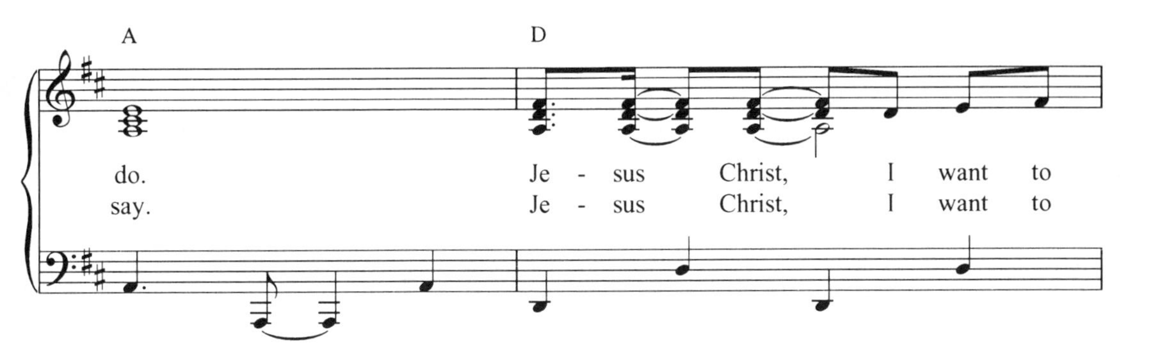
A D
do. Je - sus Christ, I want to
say. Je - sus Christ, I want to

G D G A D
D.S.
fol - low you, I want to be more like you in all I do.
fol - low you, I want to be more like you ev - 'ry day.

610 Jesus went out of his way *(Out of our way!)*

Words and Music: John Hardwick
arr. Chris Mitchell

Em Am7 B7
Chorus
Am Em
Je - sus went out of his way, out of his way,
B7 Em Am
out of his way to help o - thers! Je - sus went out of his way,
Em B7 Em
out of his way, out of his way to do right! So let's go
Am Em D
out of our way, out of our way, out of our way to help o -

G
Am
Em
- thers! So let's go out of our way, out of our way,
B7
Last time
Em
Fine
To continue
Em
out of our way to do right! right! 1. When I was
2. When I had
B7
Em
hun - gry did you feed me? When I was thirs - ty did you
no clothes, did you clothe me? When I was so sick did you
B7
give me a drink? An out - si - der, did you
look af - ter me? When in pri - son, did you
G
B7
D.C.
wel-come me or did you turn me a-way?
vi - sit me or did you turn me a-way?

611 Jesus, you knew me

Words and Music: Capt. Alan J. Price, CA
arr. Chris Mitchell

E A² E A² E A²
Je - sus, you knew me right from the start;
E A B A
Je - sus, you chose me, set me a -
E A² E A²
part. You want the best for me,
E A² E A
I know that is true, and I say
Last time to Coda
E/B B A² A/B E A 1. E A/B
'yes' to you, I'll fol-low you. Je - sus, you

2.
E
D/E
A
Je - sus, you came and you showed us a - gain how God
loves us.
Je - sus, you came and you
taught us a - gain we must turn from our sin, we must
B7sus4
turn to him.
B7
D.S.
Je - sus, you
CODA
A2
you, this is my 'yes' to you, oh I say
B
E/B
'yes' to you, I'll fol - low you.
A/B

612 Jesus, you're lovely / And I praise your name

Words and Music: *Jesus, you're lovely,* Sophie Larbalestier and Suzi de Faye;
And I praise your name, Eddie Espinosa

JESUS, YOU'RE LOVELY

F B♭6 Gm7 C F B♭6 Gm7 C
Capo 3 D G6 Em7 A D G6 Em7 A
Je - sus, you're love - ly, Je - sus, you're mine.

F B♭6 Gm7 C Dm B♭ C F
D G6 Em7 A Bm G A D
Fine
Ev - 'ry - where I go you're with me all the time.

AND I PRAISE YOUR NAME

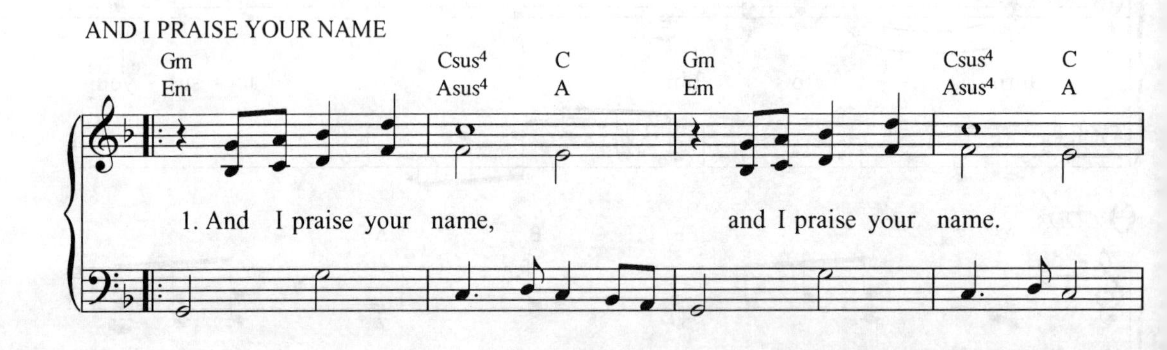

Gm Csus4 C Gm Csus4 C
Em Asus4 A Em Asus4 A
1. And I praise your name, and I praise your name.

B♭ C7 F Dm B♭ C7 F
G A7 D Bm G A7 D
You are the migh - ty God, the liv - ing Word,

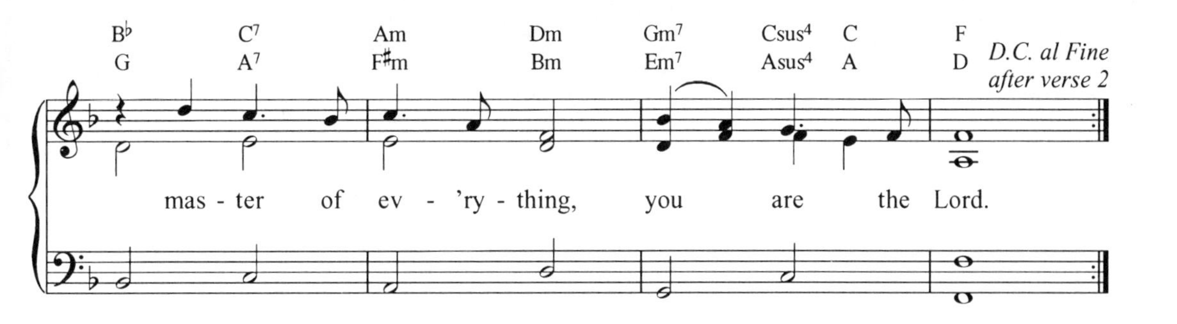
B♭ C7 Am Dm Gm7 Csus4 C F
G A7 F♯m Bm Em7 Asus4 A D
D.C. al Fine after verse 2
mas - ter of ev - 'ry - thing, you are the Lord.

2. And I love your name, and I love your name.
You are the Prince of Peace, Emmanuel,
everlasting Father, you are the Lord.

613 Jesus, your name is wonderful *(In your name)*

Words and Music: Andrew Pearson and Pauline Pearson

C G F G
Je - sus, your name is won - der - ful, Je - sus, your name is truth.
C G F 1. G
Je - sus, your name is pow - er - ful, Je - sus, we love you.
2. G Chorus F C F
you. In your name the blind will see. In your name the lame will dance.
C F Em7 Am
In your name we are set free to fol - low you. In your name,
F G C
your pow - er - ful name.

614 Keep on going

Words and Music: Capt. Alan J. Price, CA
arr. Philip Eley

(♩ = 92)
G C G
Chorus
G C
Keep on go-ing,
G C G C Em D
keep on grow - ing, keep on know-ing Je - sus bet - ter.
Last time to Coda
D.S. to repeat Chorus after v.2
G C G C G C G
Keep on go-ing, keep on grow-ing, keep on know-ing Je-sus bet-ter.
D C G
1. Let your roots go deep - er in - to Je - sus and let
2. Like a tree, be fruit - ful for Je - sus, and as

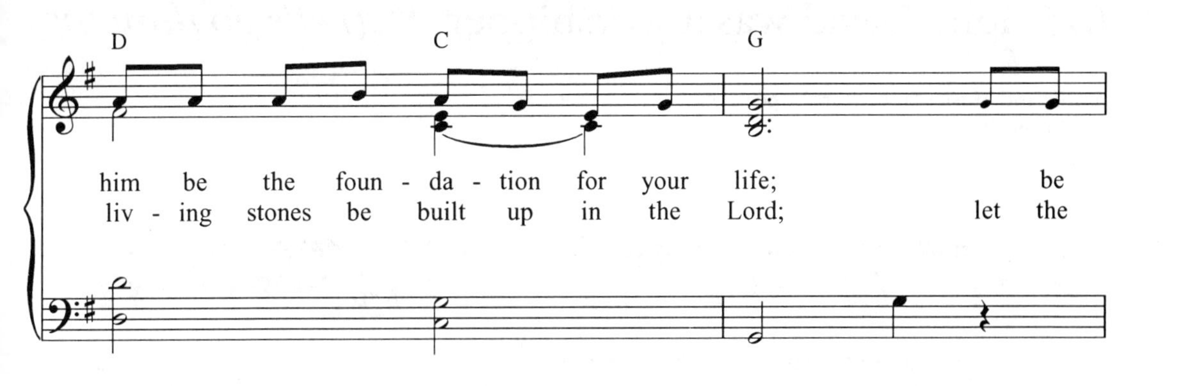
D
C
G
him be the foun - da - tion for your life; be
liv - ing stones be built up in the Lord; let the

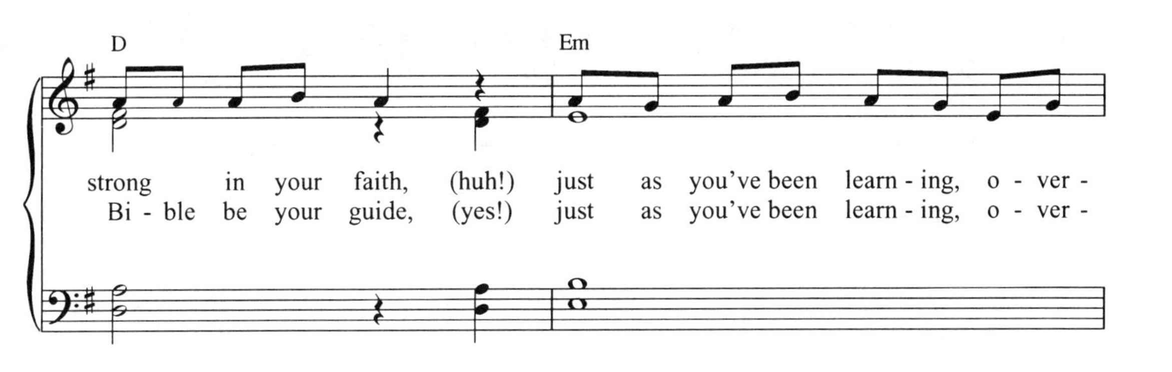
D
Em
strong in your faith, (huh!) just as you've been learn - ing, o - ver -
Bi - ble be your guide, (yes!) just as you've been learn - ing, o - ver -

A
D
flow with your praise, give the hon - our all to God.
flow with your love, live to please our Fa - ther God.

CODA
Em
A
G
C
G
bet-ter, keep on know-ing Je - sus bet-ter!

615 King David was a worshipper *(Let's go dancing)*

Words and Music: Steve Burnhope
arr. Chris Mitchell

D G D A D G D A
D G D A
Last time
D
Fine
To continue
D G2 D Asus4
1. King Da-vid was a wor-ship-per be-yond com-pare, as they
2. King Da-vid knew that danc-ing was the thing to do,
D G2 D A
say 'en fran - çais', 'ex - traor - di - naire!' The
pleas - ing to God, and pret - ty good for you,
D G2 D Asus4
queen said, 'How un - dig - ni - fied!' but he did - n't care, 'cos
give it a try and you'll see that it's true,

D G2 D A
this is what he said as he grace - ful - ly leapt in the air.
Da - vid was right when he said this is what you should do.
D Chorus G
'Let's go danc - ing, we're all gon-na go
D Bm
danc - ing, mov-in' an' a-groov-in' in praise be-fore the Lord.
Em A G
Let's go danc - ing, we're all gon-na go
D
danc - ing,
A G A D D.C.
we're gon - na dance in praise be - fore the Lord.'

616 King, King, King of the hill

Words and Music: Ruth Ranger and Trevor Ranger
arr. Chris Mitchell

Capo 3 D
F
G
E
King, King, King of the hill, show-ing ev - 'ry - bo - dy that
C
A
F
D
God loves us still. King, King, King of the hill, in
Gm7
Em7
C
A
F
D
life and in death he's the King of the hill. King of the hill.
Up
(every time)
up - on the hill - side, peo - ple there all day, Je - sus
(3rd and 4th times only)
King, King, King of the hill, show-ing ev - 'ry - bo - dy that

C
A
F
D
show-ing the way. Up up - on the hill-side, we must lis - ten still,
God loves us still. King, King, King of the hill, in
Gm7
Em7
1, 2, 3.
4.
Je - sus, King of the hill. Up King of the hill.
life and in death he's the King of the hill. King of the hill.

617 King Nebuchadnezzar

Words and Music: Susanna Levell
arr. Chris Mitchell

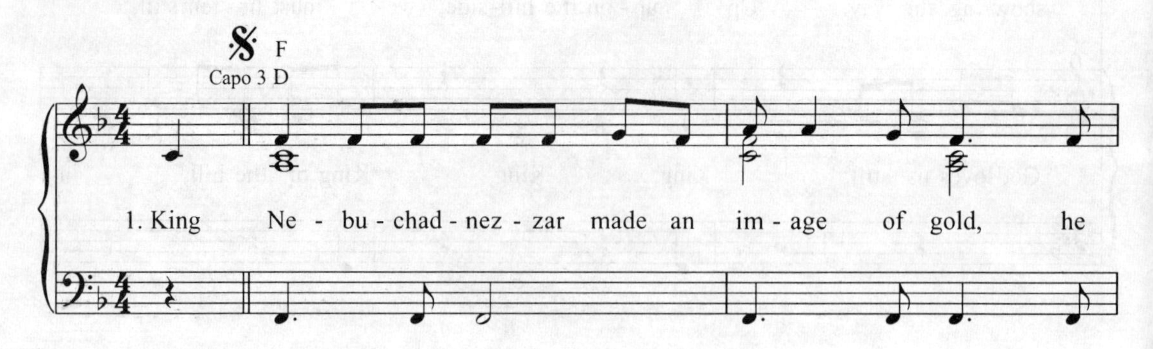

F
Capo 3 D
1. King Ne - bu - chad - nez - zar made an im - age of gold, he

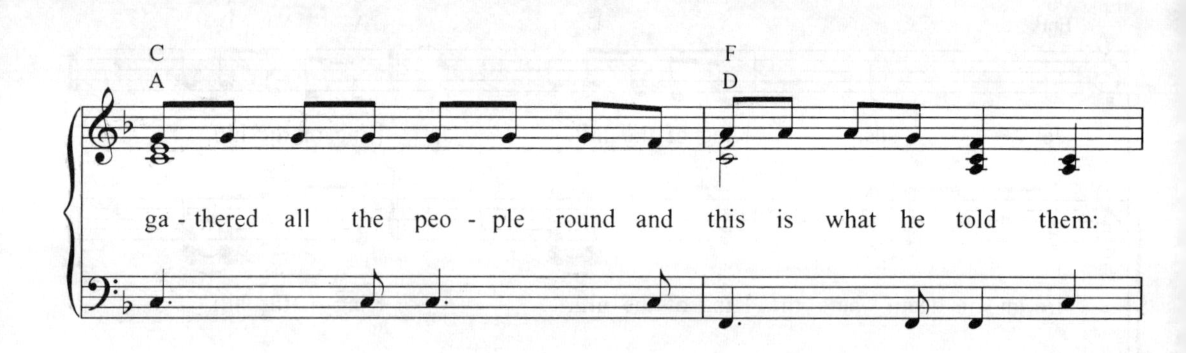

C
A
F
D
ga - thered all the peo - ple round and this is what he told them:

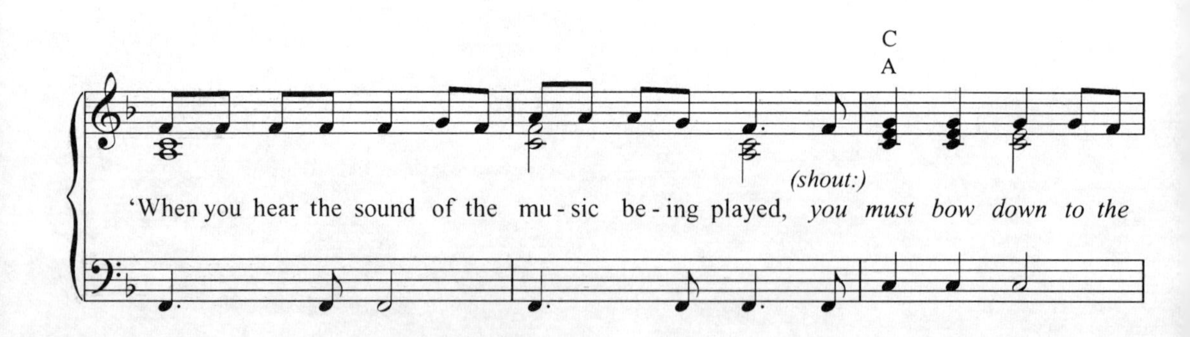

C
A
(shout:)
'When you hear the sound of the mu - sic be - ing played, you must bow down to the

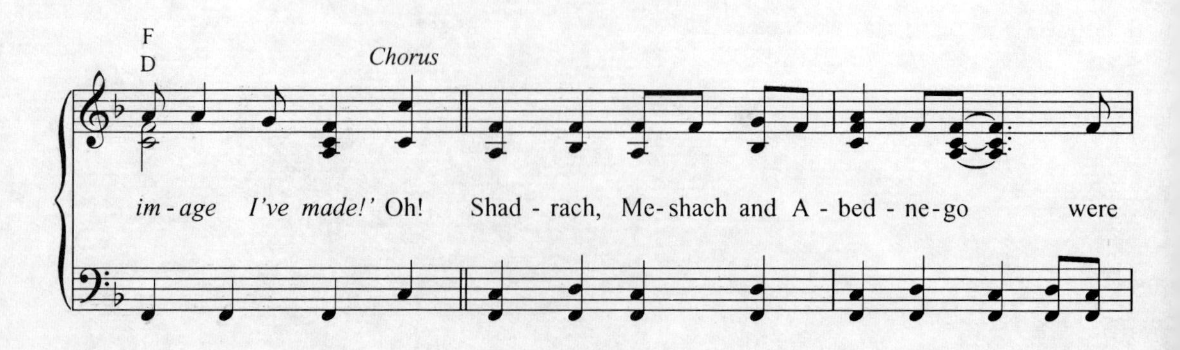

F
D
Chorus
im - age I've made!' Oh! Shad - rach, Me - shach and A - bed - ne - go were

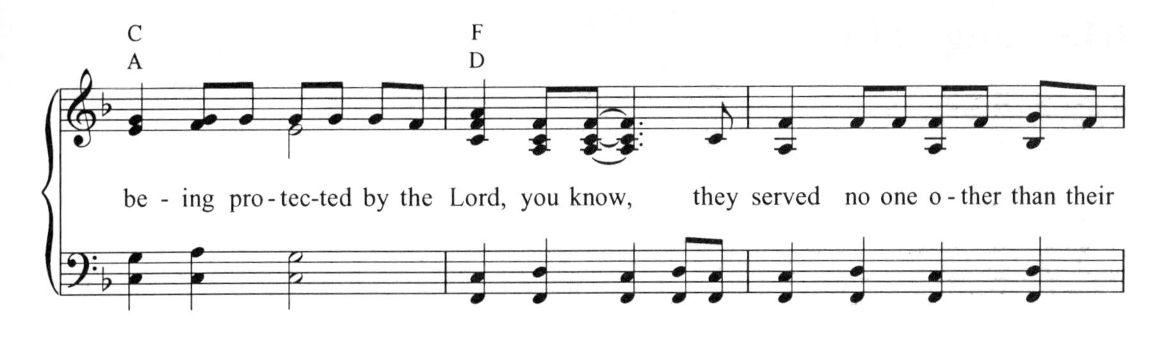
C
A
F
D
be - ing pro - tec-ted by the Lord, you know, they served no one o - ther than their

To next verse
Last time
C
A
F
D
D.S.
F
D
God a-lone, the true and liv-ing God. 2. King

2. King Nebuchadnezzar saw
   that they did not bow,
   he called his strongest soldiers
   and began to tell them how
   to tie the three men up
   and then throw them in the fire.
   'You must make sure that
   the flames burn much higher!'

3. King Nebuchadnezzar,
   when he looked in the fire,
   he jumped up with amazement
   and began to question why
   there was an extra man
   in the fire with the three
   'Your God has saved you
   and now you are free!'

618 King of love

Words and Music: Doug Horley
arr. Dave Bankhead

F
C
F
Dm7
King of love, praise you, King of love,
B♭
F
C
F
wor - ship you, King of love, thank you, I'm
1.
2.
Dm
B♭
Dm
B♭
trea - sure in your eyes.
trea - sure in your eyes.
F
C
Dm
I know my heart will love you for e - ver, I know your word, I'll
B♭
F
C
al - ways be your child. I know my soul is safe for e - ter - ni - ty, 'cos

Dm7
B♭
1.
D.C.
2.
you hold me close
in your arms.
in your arms.
G
D
Em
C
G
D
Gon-na give you all the praise I can,
gon-na give you all the thanks I can,
Em
C
in your arms I will be,
King of love hold - ing me.
G
D
Gon-na give you all the love I can,
gon-na give you all the praise I can,
E
C
in your arms I will be,
King of love hold - ing me.

G
D
Gon - na give you all the praise I can, gon - na give you all the thanks I can,
Em
C
G
King of love, King of love, I wor - ship you. King of love,
Gsus2
G
Em
C
praise you, King of love, wor - ship you,
G
Gsus2
G
Em
King of love, thank you, I'm trea - sure in your eyes.
C

619 La la la *(The la la song)*

Words and Music: Garrie-John Barnes
arr. Chris Mitchell

Chorus
E D E A E D
La la la la la la la la la la la la la la la la

Bm7 E A E D E A E
la la la la la la la la la la la la la la la la la

D Bm7 E A E D E
la la la la la la la la la la la. 1. We will re -

A E D Bm7 E
joice in the Lord, re - joice in the Lord, re - joice in the Lord al -

A E D E A E D
ways! We will re - joice in the Lord, re - joice in the Lord, re -

To continue
Last time
Chorus
Bm7 E A E D E A
joice in the Lord al - ways! La la la ways!

2. We will clap hands to the Lord . . .

3. We will sing praise to the Lord . . .

620 La la la la la

(We clap our hands and sing)

Words and Music: Capt. Alan J. Price, CA
arr. Karen Cox

(♩ = 120)
Chorus
D
A7
G
A
La la la la la, we clap our hands and sing; la la la la la, Je-sus is our King.
La la la la la, we clap our hands and sing; la la la la la,
Je-sus is our King. 1. He does-n't need a pa-lace, where we can stand and stare. He
2. He does-n't make us serve him, like a ser-vant should; he
does-n't need a big posh car to take him ev-'ry-where. (No!) Through the Ho-ly Spi-rit at
does-n't say it's ea-sy to do what's right and good. (No!) When we know he loves us, we

D
E
work in you and me, he's buil - ding his King-dom where-
want to love him too; and 'cos we want to be like him
A
A7
ev - er we may be!
that's just what we do!
Oh yeah! Oh yeah! Oh yeah! Oh yeah!
D
A7
D
La la la la la, we clap our hands and sing; la la la la la,
G A D
A7
D
Je - sus is our King. La la la la la, we clap our hands and sing;
G A D
la la la la la, Je - sus is our King.

621 Lean to the left *(Running after you)*

Words and Music: Andy Read
arr. Chris Mitchell

G7(♭3)

1. Lean to the left, lean to the right just to make sure my shoes

are on tight. Reach to the floor, reach to the sky; I'm

gon - na get rea - dy, it's near - ly time. 2. I'm gon - na get fit to run
the race, I don't wan - na fall flat on my face.
See my eyes, see me smile, I'm now gon - na jog for a

Chorus
G7
Gm7/B♭
C7
thou - sand miles.
Run-ning af - ter you (gon-na make it),
C7/B♭
G7
Gm7/B♭
C7
run-ning af - ter you (take me through it).
Run-ning af - ter you
Last time
C7/B♭
G7
To continue
C7/B♭
G7
(gon-na make it),
run-ning af - ter you.
run-ning af - ter you
G7(♭3)
(I can take it).
3. Jump to the left, jump to the right just
to make sure my legs are on tight.
Turn - ing a - round, touch-
D.S.
- ing the ground,
I would-n't stop for a
thou - sand pounds.

622 Let all the earth give praise

Words and Music: Chris Jackson
arr. Dave Bankhead

G D C D G D C
Let all the earth give praise to the Fa - ther, let all the earth give praise

D G D C D
to our God. Let all the earth re - joice and praise the Lord.

G
Last time to Coda
G C
Al - le -

D G
- lu - ia, we will

C
D
(Claps)
D.C.
clap our hands.
dance our feet.
shout A - men!

CODA
C
D
(Claps)
G
Praise
the Lord!

623 Let everything that has breath

Words and Music: Matt Redman

Driving
E Chorus
E/D♯
C♯m7
Let ev - 'ry - thing that, ev - 'ry - thing that, ev - 'ry - thing that
A
B7sus4
E
E/D♯
has breath, praise the Lord. Let ev - 'ry - thing that, ev - 'ry - thing that,
Last time
C♯m7
A
B7sus4
E
Fine
ev - 'ry - thing that has breath, praise the Lord.
To continue
A
B7sus4
F♯m7
has breath, praise the Lord.
E
E/D♯
1. Praise you in the morn - ing, praise you in the eve - ning,

C♯m7
A
praise you when I'm young and when I'm old.
E
E/D♯
Praise you when I'm laugh-ing, praise you when I'm griev-ing,
C♯m7
A
F♯m7
praise you ev-'ry sea-son of the soul. If we could see how
E/G♯
F♯m7
E/G♯
much you're worth, your pow'r, your might, your end - less love, then
F♯m7
E/G♯
A
B7sus4
D.C.
sure - ly we would ne - ver cease to praise.

2. Praise you in the heavens,
joining with the angels,
praising you for ever and a day.
Praise you on the earth now,
joining with creation,
calling all the nations to your praise.
If they could see . . .

624 Let's count to four

Words and Music: Ian Smale
arr. Chris Mitchell

E
One,
two,

three,
four.
1. Let's

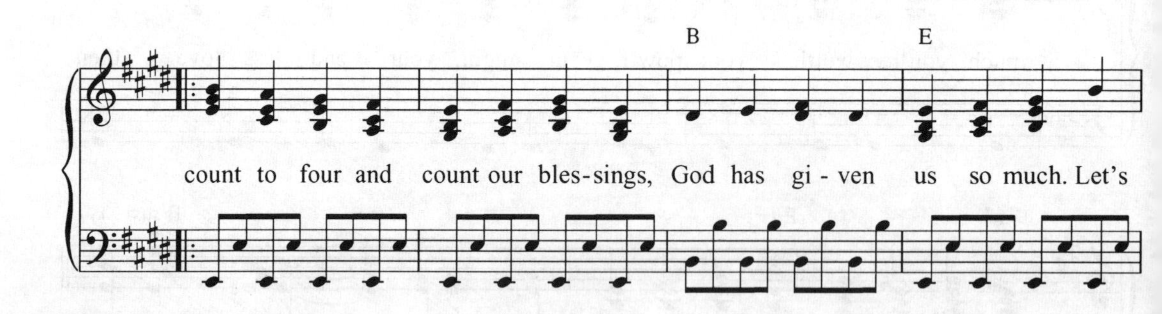
B
E
count to four and count our bles-sings, God has gi - ven us so much. Let's

B
name four things and then say 'thank you' for the Lord is

E
B
E
good to us. One,

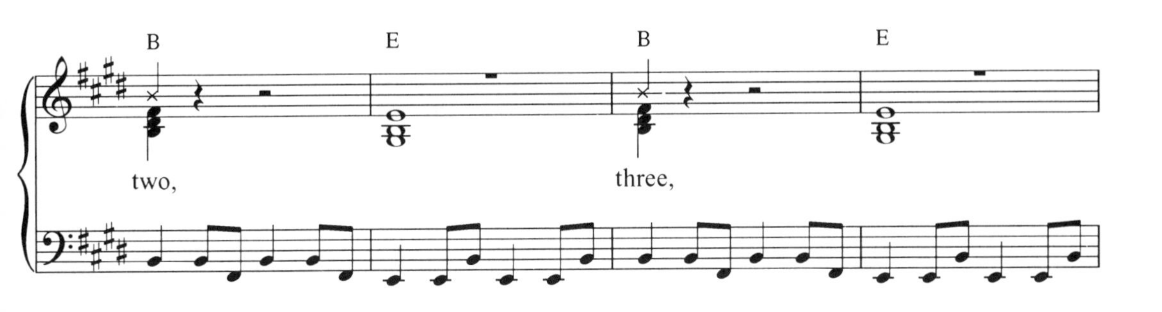
B
E
B
E
two, three,

F♯
1.
B
2.
B
E
four. 2. Let's

2. Let's count to four
   and pray for others,
   God has given us so much.
   Let's name four people we can pray for,
   for the Lord is good to us.
   One, two, three, four.

625 Let's praise God together

Words and Music: Alison Moon

Chorus
A F♯m Bm E A F♯m Bm E
Let's praise God to-ge-ther, let us clap and praise the Lord,
A F♯m Bm E A Esus4 E A D A
for he loves to hear us, he is King for e-ver-more.
Fine
D E/D C♯m7 F♯m
1. Je-sus, ho-ly is your name, high a-bove all oth-ers,
Bm7 A/E E
pow'r and glo-ry be-long to you.

Chorus 2:
Let's praise God together,
let us dance and praise the Lord,
for he loves to hear us,
he is King for evermore.

2. Jesus, mighty is your name,
high above all others,
pow'r and glory belong to you.

Running order: chorus 1, verse 1, ch.2, v.2, ch.1, ch.2.

626 Let the chimes of freedom ring

(Chimes of freedom)

Words and Music: Dave Bilbrough

With a lilting feel
A
D
E
A
1. Let the chimes of free - dom ring all a - cross the
earth; lift your voice in praise to him and
sing of all his worth, and sing of all his worth.
F♯m
1, 3.
2, 4, 5.
Chorus
live. Let all the peo - ple hear the news of the
One who comes to save: he's the Lord of all the

1.
E A D E A
D.C.
u - ni - verse, and for e - ver he shall reign.
3. In
2, 3.
A D A E D A
reign. And for e - ver - more, and for e - ver -
E D A E
more, and for e - ver - more he shall
1.
Last time
2.
A
Last time rall.
D.C.
reign. And for
5. He

2. Open wide your prison doors
   to greet the Lord of life;
   songs of triumph fill the air,
   Christ Jesus is alive,
   Christ Jesus is alive.

3. In ev'ry corner of the earth
   to ev'ry tribe and tongue,
   make known that God so loved this world
   that he gave his only Son,
   he gave his only Son.

4. Spread the news and make it plain:
   he breaks the pow'r of sin.
   Jesus died and rose again,
   his love will never end,
   his love will never end.

5. He will return in majesty
   to take his rightful place
   as King of all eternity,
   the Name above all names,
   the Name above all names.

627 Let there be singing

Words and Music: James Wright
arr. Chris Mitchell

E A E B/D♯ E
Let there be sing - ing, songs of re - joic - ing;
Let ev - 'ry na - tion sing of God's sal - va - tion;
1.
A E/G♯ F♯m E Bsus4
let there be joy through - out the earth.
this is the sea - son
2.
E/B B7 E B
to re - joice. From hea - ven to earth you
earth to
E/B B B/A E/G♯ E
came, the Son of God to reign. God's gift of
dwell, Je - sus, Em - man - u - el. God's gift of

1.
A E/G# F#m7 E B/D# C#m7 B
e - ver - last - ing love. From hea - ven to
e - ver -

2.
F#m7 A Bsus4 B A2 E A/E
last - ing love. Hal - le - lu - jah,
Hal - le - lu - jah,

E B/D# C#/E# F#m E B/D# E/G#
hal - le - lu - jah, God with us has
hal - le - lu - jah, God with us, Em -

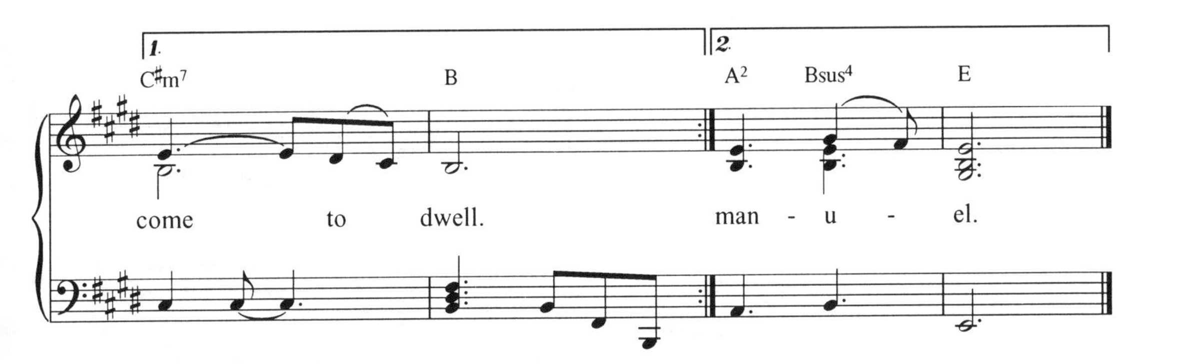
1. 2.
C#m7 B A2 Bsus4 E
come to dwell. man - u - el.

628 Let the Spirit dwell *(Celebrating in the Spirit)*

Words and Music: John Burland and John Jacobs
arr. Chris Mitchell

G2 D2
Let the Spi - rit dwell with - in our hearts,
F♯m7 G2
to ce - le - brate the won - der of our
A Em7
God. As we reach out to -
D/A A F♯7sus4 F♯7 Bm G2
ge - ther and find our strength in you, come share the
A Gm6 D
gifts of the Spi - rit.

629 Let us be grateful

Words and Music: Chris Jackson and Jill Hoffmann
arr. Dave Bankhead

G C/G G C
Let us be grate - ful, and wor-ship God
Dm/C C D Em/D D
in a way that will please him, with
C G
re - ve-rence and awe. Let us wor -
C D
- ship, let us wor - ship, let us wor -
C G
- ship with re - ve-rence and awe.

630 Let your kingdom come

Words and Music: Julia Abrahams
arr. Chris Mitchell

C7
F7
C7

G7
C7
F
F♯dim7

C/G
Am7
Dm
Dm/G
C
Chorus
C7
Let your king-dom come,

F7
C
C7
let your king - dom come.
Let your king - dom come, O Lord,

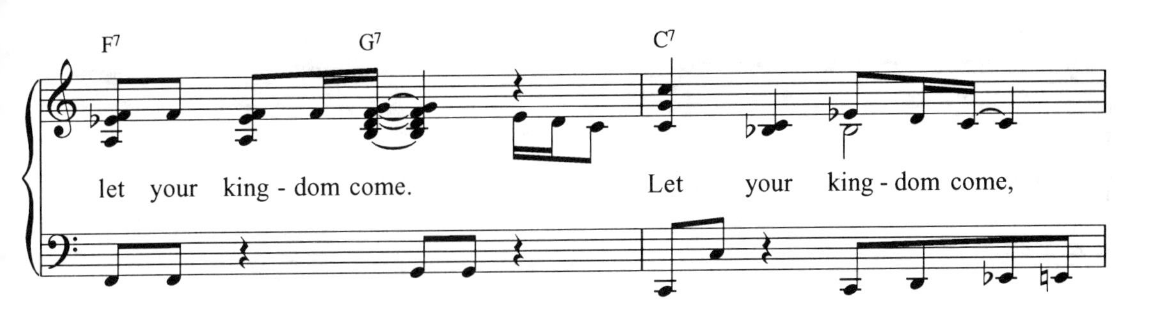
F7
G7
C7
let your king - dom come.
Let your king - dom come,

F7
F♯dim7
C/G
Am7
let your king-dom come,
let your king-dom,
let your king-dom,

Last time
To verses
Dm7
F/G
C
Fine
let your king - dom come.
let your king - dom come.
1. The

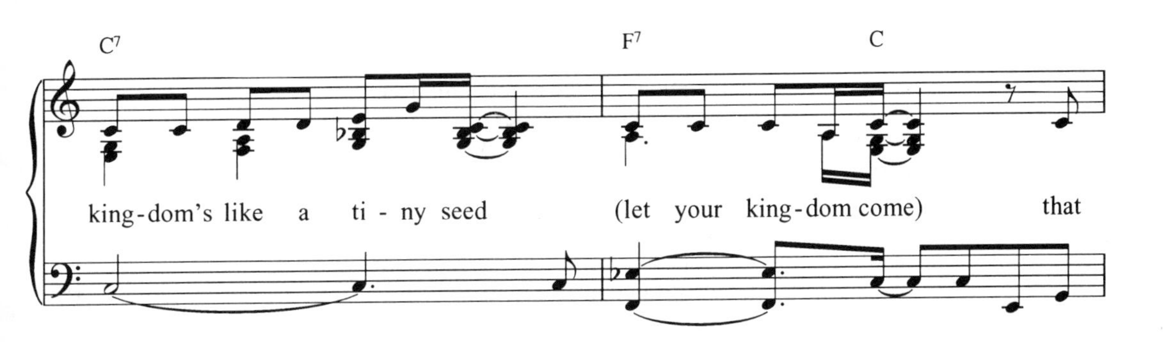
C7
F7
C
king-dom's like a ti - ny seed
(let your king-dom come)
that

C7
F7
G7
grows in - to a migh - ty tree
(let your king-dom come),
the birds

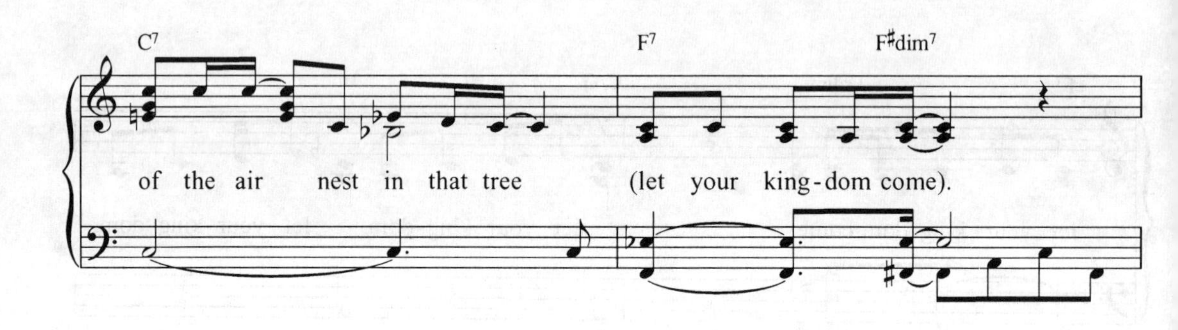
C7
F7
F#dim7
of the air
nest in that tree
(let your king-dom come).

C/G
Am7
Dm7
F/G
C
D.S.
Let your king-dom,
let your king-dom,
let your king-dom come.

2. The kingdom's like a pinch of yeast
(let your kingdom come)
that spreads throughout a mighty feast
(let your kingdom come).
From a pinch of yeast to mighty feast
(let your kingdom come).
Let your kingdom, let your kingdom,
let your kingdom come.

3. The kingdom's like a rare, rare pearl
(let your kingdom come),
the rarest pearl in all the world
(let your kingdom come).
Men sell their wealth to get that pearl
(let your kingdom come).
Let your kingdom, let your kingdom,
let your kingdom come.

631 Liar, liar

Words and Music: Christine Dalton
arr. Chris Mitchell

E
A/E
D/E
A
B
Li - ar, li - ar, pants on fire, Mum is mad, who's been bad?

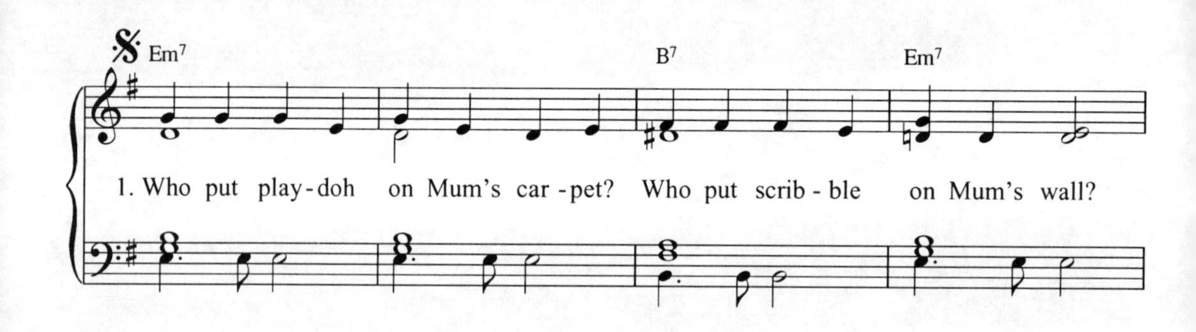
Em7
B7
Em7
1. Who put play-doh on Mum's car - pet? Who put scrib - ble on Mum's wall?

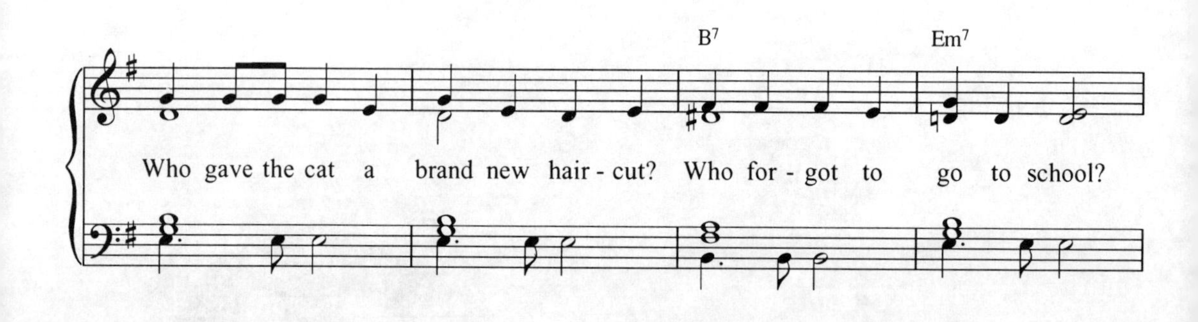
B7
Em7
Who gave the cat a brand new hair - cut? Who for - got to go to school?

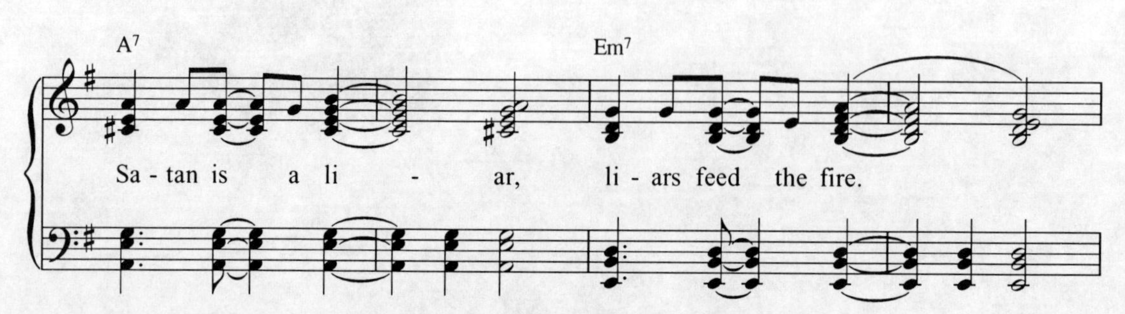
A7
Em7
Sa - tan is a li - ar, li - ars feed the fire.

A7
G
B
It is his de-sire just to hear you say:
C D G
C D G
I, I, I, I did-n't do it, no Mum, hon-
C D G
-est-ly! I, I, I, I did-n't do it.
Am7
B7
2nd time D.S.
Last time
Em
Could it be Mis-ter No-bo-dy?

2. Who put soap suds in the fish tank?
Who lost Dad's remote control?
Who put a football through the window,
trying hard to score a goal?
It is up to you, will you tell the truth?
God is proud of you when he hears you say:
I, I, I, I didn't mean it, no Mum, honestly!
I, I, I, I didn't mean it, sorry Mum, for what I've done.

632 Lord, hear my praying *(Sorrowing song)*

Words and Music: Robin Mann
arr. Chris Mitchell

F♯m
C♯7sus4
C♯7
B/C♯
C♯7
1. Lord, hear my pray - ing, lis - ten to

F♯m
Bm
F♯m
me; you know there's e - vil

G♯7/D♯
G♯7
C♯7
F♯m
in what I see. I know I'm

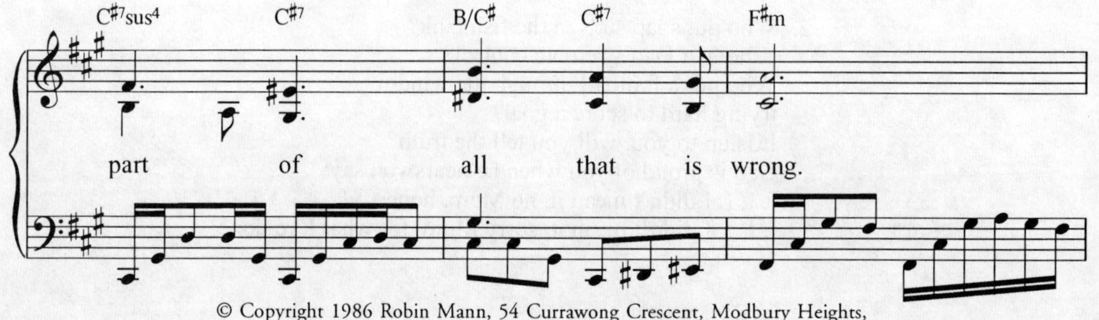

C♯7sus4
C♯7
B/C♯
C♯7
F♯m
part of all that is wrong.

Bm
F♯m
Cdim7/C♯
C♯7
F♯m
Still, won't you hear my sor - row - ing song?

Bm7
F♯sus4/A
F♯m/A
G♯7
C♯7
F♯m

2. Children are crying, hungry for food;
   sick from disease – God, are you good?
   People are homeless, lost and alone:
   God, are you hiding? Where have you gone?

3. Why do the rich ones steal from the poor?
   Why do they build their weapons of war?
   How can you stand the torture and pain,
   hope disappearing, freedom in chains?

4. Jesus, remind us that you are found
   with those who cry, with those who are bound;
   where there is suff'ring, you will be there –
   help us to follow, Lord, hear my prayer.

633 Lord, help me to tell your story

Words and Music: Tim Moyler and Donna Vann

G C G
1. Lord, help me to tell your sto - ry to those who've ne - ver heard,
help me to tell my sto - ry of what you've done for me.
so ma - ny live in dark - ness, lost in an end - less night.
C G Em
how you lived and died for us; you are
Give me cou - rage, Lord, to say how you
Help them search and find you, Lord, and fill
F Dsus4 D Chorus
the way to God.
have set me free.
them with your light.
I want to go,
G C G
Lord, in your pow - er, tell-ing the sto - ry of your name.
C Em Bm
I want to say what you said, do what you did, tell the world

1.
C
Dsus4
D
the rea - son you came.
2. Lord,
2, 3.
D
Rap
Em
Bm
You came down from hea-ven, born in a sta - ble, grew
C
D
Em
as a child in the wis-dom of God. Teach - ing and preach-ing, heal -
Bm
C
D
- ing and bless-ing, stirr - ing up an - ger; you died on a cross. Sealed
Em
Bm
C
in a tomb; burst from the grave; as - cend-ed to hea - ven and you're

D
C
F
com-ing a-gain!
I will live out your sto - ry to the glo -
G
C
- ry of your name.
I will live out your sto -
To repeat
F
G
C
- ry to the glo - ry of your name!
I will live out your sto -
To verse 3
Last time
G
D.S.
G
E♭
3. Lord,
F
E♭
Fsus²
F
G

634 Lord, I feel the heartbeat

Words and Music: Lynn Howson

Steadily
Capo 3
F D C/E A/C♯ Dm7 Bm7 C A F D
Lord, I feel the heart-beat of your love beat-ing for me.
C/F A/D B♭/F G/D F D C/E A/C♯ Dm7 Bm7
Lord, I hear you call-ing my name,
C A F D C/F A/D B♭/F G/D Chorus F D B♭ G
call-ing to me. And I am rea-dy to re-
C A Dm7 Bm7 Am7 F♯m7 B♭ G C A Dm7 Bm7 Am7 F♯m7
ceive your love, and I am rea-dy to res-pond to your call. Lord, make me

Gm7
Em7
Am7
F#m7
Dm7
Bm7
Am7
F#m7
rea - dy for your fire to fall.
To repeat
Last time
To continue
Bbsus2
Gsus2
C
A
D.C.
Bbsus2
Gsus2
F2
D2
Fine
Bbsus2
Gsus2
C
A
Bb
G
F
D
Your Spi - rit is stir - ring in us,
Asus4
F#sus4
A
F#
Dm
Bm
Bb
G
fill us once a - gain: let our hearts burn with a
F/A
D/F#
Asus4
F#sus4
1.
A
F#
D.C.
2.
A
F#
Chorus D.S.
pas - sion to glo - ri - fy your name. name. And I am

635 Lord, I need to know

Words and Music: Ian Smale

G D D7
Lord, I need to know you love me, Lord, I need to know you
G C G D
care; in the times I feel re - ject - ed,
D7 G C G
I need to know you're there. God says, 'Lis-ten, my lit - tle
C D G C
child, I'm a fa - ther who'll ne - ver leave you,

Em
Am
and though all your friends may fail you,
D
G
you can al - ways trust in me.
For you're price - less and you're
C
D
pre - cious
and your va - lue can - not be
G
Em
Am
mea - sured,
you're an heir to my king - dom,
D
D7
G
C
G
you're in my cho - sen fa - mi - ly.'

636 Lord, I wanna pause *(Pausing in your presence)*

Words and Music: Dave Godfrey

Gently
E
B7
1. Lord, I wan-na pause, pause in your pre-
E
-sence; Lord, I wan-na be
A
A7
E
still be-fore your throne. Lord,
A
E
B7
I wan-na raise my hands to you,
E
A
E
Lord, I wan-na praise the God I

B7
Chorus
E
serve: love you, Lord (love you, Lord). Al -
A E B7 E
migh - ty King, love you, Lord (love you, Lord).
A E B7
You're ev - 'ry - thing to
E
me.

2. Lord, I wanna rest, rest in your presence;
Lord, I wanna be filled up once again.
Lord, I wanna stay close to you,
Lord, I wanna say, I love you, Lord:

637 Lord, I want to worship you

Words and Music: Steve Burnhope
arr. Chris Mitchell

(♩ = c.60)
Em D Em B
Lord, I want to wor - ship you the way you want me to,

Em D Em B
Lord, I want to find your heart and be ve - ry close to you, so

G D C D G
as I close my eyes and try to con - cen - trate on you;

Em D C D Em
touch me with your Spi - rit, Lord, and fill me through and through.

G
D
Am
D
G
Lord, I want to wor - ship you,
Lord, I want to wor - ship you,

Em
D
Em
B
Em
Lord, I want to wor - ship you,
please help me wor - ship you.

638 Lord Jesus, you are faithful

Words and Music: Bev Gammon

With feeling
G/A A A/D D D/E Em
1. Lord Je - sus, you are faith - ful,
F♯m7 G
al - ways with us, ne - ver leav - ing us, Lord
Em/D D
To next verse
Last time
Je - sus.
2. Lord

2. Lord Jesus, you are blameless,
   you are perfect, you are sinless,
   Lord Jesus.

3. Lord Jesus, you are so pure,
   pure and lovely, pure and holy,
   Lord Jesus.

639 Lord, make me thankful

Words and Music: James Wright
arr. Chris Mitchell

D A7 D A7 D G
Lord, make me thank-ful and help me to see all the good things

A7 D A7 D A7
gi-ven to me, for Christ-mas par-ties and the car-ols we sing,

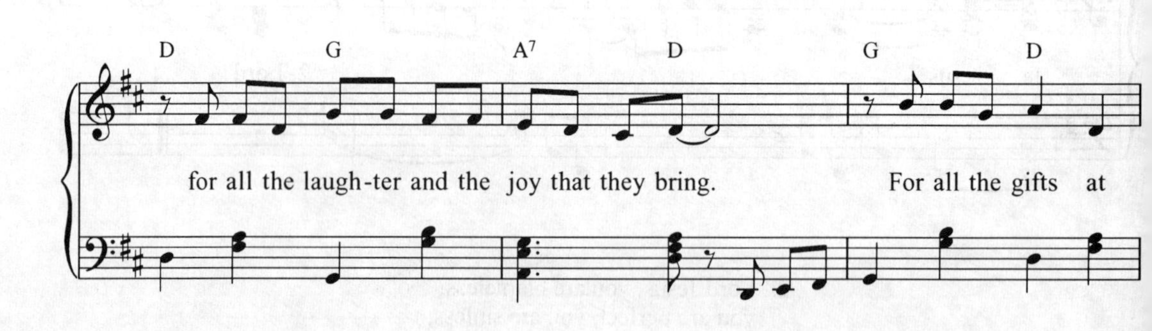
D G A7 D G D
for all the laugh-ter and the joy that they bring. For all the gifts at

G D G C D G A7
this time of year, that make our Christ-mas so full of cheer.

D A7 D A7 D A7 D
The joy of giv-ing as we re-ceive, from friends and our fa - mi - ly.
Last time
To continue
G
And we're free - ly
D A
shar - ing the good - ness of Christ - mas with one a - no -
D G D
- ther, and we're learn - ing that it's more bles-sed to give
1. 2.
E7 E7 A D A
D.C.
than it is to re-ceive. And we're

640 Lord of the future

Words and Music: Iain D. Craig

C F Gsus4 G C G7 C
1. Lord of the fu-ture, Lord of the past,
F C/E Am G C
Lord of our lives, we a - dore you. Lord of for e - ver,
G7 C F Gsus4 G 1. C F
Lord of our hearts, we give all praise to you.
Gsus4 G 2. C C/E F Gsus4 G C
you.

2. Lord of tomorrow,
Lord of today,
Lord over all, you are worthy.
Lord of creation,
Lord of all truth,
we give all praise to you.

641 Lord, our master

Words and Music: Dave Godfrey

With a 'reggae' feel
Chorus D
G
A
Lord, our mas-ter, won-der-ful is your name.

D
G
Oh Lord, our mas-ter,

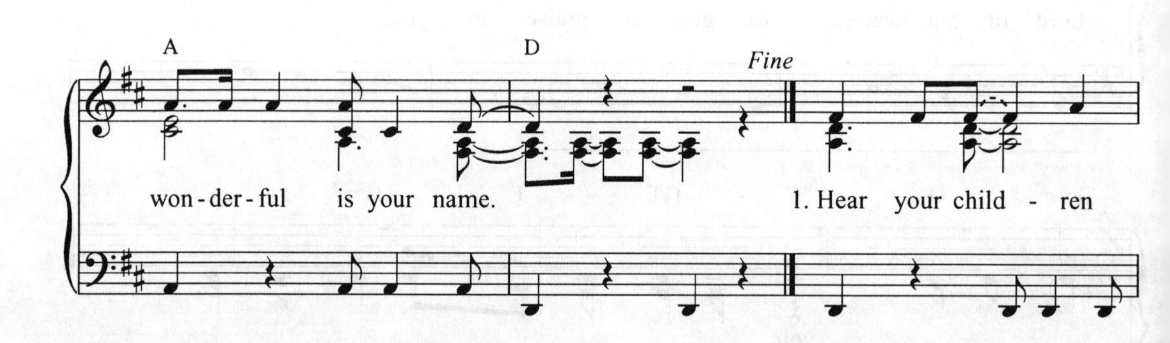

A
D
Fine
won-der-ful is your name. 1. Hear your child - ren

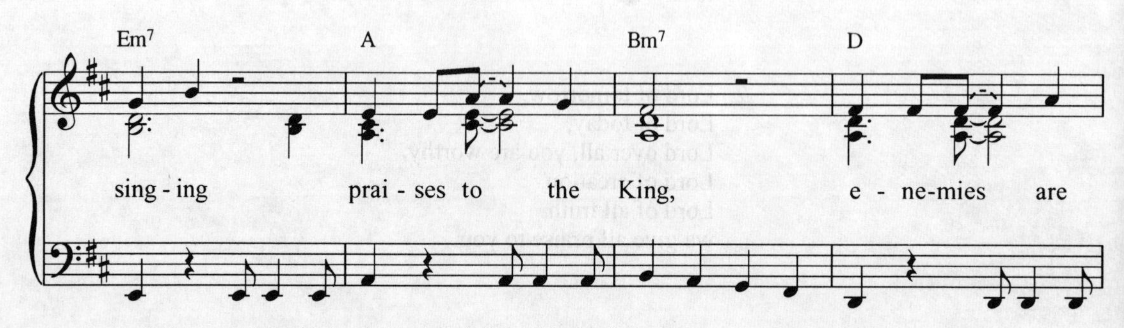

Em7
A
Bm7
D
sing-ing prai-ses to the King, e - ne-mies are

G
Em7
A
D
D.C.
si - lenced
when the child - ren
sing. And they
say:

2. I gaze into the heavens,
   when the sunlight fades:
   moon and stars are gleaming,
   so beautifully made.
   And I say . . .

3. Why are we so special,
   you care for everyone.
   You've crowned us with the glory
   of the risen Son.
   And we say . . .

4. You've given us control
   of animals like sheep:
   of birds and fish and creatures
   that live within the deep.
   And we say . . .

5. For all your mighty wonders
   and ev'rything you do,
   we will lift our voices
   and sing this song to you.
   And we say . . .

642 Lord, you know me

Words and Music: Unknown

Cheerfully (♩ = 104)
C G C G
Lord, you know me, you know ev - 'ry - thing I do. You
C G C G C C7
see me when I'm play-ing and when I'm work-ing too. You are all a - round me and
F D D7 G G7
you take care of me, e - ven in the night-time you'll still be close to me.
C G7 C F
You know what I'm think - ing and how I feel to - day.
C G/D C/E F C/G G7 C
Help me love you al - ways; you're A - O - K!

643 Lord, you see me

Words and Music: Dave Cooke and Judy Mackenzie-Dunn

Worshipfully
E
C#m7
1. Lord, you see me, Lord, you know me,
2. Lord, you're with me, all a - round me
A
E/G#
you know ev - 'ry - thing a - bout me: ev - 'ry
and your hand is here to guide me. When I
F#m7
E/G#
thought in - side my head, ev - 'ry
sit and when I stand you are
A
1.
Bsus4
B
word be - fore it's said.
ev - 'ry - where I am.
2, 3.
Bsus4
B
Chorus
A
B
Where - e - ver I go, you are. Wher - e - ver I

A B A
fly, you're there. On e - ven the far - thest star,
G♯sus4 G♯7/B♯ C♯m B A G♯m
I know you'll find me. And deep in the
A B G♯sus4 G♯7/B♯
dark - est night, you are my sun, my light:
C♯m F♯m7 E/G♯ A2
you can make the dark - ness bright when you're a-round
E C♯m A2 B D.C. E
me.

3. Lord, you made me,
and you love me,
and you're always thinking of me.
It's amazing but it's true,
and you know that I love you.

644 Lots of folk will tell you

(Jesus is the only way to God)

Words and Music: Colin Buchanan
arr. Dave Bankhead

E
F♯
1. Lots of folk will tell you that the Bi - ble is - n't true.
B
They'll say it's too old - fash - ioned, and that they
A
E
want some - thing new. But be - liev-ing bits of
F♯
this and that will ne - ver get you through 'cos
Amaj7
B
Je - sus is the on - ly way to God.

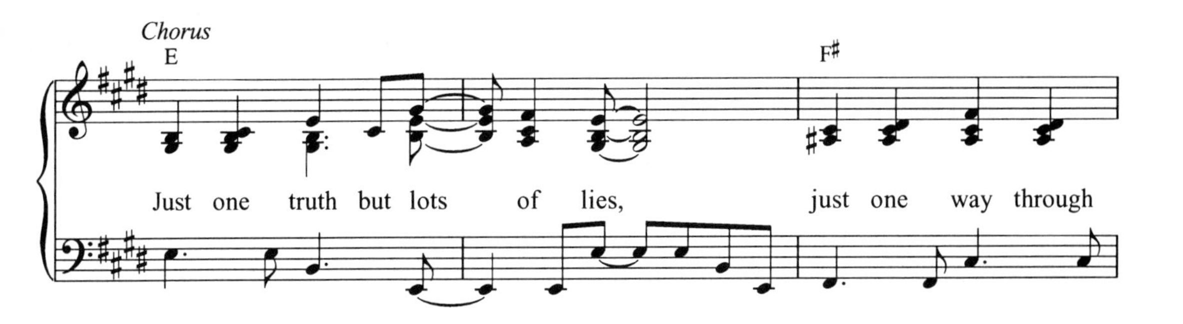
Chorus
E
F♯
Just one truth but lots of lies, just one way through

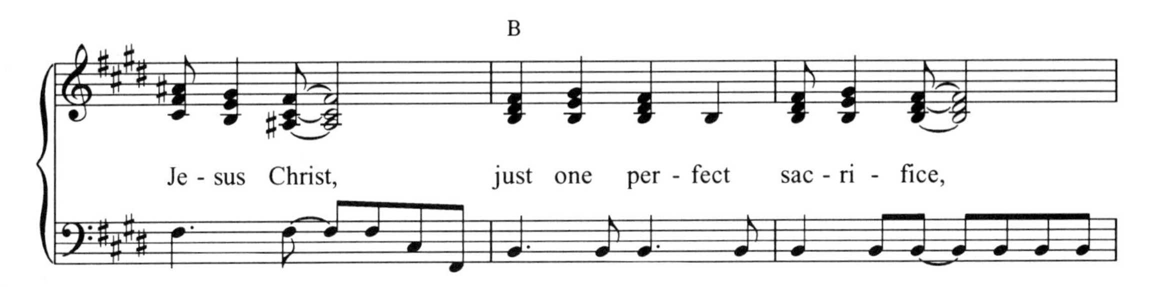
B
Je - sus Christ, just one per - fect sac - ri - fice,

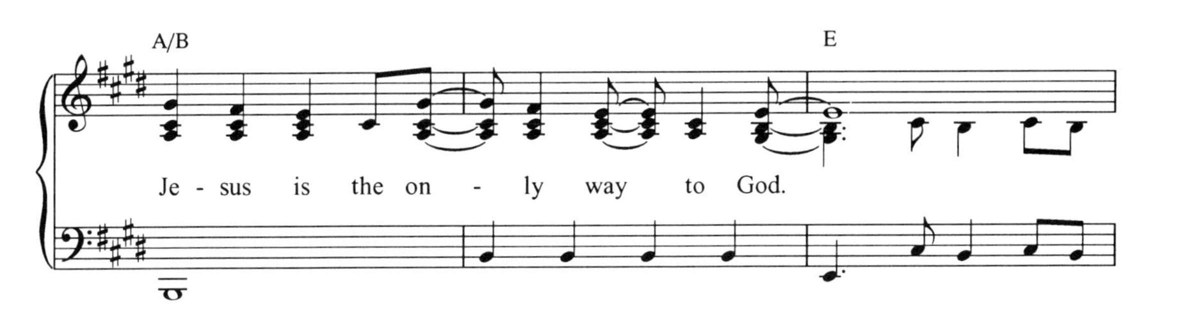
A/B
E
Je - sus is the on - ly way to God.

To verses
Last time
2. When some-one

2. When someone makes a new religion
or a new philosophy.
And they'll say what's true is true for you
and this is true for me.
But there's only one Creator
and he's given his decree
that Jesus is the only way to God.

3. Well, the devil hates the truth
and he is working to deceive.
He cooks up deadly lies
for precious people to believe.
We've got to speak the truth in love
and pray the Lord would make them see
that Jesus is the only way to God.

645 Love the Lord your God

Words and Music: Chris Jackson
arr. Dave Bankhead

Two-part round
1
D G A
Love the Lord your God with all your heart, with
D G
all your mind. Love the Lord your God
A D
with all your strength.
2
G
Love the Lord with
A D
all your heart, love the
G A D
Lord with all your strength.

646 Love you, Jesus

Words and Music: Chris Jackson
arr. Dave Bankhead

D
G
D
G
Love you, Je - sus,
I love you, Lord,

D
G
A
I love you more than words can say.

D
G
D
G
I will fol - low
where you lead,

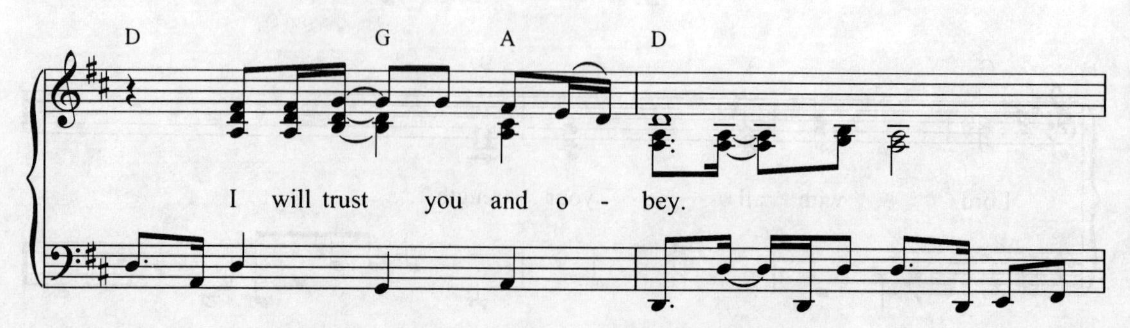
D
G
A
D
I will trust you and o - bey.

G A D
So send your Spi - rit, send your pow'r,

G A D G A
come and fill me, Lord, I pray. I am wait - ing

F♯m Bm E A A7
for you, Lord, come and have your way.

647 Made by God for God alone

Words and Music: Colin Buchanan
arr. Chris Mitchell

(♩ = 144)
To repeat/continue
Last time
G7 F C7 G G
Woah, woah.
G7 F C7 G
Made by God for God a - lone.
1.
2.
G F
1. Got - ta live your life to the praise of the gi - ver and
2. You've got - ta do ev - 'ry-thing to the praise of your mak - er, the
C7 G7
e - ve - ry breath that fills your lungs. Got - ta live your life to the
migh - ty cre - a - tor of ev - 'ry - one. You've got - ta do ev - 'ry-thing to the
F C7 G7
1st time D.S.
praise of the gi - ver, the life in - side your bones.
praise of your mak - er who holds you to - ge - ther right now.

F
C7
G
Made by God for God a - lone.
G7
F
C7
1.
G
Woah,
woah.
2.
G
G7
F
C7
3. You've got-ta come to Je - sus to be for - gi - ven, you ain't liv - in' 'til the
G7
F
deal is done. You've got - ta come to Je - sus to be for - gi - ven,
C
1.
G7
2.
G7
D.C.
put your faith in the ri - sen Son. You've got - ta ri - sen Son.

648 Make a joyful noise

Words and Music: Philip Chapman and Stephanie Chapman
arr. Dave Bankhead

Two-part round
1
G D G C Am7
Make a joy - ful noise to the Lord, make a joy - ful noise and sing out

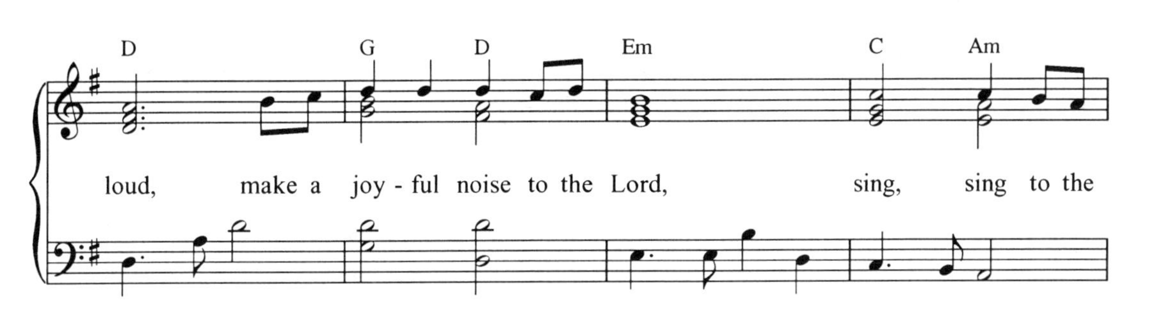
D G D Em C Am
loud, make a joy - ful noise to the Lord, sing, sing to the

G
2
D G C Am
Lord. Hal - le - lu - jah, hal - le - lu - jah, hal - le - lu - jah, sing out

D G D Em C Am G
loud. Hal - le - lu - jah, sing, sing to the Lord.

649 Marching in God's army

Words and Music: John Fryer
arr. Gillian Venton

(♩ = 140)
G C/G G C/G G C/G G D

Chorus
G
March - ing in God's ar - my, march - ing in his way.
Shoul - ders back and head held high, march - ing for our King.

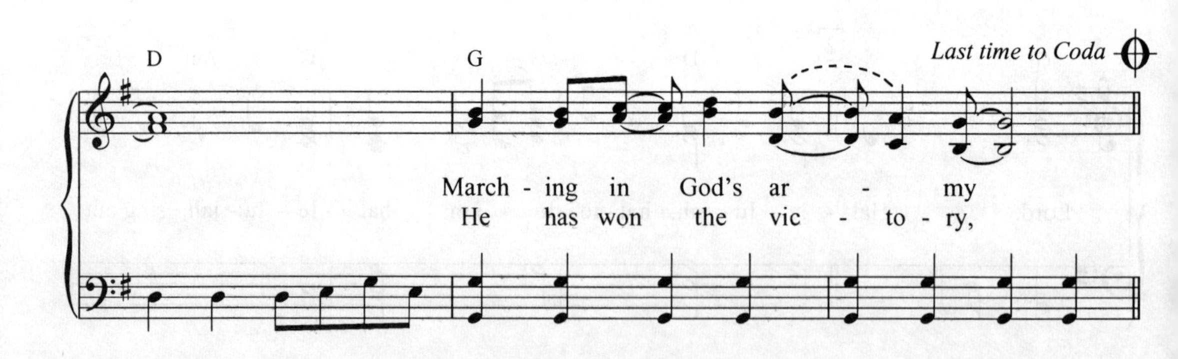
D G
Last time to Coda
March - ing in God's ar - my
He has won the vic - to - ry,

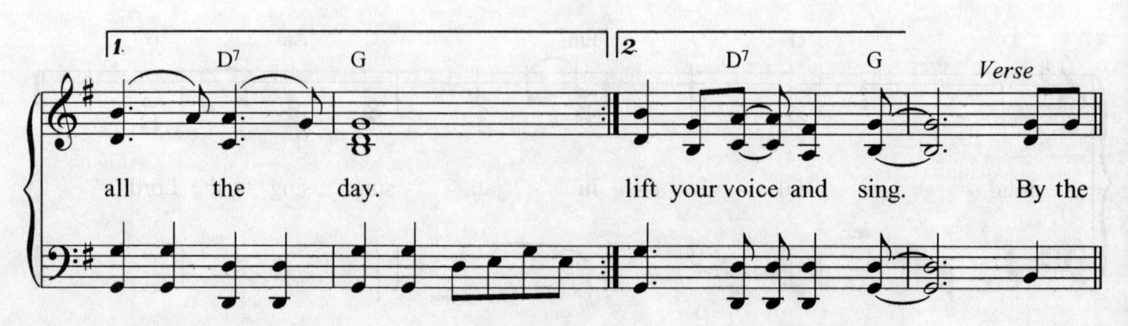
1. D7 G
all the day.
2. D7 G
Verse
lift your voice and sing. By the

C G D G
left, quick march! We're sol - diers of the Lord. By the
left, quick march! He's won the vic - to - ry. By the
1.
C G A7 D
right, quick march! The bi - ble is our sword! By the
right, quick march! And sing this song with
2.
CODA
D D.S. G D7 G
me! lift your voice and sing!

D7 G
Lift your voice and sing!

Running order: Chorus, verse, chorus twice, Coda

650 Mary shivers

(Mary's child)

Words and Music: Philip Chapman and Stephanie Chapman
arr. Dave Bankhead

(♩ = 100)
A D/A A
1. Ma - ry shi - vers, she's fright - ened, she has to
watch - ing, Jo - seph ask - ing, 'Do you
D A D
go to Beth - le - hem. Jo - seph sad - dles a don -
have a room to spare?' Ev - 'ry - one is so bu -
A D Bm E
- key, as they start a - long the road.
- sy and no one seems to care.
E7 A D/A A
Ma - ry walk - ing, so slow - ly, they have a
Ma - ry cry - ing, there is no room, so she
D A D
long, long way to go, Jo - seph walk - ing be -
lies on a bed of straw. A bright star shines like a

A
D
Bm7
E
E7
side her. Who can say what lies a - head?
dia-mond, in a dark and emp-ty sky.
Chorus
D
E
A
F♯m
Ma - ry's child is born (he is born), and
D
E
A
F♯m
D
E
this is the day, this is the day, this is the day for re -
A
F♯m
D
E
D
A
joic - ing, this is the day for re - joic - ing.
1.
2.
D
A
E
D.S.
E
A
2. Ma-ry

651 Matthew, Mark, Luke and John

(The New Testament Song)

Words and Music: Steve Burnhope
arr. Chris Mitchell

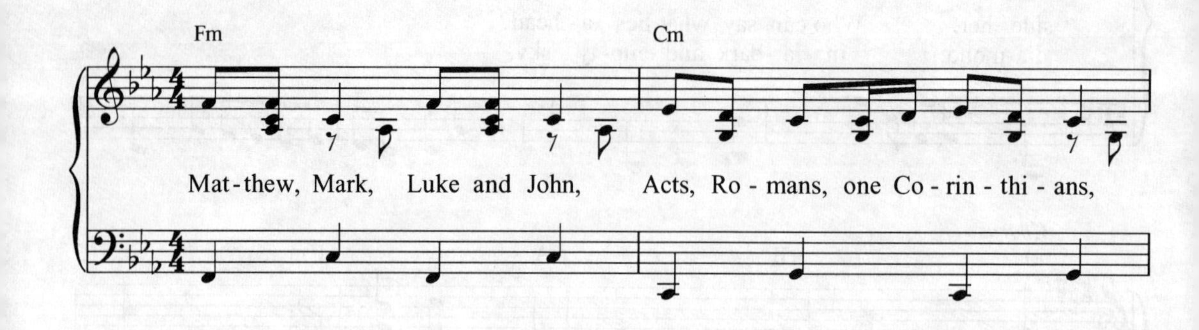
Fm
Cm
Mat-thew, Mark, Luke and John, Acts, Ro-mans, one Co-rin-thi-ans,

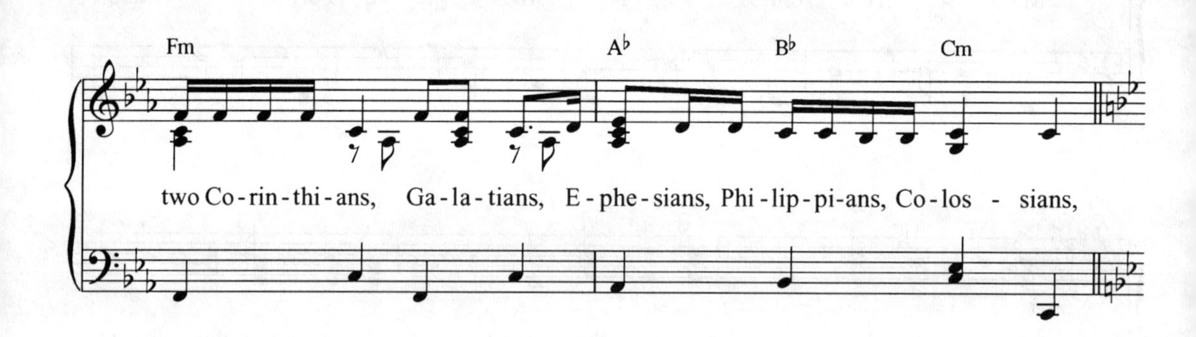
Fm
A♭
B♭
Cm
two Co-rin-thi-ans, Ga-la-tians, E-phe-sians, Phi-lip-pi-ans, Co-los - sians,

Gm
Dm
one and two Thes-sa-lo-ni-ans, one and two Ti-mo-thy,

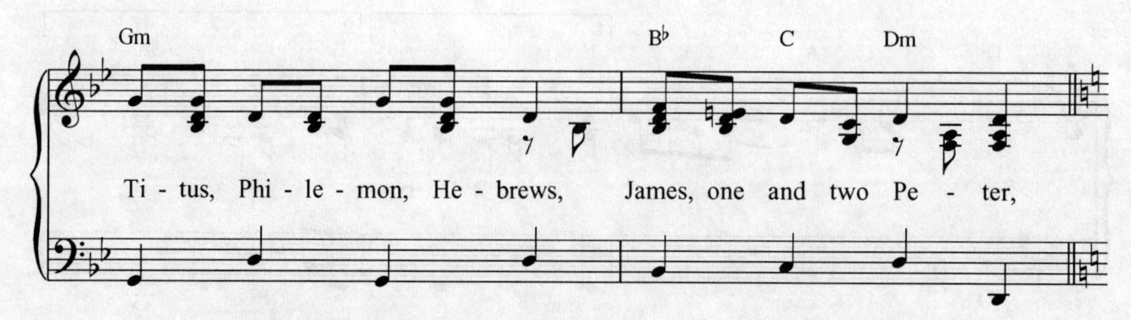
Gm
B♭
C
Dm
Ti - tus, Phi - le - mon, He - brews, James, one and two Pe - ter,

Am
Em
one, two and three John, Jude and Re - ve - la - tion,

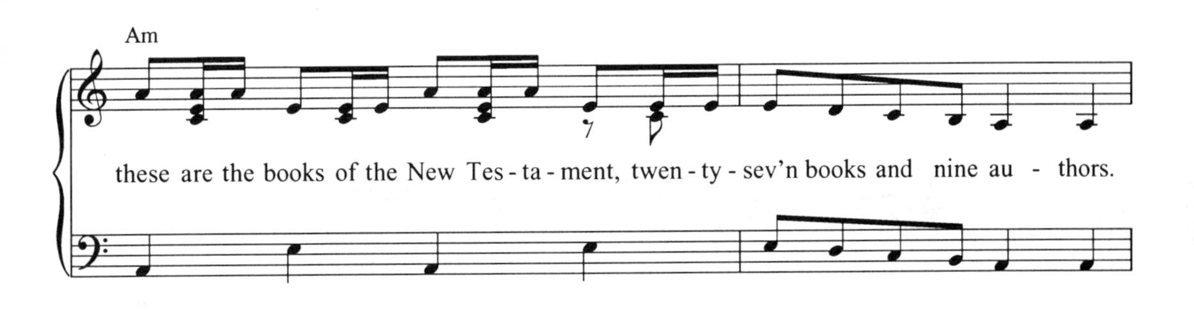
Am
these are the books of the New Tes - ta - ment, twen - ty - sev'n books and nine au - thors.

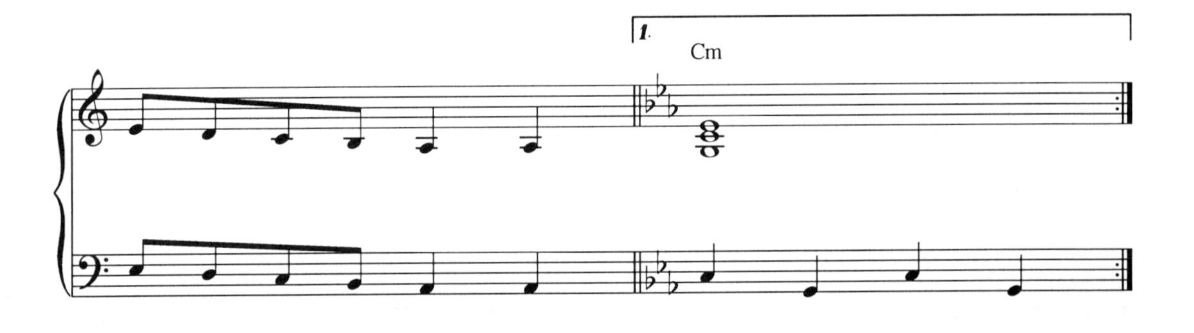
1.
Cm

2.

652 Matthew twenty-two *(Love the Lord your God)*

Words and Music: Mark Johnson and Helen Johnson
arr. Dave Bankhead

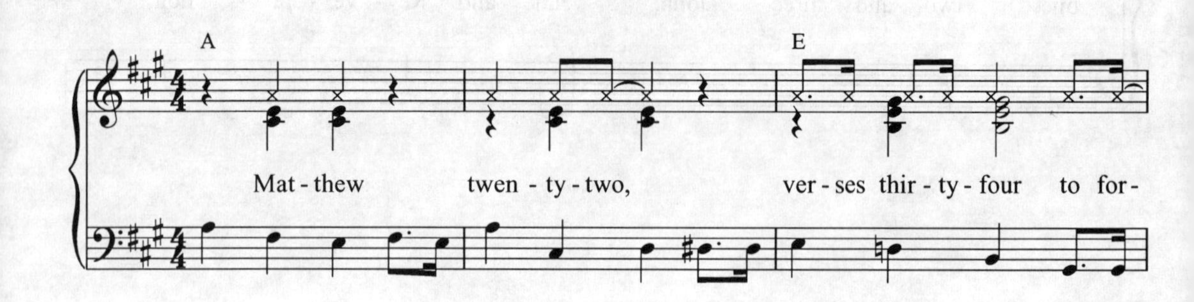
A
E
Mat - thew twen - ty - two, ver - ses thir - ty - four to for -

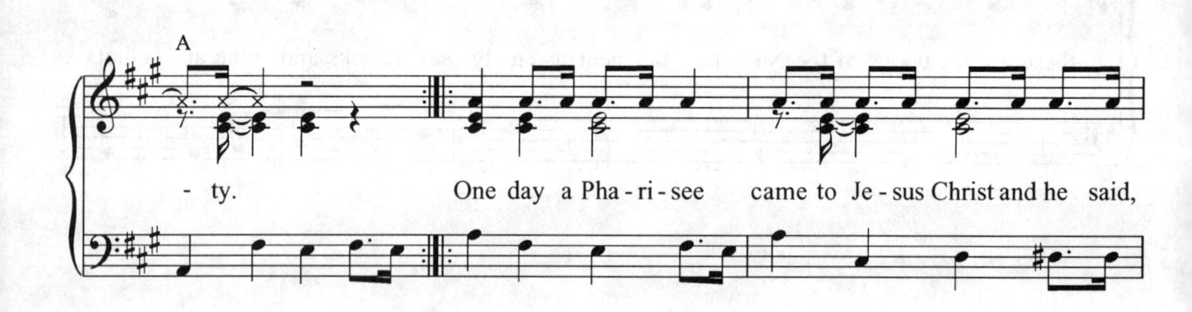
A
- ty. One day a Pha - ri - see came to Je - sus Christ and he said,

E
A
'Tell me, what's the great - est com - mand - ment?'

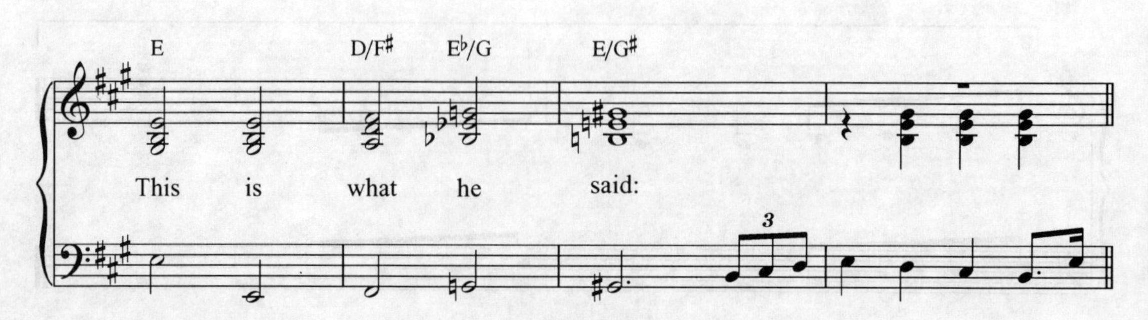
E
D/F♯
E♭/G
E/G♯
This is what he said:
3

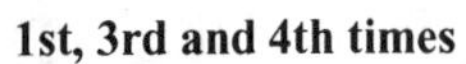
1st, 3rd and 4th times

A
Love the Lord your God with all your heart, with all your soul, with all your
2nd, 3rd and 4th times
Love your neigh - bour as your - self, and
4th time only
One day a Pha - ri - see came to Je - sus Christ and he said,
4th time only (optional)
Mat - thew twen - ty - two,

E
A
mind, with all your strength.
do to o - thers as you'd have them do to you.
'Tell me, what's the great - est com - mand - ment?'
ver - ses thir - ty - four to for - ty.

A
Love the Lord your God with all your heart, with all your soul, with all your
Love your neigh - bour as your - self, and
One day a Pha - ri - see came to Je - sus Christ and he said,
Mat - thew twent - ty - two,

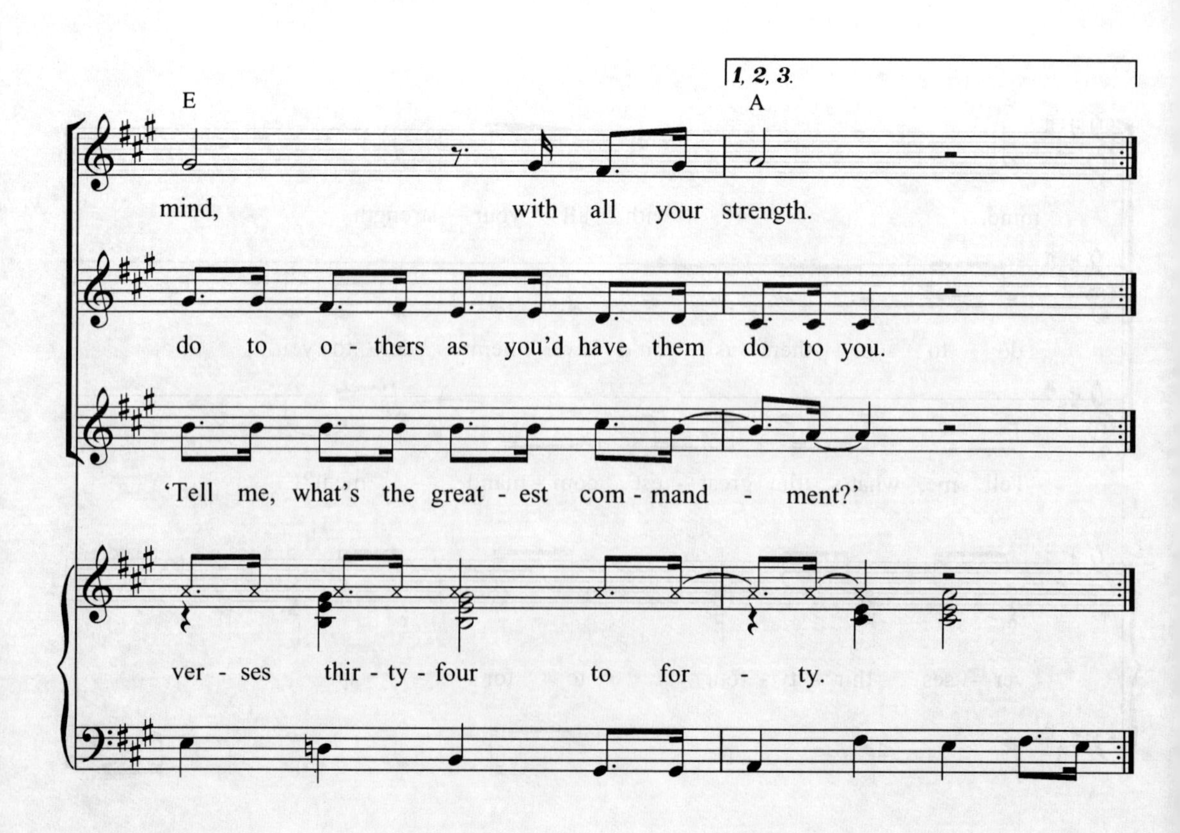
1, 2, 3.
E
A
mind, with all your strength.
do to o - thers as you'd have them do to you.
'Tell me, what's the great - est com - mand - ment?'
ver - ses thir - ty - four to for - ty.

4.
A
strength.
do to you.
- ment?'
- ty.

653 May my life be a thank-you

Words and Music: Steve Morgan-Gurr and Kay Morgan-Gurr

G
Bm
C
May my life be a thank - you for what you have
G
Bm
C
done, prais-ing you for your kind - ness in send - ing your
D
C
D
G
Son. Be - ing filled with your Spi - rit, the com - fort - ing
Em
C
D
G
One, may my life be a thank - you to you;
Em
C
D
G
may my life be a thank-you to you.

654 May my praise be sung *(I adore you)*

Words and Music: Ian Smale and Irene Smale

G D G C D
May my praise be sung with feel - ing, may my wor - ship be sin-cere,

G C G Am
may my voice de-clare Je - sus is God for all the world to

D G D G
hear. May my mind be con - stant - ly re - newed, may my

C D G C G
thoughts be clean and pure, may my life be de - di - ca - ted to

Am D C D7 G
you, whom I a - dore. I a - dore you, I a -
C D G C
dore you; there's no-thing I would
G Am D
ra - ther do than simp - ly a - dore you. I a -
C D7 G C D G
dore you, I a - dore you; I
C G Am D G
want to live my whole life through simp-ly a - dor - ing you.

655 May the Lord bless you

Words: *Book of Common Prayer*

Music: Phil Overton
arr. Chris Mitchell

D
May the Lord bless you. May the Lord keep you. May the

G D D/A A7 D
Lord make his face to shine up - on you. May the

Lord bless you. May the Lord be gra - cious. May the

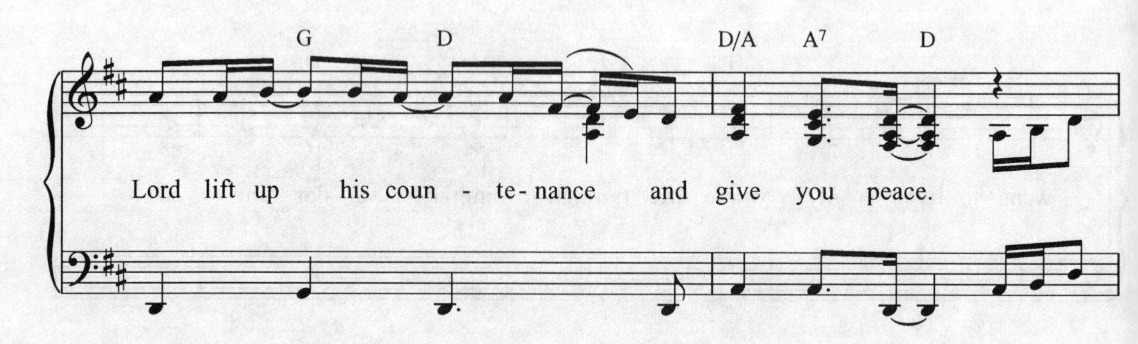
G D D/A A7 D
Lord lift up his coun - te - nance and give you peace.

Hal - le - lu - jah,
hal - le - lu - jah,

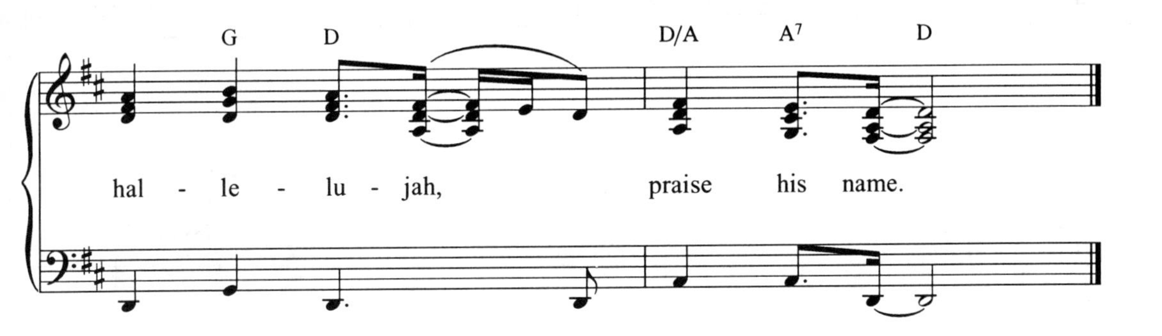
G
D
D/A
A7
D
hal - le - lu - jah,
praise his name.

656 Meekness and majesty *(This is your God)*

Words and Music: Graham Kendrick

Majestically
C
Am
Cmaj7
Am7
C
Capo 3 A
F♯m
Amaj7
F♯m7
A
1. Meek-ness and ma-jes-ty, man-hood and de-i-ty, in per-fect

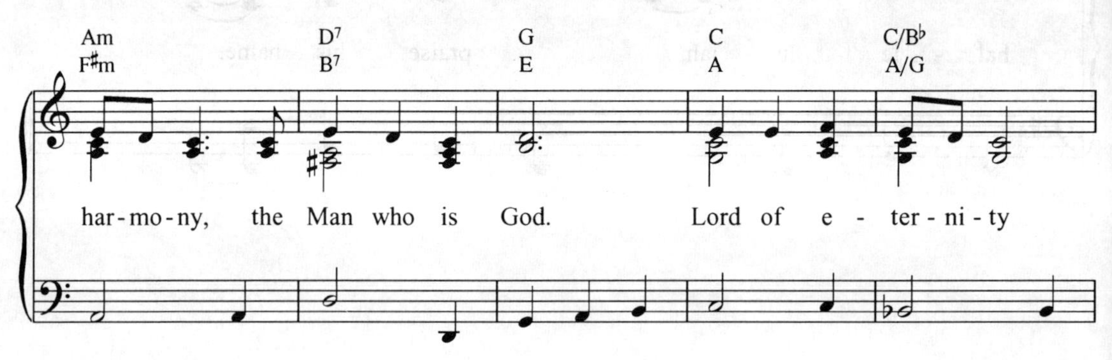
Am
D7
G
C
C/B♭
F♯m
B7
E
A
A/G
har-mo-ny, the Man who is God. Lord of e-ter-ni-ty

F
F♯dim
Em
Am
F
C/G
G
D
D♯dim
C♯m
F♯m
D
A/E
E
dwells in hu-ma-ni-ty, kneels in hu-mi-li-ty and wash-es our

C
Dm
G
E7
Am
A
Bm
E
C♯7
F♯m
Chorus
feet. O what a mys-te-ry, meek-ness and ma-jes-ty.

F F♯dim C Am Dm G
D D♯dim A F♯m Bm E
Bow down and wor - ship for this is your
To verses 2 and 3
B♭9 F G A♭
G9 D E F
God, this is your God.
Last time
Gm7 C G B♭9
Em7 A E G9
God,
F G A♭ Gm7 C
D E F Em7 A
this is your God.

2. Father's pure radiance,
perfect in innocence,
yet learns obedience
to death on a cross.
Suffering to give us life,
conquering through sacrifice,
and as they crucify
prays: 'Father forgive.'

3. Wisdom unsearchable,
God the invisible,
love indestructible
in frailty appears.
Lord of infinity,
stooping so tenderly,
lifts our humanity
to the heights of his throne.

657 Mister Noah built an ark

Words and Music: Unknown arr. David Ball

Moderato
D A
1. Mis - ter No - ah built an ark, the peo - ple thought it
a - ni - mals went in two by two, e - le - phant, gi - raffe and
D A
such a lark. Mis - ter No - ah plead - ed so, but in - to the ark they
kan - ga - roo. All were safe - ly stowed a - way, on that great and
D Chorus A
would not go. Down came the rain in tor - rents, (splish, splash)
aw - ful day. When - e - ver you see a rain - bow, when -
D
down came the rain in tor - rents, (splish, splash) down came the rain in
e - ver you see a rain - bow, when - e - ver you see a
G D A D Fine D.C.
tor - rents and on - ly eight were saved. 2. The
rain - bow, re - mem - ber God is love.

658 Monday, Tuesday

Words and Music: Andy Read
arr. Chris Mitchell

Am7 D/F# Am7
Mon-day, Tues-day, Wedn's-day, Thurs-day, Fri-day, Sa-tur-day, Sun-day, here we go.
D/F# Am7
Mon-day, Tues-day, Wedn's-day, Thurs-day, Fri-day, Sa-tur-day, Sun-day, here we go.
Last time
Fine
To continue
D7 Am7
I will praise you ev-'ry day, I will wor-ship, come what may,
D7 Am7
there is some-thing deep in-side, I will let it come out-side.

D7
Am7
Praise
you,
Lord.
D7
Am7
D.C.
Praise
you,
Lord.

659 My body is a temple of the Holy Spirit

Words and Music: Sharon E. Ward
arr. Chris Mitchell

C G7 C F C/G G7 C G7 C F
My bo-dy is a tem-ple of the Ho-ly Spi-rit. My bo-dy is a tem-ple of the
C/G G7 C F C G7 C
Ho-ly Spi-rit. My bo-dy is a tem-ple and Je-sus lives with-in it. My
C G7 C F C/G G7 C F C
bo-dy is a tem-ple of the Ho-ly Spi-rit. Keep it ti-dy, keep it clean,
G7 C G7 C F C/G G7 C
make it spar-kle, make it gleam. My bo-dy is a tem-ple of the Ho-ly Spi-rit.

660 My God is big enough

Words and Music: Frank Montgomery and Bruce Monthy
arr. Chris Mitchell

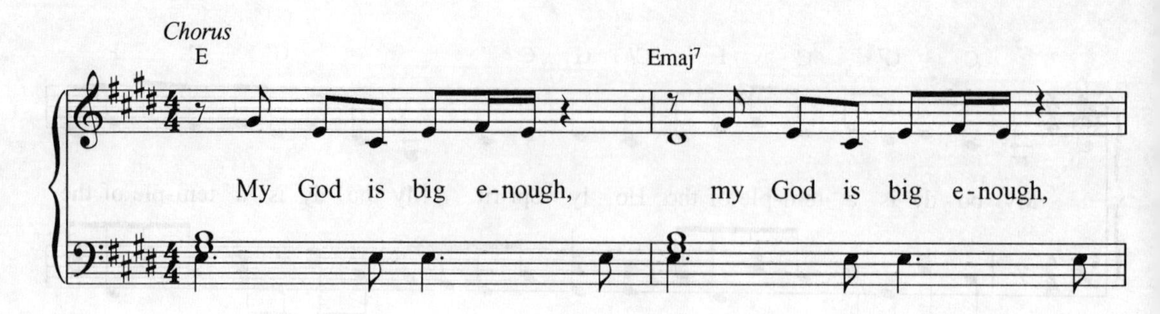
Chorus
E
Emaj7
My God is big e-nough, my God is big e-nough,

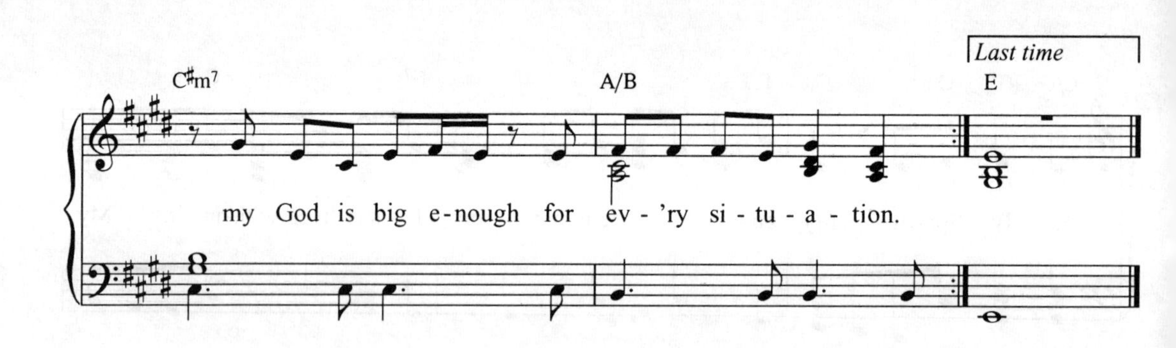
C#m7
A/B
Last time
E
my God is big e-nough for ev-'ry si-tu-a-tion.

To continue
C#m7
E7
1. No-where I'll e-ver go, no words I'll e-ver say;

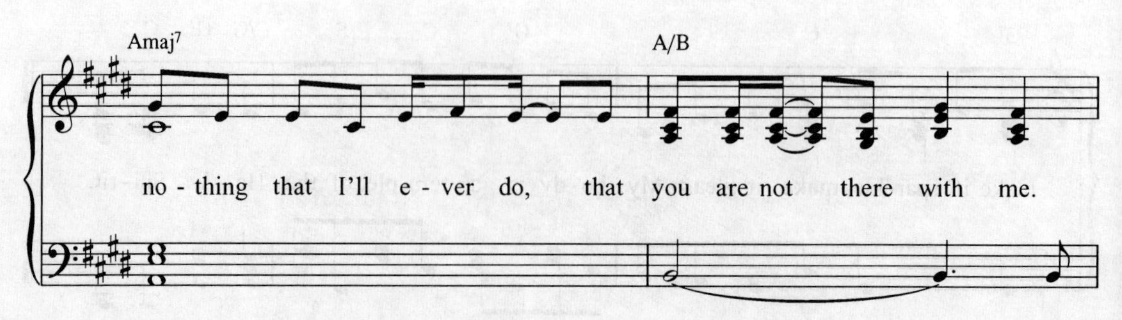
Amaj7
A/B
no-thing that I'll e-ver do, that you are not there with me.

C#m7
E7
I'm in you and you're in me, I'll ne - ver stand a - lone; no

Amaj7
A/B
D.C.
force that there will e - ver be can se - pa - rate us.

2. Deeper than the ocean,
your word is in my heart;
higher than the sky above,
your love for me is endless.
Stronger than a raging storm,
my confidence in you;
closer than the air I breathe,
you're always with me!

661 My Lord loves me

Words: Carole Pegler
Music: traditional
arr. E.J. Hume
Capo 3
Chorus
My Lord loves me and oh, the wonder I see! A rainbow shines in my window: my Lord loves me.
Verse
He died for me, on a cross at Calvary, he bore my sin and my shame when he died for me.

662 My mouth was made for worship

Words and Music: Ian Smale

Capo 3
F D C A F D C A
1. My mouth was made for wor-ship, my hands were made to
F D B♭ G (v.2) F D
raise, my feet were made for danc-ing, my life is one of
C7 A7 B♭ G F D C A F D B♭ G F D C A F D
praise to Je - sus. And all God's peo - ple said: 'A - men, hal - le - lu - jah, a - men,
B♭ G F D C A F D C A
praise and glo - ry, a - men, a - men, a - men, a - men.'

1.
2.
C7
A7
C7
A7
F
D
Wo, wo, wo, wo. 2. My
Wo, wo, wo, wo, wo.

2. My heart was made for loving,
my mind to know God's ways,
my body was made a temple,
my life is one of praise to Jesus.
And all God's people said: 'Amen,
hallelujah, amen, praise and glory,
amen, amen, amen, amen.'
Wo, wo, wo, wo, wo.

663 Never ever go *(He'll never ever go)*

Words and Music: Andy Read
arr. Chris Mitchell

Chorus
E A E
Ne-ver e-ver go, ne-ver e-ver go, ne-ver e-ver go a-
B E A E
way from me. He'll ne-ver e-ver go, ne-ver e-ver go,
B E
Fine
A
ne-ver e-ver go a-way from me. 1. Je-sus said he would ne-ver
B E A
e-ver leave me far be-hind. Je-sus cares, and he says
1. 2.
B E D.C. B E D.C.
no-thing I can do will change his mind. love you 'cos you're you. He'll

2. Jesus said he would never
ever stop from loving me.
Jesus cares, and he says
I love you 'cos you're you.
He'll...

664 Nobody's a nobody

Words and Music: John Hardwick

E
A
B7
Nobody's a nobody, believe me 'cos it's true,
E
E7
nobody's a nobody, especially not you. Nobody's a nobody and
A
B
God wants us to see that ev'rybody's somebody and
1.
2.
Fine
that means even me. I'm that means even me.
E
A
B7
no cartoon, I'm human, I have feelings, treat me right. I'm

E
not a su - per - he - ro with su - per strength and might. I'm
E7
A
not a me - ga pop star or su - per a - the - lete, but
B
E
D.C. al Fine
did you know I'm spe - cial, in fact I'm quite u - nique!

665 O come, all ye faithful

Words: possibly by John Francis Wade
trans. Frederick Oakeley and others

Music: possibly by John Francis Wade

ADESTE FIDELES Irregular and Refrain

1. O come, all ye faith - ful, joy - ful and tri - um - phant, O come ye, O come ye to Beth - le - hem;
come and be - hold him, born the king of an - gels:

Chorus

O come,
O come, let us a - dore him, O come, let us a - dore him, O come, let us a - dore him, Christ the Lord.

2. God of God,
   Light of Light,
   lo, he abhors not the Virgin's womb;
   very God, begotten not created:

3. See how the shepherds,
   summoned to his cradle,
   leaving their flocks, draw nigh with lowly fear;
   we too will thither bend our joyful footsteps:

4. Lo, star-led chieftains,
   Magi, Christ adoring,
   offer him incense, gold and myrrh;
   we to the Christ-child bring our hearts' oblations:

5. Sing, choirs of angels,
   sing in exultation,
   sing, all ye citizens of heav'n above;
   glory to God in the highest:

6. Yea, Lord, we greet thee,
   born this happy morning,
   Jesu, to thee be glory giv'n;
   Word of the Father, now in flesh appearing:

666 O come and join the dance

Words and Music: Graham Kendrick

1.
2.
Domit3 Am7/D A7/D Domit3 C/D Domit3 Domit3
1. O
(verse 3 instrumental)
D Am7 A7
come and join the dance that all be - gan so long a - go, when
shed your hea - vy load and dance your wor - ries all a - way, for
laugh - ter ring and an - gels sing and joy be all a - round, for
D Am7 D C/D D
Christ the Lord was born in Beth - le - hem.
Through
He
And
Am7 A7
all the years of dark - ness still the dance goes on and on,
came to break the pow'r of sin and turn your night to day,
O,
if you seek with all your heart he sure - ly can be found,
D Am7 D C/D D
Chorus
take my hand and come and join the song.
Men
Re -

Am7 A7
Women Re-joice! Re-joice! All
joice! Re-joice! O lift your voice and sing, and
D Am7 D C/D D
Women Re-joice! Re-joice!
o-pen up your heart to wel-come him. Men Re-joice! Re-joice! All and
1, 2, 3.
Am7 A7 D Am7 D C/D D
wel-come now your King, for Christ the Lord was born in Beth-le-hem. 2. Come
3. Instr.
4. Let
4. 5.
D C/D D D.S. D C/D D Am7
hem. Re- hem. For Christ the Lord was born in Beth-le-
D C/D D Am7 D C/D D
hem. For Christ the Lord was born in Beth-le-hem.

667 O God, you're so big

Words and Music: Steve Burnhope
arr. Chris Mitchell

C Csus4 C Csus4
1. O God, you're so big, and I feel so small, it's
C Am7 F F/G
real - ly quite a - maz - ing that you no - tice me at all, al -
C Csus4 C Csus4
though you live in hea - ven, a long, long way a - way, you're
C Am7 F G7 C
Chorus
ev - 'ry-where on earth as well and close to me each day. No

F G Dm7 C C7
won - der, Lord, I wor - ship you, 'cause no one else is like you, no
F G C Gm7/C
won - der, Lord, I wor - ship you be - cause of who you are, no
F G C G/B Am
won - der I re - ly on you, Lord, I'm reach - ing out to you, I
F Dm
wor - ship you, I wor - ship you, I
F/G
wor - ship you.
Last time
C
Fine
To continue
C
2. There are

Csus4 C Csus4
mil - lions of peo - ple liv - ing in this land, but

C Am7 F F/G
ev - 'ry sin - gle one of them, Lord, you un - der - stand, I

C Csus4 C Csus4
don't know how you do that, it's a mys - te - ry to me, but

C Am7 F G7 C
Chorus D.S.
I'm just glad that you've got time for lis - ten - ing to me. No

668 O happy day!

Words and Music: Unknown
arr. Richard Lewis

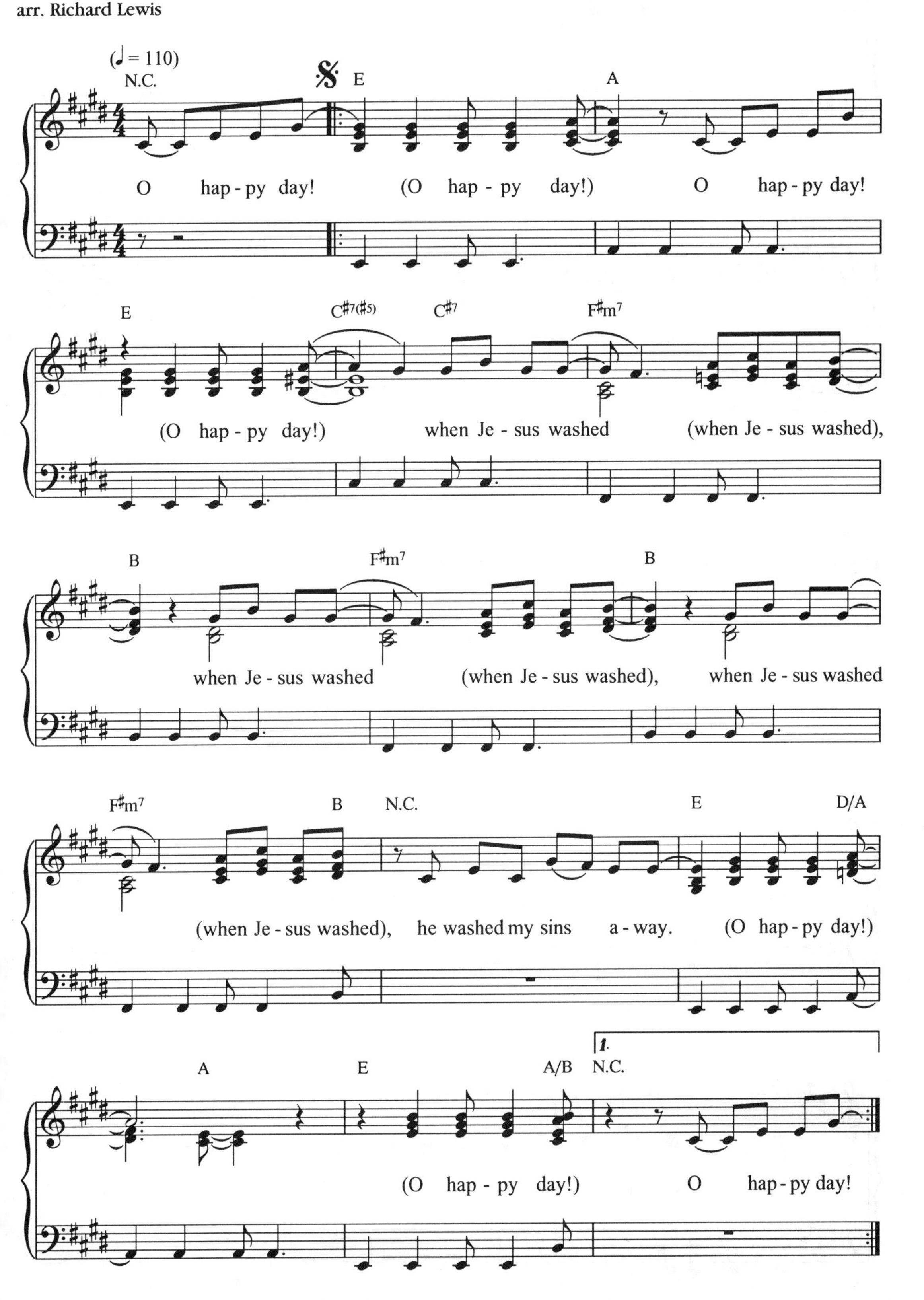

(♩ = 110)
N.C.
E
A
O hap-py day! (O hap-py day!) O hap-py day!
E
C♯7(♯5)
C♯7
F♯m7
(O hap-py day!) when Je-sus washed (when Je-sus washed),
B
F♯m7
B
when Je-sus washed (when Je-sus washed), when Je-sus washed
F♯m7
B
N.C.
E
D/A
(when Je-sus washed), he washed my sins a-way. (O hap-py day!)
A
E
A/B
1.
N.C.
(O hap-py day!) O hap-py day!

2.
F♯m
E
A
He taught me how to watch,
F♯m/A
E
A/E
E
watch and pray,
watch and pray;
N.C.
A6/B
E
and live re - joic - ing
A
E
ev - 'ry, ev - 'ry day,
1.
A/E
N.C.
A/B
Amaj7/B
D.S.
ev - 'ry day.
O hap - py day!

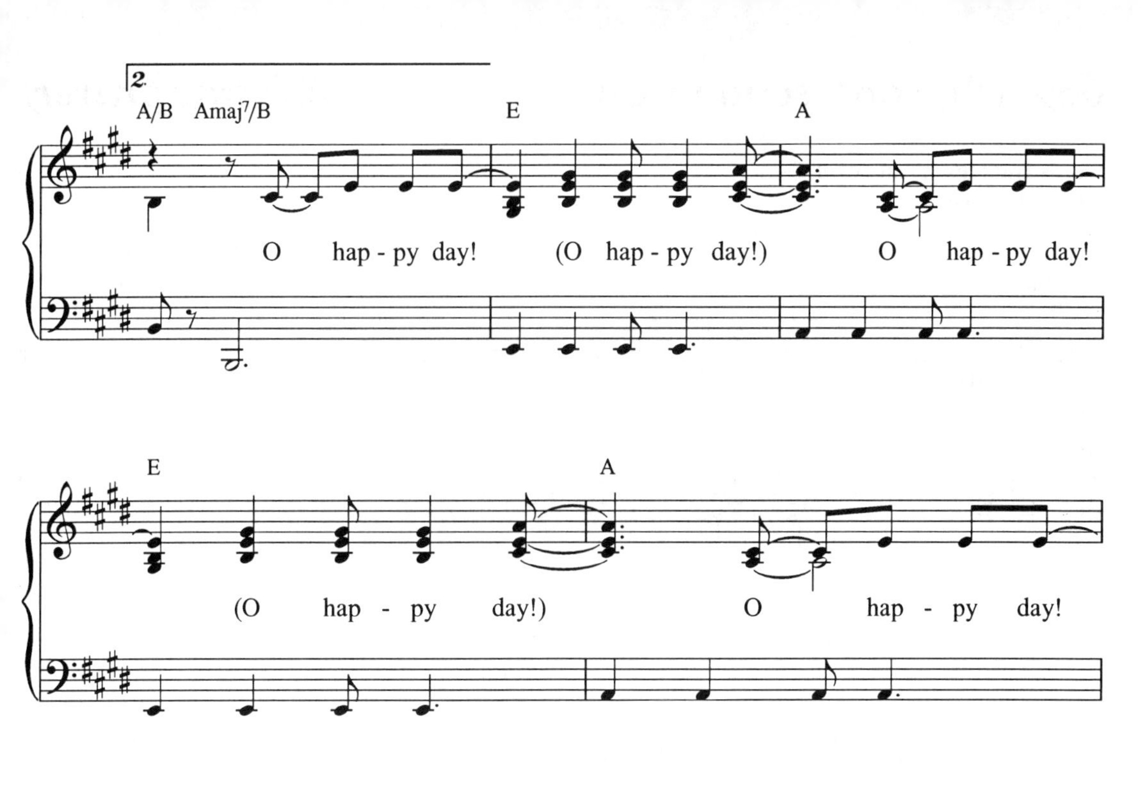
2.
A/B Amaj7/B
E
A
O hap - py day! (O hap - py day!) O hap - py day!
E
A
(O hap - py day!) O hap - py day!

E
D/A
A
D
A
E
(O hap - py day!) O hap - py day!

669 Oh, Lord, send us out *(Closing prayer)*

Words and Music: Sally Wolf
arr. Chris Mitchell

F
B♭/F
F
F/A
C7sus4
C7
Capo 3 D
G/D
D
D/F♯
A7sus4
A7
Chorus
Oh,

F
Dm
Gm7
C
C/B♭
D
Bm
Em7
A
A/G
Lord, send us out with your love to - day, let us

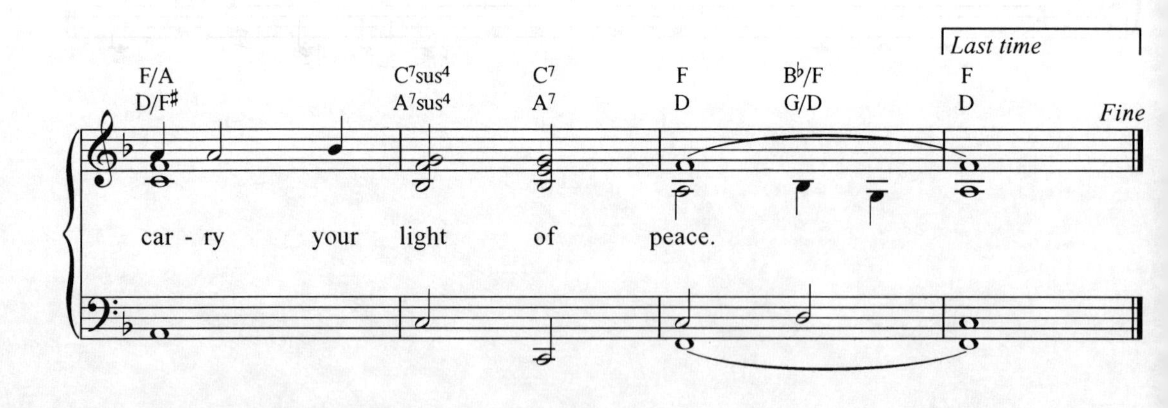

Last time
F/A
C7sus4
C7
F
B♭/F
F
D/F♯
A7sus4
A7
D
G/D
D
Fine
car - ry your light of peace.

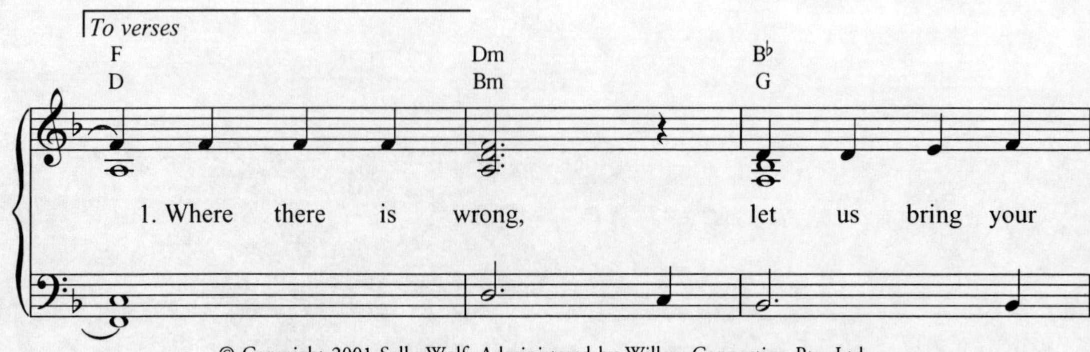

To verses
F
Dm
B♭
D
Bm
G
1. Where there is wrong, let us bring your

B♭/F F C/E Dm7 G7
G/D D A/C♯ Bm7 E7
jus - tice; where there is hun - ger, your

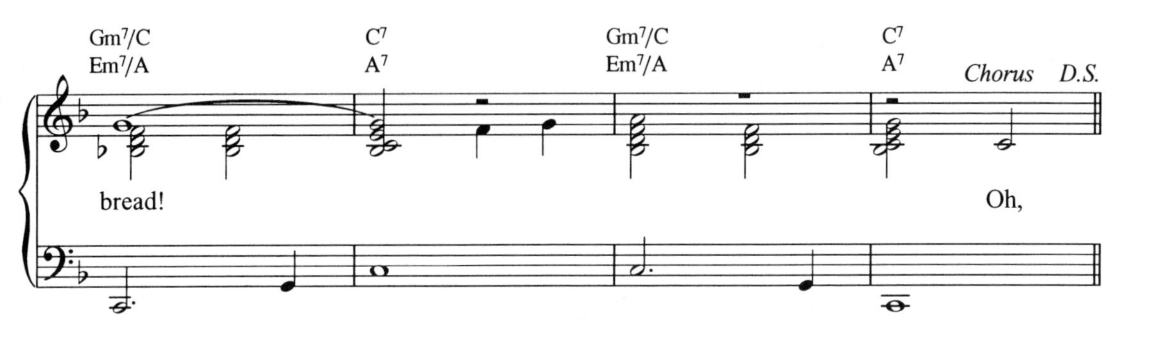
Gm7/C C7 Gm7/C C7
Em7/A A7 Em7/A A7
Chorus D.S.
bread! Oh,

2. Where there is pain,
   let us bring your comfort;
   where there is sadness, your joy!

670 Oh, praise the Lord *(Brand new song)*

Words and Music: Paul Crouch and David Mudie

F
D
Capo 3
C
A
Chorus
F
D
Oh, praise the Lord, sing a brand new song. Ev - 'ry - bo - dy join

B♭
G
C
A
F
D
in and sing a - long. Oh, praise the Lord, sing a brand new

To repeat / continue
Last time
B♭
G
C
A
F
D
F
D
Fine
song. Ev - 'ry - bo - dy join in and sing a - long.

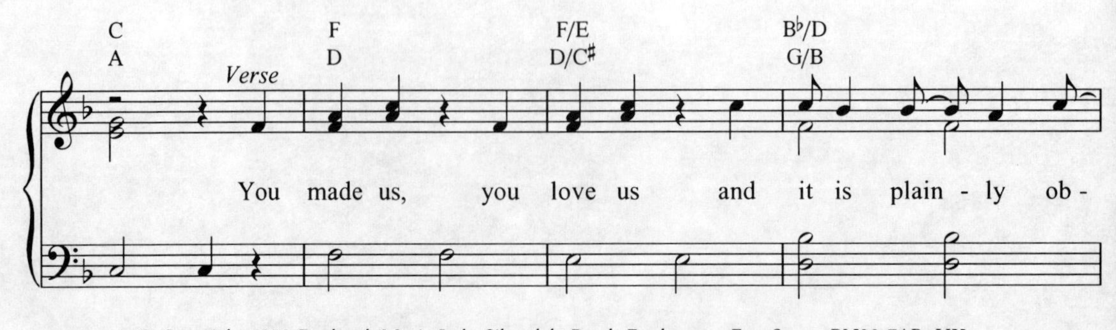

C
A
Verse
F
D
F/E
D/C♯
B♭/D
G/B
You made us, you love us and it is plain - ly ob -

F/C D/A B♭ G C A F D
- vi - ous that you can - not re - strain your gen - 'rous hand.
C A F D F/E D/C♯
So you will hold us and keep us, en -
B♭/D G/B F/C D/A B♭ G Gm7 Em7
fold us in your lov - ing arms and guide us in the pur -
C7 A7 F D D.S.
- po - ses you've planned. Oh, praise the Lord,

After the final chorus, the chorus is repeated while the following is spoken:

It's a new song we sing, it's a song for the King.
He's by our side through thick and thin.
He stooped down low to become our friend,
and he'll be with us to the end.

Chorus

671 Oh town of Bethlehem

Words and Music: James Wright
arr. Chris Mitchell

Capo 3 Bm
Dm C/D A/B B♭/D G/B
1. Oh town of Beth - le - hem be - neath the stars of heav'n, what is the sec - ret you
A7 F♯7 Dm Bm B♭maj7 Gmaj7 C A Am7 F♯m7
hold this night? God's own be - got - ten Son, hea - ven's a - noint - ed one
B♭maj7 Gmaj7 Am7 F♯m7 1. Dm Bm 2. Dm Bm C A F D Dm7 Bm7
Chorus
has come down. down. Come now and be -
Gm7 Em7 C7 A7 F D Dm7 Bm7 B♭/C G/A
hold the new-born King, glo - ry of Is - ra - el,

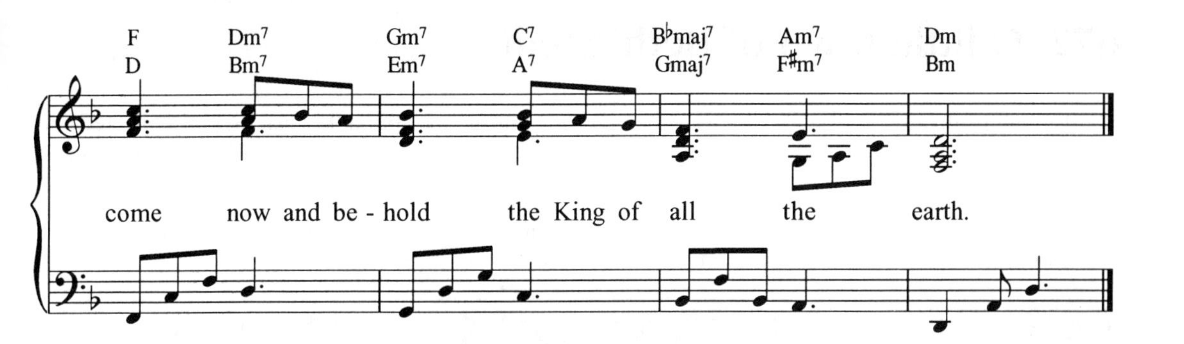
F
D
Dm7
Bm7
Gm7
Em7
C7
A7
B♭maj7
Gmaj7
Am7
F♯m7
Dm
Bm
come now and be - hold the King of all the earth.

2. Oh what a glorious plan
 that brought your love to man;
 born in a stable so cold and bare.
 From heaven's majesty
 to earth's humanity
 love came down.

672 O little town of Bethlehem

Words: Phillips Brooks, alt.
Music: traditional English melody collected and arr. Ralph Vaughan Williams
FOREST GREEN DCM
C F B♭ F Gm F Dm C Dm Gm F Gm7 C
Capo 5 G C F C Dm C Am G Am Dm C Dm7 G
1. O lit - tle town of Beth - le - hem, how still we see thee
F C F B♭ F Gm F Dm C Dm Gm F Gm7 C
C G C F C Dm C Am G Am Dm C Dm7 G
lie! A - bove thy deep and dream - less sleep the si - lent stars go
F Dm Am C F Dm C F Gm Dm
C Am Em G C Am G C Dm Am
by. Yet in thy dark streets shi - neth the e - ver - last - ing
C F B♭ F Gm F Dm C Dm Gm F Csus4 C F
G C F C Dm C Am G Am Dm C Gsus4 G C
light; the hopes and fears of all the years are met in thee to - night.

2. O morning stars, together
   proclaim the holy birth,
   and praises sing to God the King,
   and peace upon the earth.
   For Christ is born of Mary;
   and, gathered all above,
   while mortals sleep, the angels keep
   their watch of wond'ring love.

3. How silently, how silently,
   the wondrous gift is giv'n!
   So God imparts to human hearts
   the blessings of his heav'n.
   No ear may hear his coming;
   but in this world of sin,
   where meek souls will receive him, still
   the dear Christ enters in.

4. O holy child of Bethlehem,
   descend to us, we pray;
   cast out our sin, and enter in,
   be born in us today.
   We hear the Christmas angels
   the great glad tidings tell:
   O come to us, abide with us,
   our Lord Emmanuel.

2. O morning stars, together
proclaim the holy birth,
and praises sing to God the King,
and peace upon the earth.
For Christ is born of Mary,
and, gathered all above,
while mortals sleep, the angels keep
their watch of wond'ring love.

3. How silently, how silently,
the wondrous gift is giv'n!
So God imparts to human hearts
[illegible]
[illegible]
[illegible]
[illegible]
the dear Christ enters in.

4. O holy Child of Bethlehem,
descend to us, we pray;
cast out our sin, and enter in,
be born in us today.
We hear the Christmas angels
the great glad tidings tell:
O come to us, abide with us,
our Lord Emmanuel.

673 O Lord, all the world belongs to you
(Turning the world upside down)

Words and Music: Patrick Appleford

G D7 G C Em
1. O Lord, all the world be - longs to you, and
Am E Am A D D7
you are al - ways mak - ing all things new. What is
G Em Am D7
wrong you for - give, and the new life you give is what's
To next verse
Last time
G D7 G C G G
turn - ing the world up - side down. 2. The

2. The world's only loving to its friends,
   but you have brought us love that never ends;
   loving enemies too,
   and this loving with you
   is what's turning the world upside down.

3. This world lives divided and apart.
   You draw all men together and we start
   in your body to see
   that in fellowship, we
   can be turning the world upside down.

4. The world wants the wealth to live in state,
   but you show us a new way to be great:
   like a servant you came,
   and if we do the same,
   we'll be turning the world upside down.

5. O Lord, all the world belongs to you,
   and you are always making all things new.
   Send your Spirit on all
   in your church whom you call
   to be turning the world upside down.

674 O Lord, I will sing your praise *(Song of liberty)*

Words and Music: Jim Bailey

Steadily
G
D
Em
3
O Lord, I will sing your praise, O Lord, for the

C
G
D
ma - ny ways that, Lord, you have been so good to me.

C
G
O Lord, I am

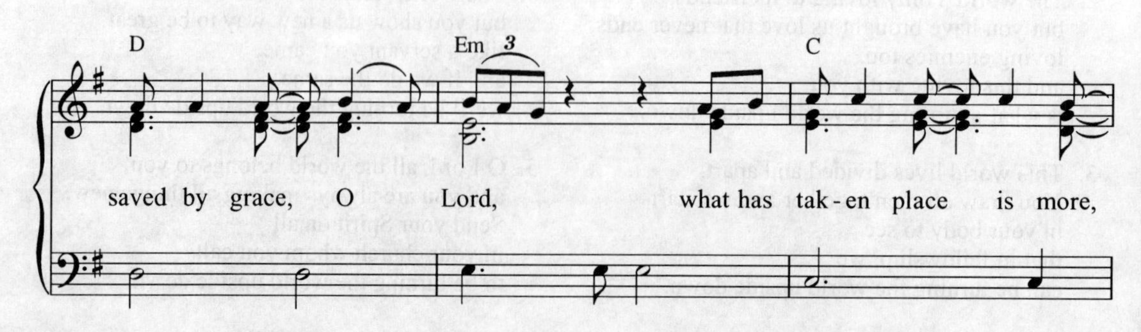

D
Em
3
C
saved by grace, O Lord, what has tak-en place is more,

G D G
so much more than I can say. Now I am
C D G C D G
saved to save, and there's no o - ther way: sal - va - tion's
C D G D G
in the name of Je - sus. You came and
C D G C D G
set me free, my song will e - ver be a song of
1. 2.
C D G D G G
li - ber - ty in Je - sus. O

675 On a cross he died *(Tomb breaker)*

Words and Music: Jennifer Reay
arr. Chris Mitchell

(♩ = 140)
Capo 3
Gm7 Em7
Fmaj7 Dmaj7
Gm7 Em7
On a cross he died, he was cru - ci - fied.
F D
He did it for us, he did it for us.
Gm7 Em7
1. Dm7 Bm7
2. Dm7 Bm7
But that's not the end of the sto - ry;
Gm Em
he was strong-er than death.
That's not the end of the sto - ry; for

F
D
Dsus4
Bsus4
D
B
e - ver he's a - live!
He is a
Gm
Em
F
D
tomb break - er,
mind shak - er;
he is a - live!
Gm
Em
He is a
death beat - er,
life greet - er;
1.
2.
F
D
Gm
Em
F
D
he is a - live!
He is a
he is a - live!
Last time
Gm
Em
D.C.
F
D
G
E
Fine
he is a - live!

676 Once in royal David's city

Words: Cecil Frances Alexander;
v.4: Michael Forster

Music: Henry John Gauntlett

IRBY 87 87 77
Capo 3
F C7 F C7 F Dm
D A7 D A7 D Bm
1. Once in roy - al Da - vid's ci - ty stood a
F Gm C F C7 F G7
D Em A D A7 D E7
low - ly cat - tle shed, where a mo - ther laid her
C7 F C F Gm C F B♭
A7 D A D Em A D G
ba - by in a man - ger for his bed: Ma - ry
F Gm C7 F B♭ F Gm C7 F
D Em A7 D G D Em A7 D
was that mo - ther mild, Je - sus Christ her lit - tle child.

2. He came down to earth from heaven,
who is God and Lord of all,
and his shelter was a stable,
and his cradle was a stall;
with the poor and meek and lowly,
lived on earth our Saviour holy.

3. And through all his wondrous childhood
day by day like us he grew;
he was little, weak and helpless,
tears and smiles like us he knew;
and he feeleth for our sadness,
and he shareth in our gladness.

4. Still among the poor and lowly
hope in Christ is brought to birth,
with the promise of salvation
for the nations of the earth;
still in him our life is found
and our hope of heav'n is crowned.

5. And our eyes at last shall see him
through his own redeeming love,
for that child so dear and gentle
is our Lord in heav'n above;
and he leads his children on
to the place where he is gone.

6. Not in that poor lowly stable,
with the oxen standing by,
we shall see him, but in heaven,
set at God's right hand on high;
when like stars his children crowned,
all in white shall wait around.

677 Our Father in heaven *(The Lord's Prayer)*

Words: based on Matthew 6:9-13;
Dave Bankhead and Mike Burn

Music: Dave Bankhead and Mike Burn

D D/F♯ A Bm G Em7
Our Fa - ther in hea - ven, hal - lowed be your

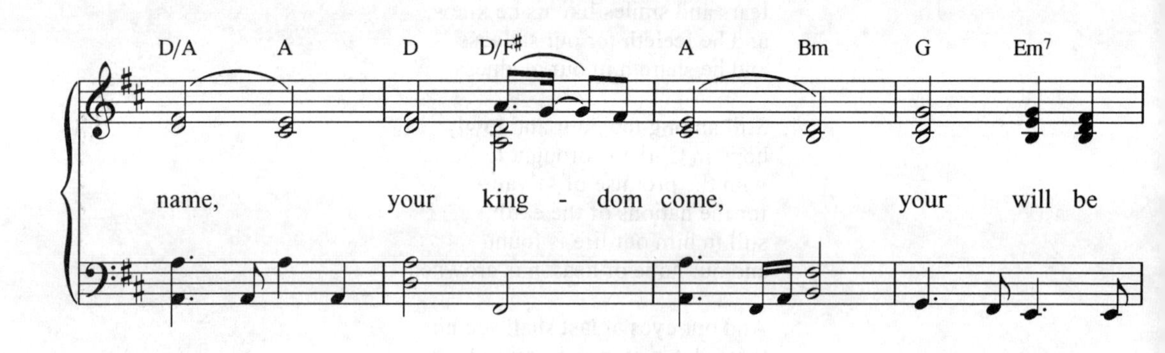

D/A A D D/F♯ A Bm G Em7
name, your king - dom come, your will be

A D D/F♯ A Bm
done on earth as it is in hea-ven;

G Em7 D/A A D D/F♯
give us to - day our dai - ly bread, and for - give us our

G A Bm A G D/F♯ A D Gmaj7 A
sins as we for - give those who sin a - gainst us.

G D/A A G
Lead us not in-to temp - ta - tion, but de-liv - er us from

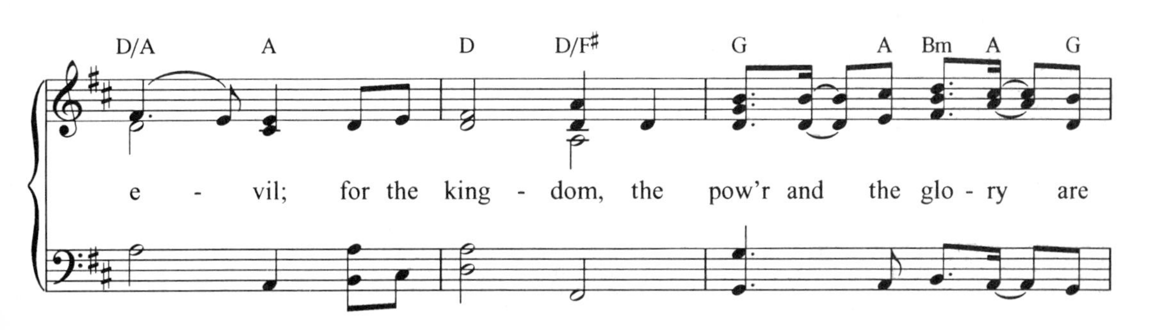
D/A A D D/F♯ G A Bm A G
e - vil; for the king - dom, the pow'r and the glo - ry are

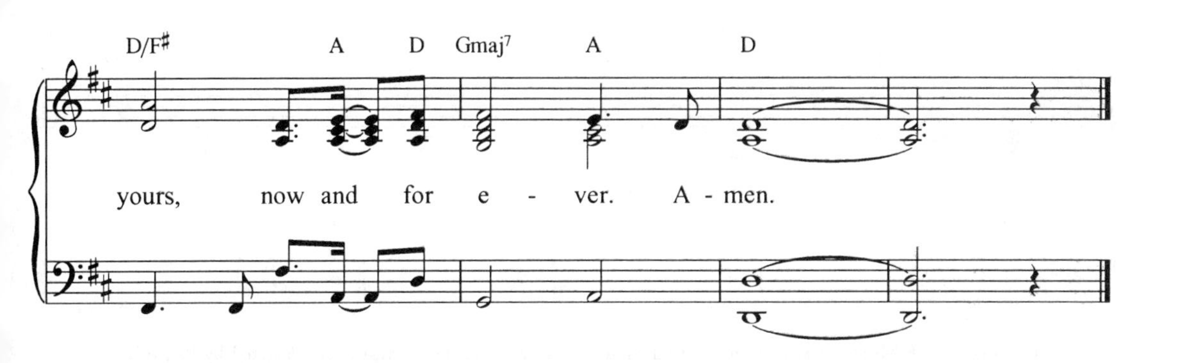
D/F♯ A D Gmaj7 A D
yours, now and for e - ver. A - men.

678 Our Father, who art in heaven *(The Lord's Prayer)*

Words: Paul Field and Stephen Deal

Music: traditional Scottish melody adapted by Paul Field and Stephen Deal

D A D D/F♯ G
Our Fa - ther, who art in hea - ven, hal - lowed be thy name. Thy
D A D/F♯ G Asus4 A D G/D
king - dom come, thy will be done on earth as in heav'n. Give
D A D D/F♯
us to - day our dai - ly bread and for - give our
lead us not to the time of trial but de - li - ver us from
G D A D/F♯
sins, as we for - give each one of those who
e - vil, for thine is the king - dom, the
1, 3.
2.
4.
Harmony
G Asus4 A D G/D D D.C. D G/D
sins a - gainst us; and
pow - er and the glo - ry. glo - ry. Let

D D/F♯ A G/B D D/F♯
all the peo - ple say 'A-men' in ev - 'ry tribe and
G G/B D D/F♯ A D/F♯
tongue; let ev - 'ry heart's de - sire be joined to
G Asus4 D G D
see the king - dom come. Let ev - 'ry hope and
A G/A D G
ev - 'ry dream be born in love a - gain; let
D A D/F♯ G A D
all the world sing with one voice, let the peo - ple say 'A - men'.

679 Our fingers that click *(Everything comes from God)*

Words and Music: Nick Harding

Capo 3
F D
Dm Bm
Gm Em
C A
F D
Gm Em
1. Our fin-gers that click come from God, our fin-gers that click
B♭ G
C A
C7 A7
F D
C A
A F♯
Dm Bm
come from God, our fin - gers that click come from God;
C A
C7 A7
1.
F D
2.
F D
ev - 'ry - thing comes from God. 2. Our God.

2. Our ears that hear . . .

3. Our feet that stamp . . .

4. Our head that nods . . .

680 Our song's about the greatest man

(The greatest man)

Words: John Lane

Music: Traditional melody, *Wild Colonial Boy,* arr. John Lane

(♩. = 108)
D
Em7/G
A
D
1. Our
song's a - bout the great - est man the world has e - ver seen. His
life was good in ev - 'ry way, not self - ish, sly or mean. The
poor folk and the child - ren en - joyed his lov - ing care, now
we can know his kind - ness too, as if we had been there.
D/F#
Em
A7

To next verse
Last time
G
A
D
D
2. Our

2. Our song's about the greatest friend,
and Jesus is his name,
he calls us all to follow him,
for that is why he came.
He knows us more than anyone;
he won't forget our names,
though we might change or let him down,
he still remains the same.

3. Our song's about the King who came
to set his people free.
He healed the sick and cured the deaf,
he helped the blind to see.
His teachings show us how to live
the way we're meant to be.
And when we make this man our King,
it's then we're really free.

4. Our song's about the one who died,
to show he loves us all.
We feel so weak to do what's right,
we often trip and fall.
But Jesus rose to show his pow'r,
now sin and death can't win,
so he can clear our wrongs away
and help us start again.

5. Our song's about the Lord who lives,
he's Ruler, Boss and King.
His death is past, this rule will last,
he's King of ev'rything.
His love won't fail, nor strength grow frail,
we always know he's there.
Don't fear what comes, he knows the way,
and we can trust his care.

6. So Jesus' love can fill our lives
as he has filled our song.
The light of all the world he is,
he shows up all that's wrong.
He gives us hope, forgives our faults
and colours all our days,
we'll open up our lives to him;
we'll give to him our praise.

681 Over all the earth *(Lord, reign in me)*

Words and Music: Brenton Brown

C G F Gsus4 C G
1. O-ver all the earth, you reign on high, ev - 'ry moun-tain stream,

F Gsus4 Am G F Gsus4
ev - 'ry sun - set sky. But my one re - quest, Lord, my on - ly aim

Dm7 F G C Chorus G F
is that you'd reign in me a - gain. Lord, reign in me,

G C G F G
reign in your pow'r o - ver all my dreams, in my dark - est hour.

Am G F G Dm7
You are the Lord of all I am, so won't you
F G C G F
reign in me a-gain.
Am G F C

2. Over ev'ry thought, over ev'ry word,
may my life reflect the beauty of my Lord;
'cause you mean more to me than any earthly thing,
so won't you reign in me again.

682 O what love

Words and Music: Capt. Alan J. Price, CA
arr. Philip Eley

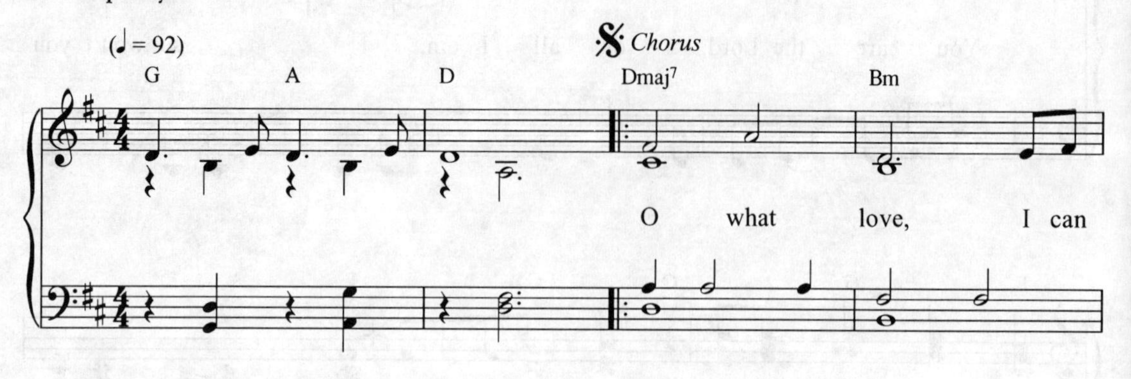

(♩ = 92)
Chorus
G
A
D
Dmaj7
Bm
O what love, I can

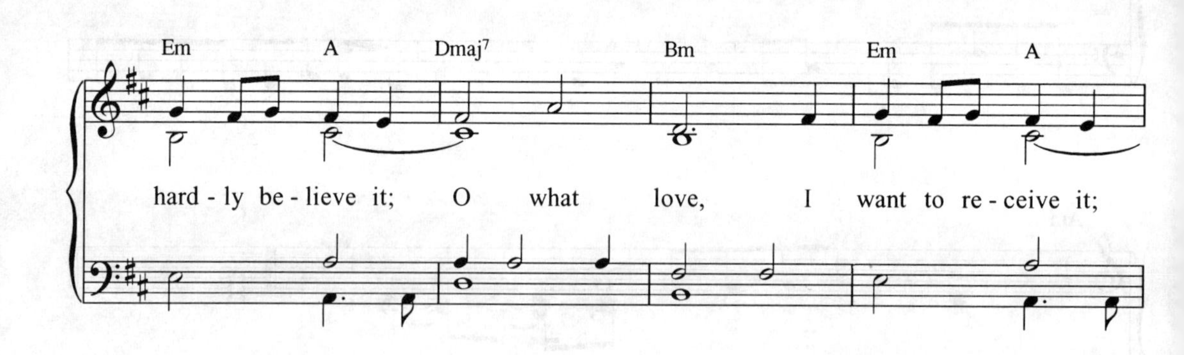

Em
A
Dmaj7
Bm
Em
A
hard - ly be - lieve it; O what love, I want to re - ceive it;

Last time to Coda
To repeat
Dmaj7
Bm
G
A
G
A
D
O what love, I just want to feel it more and more and more.

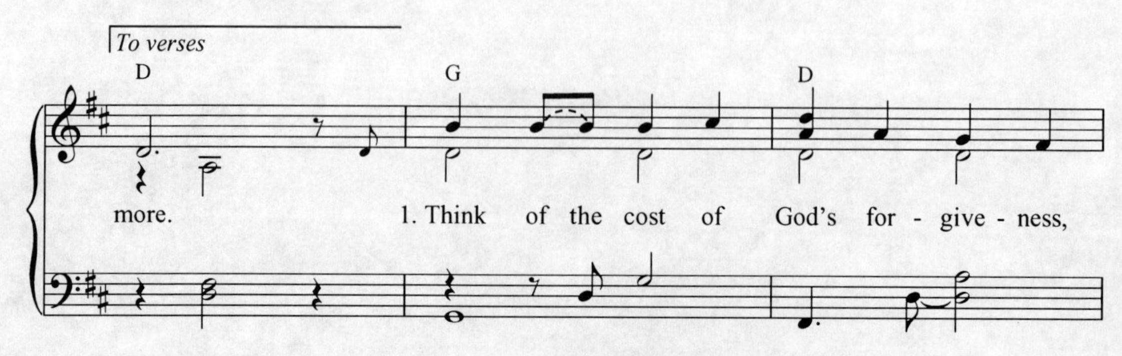

To verses
D
G
D
more. 1. Think of the cost of God's for - give - ness,

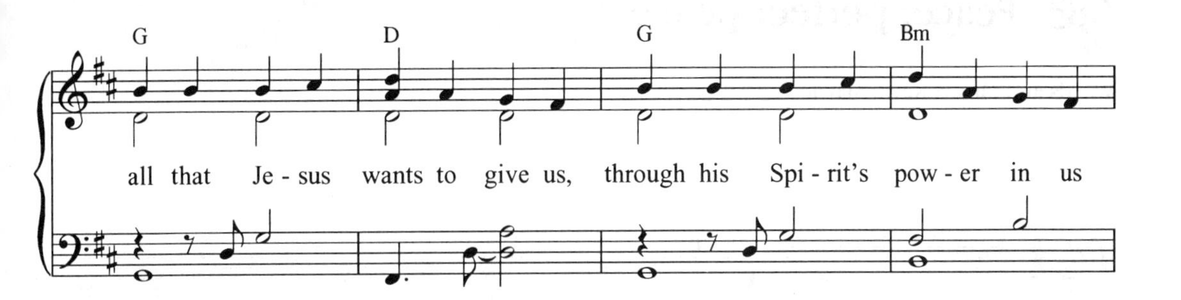
G
D
G
Bm
all that Je - sus wants to give us, through his Spi - rit's pow - er in us

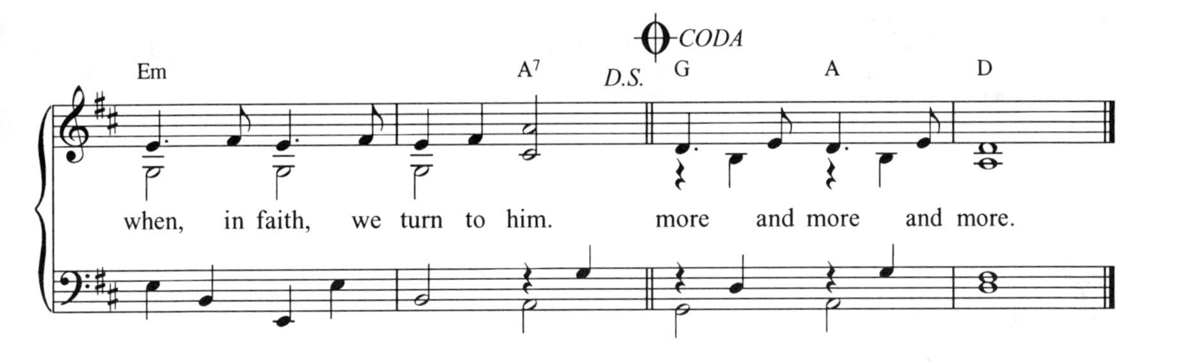
CODA
Em
A7
D.S.
G
A
D
when, in faith, we turn to him. more and more and more.

2. Before he made the world,
   God chose us to be his
   through faith in Jesus.
   He will always touch and bless us
   when, in faith, we come to him.

683 Peace, perfect peace

Words and Music: Kevin Mayhew

C
Dm/C
G/C
1. Peace, per - fect peace, is the gift of Christ our

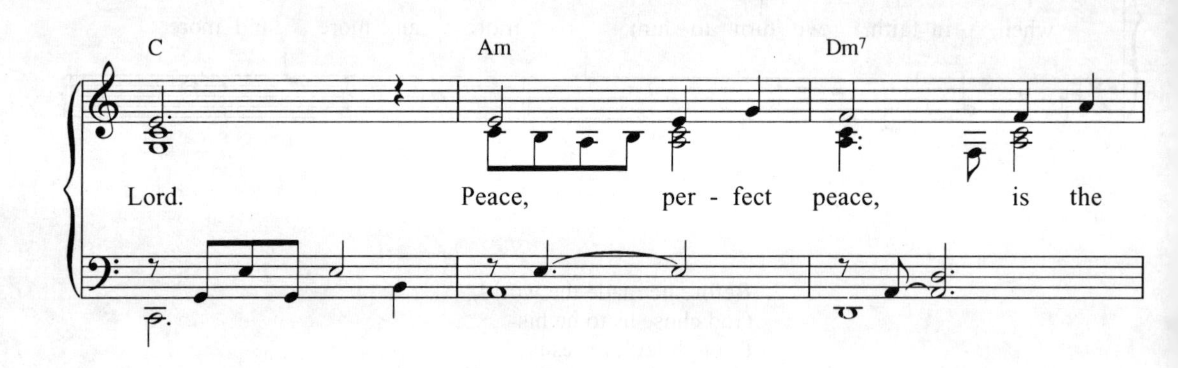

C
Am
Dm7
Lord. Peace, per - fect peace, is the

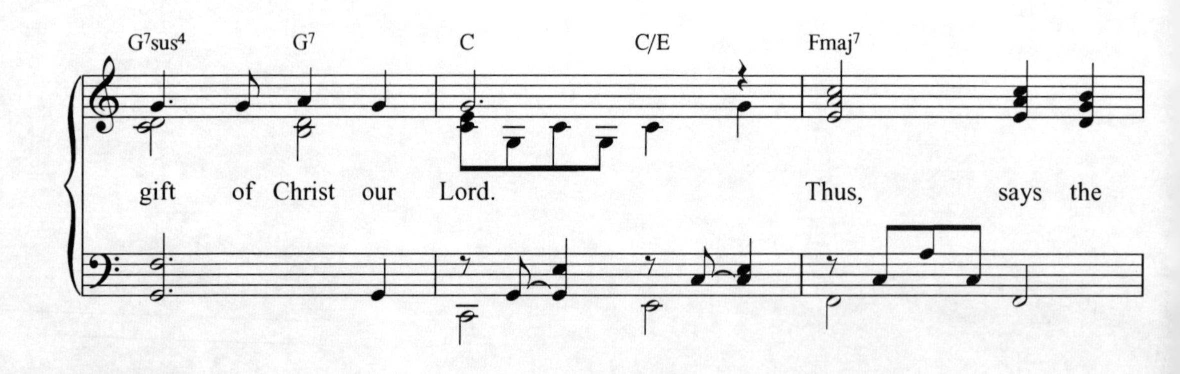

G7sus4
G7
C
C/E
Fmaj7
gift of Christ our Lord. Thus, says the

Dm7
G
C
Lord, will the world know my friends.

A7sus4 A Dm Dm7 G7sus4 G C
Peace, per - fect peace, is the gift of Christ our Lord.

2. Love, perfect love, is the gift of Christ our Lord.
Love, perfect love, is the gift of Christ our Lord.
Thus, says the Lord, will the world know my friends.
Love, perfect love, is the gift of Christ our Lord.

3. Faith, perfect faith, is the gift of Christ our Lord.
Faith, perfect faith, is the gift of Christ our Lord.
Thus, says the Lord, will the world know my friends.
Faith, perfect faith, is the gift of Christ our Lord.

4. Hope, perfect hope, is the gift of Christ our Lord.
Hope, perfect hope, is the gift of Christ our Lord.
Thus, says the Lord, will the world know my friends.
Hope, perfect hope, is the gift of Christ our Lord.

5. Joy, perfect joy, is the gift of Christ our Lord.
Joy, perfect joy, is the gift of Christ our Lord.
Thus, says the Lord, will the world know my friends.
Joy, perfect joy, is the gift of Christ our Lord.

684 People can be like a cake *(Christian cakes)*

Words and Music: Christine Dalton
arr Chris Mitchell

C Bb G C
1. Peo - ple can be like a cake – they de - cide which one to bake.
2. Christ - ian rock-cakes are the best, you won't want to be the rest.
Bb G C
Je - sus left a re - ci - pe to bake some Chris - ti - a - ni - ty.
God's in - gre - di - ents you see make us how we're meant to be.
F G
So, be - fore you cook, look in - to his book.
So, be - fore you cook, go and get the book.
F/G Chorus G7 C F C
'Cause you don't want to be a Christ - ian cream puff,
F C G7 C G
all puffed up and full of air. No, you

C F C F C
don't want to be a dough - nut Christ - ian, hole in the mid - dle –
F C G7 C
may be lit - tle but it's not all there!
F B♭ F B♭ F
Or a Christ - ian choc - 'late crack - le full of noise! Snap,
G7 C
crack - le and pop! I want to be a
F C F C G7 C
Christ - ian rock-cake, full of fruit with God on top.

F
C
I'll mix up love, joy, peace, pa - tience, kind - ness in a bowl
F
then add good - ness, faith - ful - ness, gen - tle - ness and
D7
G
D7
G
stacks of self - con - trol, stacks of self - con - trol.
C
F
C
That's the Bi - ble's re - ci - pe, Ga -
F
C
G7
C
D.C. for v.2
la - tians five: twen - ty - two, twen - ty - three.

685 Praise God, all you people *(A very short song)*

Words and Music: Dave Godfrey

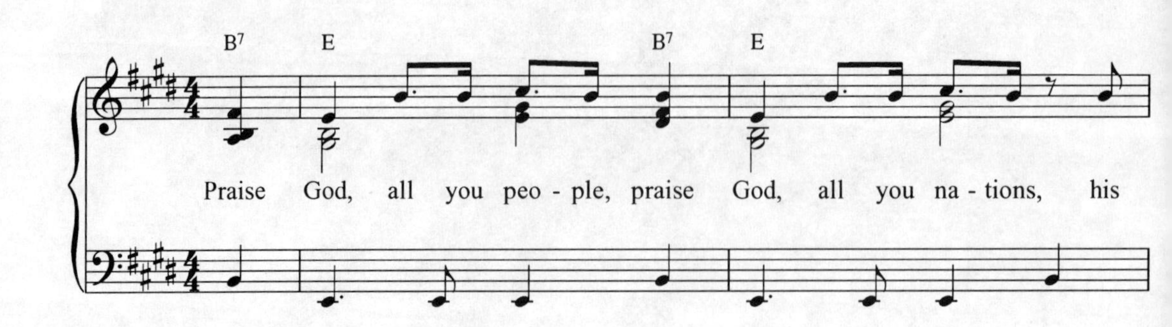
B7 E B7 E
Praise God, all you peo - ple, praise God, all you na - tions, his

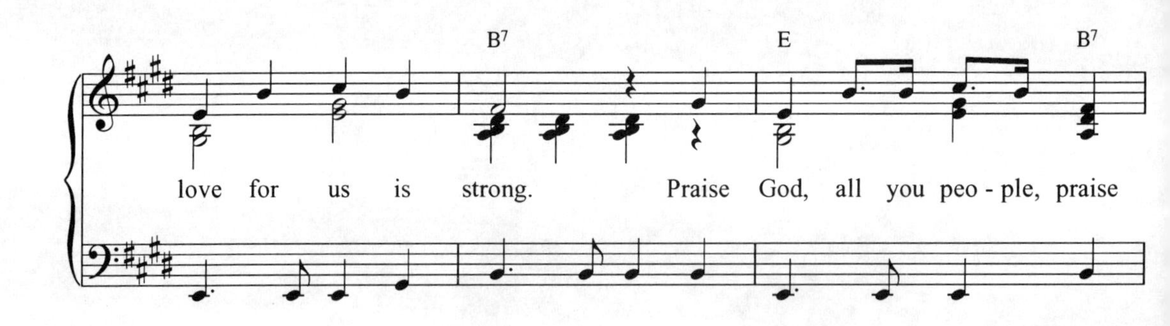
B7 E B7
love for us is strong. Praise God, all you peo - ple, praise

E B7 E B7 E B7
God, all you na - tions, his faith - ful - ness goes on (and on and

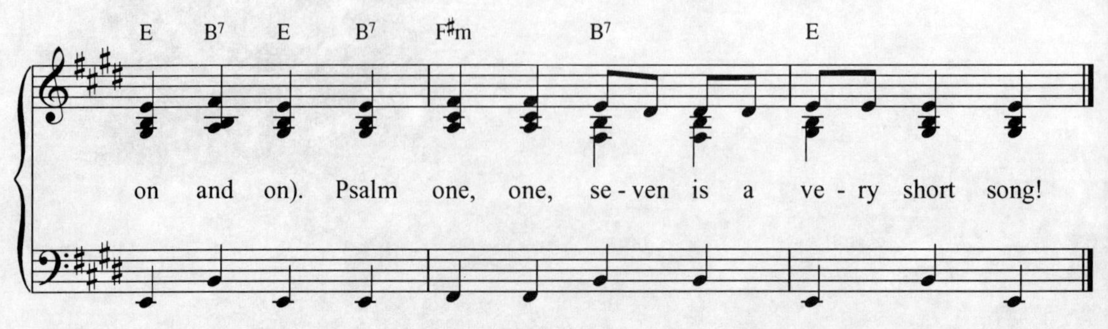
E B7 E B7 F♯m B7 E
on and on). Psalm one, one, se - ven is a ve - ry short song!

686 Praise him *(All God's faithful children)*

Words and Music: Ian Smale
arr. Chris Mitchell

E A/E E B7
1. Praise him, praise him, bring prai - ses to the Lord our God.
E A F♯ B
(Repeat verse)
All God's faith - ful child-ren must learn to praise him.
B7 E Chorus A
learn to praise him. Sing hal - le - lu, hal - le - lu, sing
E B7 E A
hal - le - lu - jah to our God. All God's faith - ful child - ren sing
F♯ B B7 E
hal - le - lu - jah, God. Sing hal - le - lu - jah, God.

2. Worship him, worship him,
bring worship to the Lord our God.
All God's faithful children
must learn to worship him.

687 Prayer can make a difference

Words and Music: Mike Burn

Chorus
Em
C
Prayer can make a dif - f'rence, prayer can make a dif - f'rence,
Am7
Bm7
Em
prayer can make a dif - f'rence, so pray!
C
Prayer can make a dif - f'rence, prayer can make a dif - f'rence,
To verse 1
To verse 2 ϕ / Last time
Am7
Bm7
Em
Em
prayer can make a dif - f'rence, so pray! 1. Through
C
D
Em
C
D
prayer our God can heal. We be - lieve in mi - ra -

Em C D G D/F♯ Em
cles; through prayer a whole si - tu - a - tion can change, through
Fmaj7 C Dsus4 D Dsus4 D
D.C.
prayer a per - son can be born a - gain.
C D Em C D
2. No - thing has such pow - er as a prayer to God my Fa -
Em C D G D/F♯ Em
- ther. There's no one else who can do what he can, I want to
F C Dsus4 D Dsus4 D
D.C.
live my life ac-cord-ing to his plan.

688 Reach to the Lord *(Hey, hey, Jesus)*

Words and Music: J. Macpherson
arr. Chris Mitchell

E D E D E
1. Reach to the Lord, reach out to the Lord. Reach to the Lord, reach out! Hey!

A D A F♯m D
Hey, hey, Je-sus, it's good to be here, reach-ing out to your

B E A D A
fa-mi-ly. Hey, hey, Je-sus, it's good to be here.

D E A D.C.
Reach to the Lord, reach out to the Lord, reach out! Hey!

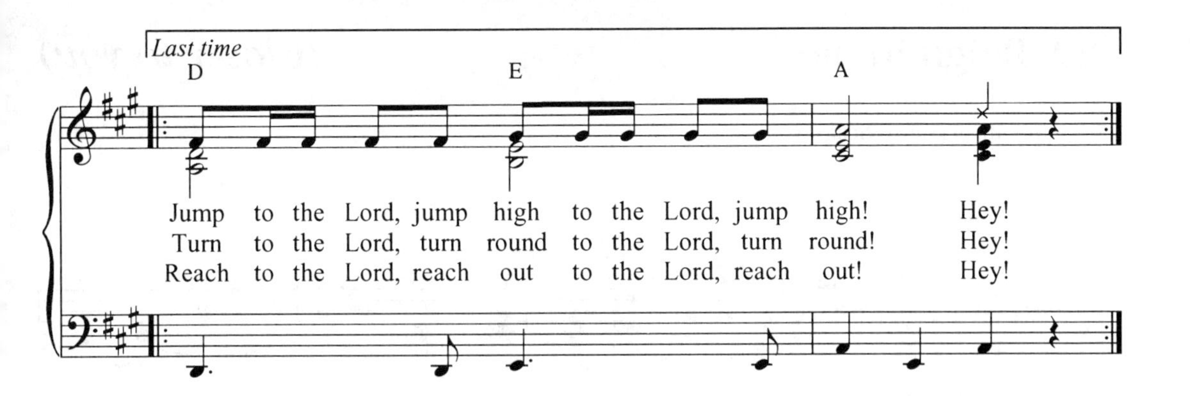
Last time
D
E
A
Jump to the Lord, jump high to the Lord, jump high! Hey!
Turn to the Lord, turn round to the Lord, turn round! Hey!
Reach to the Lord, reach out to the Lord, reach out! Hey!

2. Turn to the Lord, turn round to the Lord,
turn to the Lord, turn round! Hey! *(repeat)*
Hey, hey, Jesus, it's good to be here,
turning round with your family.
Hey, hey, Jesus, it's good to be here.
Turn to the Lord, turn round to the Lord,
turn round! Hey!

3. Jump to the Lord, jump high to the Lord,
jump to the Lord, jump high! Hey! *(repeat)*
Hey, hey, Jesus, it's good to be here,
jumping high with your family.
Hey, hey, Jesus, it's good to be here.
Jump to the Lord, jump high to the Lord,
jump high! Hey!

4. Shout to the Lord, shout loud to the Lord,
shout to the Lord, shout loud! Hey! *(repeat)*
Hey, hey, Jesus, it's good to be here,
shouting loud with your family.
Hey, hey, Jesus, it's good to be here.
Shout to the Lord, shout loud to the Lord,
shout loud! Hey!

689 Reign in me *(Closer to you)*

Words and Music: Andy Pickford

Steady 6 feel
D
Bm7
1. Reign in me, reign in me

G
D/F♯
1.
Em7
A
in all of my life, Lord, won't you reign in me.

2.
Em7
A
D
G Chorus
D/F♯
A
reign in me. Clo-ser to you is where I should

D
G
D/F♯
Em7
be, so I hear your voice and learn to o-

A
G
D/F♯
A
bey.
In all that I do,
and all that I
D
1.
Bm
G
G/B
A/C♯
D
D.C.
say,
Lord, my de - sire
is that you reign
in
me.
2.
Bm7
G
G/B
A/C♯
D
Lord, my de - sire
is that you reign in me.

2. Be with me, be with me
in all of my life, Lord,
won't you be with me.

690 Rejoice! For the Lord is reigning

Words and Music: Chris Jackson
arr. Dave Bankhead

D
G
A
D
Re - joice! For the Lord is reign - ing. Re - joice!

G
A
D
For Je - sus is King. Re - joice! For the

G
D
G
D
A
D
Fine
Lord is reign - ing, Je - sus is com - ing and he's com-ing as King.

Bm
A
G
A
Bm
A
Shout and sing to the King of cre - a - tion, shout and sing to the Lord

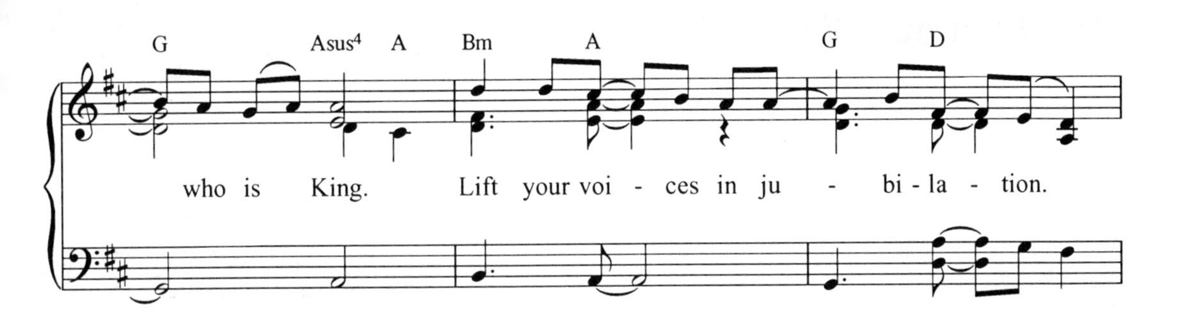
G
Asus4
A
Bm
A
G
D
who is King. Lift your voi - ces in ju - bi - la - tion.

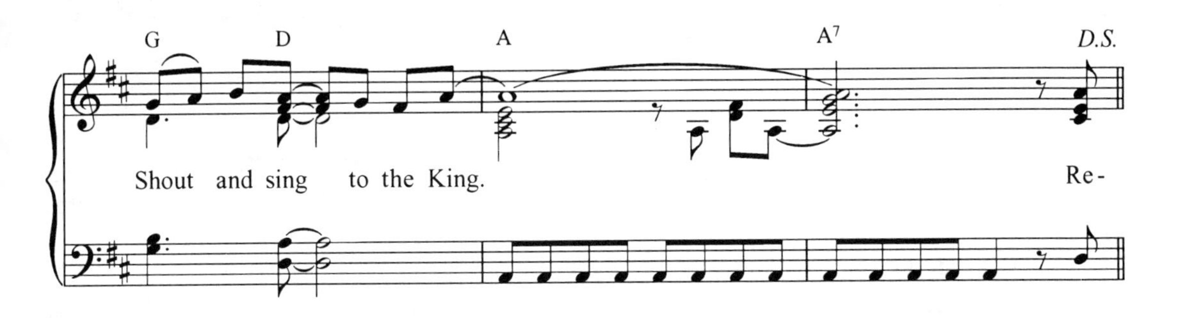
G
D
A
A7
D.S.
Shout and sing to the King. Re-

691 Rich man Zac

Words and Music: Peter Mangold arr. Chris Mitchell

E
B
1. Rich man Zac, short as can be, heard Je - sus was com - ing and he
want - ed to see. So he climbed right up a sy - ca - more tree, when
A B E B7 E
Je - sus passed that way.
2. Je - sus looked up, said 'Get
out of that tree, I want to stay at your place to - day.' So
Zac climbed down and wel - comed him in; when Je - sus passed that way.

E C7 F
3. The peo-ple who saw said 'What's he done? He's
4. Zac stood up and said to them all 'I'll
C F
gone to the house of a weal-thy man, a tax - col - lec - tor's
give half of my things to the poor, a - ny - one I've cheat - ed four
1. 2.
B♭ C F C7 F D7
place to stay.' When Je - sus passed that way.
times I'll pay.' When Je - sus passed that way.
G D G
5. Zac then heard Je - sus say, 'Sal - va - tion came to this house to - day.' He
C D
came to seek and he came to save; when Je - sus passed that way,
G Em7 C D G
when Je - sus passed that way.

692 Right at the start *(Creation song)*

Words and Music: Amanda Lofts
arr. Chris Mitchell

E
B7
1. Right at the start God made the world, he made the world, yes, he
E
B7
made the world. Right at the start God made the world,
E
oh, what a beau - ti - ful sight.

2. On day one, God made night and day,
he made night and day,
yes, he made night and day.
On day one, God made night and day,
oh, what a beautiful sight.

3. On day two, God made the sky,
he made the sky, yes, he made the sky.
On day two, God made the sky,
oh, what a beautiful sight.

4. On day three, God made land and sea,
he made plants and trees, he made land and sea.
On day three, God made plants and trees,
oh, what a beautiful sight.

5. On day four, God made sun, moon and stars,
sun, moon and stars, sun, moon and stars.
On day four, God made sun, moon and stars,
oh, what a beautiful sight.

6. On day five, God made fish and the birds,
fish and the birds, yes, fish and the birds.
On day five, God made fish and the birds,
oh, what a beautiful sight.

7. On day six, God made animals and us,
animals and us, yes, animals and us.
On day six, God made animals and us,
oh, what a beautiful sight.

8. On day seven, God had a rest,
God had a rest, God had a rest.
On day seven, God had a rest,
thank you for making the world.

693 Save me, Lord

Words and Music: Andy Read
arr. Chris Mitchell

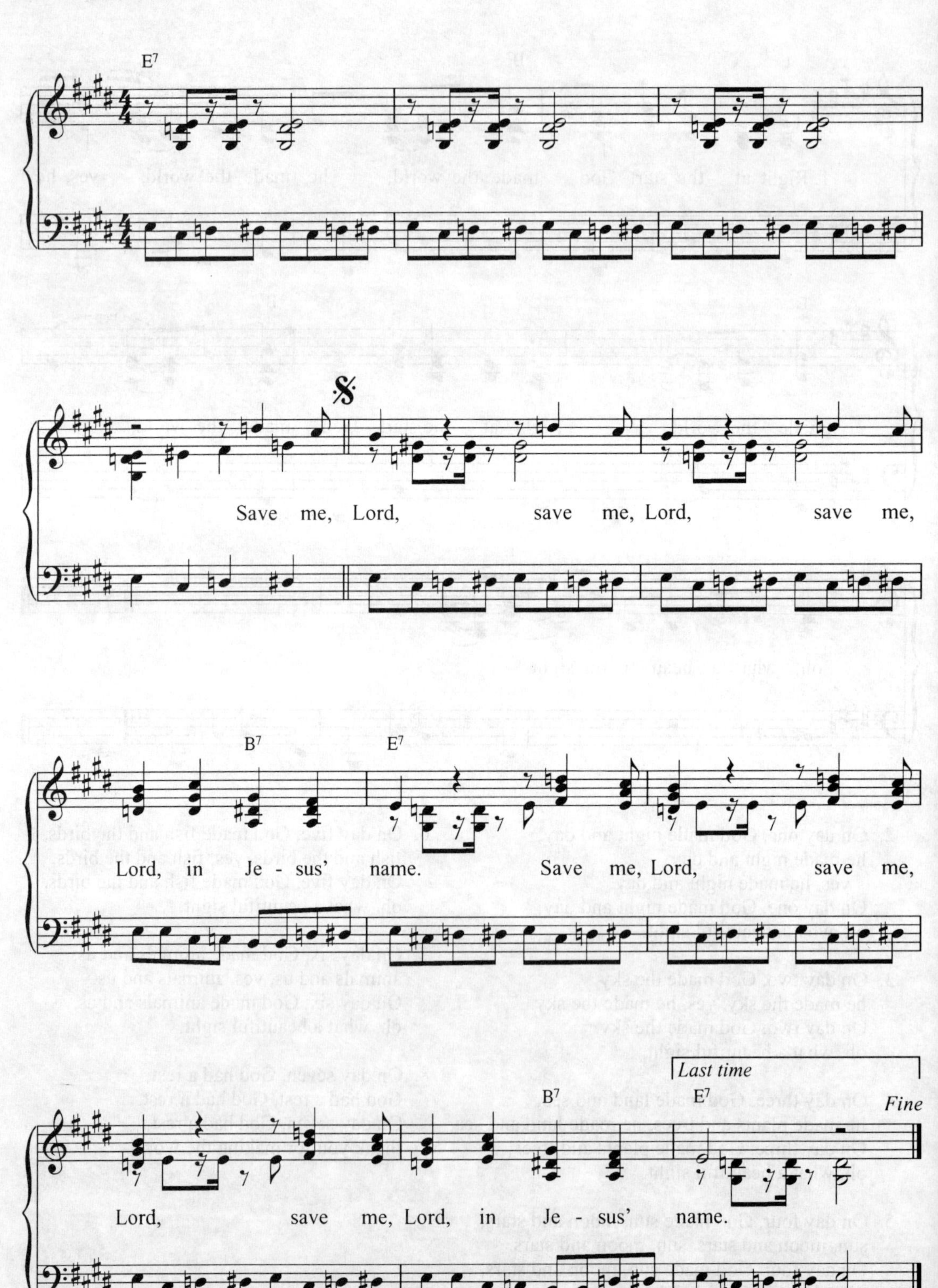
E7
Save me, Lord, save me, Lord, save me,
B7
E7
Lord, in Je - sus' name. Save me, Lord, save me,
Last time
B7
E7
Fine
Lord, save me, Lord, in Je - sus' name.

To continue
E7
name. He came to me when I was down, he came to
me when I was out,
B7
he came to me in my
E7
A7
sin, he came to me and set me free! Save me,
E7
B7
E7
D.S.

694 Say amen to the Lord

Words and Music: Laura Wright and Chris Laughlin
arr. Chris Mitchell

With a reggae feel
Chorus
Capo 3
F D
B♭ G
F D
Say a - men to the Lord for he has con - quered. Say a -
G E
C A
men to the Lord to - day. Say a -
F D
B♭ G
F D
men to the Lord for he has con - quered. Oh
C A
B♭ G
1.
2.
hip, hip, hip hoo-ray. Say a- Say
F D
C A
B♭ G
Last time to Coda
hip, hip, hip hoo - ray.

F D
B♭ G
2. 'Make way for the King of kings', say the an - gels on high.
1. See the de - vil fall - ing down on his knees,
F D
G7 E7
We see him com - ing down from out of the sky.
hear him begg - ing, 'Je - sus, please, please, please.'
C A
F D
B♭ G
He has come to save us all.
How he'd love to claim this vic - to - ry,
F D
C A
Thank you, Je - sus, Lord, my Sa -
but the bat - tle be - longs to the Lord,

B♭
G
F
D
- viour. Thank you, Je - sus,
yes, the bat - tle be - longs
C
A
B♭
G
D.S.
Lord, my Sa - viour. Say a -
D.S.
to the Lord. Say a -
CODA
G
E
C
A
Our pray'rs have not been in vain
A
F♯
D
B
so we will sing it a - gain. Say a -

G E
C A
G E
men to the Lord for he has con - quered. Say a -
A F♯
D B
men to the Lord to - day. Say a -
G E
C A
G E
men to the Lord for he has con - quered. Oh
D B
C A
1.
hip, hip, hip hoo - ray. Say a-
2.
G E
D B
Say hip, hip, hip hoo - ray.
C A
G E

695 See, amid the winter's snow

Words: Edward Caswall

Music: John Goss

HUMILITY (OXFORD) 77 77 and Refrain

Solo or Unison
G Am7 Bm C G D/F♯ C/E G G/D D
1. See, a-mid the win-ter's snow, born for us on earth be-low,

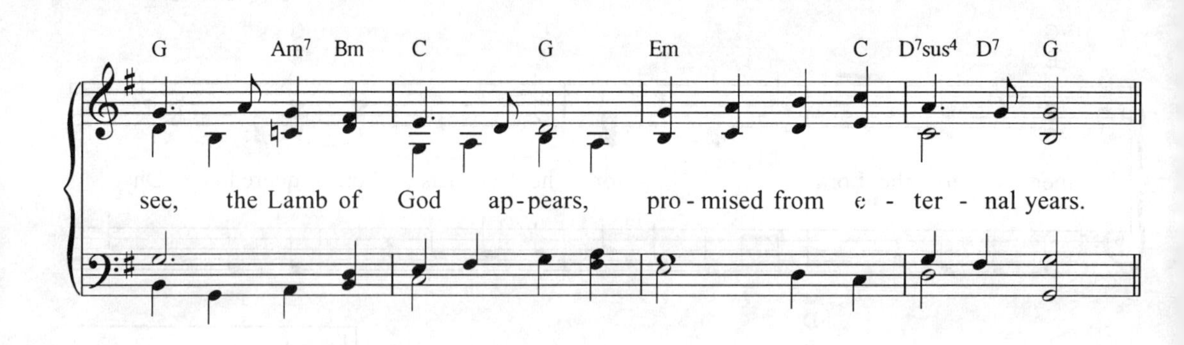
G Am7 Bm C G Em C D7sus4 D7 G
see, the Lamb of God ap-pears, pro-mised from e-ter-nal years.

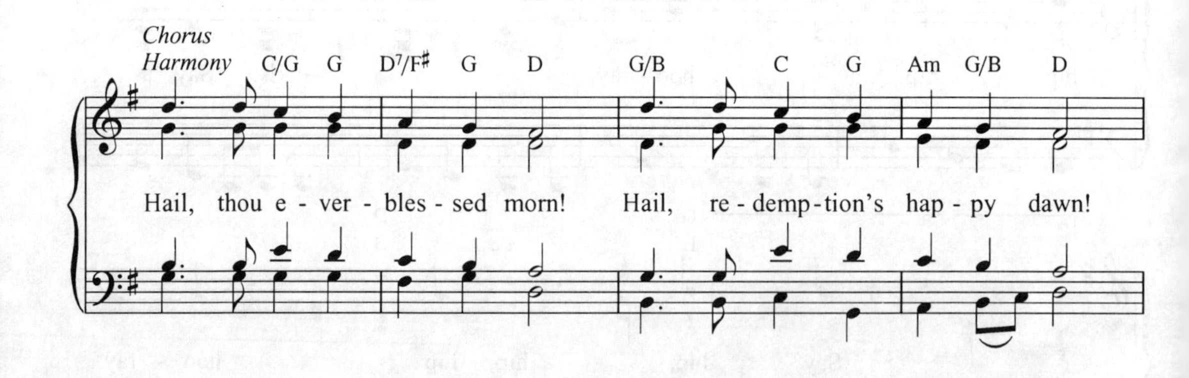
Chorus
Harmony
C/G G D7/F♯ G D G/B C G Am G/B D
Hail, thou e-ver-bles-sed morn! Hail, re-demp-tion's hap-py dawn!

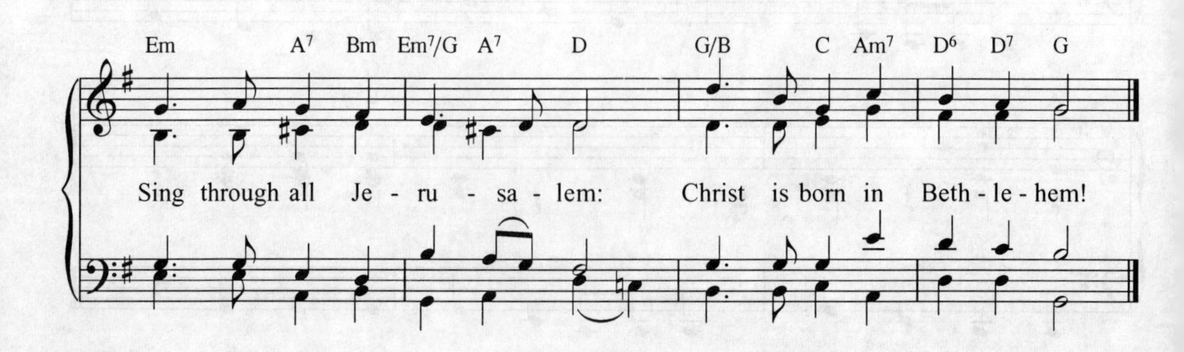
Em A7 Bm Em7/G A7 D G/B C Am7 D6 D7 G
Sing through all Je-ru-sa-lem: Christ is born in Beth-le-hem!

2. Lo, within a manger lies
he who built the starry skies,
he who, throned in heights sublime,
sits amid the cherubim.

3. Say, ye holy shepherds, say,
what your joyful news today;
wherefore have you left your sheep
on the lonely mountain steep?

4. 'As we watched at dead of night,
lo, we saw a wondrous light;
angels, singing peace on earth,
told us of the Saviour's birth.'

5. Sacred infant, all divine,
what a tender love was thine,
thus to come from highest bliss,
down to such a world as this!

6. Teach, O teach us, holy child,
by thy face so meek and mild,
teach us to resemble thee
in thy sweet humility.

696 Sheep!

Words and Music: Roger Jones
arr. Annie Routley

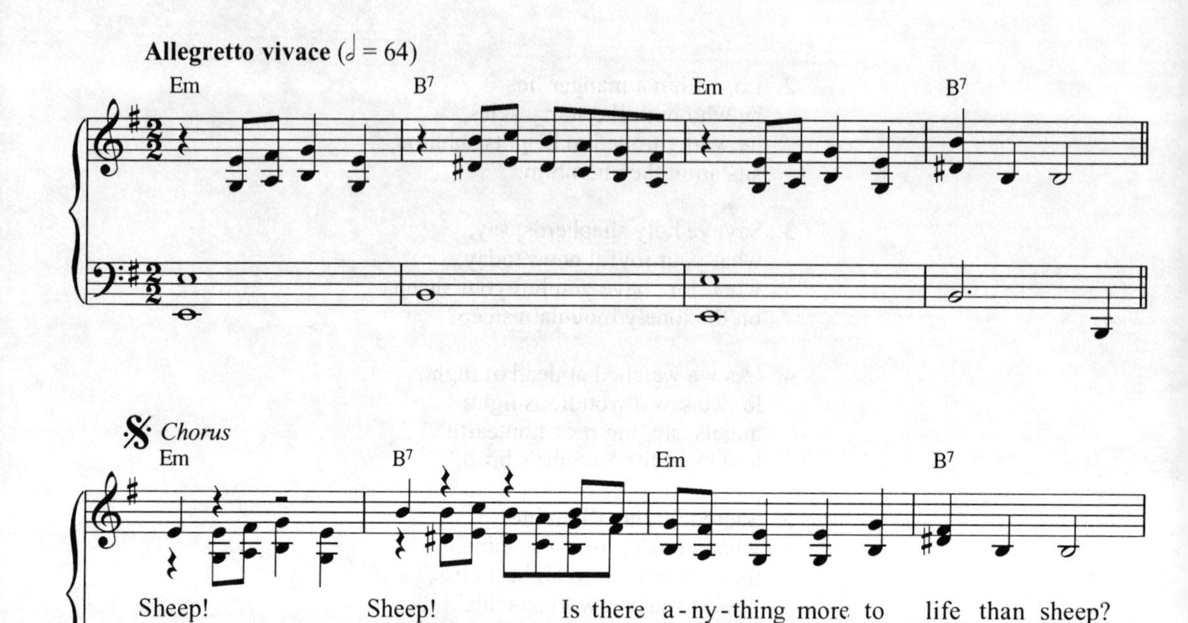
Allegretto vivace (𝅗𝅥 = 64)
Em B7 Em B7
Chorus
Em B7 Em B7
Sheep! Sheep! Is there a-ny-thing more to life than sheep?

Last time
Em B7 Em B7 Em
Fine
Sheep! Sheep! Is there a-ny-thing more than sheep?

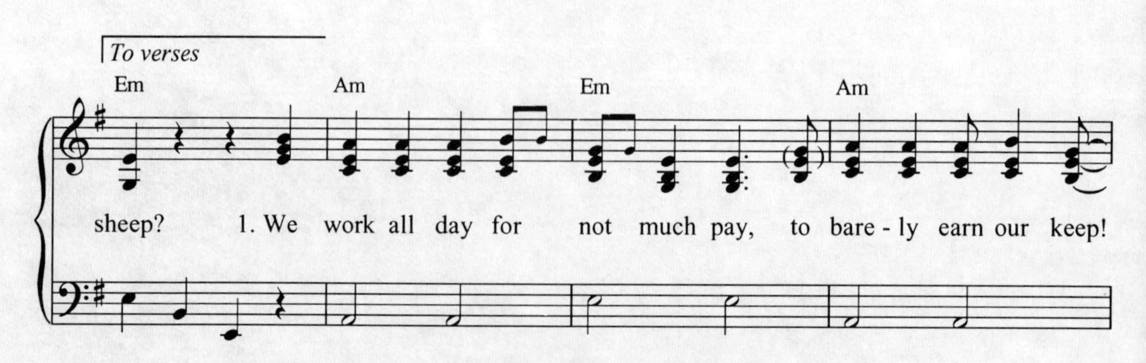
To verses
Em Am Em Am
sheep? 1. We work all day for not much pay, to bare-ly earn our keep!

Em
Am
Em
In bed at night, can you guess our plight?

Em/D♯
Em/D
Em/C♯
C
Bm
Em
D.S.
Spoken: (Yawn) I can't sleep! Sung: We end up count-ing sheep!

2. King David was a shepherd-boy,
   at night he used to keep
   his watchful eye on his flocks, but why?
   (Spoken) Someone please tell me why
   (Sung) should anyone want his sheep!

3. We go to town, but people frown
   as 'round the streets we creep.
   'Not welcome here! Out of town, d'you hear!
   (Spoken) In the fields, that's your place!
   (Sung) Go back to keep your sheep!'

4. Oompah, oompah! There's a woolly jumpah!
   No, it's just a lamb!
   What can it be? Is it plain to see?
   (Spoken) Is it him? Is it her? Is it you or me?
   (Sung) No, it's just a ewe or ram!

697 Silent night

Words: Joseph Mohr
trans. John Freeman Young

Music: Franz Grüber
arr. Colin Hand

STILLE NACHT Irregular
Capo 1
1. Silent night, holy night. All is calm,
all is bright, round yon virgin mother and child;
holy infant, so tender and mild,
sleep in heavenly
peace, sleep in heavenly peace.

2. Silent night, holy night.
Shepherds quake at the sight,
glories stream from heaven afar,
heav'nly hosts sing alleluia:
Christ the Saviour is born,
Christ the Saviour is born.

2. Silent night, holy night.
Son of God, love's pure light,
radiant beams from thy holy face,
with the dawn of redeeming grace:
Jesus, Lord, at thy birth,
Jesus, Lord, at thy birth.

698 Sing a new song

Words and Music: Dave Cooke and Paul Field

Steadily
E A B E A B E
1. Sing a new song to the Lord, all a-round the world.
All the praise that we can bring will ne-ver be e-nough.
A B E
Sing a new song to the Lord,
Tell some-bo-dy ev-'ry day the
A B E
all a-round the world.
won-der of his love.
1. 2.
Chorus
And we'll sing
A2 B C♯m
glo-ry, glo-ry, glo-ry to his name.

G♯m A G♯m
Let the beau - ty of his ho - li - ness
A D C D G
set our hearts a - flame. Let the hea - vens be glad,
C G G/B D
let the earth re - joice and sing: we'll sing
C2 G Bsus4/F♯ B
glo - ry, glo - ry, glo - ry to the
E A B E A B D.C. E
King.

2. Sing a new song to the Lord, all around the earth.
Sing a new song to the Lord, all around the earth.
He is wise and he is strong, on him we can depend.
Tell somebody ev'ry day his kingdom never ends.

699 Sing a song *(Samba praise)*

Words and Music: Gill Hutchinson

Capo 3
F
D
C/E
A/C♯
Sing a song to the Lord, be joy - ful and sing, let his praise be heard in
Em7
C♯m7
Gm
Em
C
A
ev - 'ry na - tion, won - der - ful and migh - ty is his name.
Shout the praise of the Lord, let ev -
- 'ry - one hear, there is none like him in all cre - a - tion.
Wor - ship him for e - ver. He's the same.

C/E
A/C♯
F
D
Come and praise him, for he is
C
A
Dm7
Bm7
Gm7
Em7
the King of glo - ry and he reigns on earth be - low,
C
A
F
D
in heav'n a - bove. Come and praise
C/E
A/C♯
F
D
C
A
Dm7
Bm7
him, he is wor - thy of our wor - ship and he gives
Gm7
Em7
C
A
F
D
us all his e - ver - last - ing love.

700 Sing hallelujah, hallelujah, praise the Lord

Words and Music: Ian Smale
arr. Chris Mitchell

E
A
Sing hal - le - lu - jah, hal - le - lu - jah, praise the Lord, praise the Lord.

E
B
E
Hal - le - lu - jah, praise the Lord. Sing hal - le - lu - jah, hal - le - lu - jah,

Last time
A
E
B
E
Fine
praise the Lord, praise the Lord. Hal - le - lu - jah, praise the Lord.

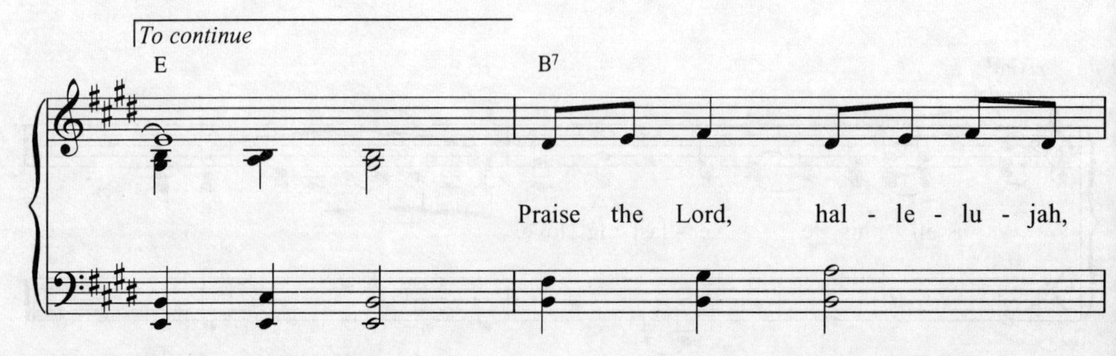

To continue
E
B7
Praise the Lord, hal - le - lu - jah,

E
B7
hal - le - lu - jah, praise the Lord. Hal - le - lu - jah, praise the Lord.

E
B7
Hal - le - lu - jah, praise the Lord.

E
F#7
B
D.S.
Hal - le - lu - jah, praise the Lord. Hal - le - lu - jah, praise the Lord. Sing

701 Sing out an Easter song

Words and Music: Mark Johnson and Helen Johnson
arr. Dave Bankhead

Chorus
C F C
Sing out an Eas - ter song, tell ev - 'ry - one that the

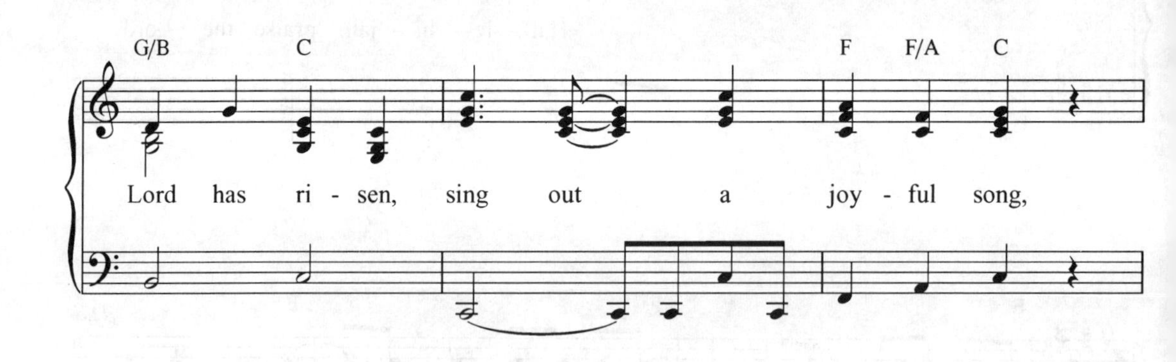

G/B C F F/A C
Lord has ri - sen, sing out a joy - ful song,

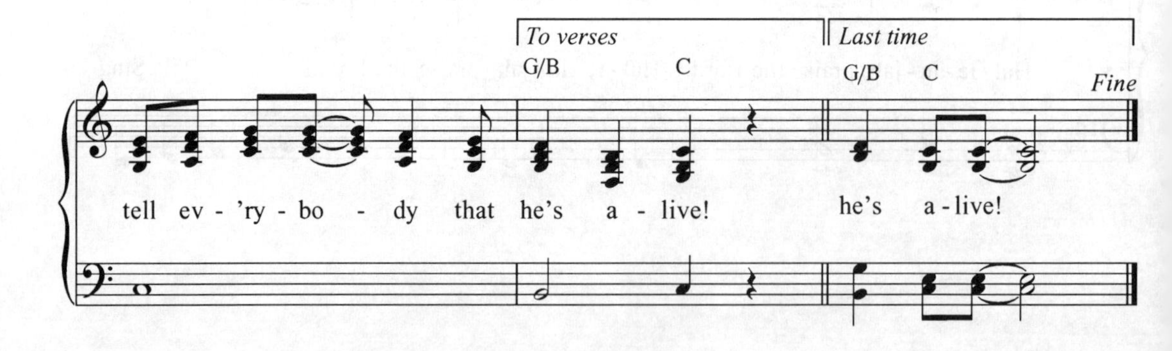

To verses
Last time
G/B C G/B C
Fine
tell ev - 'ry - bo - dy that he's a - live! he's a - live!

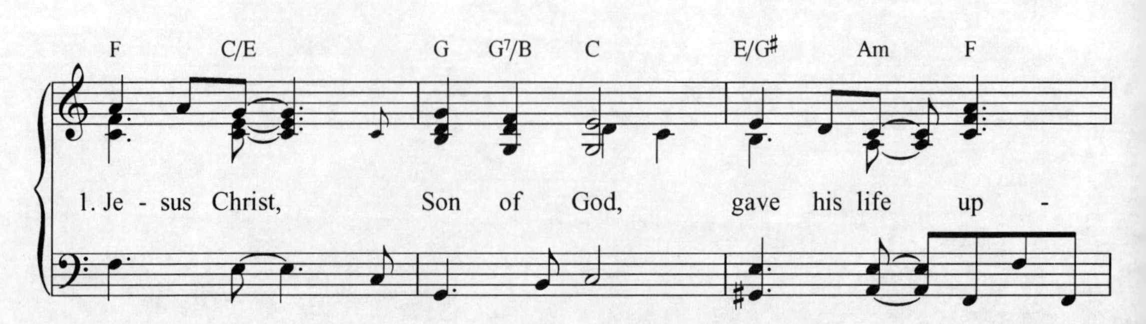

F C/E G G7/B C E/G# Am F
1. Je - sus Christ, Son of God, gave his life up -

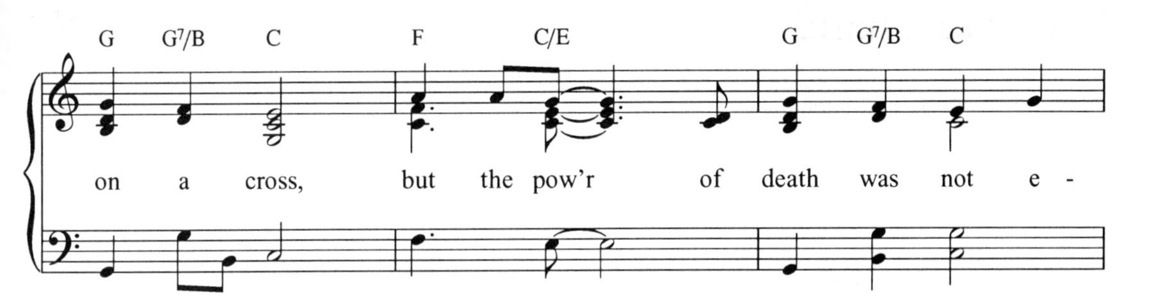
G G7/B C F C/E G G7/B C
on a cross, but the pow'r of death was not e -

D7 Gsus4 G D.C.
nough to hold him down.

2. Taken down from public view,
   he was placed inside a tomb,
   but the pow'r of love broke through
   and raised him back to life.

3. He returned to see his friends,
   showed himself alive again.
   What a day it must have been
   to have him back again!

702 Slap a hand

(Peace march)

Words and Music: J. Macpherson
arr. Chris Mitchell

C
Dm7
A7
Slap a hand and pat a back and wink an eye; you'll spread good

Dm7
G
cheer. Walk a mile and share a smile and talk it o - ver;

C
F♯dim7
G
C
all comes clear. Look and see and try to be a

Dm
A7
Dm7
Fm6
friend who lends a list - 'ning ear.

1.
C/G A7 Dm G7 C F C/E G7
Walk and talk to - ge - ther. May - be we could live in peace.

2.
C A7 Dm G7 C A7
peace. May - be we could live in peace.

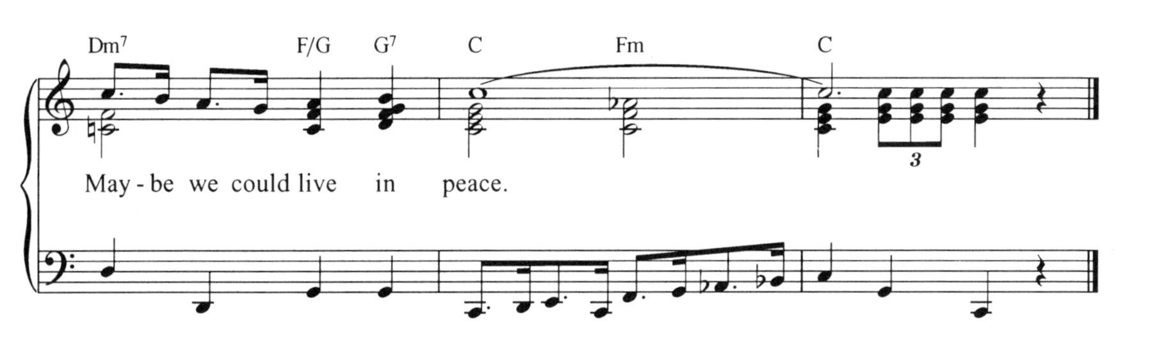
Dm7 F/G G7 C Fm C
May - be we could live in peace.
3

703 Sleep, holy child

Words and Music: James Wright
arr. Chris Mitchell

D
Em/D
1. Sleep, holy child, born on this night,
A/C♯
D
Bm7
E7
A7sus4
A7
an-gels and mor-tals bow down at this ho-ly sight.
D
Em/D
Who would have thought one born so small
A
A/G
D/F♯
Bm7
E7sus4
E7
would grow from a child to a King and be-come Sa-viour of
A
Chorus
D
A/C♯
all. Glo-ry to God, give glo-ry to God, with

Bm7
Gm/B♭
D/A
the host of hea - ven we sing, we bow down and
A7
1.
G
G/A
A7
wor - ship the new - born King.
2.
G
Gm
D
A/C♯
King. Bow down and wor - ship
G2/B
A7sus4
D
A/C♯
G2/B
A7sus4
Je - sus the King. Bow down and
D
A/C♯
G2/B
A7sus4
D
wor - ship Je - sus the King.

2. Two thousand years have passed and gone
yet we remember the night your glory shone.
Nations may rise, kingdoms may fall,
yet the light of heaven shines on
Jesus, the Saviour of all.

704 Some days are not easy *(Trust in the Lord)*

Words and Music: Tim Moyler and the Ichthus Beckenham children

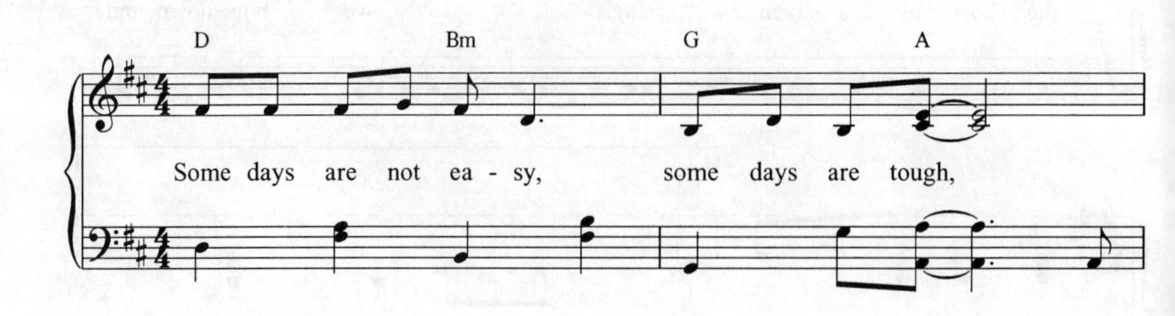
D
Bm
G
A
Some days are not ea - sy, some days are tough,

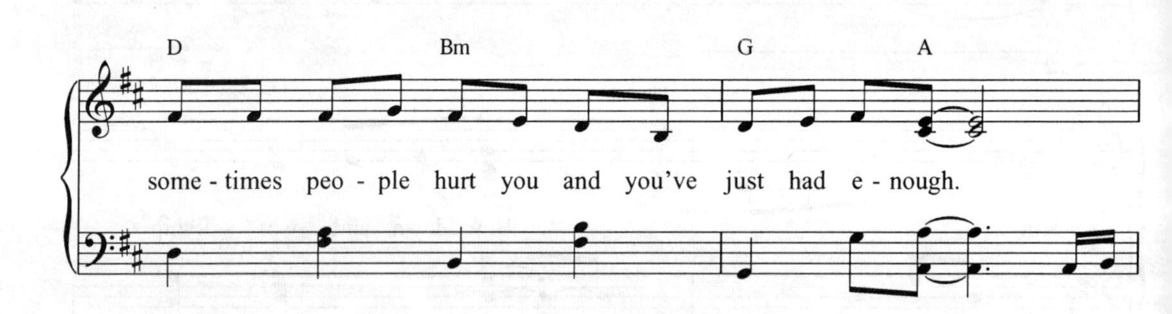
D
Bm
G
A
some - times peo - ple hurt you and you've just had e - nough.

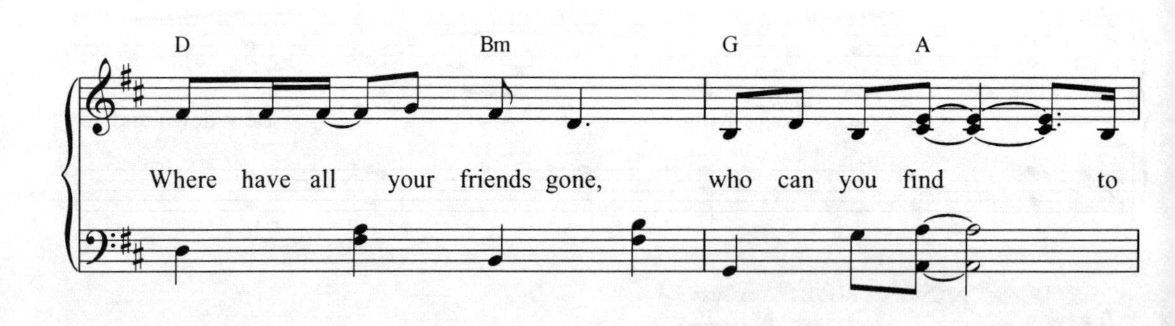
D
Bm
G
A
Where have all your friends gone, who can you find to

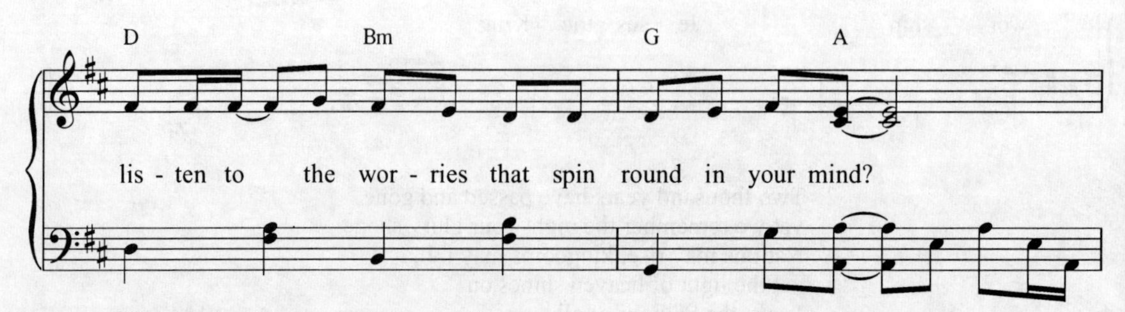
D
Bm
G
A
lis - ten to the wor - ries that spin round in your mind?

G A D Bm F♯m G
Tell me what shall I do, who can I trust?
D G A G A Chorus
Who will be with me and won't let me down? Trust in the
D A G Bm G D
Lord your God when the sun ri - ses, trust in him
A D A G Bm
when the sun sets, keep trust-ing e - ven when you feel he's not with you, 'cos
G D A7 D G D A7 D
he's al-ways near you, he pro-mi-ses. He's al-ways near you, he pro-mi-ses.

705 Sometimes I can't understand

Words and Music: Phil Chapman and Sharon Waspe
arr. Chris Mitchell

C G F
1. Some - times I can't un - der - stand and I strug - gle to
of - ten am trou - bled and wres - tle with
Sa - viour, my com - fort, he knows me through -
C G D7
see God's will and God's plan work - ing round a - bout
sin. My words and my ac - tions, my thoughts deep with -
out. He gives me his pro - mise and why should I
G F C/E F
me. And yet he still calls me with all of my
in. Lord, give me dis - cern - ment and grant me your
doubt? My rock and my shel - ter, my guide and my
C/E F C/E D7
sin to show o - ther peo - ple their way back to
peace and my vis - ion of Christ as my Sa - viour in -
friend, he loves the un - love - ly: on him I'll de -

G
To verses 2 and 3
To verse 4
C
him.
crease.
pend.
2. I
3. My

F
G
A7
4. In

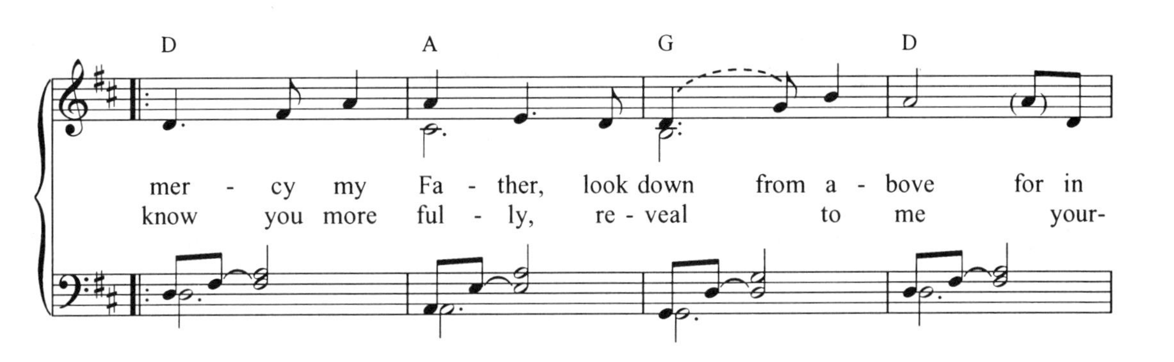
D
A
G
D
mer - cy my Fa - ther, look down from a - bove for in
know you more ful - ly, re - veal to me your-

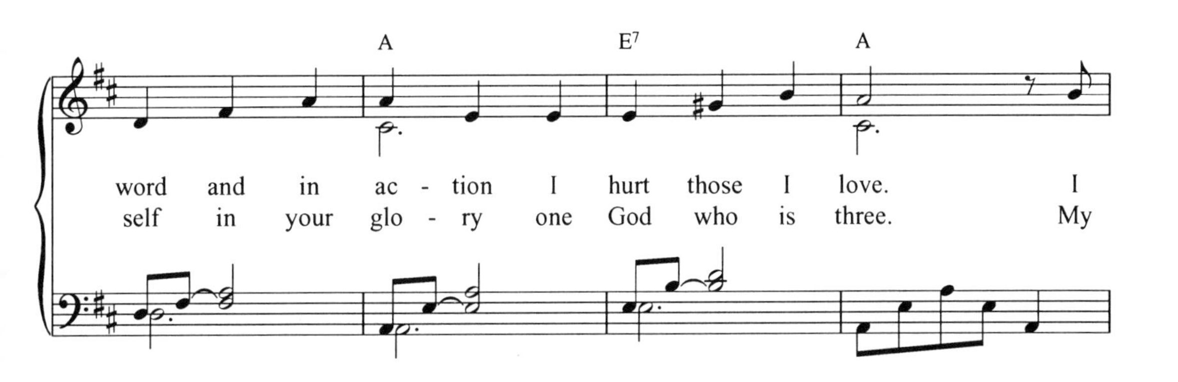
A
E7
A
word and in ac - tion I hurt those I love. I
self in your glo - ry one God who is three. My

G
D/F♯
G
D/F♯
come in re - pen - tance and ask that your grace be ex -
Fa - ther, my com-for-ter, my Sa - viour, my Lord who

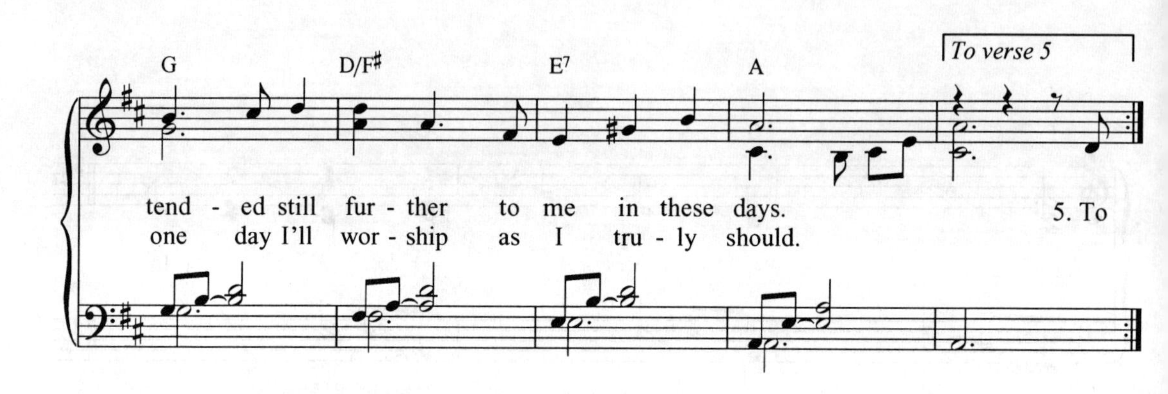
To verse 5
G
D/F♯
E7
A
tend - ed still fur - ther to me in these days.
one day I'll wor - ship as I tru - ly should.
5. To

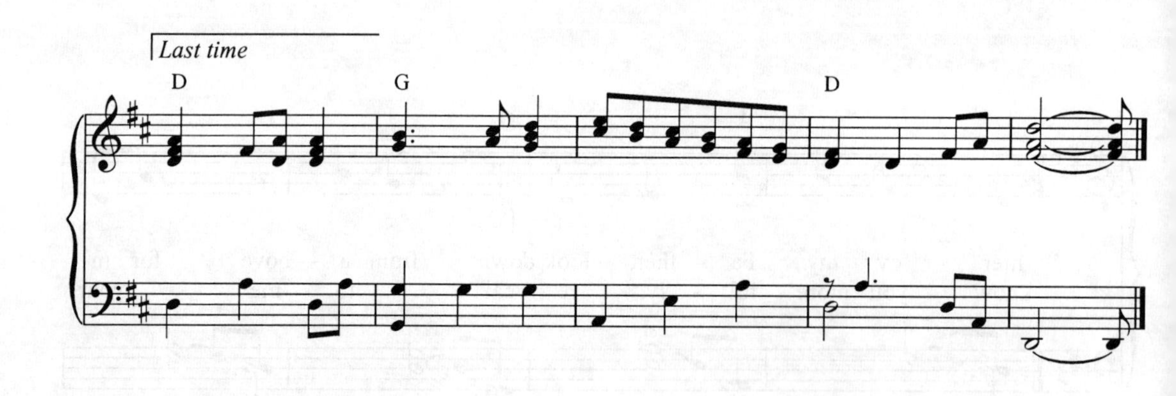
Last time
D
G
D

706 Sometimes life is an uphill climb *(Heaven's hero)*

Words and Music: Christine Dalton
arr. Chris Mitchell

E
1. Some-times life is an up-hill climb, De-vil loves work-ing
2. Pow-er Ran-gers and Su-per-man nev-er bo-ther the
B A
o-ver-time. He laughs when I do things wrong, my will-pow'r is
De-vil's plan. This is a bat-tle they can't fight bet-ween the pow'rs of
E
not that strong. Some-times life is a
dark and light. Bi-ble sto-ries
B
down-hill slide, De-vil gives me a rock-y ride. How he loves to
of-ten tell a-bout a man who con-quered Hell. Je-sus fought in his
A E
tor-ment me, Her-cu-les, please res-cue me.
Fa-ther's name and beat the De-vil at his own game.

B
A
E
A
E
Bat - man and Ro - bin, where are you? I need your mus-cles to
Je - sus, you're my cham - pi - on! Hea - ven's he - ro,
Last time to Coda
A
E
B
A
E
pull me through! What good are he - roes on T V?
God the Son. I don't need mus-cles and I don't need swords;
C
B7
E
They ne - ver come to res - cue me!
C
B7
E
D.C.
CODA
C
B7
E
just say 'Je - sus Christ is Lord.'
C
B7
E

707 Sovereign Lord

Words and Music: Phil Chapman
arr. Chris Mitchell

C2 G/B Am7 D7 G C2/G G
1. Sov - 'reign Lord, to
C2/G G2 Am7 G/B A/C♯ D
you we sing; hymns of praise to you we bring.
C2 G/B A7 D C G/B
For your good - ness true and pure seed - time and har - vest
Am7 D7 G C2 G/B Am7 D7 G
shall en - dure.

2. Rain and sun and crops preserved,
gifts to us so undeserved.
Help us better to recall
God of love who gives us all.

3. Food a-plenty by your might,
choice so varied for our delight!
For your gifts let praise be giv'n,
ev'ry meal a gift from heav'n.

708 Step out with Jesus

Words and Music: Steve Morgan-Gurr and Kay Morgan-Gurr

Country feel
Chorus
G D A
Step out with Je - sus, walk a - way from

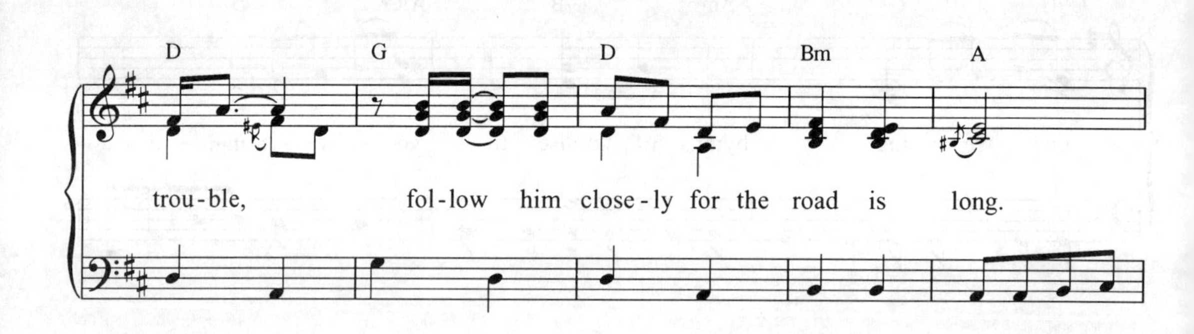

D G D Bm A
trou - ble, fol - low him close - ly for the road is long.

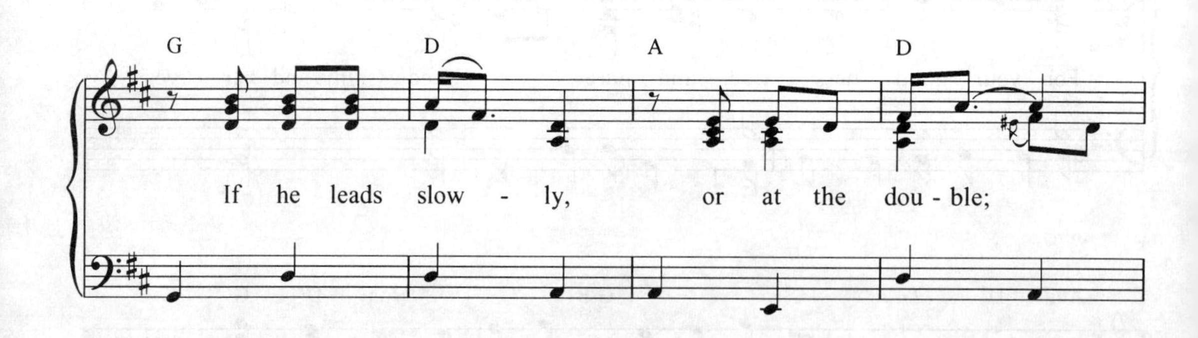

G D A D
If he leads slow - ly, or at the dou - ble;

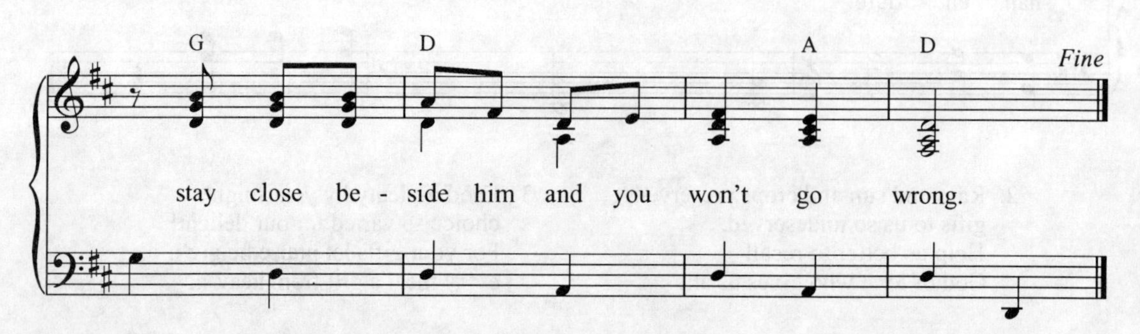

G D A D
Fine
stay close be - side him and you won't go wrong.

A
G
D
1. You need to tra - vel with im - por - tant things with you; a
A
D
map, a guide, a lamp for when it's night. We have the
A
G
D
Bi - ble, and we have the Spi - rit too, and
Bm
G
A
D.S.
close to Je - sus he will be our light, light, light.

2. You have to watch your step
as you walk through each day.
It's often hard to go against the flow.
Don't follow all the people on the easy way,
just follow Jesus, he's the way to go, go, go.

709 Sun-deedle *(Sun-deedle-day)*

Words and Music: Alex Legg

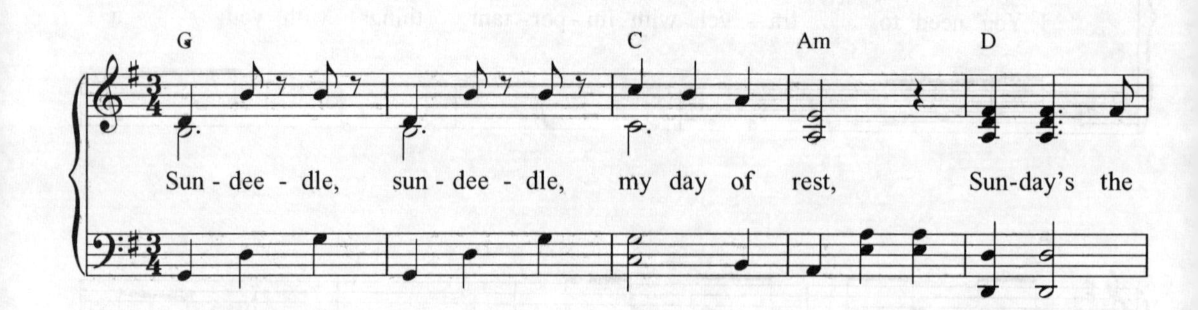
G
C
Am
D
Sun - dee - dle, sun - dee - dle, my day of rest, Sun-day's the

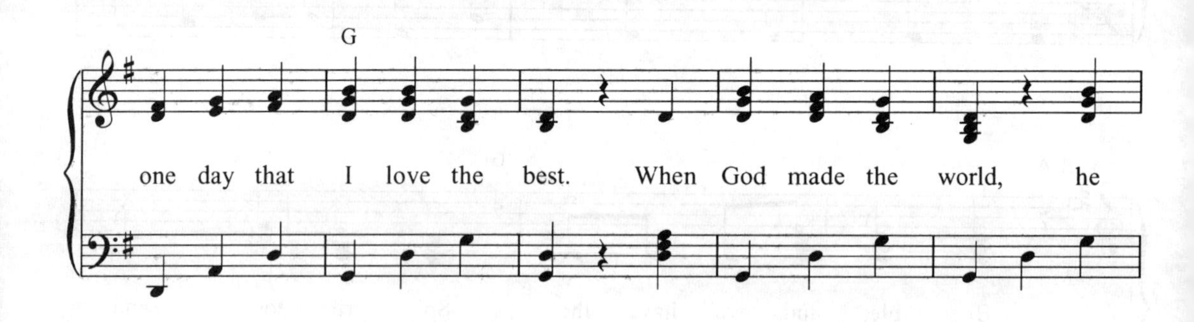
G
one day that I love the best. When God made the world, he

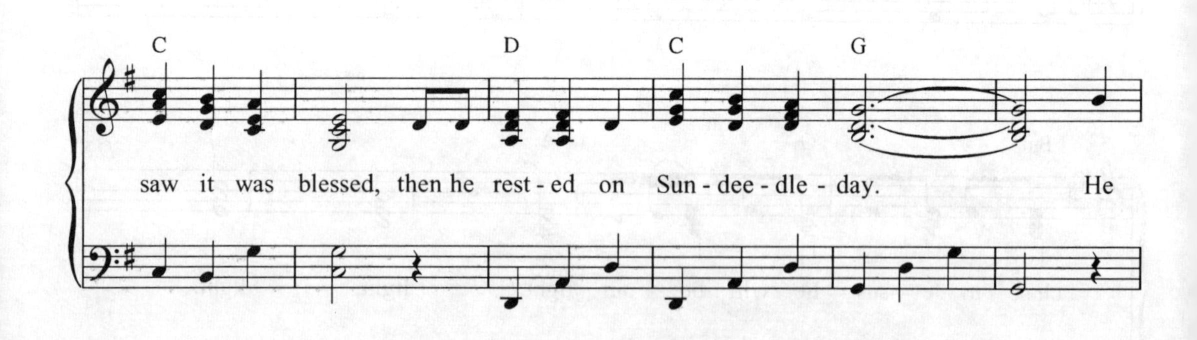
C
D
C
G
saw it was blessed, then he rest - ed on Sun - dee - dle - day. He

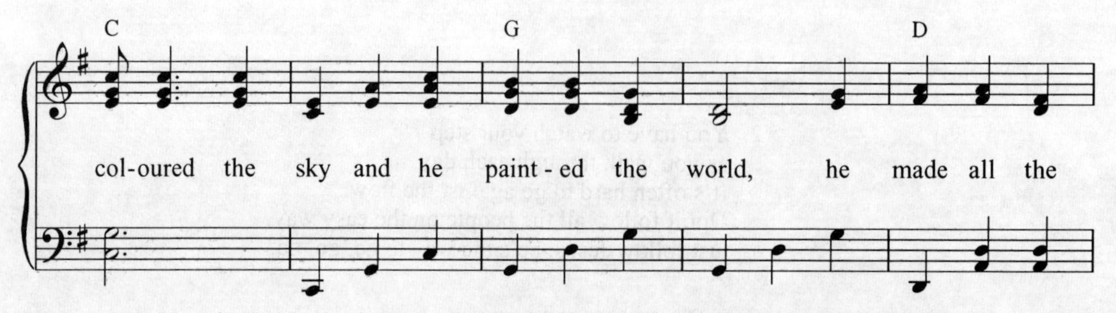
C
G
D
col-oured the sky and he paint - ed the world, he made all the

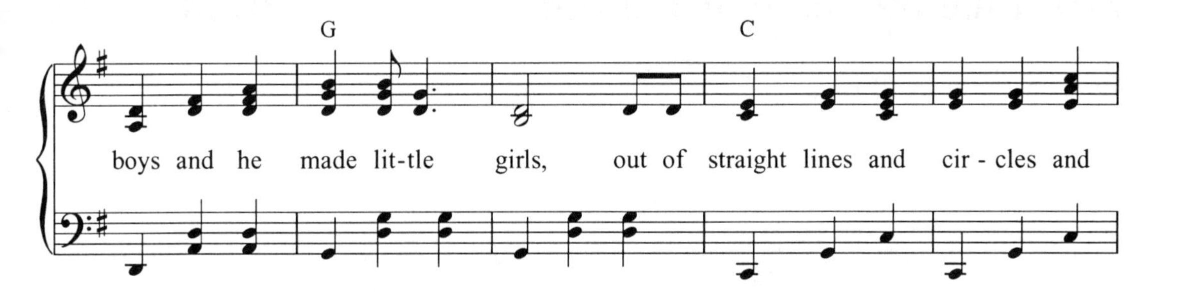
G
C
boys and he made lit-tle girls, out of straight lines and cir - cles and

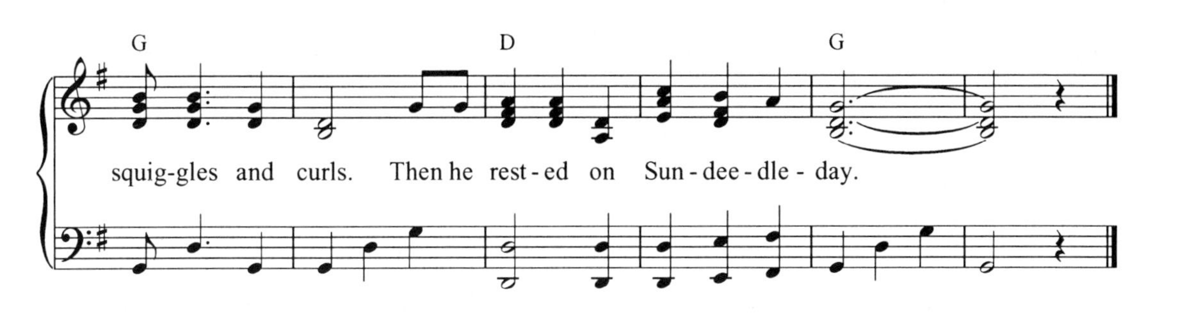
G
D
G
squig-gles and curls. Then he rest - ed on Sun - dee - dle - day.

710 Take the Bible, live it out *(God's way)*

Words and Music: Nick Harding

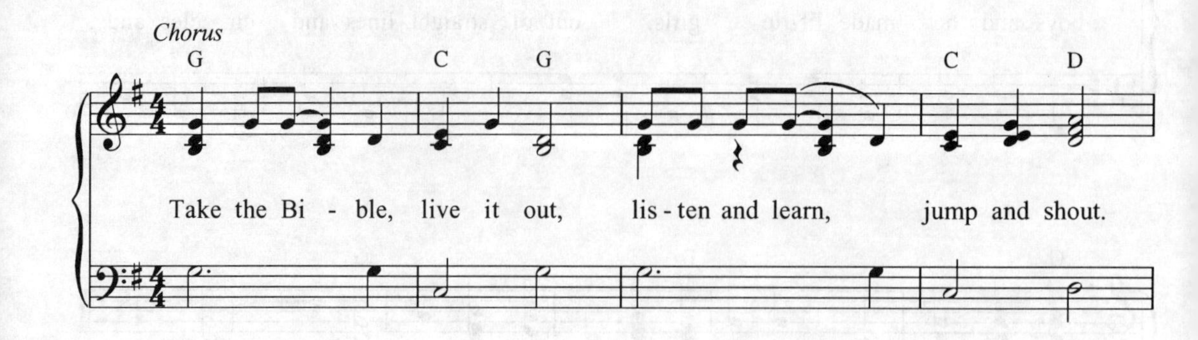
Chorus
G C G C D
Take the Bi - ble, live it out, lis-ten and learn, jump and shout.

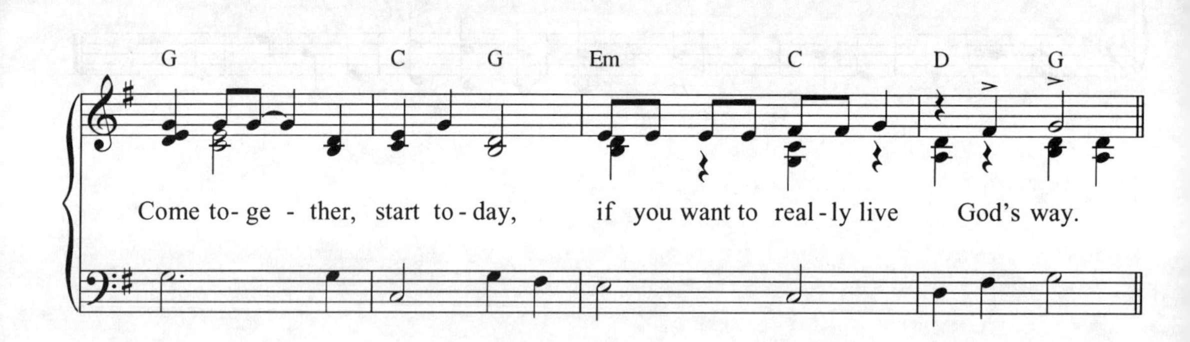
G C G Em C D G
Come to-ge - ther, start to-day, if you want to real-ly live God's way.

Verse
Em Bm Em D G
Wor - ship God and no-thing more, that's what he de - signed us for!

Em Bm Em C D G
Think of God in all you say, if you want to real-ly live God's way.

711 Teach me to trust you

Words and Music: Iain D. Craig

C G C F G
1. Teach me to trust you, Lord Je - sus,
help me to draw close to you.

C F G C Am
Let me be filled with your love and de - light,

To next verse
Last time
F G C C
Lord, may I know more of you.

2. Teach me to pray to you, Jesus,
please give me the right words to say.
Help me to pray for my friends at school,
so they may get to know you.

3. Teach me to love you, Lord Jesus,
show me the things I must do.
Help me to get to that place, O Lord,
where I can be close to you.

712 Tell me who made all of creation

(Everywhere around me)

Words and Music: Mark Johnson and Helen Johnson
arr. Dave Bankhead

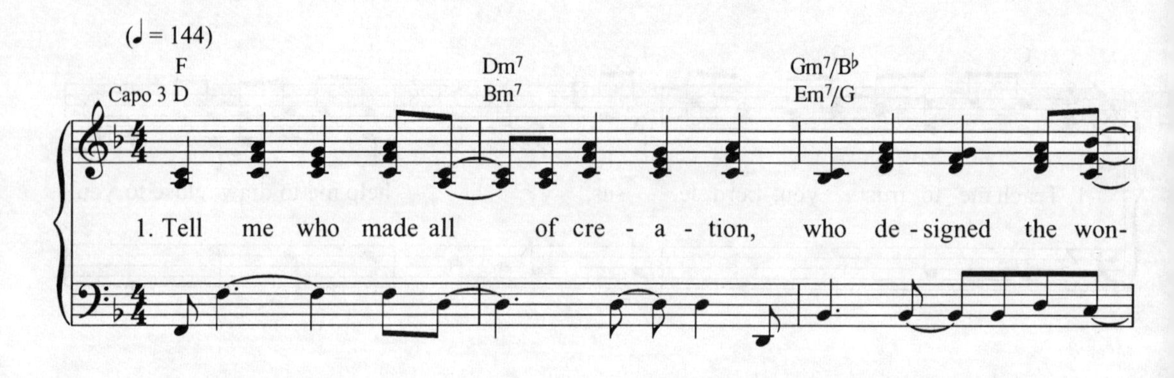
(♩ = 144)
F
Capo 3 D
Dm7
Bm7
Gm7/B♭
Em7/G
1. Tell me who made all of cre - a - tion, who de - signed the won-

C7sus4
A7sus4
C7
A7
F
D
Dm7
Bm7
- ders of na - ture? Whose i - dea was pat - tern and col - our,

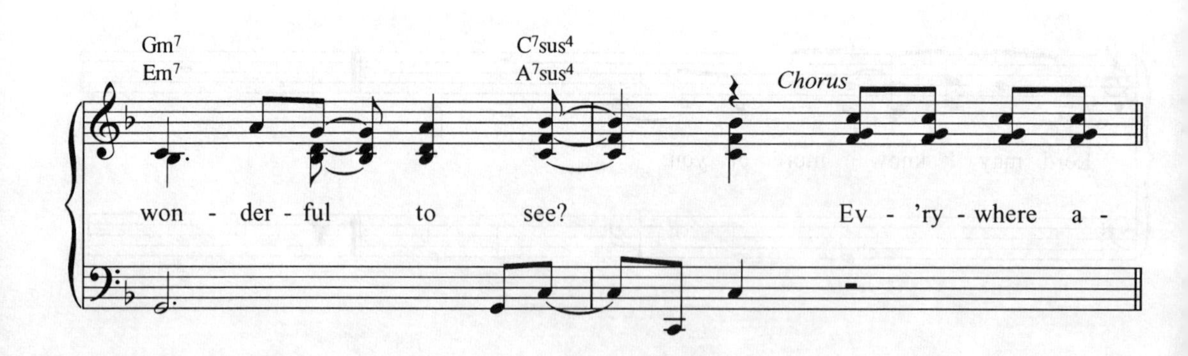
Gm7
Em7
C7sus4
A7sus4
Chorus
won - der - ful to see? Ev - 'ry - where a -

F/A
D/F♯
Dm7
Bm7
Gm7
Em7
C7sus4
A7sus4
round me, I can see the hand of God,

F/A
D/F♯
Dm7
Bm7
the e - vi-dence sur - rounds me,
in the

To repeat
To verses
Gm7
Em7
B♭/C
G/A
C7sus4
A7sus4
B♭/C
G/A
great - ness of his world.
Ev - 'ry-where a -
world.

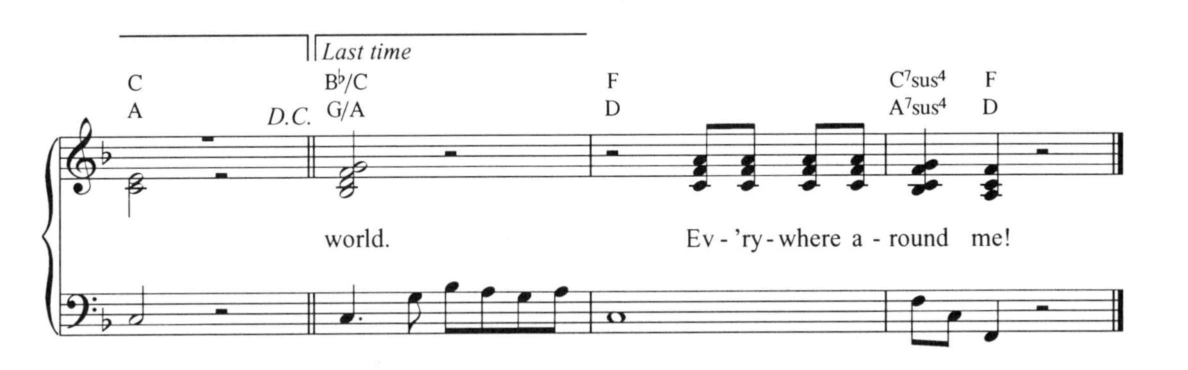
Last time
C
A
D.C.
B♭/C
G/A
F
D
C7sus4
A7sus4
F
D
world.
Ev - 'ry-where a - round me!

2. Tell me who made music and laughter,
who designed our bodies to start with?
Whose idea was thinking and feeling,
who gave life to me?

3. Don't stop looking, don't stop believing,
God is to be found when you seek him.
All creation tells of his glory
for eternity.

713 Thank you for saving me

Words and Music: Martin Smith

With a steady rhythm
Capo 2
E D B/D♯ A/C♯ A/C♯ G/B A G B⁷sus⁴ A⁷sus⁴ E D
1. Thank you for sav - ing me; what can I say?
You are my ev - 'ry-thing, I will sing your praise.
You shed your blood for me; what can I say?
You took my sin and shame, a sin - ner called by
name.
Chorus
A² G²
Great

E D Bsus4 Asus4 B A A2 G2
is the Lord. Great
E D Bsus4 Asus4 B A C♯m7 Bm7 A G
is the Lord. For we know your truth has
E D A G B A
set us free; you've
A G E D B7sus4 A7sus4 E D Esus4 Dsus4
set your hope in me.
Last time
E D B/D♯ A/C♯ A/C♯ G/B A G B7sus4 A7sus4 E D
Thank you for sav - ing me; what can I say?

2. Mercy and grace are mine, forgiv'n is my sin;
Jesus, my only hope, the Saviour of the world.
'Great is the Lord,' we cry; God, let your kingdom come.
Your word has let me see, thank you for saving me.

714 Thank you, God, for this good day

(When I consider)

Words: Kate Abba
Music: Julia Abrahams
arr. Chris Mitchell
Capo 3
F2 Gm7 F2/A Cm7 F7
D2 Em7 D2/F# Am7 D7
1. Thank you, God, for this good day and
2. Keep me warm through - out the night, en -
B♭2 B♭m6 F2/A B♭/C C7
G2 Gm6 D2/F# G/A A7
keep me safe in you, I pray. That
fold me in your shi - ning light. You
F2 Gm7 F2/A Cm7 F7
D2 Em7 D2/F# Am7 D7
you should keep me in your care is my
raised me more than is my due and
B♭2 B♭m6 F/G G7 C7
G2 Gm6 D/E E7 A7
Chorus
hope, my joy, my life, my pray'r.
give me hon - our, glo - ry too.
When I con-

F F/E♭ Dm B♭2/C
D D/C Bm G2/A
si - der the hea - vens and all you have made, the
F F/E♭ G7sus4 G7 C7sus4 C7
D D/C E7sus4 E7 A7sus4 A7
sun and the moon and the light and the shade, the
E♭/F F9/A B♭maj9
C/D D9/F♯ Gmaj9
moun - tains and ri - vers and stars up a -
E♭7 F/C F/A A♭dim7 Gm7 C7
C7 D/A D/F♯ Fdim7 Em7 A7
bove, yet you gave me your - self to me in
To verse 2
F2 F/E♭ B♭/D B♭2/C
D2 D/C G/B G2/A
love.

Last time
F/E♭
D/C
B♭/D
G/B
B♭2/C
G2/A
F
D
Fine
To continue
F
D
F/E♭
D/C
B♭maj7
Gmaj7
C
A
3. Take my hand and show me the way,
Dm7
Bm7
Dm7/C
Bm7/A
Gm9
Em9
C
A
A♭/E♭
F/C
E♭7
C7
take my heart and love me, I pray.
A♭
F
A♭7/G♭
F7/E♭
D♭maj7
B♭maj7
Show me a love, one like I've ne - ver known, for
B♭m7
Gm7
D♭
B♭
Csus4
Asus4
C
A
D.S.
your love will take me a - way. When I con -

715 Thank you, Lord

Words and Music: Andrew Pearson and Pauline Pearson

C G F G C G
1. Thank you, Lord, for the bright blue sky. Thank you, Lord, for the

F Gsus4 G C G F Gsus4
birds that fly. Thank you, Lord, for the moun-tains so high.

C Gsus4 C G C Chorus G
Thank you, Lord, for your beau - ti - ful world. Thank you, Lord,

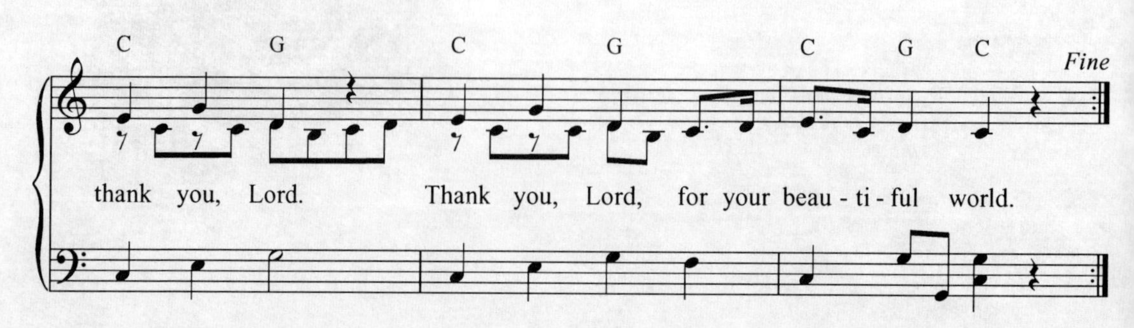
C G C G C G C
Fine
thank you, Lord. Thank you, Lord, for your beau - ti - ful world.

C G F G C G
2. Thank you, Lord, for the ve - ry blue sea. Thank you, Lord, for the

F Gsus4 G C G F Gsus4
ve - ry tall tree. Thank you, Lord, for mak-ing me 'me'.

C Gsus4 C G C
D.S.
Thank you, Lord, for your beau - ti - ful world.

716 The birds can fly and the monkeys swing

Words and Music: Ian Smale
arr. Chris Mitchell

A7
D
The
A7
birds can fly and the mon-keys swing. The fat worm wig-gles and the bee can sting. The
D
li - on roars whilst the wise owl thinks. The fox can run and the skunk just stinks. But,
A7
Lord, I am not like all these, I'm a lit - tle child just keen to please.
D
What can I do? What can I be? Je - sus says just be like me.

717 The fingers of my hand *(Finger Song)*

Words and Music: Andrew Pearson and Pauline Pearson

(♩ = 120)
C G C D Am
The fin - gers of my hand help me to un - der - stand that
F G C G C
Je - sus loves me ve - ry much, ve - ry much. The
C F G C
much. All the hairs on our heads are count - ed. All the
F G C F G
names we are called are re - cord - ed. All the things we do wrong are for -
C F G C G C
got-ten be-cause Je-sus loves me ve-ry much, ve-ry much.

718 The first Nowell

Words: from William Sandys'
Christmas Carols, Ancient and Modern, alt.

Music: traditional English melody
arr. John Stainer

THE FIRST NOWELL Irregular and Refrain

C Am G Dm/F C/E F C F C/E Cmaj7 G7/D
1. The first No - well the an - gel did say was to cer - tain poor

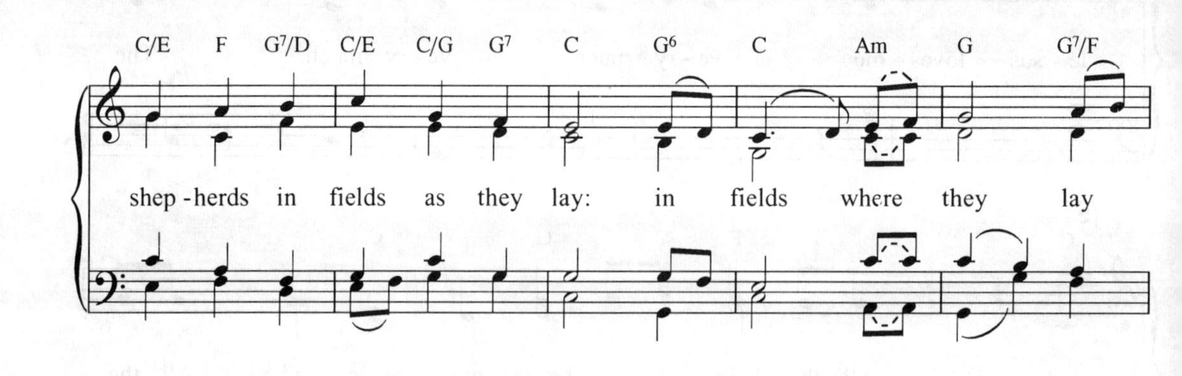

C/E F G7/D C/E C/G G7 C G6 C Am G G7/F
shep - herds in fields as they lay: in fields where they lay

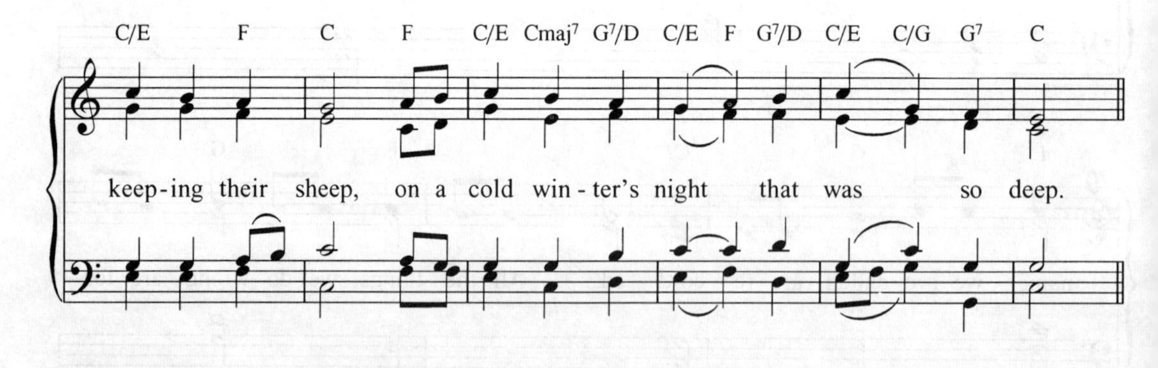

C/E F C F C/E Cmaj7 G7/D C/E F G7/D C/E C/G G7 C
keep - ing their sheep, on a cold win - ter's night that was so deep.

Chorus
G6 C Am G C F F/A C G/B
No - well, No - well, No - well, No - well,

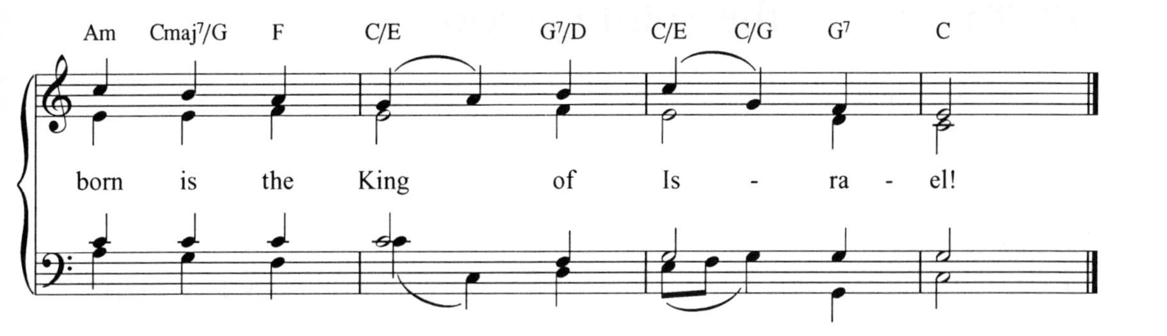
Am
Cmaj7/G
F
C/E
G7/D
C/E
C/G
G7
C
born is the King of Is - ra - el!

2. They lookèd up and saw a star,
shining in the east, beyond them far,
and to the earth it gave great light,
and so it continued both day and night.

3. And by the light of that same star,
three wise men came from country far;
to seek for a king was their intent,
and to follow the star wherever it went.

4. This star drew nigh to the north-west,
o'er Bethlehem it took its rest,
and there it did both stop and stay
right over the place where Jesus lay.

5. Then entered in those wise men three,
full rev'rently upon their knee,
and offered there in his presence,
their gold and myrrh and frankincense.

6. Then let us all with one accord
sing praises to our heav'nly Lord,
who with the Father we adore
and Spirit blest for evermore.

719 The fruit of the Spirit (Jackson)

Words and Music: Chris Jackson
arr. Chris Mitchell

Chorus
G
The fruit of the Spi - rit is love, joy, peace,

D7
C7
G
pa - tience, kind - ness and good-ness too;

gen - tle - ness and faith - ful - ness and self - con - trol.

D7
C7
G
That's what the Spi - rit will grow in you, oh, oh!

Last time
G7
Fine
Oh, yeah!

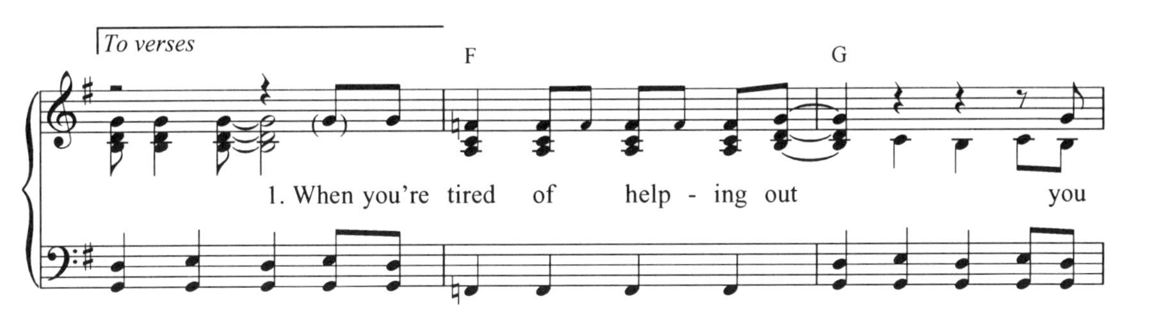
To verses
F
G
1. When you're tired of help - ing out you

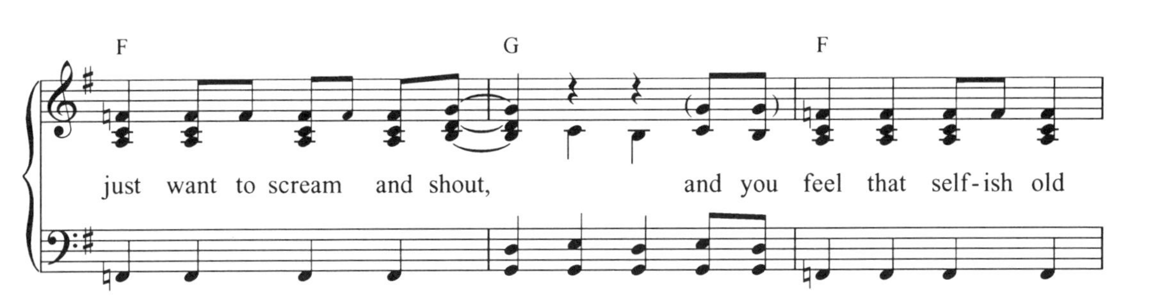
F
G
F
just want to scream and shout, and you feel that self - ish old

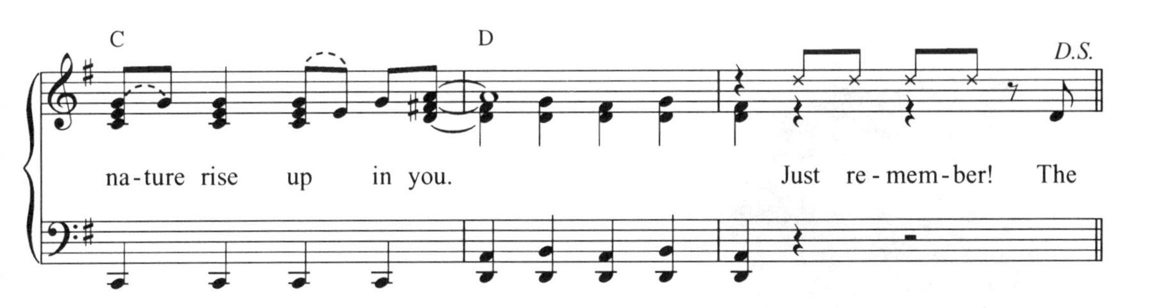
C
D
D.S.
na - ture rise up in you. Just re - mem - ber! The

2. The Spirit will give you the pow'r,
   the Spirit will give you the strength.
   He's the one who will help you stand up
   and fight the selfish nature!

720 The fruit of the Spirit

Words: based on Galatians 5:22

Music: Susanna Levell
arr. Chris Mitchell

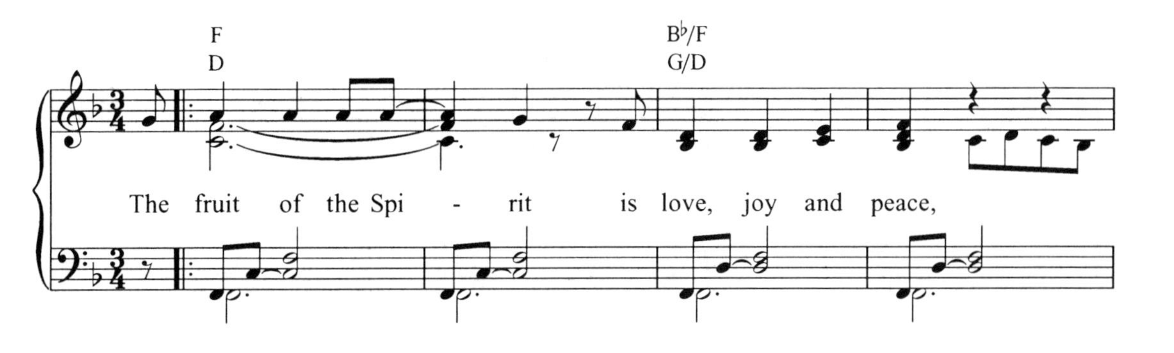
F
D
B♭/F
G/D
The fruit of the Spi - rit is love, joy and peace,

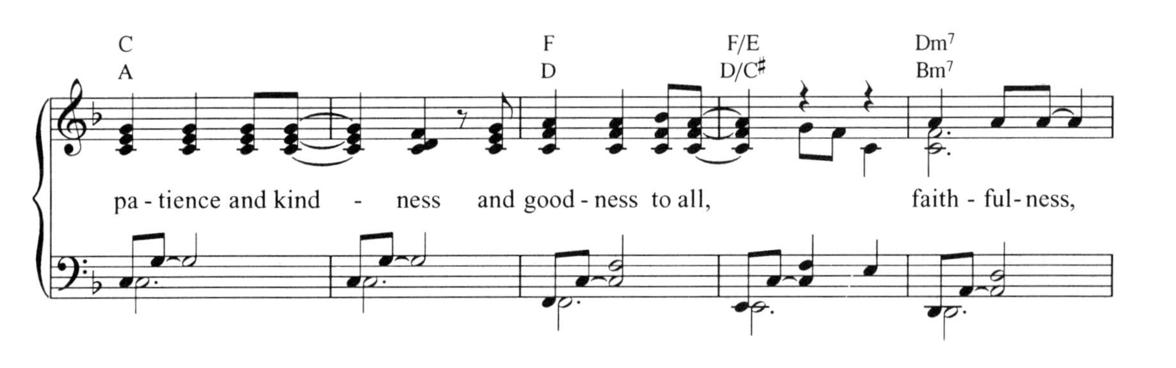
C
A
F
D
F/E
D/C♯
Dm7
Bm7
pa - tience and kind - ness and good - ness to all, faith - ful - ness,

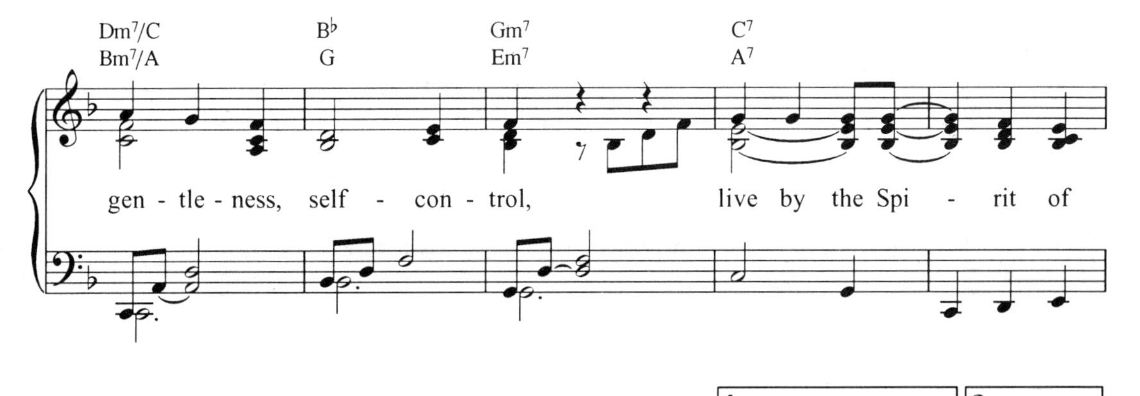
Dm7/C
Bm7/A
B♭
G
Gm7
Em7
C7
A7
gen - tle - ness, self - con - trol, live by the Spi - rit of

F2
D2
1.
2.
F
D
God. The

721 The going is hard *(It's party-time)*

Words and Music: Ian Smale
arr. Chris Mitchell

D
G
D
The go - ing is hard and the go - ing is tough. I'm

G
A7
feel - ing ex - haust - ed, I'm feel - ing rough. But I'm

D
G
D
stay - ing with Je - sus till the end of the line. 'Cause

A7
D
not long from now it will be par - ty - time. Hey,

G
yip - pee - yi - yea, hey, yip - pee - yi - yo. There's

D
A7
no look - ing back, I'm gon - na go go go. Hey,

D
G
yip - pee - yi - yo, hey, yip - pee - yi - yea. When

D/A
A7
D
Je - sus re - turns we will par - ty all day!

722 The Holy Spirit is a 'he' *(Not an 'it')*

Words and Music: Steve Burnhope
arr. Chris Mitchell

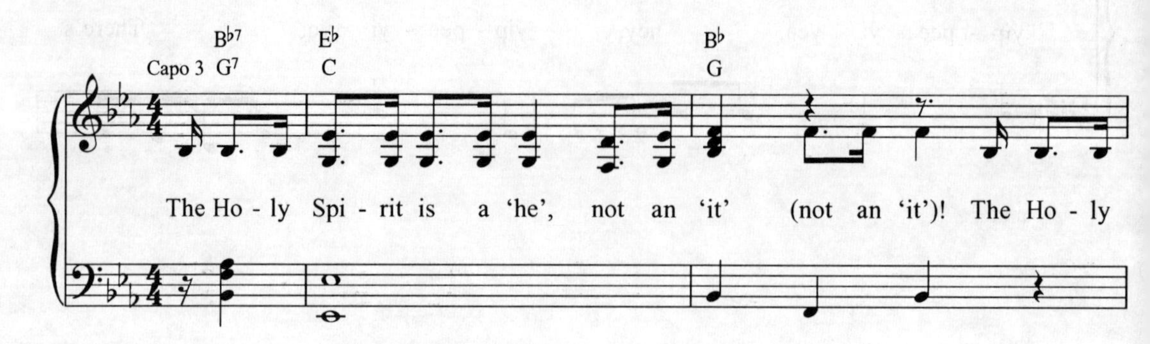

Capo 3
B♭7 G7
E♭ C
B♭ G
The Ho - ly Spi - rit is a 'he', not an 'it' (not an 'it')! The Ho - ly

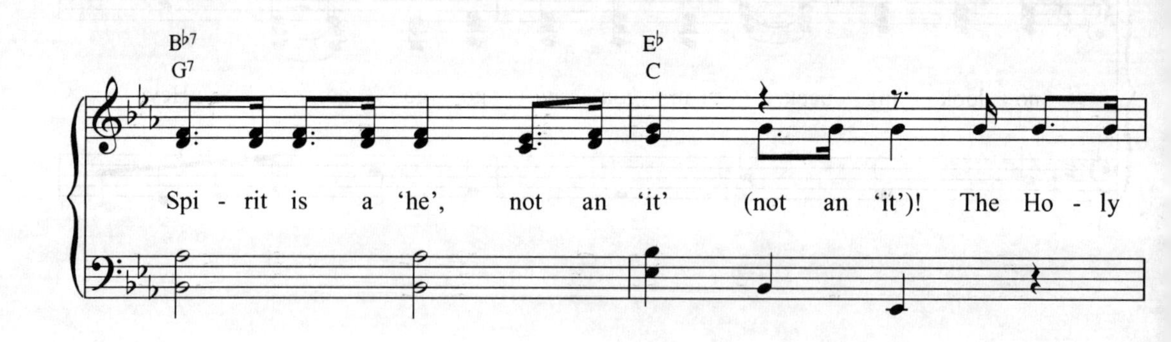

B♭7 G7
E♭ C
Spi - rit is a 'he', not an 'it' (not an 'it')! The Ho - ly

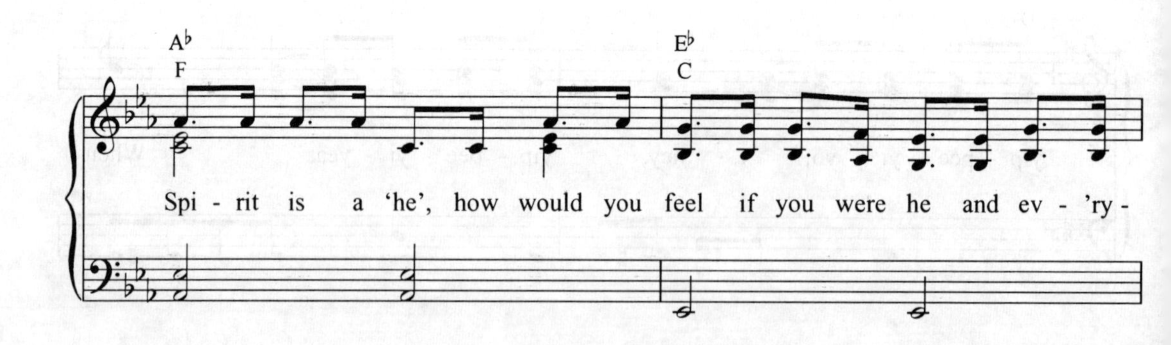

A♭ F
E♭ C
Spi - rit is a 'he', how would you feel if you were he and ev - 'ry -

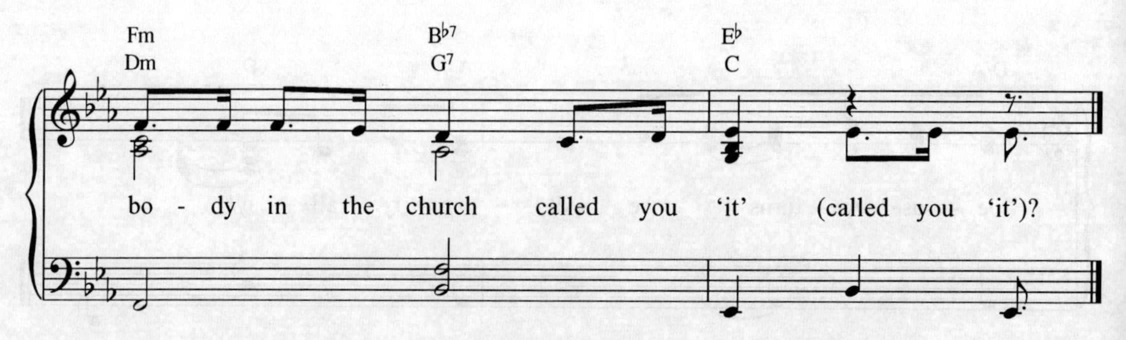

Fm Dm
B♭7 G7
E♭ C
bo - dy in the church called you 'it' (called you 'it')?

723 The Lord loves me

Words and Music: Ian Smale

B
E
The Lord loves me, he

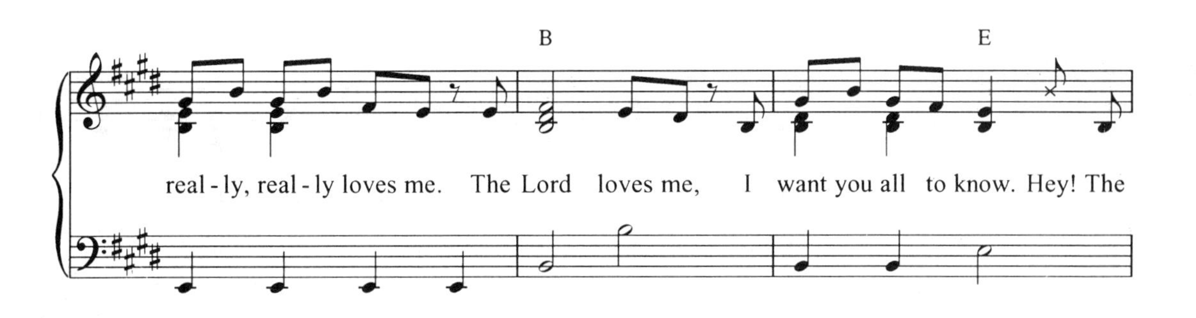
B
E
real - ly, real - ly loves me. The Lord loves me, I want you all to know. Hey! The

B
Lord loves me, he real - ly, real - ly loves me: I am his and he is mine, the

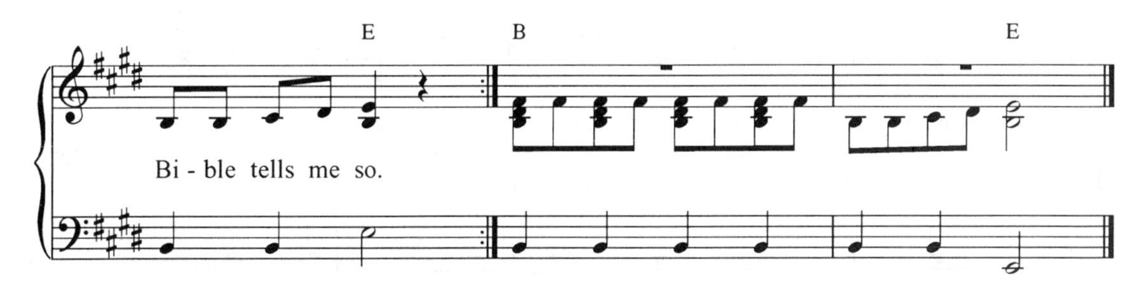
E
B
E
Bi - ble tells me so.

724 The nations around Israel

(The scarecrow and the King)

Words and Music: Dave Godfrey

Steadily
Capo 3
F D
B♭ G
C A
1. The nations around Israel had gods of wood and stone,
people in the world today make gods of many things,
Jeremiah long ago, I'll gently bow the knee,
the prophet Jeremiah said: 'Don't
though idols remain powerless to
to the God who made the universe and
make those gods your own.' Precious silver,
forgive all man's sins. Football players,
gave his life for me. Mighty Saviour,
human hands, what good can idols do? And
top pop stars are good at what they do. But
Jesus Christ, you're good at all you do. And

F
D
B♭
G
C
A
when it comes to last - ing things, this scrip - ture is true!
when it comes to last - ing things, this scrip - ture is true!
when it comes to last - ing things, I will trust in you.
Chorus
1.&2. They're like a scare-crow in a me - lon patch! Can't
3. 'Cos you're the King of all e - ter - ni - ty! You
walk, can't talk, can't do, can't do a - ny - thing
walk, and talk, you do, you do ev - 'ry - thing
that's last - ing, like a scare-crow in a
that's last - ing, you're the King of all e -
Last time to Coda
1, 2.
me - lon patch.
ter - ni - ty.
2. And the
3. Like

3.
C
A
B♭
G
C
A
Dm
Bm
B♭
G
I'll wor - ship you, wor - ship you, wor - ship

C
A
F
D
1.
2
D.S.
you, you're the King of all e - ter - ni - ty. I'll You

CODA
F
D
B♭
G
C
A
F
D

725 There is a green hill far away

Words: Cecil Frances Alexander

Music: William Horsley

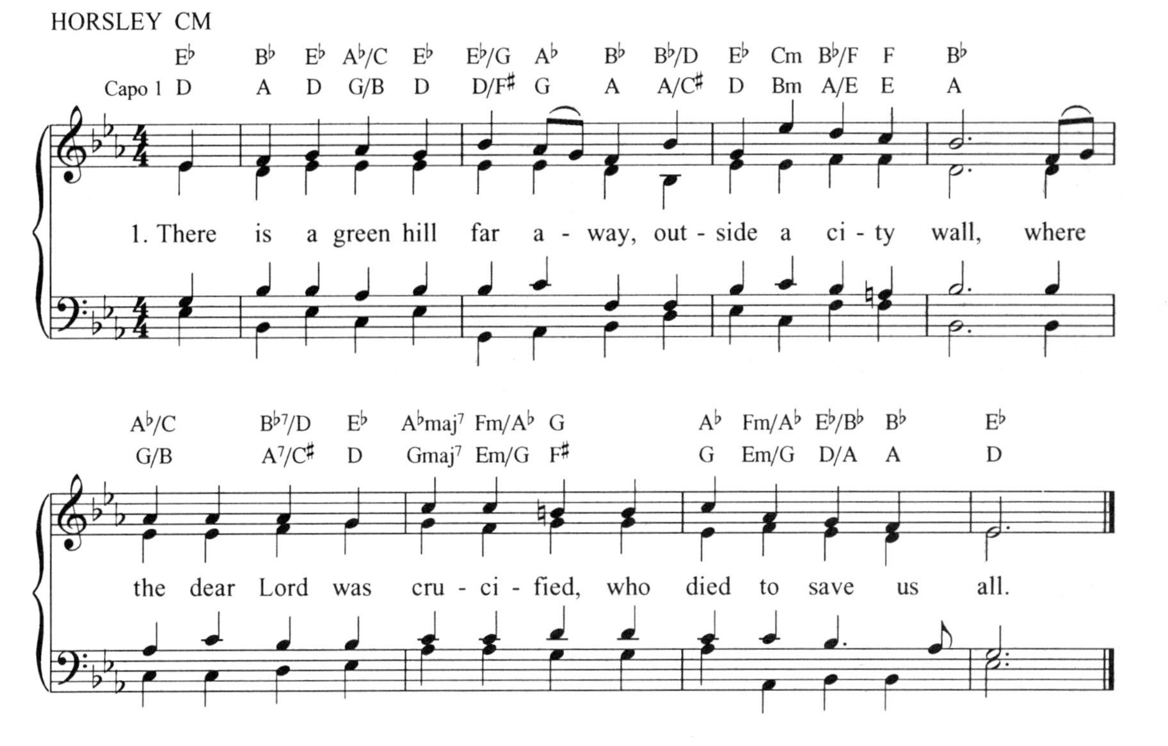
HORSLEY CM
E♭ B♭ E♭ A♭/C E♭ E♭/G A♭ B♭ B♭/D E♭ Cm B♭/F F B♭
Capo 1 D A D G/B D D/F♯ G A A/C♯ D Bm A/E E A
1. There is a green hill far a - way, out - side a ci - ty wall, where
A♭/C B♭7/D E♭ A♭maj7 Fm/A♭ G A♭ Fm/A♭ E♭/B♭ B♭ E♭
G/B A7/C♯ D Gmaj7 Em/G F♯ G Em/G D/A A D
the dear Lord was cru - ci - fied, who died to save us all.

2. We may not know, we cannot tell,
what pains he had to bear,
but we believe it was for us
he hung and suffered there.

3. He died that we might be forgiv'n,
he died to make us good;
that we might go at last to heav'n,
saved by his precious blood.

4. There was no other good enough
to pay the price of sin;
he only could unlock the gate
of heav'n, and let us in.

5. O, dearly, dearly has he loved,
and we must love him too,
and trust in his redeeming blood,
and try his works to do.

726 There is no mountain *(No mountain high enough)*

Words and Music: Charles Kirby

Bouncing march (♩ = 148)
Chorus
Capo 3
There is (clap) no moun - tain high e-nough (clap, clap) no ri - ver
wide e - nough. (clap, clap) No o - cean deep e - nough to
hide me from God's love. There is (clap) no moun - tain
high e - nough (clap, clap) no ri - ver wide e - nough. (clap,

F C7 F Dm7 B♭m6 F C7 F
D A7 D Bm7 Gm6 D A7 D
Last time to Coda
clap) No o - cean deep e-nough to hide me from God's love. (clap, clap, clap)
B♭ C C7 F C7 F B♭ Am7 C7 F C7 F
G A A7 D A7 D G F♯m7 A7 D A7 D
1. No de - sert dry e - nough, no jun - gle thick e - nough,
B♭ C C7 F C♯dim Dm D7 G F/G G7
G A A7 D A♯dim Bm B7 E D/E E7
no dark - ness black e - nough to hide me from God's
CODA
C Gm7 C9 F Gm F C7 F
A Em7 A9 D Em D A7 D
love. There is love, to hide me from God's love. (clap)

2. No king is great enough,
no army large enough,
no power strong enough
to hide me from God's love.

3. No sin is bad enough,
no troubles tough enough,
no questions hard enough
to hide me from God's love.

727 There is one

Words and Music: Sammy Horner

(♩ = 130)
Chorus
D
G
There is one who is for us, no mat-ter who's a-gainst
Bm
A
D
A
us, there is one, on-ly one, and I trust his ev-'ry word.
D
G
And there is one who is for us, no mat-ter who's a-gainst
Bm
A
D
us. There is one, on-ly one, the bles-sed, ri-sen Son.
Bm
A
D
Fine
There is one and his name is Christ the Lord.

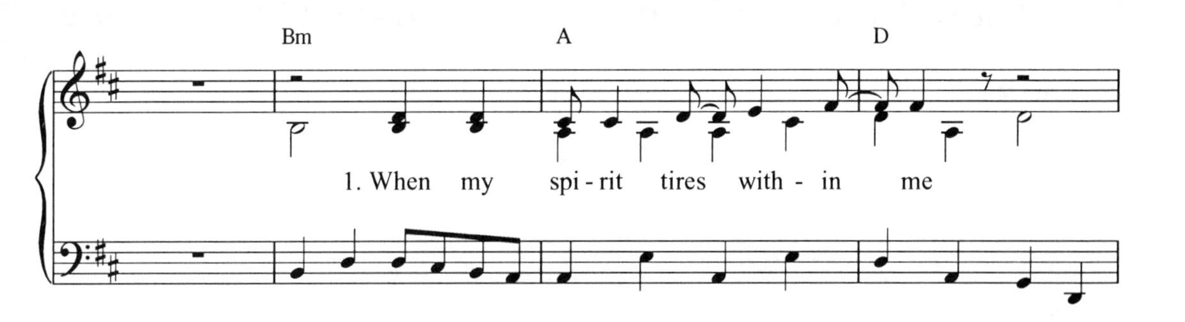
Bm
A
D
1. When my spi - rit tires with - in me

G
Em
D
it's on - ly you who knows my way.

Bm
A
D
If men have hid - den traps to snare me

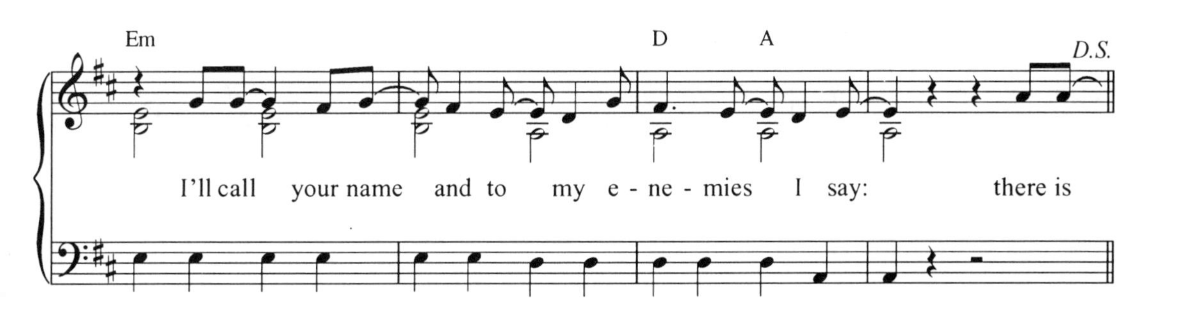
Em
D
A
D.S.
I'll call your name and to my e - ne - mies I say: there is

2. I cry to you,
you are my refuge.
You listen to me when I need
you set me free from my prison,
and that is why I praise your name,
you're great indeed.

728 There I was, walking *(The wellyboot song)*

Words and Music: Philip Chapman and Stephanie Chapman
arr. Dave Bankhead

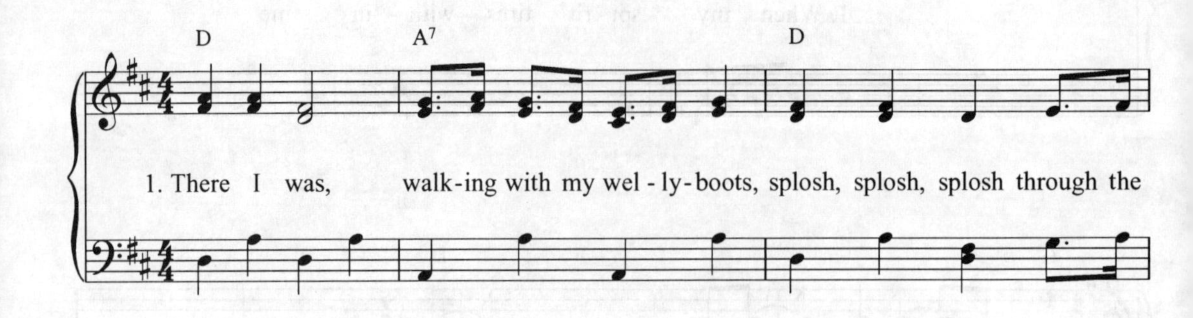
D
A7
D
1. There I was, walk-ing with my wel - ly-boots, splosh, splosh, splosh through the

A
G
D
mud. And as I was squelch-ing a - long, I

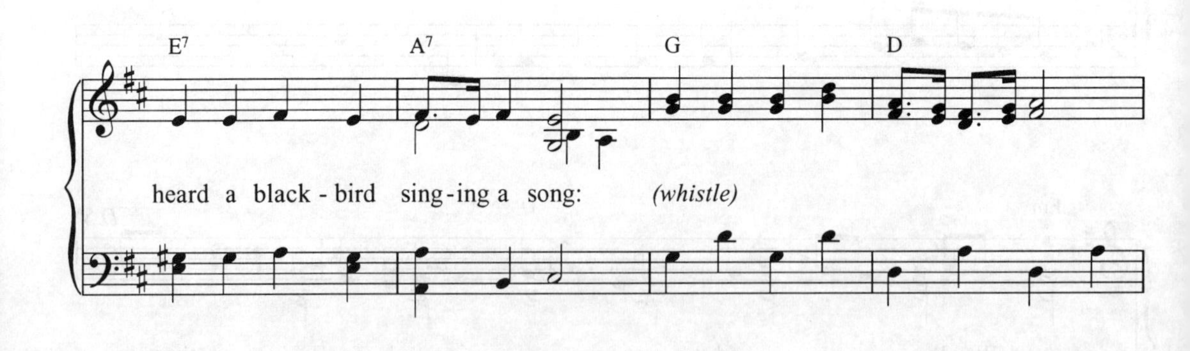
E7
A7
G
D
heard a black - bird sing-ing a song: (whistle)

A7
D
G
D

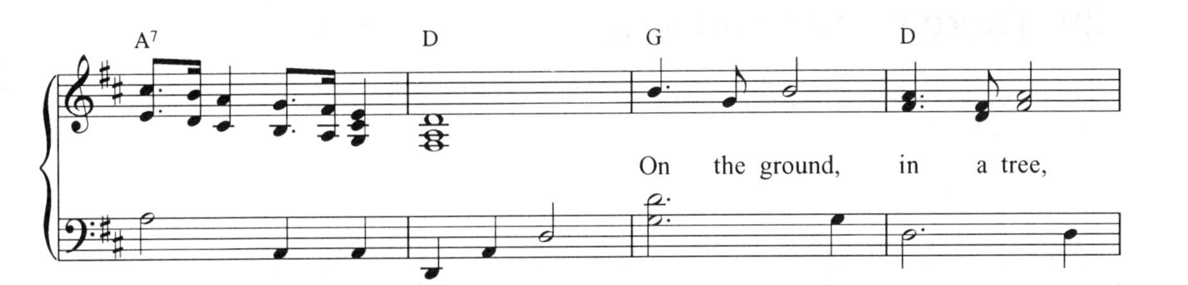
A7
D
G
D
On the ground, in a tree,

A7
D
G
D/F♯
F♯
through the air or un - der the sea, I know who - e - ver

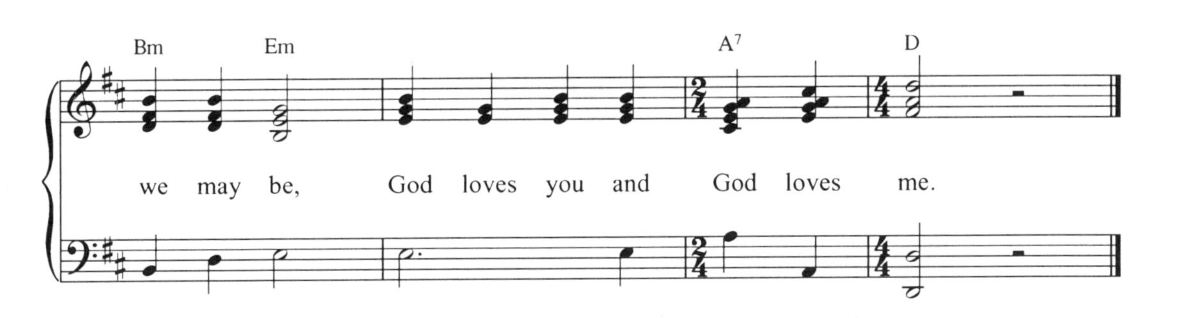
Bm
Em
A7
D
we may be, God loves you and God loves me.

2. There I was, walking with my wellyboots,
   splosh, splosh, splosh through the mud.
   And as I was squelching along,
   I heard a cow singing a song:
   moo...

Add extra verses as required.

729 There's a river flowing

Words and Music: Chris Jackson and Jill Hoffmann
arr. Dave Bankhead

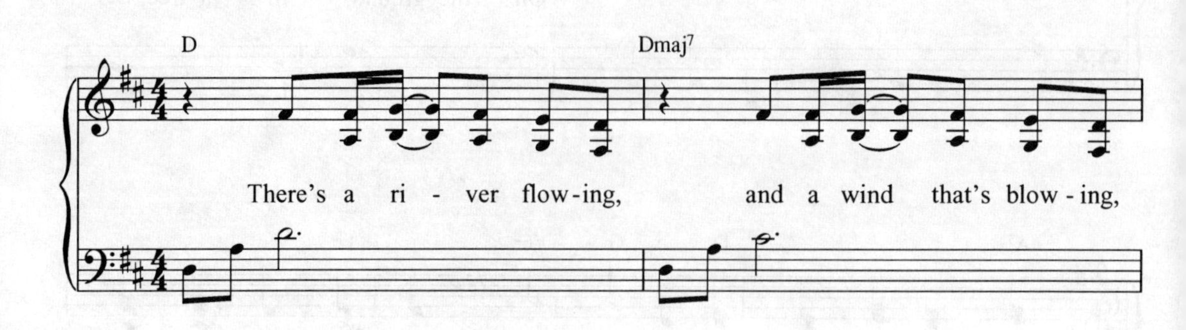
D
Dmaj7
There's a ri - ver flow-ing, and a wind that's blow-ing,

Bm
G
A
there's a fire burn-ing in our hearts.

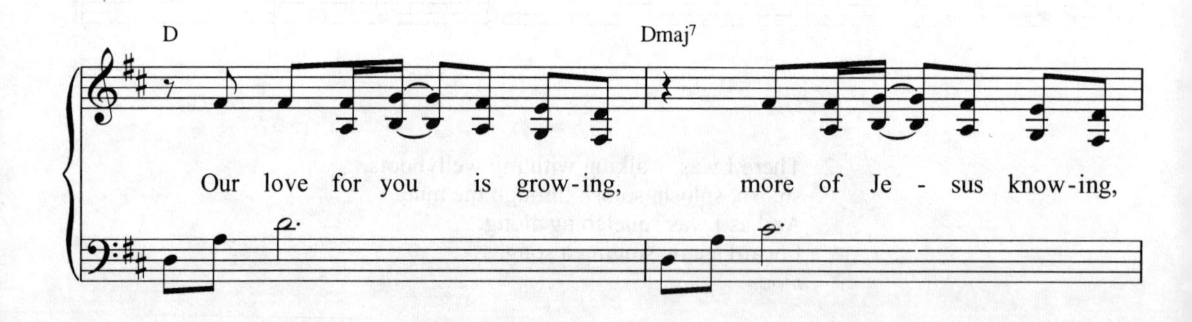
D
Dmaj7
Our love for you is grow-ing, more of Je - sus know-ing,

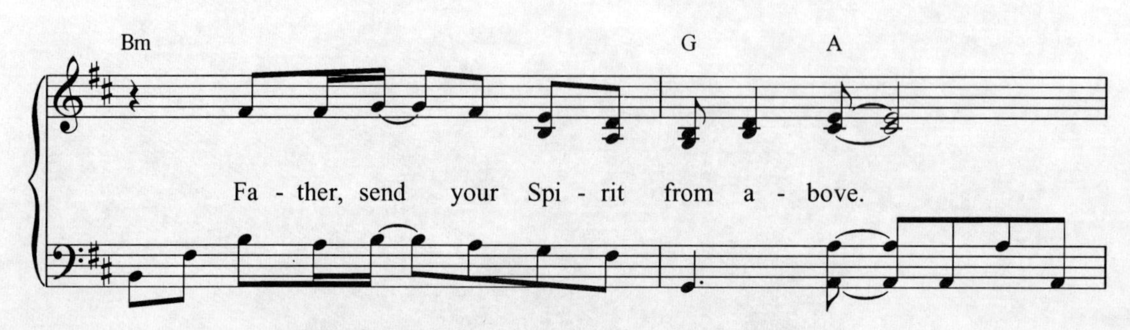
Bm
G
A
Fa - ther, send your Spi - rit from a - bove.

G/B A/C♯ D Dmaj7
Oh, come ri - ver of
Bm7 G A D
love, fill me a - gain
Dmaj7 Bm7 G A
pow - er of God, o - ver and o - ver a -
D D/F♯ G A
gain, o - ver and o - ver a -
D D/F♯ G A D
gain, o - ver and o - ver a - gain.

730 There's a special feeling

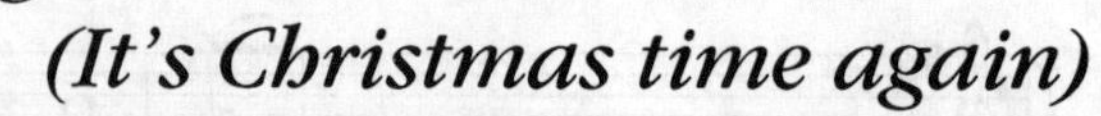
(It's Christmas time again)

Words and Music: Philip Chapman
and Stephanie Chapman

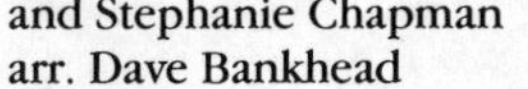
arr. Dave Bankhead

Capo 3
B♭ G
E♭ C
F D
B♭ G
1. There's a spe - cial feel - ing in the air, it's

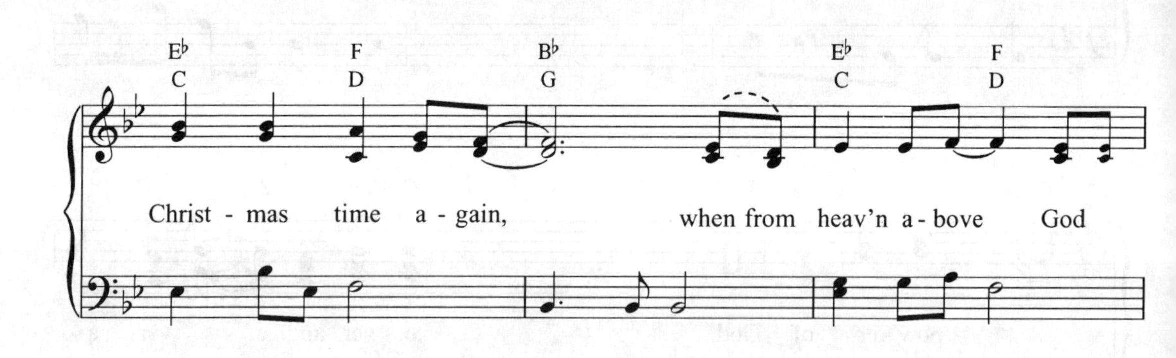
E♭ C
F D
B♭ G
E♭ C
F D
Christ - mas time a - gain, when from heav'n a - bove God

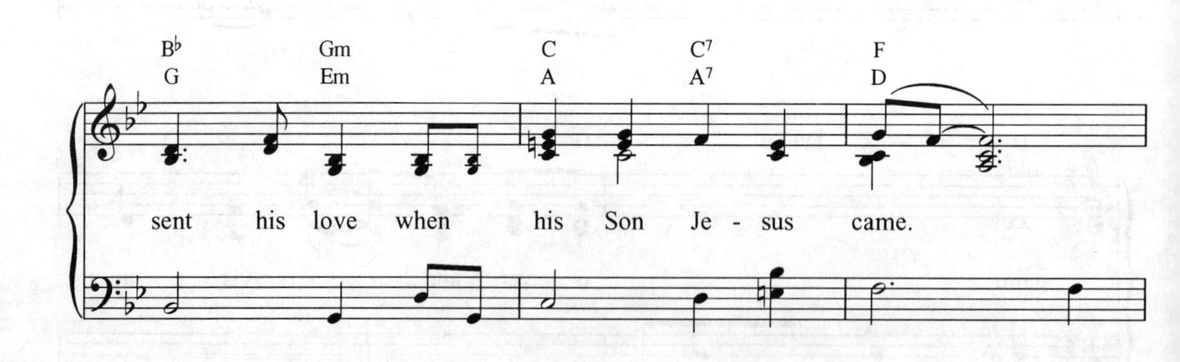
B♭ G
Gm Em
C A
C7 A7
F D
sent his love when his Son Je - sus came.

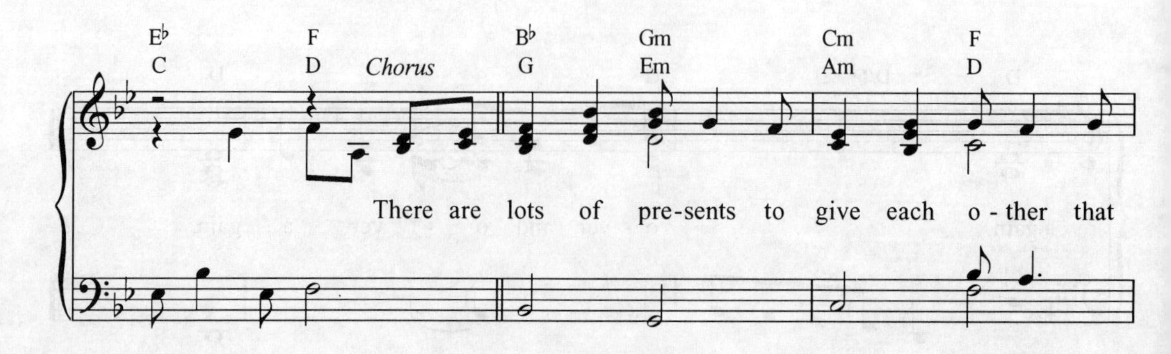
E♭ C
F D
Chorus
B♭ G
Gm Em
Cm Am
F D
There are lots of pre-sents to give each o - ther that

B♭ G
Gm Em
Dm Bm
E♭ C
Cm Am
don't need mo-ney at all, when we show our love, when they
1, 2.
3.
Dm Bm
Gm Em
E♭ C
E♭/F C/D
F D
B♭ G
Cm Am
F D
B♭ G
know we care, that's the best gift we can share. 2. Re - share.

2. Remember all that Jesus brings
   each day the whole year through,
   he gives us help and he gives us love
   and he gave his life for you.

3. So think about the ones you love
   and all that you can do
   to help them feel all your love so real,
   just as Jesus loves you too.

731 There's a star

Words and Music: James Wright
arr. Chris Mitchell

Capo 3
Chorus
B♭ F/A E♭/G F7sus4 E♭ B♭/D
G D/F♯ C/E D7sus4 C G/B
There's a star that shines so bright on this still and
There's a joy that fills the air, it's a joy that
Cm7 Fsus4 F B♭ F/A E♭/G B♭/F
Am7 Dsus4 D G D/F♯ C/E G/D
ho - ly night. Hea-ven's own be - got - ten Son
all can share. For the Sa - viour
1.
Cm7 F7 E♭/G B♭/F
Am7 D7 C/E G/D
is born this hap - py morn.
2.
of the world is
Cm7 Fsus4 F B♭ D D7/F♯
Am7 Dsus4 D G B B7/D♯
Fine
born this hap - py morn.
1. Shep - herds in the

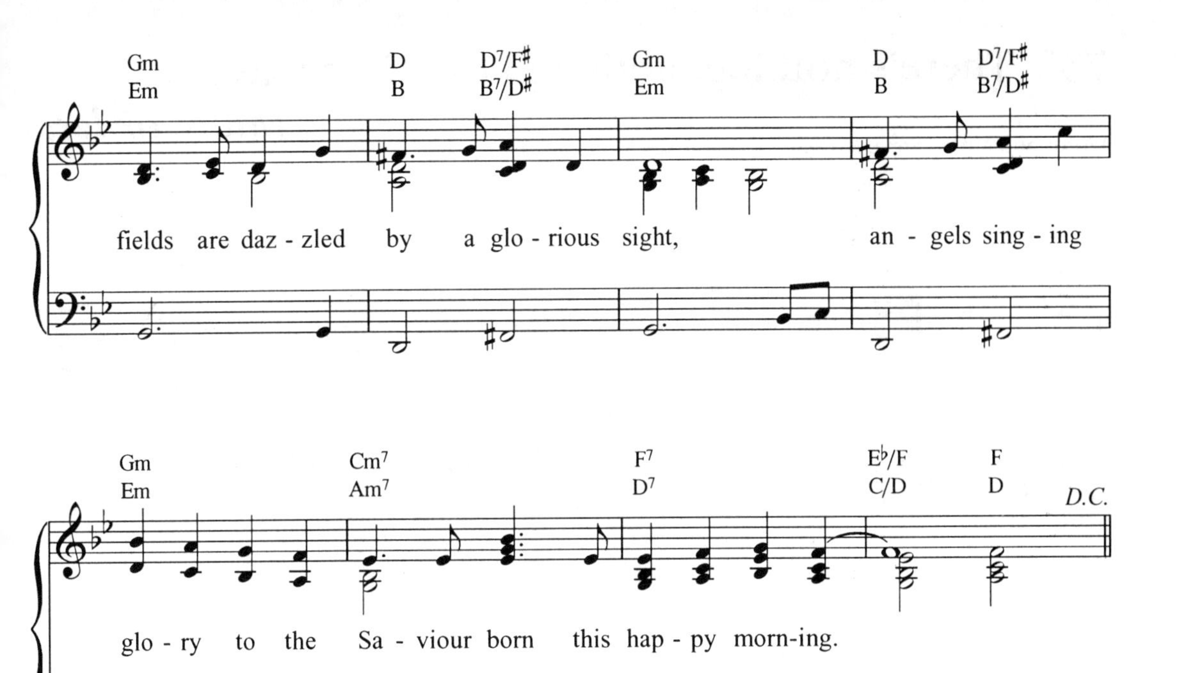
Gm D D7/F# Gm D D7/F#
Em B B7/D# Em B B7/D#
fields are daz - zled by a glo - rious sight, an - gels sing - ing
Gm Cm7 F7 E♭/F F
Em Am7 D7 C/D D
D.C.
glo - ry to the Sa - viour born this hap - py morn-ing.

2. Wise men travel far to gaze
   and worship at his feet,
   bearing precious gifts before
   the Saviour born this happy morning.

732 There's nothing, nothing I can do or say

(More or less)

Words and Music: Steve Morgan-Gurr and Kay Morgan-Gurr

G
C
1. There's no - thing, no - thing I can do or say to make God love me more.

G
He fa - thers me in such a way it

A
D7
G
lasts for e - ver - more. The Bi - ble says that

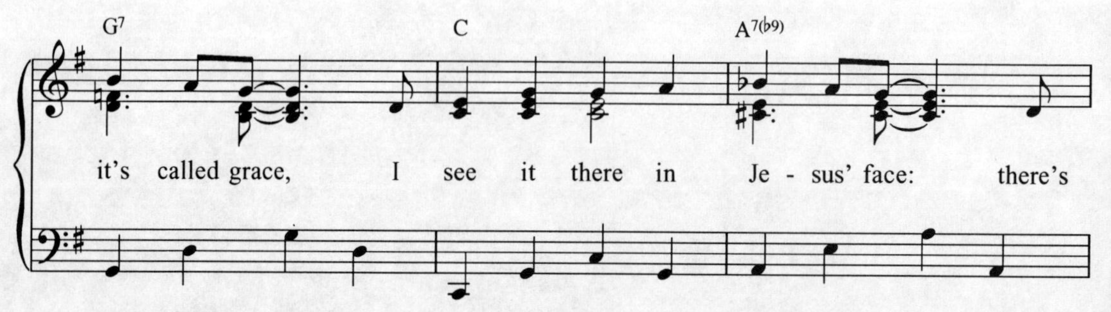
G7
C
A7(♭9)
it's called grace, I see it there in Je - sus' face: there's

G
Em
C
D
no - thing, no - thing I can do or say to make God love me more,
G
Em
C
D
1.
G
2.
G
to make God love me more.
2. There's

2. There's nothing, nothing I can do or say
to make God love me less.
I need forgiveness ev'ry day,
and Jesus' righteousness.
But when I turn to him and pray
he gives his mercy right away:
there's nothing, nothing I can do or say
to make God love me less,
to make God love me less.

733 There was a clever man *(The two builders)*

Words and Music: Amanda Lofts
arr. Chris Mitchell

Capo 3
F D
B♭ G
1. There was a cle - ver man who had a cle - ver plan to
C7 A7
F D
B♭ G
F/A D/F♯
Gm7 Em7
build a love - ly house all safe and strong. He
found a nice firm rock and went knock, knock, knock. He'd
built a love - ly house be - fore too long.
Chorus
And the light - ning flashed and the
thun - der crashed, and the wind was blow - ing and the snow was snow - ing. The
C7 E7

B♭ G
F/A D/F♯
C7 A7
F D
rain poured down, the man was safe and sound. His
(2.) rain went splash and his house went crash! His

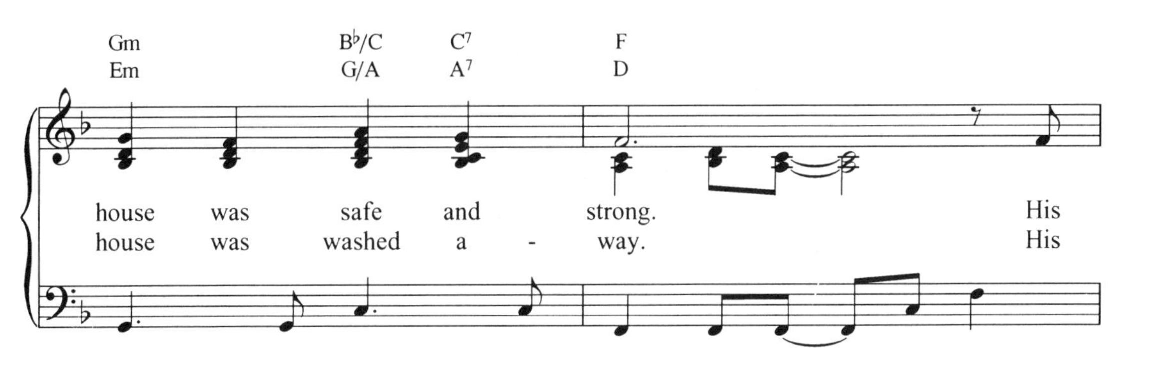
Gm Em
B♭/C G/A
C7 A7
F D
house was safe and strong. His
house was washed a - way. His

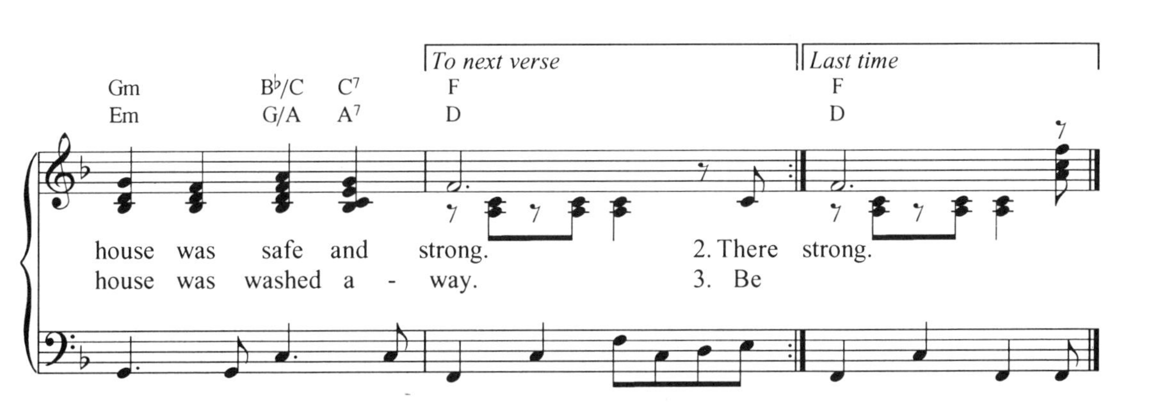
To next verse
Last time
Gm Em
B♭/C G/A
C7 A7
F D
F D
house was safe and strong. 2. There strong.
house was washed a - way. 3. Be

2. There was a silly man who had a silly plan
   to build a house as quickly as he could.
   He found some sand so flat and went splat, splat, splat.
   The silly man thought it looked quite good.

Chorus 2

3. Be like the clever man, and have a clever plan
   to listen to the things that God tells you.
   So go and find his book and look, look, look
   and do the things he's telling you to do.

Chorus 1

734 These are the days *(Days of Elijah)*

Words and Music: Robin Mark
Capo 2
A2 G2 D/A C/G A2 G2
D/A C/G A G D/A C/G
1. These are the days of E - li - jah, de -
2. These are the days of E - ze - kiel, the
A G E D A G
clar - ing the word of the Lord; and these are the days of your
dry bones be - com - ing as flesh; and these are the days of your
D/A C/G A/E G/D E D A G
ser - vant, Mo - ses, right - eous - ness be - ing re - stored. And
ser - vant, Da - vid, re - build - ing a tem - ple of praise.
C♯m Bm F♯m Em Bm7 Am7 Bm7/A Am7/G
though these are days of great tri - al, of fa - mine and dark - ness and
These are the days of the har - vest, the fields are as white in the

E D A G D/A C/G
sword, still we are the voice in the de - sert cry - ing, 'Pre-
world, and we are the lab-'rers in your vine-yard, de -
A/E G/D E D A G
Chorus
pare ye the way of the Lord.'
clar - ing the word of the Lord.
Be - hold, he comes ri - ding on the
D/A C/G A G E D
clouds, shi - ning like the sun at the trum - pet call; lift your
A G D/A C/G A G E D A G
voice, it's the year of ju - bi - lee, out of Zi - on's hill sal - va - tion comes.
D/A C/G A G D/A C/G
Last time
A G

735 These are the things we believe

Words and Music: Capt. Alan J. Price, CA
arr. Philip Eley

(♩ = 134)
Cmaj7
G9
Cmaj7
G9
Cmaj7
G9
Cmaj7
G9

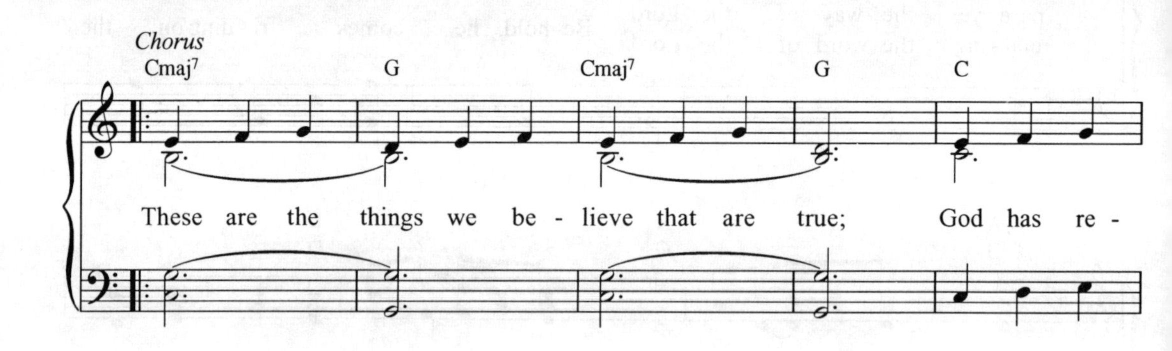

Chorus
Cmaj7
G
Cmaj7
G
C
These are the things we be - lieve that are true; God has re -

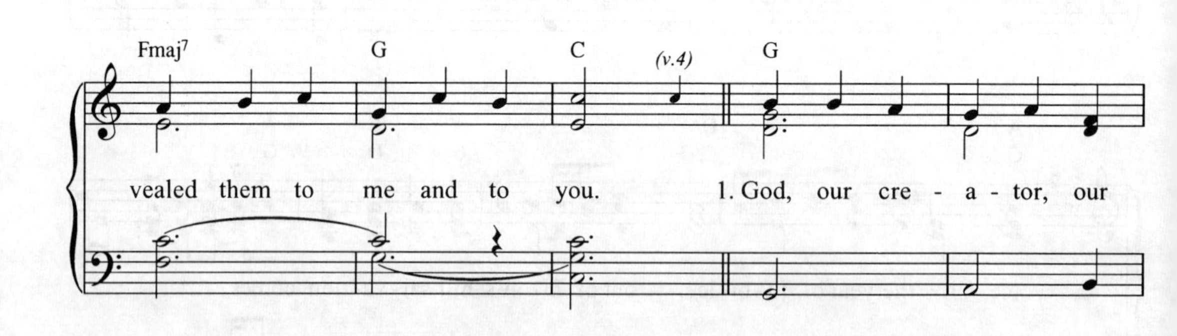

Fmaj7
G
C
(v.4)
G
vealed them to me and to you. 1. God, our cre - a - tor, our

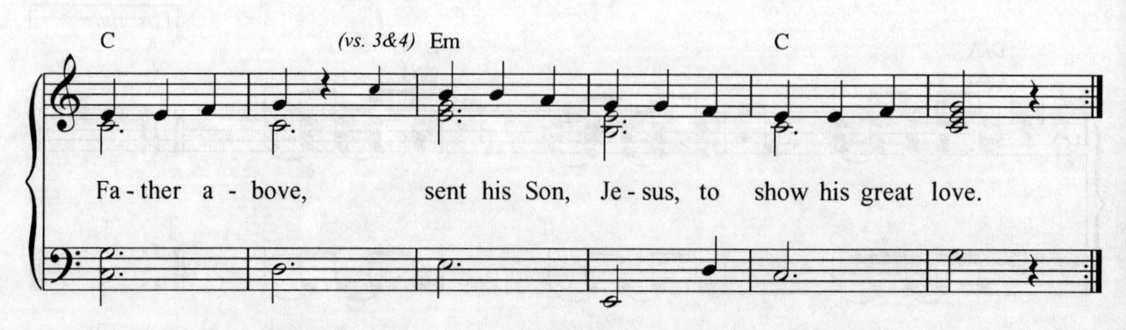

C
(vs. 3&4)
Em
C
Fa - ther a - bove, sent his Son, Je - sus, to show his great love.

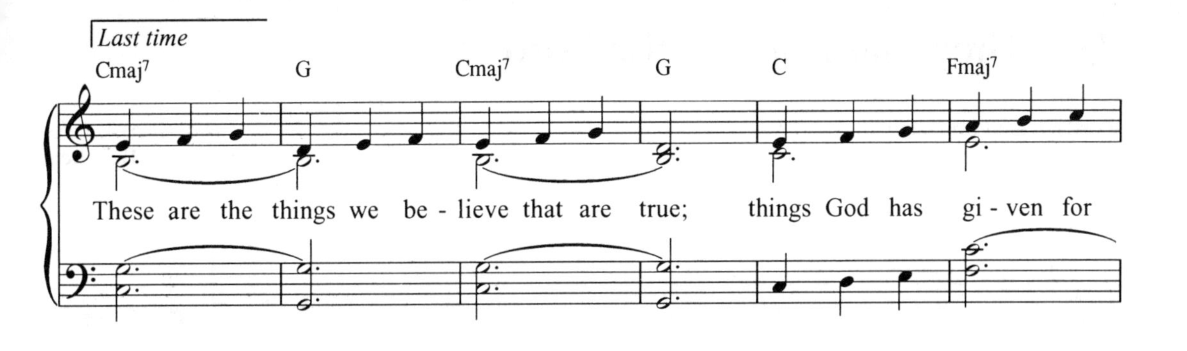
Last time
Cmaj7
G
Cmaj7
G
C
Fmaj7
These are the things we be - lieve that are true; things God has gi - ven for

G
C
Cmaj7
G9
Cmaj7
G9
me and for you.

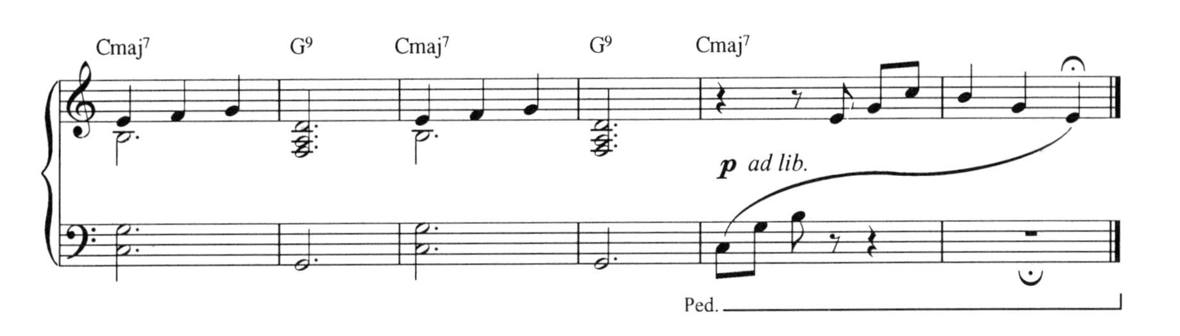
Cmaj7
G9
Cmaj7
G9
Cmaj7
p ad lib.
Ped.

2. Jesus was killed,
   though no wrong he had done;
   part of God's plan
   to forgive ev'ryone.

3. Risen from death,
   then to heaven he went,
   and just as he promised,
   the helper he sent.

4. Spirit, our helper,
   works in you and me,
   'til Jesus returns
   and with him we will be.

736 They that hope in the Lord

Words: based on Isaiah 40:31

Music: Chris Jackson
arr. Dave Bankhead

G
D
They that hope in the Lord
shall re - new their

G
D
strength,
they that hope in the Lord,

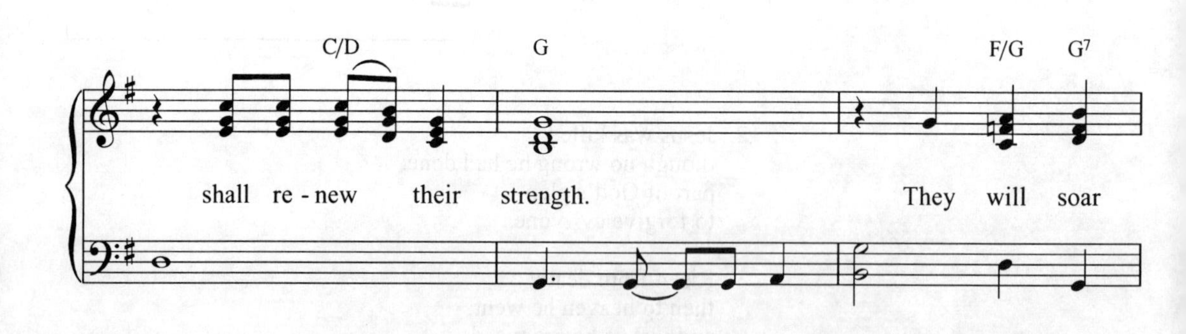
C/D
G
F/G
G7
shall re - new their strength.
They will soar

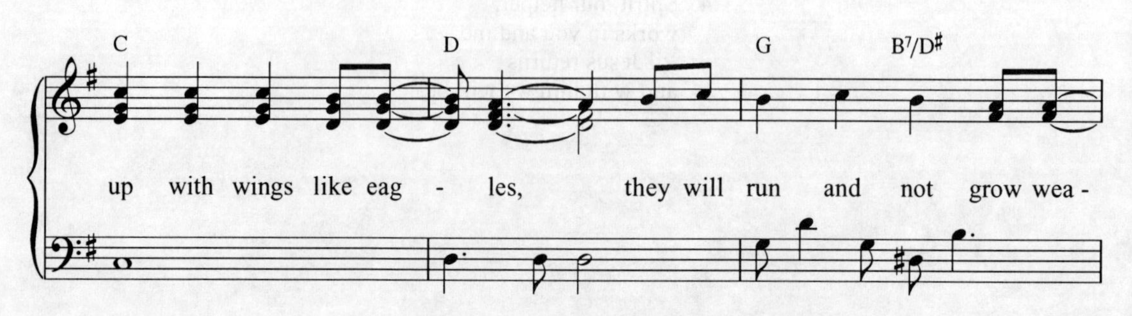
C
D
G
B7/D#
up with wings like eag - les,
they will run and not grow wea -

Em
D
- ry, they will walk,
and not faint.

G
F/G
G7
C
They will soar up with wings like eag -

D
G
B7/D♯
Em
- les, they will run and not grow wea - ry, they will

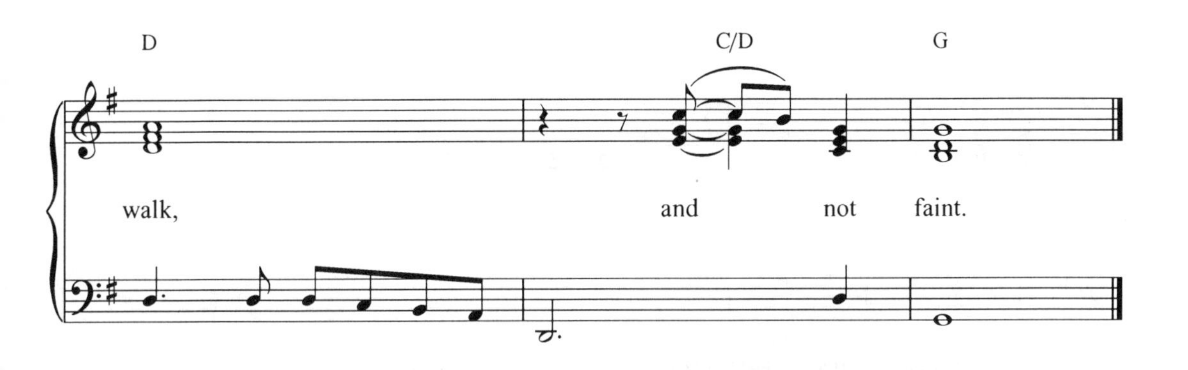
D
C/D
G
walk,
and not faint.

737 This Child

Words and Music: Graham Kendrick

Calypso
D
G
A7

D
G
1. This Child, se - cret - ly comes in the night, O this

A7
D
Child, hi-ding a hea - ven - ly light, O this Child, com-ing to us

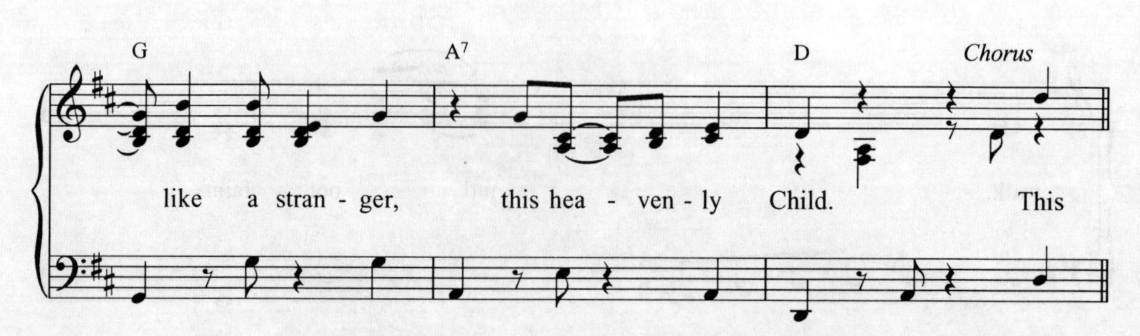
G
A7
D
Chorus
like a stran - ger, this hea - ven - ly Child. This

G
D
A7
Child, hea-ven come down now to be with us here, hea-ven-ly love
D
G
D
and mer - cy ap - pear, soft-ly in awe and won - der come
Asus4
A
1, 2.
D
near – to this hea - ven - ly Child.
3.
D
D.S.
4.
D
2. This Child. This Child.
3. This

2. This Child, rising on us like the sun,
   O this Child, given to light everyone,
   O this Child, guiding our feet on the pathway
   to peace on earth.

3. This Child, raising the humble and poor,
   O this Child, making the proud ones to fall;
   O this Child, filling the hungry with good things,
   this heavenly Child.

738 This is a noisy song *(Song to Jesus)*

Words and Music: Andrew Pearson and Pauline Pearson

D G D
1. This is a noi - sy song, a noi - sy song to Je - sus.
A G D
This is a noi - sy song, that I can sing to him.

2. This is a clapping song . . .

3. This is a marching song . . .

4. This is a quiet song . . .

5. This is a noisy song . . .

739 Those who put their hope in the Lord

Words: based on Isaiah 40:31

Music: John Hardwick
arr. Dave Bankhead

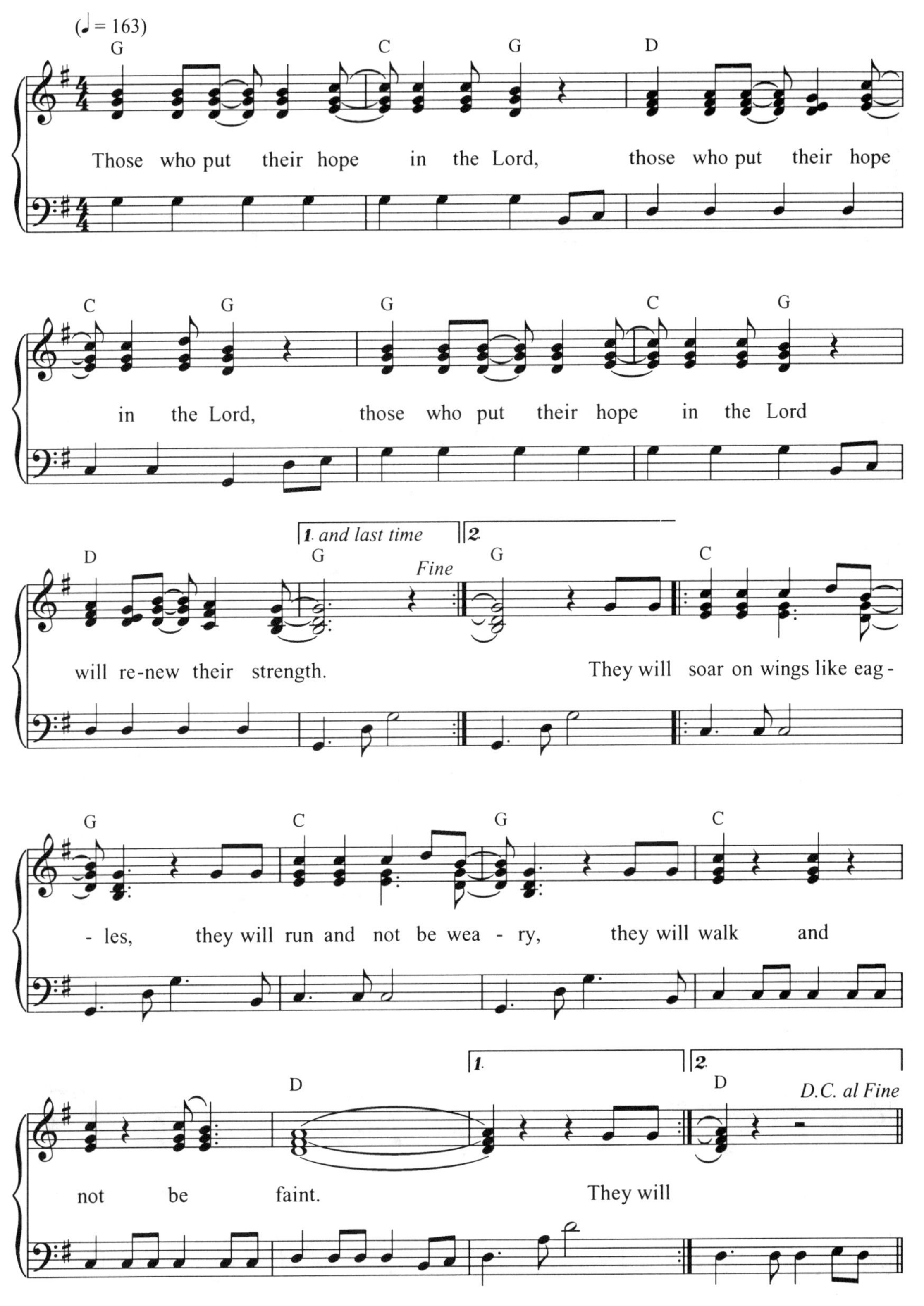

(♩ = 163)
G C G D
Those who put their hope in the Lord, those who put their hope
C G G C G
in the Lord, those who put their hope in the Lord
1. and last time
2.
D G G C
Fine
will re-new their strength. They will soar on wings like eag-
G C G C
-les, they will run and not be wea-ry, they will walk and
1.
2.
D D
D.C. al Fine
not be faint. They will

740 Though I am little *(In all things)*

Words and Music: Iain D. Craig

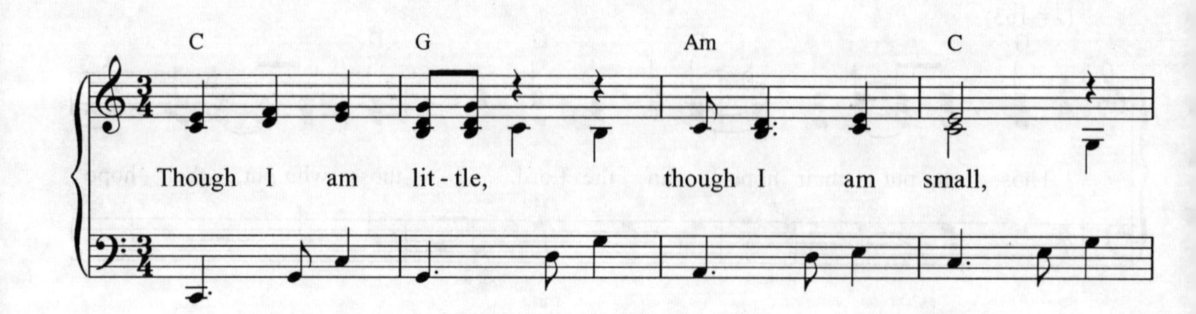
C
G
Am
C
Though I am lit - tle,
though I am small,

G
C
G
Lord, I can trust you in all things.

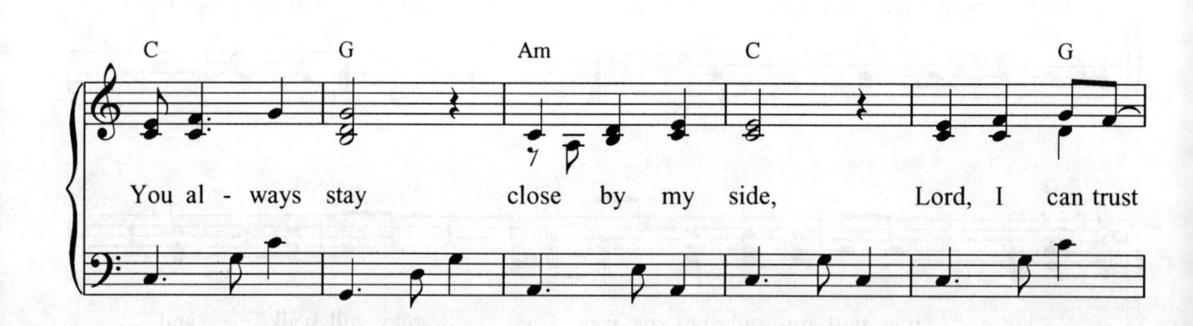
C
G
Am
C
G
You al - ways stay close by my side, Lord, I can trust

C
G
F
you in all things. You ne - ver leave

G C A
me, I'm ne-ver a-lone. When I sit at your feet I am

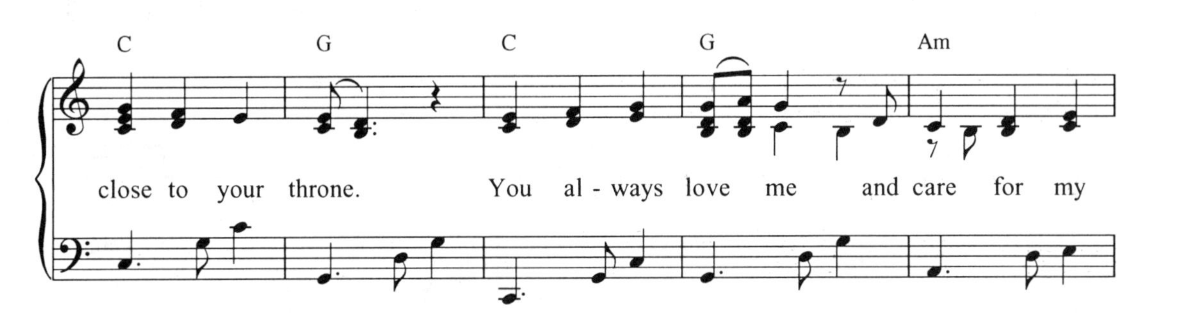
C G C G Am
close to your throne. You al-ways love me and care for my

C G C
needs. Lord, I can trust you in all things.

741 Three, nine, thirty-nine

Words and Music: Ian Smale

G G C G
1. Three, nine, thir - ty - nine,
C G G D G
thir - ty - nine books are in the Old Tes - ta - ment. Two, se - ven,
C G C D G D7 G
Chorus
twen - ty - sev'n, but there's on - ly twen - ty - se - ven in the New. But
D G C
just one ho - ly God could bring the book to life and pro - mise
G D G
ev - 'ry word is true. The one and on - ly liv - ing God told the

A7
D7
E♭
wri - ters what they should and should - n't do.
A♭
D♭
A♭
D♭
A♭
2. Two, eight, twen - ty - eight, o - ver twen - ty - eight au - thors in the
A♭
E♭
A♭
D♭
A♭
Old Tes - ta - ment, but just nine, on - ly nine, there are
D♭
E♭
A♭
E♭7
A♭
Chorus
E♭
on - ly nine au - thors in the New. But just one
A♭
D♭
ho - ly God could bring the book to life and pro - mise

A♭
E♭
A♭
ev - 'ry word is true. The one and on - ly liv - ing God told the
B♭7
E♭7
E7
wri - ters what they should and should - n't do.
A
D
A
3. Two, com - ma, nought, nought, nought, two
D
A
E
A
thou - sand years are co - vered in the Old Tes - ta - ment, but e - ven less than
D
A
D
E
one, nought, nought, less than one hun - dred years are co - vered in the

A E7 A Chorus E A
New. But just one ho - ly God could
D A E
bring the book to life and pro - mise ev - 'ry word is true. The
A
one and on - ly liv - ing God told the
1.
B7 E7
wri - ters what they should and should - n't do. But
2.
B7 E7 A
wri - ters what they should and should - n't do.

742 Tick tock goes the clock *(Sound song)*

Words and Music: J. Macpherson

Clock-rock! (♩ = 152)
E
*
Leader
E
Group 1
1. Tick tock goes the clock, *tick tock, tick*
Leader
B
Group 2
Leader
tock. Drip - a - drip goes the tap, *drip - a - drip, drip - a - drip.* Croak, croak goes the
Group 3
Leader
E
Groups 1, 2 and 3
frog, *croak, croak, croak, croak.* That's the sound of the night. *Tick tock, tick*
Drip - a - drip, drip - a-
Croak, croak, croak,
1, 3, 5,
Leader
tock, tick tock, tick tock, tick tock, tick tock. 2. Brr, brr goes the
drip, drip-a-drip, drip-a - drip, drip-a-drip, drip-a - drip.
croak, croak, croak, croak, croak, croak, croak, croak, croak.
2, 4, 6,
Leader
A
Groups
Leader
dong.
plates. Let ev - 'ry - thing, *let ev - 'ry - thing* that makes a
house.

* *Pitched wood-blocks (optional throughout)*

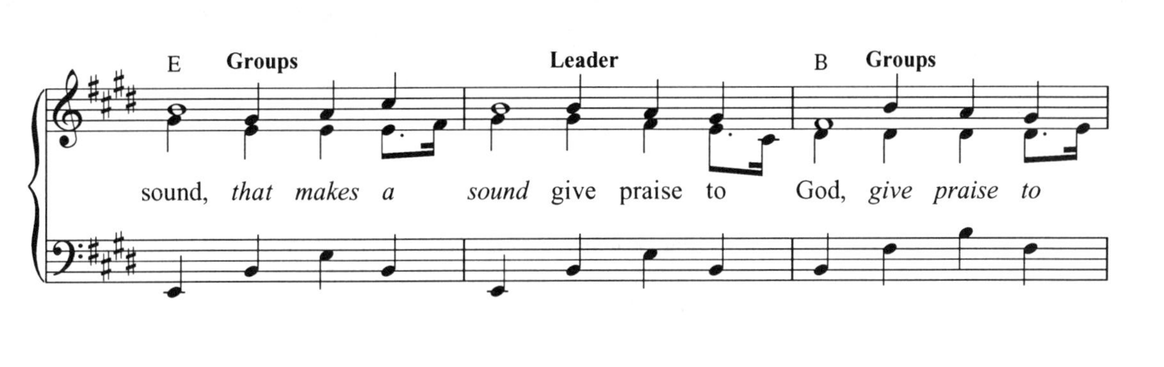
E Groups
Leader
B Groups
sound, that makes a sound give praise to God, give praise to

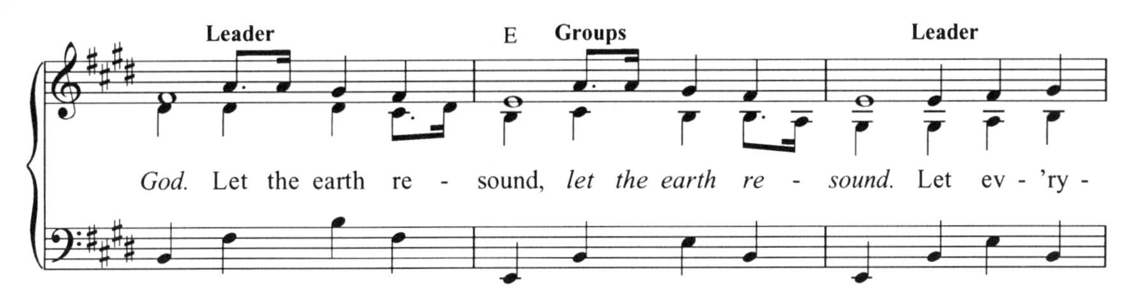
Leader
E Groups
Leader
God. Let the earth re - sound, let the earth re - sound. Let ev - 'ry -

A Groups
Leader
E Groups
thing, let ev - 'ry - thing that lives and breathes, that lives and

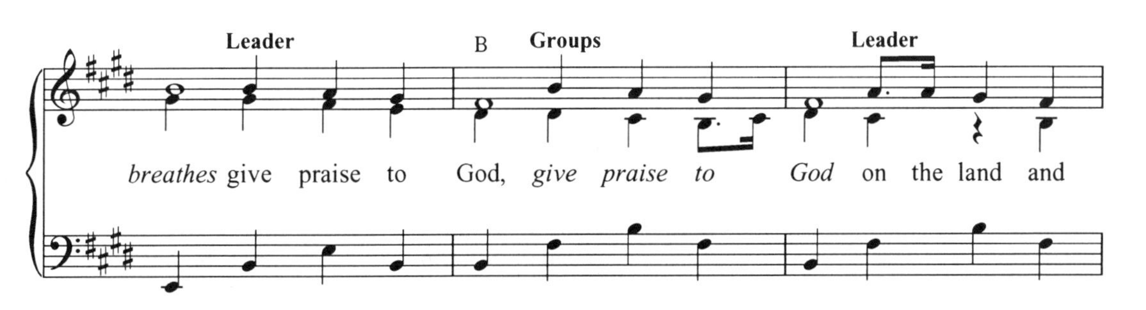
Leader
B Groups
Leader
breathes give praise to God, give praise to God on the land and

To next verse
Last time
E Groups
Leader
Leader
sea, on the land and sea. 3. Woo, woo goes the on the land and sea.

2. Brr, brr goes the phone,
brr, brr, brr, brr.
Ding dong goes the door,
ding dong, ding dong.
Clatter, clatter go the plates,
clatter, clatter, clatter, clatter.
That's the sound of the house.

Chorus

3. Woo, woo goes the horn,
woo, woo, woo, woo,
'All aboard,' goes the guard,
'all aboard, all aboard.'
Clacketty clack go the wheels,
clacketty clack, clacketty clack.
That's the sound of the train.

4. Breep, breep goes the ref,
breep, breep, breep, breep.
Boing, boing goes the ball,
boing, boing, boing, boing.
Hip hooray goes the crowd,
hip hooray, hip hooray.
That's the sound of the game.

Chorus

5. Boom, boom goes the bass,
boom, boom, boom, boom.
Rat-a-tat goes the drum,
rat-a-tat, rat-a-tat.
Tweedle dee goes the fife,
tweedle dee, tweedle dee.
That's the sound of the band.

6. Wark, wark goes the crow,
wark, wark, wark, wark.
Moo, moo goes the cow,
moo, moo, moo, moo.
Oink, oink goes the pig,
oink, oink, oink, oink.
That's the sound of the farm.

Chorus

743 Tick, tock, tick, tock

Words and Music: Capt. Alan J. Price, CA

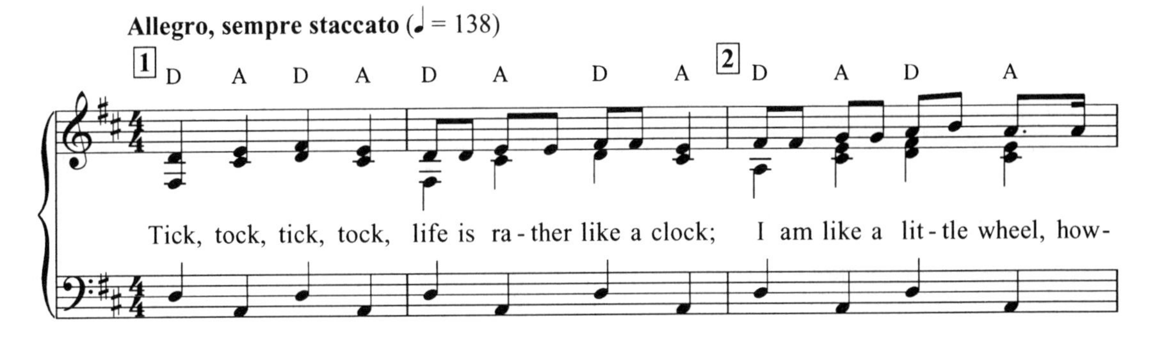
Allegro, sempre staccato (♩ = 138)
1
D A D A D A D A
2
D A D A
Tick, tock, tick, tock, life is ra - ther like a clock; I am like a lit - tle wheel, how-

D A D A
3
D A D A
e - ver big or small I feel; God can use me in his plan,

D A D A
4
D A D A D A D A
I can serve him as I am; is - n't it good? Is - n't it good?

This may be sung as a round,
with entries indicated by numbers.

744 Touch a finger *(Every bit of you is special)*

Words and Music: Doug Horley
arr. Dave Bankhead

D A
Touch a fin - ger, touch a thumb, touch a wrist, touch an el-
D A
- bow, touch a shoul - der, touch a head, ev - 'ry bit of you is
touch an ear,
D
1.
2.
A
spe - cial. Touch a fin - If you're short and fat, or
D A D A
tall and thin, got knob - b - ly knees or fif - teen chins; does - n't mat - ter just what
D Em D A/C♯ Bm7 A
shape you're in, God loves you as you are. Touch a fin-

D A D
- ger, touch a thumb, touch a wrist, touch an el - bow, touch a shoul-
A D
- der, touch an eye - brow, ev - 'ry bit of you is spe-cial.
A
Touch a toe, touch an an - kle, touch a knee, touch a hip,
D A
touch a back, bump a bot - tom, touch a nose;
D G A G D
touch lips!

745 Turn to the Lord

Words and Music: Andy Read
arr. Chris Mitchell

Chorus
E7 A7 E7 A7
Turn to the Lord, turn to the Lord,
E7 A7 E7
turn to the Lord and praise him.
A7 E7 A7
Turn to the Lord, turn to the Lord,
Last time to Coda
To repeat
To continue
E7 A7 E7 E7
turn to the Lord and praise him. praise him. 1. For he is
2. From my
E7 A7 B7
good, for he is kind, he has pow-er to de-li-ver me.
fear, from my sin, he has pow-er to de-li-ver me.

E7
He is ho - ly, full of mer - cy, he has
He is love, he is light, he has
A7
B7
E7
D.C.
CODA
pow - er to de - li - ver me.
pow - er to de - li - ver me.
praise him.
Praise him!
Praise him!
Pow - er to de - li - ver me.
To repeat
Last time
Fine
To continue
Bop bop boo - wop,
bop bop boo - wop,
bop bop boo - wop,
bop bop bop bop bop.
2nd time D.S.

746 Unto us a child is born

Words and Music: Mark Johnson and Helen Johnson
arr. Dave Bankhead

(♩ = 96)
Capo 3
Chorus
F D
Dm7 Bm7
Gm7 Em7
B♭ G
B♭/C G/A
Un - to us a child is born, un - to us a Son is gi - ven.
To repeat
C7 A7
He shall reign in all the earth, he will be called Em - man - u - el!
Last time
To verses
Fine
he will be called Em - man - u - el!
he will be called Em - man - u - el!
Csus4 Asus4
C A
1. An - gel voi - ces sing, hal - le - lu - jahs ring, for to-

A
F♯
A/C♯
F♯/A♯
Dm
Bm
C
A
C/E
A/C♯
F
D
day in Beth - le - hem the love of God has come to men, the

B♭
G
F/A
D/F♯
Gm7
Em7
F
D
C
A
B♭ F/A Gm7
G D/F♯ Em7
D.C.
Sa - viour of the world is Christ the King!

2. Leave your cares aside,
   seek and you will find,
   for today in Bethlehem
   the love of God has come to men,
   the Saviour of the world is Jesus Christ!

3. Come, let us adore,
   now and evermore,
   for today in Bethlehem
   the love of God has come to men,
   the Saviour of the world is Christ the Lord!

747 We are a new generation *(New generation)*

Words and Music: John Hardwick
arr. Chris Mitchell

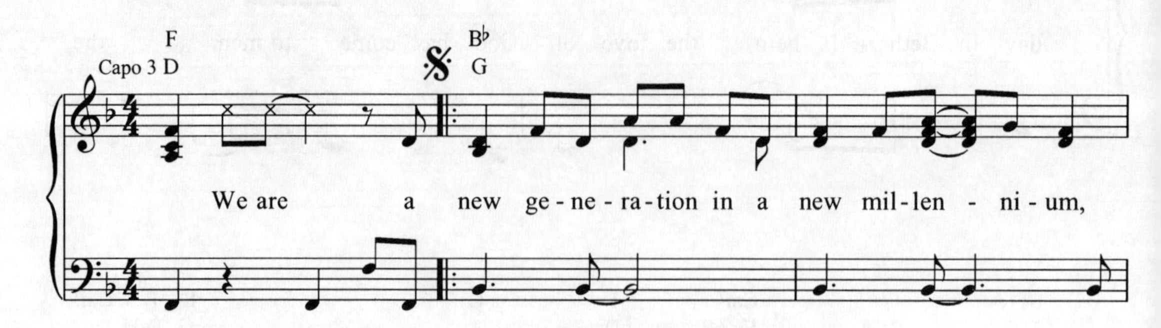
F
D
Capo 3 D
B♭
G
We are a new ge-ne-ra-tion in a new mil-len - ni-um,

F
D
B♭
G
want-ing to do what is right. We are a new ge-ne-ra-tion in a

G7
E7
C
A
new mil-len - ni-um, walk-ing in God's light. We are a

B♭
G
F
D
new ge-ne-ra-tion in a new mil-len - ni-um, not know-ing what the fu-ture holds.

Dm7
Bm7
B♭
G
We are a new ge-ne-ra-tion in a new mil-len-ni-um,
To repeat
Last time
F
D
Fine
put-ting our hope in the Lord. We are a Lord.
To continue
C
A
Lord. Some put their hope in rich-es, some
put their hope in fame. Some put their hope in good
looks; but that seems such a shame. I'm

C
A
B♭
G
put - ting my hope in the one thing that has a gua - ran - tee.
F
D
C
A
I'm put - ting my hope in Je -
G
E
C
A
- sus; he is the one for me! He's the
N.C.
same yes - ter - day, to - day and for e - ver and his
1.
2.
D.S.
love lasts e - ter - nal - ly. He's the We are a

748 We are God's chosen, holy nation

(Rising generation)

Words and Music: Dave Bankhead and Mike Burn

D A/C♯
Chorus
Bm
A
D
D/F♯
We are God's cho - sen, ho - ly na - tion, we be -

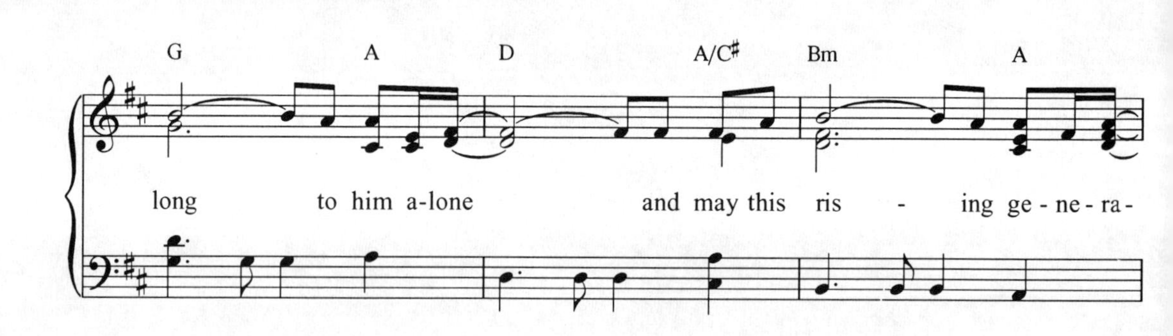
G
A
D
A/C♯
Bm
A
long to him a-lone and may this ris - ing ge - ne - ra -

D
D/F♯
G
A
Bm
D/F♯
- tion wor - ship Christ up - on his throne, wor - ship

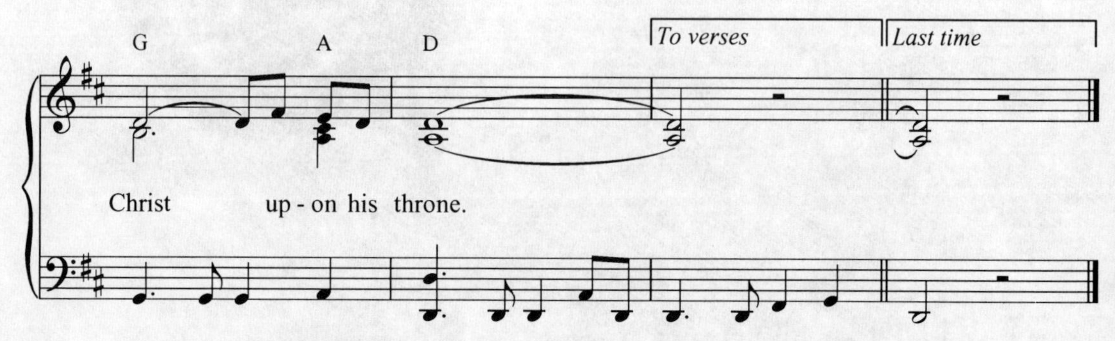
G
A
D
To verses
Last time
Christ up - on his throne.

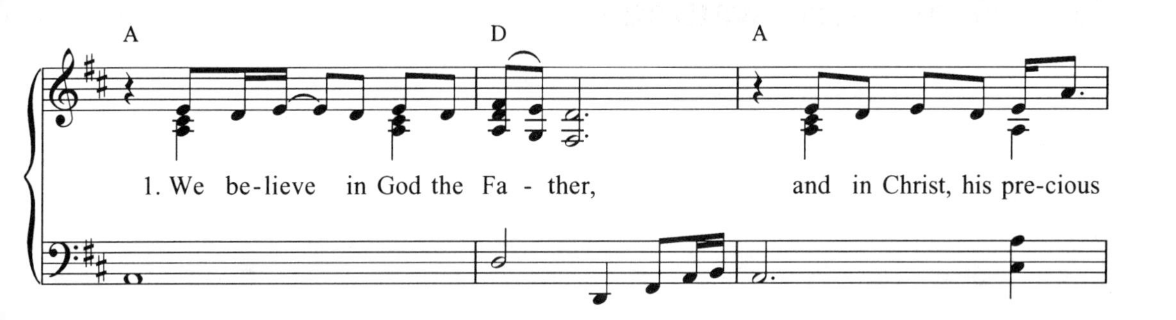
A
D
A
1. We be-lieve in God the Fa - ther,
and in Christ, his pre-cious

D
A
Bm
Son.
We be-lieve he died to save us,

G6
Em7
Asus4
A
Chorus
D.S.
came to call us as his own.
We are God's

2. We believe he sends his Spirit
on us now with gifts of power.
Hear the Spirit calling out to us,
where he leads us we will go.

749 We are here, waiting

Words and Music: Capt. Alan J. Price, CA
arr. Philip Eley

(♩ = 94)
D
F♯m

Bm
G
3
D
1. We are

D
F♯m
Bm
1.&2. here, wait-ing, we are here, seek-ing, we are here,
1.&2. here, need-ing, we are here, ask - ing, we are here,

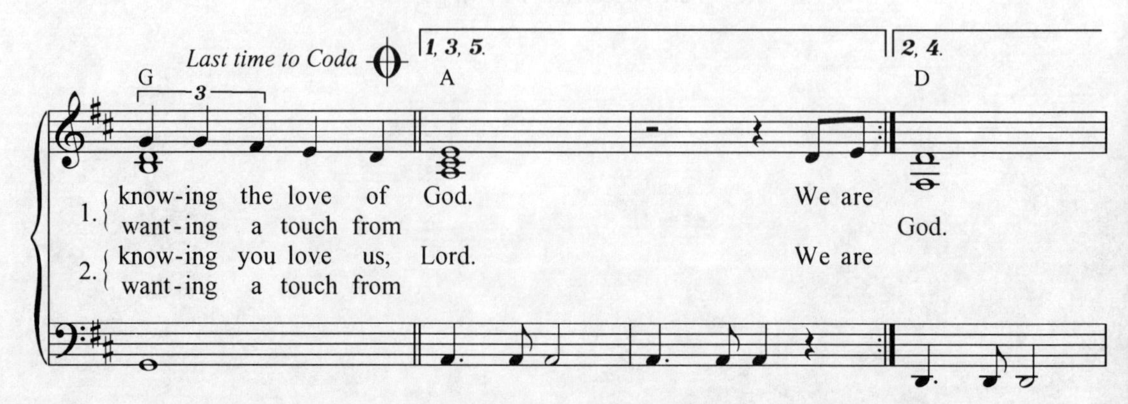

Last time to Coda
1, 3, 5.
2, 4.
G
3
A
D
1. know-ing the love of God. We are
want-ing a touch from God.
2. know-ing you love us, Lord. We are
want-ing a touch from

Chorus
G
D
The touch of his Son, Je - sus Christ, the touch of his

G
D
G
E7
Spi - rit, Lord of life: the touch of our God to make us all that he wants us to

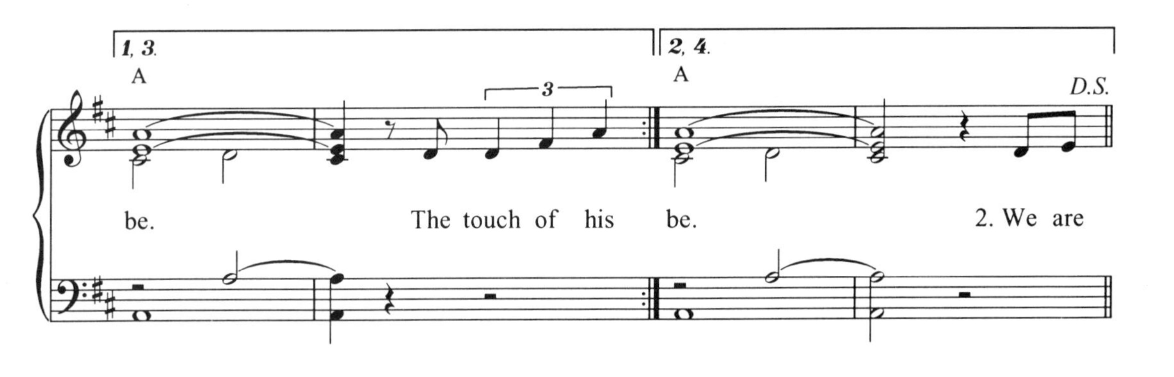
1, 3.
2, 4.
A
A
D.S.
be. The touch of his be. 2. We are

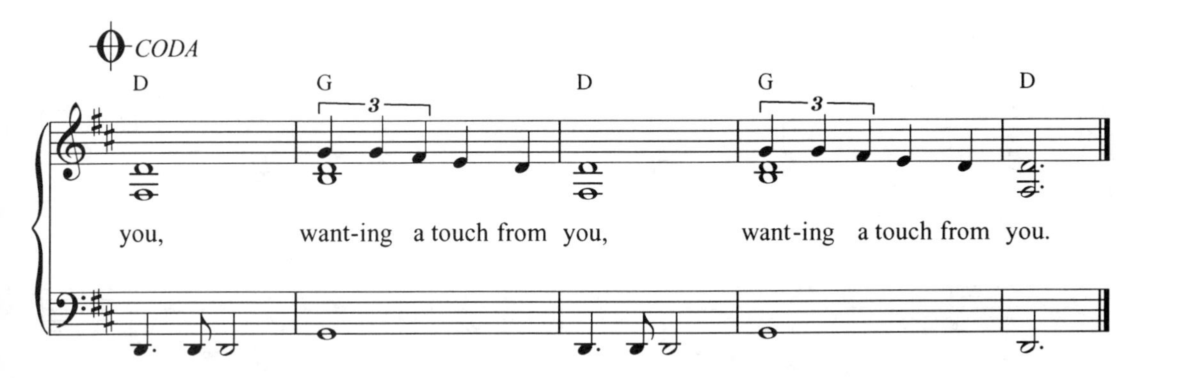
CODA
D
G
D
G
D
you, want-ing a touch from you, want-ing a touch from you.

750 We are in the army *(The power of God's word)*

Words and Music: Margaret Carpenter
arr. Dave Bankhead

Gm D7 Gm D Gm D7 Gm D
Capo 3 Em B7 Em B Em B7 Em B
1. We are in the ar - my, the ar - my of the Lord,

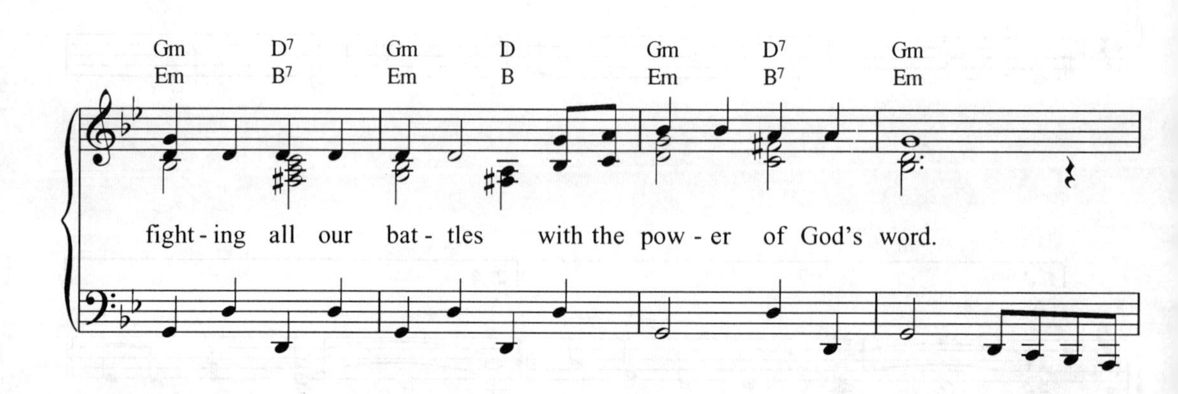
Gm D7 Gm D Gm D7 Gm
Em B7 Em B Em B7 Em
fight - ing all our bat - tles with the pow - er of God's word.

Chorus
Descant
Gm D7 Gm D Gm D7 Gm D
Em B7 Em B Em B7 Em B
Hel - met of sal - va - tion, sword of the Spi - rit high, the
Chorus
We are in the ar - my, the ar - my of the Lord,

Gm D7 Gm D Gm D7 Gm
Em B7 Em B Em B7 Em
shield of faith pro - tect - ing us from the de - vil's ug - ly lies.
fight-ing all our bat - tles with the pow - er of God's word.
D Gm D Gm
B Em B Em

2. Devil, you're a liar
and we know all your tricks.
We are not deceived by you,
'cos Jesus' got you licked.

751 We are marching along in the power of God

Words and Music: Ian Smale
arr. Chris Mitchell

C
G7
C
We are

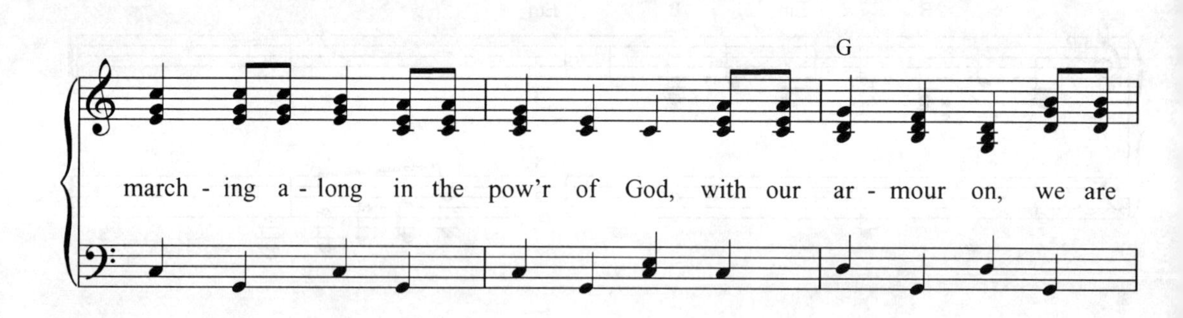
G
march - ing a - long in the pow'r of God, with our ar - mour on, we are

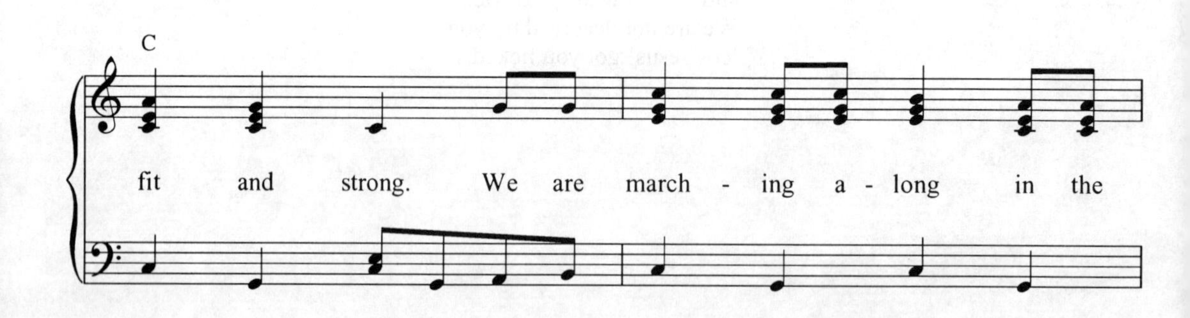
C
fit and strong. We are march - ing a - long in the

G7
C
pow'r of God, we are sol-diers, lit - tle sol-diers of the King.

752 We are warriors

Words and Music: Doug Horley

(♩ = 100)
Chorus
Capo 1
Fm Em
E♭/F D/E
We are war-ri-ors, gon-na fight and we're gon-na pray;
B♭/F A/E
B♭m/D♭ Am/C
Cm7 Bm7
Fine
we are war-ri-ors, gon-na fight and we're gon-na pray, (yeah.)
(omit last time)
Verse
E♭ D
B♭ A
Fm Em
Kick-ing down the strong-holds of the e-ne-mies of God,
E♭ D
B♭ A
Fm Em
E♭ D
we are gon-na see mi-ra-cles: cry-ing to our King,
B♭ A
E♭ D
C B
C7 B7
D.C.
plead-ing for this na-tion we de-clare we're gon-na break through. 'Cause,

753 We can heal our world *(Heal our world)*

Words and Music: Terry Tarsiuk
arr. Chris Mitchell

Chorus
D
A
We can heal our world, we can show the
We can heal our world, we can love them

G
D/F#
A
love of Je - sus. We can heal our world,
through their sor - row. We can heal our world,

G
D2
we can say he tru - ly frees us. 1. Lost,
we can give a bright to - mor - row.

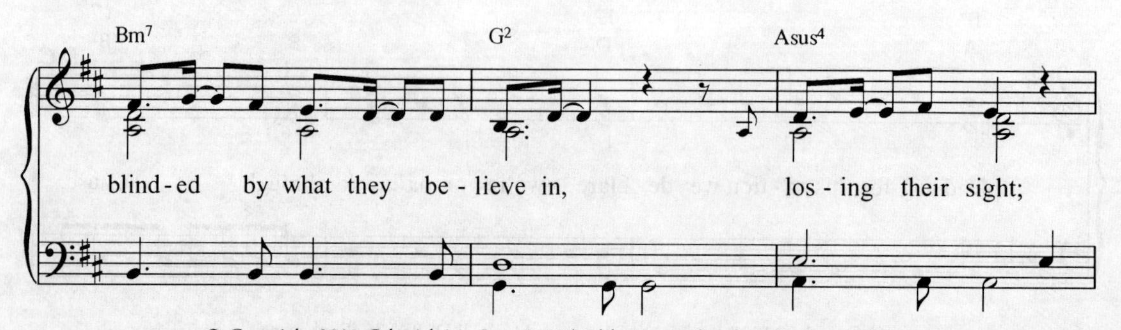
Bm7
G2
Asus4
blind - ed by what they be - lieve in, los - ing their sight;

D2
Bm7
G2
lost, stumb-ling a-lone in the dark-ness in

Asus4
G2
A2
search of the light; you, on - ly you can

Bm7
A/C♯
G2
A2
real-ly e - ver sa - tis-fy, you, on - ly you are the

Bm7
A/C♯
D.C.
D2
ans-wer to their hurt - ing cry!

2. Hearts as dry as the sunburned desert,
in need of the rain;
hearts so bruised by the blows of indiff'rence
they feel so much pain;
you, only you can really ever satisfy,
you, only you are the answer to their hurting cry!

754 We dance to praise the Lord

Words and Music: Chris Wyman and Tony Cooke
arr. Chris Mitchell

D
G
We dance to praise the Lord! We dance to

D
bless his name! We dance to praise the name of

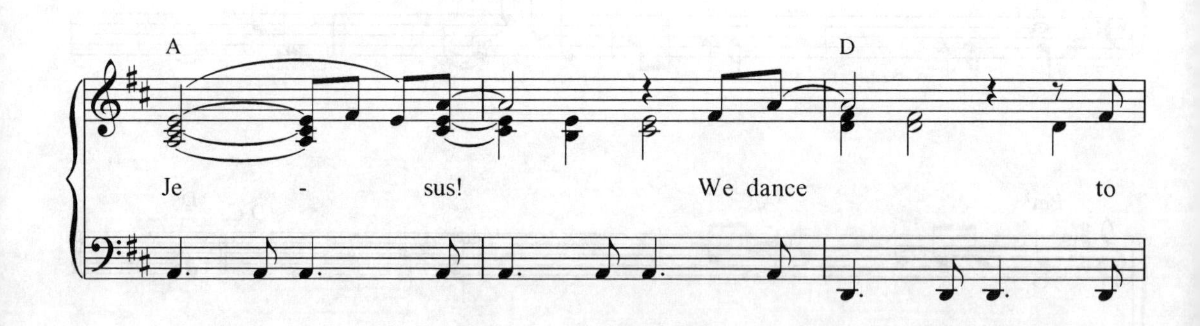

A
D
Je - sus! We dance to

G
praise you, Lord! We dance to bless your name! We dance

D
A
D
Fine
to praise your name, Lord Je - sus!

A
D
Lift your hands in - to the air!

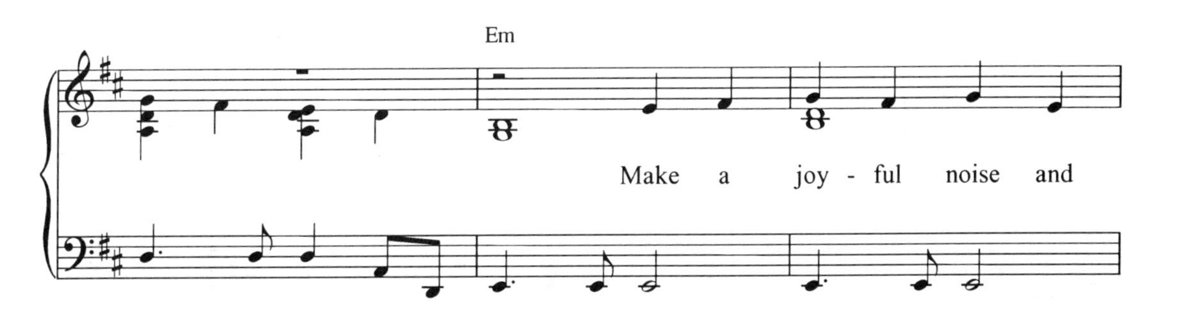
Em
Make a joy - ful noise and

D/F♯
G
G♯
A
D.S.
dance be - fore the Lord!
We dance

755 We have a mega-story *(Good news)*

Words and Music: Andrew Rayner and Wendy Rayner
arr. Chris Mitchell

C2 Am7 Dm7 G
1. We have a me-ga-sto-ry, a head-line for the world,
C F C/E
that Je-sus loves and cares for us, for
Dm7 Gsus4 C2
ev-'ry boy and girl. So we'll broad-cast all a-bout
Am7 F G Am
it with ac-tion, light and sound. We
Dm7 C/E F Gsus4
need to tell ev-'ry-one the best news has been found.

G
Chorus
Am7
Dm7
Em7
Good news, Je - sus loves you. We'll
Am7
Dm7
Em7
Am7
shout it loud and clear. Good news, Je - sus loves
Dm7
Em7
F
G
To repeat
C2
Chorus
G
you, it's the best news you can hear. Good
To verse 2
C2
D.S.
Last time
C2
2. Now

Optional Christmas verse:

2. Now love came down at Christmas,
for God loves ev'ryone.
'Cause we all need forgiveness,
he gave his only Son.
So come on, ev'rybody,
let's worship him and sing.
We need to tell ev'ryone
that Jesus is the King.

756 We have been called

Words and Music: Terry Tarsiuk
arr. Chris Mitchell

E
B
We have been called a cho - sen ge - ne - ra - tion,
A
F♯m7
Bsus4
E
B
a roy - al priest - hood, a ho - ly na - tion. We have been called his own
A
spe - cial peo - ple; we will pro - claim the prai -
F♯m7
Bsus4
E2
Fine
- ses of his mar - vel - lous light.
E
B/D♯
C♯m7
B
Lord, my life is a song since you came a - long

A2 E/G♯ F♯m7 A/B E B/D♯
and now I be-long to you on - ly. Lord, how awe-some you are,
C♯m7 B A2 E/G♯ F♯m7 A/B
how bet-ter by far, bright and morn - ing star and you know me!
F♯m7 E/G♯ A
Who would e - ver be-lieve that some-one like me could e - ver
E/B B C♯m7 B/D♯
know some-one like you, who spoke and the dark -
E G♯m7 A2 F♯m7
- ness had to flee and you've shown us,
Bsus4 B D.C.
and you've told us.

757 We have come

Words and Music: Capt. Alan J. Price, CA
arr. Chris Mitchell

Cmaj7
Em7
F
We have come, we are here to en - ter the pre-sence of a
F/G G F/G G
Cmaj7
Em7
ho - ly God. We have come, we are here to
F
F/G G F/G G
Am Em7
en - ter the pre-sence of a ho - ly God. In the name of Je - sus,
F G
Am Em7
F
hear us as we pray; come, Ho - ly Spi - rit, teach us what to say.
G
Cmaj7
Em7
We have come, we are here to

F F/G G F/G G Cmaj7
pray in the pre-sence of a ho - ly God. We have come,
Em7 F C
we are here to pray in the pre-sence of a ho - ly God, to
F C F C D.C.
pray in the pre-sence of a ho - ly God.
Am Cmaj7
This is a ho - ly place, where Je - sus meets us now.
Am Cmaj7 Fine
This is a ho - ly place, where the Spi - rit moves us now.

758 Well, if you love the Lord

(You got to do what the Lord say)

Words and Music: Colin Buchanan

Jamaican half-time (𝅗𝅥 = 76)
E
B7
1. Well, if you love the Lord
E
A
E
you can sing and shout.
some - times you glad.
and Je - sus cry.
B7
E
A
And if you love the Lord
If you love the Lord
Je - sus hurt
you can dance a - bout.
some - times you sad.
and Je - sus die.
E
A
But if you love the Lord
If you love the Lord
But he rose from the dead

C♯m
A
well you'd bet - ter o - bey, 'cause
well you'd bet - ter o - bey, 'cause
'cause he o - bey, you know,
E/B
B7
E
Chorus
A
you got to do what the Lord say.
you got to do what the Lord say. You got to do, wack - a -
he al - ways do what the Lord say.
E
B7
E
do, wack - a - do, you got to do what the Lord say.
A
E
You got to do, wack - a - do, wack - a - do, you got to do what the
To next verse
Last time
B7
E
B7
E
Lord say. 2. Well, if you love the Lord
3. Well, Je - sus laugh

759 Well, I need to move this mountain

(You've gotta have faith)

Words and Music: Dave Cooke

Moderato
G
2. need to take my dog for a walk, but I
1.&4. Well, I need to move this moun - tain, but I've
3. want to learn to love my friends, but
C
D
have - n't got a dog. And I
on - ly got a tooth - pick. And I
some - times find that hard. And I
G
want to go fish - ing for a ve - ry big fish, but all I've
need to move this o - cean, but I've
want to do the right thing, but some -

C D G
got is a piece of string. And I want to sing so sweet - ly but I
on - ly got a jug. And I'm gon - na build a build - ing, but
times things get in the way. And I want to do what my God wants, be
C Am
sound just like a frog. You've got - ta have
all I've got is one brick. You've got - ta have
al - ways on my guard. You've got - ta have
1.
C G
faith, that's right, you've got - ta have faith. 2. Well, I
2.
C G
To Bridge
faith, that's right, yes sir, O - K, you've got - ta have faith.

3.
C
faith, that's right, yes sir, O - K, I said that's right, you've got - ta have
G
D.S.
4.
C
faith. 4. Well, I faith, that's right, yes sir, O - K, I said that's
G
Repeat 4 times
right, what's right? that's right! You've got - ta have faith, you've got - ta have
BRIDGE
Fine
C G C D
faith. Faith as small as an in - sect's nose, as small as a mus - tard seed;
C G A D
D.S.
faith as ti - ny as a cen - ti - pede's toes, that's how much you need. 3. Well, I

760 We'll walk the land *(Let the flame burn brighter)*

Words and Music: Graham Kendrick

With a strong rhythm
Capo 3
F C F
D A D
1. We'll walk the land with hearts on fire; and ev - 'ry
years, and still the flame is burn - ing
truth, speak out for love; in Je - sus'
B♭ Gm
G Em
step will be a prayer. Hope is ris - ing, new day
bright a - cross the land. Hearts are wait - ing, long-ing,
name we shall be strong, to lift the fal - len, to save the
Dm Gm C7 F C
Bm Em A7 D A
1.
dawn-ing; sound of sing - ing fills the air. 2. Two thou-sand
ach - ing, for a - wak - 'ning once a - gain.
child-ren, to fill the na - tion with your song.
2, 3.
Chorus
F/C F
D/A D
Let the flame burn bright - er in the heart of the dark - ness, turn-ing

B♭
G
C
A
Gm
Em
night to glo-rious day. Let the song grow loud - er, as our love grows
Dm
Bm
3rd time to Coda
C
A
B♭
G
Dm7
Bm7
C
A
F
D
B♭
G
strong - er; let it shine! Let it shine!
1.
2.
Dm7
Bm7
C
A
D.C.
Dm7
Bm7
C
A
Chorus
D.S. al Coda
3. We'll walk for
Let the flame burn
To end
Dm7
Bm7
C
A
B♭
G
Dm7
Bm7
C
A
F
A
B♭
G
Let it shine! Let it shine!
CODA
Dm7
Bm7
B♭
G
C
A
F
D
Fine
C
A
B♭
G
Dm7
Bm7
D
A
D.S. al Fine
shine! Let the flame burn

761 Well, you don't have to hear *(Listen)*

Words and Music: Gerry Holmes

With an easy 'country' swing (♩ = 120)
C C/E F G C
Well, you don't have to hear to
G C F G
lis - ten, you don't have to see to un - der - stand. 'Cause
Last time to Coda
Am Em F C Dm Dm/F
deep in - side God has sup - plied a lit - tle way of
G C G
know - ing. And you don't have to touch to have feel - ings, you
C F G Am Em
don't have to smell to know lunch is near, 'cause deep in - side God

F
C
Dm
G
has sup-plied a lit-tle seed that's grow-ing.
Em
F
Big peo-ple find it hard-er all the time to lis-ten to the
C
Em
3
in-side. 'Cause most peo-ple say it's the cle-ver-est way to
F
G
D.S. al Coda
trust what's on the out - side! But you
CODA
G
C C/E F F/D G C
know-ing, hey yeah, yeah!

762 We need to know the Bible

Words and Music: Steve Burnhope
arr. Chris Mitchell

(vs. 2 and 3)
(v.3 only)
E
A2
1. We need to know the Bi - ble, if we want to know the Lord, it
F♯m
B7
A
B7
E
is - n't just a big old book, the Bi - ble is God's word, it
A
E/G♯
B
E
does - n't just have sto - ries ('though the ones it has are true)
F♯m
B
A
B
E
Chorus
God put in all kinds of things to speak to me and you. It reach-es

B7
E
down in - to the soul, it reach - es up in - to the mind, it
A
E
F♯m7
B
reach - es deep in - to the parts that o - ther books can - not find, our
A2
B
E
C♯m7
spi - rits leap with - in us when we hear the word of God, that's
A2
B
why we need to know the Bi - ble if we
To next verse
A
B
E
want to know the Lord.
Last time
A
B
E
want to know the Lord.

2. There are sev'ral other ways
God can speak to us,
it may be when we're praying,
or through somebody else,
we should keep on praying
and list'ning to our friends,
but we need to know the Bible
to know what God intends.

3. God has many purposes
to accomplish through his word,
it helps us understand him,
and how much he loves the world,
it tells us when we're going wrong
and helps us find the way,
so when others ask, 'What is that book?'
this is what to say:

763 We're God's family

(One for others)

Words: Monica O'Brien

Music: Trisha Watts
arr. Chris Mitchell

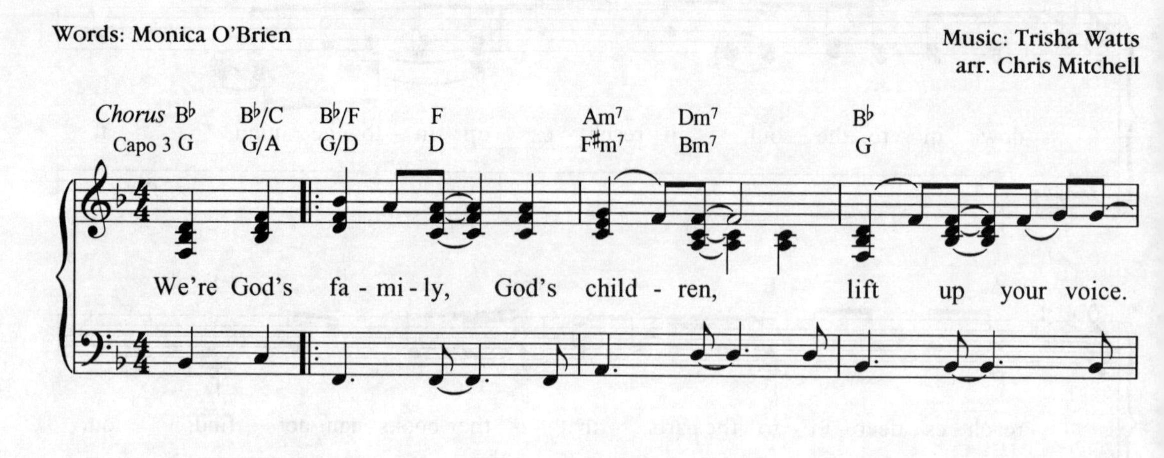
Chorus B♭ B♭/C B♭/F F Am7 Dm7 B♭
Capo 3 G G/A G/D D F♯m7 Bm7 G
We're God's fa - mi - ly, God's child - ren, lift up your voice.

B♭/C B♭/F F Am7 Dm7
G/A G/D D F♯m7 Bm7
We're God's fa - mi - ly, God's cho - sen,

G7 Csus4 C B♭/F F
E7 Asus4 A G/D D
let your heart re - joice! U - ni - ted in the

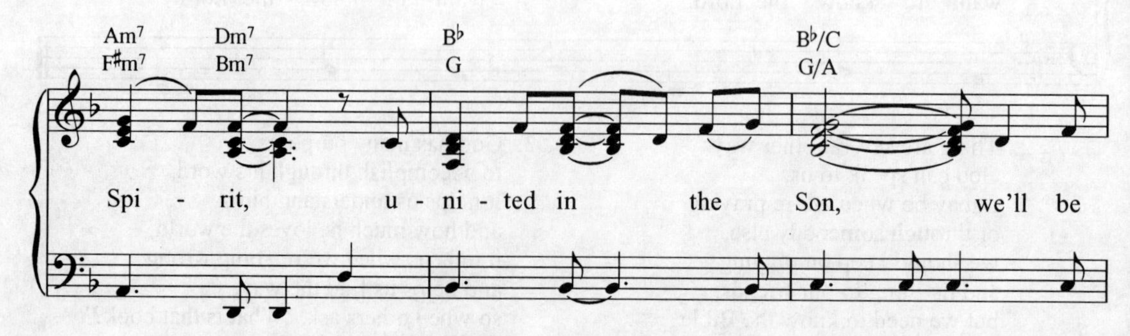
Am7 Dm7 B♭ B♭/C
F♯m7 Bm7 G G/A
Spi - rit, u - ni - ted in the Son, we'll be

B♭/F F Am7 Dm7 B♭ C F B♭/F F B♭/F
G/D D F♯m7 Bm7 G A D G/D D G/D
one for o - thers! One in the Lord!
F B♭/F F C/F F
D G/D D A/D D
1. Have you
2. We are
B♭/C F
G/A D
e - ver been lone - ly, be -
long - ing for whole-ness. Ex -
Dm Dm7/C B♭
Bm Bm7/A G
wild - ered by the way in which life's go - ing?
pand our minds to know the heart of Je - sus.
C Am7 Dm7
A F♯m7 Bm7
Know it is true, some-one is lov - ing you. To -
Show us the way, re - veal it this day. To -

B♭ C F
G A D
ge - ther we'll see it through. Re -
ge - ther as one we'll stay,

B♭ C Am7 Dm7
G A F♯m7 Bm7
mem - ber the hope that's been gi - ven to you. So
claim - ing the joy we've found in your name. So

B♭maj7
Gmaj7
reach out! Reach out! This way is true.
reach out! Reach out! We pro - claim.

B♭/C
G/A
1.
C
A
Chorus
We're God's
2.
C
A
F
D

764 We're going deep *(Deep, under the ocean)*

Words and Music: Dave Godfrey

Steadily
F
Capo 3 D
1. We're go - ing deep, deep, deep un - der the o - cean, we're go - ing

Gm7
Em7
F/A
D/F♯
deep, deep, deep un - der the sea, we're go - ing deep, deep, deep in search of

B♭
G
1.
C
A
last - ing trea - sure, kept un - der the waves for me. 2. We're go - ing

2, 3.
F
D
C
A
F
D
Chorus
B♭
G
pro - mi - ses that he can be found. It's not pi - rate loot, or

F/A
D/F♯
E♭
C
Gm7
Em7
F
D
an - cient wrecks, it's price - less what we seek. It's
B♭
G
F/A
D/F♯
G
E
G7
E7
last - ing trea-sure, a friend for e - ver, strength when we feel
To verse 3
Last time
C
A
C7
A7
D.S.
weak. 3. So we'll go

2. We're going deep, deep, deep no fear of danger,
   we're going deep, deep, deep just hear the sound,
   of the deep, deep, deep where the Lord of the sea
   promises that he can be found.

3. So we'll go deep, deep, deep under the ocean,
   and we'll go deep, deep, deep until we know,
   all the deep, deep love that he has for us:
   deep is just where we have to go.

765 We're gonna build our lives *(Solid rock)*

Words and Music: Andrew Pearson and Pauline Pearson

Rock 'n' roll feel
Chorus
E
We're gon - na build our lives on a sol - id rock,
B7
E
build our lives on a sol - id rock, we're gon - na build our lives on a
A
Last time to Coda
E
B7
1.
E
sol - id rock, on Je - sus Christ the Lord. We're gon - na
2.
E
E7
Verse
A
We'll o - bey all he has to say and
E
F♯m
do what he wants us to do, then our lives will

B7
Chorus
D.S.
be se-cure: Je - sus liv - ing in me and you. We're gon - na
CODA
B7
E
B7
E
Je - sus Christ the Lord, on Je - sus Christ the Lord, on
B
B7
E
E7
Je - sus Christ the Lord. We said it's on
A
B7
A
Je - sus, on - ly on Je - sus, we're gon - na build our
B
1.
E
E7
2.
E7
lives a - lone. We said it's on lone.

766 We're gonna tell the world

Words and Music: Garrie-John Barnes
arr. Chris Mitchell

G
1. We're gon - na tell the world a - bout Je - sus! We're
2. God is build - ing up his king - dom; does he

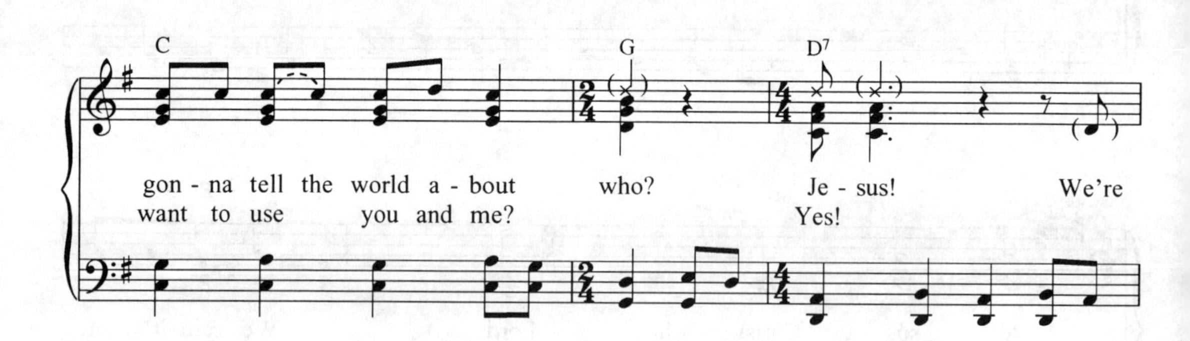

C
G
D7
gon - na tell the world a - bout who? Je - sus! We're
want to use you and me? Yes!

G
gon - na tell the world a - bout Je - sus! And
God is build - ing up his king - dom to

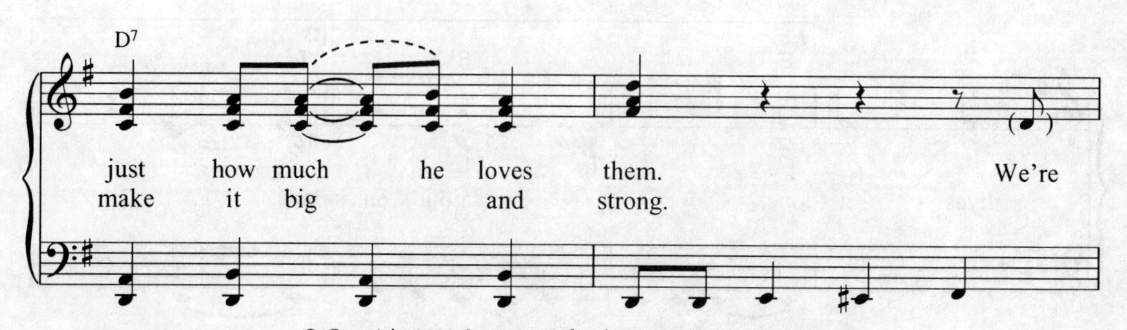

D7
just how much he loves them. We're
make it big and strong.

G
gon - na tell the world a - bout Je - sus! We're
God is build - ing up his king - dom; does he
C
G
gon - na tell the world a - bout who?
want to use you and me?
D7
G
Je - sus! We're gon - na tell the world a - bout, dance
Yes! God is gon - na build it up, ne -
C
G
D7
and sing and shout a - bout, we're gon - na tell the world a - bout Je -
- ver gon - na give it up, God is build - ing up his king -
G
1.
2.
- sus!
- dom.

767 We're meeting with Jesus

Words and Music: Capt. Alan J. Price, CA
arr. Chris Mitchell

Chorus
A7
D
G
A
We're meet-ing with Je - sus, meet-ing the King, as we wor-ship to -

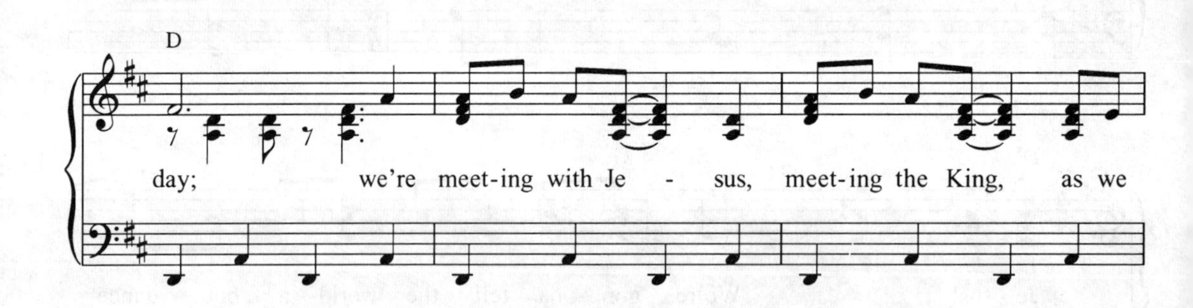
D
day; we're meet-ing with Je - sus, meet-ing the King, as we

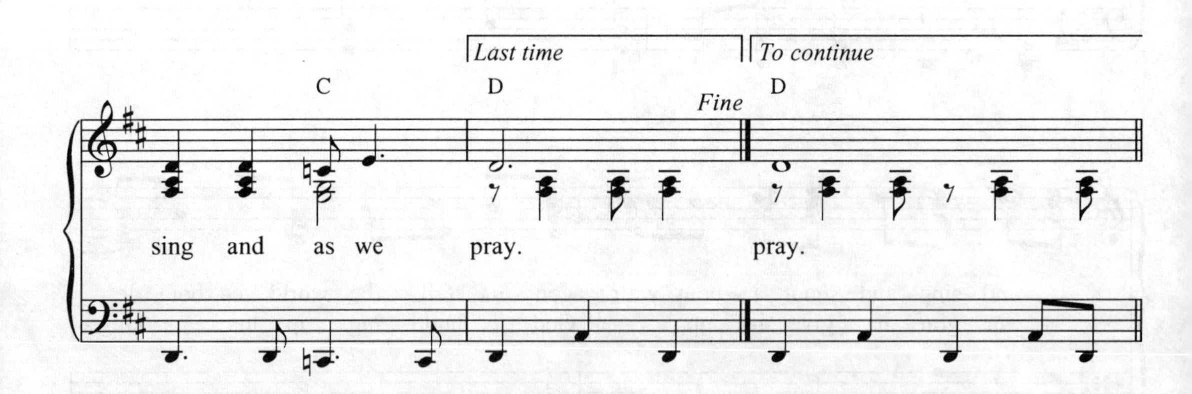
Last time
To continue
C
D
Fine
D
sing and as we pray. pray.

Gm
Verse
D
Je - sus knows our deep - est thoughts,

Gm
the hopes and fears deep in -

D
Gm
side;
he longs to

D
Bm7
E7
be our clo - sest friend,
this King with

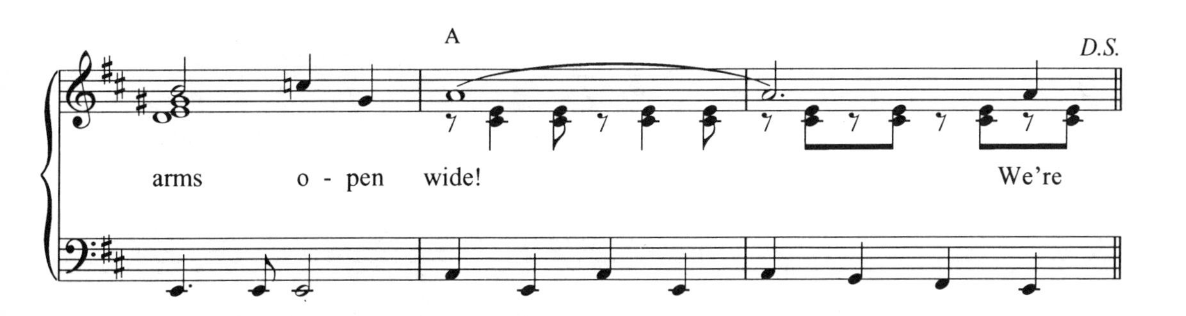
A
D.S.
arms o - pen wide!
We're

768 We're not too young *(Not too young)*

Words and Music: J.D. Bullen

F
D
B♭
G
F
D
B♭
G
Capo 3
1. We're not too young to read a-bout the sto-ries in his

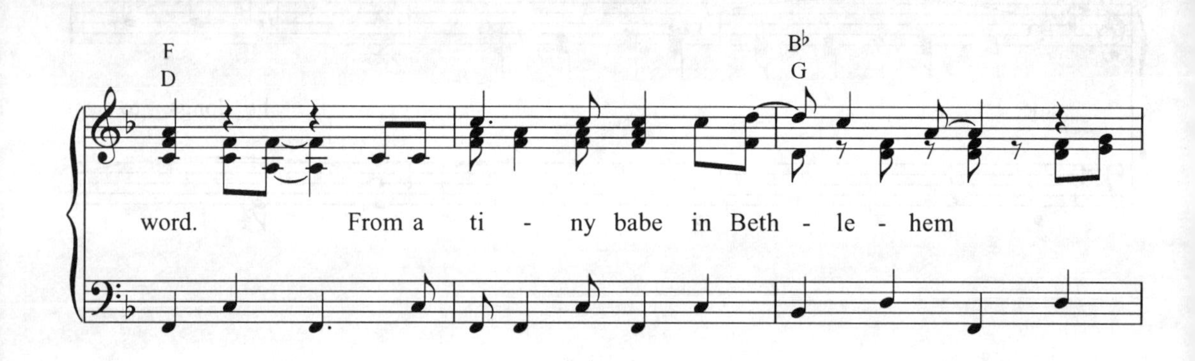
F
D
B♭
G
word. From a ti - ny babe in Beth - le - hem

G
E
C
A
F
D
to the ri-sen Lord, feed-ing of five thou-

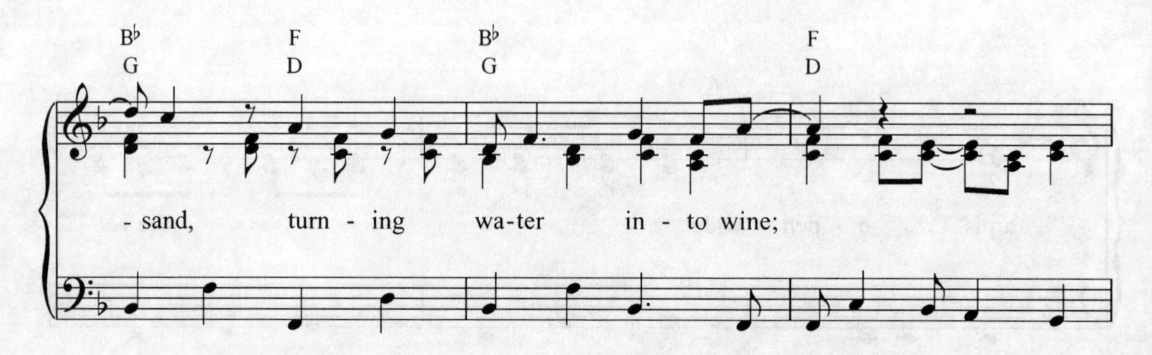
B♭
G
F
D
B♭
G
F
D
- sand, turn - ing wa-ter in - to wine;

B♭
F
C
G
D
A
this is God's Son Je - sus, he's a friend of
F
D
Chorus
B♭
G
F
D
mine. We're not too young, not too young,
B♭
G
G
E
C
A
we're not too young, not too young,
F
D
B♭
G
F
D
D
B
not too young. We're not too young,
B♭
G
C
A
B♭
G
C
A
F
D
Fine
N-T-Y for J-E-S-U-S, Je - sus.

F D Bb G F D Bb G
2. Not yet old e - nough to vote, or to take G C S Es,
F D Bb G
we can't stay up all night to watch T V.
G E C A F D
Can't drive cars, get mar-
Bb G F D Bb G F D
- ried, or fly an ae - ro - plane, we can know for sure
Bb G F D C A F D
Chorus D.S. al Fine
that Je - sus loves us just the same. We're not too

769 We're raising the roof for Jesus

Words and Music: Phil Overton
arr. Chris Mitchell

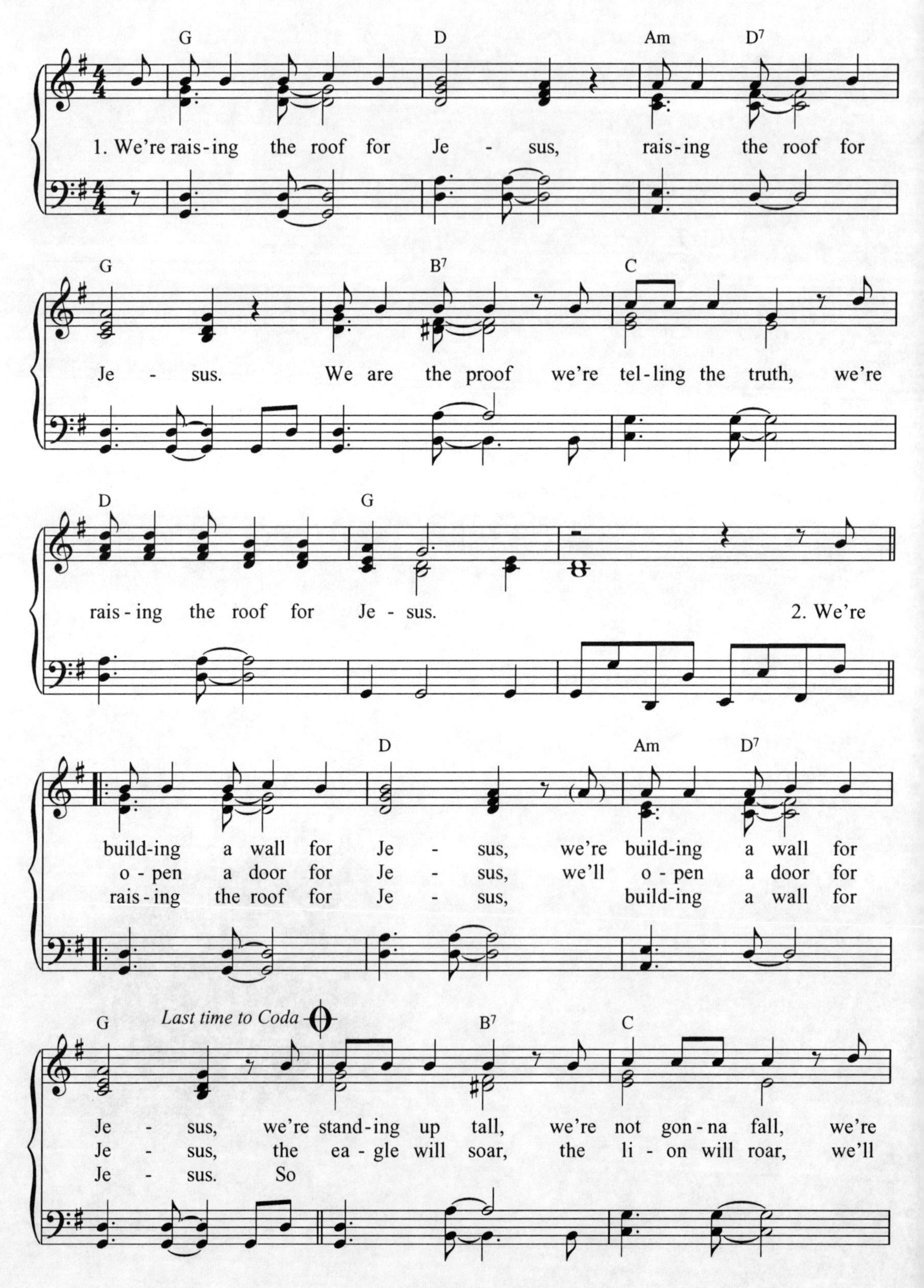
G D Am D7
1. We're rais-ing the roof for Je - sus, rais-ing the roof for
G B7 C
Je - sus. We are the proof we're tel-ling the truth, we're
D G
rais-ing the roof for Je - sus.
2. We're
D Am D7
build-ing a wall for Je - sus, we're build-ing a wall for
o-pen a door for Je - sus, we'll o-pen a door for
rais-ing the roof for Je - sus, build-ing a wall for
G Last time to Coda B7 C
Je - sus, we're stand-ing up tall, we're not gon-na fall, we're
Je - sus, the ea-gle will soar, the li-on will roar, we'll
Je - sus. So

D
Am/G G
C
G
build-ing a wall for Je - sus.
3. We'll
o - pen a door for Je - sus.
4. We're
CODA
B7
C
G
B7
get off the floor and don't be a bore! Give it some more – it
C
G
B7
C
is - n't a chore. The ea - gle will soar, the li - on will roar! We'll
D
o - pen a door
Am/G G
C
G
for Je - sus.

770 We're the kids of the King

Words and Music: Chris Jackson
arr. Dave Bankhead

G
Em
C
D
We're the kids of the King,

G
Em
C
D
G
Em
that's why we dance and sing,
we're the kids, we're the

Last time to Coda
C
D
G
Em
C
D
kids, we're the kids of the King.
Oh yeah!
Oh yeah!

G
Em
C
G/D
D
Come on ev - 'ry - bo - dy, and join the ce - le - bra - tion,

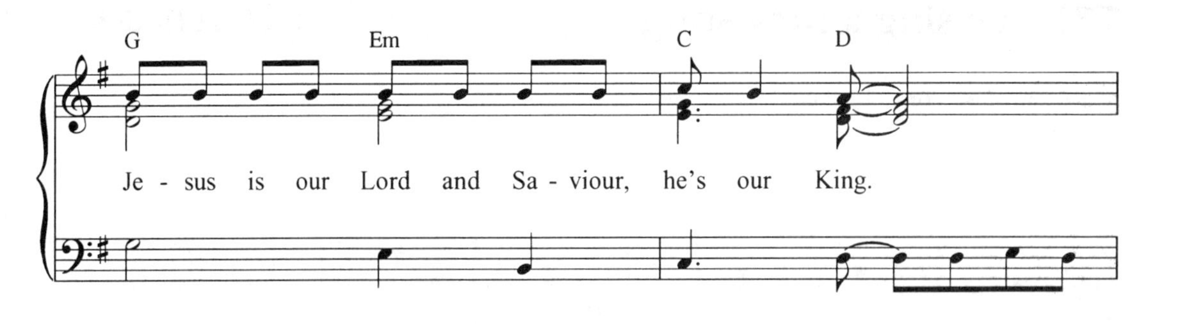
G
Em
C
D
Je - sus is our Lord and Sa - viour, he's our King.

G
Em
C
D
Clap your hands, dance your feet and shout a - loud to the Lord,

G
Em
C
D
G
Em
Praise the Lord! to the Lord.

CODA
C
D
D.C.
G
Praise the Lord! We're the kids of the King! Yeah!

771 We sing a new song *(Sing a new song)*

Words and Music: Terry Tarsiuk
arr. Chris Mitchell

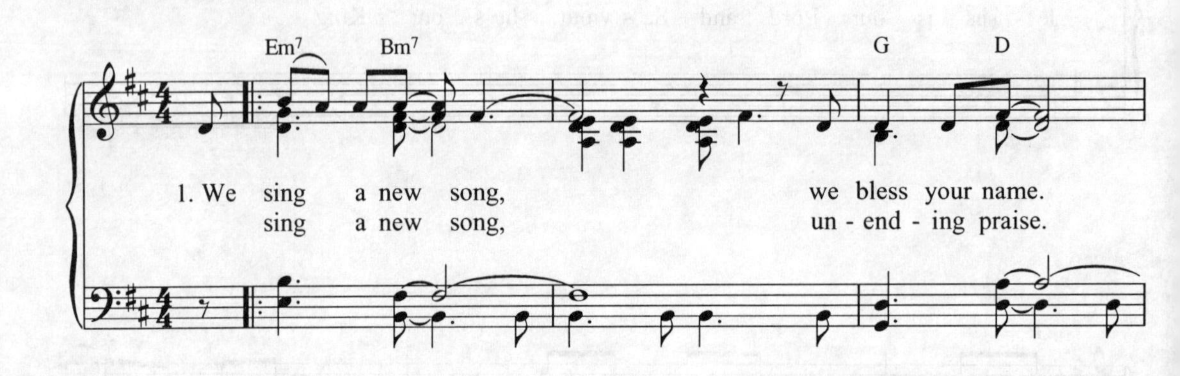
Em7 Bm7 G D
1. We sing a new song, we bless your name.
sing a new song, un - end - ing praise.

Em7 Bm7
We sing a new song, we
I sing a new song, of e -

G D Em7 Bm7
fan the flame. The flame is burn - ing,
ter - nal grace. Your voice like hon - ey,

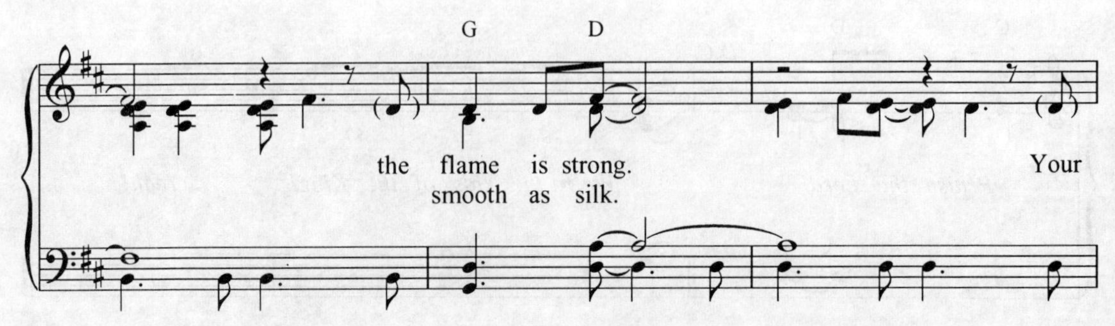
G D
the flame is strong. Your
smooth as silk.

Em7
Bm7
G
D
love's a fire,
your love's my song.
Says you love me,
I'm in your will.

A/C♯
Bm7
G
Hal - le - lu - jah,
Glo - ry to God,

A/C♯
D
A/C♯
Bm7
G
hal - le - lu - jah,
hal - le - lu - jah,
glo - ry to God,
glo - ry to God,

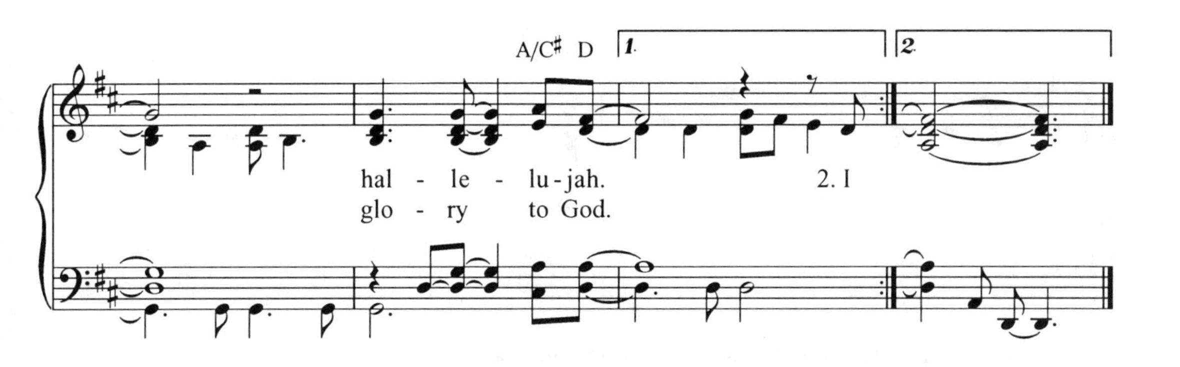
A/C♯
D
1.
2.
hal - le - lu - jah.
2. I
glo - ry to God.

772 We stand together

Words and Music: Paul Crouch and David Mudie
arr. Chris Mitchell

A Chorus A/C♯ D E
We stand to-ge - ther with our feet up - on a rock,
A A/C♯ D E
we stand to-ge - ther with our feet up-on a rock,
A A/C♯ D E
we stand to-ge - ther with our feet up - on a rock,
G D/F♯ E A
it's a rock which ne - ver can be moved,
Last time To continue
G D/F♯ E A Fine A
it's a rock which ne - ver can be moved. moved.

D
A
1. Moun - tains may crum - ble, storms may lash and rage,
D
E
but this rock ne - ver shall be moved.

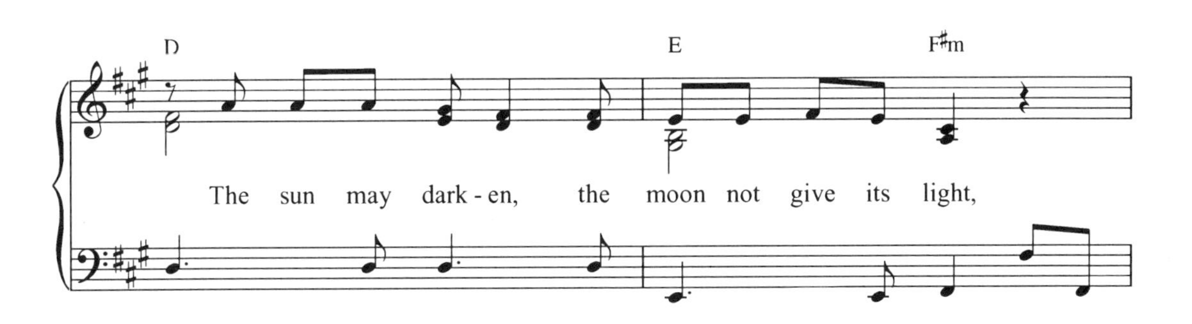
D
E
F#m
The sun may dark - en, the moon not give its light,

B
B/D#
E
D.C.
but this rock ne - ver shall be, ne - ver shall be moved!

2. Our friends may fail us and disappointments come,
but this rock never shall be moved!
You may start wondering what it's all about,
but this rock never shall be moved.

773 What a mighty God we serve

Words and Music: Unknown
arr. Chris Mitchell

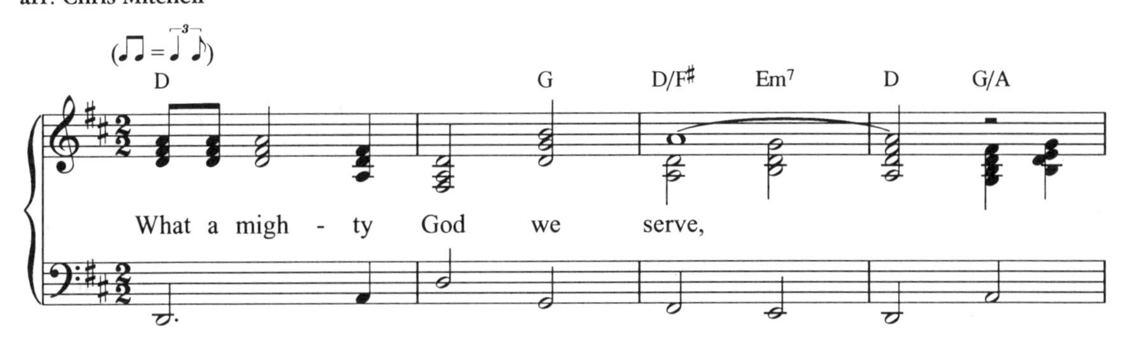

D
G
D/F♯
Em7
D
G/A
What a migh - ty God we serve,

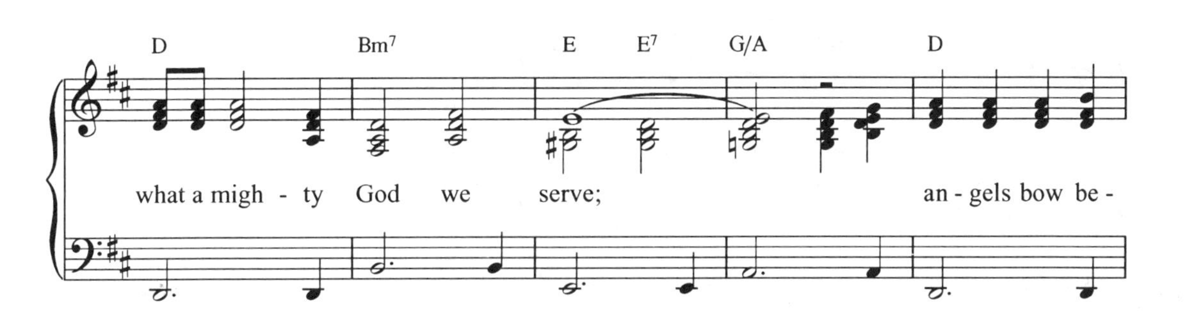

D
Bm7
E
E7
G/A
D
what a migh - ty God we serve;
an - gels bow be -

D7/F♯
Gmaj9
C9
D/A
G/A
fore him,
hea-ven and earth a - dore him,
what a migh - ty

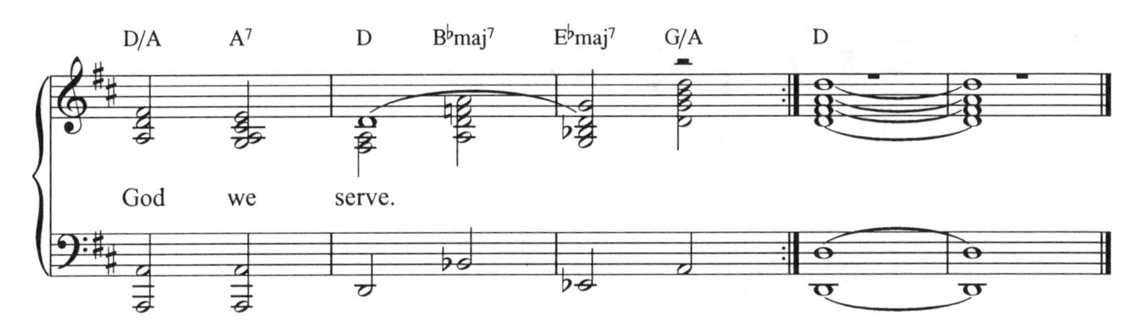

D/A
A7
D
B♭maj7
E♭maj7
G/A
D
God we serve.

774 What wondrous love is this

(Upon a cross of shame)

Words and Music: James Wright
arr. Chris Mitchell

E E/G♯ Asus2 A/C♯ B/D♯
1. What won-drous love is this from heav'n to earth come
2. What won-drous pow'r is this that held you to that
3. Your blood for e - ver flows, a ne - ver-fail - ing
E E/G♯ Asus2 Bsus4 B
down? The great - est gift of all was gi - ven,
cross? Not the a - go - ny of thorns and nails,
stream of for-give - ness, of pow'r and cleans - ing.
E E/G♯ Asus2 B Cdim
the ho - ly Lamb of God was lift - ed up to
but e - ver-last - ing love and waves of ho - ly
And your cross for e - ver stands from age to age the
1.
C♯m F♯m7 B7sus4 B
die that we might have life.
2, 3.
C♯m F♯m7
grace poured out for us
same, draw-ing all men to

Bsus4
B
E
Chorus
E/G#
A
all.
you.
Up - on a cross of shame you bled and died,
E
B
A/C#
B/D#
E
E/G#
poured out your life with arms o - pen wide, and there you
A
E/G#
hung with a heart full of love poured out for all the world,
B
A/C#
B/D#
B
with a heart full of love.
1.
2.
E
E/G#
A2
A/C# B/D#
D.C. for v.3
A2
A/C#
B/D#
Poured out for all the world,

E
E/G♯
A2
A/C♯
B/D♯
with a heart full of love;

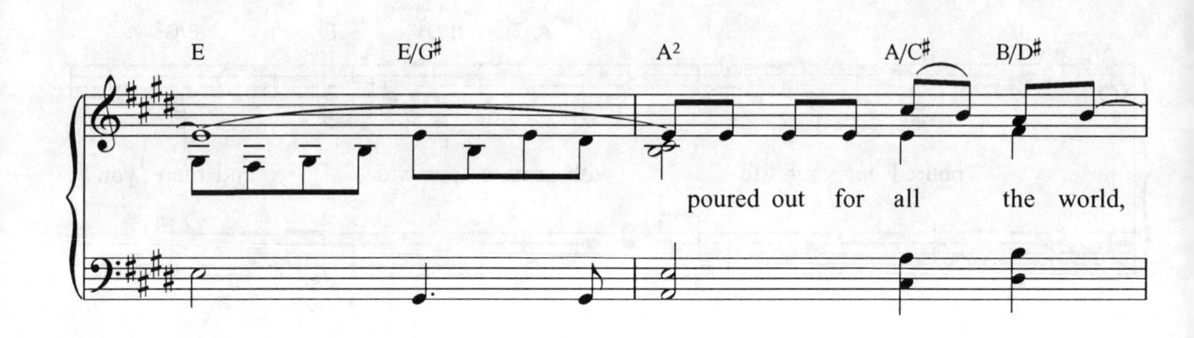
E
E/G♯
A2
A/C♯
B/D♯
poured out for all the world,

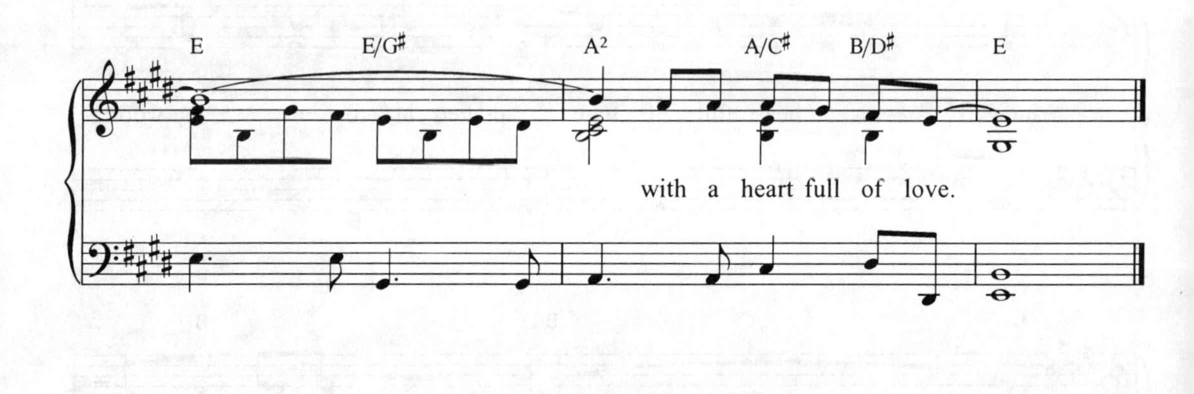
E
E/G♯
A2
A/C♯
B/D♯
E
with a heart full of love.

775 When I smile or rub my hair *(God is there)*

Words and Music: Nick Harding
arr. Dave Bankhead

F Dm Gm C
Capo 3 D Bm Em A
1. When I smile or rub my hair, when my arms wave
F A Dm
D F♯ Bm
ev - 'ry - where, when I jump high in the air,
B♭ F/C C F Dm B♭ Csus4 C F
G D/A A D Bm G Asus4 A D
I know God is there, oh yes, I do! I know God is there.

2. When I've had a nasty scare,
when there's no one anywhere,
when my best friend will not share,
I know God is there,
oh yes, I do!
I know God is there.

776 When Jesus taught his friends to pray *(Forgiven)*

Words and Music: Steve Morgan-Gurr and Kay Morgan-Gurr

E B F♯m B E F♯
Capo 2 D A Em A D E
1. When Je - sus taught his
B E F♯ B
A D E A
friends to pray, he taught them how to live: for -
E F♯ G♯m F♯ E B
D E F♯m E D A
gi - ving oth - ers the same way they'd like him to for -
F♯ E F♯ B
E D E A
Chorus
give. And if we know that we're for - gi - ven, we'll want to

E F♯ B E F♯
D E A D E
3
show it by our love, and try to grow to be like
G♯m F♯ E F♯ 1. B 2. B
F♯m E D E A A
3
we should be, liv-ing to please our God a - bove. 2. When bove.

2. When we forgive, it helps us see
what Father God has done:
forgiving you, forgiving me,
through Jesus, his dear Son.

777 When the fists are flying

(A whole lotta self-control)

Words and Music: Colin Buchanan

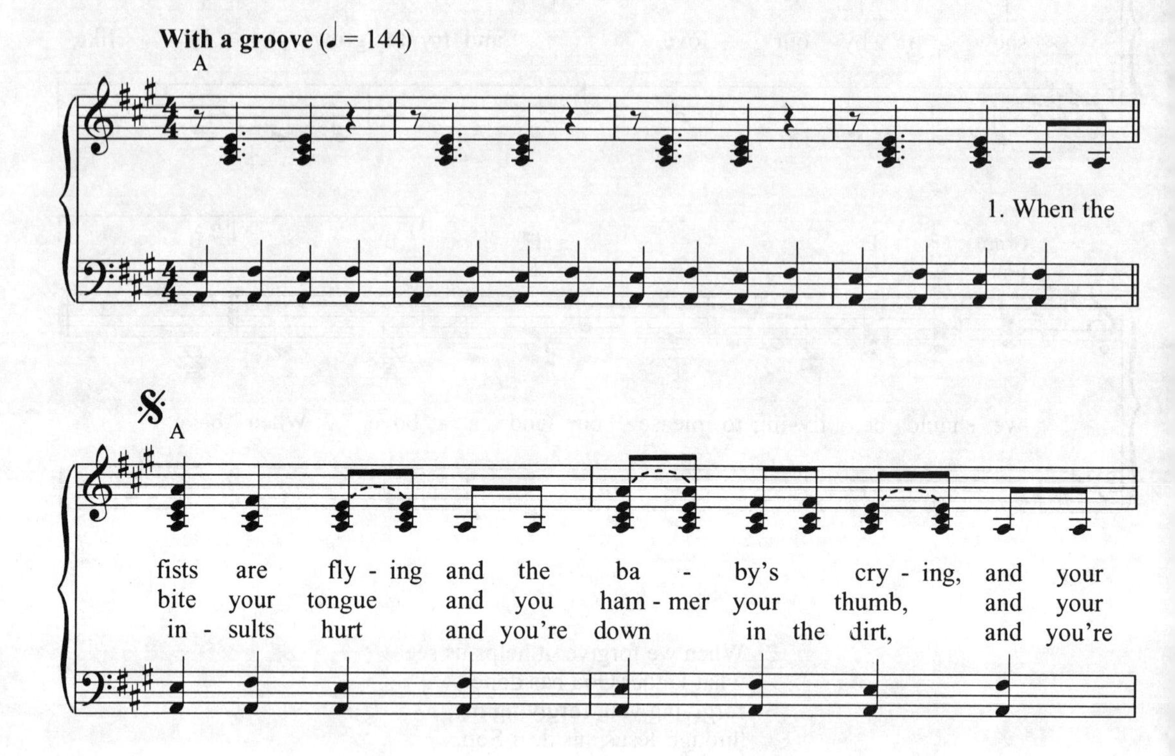
With a groove (♩ = 144)
A
1. When the
A
fists are fly - ing and the ba - by's cry - ing, and your
bite your tongue and you ham - mer your thumb, and your
in - sults hurt and you're down in the dirt, and you're

blood's at a hun - dred de - grees. When the
brain is start - ing to ache. When the
just a - bout to rant and rave, re -

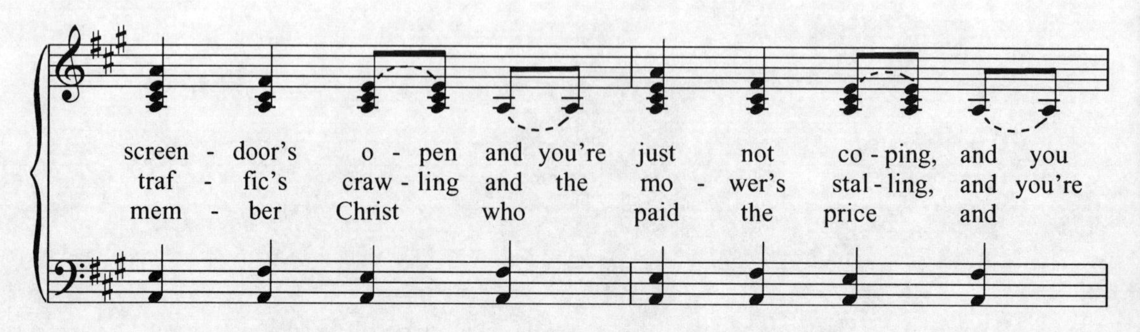
screen - door's o - pen and you're just not co - ping, and you
traf - fic's craw - ling and the mo - wer's stal - ling, and you're
mem - ber Christ who paid the price and

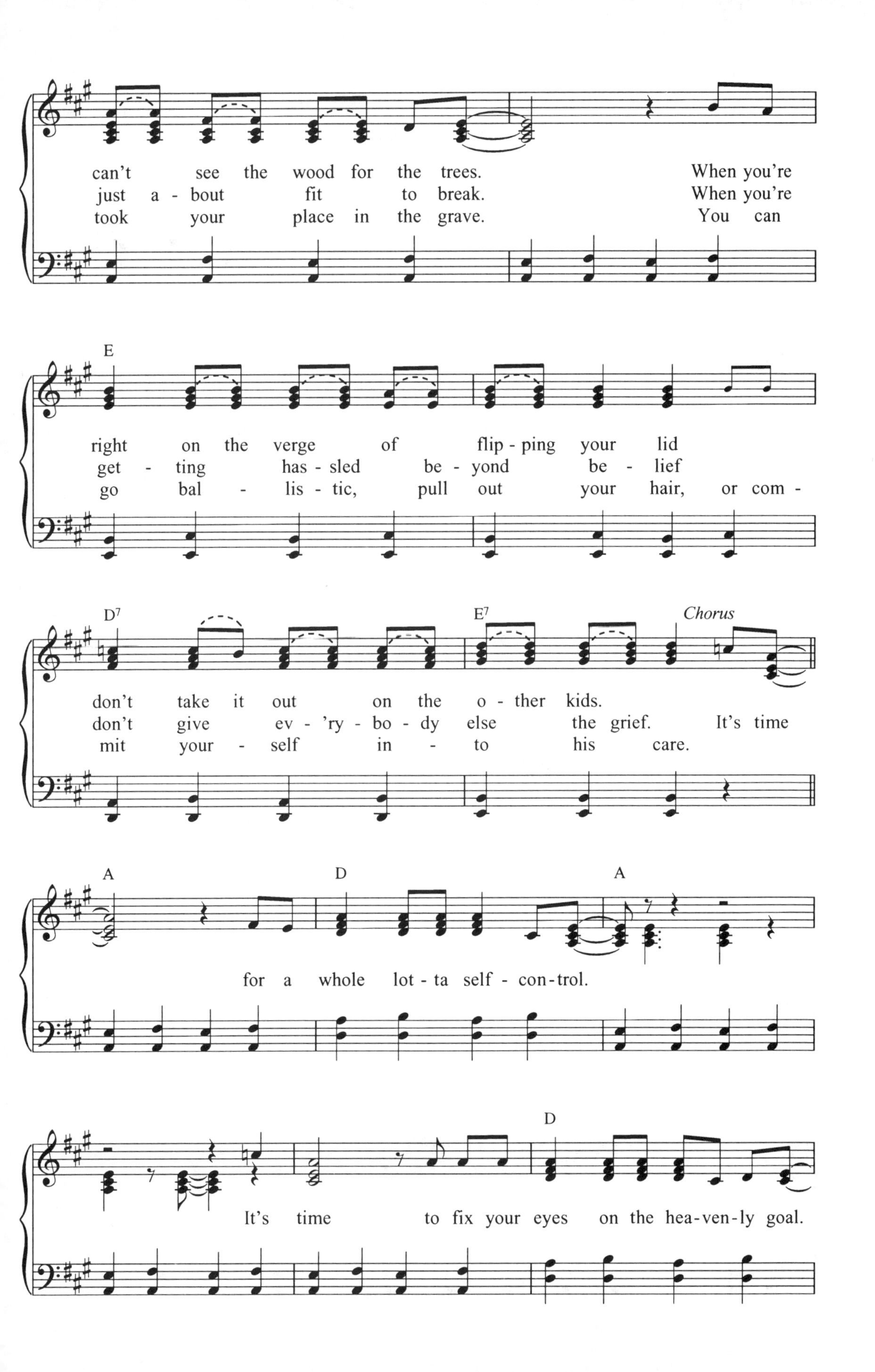

can't see the wood for the trees. When you're
just a - bout fit to break. When you're
took your place in the grave. You can
E
right on the verge of flip - ping your lid
get - ting has - sled be - yond be - lief
go bal - lis - tic, pull out your hair, or com -
D7
E7
Chorus
don't take it out on the o - ther kids.
don't give ev - 'ry - bo - dy else the grief. It's time
mit your - self in - to his care.
A
D
A
for a whole lot - ta self - con - trol.
D
It's time to fix your eyes on the hea - ven - ly goal.

A
C
It's time to keep in
D7
step with the Spi - rit, if you've gone and put your big foot in it. Con -
F
E
Last time to Coda
fess your sin and con - si - der the good of your soul. And
D
C
D
A
pray for a whole lot - ta self - con - trol.
D.S.
2. When you
3. When the

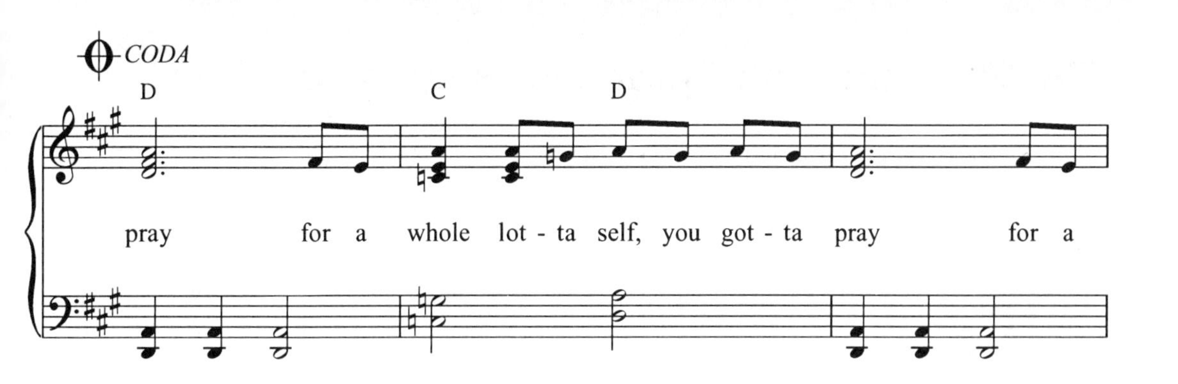
CODA
D
C
D
pray for a whole lot - ta self, you got - ta pray for a

C
D
C
D
whole lot - ta self, you got - ta pray for a whole lot - ta self - con - trol.

A

778 When the Holy Spirit comes upon you

Words and Music: Chris Jackson and Jenny-Jenny Jackson
arr. Dave Bankhead

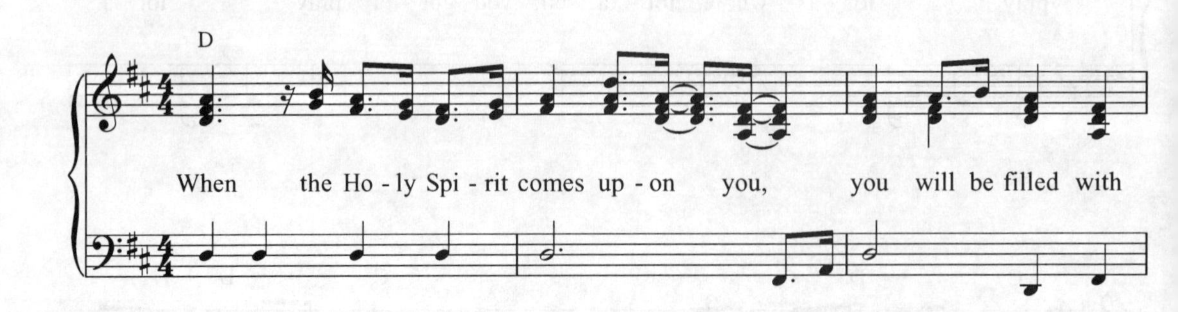
D
When the Ho - ly Spi - rit comes up - on you, you will be filled with

A
D
pow - er. When the Ho - ly Spi - rit comes up - on you,

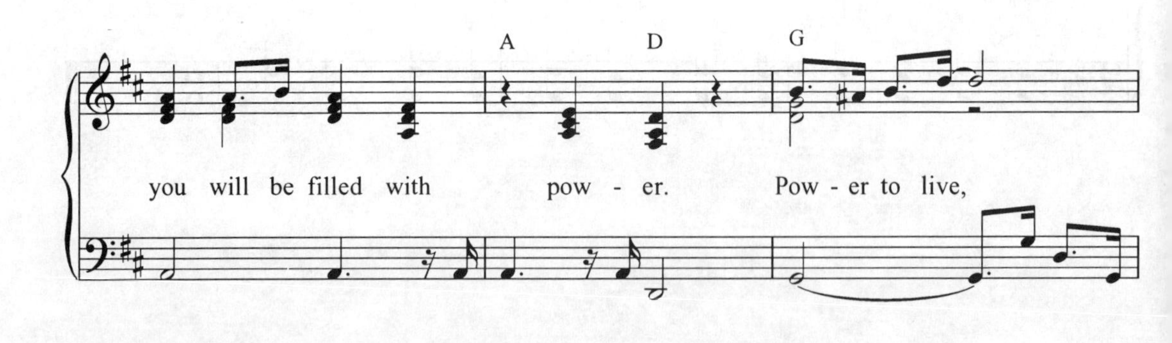
A
D
G
you will be filled with pow - er. Pow - er to live,

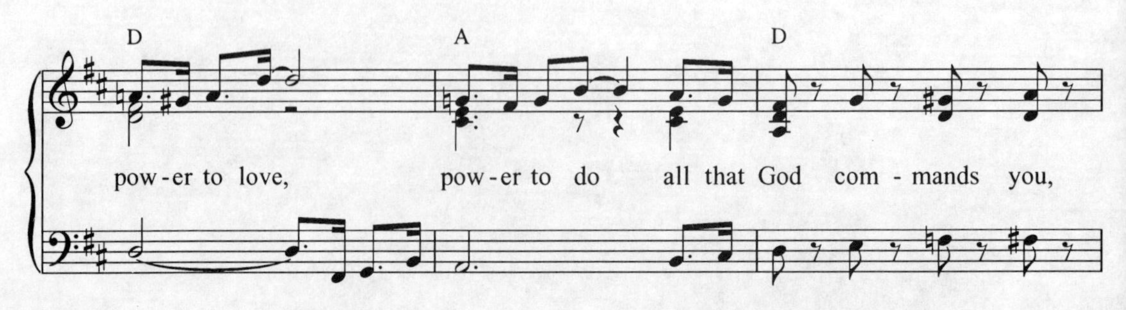
D
A
D
pow - er to love, pow - er to do all that God com - mands you,

G
D
A
pow - er to speak,
pow - er to heal,
pow - er
3

A7
D
to fight the e - ne - my.

779 When the music fades *(The heart of worship)*

Words and Music: Matt Redman

E
B/D♯
1. When the mu - sic fades, all is stripped a - way,
2. King of end - less worth, no one could ex - press
F♯m7
Bsus4
E
and I simp - ly come. Long - ing just to bring
how much you de - serve. Though I'm weak and poor
B/D♯
F♯m7
some - thing that's of worth, that will bless your heart.
all I have is yours, ev - 'ry sin - gle breath.
B7sus4
B7
F♯m7
E/G♯
B
I'll bring you more than a song, for a song in it - self
F♯m7
E/G♯
B
is not what you have re - quired.

F#m7
E/G#
B
You search much deep - er with - in,
through the way things ap - pear;
F#m7
E/G#
B
you're look - ing in - to my heart.
Chorus
E
B/D#
F#m7
I'm com-ing back to the heart of wor - ship, and it's all a - bout you,
Amaj7
B
E
B/D#
E/B
B
all a - bout you, Je - sus. I'm sor - ry, Lord, for the thing I've made it, when it's
F#m7
Amaj7
Amaj7/B
B
E
all a - bout you, all a - bout you, Je - sus.

780 When the sky turned black

(Good Fri, Good Fri, Good Friday)

Words and Music: Gerry Holmes

Energetically (♩ = 135)
Capo 3
Chorus
1. When the sky turned black and Je - sus cried,
that was a kind of vic - to - ry.
When the tem - ple cur - tain was
ripped a - part,
that was a sign for you and me.
It was a
Good Fri-, Good Fri-, Good Fri - day,
it was a Good Fri-, Good Fri - day.

Dm
Bm
C
A
It was a Good Fri-, Good Fri-, Good Fri - day, it was a
Good Fri-, Good Fri - day.
1.
2. When his
2, 3.
G/D
E/B
D.S.
3. When there's
2

2. When his friends all turned and ran away,
   the soldiers nailed his hands and feet.
   On a lonely hill on a lonely day,
   Jesus died for you and me.

2nd Chorus: On a Good Fri, Good Fri, Good Friday. (repeat)

3. When there's hat parades and Easter eggs
   and hot cross buns are in the stores
   we remember Jesus on the cross,
   we remember who he suffered for.

3rd Chorus: Remember Good Fri, Good Fri, Good Friday. (repeat)

781 Where the presence of the Lord is

Words and Music: Chris Jackson and Jill Hoffmann
arr. Chris Mitchell

Em
Where the pre - sence of the Lord is, there is free -

B7
Em
dom, free - dom, free -

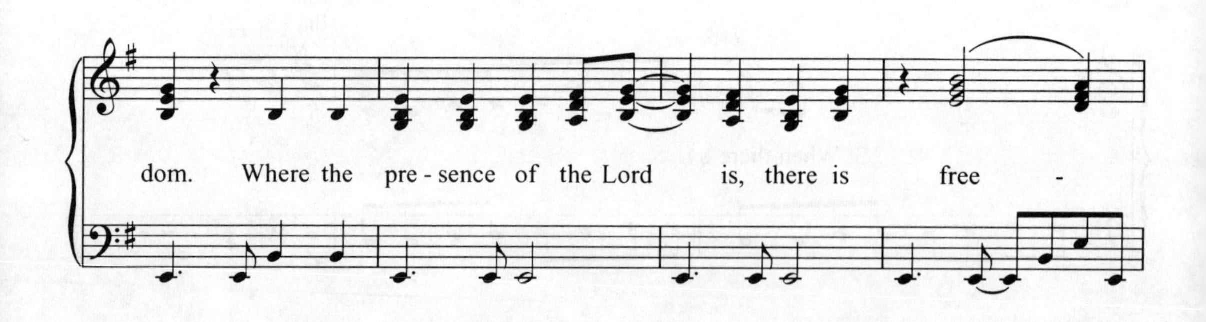
dom. Where the pre - sence of the Lord is, there is free -

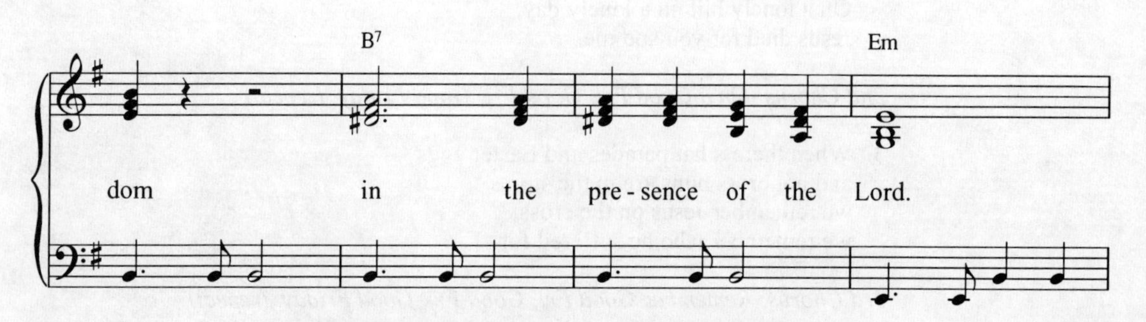
B7
Em
dom in the pre - sence of the Lord.

E7
Am
There is heal - ing and for - give - ness, there is
Em
B7
free - dom and re - lease. There is joy and peace and laugh -
Em
E7
Am
- ter that will ne - ver cease. So let's give him all our wor -
Em
B7
- ries; let us give him all our fears, for we know that he is with
Em
us and we know he al - ways hears.

782 While shepherds watched

Words: Nahum Tate, alt. Music: from Este's *Psalter* (1592)

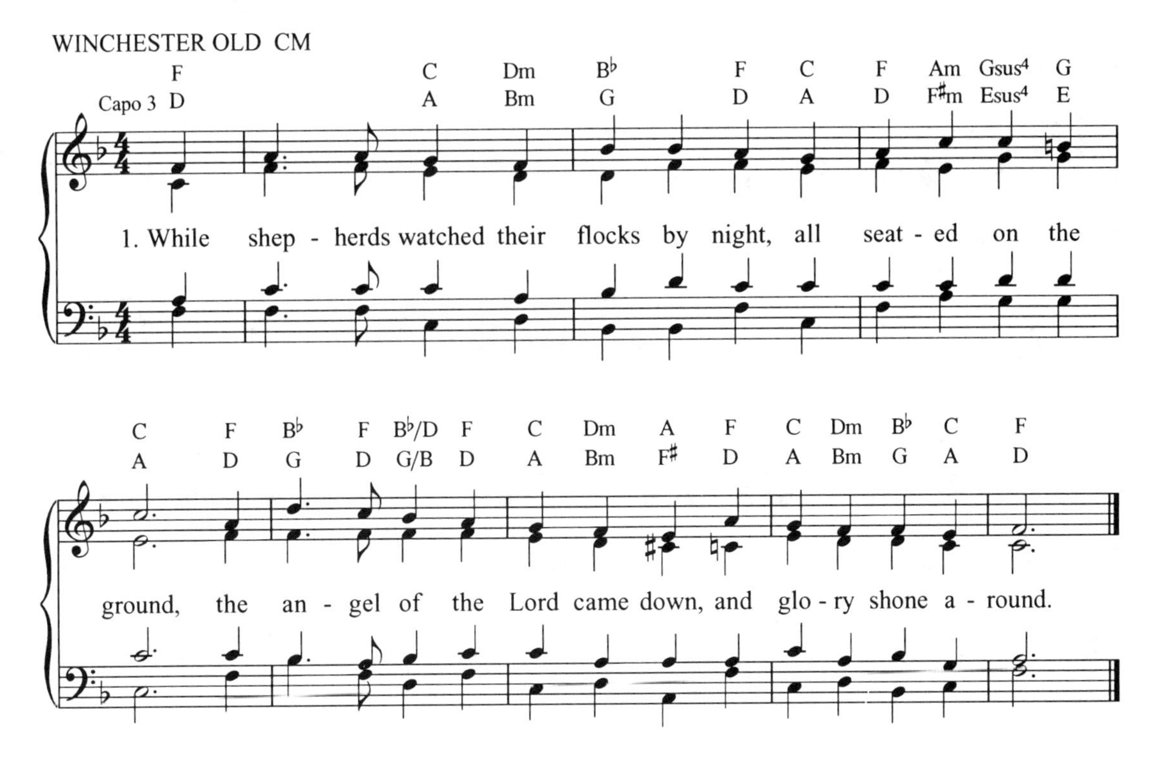
WINCHESTER OLD CM
Capo 3
F C Dm B♭ F C F Am Gsus4 G
D A Bm G D A D F♯m Esus4 E
1. While shep - herds watched their flocks by night, all seat - ed on the
C F B♭ F B♭/D F C Dm A F C Dm B♭ C F
A D G D G/B D A Bm F♯ D A Bm G A D
ground, the an - gel of the Lord came down, and glo - ry shone a - round.

2. 'Fear not,' said he, (for mighty dread
had seized their troubled mind);
'glad tidings of great joy I bring
to you and all mankind.

3. 'To you in David's town this day
is born of David's line
a Saviour, who is Christ the Lord;
and this shall be the sign:

4. 'The heav'nly babe you there shall find
to human view displayed,
all meanly wrapped in swathing bands,
and in a manger laid.'

5. Thus spake the seraph, and forthwith
appeared a shining throng
of angels praising God, who thus
addressed their joyful song:

6. 'All glory be to God on high,
and to the earth be peace,
goodwill henceforth from heav'n to earth
begin and never cease.'

783 Who paints the skies? *(River of fire)*

Words and Music: Stuart Townend

Rhythmically
G D G
Leader
1. Who paints the skies in - to glo - rious day?
Who shapes the val - leys and brings the rain?
C G
All
On - ly the splen - dour of Je - sus.
Leader
Who breathes his life in - to
Who makes the des - ert to
D G D G
fists of clay?
live a - gain?
All
On - ly the splen - dour of Je - sus.
D G C
Teach ev - 'ry na - tion his marv - 'llous ways;
D
each ge - ne -

G C D
ra - tion shall sing his praise.
Chorus
G C D
He is won-der - ful, he is glo-ri - ous, clothed in right-eous - ness,
C D G C
full of ten-der - ness. Come and wor - ship him, he's the Prince of life,
D C D G
he will cleanse our hearts in his ri-ver of fire.

2. Who hears the cry of the barren one?
   Only the mercy of Jesus.
   Who breaks the curse of the heart of stone?
   Only the mercy of Jesus.
   Who storms the prison and sets men free?
   Only the mercy of Jesus.
   Purchasing souls for eternity?
   Only the mercy of Jesus.

784 Why do fish swim instead of sink?

Words and Music: Susie Hare

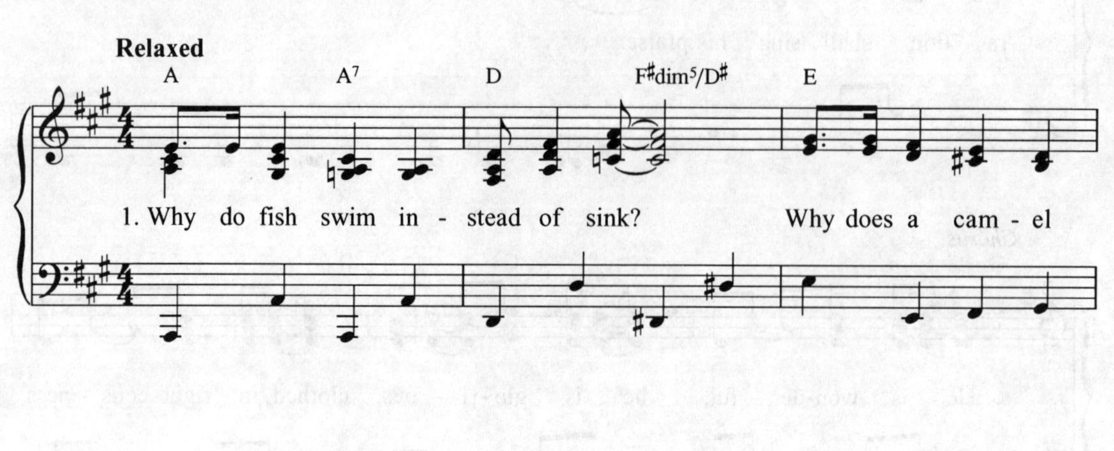
Relaxed
A
A7
D
F#dim5/D#
E
1. Why do fish swim in - stead of sink? Why does a cam - el

A
A#dim5
E7/B
E7
A
A7
D
F#dim5/D#
store its drink? Why do hens cluck in - stead of coo?

E
A
Aaug5
Chorus
D
F#dim5/D#
Why do cats purr in - stead of moo? Well, I don't know why they

A/E
F#
Bm7
E7
A
A7
do it, so it's no good ask - ing me. It's the

D
F♯dim5/D♯
A/E
F♯
Bm7
E7
A
way that God has made them, and it just comes nat - ural-ly!

2. Why do bees buzz instead of bark?
   Why does an owl see in the dark?
   Why do birds fly instead of walk?
   Why do pigs grunt instead of talk?

3. Why do sheep chew instead of peck?
   Why do giraffes have great long necks?
   Why do mice squeak instead of roar?
   Why does a woodworm eat the door?

785 Will you follow

Words and Music: Nick Harding

D7 G C D G
1. Will you fol - low the Shep-herd who knows the way? Will you
G C D C B
fol - low the King from a - bove? Will you fol - low the Shep-herd
Em D C D G
ev - 'ry day? Will you fol - low the God of love?
G Chorus Em D B A7 D
I will fol-low the God of love, I will fol - low
1. 2. 3.
G G D7 D.S. G
him. him. 2. Will you him.

2. Will you look for the light that shows the way?
Will you look for the King from above?
Will you look for the Light of the World today?
Will you look for the God of love?

I will look for the God of Love,
I will look for him. *(x2)*

786 With all of my heart *(I love you, Lord)*

Words and Music: Andy Read
arr. Chris Mitchell

G
C
D
With all of my heart I love you, Lord; with all of my soul

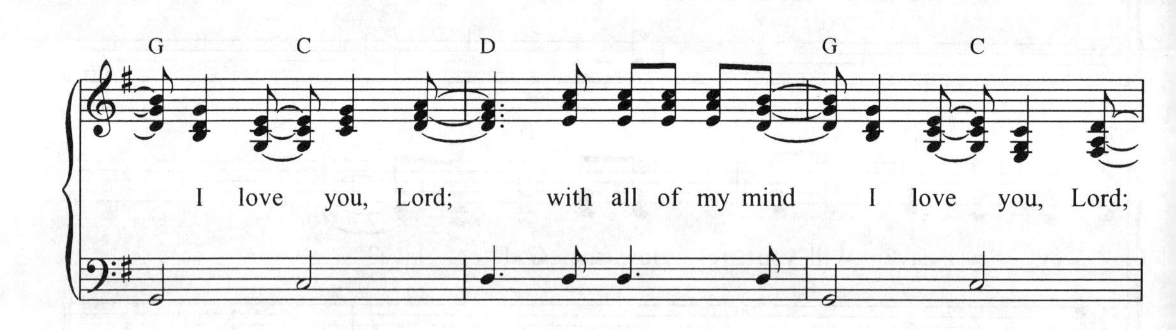

G
C
D
G
C
I love you, Lord; with all of my mind I love you, Lord;

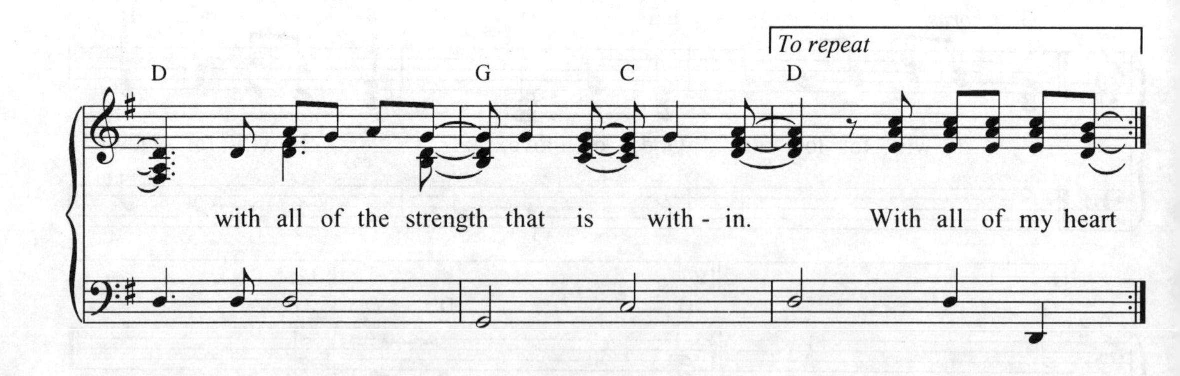

To repeat
D
G
C
D
with all of the strength that is with - in. With all of my heart

Last time
To continue
D
G
Fine
D
Yeah! There is

Em7 D/F♯ G Am7
no great - er thing I could do in all my life,
D Em7 D/F♯ G Dsus4
there is no great - er cost to make.
D Em7 D/F♯ G
There is no great - er joy that you
Am7 D Bm7 Em7 Am7
want to give to me when I have you reign-
D Em7 D D.S.
- ing in my life. With all of my heart

787 With all of my heart I will praise

Words and Music: James Wright
arr. Chris Mitchell

D
G
D/A
A7
1. With all of my heart I will praise.
D
G
D/A
A7
With all of my heart I will praise.
D
G
D/F#
G
With all of my heart I will lift up his ho - ly name.
Last time to Coda
D/A
A7
D
G
1.
D/A
A7
With all of my heart I will praise.
2
D/A
G
D
A
G
With all of my be - ing I will re-joice in the Lord.

D G D G D A
With all of my be - ing
G A G/A A G/A
D.C. for next verse
I will give praise to the name of Je - sus.
CODA
D G D/A A7
Praise the Lord, hal - le - lu - jah.
D G D/A A7
Praise the Lord, hal - le - lu - jah.
D G D/A A7 D G
Praise the Lord, hal - le - lu - jah. Praise the Lord, hal - le - lu -
D/A A7 D G D
jah. Praise the Lord,

2. With all of my breath I will sing . . .

3. With both of my hands I will clap . . .

4. With both of my feet I will jump . . .

5. With all of my body I'll dance . . .

788 With just one touch

Words and Music: Martin Cooper

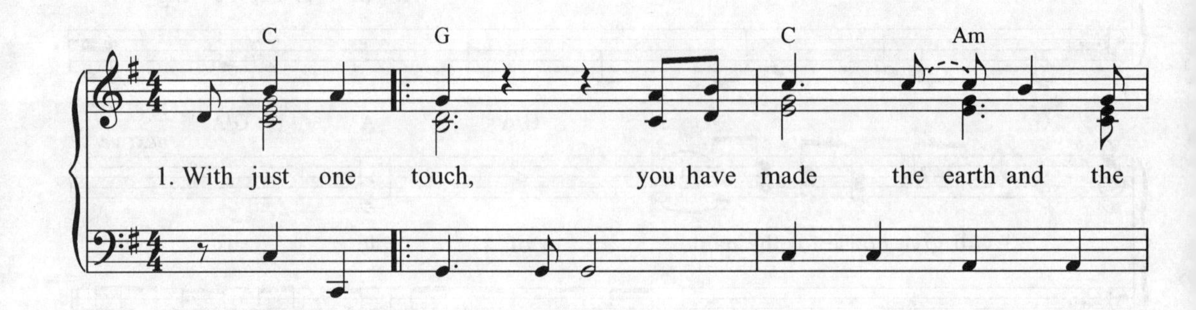

C G C Am
1. With just one touch, you have made the earth and the

D G D Em D G C G
sea. With just one breath you cre-

C Am D Am
a-ted the sun and the sky, and you have made all the

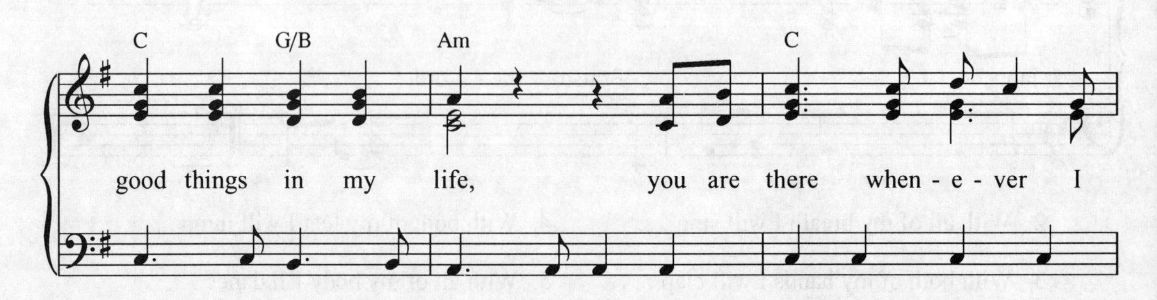

C G/B Am C
good things in my life, you are there when-e-ver I

D
Chorus
G
D/F#
Em7
cry. For you are Lord of all, and your

C
G
D
D/F#
Em7
love goes on for e - ver; you are Lord of all, and my

1.
2.
C
G
D
G
C
G
life I will sur - ren - der to you. 2. And in my

2. And in my life
I will sing my praise to you,
and with my lips
I will only say things that are true,
and I will speak of the good things you have made,
you are with me every day.

789 Wobble your knees

Words and Music: Olivia Johnson

C
F
Wob-ble your knees, wig-gle your nose, look with your eyes and
C
F
lis - ten with your ears, ’cos God is all a-round us, and he loves
G
1.
you and me and you and you and you. So
2.
C
you and you and you and me.

790 Worship the King

Words and Music: Chris Jackson
arr. Dave Bankhead

E A E A
Wor-ship the King, your prai - ses bring
No need to fear, you can draw near,
E A B
right in - to the pre - sence of the Lord.
and stand in the pre - sence of the Lord.
E A E
Say - ing 'I love you, Lord', say - ing 'I
A E A
love you, Lord', say - ing 'I love you,
B
Lord'.
1. A/B B
2. B E
'I love you, Lord'.

791 Wow! That's amazing

Words and Music: Phil Chapman
arr. Chris Mitchell

Chorus
D
A7
G
D/F♯
A
Wow! That's a - maz - ing. Wow! That's fan - tas - tic. When
Je - sus died, he died to for - give me.
Wow! That's a - maz - ing. Wow! That's fan - tas - tic. God's
love for us is big as big can be.
Fine
1. The Bi - ble says we all do wrong things,

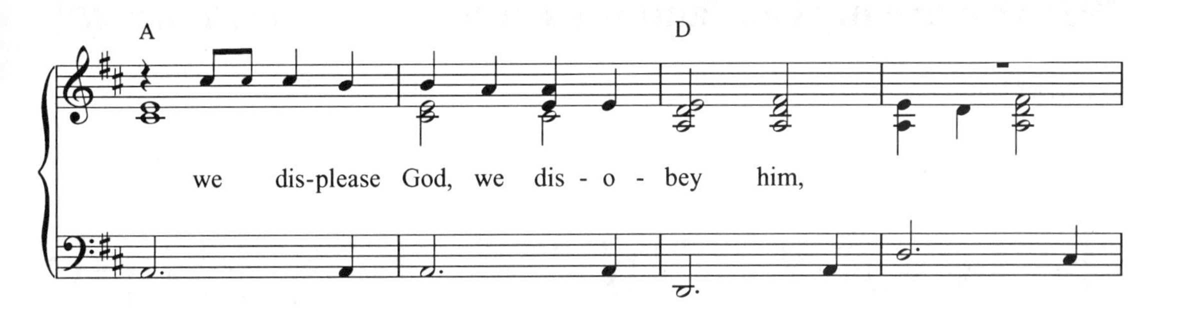
A
D
we dis-please God, we dis - o - bey him,

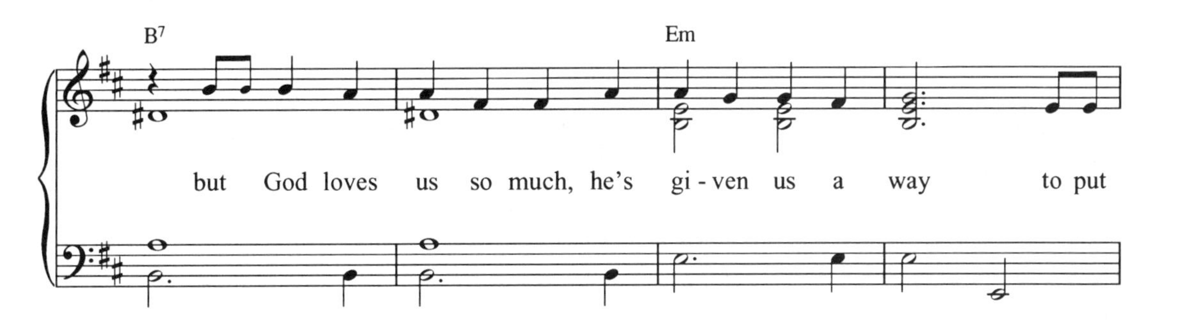
B7
Em
but God loves us so much, he's gi - ven us a way to put

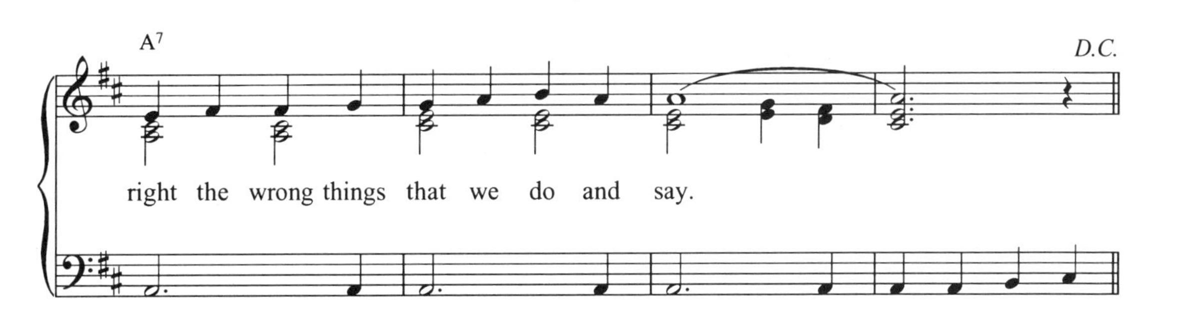
A7
D.C.
right the wrong things that we do and say.

2. God sent his Son, his name is Jesus,
   he died upon a cross to save us.
   There is no other way to gain eternal life
   and to be with God in heaven when we die.

3. I must trust Jesus as my Saviour,
   live my life for him, change my behaviour.
   He says he will forgive me, of that I can be sure,
   and I'll live with him in heav'n for evermore!

792 You are my God and my Father *(Fill me up!)*

Words and Music: Chris Jackson

Brightly
E
B
A
You are my God and my Fa - ther; you are my Lord and my King.
B
E
B
You are my friend and my Sa - viour;
A
B
E
C♯m
I will lift my voice and sing; fill me up and let your
A
B
E
C♯m
A
B
Spi-rit flow, fill me up, let the love of Je-sus show, 'cause I
E
C♯m
A
B
want to be like Je - sus, he's my King.

793 You are the potter

Words and Music: Paul Crouch and David Mudie

Slow 4
Capo 3
F Am7 Gm7 F
D F#m7 Em7 D
You are the pot - ter, I am the clay,
Dm Gm F/A B♭ Csus4 C
Bm Em D/F# G Asus4 A
your hands are work - ing in my life day by day,
Am7 Dm7 Gm7 B♭m
F#m7 Bm7 Em7 Gm
and as they are mov - ing I am made a - new,
F Am7 Gm7 B♭/C
D F#m7 Em7 G/A
built up and mould - ed 'til I'm clo - ser to the im - age of
F Am7 B♭ Csus4 C F
D F#m7 G Asus4 A D
you.

794 You came from heaven's splendour

(Jesus, almighty Saviour)

Words and Music: James Wright
arr. Chris Mitchell

Capo 3
F B♭/F F B♭/D
D G/D D G/B
1. You came from hea - ven's splen - dour to earth's hu - ma -
C/E F C F/C C B♭
A/C♯ D A D/A A G
- ni - ty, heal - ing the bro - ken - heart - ed, sett - ing them
Csus4 C F B♭/F F B♭/D
Asus4 A D G/D D G/B
free. But for the joy that fol - lowed, you gave up ev -
C/E F C F/C C B♭
A/C♯ D A D/A A G
- 'ry - thing; death on a curs - ed cross that we might have
Csus4 C F B♭/F F B♭/F
Asus4 A D G/D D G/D
Chorus
life. Je - sus, al - migh - ty Sa - viour, you rose up from

F Csus4 C F B♭/F F B♭
D Asus4 A D G/D D G
the dead, vic - to - ri - ous, tri - um - phant, just like you
Csus4 C F B♭/F F B♭/F
Asus4 A D G/D D G/D
said. In re - sur - rec - tion pow - er, the grave you o -
F Csus4 C F B♭/F F
D Asus4 A D G/D D
- ver - came, and now you sit in hea - ven, for
B♭ Csus4 C F B♭2
G Asus4 A D G2
e - ver - more to reign.
Dm7 C/E F/A B♭2 F2 F
Bm7 A/C♯ D/F♯ G2 D2 D
D.C.

2. There in the tomb your broken
body in silence lay,
but for three days, three nights
it did not see decay.
You had a greater purpose,
you had a greater plan,
that through the death of one man
all might have life.

795 You can tell the Lord that you love him

Words and Music: Colin Buchanan
arr. Chris Mitchell

Chorus
G G/D D7
You can tell the Lord that you love him a - ny time.
G
You can tell the Lord that you need him
G/D D7 G C D G
a - ny time. Thank him for his love and care,
Em7 C D
shoot him up an ar - row prayer.
Last time to Coda
G G/D D7 G
You can tell the Lord that you love him a - ny time.

D/G G C/G G C D G
C/G G D
1. In the mid - dle of what - e - ver you're
2. When you're hap - py as Lar - ry, when you're
Em C D7
do - ing at school, at lunch when you're kick - in' the ball.
full of joy, when you're blown out by the view.
G D
When you're chas - ing your mates all
Give thanks to the God who's
Em C D
1.
D.C.
o - ver the place you can talk to the Lord of all.
show-ered his bles-sings, show-ered his bles-sings on

2
CODA
D.C. al Coda
D
G
you, and you, and you, and You can tell the Lord

C
G/D
C/D
that you love him. You can tell the Lord that you need him.

G
G/D
D7
You can tell the Lord that you love him a - ny time.

G D/G G C/G G C D G C/G G

796 You can't stop rain from falling down

(You can't stop God from loving you)

Words: J. Gowans
Music: J. Larsson
arr. Chris Mitchell
Em7 A7 D Em7 A7
1. You can't stop rain from
Em7 A7 D
fall - ing down, pre - vent the sun from shi - ning, you
Em7 A7 Em7 A7 D
can't stop spring from com - ing in, or win - ter from re -
C/D D7 G F# Bm B7
sign - ing. Or still the waves or stay the winds, or

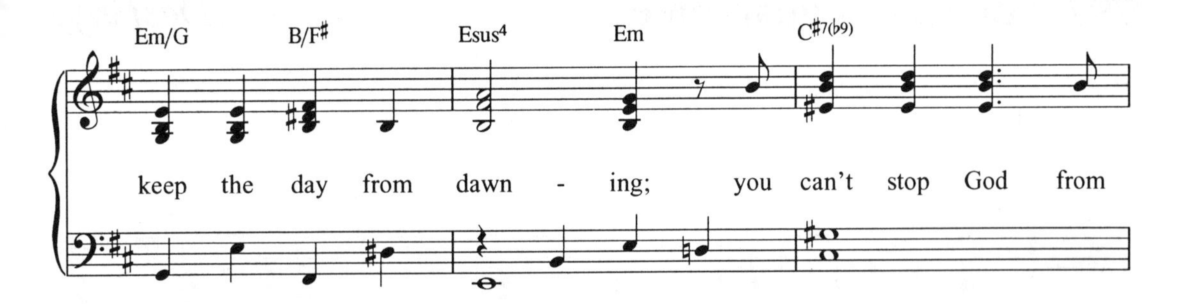
Em/G
B/F♯
Esus4
Em
C♯7(♭9)
keep the day from dawn - ing; you can't stop God from

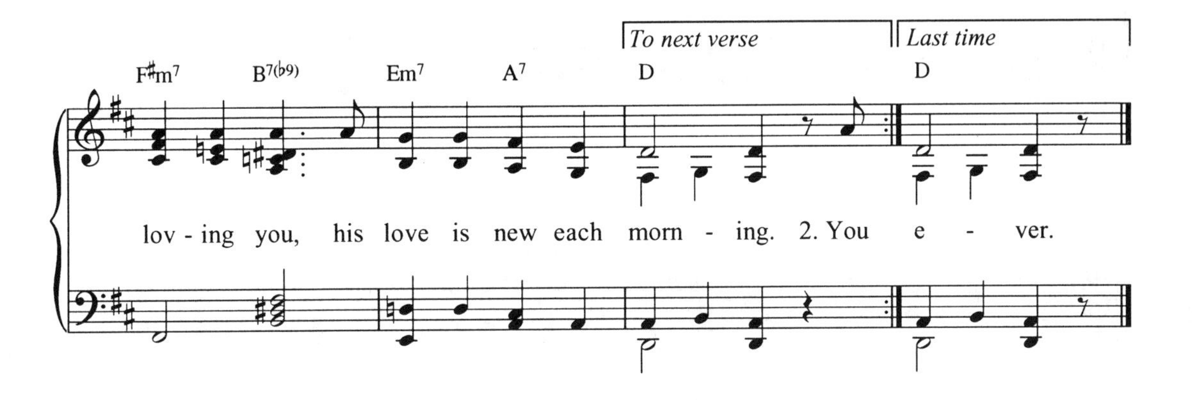
To next verse
Last time
F♯m7
B7(♭9)
Em7
A7
D
D
lov - ing you, his love is new each morn - ing. 2. You e - ver.

2. You can't stop ice from being cold,
   you can't stop fire from burning;
   or hold the tide that's going out,
   delay its sure returning.
   Or halt the progress of the years,
   the flight of fame and fashion;
   you can't stop God from loving you,
   his nature is compassion.

3. You can't stop God from loving you,
   though you may disobey him;
   you can't stop God from loving you,
   however you betray him.
   From love like this no pow'r on earth
   the human heart can sever;
   you can't stop God from loving you,
   not God, not now, nor ever.

797 You gave a guarantee *(Destiny)*

Words and Music: Terry Tarsiuk
arr. Chris Mitchell

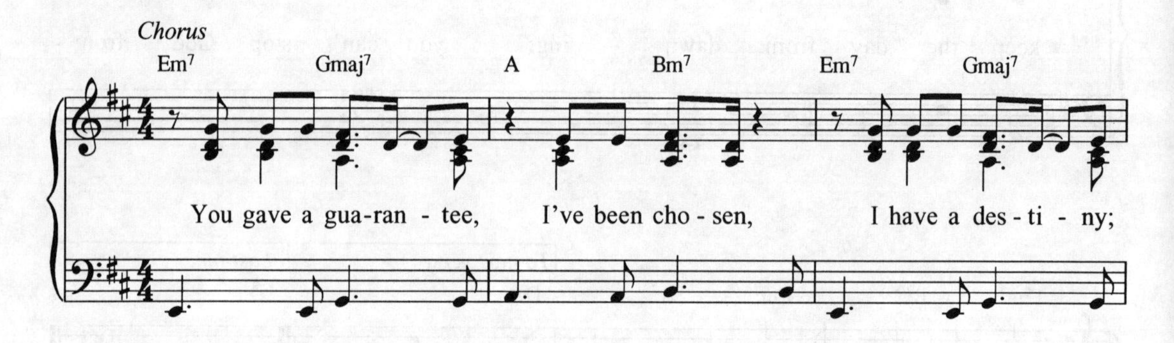
Chorus
Em7
Gmaj7
A
Bm7
Em7
Gmaj7
You gave a gua - ran - tee, I've been cho - sen, I have a des - ti - ny;

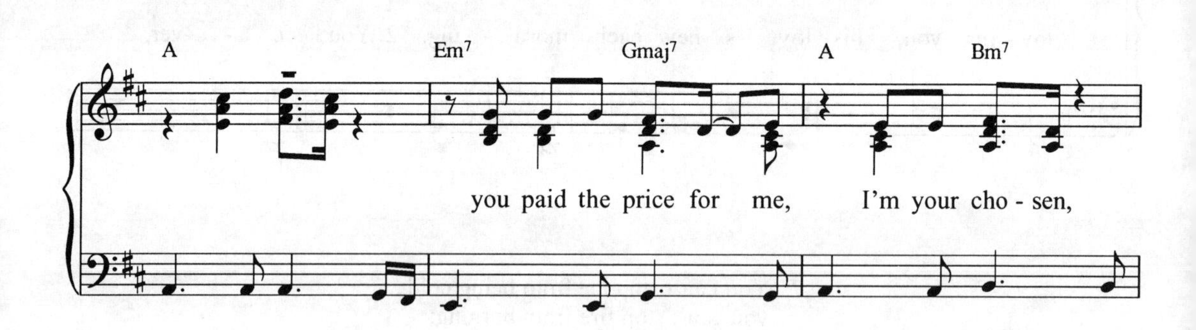
A
Em7
Gmaj7
A
Bm7
you paid the price for me, I'm your cho - sen,

Em7
Gmaj7
A
Last time
Fine
I have a des - ti - ny.

To continue
Bm7
Verse
G2
D/A
A
Cho - sen in you be - fore the world be - gan;

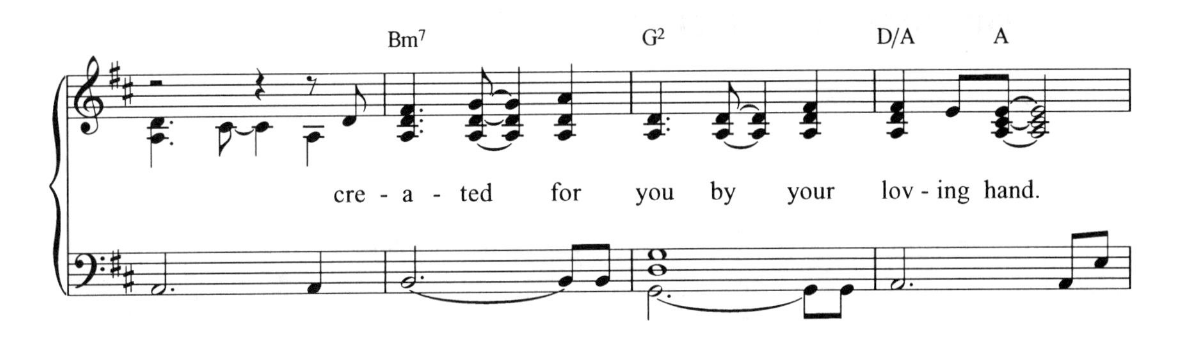
Bm7 G2 D/A A
cre - a - ted for you by your lov - ing hand.

D/F♯ G2 D Em7
I have been blessed so I give you my best

A F♯m7 G
and I live with the joy of

D/A Asus4 A D.C.
know - ing I give you plea - sure.

798 You need to natter to God

Words and Music: Doug Horley

(♩ = 83)
Verse
Capo 3 D
F
C
A
You need to nat-ter to God, be-cause you mat-ter to God,
Gm
Em
Dm
Bm
Gm
Em
1.
F
D
C
A
be-cause he loves to hear just what you are think - ing.
2.
F
D
C
A
Chorus
B♭
G
F
D
think - ing. His heart leaps ev - 'ry time he hears you talk - ing,
B♭
G
F
D
his heart leaps ev - 'ry time he hears you sing. He's

B♭
G
Dm
Bm
Gm
Em
so thrilled when you tell him that you love him, keep talk, talk,

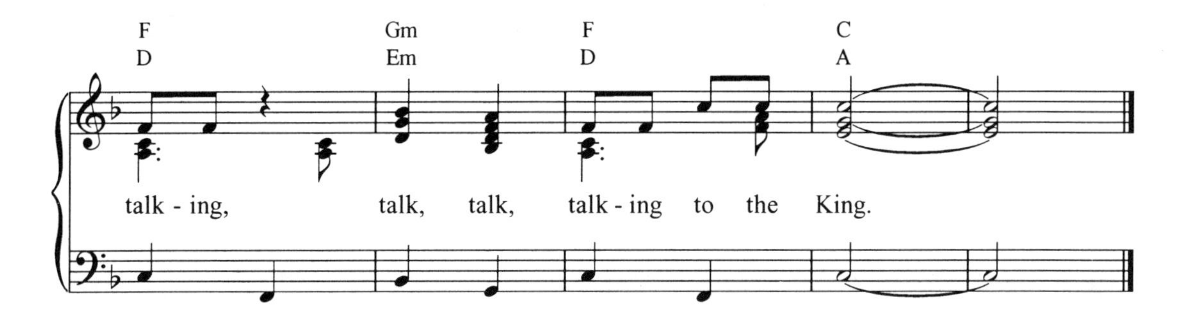
F
D
Gm
Em
F
D
C
A
talk - ing, talk, talk, talk - ing to the King.

799 You offer a way *(Still the storm)*

Words and Music: Nick Harding

D G Em D B C Dsus4 D

Gsus4 G Em D B
1. You of - fer a way to live day by day in peace

C A G D G Em
and in pu - ri - ty, but Je - sus, I know that I

D B C A G D C D
Chorus
need to grow to love you com - plete - ly. From all fears,

Bdim Em F D G C D
pain and tears, Je-sus, set me free. When I'm shout-ing,

1. 2.
Bdim Em F D Gsus4 G Gsus4 G
fear-ing, doubt-ing, still the storm in me.

2. I know deep inside
the times I have tried
to change, but I stay the same,
so now I give way
and offer today
my life, as you call my name.

800 You're a mighty God

Words and Music: Gerry Holmes
arr. Chris Mitchell

(♩ = 140)
C Am Dm7 G Dm7 G
You're a migh - ty God, yes, and migh - ty strong, who can change the world, e-ven
C F G C Am Dm7 G
beat King Kong, and you care for us in so ma - ny ways. If we
Dm7 G C G7 C
trust and pray we will grow and change.

801 You ride on the wings of the wind *(Psalm 104)*

Words and Music: Paul Field

G
Chorus
Am
C
D
You ride on the wings of the wind,
C
D
you are won-der-ful, Lord. The glo-ry is yours.
G
Am
C
D
All of cre-a - tion be - gins
C
D
by your wis-dom and might; clothed in ma - jes -
G
D/F#
Em
D
C
D
ty and light you ride on the wings of the wind.

G
Am7
G/B
C
D
1. When I
hear the voice of your thun - der, when I
see your light - ning in the sky, by the
light of ev - 'ry star I see how won - der - ful you are.
Em
Em/D
C/D
Em7
E7
B7
All my life I will sing your praise.

2. By the moon you measure the seasons,
by the sun you measure out the days:
all of nature plays a part,
bringing heaven to my heart.
All my life I will sing your praise.

802 Your love

Words and Music: Dave Godfrey

Driving beat
Chorus
E
A
E
Your love, O Lord, is high - er than the moun - tains. Your

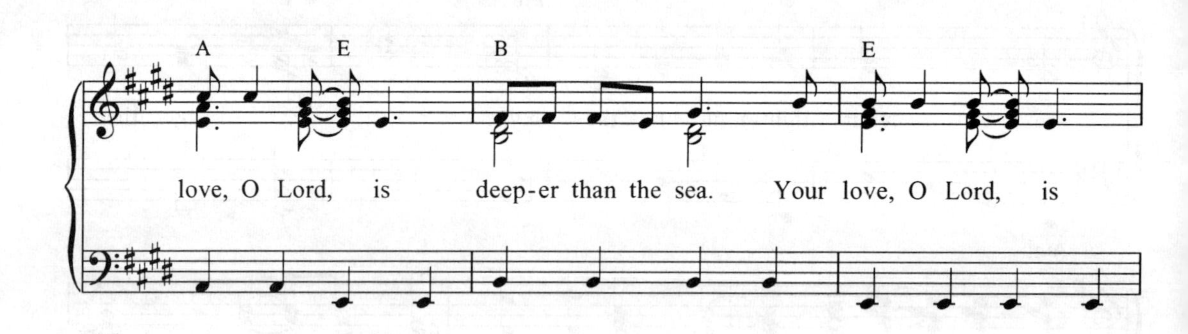
A
E
B
E
love, O Lord, is deep-er than the sea. Your love, O Lord, is

A
E
A
E
wi - der than the u - ni - verse, your love, O Lord, it

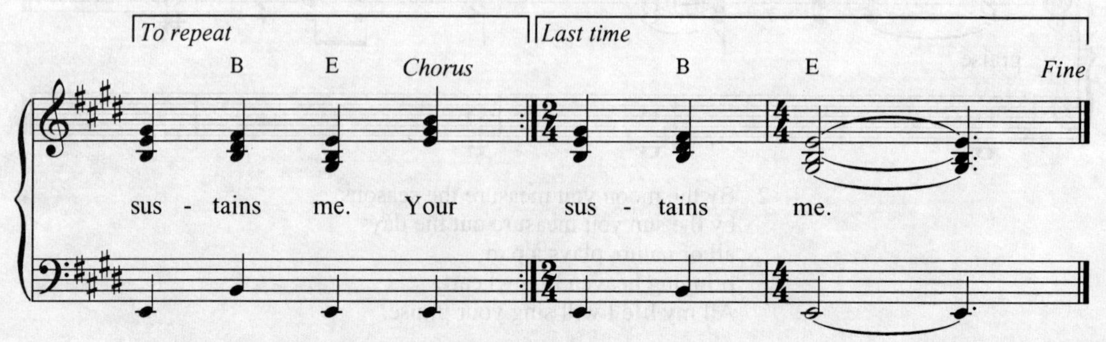
To repeat
Last time
B
E
Chorus
B
E
Fine
sus - tains me. Your sus - tains me.

To verses
B E B
sus - tains me. 1. You are love,
C♯m A B C♯m E
kind and pa-tient, migh - ty arms pro - tect me to - day.
A E A E A
As I am, I'm loved by you, so when I feel my feet a - slip - ping,
B
D.S.
I'll just say that your

2. Nothing, Lord, in all creation
could ever take your love away.
I'm so glad I'm loved by you,
so when I feel my feet a-dancing,
I'll just say that your love . . .

803 Your love is amazing *(Hallelujah)*

Words and Music: Brian Doerksen and Brenton Brown
arr. Chris Mitchell

G/B
1. Your love is a - maz - ing, stea - dy and un - chang -
- ing, I can feel it ri -

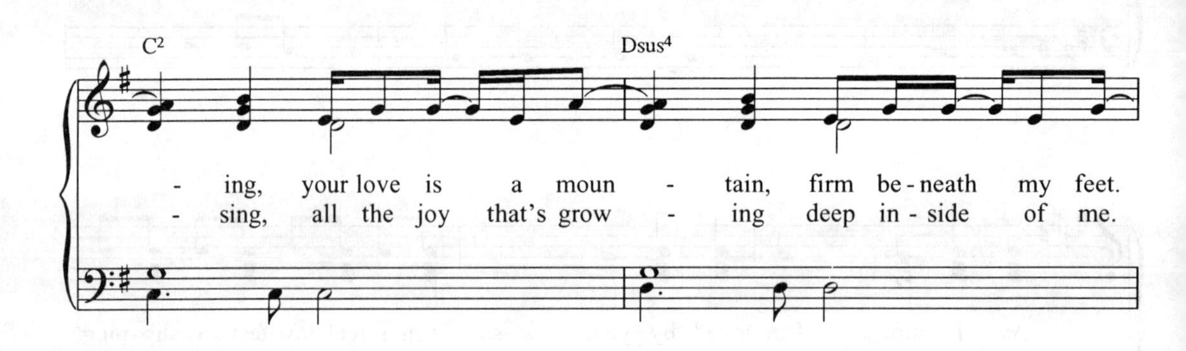
C²
Dsus⁴
- ing, your love is a moun - tain, firm be - neath my feet.
- sing, all the joy that's grow - ing deep in - side of me.

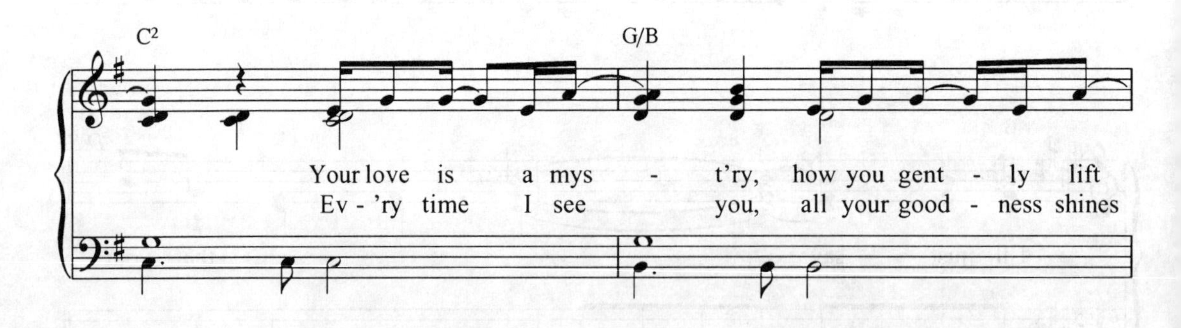
C²
G/B
Your love is a mys - t'ry, how you gent - ly lift
Ev - 'ry time I see you, all your good - ness shines

C²
Dsus⁴
me, when I am sur - round - ed, your love car - ries me.
through, I can feel this God - song, ri - sing up in me.

C2
Chorus
G
Hal - le - lu - jah,
hal - le - lu -
D
Em7
- jah,
hal - le - lu - jah,
C2
G
your love makes me sing.
Hal - le - lu - jah,
hal - le - lu -
D
Em7
C2
- jah,
hal - le - lu - jah,
your love makes me sing.
1.
Last time
G
Fine
2. Your love is sur - pris -

2.
D
Em7
Yes, you make me sing.
D/F#
C2
Lord, you make me sing, sing, sing.
D
Em7
D/F#
D.S.
How you make me sing.
Hal - le - lu -

804 You've gotta be fit *(Fit for the King)*

Words and Music: Brian Edgeley

Chorus
G7
C
You've got - ta be fit (fit!) for the King, giv - ing your

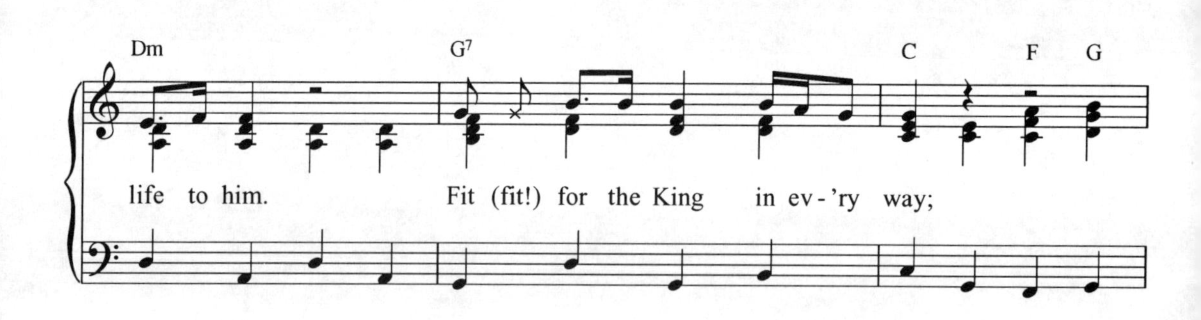
Dm
G7
C F G
life to him. Fit (fit!) for the King in ev - 'ry way;

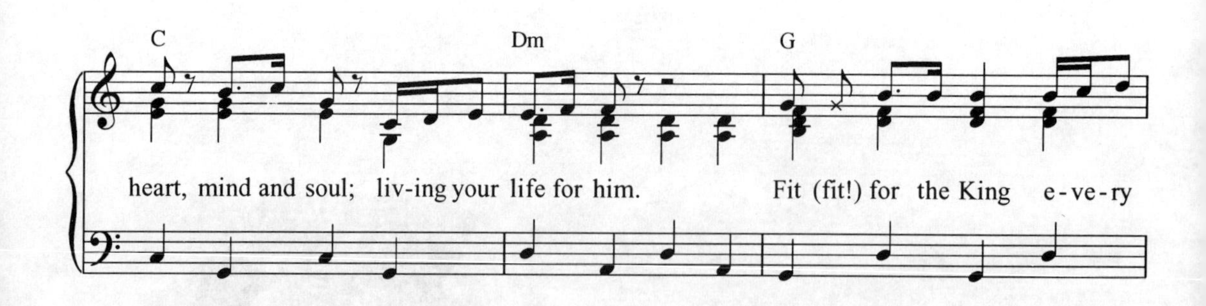
C
Dm
G
heart, mind and soul; liv-ing your life for him. Fit (fit!) for the King e - ve - ry

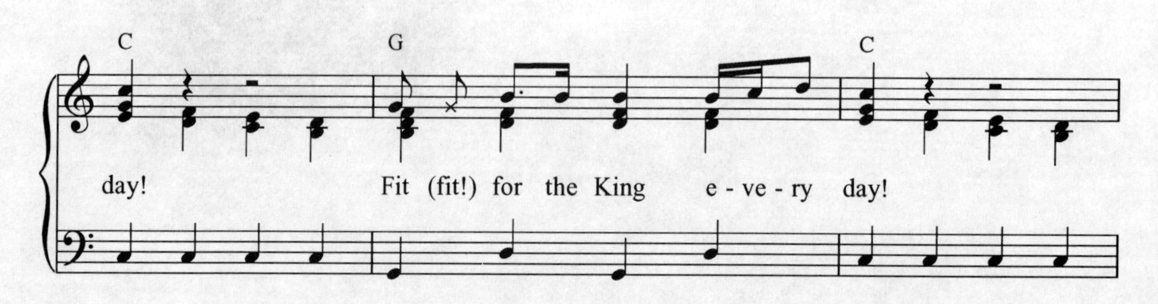
C
G
C
day! Fit (fit!) for the King e - ve - ry day!

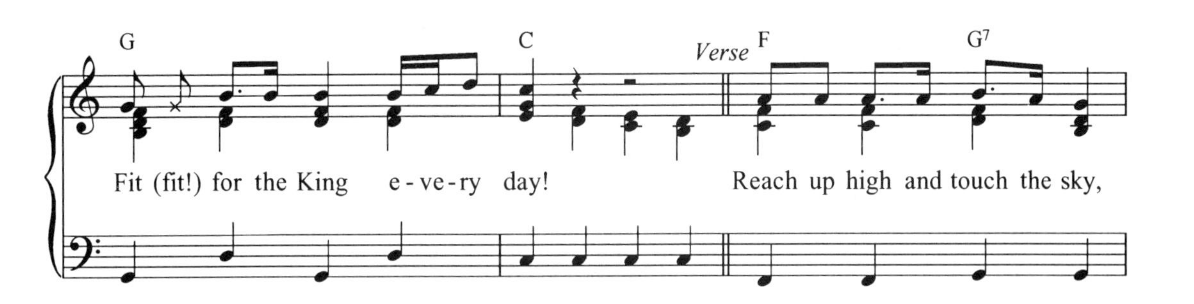
G C *Verse* F G7
Fit (fit!) for the King e-ve-ry day! Reach up high and touch the sky,

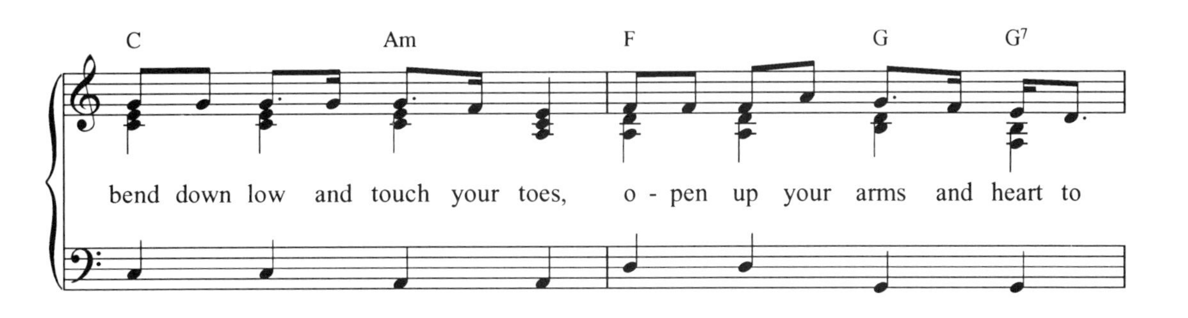
C Am F G G7
bend down low and touch your toes, o-pen up your arms and heart to

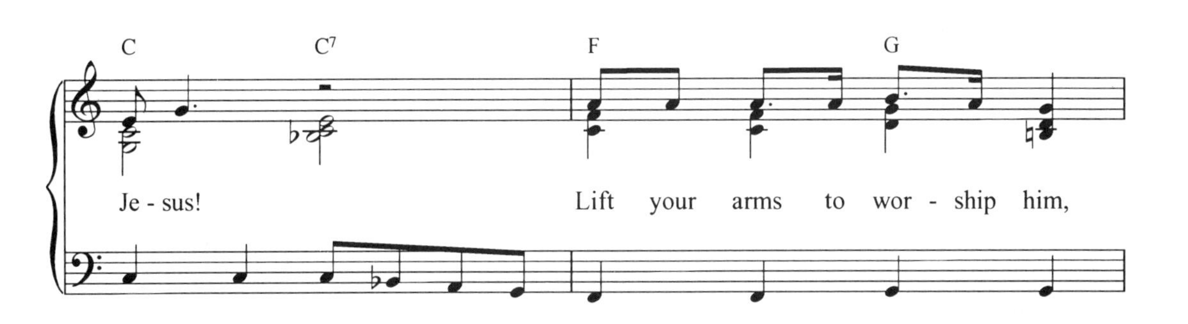
C C7 F G
Je-sus! Lift your arms to wor-ship him,

C Am Dm G G7 C
clap your hands to praise him; o-pen up your heart and mind to him.

805 You've touched my life

Words and Music: John Matheson
arr. Chris Mitchell

Capo 3
B♭/C G/A F D Gm7 Em7
You've touched my life, I can ne-ver be the same.
C A Gm7 Em7 B♭/C G/A C7 A7 Fsus4 Dsus4 F D
You've touched my life, you're in my heart to reign.
B♭/C G/A Cm7/F Am7/D F7 D7 B♭ G
You've touched my life, all glo-ry to your name.
Gm7 Em7 F/C D/A C A C/B♭ A/G Am F♯m
You've touched my life,
Dm7 Bm7 F/C D/A C A B♭/C G/A F D
you've touched my life.

806 You won't get to heaven

Words and Music: Doug Horley
arr. Chris Mitchell

A
1. You won't get to hea-ven on the back of a ca-mel and you
D A
won't get to hea-ven on a sheep. You won't get to hea-ven on a
B E
dou-ble deck-er bus, and you won't get to hea-ven in a jeep. A
A D
po - go stick will on - ly make you feel sick and you can't drive there in a
A
car. A rock-et in your pock-et might make you see stars but it

E7
A
Chorus
D
A
sure won't get you that far. There's on - ly one way (one way), one way (one way),
E
A
D
you can get to hea-ven, oh yeah! There's on - ly one way (one way),
A
E
D
one way (one way), that's through God's Son Je - sus.
A
To next verse
Last time
He's the on-ly way.
2. You

Melodies for verses 2 and 3 are given overleaf

2. You won't get to heaven by looking real good
   and you won't get to heaven 'cos you're slick.
   You won't get to heaven by jumping from a plane
   and by flapping your arms real quick.
   A flight or a kite or an elastic band
   might whizz you through the air.
   Or you could scuttle in a shuttle right over the moon,
   but it still won't get you there.

3. You won't get to heaven by saying you're a Christian
   and you won't get to heaven 'cos you're good.
   You won't get to heaven just by going to a church
   though many may think you could.
   A mum or a dad or a sister who loves Jesus
   won't get you there, it's true.
   Oh, you're in favour with the Saviour but this you gotta know,
   you need to find him just for you.

Verse 2
2. You won't get to hea - ven by look - ing real good and you
won't get to hea - ven 'cos you're slick. You won't get to hea-ven by
jump - ing from a plane and by flap - ping your arms real quick. A
flight or a kite or an e - las - tic band might whizz you through the air.
Or you could scut - tle in a shut - tle right o -
Chorus D.S.
- ver the moon, but it still won't get you there. There's on - ly
Verse 3
3. You won't get to hea - ven by say - ing you're a Christ - ian, and you
won't get to hea - ven 'cos you're good. You won't get to hea - ven just by
go - ing to a church though ma - ny may think you could. A
mum or a dad or a sis - ter who loves Je - sus won't get you there, it's
true. Oh, you're in fa - vour with the Sa - viour but this
Chorus D.S.
you got - ta know, you need to find him just for you. There's on - ly

Indexes

Index of Songwriters, Authors, Composers and Arrangers

Arrangers are shown indented and in italics

Scriptural Index

Key Word Index

The key word categories appear alphabetically and are cross-referenced to make it as easy as possible for worship leaders to find songs and hymns suitable for various themes and occasions.

Index of First Lines and Titles

This index gives the first line of each hymn. If a hymn is known by an alternative title, this is also given, but indented and in italics.

kidsource Music Edition

kidsource
super songs for church and school
compiled by Capt. Alan Price, CA

1470154 1 84003 310 X

kidsource Combined Words

kidsource
super songs for church and school
compiled by Capt. Alan Price, CA

1470152 1 84003 344 6

the source Music Edition

the source
the definitive worship collection compiled by
Graham Kendrick
adoration
worship

1470104 1 84003 120 4

the source 2 Music Edition

the source
2
the worship collection compiled by
Graham Kendrick
worship

1470105 1 84003 724 5

the source Combined Words

the source
the worship collection compiled by
Graham Kendrick
adoration
worship

1470102 1 84003 726 1